CW00566943

China Arbitration Yearbook

Series Editor

Yifei Lin, Shenzhen, Guangdong, China

Yifei Lin

China Arbitration Yearbook (2021)

 Springer

Yifei Lin
Yi & Partners
Shenzhen, China

ISSN 2524-8618   ISSN 2524-8626 (electronic)
China Arbitration Yearbook
ISBN 978-981-19-1286-3   ISBN 978-981-19-1284-9 (eBook)
https://doi.org/10.1007/978-981-19-1284-9

This Springer imprint is published by the registered company Springer Nature Singapore Pte Ltd.
The registered company address is: 152 Beach Road, #21-01/04 Gateway East, Singapore 189721,
Singapore

Preface

Arbitration in China is evolving rapidly, with domestic caseloads reaching 400,000 in 2020. An increasing number of people are involved in arbitration and are concerned about common or controversial issues related to Chinese arbitration. By the time this book was finalized, the Ministry of Justice of P. R. China had just released an Arbitration Law draft for comments to the public.

This series principally addresses the law and practice of commercial arbitration in China mainland and is intended to provide cases, materials and commentary on the main issues arising in Chinese arbitration. It aims to help arbitration practitioners, judges, lawyers, researchers and anyone interested in China arbitration from any jurisdiction to know more about and make use of China arbitration as a dispute resolution method.

This is a book about Chinese arbitration, with many decisions, rulings and interpretations rendered by China's courts in recent years. In this sense, this volume may be regarded as a case book. As all the cases are introduced in English, errors, omissions and confusion may arise due to the translation. In addition, confidential or privacy treatments are made in some cases. We may just use Pinyin instead of literally or officially English name of the parties in some decisions by Chinese courts. Additionally, in some cases, introduction or background may be too simple for readers to understand fully, and for some cases arranged in one chapter, it may be more relevant to be discussed in other chapters from other perspectives. All these may not give you the best reading experience or absolute correct understanding. Readers are encouraged to provide criticisms, comments, suggestions and queries.

This volume would never have been completed without the able assistance from my colleagues, friends and those readers who always support me. I particularly acknowledge the time and contributions of Susan Finder, Ye Shanshan, Ma Huilian, Gu Dai, Liu Xiaorong, Li Jiefei, Cai Haiying, Wang Shuai and Sun Jingqu, who helpfully assisted in preparing the drafts, reviewed some of the chapters, provided relevant materials and/or handled some administrative matters. I also owe thanks for the assistance of those friends and editors in Springer, especially Lydia, who is the editor of this book.

Before I finalized this volume, Yi & Partners, as a boutique law firm founded by myself and some colleagues, ran for nearly 4 years. It still works with the CNARB Arbitration Institute to practice and research in the field of dispute resolution and arbitration. This series on China arbitration is one of its tasks. Anyone with common interest is welcome to contact me for discussion or future cooperation via lyf@yipartners.com.

Shenzhen, China   Yifei Lin
October 2021

Contents

1   Judicial Review of Arbitration Agreement: General   1
   1.1   Nonexistence of Arbitration Agreement   1
   1.2   Multi-tiered Disputes Resolution Clause   7
   1.3   Transfer of Contract Rights   10
   1.4   Standard Form Contract   13
   1.5   The Dismissal of Law Suits *Ex Officio*   20
   1.6   The Principle of Independence of Arbitration Clauses   24

2   Multiple Contracts and Conflicting Dispute Resolution Provisions   31
   2.1   "Arbitration or litigation" Clause   31
   2.2   "May" Apply for Arbitration   33
   2.3   "First Arbitration then Litigation" Clause   36
   2.4   Multiple Related Agreements   39
   2.5   Main Contract and Guarantee Contract   43
   2.6   Unilateral Document   47
   2.7   Unilateral Commitment Letter   50

3   Arbitration Institution and Place   55
   3.1   Nationality of Arbitral Awards Made by Foreign Arbitration Institutions in Mainland   55
   3.2   Inaccurate Arbitration Institution Name   59
   3.3   "Local" Arbitration Commission   62
   3.4   The Scope of "Local"   64
   3.5   Arbitration Agreement with Arbitration Rules Only   67

4   Parties   71
   4.1   Nonsignatory to Property Service Contract   71
   4.2   Joint Venture Which is Nonsignatory to Joint Venture Contract   74
   4.3   Insurance Subrogation Claimant   76
   4.4   Heir   83

4.5	Deregistered Enterprise	86
4.6	Governmental Organ	89
4.7	Headquarters and Branch	97

5   Arbitrator and Tribunal 103
5.1	Colleagueship	103
5.2	Conflict of Identity Between Arbitrators and Agents	105
5.3	Time Limit for Challenge	108

6   Arbitral Procedures 115
6.1	Arbitral Procedures and Judicial Procedures	115
6.2	The Service of Arbitral Award	118
6.3	No Telephone Number	120
6.4	Negotiation	123
6.5	Delay in Amending the Claim or Producing Evidence	126
6.6	Time Limit for Rendering the Award	129

7   Evidence 133
7.1	Authenticity of Evidence	133
7.2	Collection of Evidence	135
7.3	Determination of Evidence	138
7.4	Allocation of Burden of Proof	140
7.5	Concealment of Evidence	144

8   Arbitrability and Arbitral Scope 147
8.1	Arbitration Involving Criminal Case	147
8.2	Filing Litigation to Circumvent Arbitration Clause	150
8.3	Reasonable Expenses for Case Handling	155
8.4	Contracts in Which the Name and the Actual Legal Relationship Are Inconsistent	158
8.5	Adjustment of Liquidated Damages	161
8.6	Beyond the Scope of Arbitration	163

9   Arbitral Awards and Decisions 167
9.1	Determination and Standards of Repeated Arbitration	167
9.2	Dismissal of Repeated Arbitration	171
9.3	Non-enforceability Due to the Nonspecific Content of Awards	176
9.4	Consequences of Revocation or Non-enforcement of Awards	179
9.5	Cancellation of Mediation Statement	182
9.6	Application of Persons Not Involved in the Case of Non-enforcement of the Arbitral Award	192
9.7	Application of Persons Not Involved in the Case for Non-enforcement of Mediation Statement	198
9.8	Arbitral Awards Made by "Pre-arbitration"	203

10 Public Policy 211
    10.1 Violation of Mandatory Provisions of Laws 211
    10.2 Violation of Policy Documents 215
    10.3 Conflicts with Effective Rulings of Courts 218

11 Main China Arbitration Institutions and Judicial Review
Decisions 225
    11.1 Arbitration Agreements 226
    11.2 Party to Arbitration 233
    11.3 Arbitration Institution 234
    11.4 Arbitration Proceedings 237
    11.5 The Scope of Judicial Review: Substances and Procedures 243
    11.6 Arbitral Scope and Beyond the Scope of Submission
         to Arbitration 246
    11.7 Arbitrability and Public Policy 247
    11.8 Others 250

12 Recognition and Enforcement of New York Convention
Awards in China 253
    12.1 General Introduction 254
    12.2 Validity of Arbitration Agreements 281
    12.3 Due Process 290
    12.4 The Scope of Arbitration 295
    12.5 Composition of Arbitral Tribunal and Arbitration
         Proceedings 298
    12.6 Validity of the Arbitral Award 308
    12.7 Arbitrability and Public Policy 310
    12.8 Conclusion 316

Official Replies by the Supreme People's Court Concerning
Arbitration in China 317

Table of Abbreviations and Short Forms

AAA	American Arbitration Association
AFI	Association of Food Industries
Arbitration Law (Draft for Comments)	Arbitration Law of the People's Republic of China (2021) (Draft for Comments)
Arbitration Law Interpretation	Interpretation of the Supreme People's Court on Certain Issues Concerning the Application of the Arbitration Law of the People's Republic of China
Arbitration Law	Arbitration Law of the People's Republic of China
BelCCI	International Arbitration Court of the Belarusian Chamber of Commerce and Industry
China	People's Republic of China
CICC	China International Commercial Court
CIETAC	China International Economic and Trade Arbitration Commission
Civil Code	Civil Code of People's Republic of China
Civil Procedure Law Interpretation	Interpretation of the Supreme People's Court concerning the Application of the Civil Procedure Law of the People's Republic of China
Civil Procedure Law	Civil Procedure Law of the People's Republic of China
Co.	Company
Contract Law	Contract Law of the People's Republic of China
Corp.	Corporation
ed.	Edition
etc.	Et cetera

FAI	The Arbitration Institute of the Finland Chamber of Commerce
FOSFA	The Federation of Oils, Seeds and Fats Association Ltd.
GAFTA	The Grain and Feed Trade Association
HKIAC	Hong Kong International Arbitration Centre
Hong Kong	Hong Kong Special Administrative Region
i.e.	Id est (that is)
IBA	International Bar Association
ICA	International Cotton Association
ICC	International Court of Arbitration of the International Chamber of Commerce
ICDR	International Centre for Dispute Resolution
JCAA	Japan Commercial Arbitration Association
KCAB	Korean Commercial Arbitration Board
L.P.	Limited Partnership
LCIA	London Court of International Arbitration
LMAA	London Maritime Arbitrators Association
Ltd.	Limited
Macao	Macao Special Administrative Region
Model Law	UNCITRAL Model Law on International Commercial Arbitration
New York Convention	Convention on the Recognition and Enforcement of Foreign Arbitral Awards
No./Nos.	Number/Numbers
p./pp.	Page/Pages
RFCC	International Commercial Arbitration Court at the Russian Federation Chamber of Commerce
SCC	Arbitration Institute of the Stockholm Chamber of Commerce
SCIA	Shenzhen Court of International Arbitration
SIAC	Singapore International Arbitration Centre
SICOM	Singapore Commodity Exchange Limited
SPC	Supreme People's Court of China
UK	United Kingdom
UNCITRAL	United Nations Commission on International Trade Law
v.	Versus (against)

Table of Cases

Chapter 1

1.1 Nonexistence of Arbitration Agreement

Luck Treat Ltd. v. Zhong Yuan Cheng Commercial Investment Holdings Co., Ltd. (2019) Zui Gao Fa Min Te No. 1

Shibing Yuanxin Real Estate Development Co., Ltd. of Guizhou Province v. Yingtan Fenghua Construction Engineering Co., Ltd. (2018) Yu Min Zhong No. 568

Liao v. Zhang (2019) Yu Min Zhong No. 77

Huang v. Yuanzheng Small Loan Co., Ltd., Wanzhou District, Chongqing City (2018) Yu Min Zhong No. 386

Chongqing Bayue Construction and Installation Engineering Co., Ltd. v. Chongqing Weiping Real Estate Development Co., Ltd. (2018) Yu Min Zhong No. 569

University of Science and Technology of China v. Anhui Sanjian Engineering Co., Ltd. (2018) Wan Min Te No. 1

Ge v. Zhejiang Xinhua Commodity Exchange Center Co., Ltd. (2019) Zhe 02 Min Te No. 20

Yue v. Qian (2019) Su 11 Min Te No. 3

Guoji Construction Group Co., Ltd. v. Shanghai Zhenxing Tourism Co., Ltd. (2018) Qiong 01 Min Te No. 144

China Development Bank Securities Co., Ltd. v. Shanghai Huaxin International Group Ltd. (2019) Jing 04 Min Te No. 387

Lin v. Sifang Yufeng Investment Co., Ltd., et al. (2019) Jing 04 Min Te No. 198

Pan v. Beijing Xicheng Branch of Shenzhen Zhenai Information Technology Co., Ltd. (2019) Jing 04 Min Te No. 180

Wang v. Shenzhen Chuangdongfang Fuben Investment Enterprise(L.P.), et al. (2019) Jing 04 Min Te No. 174

Shanxi Gas Industry Group Co., Ltd. v. Linklaters (2015) Si Zhong Min (Shang) Te Zi No. 327

Hengfeng Real Estate Co., Ltd. v. Beijing Urban Construction Real Estate Development Co., Ltd., et al. San Zhong Min Te Zi No. 09095

Shanghai Zhongyun Asset Management Co., Ltd., et al. v. Chen, et al. (2015) San Zhong Min (Shang) Te Zi No. 10138

Shanghai Fengqing Chemical Co., Ltd. v. Shanghai Branch of DBS Bank (China) Limited (2016) Jing 02 Min Te No. 94

Yang v. Yangpu China Railway Xinlong Trading Co., Ltd. (2013) Yi Zhong Min Te Zi No. 9618

Henan Yawen Hotel Co., Ltd. v. Tengsheng Building Decoration Co., Ltd (2019) Yu 01 Min Te No. 15

Huizhou International Container Terminal Co., Ltd. v. Guangzhou Ronghaitai Dredging Engineering Co., Ltd. (2018) Yue 01 Min Te No. 1220

Guangzhou Baijiaxin Group Co., Ltd. v. Guangzhou Zhujiang Sub-branch of Agricultural Bank of China Co., Ltd. (2018) Yue 01 Min Te No. 1230

Huang v. Guangzhou Zhongyong Small Loan Co., Ltd. (2019) Yue 01 Min Te No. 555

Shenzhen Hongguangyang Vacuum Technology Co., Ltd. v. Li (2013) Shen Zhong Fa She Wai Zhong Zi No. 46

Shanghai Xiangfu Real Estate Development Co., Ltd. v. Hangzhou Binjiang Real Estate Group Co., Ltd. (2018) Hu 02 Min Te No. 458

The People's Government of Hunan Province, et al. v. Triumph International Investment (Macau) Co., Ltd., et al. (2015) Chang Zhong Min Wu Zhong Zi No. 01749

Fuzhou Haisheng Property Management Service Co., Ltd. v. Shang (2014) Rong Min Ren Zi No. 2

Huzhou Fengrun Real Estate Co., Ltd. v. Li Zhe 06 Min Te No. 23

Hangzhou Hanxin Machinery Manufacturing Co., Ltd. v. Zhejiang Huanyu Construction Group Co., Ltd. (2011) Zhe Shao Zhong Que Zi No. 6

Wuxi Wantong Real Estate Development Co., Ltd. v. Changzhou Jiacheng Construction Engineering Co., Ltd., et al. (2015) Xi Min Zhong Shen Zi No. 00381

Xu v. High-tech Sub-branch of Chongqing Three Gorges Bank Co., Ltd. (2016) Yu 01 Min Te No. 1009

Shanghai Siemens High Voltage Switchgear Co., Ltd. v. Wuxi Branch of China Pacific Property Insurance Co., Ltd. Hu 74 Min Te No. 10

Shenhua Coal Transportation and Marketing Co. v. Marinick Shipping Co. (2013) Min Si Ta Zi No. 4.

1.2 Multi-tiered Disputes Resolution Clause

Shandong Hongxingyuan Food Co., Ltd., et al. v Suqian Zhongshan Tianrui Liding Venture Capital Center (L.P.) (2018) Jing 04 Min Te No. 146 (1).

National Company (State X) v. (1) Company A (State Y), (2) Company B (State X), (3) Company C (State X), ICC Case No. 11490

State Joint Stock Company (Uzbekistan) v. State agency (India), Final Award, ICC
    Case No. 14667, 2011
Runhe Development Co., Ltd.'s application for non-enforcement of arbitral awards
    (2008) Min Si Ta Zi No. 1

1.3 Transfer of Contract Rights

Beijing Saiaotu Technology Development Co., Ltd. v. Zhang (2018) Jing 04 Min Te
    No. 235
Chongqing Bishan Jinchun Small Loan Co., Ltd. v. Chongqing Rail Transit (Group)
    Co., Ltd. (2017) Yu 0120 Min Chu No. 2096
Kunshan Xingsheng Construction Development Co., Ltd. v. Shanghai Hengtai Law
    Firm (2017) Su 05 Min Te No. 61
Weiming Composite Materials (Huai'an) Co., Ltd. v. Zhang (2017) Su 08 Min Te
    No. 75
Taiyuan Jinxiang Enterprise Management Consulting Co., Ltd. v. Xinjiang Daming
    Animal Husbandry Co., Ltd., et al. (2016) Zui Gao Fa Min Xia Zhong No. 273

1.4 Standard Form Contract

Chen v. Beijing HB World Network Technology Co., Ltd. (2017) Jing 03 Min Te
    Jian No. 8
Ya'an Dayuan Real Estate Development Co., Ltd. v. Ya'an Municipal Bureau of
    Land and Resources (2017) Zui Gao Fa Min Zhong No. 91
Qiu, et al. v. Kunming Bangsheng Real Estate Development Co., Ltd. (2009) Kun
    Min Yi Chu Zi No. 1
Li v. Jining Center Branch of AXA Tianping Property Insurance Co., Ltd. (2016) Lu
    11 Min Xia Zhong No. 90
Qiu, et al. v. Kunming Bangsheng Real Estate Development Co., Ltd. (2009) Kun
    Min Yi Chu Zi No.1
Bai v. Taiyuan Yingze Branch of the People's Insurance Company of China (2016)
    Jin 11 Min Xia Zhong No. 55
Chen v. Beijing HB World Network Technology Co., Ltd. (2017) Jing 03 Min Te
    Jian No. 8
Yang v. Huaihua Central Branch of the Bank of China Insurance Co., Ltd. (2014)
    Huai Zhong Min Er Zhong Zi No. 91
Luohe Branch of China XXXX Insurance Co., Ltd. v. Linying County Branch of
    Luohe City XX Company (2009) Luo Min Er Zhong Zi No. 147
Ya'an Dayuan Real Estate Development Co., Ltd. v. Ya'an Municipal Bureau of
    Land and Resources (2017) Zui Gao Fa Min Zhong No. 91

1.5 The Dismissal of Law suits *Ex Officio*

Hu v. Wang, et al. (2018) E 01 Min Zhong No. 5438
Wang, et al. v. Hubei Chenggong Real Estate Development Co., Ltd., et al. (2018) E
    01 Min Zhong No. 5174
Song v. Zhumadian Xinghai Real Estate Co., Ltd., et al. (2019) Yu 01 Min Zhong
    No. 4497

1.6 The Principle of Independence of Arbitration Clauses

Singapore Yideman Asia Pte. Ltd. v. Wuxi Huaxin Cocoa Food Co., Ltd. (2001) Min
    Si Ta Zi No. 43

Chapter 2

2.1 "Arbitration or litigation" Clause

Reply of the SPC on the Request for Instructions on Determining the Validity of the
    Foreign Arbitration Clause between Wang v. Dongguan Weiyang Sports Equip-
    ment Co., Ltd. et al. (2012) Min Si Ta Zi No. 52 Reply of the SPC on the Request
    for Instructions on the Validity of the Arbitration Clause in the Contract Termi-
    nation Dispute between Yanzhou Haoke Weibo Mining Engineering Co., Ltd. v.
    A. WEBERS. A. et al. (2009) Min Si Ta Zi No.19
Wuhan Weisidun Network Technology Co., Ltd. v. Shichuang Home Decoration
    Group (Lanzhou) Co., Ltd. (2019) Er 01 Min Te No.282
Xian v. Guangzhou Shangjian Decoration Design Co., Ltd. (2019) Yue 01 Min Xia
    Zhong No.231

2.2 "May" Apply for Arbitration

Licheng Yibo Aluminum Alloy Processing Plant v. Shenzhen Hongtao Decoration
    Co., Ltd. (2019) Lu 01 Min Te No.46
Reply of SPC on the Request for Instructions in the Case of Anhui Hefei United
    Power Generation Co., Ltd. v. Alstom Power Generation Co., Ltd. (2003) Min Si
    Ta Zi No.7
Beijing Branch of the People's Property Insurance Co., Ltd. v. Licheng Tongda
    Mining Co., Ltd. (2014) Chang Min Zhong Zi No.00919
China Light Sanlian International Trade Co., Ltd. v. Tata International Metals (Asia)
    Limited (2017) Jing 04 Min Te No.23
Zhongshan Ganghong Building Materials Co., Ltd., v. China Railway Seventh
    Bureau Group Zhengzhou Engineering Co., Ltd. (2018) Yue 20 Min Te No.176

Shanghai Hanshu Cosmetics Co., Ltd. v. NBA Ssports Culture Development (Beijing) Co., Ltd. (2020) Jing 04 Min Te No.20
Tian v. Xiong,(2020) Yu 01 Min Te No.17 Liu v. Diantong Angel (Shanghai) Investment Co., Ltd. (2015) Er Zhong Min Te Zi No.03923

2.3 "First Arbitration Then Litigation" Clause

Jiangsu Jinxia Construction Group Co., Ltd., v. Shanxi Yirong Real Estate Development Co., Ltd. (2019) Zui Gao Fa Min Zhong No.279
Inner Mongolia Jixiang Coal Industry Co., Ltd. v. Tianjin Metallurgical Group Trading Co., Ltd., (2013) Min Er Zhong Zi No.81
Sichuan Lanjun Land Industrial Co., Ltd. v. Zigong No.1 Construction Engineering Company (2014) Mian Min Zhong Zi No.26
Anhui Dilong Pipeline Trenchless Engineering Co., Ltd. v. Nanjing Hongkun Telecom Engineering Design Co., Ltd. (2017) Su Min Shen No. 4452
Beijing Xinhua Multimedia Data Co., Ltd. v. Urumqi Shengshi Weimi Media Information Technology Co., Ltd., (2019) Jing 04 Min Te No.382

2.4 Multiple Related Agreements

Jiangsu Suzhong Construction Group Co., Ltd., v. Handan JIAYE Real Estate Development Co., Ltd. (2017) Zui Gao Fa Min Xia Zhong No.76
Zeng v. Xiamen Junhao Real Estate Development Co., Ltd., (2016) Min 02 Min Zhong No.1303
Handan Second Construction and Installation Co., Ltd. v. Mingmen Real Estate (Anyang) Co., Ltd., (2015) Han Shi Zhi Yi Zi No.00125
Beijing Normal University Anbo Education Technology Co., Ltd. v. Changsha Yaxing Real Estate Development Co., Ltd. (2014) Min Yi Zhong Zi No.24
Beijing Zhonghai Wobang Energy Investment Co., Ltd. v. Shanxi Dingsheng Construction and Installation Engineering Co., Ltd. (2016) Shan 01 Min Te No.270
Hunan Huaxia Construction Co., Ltd. v. Changde Arts and Crafts School, (2015) Zhi Shen Zi No.33

2.5 Main Contract and Guarantee Contract

Beijing Allianz Real Estate Development Co., Ltd. v. Beijing Anhengda Investment Co., Ltd. et al. (2014) Min Er Zhong Zi No.00084
China Construction Bank Co., Ltd. Zhejiang Branch Business Department v. Xue et al. (2015) Hang Xia Shang Chu Zi No.00953

Reply of the SPC on the Request of Yulin Intermediate People's Court for Instructions
    Not to Enforce the Foreign Arbitration Case of Dongxun Investment Co., Ltd.
    (2006) Min Si Ta Zi No.24
Reply of the SPC to the Request for Instructions on the Application of Chengdu
    Youbang Stationery Company and Wang Guojian for Revocation of Arbitral
    Award No. 601 [2011] of Shenzhen Arbitration Commission (2013) Min Si Ta Zi
    No.9

2.6 Unilateral Document

China National Complete Equipment Import and Export Tianjin Company v.
    Shandong Xinhua Pharmaceutical Group Co., Ltd. (2013) Zhi Jian Zi No.182

2.7 Unilateral Commitment Letter

Guangxi Investment Group International Co., Ltd.v. Guangxi Jiahe Investment Co.,
    Ltd. and Guangxi Investment Group Hengyuan Trading Co., Ltd. (2019) Zui Gao
    Fa Min Xia Zhong No.19

Chapter 3

3.1 Nationality of Arbitral Awards Made by Foreign Arbitration Institutions in Mainland

Brentwood Industries, Inc. (U.S.A) v. Guangdong Faanlong Machinery Equipment
    Engineering Co., Ltd. (2015) Sui Zhong Fa Min Si Chu Zi No.62

3.2 Inaccurate Arbitration Institution Name

Reply of the SPC to the Request for Instructions on Determining the Force of an
    Arbitral Agreement (2005) Min Si Ta Zi No.52
International Entertainment Overseas Co., Ltd. v. Hangzhou Little Donkey Sports
    Brokerage Co., Ltd. (2013) Min Si Ta Zi No.53
Jiujiang Hongbai Industry and Trade Co., Ltd., v. Jiujiang Shengchaoxinye Tech-
    nology Co., Ltd. (2018) Gan Min Zhong No.112
Qingdao Antaixin Group Co., Ltd. v. Chalco International Engineering Equipment
    Co., Ltd. et al. (2017) Jing 02 Min Te No.228
National Technology Co., Ltd. v. Epekson Microelectronics Co., Ltd. (2014) Shen
    Zhong Fa She Wai Zhong Zi No.32

3.3 "Local" Arbitration Commission

Du v.Jiangxi Tianma Investment Real Estate Co., Ltd. (2018) Gan Min Zhong No.460

Gansu PetroChina Kunlun Gas Construction and Installation Investment Co., Ltd. v. Lanzhou Xiaoshaomenwai Central Heating Station (2018) Gan Min Zai No.5

Beijing Zhonghai Wobang Energy Investment Co., Ltd. v. Shaanxi Dingsheng Construction and Installation Engineering Co., Ltd. (2016) Shan 01 Min Te No.270

Sanya Lanwan Engineering Co., Ltd. v. Tianjin Xin'an Construction Engineering Co., Ltd. (2015) Qiong Li Yi Zhong Zi No.106

3.4 The Scope of "Local"

Jinghan Real Estate Group Co., Ltd. v. Langdu International Consulting (Beijing) Co., Ltd. (2020) Jing 01 Min Xia Zhong No.36

Northwest Construction Co., Ltd. v. Xi'an Shengjie Construction Engineering Co., Ltd. (2018) Shan 01 Min Te No.381

Liuzhou Longsheng Entertainment Management Co., Ltd. v. Guangxi Yingxuetang Pension Service Co., Ltd. (2019) Gui 02 Min Xia Zhong No.9

Sichuan Minzheng Construction Co., Ltd. v. Sichuan Taicheng Real Estate Development Co., Ltd. (2018) Chuan 13 Min Xia Zhong No.81

Pucheng Lvyuan Real Estate Co., Ltd. v. Pucheng County Bureau of Land and Resources of Shaanxi Province (2015) Min Yi Zhong Zi No.351

3.5 Arbitration Agreement with Arbitration Rules Only

Panjin Liaohe Oilfield Kaite Petroleum Equipment Co., Ltd., v. Bohai equipment Liaohe Heavy Industry Co., Ltd. (2017) Zui Gao Fa Min Xia Zhong No.255

Hebei Zhongxing Automobile Manufacturing Co., Ltd. v. Automotive Gate FZCO (2011) Shi Min Li Cai Zi No.00002

Reply of the SPC to the Request for Instructions on the Case concerning the Application of Züblin International GmbH and Wuxi Woke General Engineering Rubber Co., Ltd. For Determining the Validity of the Arbitration Agreement (2003) Min Si Ta Zi No.23

Reply of the SPC to the Request forInstructions on the Validity of an Arbitration Clause in a Sales Contract Dispute between Cangzhou Donghong Packing Material Co., Ltd. and France DMT Ltd. (2006) Min Si Ta Zi No.6

Reply of the SPC to the Request forInstructions on Contract Dispute between Taizhou Haopu Investment Company and Wicor Holding AG (2012) Min Si Ta Zi No.6

Reply of the SPC to the Request for Instructions on the Validity of the Arbitration Clause in the Case concerning the Dispute over the Sale and Purchase Contract between Ningbo Beilun Licheng Lubricating Oil Co., Ltd. and Formal Venture Corp. (2013) Min Si Ta Zi No.74

Chapter 4

4.1 Nonsignatory to Property Service Contract

C v. Shenzhen LM Property Management Co., Ltd. (2018) Yue 03 Min Te No. 245
Fang v. Guangzhou Jinhe Property Co. Ltd. (2014) Shui Zhong Fa Zhong Shen Zi
    No. 12
Jiao v. Beijing Kailai Property Management Co., Ltd. Guangzhou Branch (2018)
    Yue 01 Min Te No. 397, 398, 399, 400
Shi v. Guangzhou Panyu Junbang Property Management Co., Ltd. (2017) Yue 01
    Min Te No. 478
Liu v. Hainan Guanghua Jingrui Property Service Co., Ltd. (2014) Hai Zhong Fa
    Zhong Zi No. 34
Chen v. Fuzhou Rongqiao Property Management Co., Ltd. (2019) Min 01 Min Te
    No. 77
You v. Huaian Anzhongyuan Property Service Co., Ltd. (2018) Su 08 Min Te No. 14
Li v. Chongqing Yicai Property Management Co., Ltd. (2019) Yu 01 Min Te No. 91

4.2 Joint Venture Which is Nonsignatory to Joint Venture Contract

U.S.A. Huaying Company, Ltd. v. Haicheng Zhisheng Magnesium Products Co.,
    Ltd. (2017) Zui Gao Fa Min Zai No. 76

4.3 Insurance Subrogation Claimant

PICC Guangzhou Branch v. Harbin Electric Company Limited (2019) Zui Gao Fa
    Min Shen No. 236
TONGBAO (HONG KONG) OCEANIC CO. LIMITED v. China Continent Insur-
    ance Shanghai Branch (2017) Zui Gao Fa Min Xia Jian No.2
CPWorldPteLtd, MitsuiO.S.K.Lines, Ltd. v. Ping An Property & Casualty Insurance
    Company of China Shenzhen Branch (2015) Yue Gao Fa Li Min Zhong Zi No.
    602
Beijing Xiangheli International Shipping Co., Ltd. v. PICC Beijing Branch (2015)
    Lu Min Xia Zhong Zi No. 28
Zhuhai Hengji Daxin International Chemical Storage Co., Ltd. v. Ping An Property &
    Casualty Insurance Company of China Guangdong Branch (2014) Yue Gao a Li
    Min Zhong Zi No. 1875
China Continent Insurance Beijing Branch v. China Pacific Shipping Co., Ltd. (2014)
    Jin Hai Fa Shang Chu Zi No. 424-1
Beijing Xiangheli International Shipping Co., Ltd. v. PICC Beijing Branch (2014)
    Lu Min Xia Zhong Zi No. 540

TYANANAVIGATIONLTD v. PICC Beijing Branch (2014) Lu Min Xia Zhong Zi
   No. 547
Shenzhen Daguangfa Logistics Co., Ltd. v. PICC Shenzhen Branch (2013) Shen
   Zhong Fa Shang Zhong Zi No. 2313
Nondisclosed Party v. Nondisclosed Party (2011) Shen Zhong Fa Min Si Zhong Zi
   No. 245
Nondisclosed Party v. Nondisclosed Party (2008) Zhe Min Gao Zhong Zi No. 65
Nondisclosed Party v. Nondisclosed Party (2008) Zhe Min Gao Zhong Zi No. 149
Chongqing ABB Transformer Co., Ltd. v. Ping An Insurance Company of China
   Jiangsu Branch (2015) Su Shang Xia Zhong Zi No. 00101
Hubei Anjie Logistics Co., Ltd. v. Zurich Property Insurance (China) Co., Ltd.
   (2015)Er Zhong Min Te Zi No. 10119
Shenzhen South China Shipping Freight Co., Ltd. v. Dubang Property Insurance Co.,
   Ltd. Shenzhen Branch (2012) Shen Zhong Fa She Wai Zhong Zi No. 203
Beijing Branch of China Pacific Insurance (Group) Co., Ltd. v. China COSCO Logis-
   tics Co., Ltd., Tianjin Zhenhua Shipping Agency Co., Ltd. and Nile Dutch Africa
   Line B.V. (2009) Min Si Ta Zi No.11
China Ping An Property Insurance Co., Ltd. Sichuan Branch v. Beijing Xiangheli
   International Shipping Co., Ltd. and Jifa Shipping Co., Ltd. (2009) Min Si Ta Zi
   No.39
The Xiamen Branch of the People's Insurance Company of China v. The China-
   Poland Shipping Company (2004) Min Si Ta Zi No.43
The Shenzhen Branch of the People's Insurance Company of China, Ltd. v.
   Guangzhou Ocean Shipping Co., Ltd. (2005) Min Si Ta Zi No.29

4.4 Heir

Chen v. the Panyu branch of Guangzhou Rural Commercial Bank Co., Ltd. (2019)
   Yue 01 Min Te No. 1179
Jin et al. v. Jianyin Cultural Industry Equity Investment Fund (Tianjin) Co., Ltd.
   (2015) Er Zhong Min Te Zi No. 00437
Li v. the Industrial and Commercial Bank of China Co., Ltd. Liaoyuan Dongfanghong
   Sub-branch, (2016) Ji 04 Min Te No. 3
Zhu v. Li (2018) Jing 04 Min Te No. 117

4.5 Deregistered Enterprise

Li v. the Land Acquisition and Reserve Center of Zhijiang City (2017) Zui Gao Fa
   Min Shen No. 4911

4.6 Governmental Organ

Bazhong Municipal Government v. Sichuan Bawan Highway Co., Ltd. (2017) Jing 02 Min Te No. 11

Huixian Municipal Government v. Henan Xinling Highway Construction Investment Co., Ltd. (2015) Min Yi Zhong Zi No. 244

Yilin Town Government of Funing County v. Kaifa Xinquan Sewage Treatment (Funing) Co., Ltd. (2017) Jing Min Te No. 272

Dalian Chunbin Wood Industry Co., Ltd. v. Dalian Jinpu New District Urban and Rural Construction Bureau (2016) Liao 02 Min Te No. 78

Mingfa Group Wuxi Real Estate Development Co., Ltd. v. Wuxi Municipal Bureau of Land and Resources (2017) Su 02 Min Te No. 209

Fuzhou Phoenix Housing Acquisition and Engineering Office v. Fuzhou Hengxing Binhai Real Estate Co., Ltd.(2016) Min 02 Min Te No. 52

Zhangpu Zhonghuan Tianchuan Environmental Protection Water Co., Ltd. v. Zhangpu County Environmental Protection Bureau (2015) Min Shen Zi No. 3013

Anqing Municipal Land and Resources Bureau v. Anqing Muncipal Yingchun Real Estate Development Co., Ltd. (2017) Wan 08 Xing Xia Zhong No.1

Xu v. Song (2015) Zhe Jia Zhong Che Zi No. 16.

Jiaxing Municipal Bureau of Land and Resources v. Jiaxing Auchan Supermarket Co., Ltd. (2016) Zhe 04 Min Te No. 4

Shanxi Kailaisike Yaoci Culture Co., Ltd. v. Tongchuan Municipal Bureau of Land and Resources (2018) Shan 02 Min Te No. 4

4.7 Headquarters and Branch

Lanzhou New District Jiabo Cultural Development Co., Ltd. v. Guangzhou Boxia Architectural Design and Research Institute Co., Ltd. and its Lanzhou Branch (2018) Gan Min Zhong No. 453

Zhuang v. Jiangsu Shuntong Construction Group Co., Ltd. Changzhou Branch (2017) Su Zhi Fu No.240

Beijing Huahong Integrated Circuit Design Co., Ltd. v. Chengdu Qidong Youshi Technology Co., Ltd, (2017) Jing 01 Zhi Yi No. 48

Huang v. Shanxi Fourth Construction Group Co., Ltd.Sichuan Branch (2016) Chuan Zhi Fu No. 41

Chapter 5

5.1 Colleagueship

Beijing Liumingju Catering Management Co., Ltd. v. Beijing Beiguang Electronic Group Co., Ltd. (2019) Jing 04 Min Te No. 227

Guangzhou Mola Network Technology Co., Ltd. v. Tianjin Jiawu Warehousing Co., Ltd. & Guangzhou Yiruier Network Technology Co., Ltd. (2015) Hu Er Zhong Min Si (Shang) Che Zi No. 1.

Aba Prefecture Ciyun Ethnic Culture Co., Ltd. v. Dongguan Kaichuang Laser Technology Co., LTD. (2017) Yue 18 Min Te No. 9

Chifeng Urban Construction Investment (Group) Co., Ltd. v. Beijing Ouandihezhong Architectural Design Consulting Co., Ltd. (2017) Nei 04 Min Te No. 23

Anhui Wanji Real Estate Group Co., Ltd. v. Anhui Anchao Construction Engineering Co., Ltd. (2015) He Min Zhong Zi No. 00124

5.2 Conflict of Identity Between Arbitrators and Agents

Zhang v. Gu (2017) Su 02 Zhi Yi No. 93

Huaibei Changyuan CoalGangue Comprehensive Utilization Co.,Ltd. v. Suixi branch of Lianyungang East China Sea Construction and Installation Engineering Co., Ltd. (2017) Wan 06 Min Te No. 29

China Oriental Minsheng Investment Co., Ltd. v. Wan&Meng (2017) Gan 01 Min Te No. 31

Nanchang Huayu Building Industrial Co., Ltd. v. Jiangxi Dingchang Construction Engineering Co., Ltd. (2016) Gan 01 Min Te No. 62

Shanxi Construction Engineering (Group) Corporation v. Mengcheng Wanfo Shang-ping Co., Ltd. (2017) Wan 06 Min Te No. 59

Huang & Guo v. Li (2017) Qiong 01 Min Te No. 7

5.3 Time Limit for Challenge

Beijing Fuji Standard Dealer Circulation Information Technology Co., Ltd. and Tianjin Oriental Fuhai Equity Investment Fund Partnership (Limited partnership), et al. (2020) Jing 04 Min Te No. 114

Tianjin Huawu Trading Co., Ltd. and Tianjin Branch of China Export Credit Insurance Co., Ltd. (2018) Jing 04 Min Te No. 42

Chongqing Ganglong Industry and Trade (Group) Co., Ltd. v. Peng, (2018) Yue 08 Min Te No. 46

Nanjing Runzhao New Energy Technology Co., Ltd. v. Jiangsu Huwu Construction Group Co., Ltd.& Jiangsu Longkun Group Co., Ltd., et al. (2020) Su 10 Min Te No. 5

Hengyang Hongyu Construction Engineering Co., Ltd. v. Hengyang Yiyuan Real Estate Development Co., Ltd & Hunan Yinhai Real Estate Co., Ltd. (2020) Xiang 04 Min Te No. 1

China Construction Seventh Bureau Construction Decoration Engineering Co., Ltd. v. Ningbo Hongshan high-tech Panel Co., Ltd. (2016) Zhe 02 Min Te No. 113

Chapter 6

6.1 Arbitral Procedures and Judicial Procedures

Yangshuo Yuerong Hotel Co., Ltd. & Shanghai Zhongning Building Installation
  Senior Decoration Co., Ltd. (2018) Jing 04 Min Te No. 43
Guangdong Precious Metals Trading Center Co., Ltd. v. Guangdong Zhaoxin
  Precious Metals Trading Co., Ltd. (2018) Yue 01 Min Te No. 638
Hexing Glass Aluminum (Shanghai) Co., Ltd. v. Suzhou Industrial Park Sudong
  Glass Technology Co., Ltd. (2015) Hu Yi Zhong Min Si (Shang) Che Zi No. 50

6.2 The Service of Arbitral Award

Fairdeal Supplies Ltd. v. Shanxi Coal Import & Export Group Co., Ltd. (2018) Ji
  01Minchu No. 921
Japan Shin-Etsu Chemical Industry Co. Ltd. v. Jiangsu Zhongtian Technology Co.
  Ltd (2007) Min Si Ta Zi No. 26
JapanShin-etsu Chemical Industry Co.,Ltd v. Tianjin Xinmao Science & Technology
  Co.,Ltd (2007) Min Si Ta Zi No. 18
Mengadolado Co., Ltd. v. Zhejiang Zhancheng Construction Group Co., Ltd (2009)
  Min Si Ta Zi No. 46

6.3 No Telephone Number

Tianjin Minghongjia Mechanical & Electrical Trading Co. Ltd. v. Qingdao Renyuan
  Environmental Equipment Co. Ltd. (2019) Jing 04 Min Te No. 153
Sichuan Tianzhihui Construction Engineering Co., Ltd. v. Chongqing Zhixiang
  Pavement Technology Engineering Co., Ltd. (2019) Yu 01Min Te No. 308
Hainan Gusheng Industrial Investment Co., Ltd. v. Beijing Renji Real Estate
  Development Group Co., Ltd. (2018) Jing 03 Min Te No. 70

6.4 Negotiation

Jiang v. Li(2019) Jing 04 Min Te No. 310.
Liqi Investment Co. Ltd. v. LI (2014) Hui Zhong Fa Min Si Chu Zi No. 24.
Gu v. Zhejiang Zhongke Donghai Venture Capital Partnership (Limited Partnership),
  et al. (2016) Jing 02 Min Te No. 78
Cui v. Shanghai Guochun Venture Capital Co., Ltd. (2019) Hu 01 Min Te No. 250

6.5 Delay in Amending the Claim or Producing Evidence

Xia v. Beijing Yingsheng Asset Management Co., Ltd (2018) Jing 04 Min Te No. 306

6.6 Time Limit for Rendering the Award

Shenzhen Qianhai Jinshan Financial Services Co., Ltd. v. Shenzhen Tianyi Network Technology Co., Ltd (2013) Yue 03 Min Te No. 772
MohammedEnterprises (T) Ltd. v. Yiqi Africa Investment Co.Ltd. (2017)Jing 04 Min Te No. 41
Shenzhen Qianhai Jinshan Financial Services Co., Ltd. v. Shenzhen Tianyi Network Technology Co., Ltd. (2013) Yue 03 Min Te No 772

Chapter 7

7.1 Authenticity of Evidence

Nanyang Real Estate (Nanjing) Co., Ltd. v. Nanjing Jianghong Property Development Co., Ltd. (2018) Su 01 Min Te No. 237

7.2 Collection of Evidence

Zhang et al. v.Wang et al.(2019) Jing 04 Min Te No. 92.
Shanghai Shengjiu Investment Management Co., Ltd. v. Tianjin Jiajing Investment Consulting Co., Ltd. (2018) Jing 02 Min Te No. 2
Shanxi Yulongfeng Grain Purchase and Sale Co., Ltd. v. Beijing Huangcheng Cereals and Oils Co., Ltd. (2017) Jing 02 Min Te No. 171

7.3 Determination of Evidence

Beijing Heli Jinqiao System Integration Technology Co., Ltd. v. Beijing Xinli Hengfeng Technology Development Co., Ltd. (2018) Jing 04 Min Te No.88

7.4 Allocation of Burden of Proof

Beijing Bei'ao Shengdian International Cultural Development Co., Ltd. v. Beijing Beite Shengdi Technology Development Co., Ltd. Second Branch (2019) Jing 04 Min Te No.88

China Construction Railway Construction Co., Ltd. v. Shanxi Rongquan Industrial
    Co., Ltd. (2019) Jing 04 Min Te No.31

7.5 Concealment of Evidence

Beijing Jinqiao Investment Co., Ltd. et al. v. Yishuo Holdings Co., Ltd. et al. (2018)
    Jing 04 Min Te No.23

Chapter 8

8.1 Arbitration Involving Criminal Case

CITIC Securities Co., Ltd. v. Qian (2020) Jing 04 Min Te No.187.
Sinopec International Petroleum Exploration and Development Co., Ltd. v. UNI-
    TOPAsiaInvestmentLimited (2017) Jing 04 Min Te No. 39

8.2 Filing Litigation to Circumvent Arbitration Clause

Fuzhou Gulou District Housing Security and Real Estate Administration and Fuzhou
    Gulou District Construction Investment Management Center v. Fuzhou Hengxing
    Binhai Real Estate Co., Ltd. et al. (2019) Zui Gao Fa Min Zhong No. 188
Asia Optical Co., Inc. and Dongguan Xintai Optical Co., Ltd. v. Fujifilm Corpora-
    tion, Fujifilm (China) Investment Co., Ltd., Fujifilm (China) Investment Co., Ltd.
    Shenzhen Branch and Fujifilm Optoelectronics (Shenzhen) Co., Ltd. (2019) Zui
    Gao Fa Shang Chu No.2
Zhao v. Shenzhen Construction Industry Group Co., Ltd. and Nanjing Dingzheng
    Real Estate Co., Ltd. (2019) Su 01 Min Zhong No. 686
BHMINGING&PETROLEUMPTELTD v. Zhejiang Tianlu Energy Co., Ltd. (2017)
    Zhe 72 Min Chu No. 445.
Wang v. Qi(2018) Jing 02 Min Zhong No. 8902
SwissSingaporeOverseasEnterprisesPteLed v. Beijing Huitiansheng Agricultural
    Production Co., Ltd.and Li (2017) Lu 02 Min Chu No.88
Hua and Zeng v. Wen, Zhou, Shenzhen Litaihua Investment Management Co., Ltd.
    and Shenzhen Taikeyuan Trading Co., Ltd. (2016) Yue 03 Min Zhong No. 12015

8.3 Reasonable Expenses for Case Handling

Jia v. CITIC Securities Co., Ltd.(2018) Jing 04 Min Te No. 121
He v. Chengliwei Industrial Co., Ltd., Zhuhai Zhu'ao Cross-border Industrial Zone
    (2016) Yue 01 Min Te No. 155

Taixing Pharmaceutical Packaging Materials Co., Ltd. v. Air Products (Nanjing) Gas
   Co., Ltd. (2016) Jing 02 Min Te No. 85
Cao v. Chongqing Tanshi Finance Guarantee Co., Ltd. (2017) Yu 01 Min Te No. 822
Sichuan Yuqiao Iron Tower Co., Ltd. v. Sichuan Guanghan Eleventh Construction
   Engineering Co., Ltd. (2018) Chuang 06 Min Te No. 11

8.4 Contracts in Which the Name and the Actual Legal Relationship are Inconsistent

Hunan Tuotian Energy Saving Control Technology Co., Ltd. v. Changsha Machine
   Tool Co., Ltd. (2016) Xiang 01 Min Te No. 26
Huang and Mu v. Tianshui Hongye Real Estate Development Co., Ltd. (2012) Tian
   Zhi Zi No.02
Xianyang Guangyu Real Estate Development Co., Ltd. v. The 141st Division of the
   Shanxi Army Reserve Infantry of the Chinese People's Liberation Army, (2018)
   Shan 04 Min Te No.5
Reply of the SPC on Request for Instructions ReEnforcement of Award No. 224
   (2007) of China International Economic & Trade Arbitration Commission. (2008)
   Min Si Ta Zi No.34

8.5 Adjustment of Liquidated Damages

Hunan Lifeng Business Management Co., Ltd. v. Changsha Yangfan Real Estate
   Development Co., Ltd. (2020) Xiang 01 Min Te No.66
Guizhou Xinshengchang Real Estate Co., Ltd. v. Land and Resources Bureau of
   Dejiang County of Guizhou Province (2017) Zui Gao Fa Min Shen No. 4029
Hubei Jinliwu Real Estate Co., Ltd. v. Shenzhen Depusch Education Technology
   Co., Ltd. (2017) Zui Gao Fa Min Shen No. 177
Beijing Yuankun Law Firm v. Beijing Urban Construction Far East Construction
   Investment Group Co., Ltd. (2016) Jing Min Zai No.11
Xi'an Dapeng Biotechnology Co., Ltd. v. Shanxi Huayu Industrial Co., Ltd. and
   Xi'an Jingyi Property Management Co., Ltd. (2014) Min Shen Zi No. 2159
Chen v. Tang(2020) Jing 04 Min Te No. 325

8.6 Beyond the Scope of Arbitration

Reply of the SPC to the Request for Instructions on the Case Involving Wang Guolin's
   Application to Revoke Arbitral Award No. 3 (2012) of the China International
   Economic and Trade Arbitration Commission South China Sub-commission
   (2013) Min Si Ta Zi No. 8
Ruihuan Education Investment Management Co., Ltd. v. Shanxi Dade Education
   Industry Development Co., Ltd. et al. (2017) Jing 02 Min Te No. 14

Liu and Gao v. Zhongjing Industry (Group) Co., Ltd. (2018) Hu 01 Min Te No.129
CHENCO ChemicalEngineeringandConsultingGMBH v. DFD Chemical Co., Ltd.
    (2015) Xin Zhong Min San Chu Zi No. 53
Bright Morning Limited v. Yixing Leqi Textile Group Co., Ltd. (2016) Su 02 Xie
    Wai Ren No.1
IPCathayII L.P. v. Zhou et al.(2016) Jing 04 Ren Gang No.2

Chapter 9

9.1 Determination and Standards of Repeated Arbitration

Guan v. CNBM Information Technology Co., Ltd. (2019) Jing 04 Min Te No. 159
Guangzhou Hongyang Bags Co., Ltd. v. Zhongshan Branch of Bohai Bank Co., Ltd.
    (2018) Yue 01 Min Te No. 355
China Securities Co., Ltd. v. Yu(2019) Jing 04 Min Te No. 439.
Liaoning Hexin Decoration Engineering Co., Ltd. v. Zhang et al. (2016) Zui Gao Fa
    Min Zai No. 249
Li v. Lin(2018) Zui Gao Fa Min Shen No. 3879.
Chongqing Urban Construction Holdings (Group) Co., Ltd. v. Chongqing Qijiang
    Branch of Sichuan Tianxin Road and Bridge Engineering Co., Ltd. (2017) Yu 01
    Min Te No. 761
Zhuzhou First General Machinery Factory of Hunan Province v. Crane Branch of
    Zoomlion Engineering (2015) Chang Zhong Min Wu Zhong Zi No. 01994

9.2 Dismissal of Repeated Arbitration

Shandong Charming Culture and Entertainment Management Co., Ltd. v. Goldstone
    China Investment 2 Co., Ltd. (2017) Jing 04 Min Te No. 45
Guangzhou Hongyang Bags Co., Ltd. v. Zhongshan Branch of Bohai Bank Co., Ltd.
    (2018) Yue 01 Min Te No. 355
Shen v. Zhao et al.(2012) Zhe Jia Zhong Che Zi No. 2.
Tengxun Entertainment Co., Ltd. et al. v. Shanghai Tianhong Real Estate Investment
    Co., Ltd. (2015) Hu Er Zhong Min Si (Shang) Che Zi No. 58
A New Energy Development Co., Ltd. v. B Technology Co., Ltd. Administered by
    SCIA in 2020

9.3 Non-enenforceability Due to the Nonspecific Content of Awards

Lin v. Li(2017) Yue 01 Min Te No. 273
Wu (1) v. Wu (2)(2018) Zui Gao Fa Min Shen No. 5058
Shanghai Miao Ma Car Rental Co., Ltd. v. Le (2018) Hu 01 Min Te No. 471

9.4 Consequences of Revocation or Non-enforcementof Awards

Qingdao Yonghong Sports Tourism Resort Co., Ltd. v. Natural Resources Bureau of Huangdao District of Qingdao City (2019) Zui Gao Fa Min Zhong No. 1893

Inner Mongolia Huineng Coal Chemical Co., Ltd. v. Shanghai Blower Works Co., Ltd. (2017) Nei 06 Min Zhong No. 1144

Wang v. Liu (2017) Shan 02 Min Zhong No. 218

Huatong Electromechanical Group Co., Ltd. v. Ye (2017) Zhe Min Zai No. 345

9.5 Cancellation of Mediation Statement

Xinyu Zhongchuang Mining Co., Ltd. v. Ganxi Geological and Mineral Exploration and Development Institute of Jiangxi Geological Exploration Bureau (2019) Gan Min Te No. 2.

Cui v. Xu (2017) Lu Min Zhong No. 659

Hongtai Real Estate Development Co., Ltd. of Hanzhong City v. Hanshui Construction Engineering Co., Ltd. of Hanzhong City (2017) Shan 07 Min Te No. 5

Li v. Liu (2016) Jin Min Zhong No. 438

Li v. Ma, et al (2018) Yun 06 Min Zhong No. 1441

Lishui Liming Specialized Middle School v. Luo, et al. (2017) Zhe 11 Min Te No. 3

Ren, et al. v. Neihuang Forest Farm of Henan (2015) An Zhong Min Yi Chu Zi No. 87

Wei v. Liu (2016) Wan 06 Min Te No. 13

Xiaoyi Jinda Coal Coke Co., Ltd. v. Wu (2015) Jin Min Zhong Zi No. 416

Qin v. Li (2015) E Min Li Shang Zi No. 00337

Zhejiang XX Construction Engineering Co., Ltd. v. Zhejiang XX Clothing Co., Ltd (2012) Zhe Min Zai Zi No. 49

Zunyi Oriental Construction and Installation Co., Ltd. v. Guizhou Zhongjie New Energy Development Co., Ltd. (2018) Qian Min Zhong No. 1149

Han v. Jin (2015) Ji Zhong Min Zhong Zi No. 4

Liao v. X (2018) Yue Min Zhong No. 1868

Residents Committee of Lianhu Community, Dongdajie Street Office, Hantai District v. Hanzhong Hongtai Real Estate Development Co., Ltd., et al. (2017) Shan 07 Min Te No. 16

Wang v. Hanzhong Hongtai Real Estate Development Co., Ltd., et al. (2017) Shan 07 Min Te No. 15

9.6 Application of Persons Not Involved in the Case for Non-enforcement of Arbitral Award

Chen v. Zeng (2015) Shen Zhong Fa She Wai Zhong Zi No. 154

Ningming County Jiade Jinghua Real Estate Co., Ltd. v. Fourth Construction Engineering Company of Dianbai County, Guangdong Province (2017) Yue 01 Min Te No. 792

Zhuhai Guojia Education Investment Co., Ltd. v. Zhuhai Campus of Beijing Normal University (2014) Zhu Zhong Fa Min Si Zhong Zi No. 7

Liao v. Wen et al.(2018) Yue Min Zhong No. 1868

Shanxi Ruida Real Estate Development Co., Ltd. v. Dacheng Property Management Co. (2018) Shan Min Zhong No. 628

Residents Committee of Lianhu Community of Dongdajie Street Office of Hantai District v. Hanzhong Hongtai Real Estate Development Co., Ltd., et al. (2017) Shan 07 Min Te No. 16

Wang v. Hanzhong Hongtai Real Estate Development Co., Ltd., et al. (2017) Shan 07 Min Te No. 15

Guo v. Jiangsu Horse Club Real Estate Co., Ltd.(2014) Su Min Zhong Zi No. 203

Siemens Financial Leasing Co., Ltd. et al. v. Bankruptcy Liquidation Group of Jiangxi Hongwang Automobile Brake Manufacturing Co., Ltd., et al. (2018) Gan Zhi Fu No. 52

9.7 Application of Persons Not Involved in the Case for Non-enforcement of Mediation Statement

Zhen v. Hefei Anbang Property Management Co., Ltd. (2018) Wan 01 Zhi Yi No. 80

Tianjin Hengzeng Real Estate Development Co., Ltd. v. Zhang, (2016) Zui Gao Fa Zhi Jian No. 443

Guangzhou Hongsheng Solar Technology Co., Ltd. v. Guangzhou Youqing Daily Chemical Industry Co., Ltd. (2016) Yue 01 Zhi Yi No. 290

Bai v. Handan Rongbang Industrial Group Co., Ltd., et al. (2015) Han Shi Zhi Yi Zi No. 00135

Beijing Jingdeyuan Real Estate Development Co., Ltd. v. Taiyuan Daidler Enterprise Management Consulting Co., Ltd. (2013) Gao Zhi Fu Zi No. 104

Lingshui Yunhai Investment Co., Ltd. v. Sun (2018) Qiong 72 Zhi Yi No. 33

Liu v. Hou(2018) Lu 01 Zhi Yi No. 82

9.8 Arbitral Awards made by "Pre-arbitration"

Huizhong Litong Investment Management (Beijing) Co., Ltd. v. Chou (2018) Yue Zhi Fu No. 206

Shenzhen Xiaoniu Online Internet Information Consulting Co., Ltd. v. Bie (2017) E 10 Zhi No. 88

Shenzhen Xiaoniu Online Internet Information Consulting Co., Ltd. v. Zhang (2018) Liao 14 Zhi No. 38

Chapter 10

10.1 Violation of Mandatory Provisions of Laws

Beijing Polestar Travel Technology Co., Ltd. v. Sichuan Jinlicheng Clothing Co., Ltd. (2018) Jing 03 Min Te No. 46

Beijing Zhongxin Zhirong Investment Fund Management Co., Ltd. v. Ma (2018) Jing 03 Min Te No. 113

Beijing Grand Metropark Hotel Co., Ltd. v. Qinhuangdao Bohai Aluminum Curtain Wall Decoration Engineering Co., Ltd. (2018) Jing 04 Min Te No. 250

Dongying Jinmeng Construction &Installation Co., Ltd. v. Shandong Zhonghai Liqun Real Estate Co., Ltd. (2016) Lu 05 Min Te No. 9

Wuhan Chaofan Logistics (Ezhou) Co., Ltd., et al. v. CCCC Second Harbor Engineering Co., Ltd. (2015) E Wu Han Zhong Zhong Jian Zi No. 00159

Jiangsu Taishengda Construction Engineering Co., Ltd. v. Yancheng Dadi Real Estate Co., Ltd. (2014) Yan Min Zhong Shen Zi No. 0015

Huaxin Petroleum (Guangdong) Co., Ltd. v. Guangdong Zhongyu Energy Development Co., Ltd. (2013) Sui Zhong Fa Zhong Shen Zi No. 95

10.2 Violation of Policy Documents

Yang, et al. v. Ji(2019) Hu 01 Min Te No. 639

Shenzhen Qianhai Chengyue Asset Management Co., Ltd. v. Wang, et al. (2020) Jing 04 Jing Te No. 193

10.3 Conflicts with Effective Rulings of Courts

Reply to the Request for Instructions concerning the Applicant Castel Electronics Pty Ltd.'s Application for Recognition and Enforcement of Foreign Arbitral Awards (2013) Min Si Ta Zi No. 46

Automotive Gate FZCO, et al. v. Hebei Zhongxing Automobile Manufacturing Co., Ltd. (2017) Jing 04 Min Te No. 45

Hemofarm DD, et al. v. Jinan Yongning Pharmaceutical Co., Ltd. (2008) Min Si Ta Zi No. 11

Wicor Holding AG v. Taizhou Hope Investment Co., Ltd., (2015) Tai Zhong Shang Zhong Shen Zi No. 00004

Reply of the SPC to the Request for Instructions on the Non-Enforcement of the No. 18295/CYK Arbitral Award of ICC, (2016) Zui Gao Fa Min Ta No. 8

Reply of the SPC to the Request for Instructions on the Application of Castel Electronics Pty Ltd. of Recognition and Enforcement of Foreign Arbitral Award (2013) Min Si Ta Zi No. 46

Chapter 11

11.1 Arbitration Agreements

Wang v. Shenzhen Petrochemical Exchange Co., Ltd. & Shenzhen Qianhai Oil Laifu
    Petrochemical Investment Co., Ltd. & Guangzhou Helibao Payment Technology
    Co., Ltd. (2018) Yue 03 Min Zhong No. 8900
Shi v. Shenzhen Qianhai Yixiang Times Business Service Co., Ltd. (2018) Xiang
    0111 Min Chu No. 443
Shenzhen Qianhai Yinghua Fund Management Partnership (L.P.) v. Zhu (2018) Yue
    03 Min Chu No. 616
Shenzhen Xingyang Chemical Co., Ltd. v. Suining Yingchuangli Electronic Tech-
    nology Co., Ltd. (2018) Chuang 09 Min Xia Zhong No.3
Tianjin Zhongse International Trade Co., Ltd. v. Hongda International Trade Co.,
    Ltd. (2017) Jing Min Zhong No. 494
Taoyun (Beijing) Investment Fund Management Co., Ltd. & Shenzhen Taoyun Equity
    Investment Fund Management Center (L.P.) v. Zhang (2018) Jing 04 Min Te No.
    215
Tianjin Zhongse International Trade Co., Ltd. v. Hongda International Trade Co.,
    Ltd. (2017) Jing Min Zhong No. 494
Cao v. Zheng (2018) Yu 13 Min Zhong No.4713
Zhu v. Shenzhen Hehui Automobile Trade Co., Ltd. & Yougu (Shanghai) Information
    Technology Co., Ltd. (2018) Yue 03 Min Zhong No.511
Shanmei Coal Import and Export Co., Ltd. v. SINOSTEEL International Macao
    Offshore Business Service Co., Ltd. (2018) Lu Min Xia Zhong No.402.
Wenzhou Huazheng Packaging Co., Ltd. v. MARKENIMAS (Shanghai) Label
    Technology Co., Ltd. (2017) Zhe 03 Min Zhong No. 5536
Greenland Holding Group Co., Ltd. v. Beijing Dongfangjinhong Real Estate Co.,
    Ltd. (2018) Jing Min Xia Zhong No.41

11.2 Party to Arbitration

Harbin Electric Co., Ltd. v. The Guangzhou Branch of People's Property Insurance
    Co., Ltd. (2019) Zui Gao Fa Min Shen No.236
Henan Xinxiang Comprehensive Trade Co., Ltd. v. Guotou Coal Co., Ltd. & Henan
    Xinxing Coal Industry Co., Ltd. (2017) Jing 0101 Min Chu No.14520

11.3 Arbitration Institution

Guangzhou Xingyi Exhibition Service Co., Ltd. v. Shanghai Junjue Exhibition
    Service Co., Ltd. (2018) Yue 01 Min Zhong No. 2811

Li v. Shenzhen Hongde Mingjiang Decoration Design Engineering Co., Ltd. (2018) Yue 03 Min Zhong No. 19616

Chongqing Education Construction (Group) Co., Ltd. v. Chongqing Meijing Fireproof Material Co., Ltd. (2018) Yu 05 Min Te No. 125

Dongfang Rili (Chengdu) Electronic Control Equipment Co., Ltd. v. Guangzhou Shengying Automatic Control System Co., Ltd. (2018) Chuan 01 Min Te No. 21

11.4 Arbitration Proceedings

Yang & Ye v. Chen & Shenzhen Puyi Battery Technology Co., Ltd. (2018) Yue 03 Min Te No. 214

Puhua Youke (Beijing) Technology Co., Ltd. v. ILAC systems (Hong Kong) Co., Ltd. (2017) Jing 04 Min Te No. 47

Nanchang Zhongqun Garment Co., Ltd. v. Shenzhen Yidatong Enterprise Service Co., Ltd. (2018) Yue 03 Min Te No. 228

Dongguan Haichuan Chemical Co., Ltd. & Chen v. Shenzhen Jiasheng Supply Chain Co., Ltd. (2018) Yue 03 Min Te No. 46

Xiamen Tuoyuan Import & Export Co., Ltd. & Gong v. Shenzhen Yidatong Enterprise Service Co., Ltd. (2018) Yue 03 Min Te No. 204

Hebei Huamao Asset Management Co., Ltd. v. Zhang (2018) Ji 01 Zhi Yi No. 319

Beijing Hongan Construction Decoration Engineering Co., Ltd. v. Shibaishi (Shanghai) Construction Engineering Co., Ltd. (2018) Hu 02 Min Te No. 1.

Zhongshan Century Tuoda Advertising Co., Ltd. v. Zhongshan Kangda Clinic & Wang (2018) Yue 20 Min Te No. 13

Harbin Aowu Mechanical and Electrical Equipment Co., Ltd. v. Harbin Aowu Mechanical and Electrical Equipment Co., Ltd., et al. (2018) Jing 04 Min Te No. 212

Shanghai Pujing Chemical Technology Co., Ltd. v. Henan Shunda New Energy Technology Co., Ltd. (2018) Jing 04 Min Te No. 352

11.5 The Scope of Judicial Review: Substances and Procedures

Shanghai Yuanpu Investment Management Co., Ltd. v. Li Yue 03 Min Te No. 80Shanghai Yuanpu Investment Management Co., Ltd. v. Li Yue 03 Min Te No. 80

Dongguan Haichuan Chemical Co., Ltd. & Chen v. Shenzhen Jiasheng Supply Chain Co., Ltd. (2018) Yue 03 Min Te No. 46

Shenzhen YapaiOpto Electronic Devices Co., Ltd. v. Shenzhen Xinfeitong Optoelectronics Technology Co., Ltd. & Dongguan Xinfeitong Optoelectronics Technology Co., Ltd. (2018) Yue 03 Min Te No. 254

Guangzhou branch of Minsheng Banking Co., Inc. v. Zhang (2018) Yue Zhi Jian No. 63

Liao v. Wen (2018) Yue Min Zhong No. 1868

11.6 Arbitral Scope and Beyond the Scope of Submission to Arbitration

Shenzhen Shantou Special Cooperation Zone Dianjin Technology Co., Ltd. v.
    Shenzhen-Shantou Special Cooperation Zone Management Service Co., Ltd.
    (2017) Yue 03 Min Te No. 904
Shenzhen Dajiayi Industrial Development Co., Ltd. v. Guangzhou Chuangxi Property
    Management Co., Ltd. (2017) Yue 03 Min Te No. 773

11.7 Arbitrability and Public Policy

Tan v. Zhang, et al. (2018) Yue Min Zai No. 271
Shanghai Yuanpu Investment Management Co., Ltd. v. Li (2018) Yue 03 Min Te No.
    80
Beijing Pengyucheng Technology Development Co., Ltd. v. Jianwei Software
    Technology (Shanghai) Co., Ltd. (2018) Jing 01 Zhi Yi No.53

11.8 Others

Zhang, et al. v. Shenzhen Zhonghe Chunsheng Yihao Equity Investment Fund
    Partnership (L.P.) (2017) Yue 03 Min Chu No. 2618
Shenzhen-Shantou Special Cooperation Zone Dianjin Technology Co., Ltd.v.
    shenzhen-Shantou Special Cooperation Zone City Integrated Service Co., Ltd.
    (2018) Yue 15 Zhi Yi No. 3

Chapter 12

12.1 General Introduction

First Investment Corp. (Marshall Island) v. Fujian Mawei Shipbuilding Ltd.,Fujian
    Shipbuilding Industry Group Co., Ltd. (2006) Xia Hai Fa Ren Zi No. 1
Shin-Etsu Chemical Co., Ltd. v. Jiangsu Zhongtian Technology Co., Ltd. (2007) Su
    Min San Ta Zi No. 0002
China Shipping Development Co., Ltd. Freighter Co. v. Anhui Technology Imp. &
    Exp. Co., Ltd. (2006) Wu Hai Fa Shang Zi No. 13
Shin-Etsu Chemical Co., Ltd. v. Tianjin Xinmao Science & Technology Co., Ltd.
    (2006) Jin Gao Min Ta Zi No. 0006
Hemofarm DD, MAG International Trade Holding DD, Suramu Media Ltd. v. Jinan
    Yongning Pharmaceutical Co., Ltd. (2007) Lu Min Si Ta Zi No. 12
Lifu Candy (Shanghai) Co., Ltd. v. Shanghai Lianfu Food Co., Ltd. (2008) Hu Er
    Zhong Min Wu (Shang) Chu Zi No. 19

Voest-Alpine International Trading USA Corp. v. Jiangsu Provincial Foreign Trade Corp. (2008) Ning Min Wu Chu Zi No. 43

Samyoung System v. Li (2009) Hu Er Zhong Min Ren (Wai Zhong) Zi No. 1

GRDMinproc Ltd. v. Shanghai Flyingwheel Industry Co., Ltd. (2007)HuYi Zhong Min Wu (Shang) Chu Zi No. 116

I. Schroeder KG. (GmbH & Co.) v. Jiangsu Huada Food Industry Co., Ltd. (2009) Zhen Min San Zhong Zi No. 2

East Land Property Pte. Ltd. v. Zhejiang Xinxing Rubber Co., Ltd. (2009) Zhe Tai Zhong Que Zi No. 4

Noble Resource Pte. Ltd. v. Zhoushan Zhonghai Grain and Oil Industry Co., Ltd. (2007) Zhe Zhi Ta Zi No. 4

Concordia Trading B.V. v. Nantong Gangde Grease Co., Ltd. (2009) Su Min San Zhong Shen Zi No. 0001

American Foreign Trading Corp. v. Shenzhen Lionda Group Co., Ltd., et al. (2008) Yue Gao Fa Min Si Ta Zi No. 11

Wu v. Zhang (2009) Lu Min Si Ta Zi No. 2

Lehua MeilanHolding Co., et al. v. Tianjin Jiashijie Group Co., Ltd., et al. (2008) Jin Gao Min Si Ta Zi No. 0004

Addax Bv v. China-Base Ningbo Foreign Trade Co., Ltd. (2009) Zhe Zhi Ta Zi No. 2

Tianrui Hotel Investment Co., Ltd. v. Hangzhou Yiju Hotel Management Co., Ltd. (2010) Zhe Shang Wai Ta Zi No. 3

Tianrui Hotel Investment Co., Ltd. v. Hangzhou Heju Hanting Hotel Management Co., Ltd. (2010) Zhe Shang Wai Ta Zi No. 2

Tianrui Hotel Investment Co., Ltd. v. Hangzhou Heting Hotel Management Co., Ltd. (2010) Zhe Shang Wai Ta Zi No. 1

Mon Eldorado Co., Ltd. v. Zhejiang Zhancheng Construction Group Co., Ltd. (2009) Zhe Shao Min Que Zi No. 1

Shin-Etsu Chemical Co., Ltd. v. Jiangsu Zhongtian Technology Co., Ltd. (2010) Su Zhi Min Zhong Shen Zi No. 0002

DMT S.A. v. Chaozhou Huaye Packaging Materials Co., Ltd., et al. (2010) Yue Gao Fa Min Si Ta Zi No. 2

Louis Dreyfus CommoditiesAsia Co., Ltd. v. Guangdong Fuhong Oil Products Co., Ltd. (2009) Yue Gao Fa Min Si Ta Zi No. 10

Subway International B.V. v. Beijing Tepu Food Co., Ltd. (2011) Jing Gao FaNo. 157

Western Bulk Pte. Ltd. v. Beijing Sinosteel Tiantie Iron & Steel Trading Co., Ltd. (2010) Jin Hai Fa Que Zi No. 6

ALSTOM Technology Ltd. v. Zhejiang University New Technology Co., Ltd. (2012) Zhe Shang Wai Que Zi No. 1

Beijing Chaolai Xinsheng Sports & Leisure Co., Ltd. v. Beijing Suowang Zhixin Investment Consulting Co., Ltd. (2013) Jing Gao Fa No. 388

"Angfohuapin" Joint Venture Co., Ltd. v. Henan Haofeng Chemical Co., Ltd. (2012) Zheng Min San Chu Zi No. 37

Royal Food Import Co. v. Ningbo Youngor International Trade and Transportation Co., Ltd. (2012) Zhe Yong Zhong Que Zi No. 3

Proton Motors (China) Co., Ltd. v. Jinxing Heavy Industry Manufacturing Co., Ltd. (2012) Yue Gao Fa Zhong Fu Zi No. 3

Ruierma Food Co., Ltd. v. Zhanjiang Guanya Food Co., Ltd. (2011) Yue Gao Fa Min Si Ta Zi No. 15

Castel Electronics Pty Ltd. v. TCL Air Conditioner (Zhongshan) Co., Ltd. (2012) Yue Gao Fa Zhong Fu Zi No. 7

Allenberg Cotton Co. v. Ningbo Youngor International Trade and Transportation Co., Ltd. (2014) Zhe Shang Wai Que Zi No. 1

Daewoo Shipbuilding & Marine Engineering Co., Ltd. v. AlphaElephantInc., et al. (2014) Xia Hai Fa Ren Zi No. 14

CAIInternationalInc. v. Daxinhua Logistics Holdings (Group) Co., Ltd. (2014) Jing Hai Fa Que Zi No. 1

Jess Smith & Sons Cotton, LLC v. Wuxi Natural Textile Industry Co., Ltd., et al. (2013) Xi Shang Wai Zhong Shen Zi No. 0007

Ksenja Pte. Ltd. v. Guan (2014) Shen Zhong Fa She Wai Chu Zi No. 119

SK Networks Co., Ltd. v. Shanghai Pan Pacific Group Co., Ltd. (2014) Hu Yi Zhong Min Ren (Wai Zhong)Zi No. S1

Rick Steven Brouman v. Beijing Yadu Indoor Environmental Protection Technology Co., Ltd. (2014) Yi Zhong Min Te Zi No. 878

Spring Maritime Ltd.v. Shandong Haina Real Estate Co., Ltd. (2013) Qing Hai Fa Hai Shang Chu Zi No. 1032

Gloria Jones Co. v. Wuxi Dongxiang Knitting Textile Co., Ltd. (2014) Xi Shang Wai Zhong Shen Zi No. 0004

Xiamen Hongxin Shipping Co., Ltd. v. Wuhan Iron and Steel Group International Economic and Trade Corporation (2014) Wu Hai Fa Ta Zi No. 00042

Marumo Corp v. Beijing Delin Golf Sports Development Co., Ltd. (2013) Er Zhong Min Te Zi No. 12593

Summer Maritime Ltd. v. Shandong Haina Real Estate Co., Ltd. (2014) Qing Hai Fa Hai Shang Chu Zi No. 721

Trust Bridge Pte. Ltd. v. Qingdao Yongxinda Petrochemical Co., Ltd. (2014) Qing Ren Zhi Zi No. 1

Allenberg Cotton Co. v. Anhui Yuhua Textile Co., Ltd. (2014) He Min Te Zi No. 00001-3

Olam International Ltd. v. Jingshan Weijia Textile Enterprise Co., Ltd. (2013) EJing Men Min San Chu Zi No. 00019

Australia CBH Grain Co., Ltd. v. Hebei Sihai Development Co., Ltd. (2013) Shi Min Wu Chu Zi No. 00525

German Schuleda Co. v. China Dandong Junao Food Co., Ltd. (2012) Dan Min San Te Zi No. 00001

Toyoshima & Co., Ltd. v. Shandong Zouping Shenghe Textile Co., Ltd. (2014) Bin Zhong Min Er Wai Zi No. 1

Queensland Cotton Corporation Pty Ltd. v. Jiangyin Huafu Textile & Clothing Corporation Ltd. (2013) Xi Shang Wai Zhong Shen Zi No. 0002

TactCommunications, Inc.v. Quanzhou Cardinu Travel Products Co., Ltd. (2013) Quan Min Ren Zi No. 35

JacobsonGolfCourseDesign,Inc. v. Sihui Zhenhuiyuan Property Development Co., Ltd., et al. (2015) Zhao Zhong Fa Min Yi Zhong Zi No. 26

Jess Smith & Sons Cotton, LLC v. Wuxi Natural Textile Industry Co., Ltd., et al. (2013) Xi Shang Wai Zhong Shen Zi No. 0007

MinajHoldingsLimited v. Rizhao Qihan International Import & Export Trade Co., Ltd. (2014) Ri Min San Chu Zi No. 10

Allenberg Cotton Co. v. Jiangsu Nijiaxiang Group Co., Ltd. (2013) Xi Shang Wai Zhong Shen Zi No. 0009

Super Sonic Imagine S.A. v. Beijing Huaxing Yuanda International Technology Co., Ltd. (2015) Si Zhong Min (Shang)Te Zi No. 00195

Arkitema K/S v. Cui (2015) Si Zhong Min (Shang)Te Zi No. 57

Krasilnikov Sergei Vitalyevich v. Heilongjiang Xinghe Dadao Automobile Trade Co., Ltd. (2015) Hei Zhong She Wai Shang Cai Zi No. 1

Noble Resources Pte. Ltd. v. Carrad Holding Co., Ltd. (2015) De Zhong Min Chu Zi No. 3

Li v. Yanshan County Yonghui Steel Pipe Co., Ltd. (2015) Cang Min Te Zi No. 13

LouisDreyfus Australia Ltd. v. Jiangsu Nijiaxiang Group Co., Ltd. (2013) Xi Shang Wai Zhong Shen Zi No. 0003

Ostin Ltd. v. Zhejiang Huateng Clothing Co., Ltd. (2015) Zhe Shao Zhong Que Zi No. 3

Siemens International Trading (Shanghai) Co., Ltd. v. Shanghai Golden Land Co., Ltd. (2013) Hu Yi Zhong Min Ren (Wai Zhong)Zi No. 2

Trinity Bulk Shipping Ltd. v. Jiangsu Huihong International Group Native Product Import & Export Co., Ltd., et al. (2015) EGao Fa No. 283

FSG Automotive Holding AG v. Wuhan Fanzhou Machinery Manufacturing Co., Ltd. EGao Fa No. 405

Spliethoff's Bevrachtingskantoor B.V. v. China Electronics Import &Export Shandong Co.,et al. (2015) Lu Min Si Ta Zi No. 6

COSCO Bulk Transport Co., Ltd. v. Jiangsu Fumet International Trade Co., Ltd. (2014) Wu Hai Fa Ta Zi No. 00038

Trafigura Pte. Ltd. v. Guangzhou China Coal South China Sales Co., Ltd. (2015) Sui Zhong Fa Min Si Chu Zi No. 4

Toyoshima & Co., Ltd. v. Qingdao Yinxia Trading Co., Ltd (2014) Qing Ren Zhi Zi No. 2

GEAHeatExchangers,Inc. v. Guangdong Changying Heavy Industry Co.,Ltd. (2015) Fo Zhong Fa Min Er Zhong Zi No. 7

Fukui Bank Co. v. Shanghai Yekao Optical Co., Ltd. (2014) Hu Er Zhong Min Ren (Wai Zhong)Zi No. 1

Ecom Agroindustrial Asia Pte. Ltd. v. Qingdao Jinchangjiang Group Penglai Textile and Garment Co., Ltd. (2015) Lu Min Si Ta Zi No. 1

Toyoshima & Co., Ltd. v. Gaomi Luyuan Textile Co., Ltd. (2015) Lu Min Si Ta Zi No. 2

Toyoshima & Co., Ltd. v. Changyi Kunfu Textile Co., Ltd. (2015) Lu Min Si Ta Zi
    No. 3
Paul Reinhart AG v. Hubei Qinghe Textile Co., Ltd. EGao Fa No. 518
Glencore Grain B.V. v. Shandong Jinhe Cotton & Linen Co., Ltd. (2015) Ji Shang
    Wai Chu Zi No. 8
Olam International Ltd. v. Wuxi Natural Textile Industry Co., Ltd. (2015) Xi Shang
    Wai Zhong Shen Zi No. 4
Noble Resource Pte. Ltd. v. Hubei Qinghe Textile Co., Ltd. (2015) EYi Chang Zhong
    Min Ren Zi No. 00001
Plexus Cotton Ltd. v. Carrad Holding Co., Ltd. (2016) Lu 14Xie Wai Ren No. 1
LH Asian Trade Finance Fund Ltd. v. Zhengzhou Aluminum Co., Ltd. (2014) Zheng
    Min San Chu Zi No. 50
Singapore Huacheng Holdings Co., Ltd. v. Anhui Huantai Metal Mineral Import
    &Export Co., Ltd. (2015) He Min Te Zi No. 00004
ADM Asia-Pacific Trading Pte. Ltd. v. Shandong Yahe Agriculture Co., Ltd. (2017)
    Lu 11Xie Wai Ren No. 2
AOT Trading AG v. Jiangsu Huihong International Group Zhongding Holding Co.,
    Ltd. (2016) Su 01Xie Wai Ren No.2
BBC Chartering & Logistic GmbH & Co. KG v. Shanghai Furui International Freight
    Forwarding Co., Ltd. (2015) Hu Hai Fa Min Ren Zi No. 2
WicorHoldingAG v. Taizhou Haopu Investment Co., Ltd. (2015) Tai Zhong Shang
    Zhong Shen Zi No. 00004
J & D IB Co v.Tian, et al. (2015) Yan Zhong Min San Chu Zi No. 858
Olam International Ltd. v. Zibo Yinhua Cotton & Linen Co., Ltd. (2015) Zi Min Te
    Zi No. 1
Glencore International AG v. Zhejiang Qiying Energy Chemical Co., Ltd. (2014)
    Zhe Yong Zhong Que Zi No. 1
Jiangyin Huacheng Industrial Co., Ltd. v. Pipavav Defense and Offshore Engineering
    Co., Ltd (2016) E72Xie Wai Ren No. 4
Clavon Engineering Pte. Ltd. v. Pipavav Defense and Offshore Engineering Co., Ltd
    (2016) E72Xie Wai Ren No. 3
Noble Resource Pte. Ltd. v. Zhejiang Xiongsheng Industrial Co., Ltd. (2014) Zhe
    Shao Zhong Que Zi No. 1
United Company for Ginning and Cotton Export Co. v. Wuxi Natural Green Fiber
    Technology Co., Ltd. (2013) Xi Shang Wai Zhong Shen Zi No. 0005
Schiffahrts-GesellschaftMS "MENTOR" mbh & Co. KG v. Da Xinhua Shiping
    (Yantai) Co., Ltd. (2015) Qing Hai Fa Hai Shang Chu Zi No. 1552
Tajco A/S v. JanSzklany (2015) Shen Zhong Min Si Te Zi No. 29 Remote Wireless
    Information Technology Co., Ltd. v. Beijing Guangxin Jiashi Technology Co.,
    Ltd. (2014) San Zhong Min (Shang)Te Zi No. 12398
Johannm.K.Blumenthal GmbH & Co. KG v. Jiangsu Rongsheng Heavy Industry
    Co., Ltd. (2015) Hu Hai Fa Min Ren Zi No. 3
Compass Cotton B.V. v. Shandong Yanggu Shunda Textile Co., Ltd. (2014) Liao
    Min Wu Chu Zi No. 4

BBC Chartering & Logistic GmbH & Co. KG v. Zhenjiang Aihai Ship Industry Co., Ltd. (2016) E72Xie Wai Ren No. 2

BrightMorningLimited. v. Yixing Leqi Textile Group Co., Ltd. (2016) Su 02Xie Wai Ren No. 1

SPS European Chemicals Co v. Panjin Heyun Industrial Group Co., Ltd. (2016) Liao 02Xie Wai Ren No. 12

Oman Shipping Co. Soac v. Jiangsu Rongsheng Heavy Industry Co., Ltd. (2017) E72Xie Wai Ren No.1

Chenco Chemical Engineering and Consulting GmbH v. Do-Fluoride Chemicals Co., Ltd. (2015) Xin Zhong Min San Chu Zi No. 53

Russian Season Ltd. v. Yongkang Tefan Import & Export Co., Ltd. (2016) Zhe 07Xie Wai Ren No. 3

Rich Islands Ltd. v. Jiangsu Rongsheng Heavy Industry Co., Ltd. (2017) E72Xie Wai Ren No. 2

Royal Food Import Corp. v. Suqian Canned Food Co., Ltd. (2016) Su 13Xie Wai Ren No. 1

Caravel Shipping Ltd. v. Shandong Yahe Agriculture Co., Ltd., et al. (2017) Lu 72Xie Wai Ren No. 1

Rhine Star Ltd. v. Jiangsu Rongsheng Heavy Industry Co., Ltd. (2017) E72Xie Wai Ren No. 5

Plexus Cotton Ltd. v. Jiangsu Jinfang Industrial Co., Ltd. (2014) Yan Shang Wai Zhong Shen Zi No. 00001

Rex Commodities Pte. Ltd. v. Qingdao Haiyunda Economic and Trade Co., Ltd. (2017) Lu 02Xie Wai Ren No. 4

Subway International B.V. v. Hangzhou Jiazhong Trading Company (2017) Zhe 01Xie Wai Ren No. 1

Top Grand Ltd. v. Jiangsu Rongsheng Heavy Industry Co., Ltd. (2017) E72Xie Wai Ren No. 4

Valmet, Inc. v. Zhejiang Purek Special Paper Co., Ltd. (2017) Zhe 04Xie Wai Rem No. 1

Season Navigation Ltd. v. Jiangsu Rongsheng Heavy Industry Co., Ltd. (2017) E72Xie Wai Ren No. 6

HyundaiGlovisCo., Ltd. v. Zhejiang Qiying Energy Chemical Co., Ltd. (2015) Zhe Yong Zhong Que Zi No. 3

Xinhe Marine Co., Ltd. v. Dalian Xinhe Ship Material Supply Co., Ltd. (2016) Liao 02Xie Wai Ren No. 2

Columbia Grain Trading Inc. v. Shandong Shenying Coal Trading Co., Ltd. (2017) Lu 11Xie Wai Ren No. 1

West Ocean Shipping Co., Ltd. v. Shenzhen Nanhai Shipping Co., Ltd. (2017) Yue 72Xie Wai Ren No. 1

China Aviation Oil (Singapore) Co., Ltd. v. Chengdu Xinhuaxin Chemical Materials Co., Ltd. (2017) Chuan 01Xie Wai Ren No. 1

Wollema-absalia Movo Ltd., Republic of Tatarstan, Russian Federation v. Jinzhou Dongfeng Machinery Co., Ltd. (2016) Ji Xie Wai Ren Zi No. 1

Semimaterials Co., Ltd. v. Henan GCL Solar Technology Co., Ltd. (2016) Yu Min
    Ta No. 2
Core White Ltd. v. Jiangsu Rongsheng Heavy Industry Co., Ltd. (2017) E72Xie Wai
    Ren No. 3
Noble Resources International Pte. Ltd. v. Shanghai Xintai International Trade Co.,
    Ltd. (2016) Hu 01Xie Wai Ren No. 1
Golden Agriculture International Pte. Ltd. v. Shandong Changhua Industrial Devel-
    opment Co., Ltd. (2017) Lu 11Xie Wai Ren No. 4
Louis Dreyfus Commodities Suisse SA v. Ningbo Qiancheng Import & Export Co.,
    Ltd. (2015) Zhe Yong Zhong Que Zi No. 5
China Land Shipping Pte. Ltd. v. Conor Shipping Co., Ltd. (2018) Jin 72Min Te No.
    2

12.2 Validity of Arbitration Agreements

Reply of the SPC to the Request for Instruction of High People's Court of Jiangsu
    Province on the Case Concerning the Application of Plexus Cotton Ltd. for Recog-
    nition and Enforcement of the UK Arbitral Award rendered by the ICA, Zui Gao
    Fa Min Ta No. 31
Voest-Alpine International Trading USA Corp. v. Jiangsu Provincial Foreign Trade
    Corp. (2008) Ning Min Wu Chu Zi No. 43
Reply of the SPC to the Request for Instruction on the Case Concerning the Appli-
    cation of Concordia Trading B.V. for Recognition and Enforcement of the No.
    3948 Arbitral Award rendered by the FOSFA (2009) Min Si Ta Zi No. 22
Reply of the SPC to the Request for Instruction on the Case Concerning the Applica-
    tion of Allenberg Cotton Co. for Recognition and Enforcement of Foreign Arbitral
    Awards against Ningbo Youngor International Trade and Transportation Co., Ltd.
    (2014) Min Si Ta Zi No. 32
Jess Smith & Sons Cotton, LLC v. Wuxi Natural Textile Industry Co., Ltd. and Wuxi
    Natural Green Fiber Technology Co., Ltd. (2013) Xi Shang Wai Zhong Shen Zi
    No. 0007
Allenberg Cotton Co. v. Jiangsu Nijiaxiang Group Co., Ltd. (2013) Xi Shang Wai
    Zhong Shen Zi No. 0009
Louis Dreyfus Australia Ltd. v. Jiangsu Nijiaxiang Group Co., Ltd. (2013) Xi Shang
    Wai Zhong Shen Zi No. 0003
Plexus Cotton Ltd. v.Jiangsu Jinfang Industrial Co., Ltd. (2014) Yan Shang Wai
    Zhong Shen Zi No. 00001
Reply of the SPC to the Request for Instruction on the Case Concerning the Applica-
    tion of Western Bulk Pte. Ltd. for Recognition and Enforcement of a UK Arbitral
    Award. (2012) Min Si Ta Zi No. 12
Australia CBH Grain Co., Ltd. v. Hebei Sihai Development Co., Ltd. (2013) Shi Min
    Wu Chu Zi No. 00525
Louis Dreyfus Commodities Suisse SA v. Ningbo Qiancheng Import & Export Co.,
    Ltd. (2015) Zhe Yong Zhong Que Zi No. 5

Reply of the SPC to the Report Concerning the Non-Recognition of the No. 73/23-06 Arbitral Award made by the Court of Arbitration of Mongolia. (2009) Min Si Ta Zi No. 46

Reply of the SPC to the Request for Instruction of High People's Court of Shandong Province on the Case Concerning the Application of Toyoshima & Co., Ltd. for Recognition and Enforcement of Foreign Arbitral Award against Changyi Kunfu Textile Co., Ltd. (2015) Min Si Ta Zi No. 31

Olam International Ltd. v. Jingshan Weijia Textile Enterprise Co., Ltd. (2013) E Jing Men Min San Chu Zi No. 00019

Jess Smith v. Jihua 3509 Textile Co., Ltd. (2014) E Xiao Gan Zhong Min Wai Chu Zi No. 00001.

Compass Cotton B.V. v. Shandong Yanggu Shunda Textile Co., Ltd. (2014) Liao Min Wu Chu Zi No. 4

Reply of the SPC to the Request for Instruction on the Case Concerning the Application of Beijing Chaolai Xinsheng Sports & Leisure Co., Ltd. for Recognition of No. 12113-0011 and No. 12112-0012 Arbitral Awards rendered by the KCAB (2013) Min Si Ta Zi No. 64

Siemens International Trading (Shanghai) Co., Ltd.v. Shanghai Golden Land Co., Ltd. (2013) Hu Yi Zhong Min Ren (Wai Zhong) Zi No. 2

Lifu Candy (Shanghai) Co., Ltd. v. Shanghai Lianfu Food Co., Ltd. (2008) Hu Er Zhong Min Wu (Shang) Chu Zi No. 19

GRD Minproc Ltd. v. Shanghai Flyingwheel Industry Co., Ltd. (2007) Hu Yi Zhong Min Wu (Shang) Chu Zi No. 116

Reply of the SPC to the Request for Instruction on the Case Concerning the Application of Proton Motors (China) Co., Ltd. for Recognition and Enforcement of Foreign Arbitral Awards against Jinxing Heavy Industry Manufacturing Co., Ltd (2013) Min Si Ta Zi No. 28

Tact Communications, Inc. v. Quanzhou Cardinu Travel Products Co., Ltd. (2013) Quan Min Ren Zi No. 35

Spring Maritime Ltd. v. Shandong Haina Real Estate Co., Ltd. (2013) Qing Hai Fa Hai Shang Chu Zi No. 1032

12.3 Due Process

Reply of the SPC to the Request for Instruction on the Case Concerning the Application of "Angfohuapin" Joint Venture Co., Ltd. for Recognition and Enforcement of the Arbitral Award rendered by the BelCCI (2012) Min Si Ta Zi No. 42

Reply of the SPC to the Request for Instruction on the Case Concerning the Recognition and Enforcement of No. 26-435-08 Arbitral Award rendered by the American Dispute Resolution Centre (2011) Min Si Ta Zi No. 21

Reply of the SPC to the Report on Non-Recognition of the No. 04-05 Tokyo Arbitral Award rendered by the JCAA. (2007) Min Si Ta Zi No. 26 Reply of the SPC on

Non-Recognition of the No. 05-03 Tokyo Arbitral Award rendered by the JCAA. (2008) Min Si Ta Zi No. 18

Mon Eldorado Co., Ltd. v. Zhejiang Zhancheng Construction Group Co., Ltd. (2009)
    Zhe Shao Min Que Zi No. 1
Last Land Property Pte. Ltd. v. Zhejiang Xinxing Rubber Co., Ltd. (2009) Zhe Tai
    Zhong Que Zi No. 4
Reply of the SPC to the Request for Instruction on the Case Concerning the Appli-
    cation of China-Base Ningbo Foreign Trade Co., Ltd. for Non-Enforcement of
    the Arbitral Award rendered by the HKIAC, (2009) Min Si Ta Zi No. 42
GEA Heat Exchangers, Inc. v. Guangdong Changying Heavy Industry Co., Ltd.
    (2015) Fo Zhong Fa Min Er Zhong Zi No. 7 Reply of the SPC to the Request for
    Instruction on the Case Concerning the Application of Ruierma Food Co., Ltd.
    for Recognition and Enforcement of Foreign Arbitral Awards against Zhanjiang
    Guanya Food Co., Ltd. (2013) Min Si Ta Zi No. 40
Western Bulk Pte. Ltd. v. Beijing Sinosteel Tiantie Iron & Steel Trading Co., Ltd.
    (2012) Min Si Ta Zi No. 12

12.4 The Scope of Arbitration

Reply of the SPC to the Request for Instructions on the Non-Recognition and Non-
    Enforcement of an Arbitral Award of the ICC. (2008) Min Si Ta Zi No. 11
Jess Smith v. Wuxi Natural&Wuxi Green Fiber (2013) Xi Shang Wai Zhong Shen
    Zi No. 0007
Reply of the SPC to the Request for Instruction on the Case Concerning the Appli-
    cation of Trinity Bulk Shipping Ltd. for Recognition and Enforcement of London
    Arbitral Award against Jiangsu Huihong International Group Native Product
    Import & Export Co., Ltd. AndYangzhou Huamei Shipping Industry Co., Ltd.
    (2015) Min Si Ta Zi No. 34
Reply of the SPC to the Request for Instruction on the Case Concerning the Applica-
    tion of Spliethoff's Bevrachtingskantoor B.V. forRecognition and Enforcement of
    the HULL XXK06-039 Foreign Arbitral Awardrendered by a Tribunal in London,
    UK, Min Si Ta Zi No. 48 BrightMorningLimited v. Yixing Leqi Textile Group
    Co., Ltd. (2016) Su 02 Xie Wai Ren No. 1
Reply of the SPC to the Request for Instruction of High People's Court of Jiangsu
    Province on the Case Concerning the Application of Bright Morning Limited for
    Recognition and Enforcement of the ARB130/11/MJL Arbitral Award rendered
    by the SIAC against Yixing Leqi Textile Group Co., Ltd. (2017) Zui Gao Fa Min
    Ta No. 44
Chenco Chemical Engineering and Consulting GmbH v. Do-Fluoride Chemicals Co.,
    Ltd. (2015) Xin Zhong Min San Chu Zi No. 53
Reply of the SPC to the Request for Instruction of High People's Court of Henan
    Province on the Case Concerning the Application of Chenco Chemical Engi-
    neering and Consulting GmbH for Recognition and Enforcement of Foreign Arbi-
    tral Award against Do-Fluoride Chemicals Co., Ltd. (2016) Zui Gao Fa Min Ta
    No. 66

GRD Minproc Ltd. v. Shanghai Flyingwheel Industry Co., Ltd. (2007) Hu Yi Zhong Min Wu (Shang) Chu Zi No. 116

12.5 Composition of Arbitral Tribunal and Arbitration Proceedings

Bright Morning Limited. v. Yixing Leqi Textile Group Co., Ltd. (2016) Su 02 Xie Wai Ren No. 1

Marumo Corp. v. Beijing Delin Golf Sports Development Co., Ltd. (2013) Er Zhong Min Te Zi No. 12593

First Investment Corp. (Marshall Island) v. Fujian Mawei Shipbuilding Ltd.&Fujian Shipbuilding Industry Group Co., Ltd. Xia Hai Fa Ren Zi No. 1

Reply of the SPC on the Application of First Investment Corp. (Marshall Island) for the Recognition and Enforcement of the Arbitral Award rendered by an ad hoc Tribunal, (2007) Min Si Ta Zi No. 35

Reply of the SPC to the Request for Instructions of the Case Concerning theApplication of China Shipping Development Co., Ltd. Freighter Co. for Recognition and Enforcement of London Arbitral Award (2008) Min Si Ta Zi No. 17

Lehua Meilan Holding Co., et al. v. Tianjin Jiashijie Group Co., Ltd., et al. (2009) Min Si Ta Zi No. 38

Western Bulk Pte. Ltd. v. Beijing Sinosteel Tiantie Iron & Steel Trading Co., Ltd. Jin Hai Fa Que Zi No. 6

Reply of the SPC to the Request for Instruction on the Case Concerning the Application of Western Bulk Pte. Ltd. for Recognition and Enforcement of a UK Arbitral Award (2012) Min Si Ta Zi No. 12

Reply of the SPC to the Request for Instruction on the Case Concerning the Application of ALSTOM Technology Ltd. for Recognition and Enforcement of Foreign Arbitral Award against Zhejiang University New Technology Co., Ltd., (2012) Min Si Ta Zi No. 54

Noble Resources International Pte. Ltd. v. Shanghai Xintai International Trade Co., Ltd. (2016) Hu 01 Xie Wai Ren No. 1

Reply of the SPC to the Request for Instruction of High People's Court of Shandong Province on the Case Concerning the Application of Toyoshima & Co., Ltd. for Recognition and Enforcement of Foreign Arbitral Award against Gaomi Luyuan Textile Co., Ltd. (2015) Min Si Ta Zi No. 30

Shin-Etsu Chemical Co., Ltd. v. Jiangsu Zhongtian Technology Co., Ltd. (2007) Min Si Ta Zi No. 26

Shin-Etsu Chemical Co., Ltd. v. Tianjin Xinmao Science &Technology Co., Ltd. (2008) Min Si Ta Zi No. 18

Reply of the SPC to the Request for Instruction on the Case Concerning the Non-Enforcement of the No. 07-11 Arbitral Award rendered by the JCAA (2010) Min Si Ta Zi No. 32

Reply of the SPC to the Request for Instruction on the Non-Recognition and Non-Enforcement of the 12330/TE/MW/AVH Arbitral Award rendered by the ICC in Lausanne (2009) Min Si Ta Zi No. 38

Gloria Jones Co. v. Wuxi Dongxiang Knitting Textile Co., Ltd. (2014) Xi Shang Wai
    Zhong Shen Zi No. 0004
Jess Smith & Sons Cotton, LLC v. Jihua 3509 Textile Co., Ltd. (2014) E Xiao Gan
    Zhong Min Wai Chu Zi No. 00001.
Glencore International AG v. Zhejiang Qiying Energy Chemical Co., Ltd. (2014)
    Zhe Yong Zhong Que Zi No. 1
Ksenja Pte. Ltd. v. Guan Ke (2014) Shen Zhong Fa She Wai Chu Zi No. 119.
Tajco A/S v. Jan Szklany (2015) Shen Zhong Min Si Te Zi No. 29
Oman Shipping Co. Soac v. Jiangsu Rongsheng Heavy Industry Co., Ltd. (2017) E
    72 Xie Wai Ren No.1
Reply of the SPC to the Request for Instruction of High People's Court of Henan
    Province on the Case Concerning the Application of Chenco Chemical Engi-
    neering and Consulting GmbH for Recognition and Enforcement of Foreign Arbi-
    tral Award against Do-Fluoride Chemicals Co., Ltd (2016) Zui Gao Fa Min Ta
    No. 66
Hyundai Glovis Co., Ltd. v. Zhejiang Qiying Energy Chemical Co., Ltd. (2015) Zhe
    Yong Zhong Que Zi No. 3

12.6 Validity of the Arbitral Award

Reply of the SPC to the Request for Instruction on the Case Concerning the Appli-
    cation of Paul Reinhart AG for Recognition and Enforcement of Foreign Arbitral
    Award against Hubei Qinghe Textile Co., Ltd. (2016) Zui Gao Fa Min Ta No. 11
Reply of the SPC to the Request for Instruction on the Case Concerning the Appli-
    cation of Noble Resource Pte. Ltd. for Recognition and Enforcement of Foreign
    Arbitral Award against Hubei Qinghe Textile Co., Ltd. (2016) Zui Gao Fa Min
    Ta No. 12
Ksenja Pte. Ltd. v. Guan Ke (2014) Shen Zhong Fa She Wai Chu Zi No. 119
Noble Resource Pte. Ltd. v. Zhejiang Xiongsheng Industrial Co., Ltd. (2014) Zhe
    Shao Zhong Que Zi No. 1
Olam International Ltd. v. Jingshan Weijia Textile Enterprise Co., Ltd. (2013) E Jing
    Men Min San Chu Zi No. 00019
Olam International Ltd. v. Zibo Yinhua Cotton & Linen Co., Ltd. (2015) Zi Min Te
    Zi No. 1
Rex Commodities Pte. Ltd. v. Qingdao Haiyunda Economic and Trade Co., Ltd.
    (2017) Lu 02 Xie Wai Ren No. 4

12.7 Arbitrability and Public Policy

Reply of the SPC to the Request for Instruction on the Case Concerning the Appli-
    cation of Non-Recognition and Non-Enforcement of the Arbitral Award rendered
    by the Court of Arbitration of Mongolia (2009) Min Si Ta Zi No. 33

Reply of the SPC to the Request for Instructions on the Non-Recognition and Non-Enforcement of an Arbitration Award of the ICC (2008) Min Si Ta Zi No. 11

Wicor Holding AG v. Taizhou Haopu Investment Co., Ltd. (2015)Tai Zhong Shang Zhong Shen Zi No. 00004

Reply of the SPC to the Request for Instruction on the Case Concerning the Non-Enforcement of No. 18295/CYK Arbitral Award rendered by the ICC, (2016) Zui Gao Fa Min Ta No. 8

Reply of the SPC to the Request for Instruction on the Case Concerning the Application of Castel Electronics Pty Ltd. for Recognition and Enforcement of Foreign Arbitral Awards (2013) Min Si Ta Zi No. 46

Tianrui Hotel Investment Co., Ltd. v. Hangzhou Yiju Hotel Management Co., Ltd. (2010) Min Si Ta Zi No.18

Spring Maritime Ltd. v. Shandong Haina Real Estate Co., Ltd. (2013) Qing Hai Fa Hai Shang Chu Zi No. 1032

Summer Maritime Ltd. v. Shandong Haina Real Estate Co., Ltd. (2014) Qing Hai Fa Hai Shang Chu Zi No. 721

Jacobson Golf Course Design Inc. v. Sihui Zhenhuiyuan Property Development Co., Ltd. & Sihui Huiguan Investment Co., Ltd. (2015) Zhao Zhong Fa Min Yi Zhong Zi No. 26

China Aviation Oil (Singapore) Co., Ltd. v. Chengdu Xinhuaxin Chemical Material Co., Ltd. (2017) Chuan 01 Xie Wai Ren No. 1

Reply of the SPC to the Request for Instruction on the Case Concerning the Application of Western Bulk Pte. Ltd. for Recognition and Enforcement of a UK Arbitral Award. (2012) Min Si Ta Zi No. 12

Reply of the SPC to the Request for Instructions of the Case Concerning the Application of GRD Minproc Ltd. for Recognition and Enforcement of Arbitral Award rendered by the SCC, (2008) Min Si Ta Zi No. 48

Noble Resource Pte. Ltd. v. Zhejiang Xiongsheng Industrial Co., Ltd. (2014) Zhe Shao Zhong Que Zi No. 1

Official Replies by the Supreme People's Court Concerning Arbitration in China

1. Reply of the Supreme People's Court to the Request for Instructions of the High People's Court of Hunan Province on the Case Concerning the Application of the People's Government of Hunan Province and the Department of Transportation of Hunan Province for Confirmation of the Validity of the Arbitration Agreement against Victory International Investment (Macau) Co., Ltd. and Hunan Victory Changtan West Line Highway Co., Ltd.
September 28, 2016
(2016) Zui Gao Fa Min Ta No. 70

2. Reply of the Supreme People's Court to the Request for Instructions on the Case Concerning the Application of China United Communications (Holdings) Co., Ltd. for the Recognition and Enforcement of an Arbitral Award Made by Hong Kong International Arbitration Center
September 19, 2016
(2016) Zui Gao Fa Min Ta No. 63

3. Reply of the Supreme People's Court to the Request for Instructions of the High People's Court of Beijing on the Case Concerning the Application of COFCO Wines Co., Ltd. for Confirmation of the Validity of Arbitration Agreement
September 14, 2016
(2016) Zui Gao Fa Min Ta No. 87

4. Reply of the Supreme People's Court to the Request for Instructions of the High People's Court of Shandong Province Regarding the Validity of the Arbitration Agreement in the Sales Contract between Shandong Huarui Road Materials Co., Ltd. and Mabong Co., Ltd.
May 26, 2016
(2016) Zui Gao Fa Min Ta No. 60

5. Reply of the Supreme People's Court to the Request for Instructions Regarding the Establishment of the Arbitration Agreement in the Disputes Arising from the Inspection Contract between ACE O.C.T.G Co., Ltd., Wuhan Branch of

General Standard Technical Service Co., Ltd. and General Standard Technical Service Co., Ltd.
May 27, 2016
(2016) Zui Gao Fa Min Ta Zi No. 53

6. Reply of the Supreme People's Court to the Request for Instructions on the Case Concerning the Application of Paul Reinhart AG for Recognition and Enforcement of Foreign Arbitral Award against Hubei Qinghe Textile Co., Ltd.
May 26, 2016
(2016) Zui Gao Fa Min Ta No. 11

7. Reply of the Supreme People's Court to the Request for Instructions of the High People's Court of Jiangsu Province Regarding the Validity of the Arbitration Agreement in the Case on Disputes Arising from Sales Contract between Hong Kong Baiteng Trading Co., Ltd. and Yunnan Jiahui Import and Export Co., Ltd.
May 25, 2016
(2016) Zui Gao Fa Min Ta No. 10

8. Reply of the Supreme People's Court to the Request for Instructions on the Case Concerning the Application of J & D IB Co. for Recognition of a Foreign Arbitral Award
May 17, 2016
(2016) Zui Gao Fa Min Ta No. 38

9. Reply of the Supreme People's Court to the Request for Instructions in the Case Concerning the Non-Enforcement of the Arbitral Award Made by ICC
March 22, 2016
(2016) Zui Gao Fa Min Ta No. 8

10. Reply of the SPC to the Request for Instructions on the Case Concerning the Application of Spliethoff's Bevrachtingskantoor B.V. for Recognition of the HULL XXK06-039 Arbitral Award rendered by an Arbitral Tribunal in London, UK
December 25, 2015
(2015) Min Si Ta Zi No. 48

11. Reply of the Supreme People's Court to the Request for Instructions on the Case Concerning the Application of FSG Automotive Holding AG for Recognition and Enforcement of No. SCH-5239 Arbitral Award rendered by the Arbitration Center of the Austrian Federal Economic Association against Wuhan Fanzhou Machinery Manufacturing Co., Ltd.
December 24, 2015
(2015) Min Si Ta Zi No. 46

12. Reply of the Supreme People's Court to the Request for Instructions on the Case Concerning the Application of Dong Cheng International Trade Co., Ltd. for Enforcement of a Foreign-Related Arbitral Award
December 9, 2015
(2015) Min Si Ta Zi No. 53

13. Reply of the Supreme People's Court to the Request for Instructions on the Case Concerning the Application of Trinity Bulk Shipping Ltd. for Recognition and Enforcement of London Arbitral Award against Jiangsu Huihong International Group Native Product Import & Export Co., Ltd. and Yangzhou Huamei Shipping Industry Co., Ltd.
November 27, 2015
(2015) Min Si Ta Zi No. 34

14. Reply of the Supreme People's Court to the Request for Instructions of the High People's Court of Beijing on the Case Concerning the Application of CGCOC Group for Revocation of the [2015] Zhong Guo Mao Zhong Jing Cai Zi No. 0377 Arbitral Award made by CIETAC
October 26, 2015
(2015) Min Si Ta Zi No. 39

15. Reply of the Supreme People's Court to the Request for Instructions on the Case Concerning the Application of Siemens International Trading (Shanghai) Co., Ltd. for Recognition and Enforcement of a Foreign Arbitral Award
October 10, 2015
(2015) Min Si Ta Zi No. 5

16. Reply of the Supreme People's Court to the Request for Instructions of the High People's Court of Shanghai on the Case Concerning the Revocation of the (2013) Hu Mao Zhong Cai Zi No. 415 Arbitral Award Made by Shanghai International Economic and Trade Arbitration Commission
October 9, 2015
(2015) Min Si Ta Zi No. 8

17. Reply of the Supreme People's Court to the Request for Instructions of the High People's Court of Guangdong Province on the Case Concerning the Application of Dongguan Haoqing Paper Co., Ltd. et al., for Non-Enforcement of an Arbitral Award
October 9, 2015
(2015) Min Si Ta Zi No. 35

18. Reply of the Supreme People's Court to the Request for Instructions of the High People's Court of Shandong Province on the Case Concerning the Application of Toyoshima Stock Co., Ltd. for Recognition and Enforcement of a Foreign Arbitral Award Against Gaomi Luyuan Textile Co., Ltd.
September 24, 2015
(2015) Min Si Ta Zi No. 30

19. Reply of the Supreme People's Court to the Request for Instructions of the High People's Court of Shandong Province on the Case Concerning the Application of ECOMAGROINDUSTRIALASIAPTELTD for Recognition and Enforcement of the Arbitral Award Made by International Cotton Association
September 24, 2015,
(2015) Min Si Ta Zi No. 29

20. Reply of the Supreme People's Court to the Request for Instructions of the High People's Court of Shandong Province on the Case Concerning the Application

of Toyoshima Co., Ltd. for Recognition and Enforcement of a Foreign Arbitral Award against Shandong Changyi Kunfu Textile Co., Ltd.
September 24, 2015
(2015) Min Si Ta Zi No. 31

21. Reply of the Supreme People's Court to the Request for Instructions on the Case Concerning the Application of Haomei Co., Ltd. for Confirmation of the Validity of an Arbitration Agreement
September 24, 2015
(2015) Min Si Ta Zi No. 36

22. Reply of the Supreme People's Court to the Request for Instructions Concerning the Validity of a Foreign-Related Arbitration Agreement in the Voyage Charter Dispute between China North Shipping Logistics Co., Ltd. and Benxi Beiying Steel Group Import and Export Co., Ltd.
September 21, 2015
(2015) Min Si Ta Zi No. 22

23. Reply of the Supreme People's Court to the Request for Instructions on the Case Concerning the Application of Petroleum Engineering General Contracting Branch of CNPC Bohai Drilling Engineering Co., Ltd. for Confirmation of the Validity of an Arbitration Agreement
August 17, 2015
(2015) Min Si Ta Zi No. 23

24. Reply of the Supreme People's Court to the Request for Instructions on the Case Concerning the Application of Chongqing Pulefei Import & Export Co., Ltd. for Non-Enforcement of an Arbitral Award
July 22, 2015
(2015) Min Si Ta Zi No. 11

25. Reply of the Supreme People's Court to the Request for Instructions on the Case Concerning the Application of Jiarui Shipping Co., Ltd. for Non-Enforcement of a Foreign-Related Arbitral Award in the Voyage Charter Dispute against Sichuan Beifang Qinyuan Bioengineering Co., Ltd.
September 26, 2014
(2014) Min Si Ta Zi No. 41

26. Reply of the Supreme People's Court to the Request for Instructions on the Case Concerning the Application of Hainan Lion City Tourism Development Co., Ltd. for Non-Enforcement of an Arbitral Award
July 31, 2014
(2014) Min Si Ta Zi No. 37

27. Reply of the Supreme People's Court to the Request for Instructions on the Case Concerning the Application of Allenberg Cotton Co., Ltd. for Recognition and Enforcement of a Foreign Arbitral Award against Ningbo Youngor International Trade & Transportation Co., Ltd.
July 31, 2014
(2014) Min Si Ta Zi No. 32

28.   Reply of the Supreme People's Court to the Request for Instructions on the Case Concerning Non-Recognition and Non-Enforcement of the No. 2/11 Arbitral Award rendered by the Waren-Verein Der Hamburger Borse E.V.
      June 30, 2014
      (2014) Min Si Ta Zi No. 31
29.   Reply of the Supreme People's Court to the Request for Instructions on the Case Concerning the Application of Shi Dong Rubber Co., Ltd. for Non-Enforcement of a Foreign-related Arbitral Award against Triangle Tire Co., Ltd.
      March 22, 2013
      (2013) Min Si Ta Zi No. 12
30.   Reply of the Supreme People's Court to the Request for Instructions on the Case Concerning the Application of Chengdu Youbang Stationery Co., Ltd. and Wang Guojian for the Revocation of the (2011) Shen Zhong Cai Zi No. 601 Arbitral Award Made by Shenzhen Arbitration Commission
      March 20, 2013
      (2013) Min Si Ta Zi No. 9
31.   Reply of the Supreme People's Court to the Request for Instructions on the Case Concerning the Application of Wang Guolin for the Revocation of the (2012) Zhong Guo Mao Zhong Shen Cai Zi No. 3 Arbitral Award Made by China International Economic and Trade Arbitration Commission South China Sub-commission
      February 26, 2013
      (2013) Min Si Ta Zi No. 8
32.   Reply of the Supreme People's Court to the Request for Instructions on the Case Concerning the Application of Ecom USA. Inc. for Enforcement of a Foreign-Related Arbitral Award
      February 6, 2013
      (2013) Min Si Ta Zi No. 3
33.   Reply of the Supreme People's Court to the Request for Instructions on the Case Concerning the Application of Northern Wanbang Logistics Co., Ltd. for the Revocation of the (2012) Hai Zhong Jing Cai Zi No. 001 Arbitral Award
      January 22, 2013
      (2013) Min Si Ta Zi No. 5
34.   Reply of the Supreme People's Court to the Request for Instructions on the Case Concerning the Application of "Angfohuapin" Joint Venture Co., Ltd. for Recognition and Enforcement of an International Arbitral Award Made by the Belarusian Chamber of Commerce and Industry
      November 2, 2012
      (2012) Min Si Ta Zi No. 42
35.   Reply of the Supreme People's Court to the Request for Instructions on the Case Concerning the Application of Singapore Zhongtian Investment (Group)

Co., Ltd. for Revocation of an Arbitral Award Made by China International
Economic and Trade Arbitration Commission
October 25, 2012
(2012) Min Si Ta Zi No. 47

36.   Reply of the Supreme People's Court to the Request for Instructions on the
      Case Concerning the Application of Western Bulk Pte. Ltd. for Recognition
      and Enforcement of an UK Arbitral Award
      May 21, 2012
      (2012) Min Si Ta Zi No. 12

37.   Reply of the Supreme People's Court to the Request for Instructions on the Case
      Concerning the Recognition and Enforcement of the No. 26-435-08 Arbitral
      Award Made by Dispute Resolution Center of the United States
      June 30, 2011
      (2011) Min Si Ta Zi No. 21

38.   Reply of the Supreme People's Court to the Request for Instructions on the
      Case Concerning the Revocation of the (2009) CIETACBJ No. 0355 Award
      Made by China International Economic and Trade Arbitration Commission
      April 22, 2011
      (2011) Min Si Ta Zi No. 13

39.   Reply of the Supreme People's Court to the Request for Instructions on the
      Case Concerning the Revocation of the (2010) Zhong Guo Mao Zhong Jing
      Cai Zi No. 0159 Award Made by China International Economic and Trade
      Arbitration Commission
      December 2, 2010
      (2010) Min Si Ta Zi No. 49

40.   Reply of the Supreme People's Court to the Request for Instructions on the Case
      Concerning the Application of DMTCo., Ltd. (France) for Recognition and
      Enforcement of a Foreign Arbitral Award against Chaozhou Huaye Packaging
      Materials Co., Ltd. and Chao'an Huaye Packaging Materials Co., Ltd.
      October 12, 2010

41.   Reply of the Supreme People's Court to the Request for Instructions on the
      Case Concerning the Application of Louis Dreyfus Commodities (Asia) Co.,
      Ltd. for Recognition and Enforcement of the No. 3980 Arbitral Award Made
      by Federation of Oils, Seeds and Fats Associations
      October 10, 2010
      (2010) Min Si Ta Zi No. 48

42.   Reply of the Supreme People's Court to the Request for Instructions on the Case
      Concerning the Non-Recognition of the No. 07-11 Arbitral Award Rendered
      by Japan Commercial Arbitration Association in Tokyo
      June 29, 2010
      (2010) Min Si Ta Zi No. 32

43.   Reply of the Supreme People's Court to the Request for Instructions Regarding
      the Non-Enforcement of the [2008] Zhong Guo Mao Zhong Jing Cai Zi

No. 0379 Arbitral Award Made by China International Economic and Trade Arbitration Commission
May 27, 2010
(2010) Min Si Ta Zi No. 21

44.   Reply of the Supreme People's Court to the Request for Instructions on the Case Concerning the Application of Tianrui Hotel Investment Co., Ltd. for Recognition of An Arbitral Award against Hangzhou Yiju Hotel Management Co., Ltd.
May 18, 2010
(2010) Min Si Ta Zi No. 18

45.   Reply of the Supreme People's Court to the Request for Instructions on the Case Concerning the Application of McLane Group International Trading Company of the United States and its Beijing Representative Office for the Revocation of the [2008] Xia Zhong Cai Zi No. 0379 Arbitral Award
December 16, 2009
(2008) Min Si Ta Zi No. 43

46.   Reply of the Supreme People's Court to the Report of Review on the Case Concerning the Application of China-Base Ningbo Foreign Trade Co., Ltd. for Non-Enforcement of an Arbitral Award Made by Hong Kong International Arbitration Center
December 9, 2009
(2009) Min Si Ta Zi No. 42

47.   Reply of the Supreme People's Court to the Report Concerning the Non-Recognition of the No. 73/23-06 Arbitral Award Made by Court of Arbitration of Mongolia
December 8, 2009
(2009) Min Si Ta Zi No. 46

48.   Reply of the Supreme People's Court to the Report of Request for Instructions on the Case Concerning the Application of Ningbo Yongxin Auto Component Manufacturing Co., Ltd. for the Revocation of the Yong Zhong Cai Zi [2007] No. 44 Arbitral Award Made by Ningbo Arbitration Commission
October 29, 2009
(2009) Min Si Ta Zi No. 45

49.   Reply of the Supreme People's Court to the Report of Request for Instructions on the Case Concerning the Application of Zhoushan Zhonghai Cereal & Oil Industry Co., Ltd. for Non-Enforcement of an Arbitral Award Made by Hong Kong International Arbitration Center
March 18, 2009
(2009) Min Si Ta Zi No. 2

50.   Reply of the Supreme People's Court to the Request for Instructions Concerning the Revocation of the [2008] Zhong Guo Mao Zhong Jing Cai Zi No. 0044 Award Made by China International Economic and Trade Arbitration Commission
March 18, 2009
(2009) Min Si Ta Zi No. 1

51. Reply of the Supreme People's Court to the Request for Instructions on the Case Concerning the Application of GRD Minproc Co., Ltd. for Recognition and Enforcement of an Arbitral Award Made by the Arbitration Institute of the Stockholm Chamber of Commerce
March 13, 2009
(2008) Min Si Ta Zi No. 48

52. Reply of the Supreme People's Court to the Request for Instructions on the Case Concerning the Application of Subway International B.V. for Recognition and Enforcement of the No. 50/114/T/00171/07 Arbitral Award Made by the International Arbitral Tribunal of International Center for Dispute Resolution
February 26, 2009
(2008) Min Si Ta Zi No. 47

53. Reply of the Supreme People's Court to the Request for Instructions in the Case Concerning the Application of Changsha Xinye Industrial Co., Ltd. for Revocation of an Arbitral Award against Metals Plus International Co., Ltd. of the United States
November 18, 2008
(2007) Min Si Ta Zi No. 43

54. Reply of the Supreme People's Court to the Request for Instructions on the Case Concerning the Revocation of an Arbitral Award between Korea Daesung G-3 Co., Ltd. and Changchun Yuanda Auto Engineering Trade Co., Ltd.
October 21, 2008
(2008) Min Si Ta Zi No. 28

55. Reply of the Supreme People's Court to the Request for Instructions Concerning the [2007] Zhong Guo Mao Zhong Hu Cai Zi No. 224 Arbitral Award Shall Not be Enforced
September 12, 2008
(2008) Min Si Ta Zi No. 34

56. Reply of the Supreme People's Court to the Report Concerning the Ruling of Non-Recognition and Non-Enforcement of the No. 05-03 Arbitral Award Made by Japan Commercial Arbitration Association in Tokyo
September 10, 2008
(2008) Min Si Ta Zi No. 18

57. Reply of the Supreme People's Court to the Report of Request for Instructions on the Case Concerning the Application of China Shipping Development Co., Ltd. Freight Company for Recognition of an Arbitral Award Made in London
August 6, 2008
(2008) Min Si Ta Zi No. 17

58. Reply of the Supreme People's Court to the Request for Instructions on the Case Concerning the Application of Yang Zhihong for Revocation of a Hong Kong-Related Arbitral Award Made by Guangzhou Arbitration Commission
July 24, 2008
(2008) Min Si Ta Zi No. 21

59. Reply of the Supreme People's Court to the Request for Instructions on the Case Concerning the Application of Weibei Hongli Co., Ltd. for the Revocation of a Foreign-Related Arbitral Award Made by Zhuhai Arbitration Commission
May 27, 2008
(2008) Min Si Ta Zi No. 2
60. Reply of the Supreme People's Court to the Report of Review on the Case Concerning the Application of Runhe Development Co., Ltd. for Non-Enforcement of an Arbitral Award
May 8, 2008,
(2008) Min Si Ta Zi No. 1
61. Reply of the Supreme People's Court to the Report Concerning the Non-Recognition of the Tokyo No. 04-05 Arbitral Award Made by Japan Commercial Arbitration Association
March 3, 2008,
Min Si Ta Zi No. 26
62. Reply of the Supreme People's Court to the Request for Instructions Regarding the Non-Enforcement of the Arbitral Award between Hong Kong Eurasian Technology Co. v. Xinjiang Hops Co., Ltd.
November 28, 2007
(2006) Min Si Ta Zi No. 48

Chapter 1
Judicial Review of Arbitration Agreement: General

1.1 Nonexistence of Arbitration Agreement

In China's arbitration practice, if there is no arbitration agreement, in principle, the arbitration institution will not accept the corresponding disputes. Under normal circumstances, a party claiming that there is no arbitration agreement may ask the court or the arbitration institution to confirm that there is no arbitration agreement. If the application is submitted to the court, pursuant to the Provisions on Causes of Action in Civil Cases that came into effect on April 1, 2011, there are only two causes of action for arbitration procedures, which are the application for confirmation of the validity of arbitration agreements and the application for revocation of arbitral awards.[1]

Among them, the legal basis for applying for confirmation of the validity of arbitration agreements is Article 20 of the Arbitration Law, which stipulates that "If a party challenges the validity of the arbitration agreement, he may request the arbitration institution to make a decision or apply to the people's court for a ruling. If one party requests the arbitration institution to make a decision and the other party applies to the people's court for a ruling, the people's court shall give a ruling. A party's challenge of the validity of the arbitration agreement shall be raised prior to the first hearing of arbitral tribunal.".

However, the problem that often arises in practice is whether a party may file a lawsuit in the cause of action of the application for confirmation of the validity of arbitration agreements, requesting the court to confirm that the arbitration agreement does not exist at all or is not binding on it. In other words, does the existence of an arbitration agreement fall within the scope of the court's review of the validity of the

---

[1] Notice of the SPC on Issuing the Revised Provisions on Causes of Action in Civil Cases, Fa [2011] No. 42.

This Chapter is coauthored with Ye Shanshan, associate of Yi & Partners Law Firm.

© The Author(s), under exclusive license to Springer Nature Singapore Pte Ltd. 2022
Y. Lin, *China Arbitration Yearbook (2021)*, China Arbitration Yearbook,
https://doi.org/10.1007/978-981-19-1284-9_1

arbitration agreement? However, there is no specific stipulation on this issue, which results in different views and judicial practices.

The following case is the first arbitration judicial review case published by the CICC thus far, and it is of guiding significance regarding this issue.

Luck Treat Ltd. v. Zhong Yuan Cheng Commercial Investment Holdings Co., Ltd.[2]

The 100% equity in Newpower Enterprises Inc. held by Luck Treat Ltd. was listed on the China Beijing Equity Exchange for sale, and Zhong Yuan Cheng Commercial Investment Holdings Co., Ltd. ("Zhong Yuan Cheng") was confirmed as the sole qualified prospective transferee. Thereafter, the parties conducted negotiations on the Equity Transfer Contract and the Debt Settlement Agreement. Both of the initialized versions of the Equity Transfer Contract and the Debt Settlement Agreement concluded by both parties during the negotiation provided that "The disputes concerning the interpretation or performance of this contract shall be resolved through negotiation between the parties; if the negotiation fails, it shall be submitted to the SCIA for arbitration."

Afterwards, the two parties could not reach an agreement on the content of the other terms of the contract, and Luck Treat Ltd. issued a Letter of Notice to Zhong Yuan Cheng to formally notify the cancellation of the transaction. On April 4, 2018, Zhong Yuan Cheng filed an application for arbitration with the SCIA in accordance with the arbitration clauses in the initialized version of the Equity Transfer Contract and the Debt Settlement Agreement against Luck Treat Ltd. and others as corespondents. Prior to hearing before the arbitral tribunal, Luck Treat Ltd. filed a lawsuit with Shenzhen Intermediate People's Court of Guangdong Province, applying for confirmation that the arbitration agreement did not exist.

The SPC considered that this case and the connected cases have great legal significance, and the hearing conducted by the CICC will be conducive to the consistent application of the law and the improvement of efficiency of dispute resolution, so the SPC ruled that this case shall be heard by the First International Commercial Court of the SPC.[3]

Luck Treat Ltd. argued that the parties did not reach agreement on the texts of the Equity Transfer Contract and the Debt Settlement Agreement, let alone signed them, and thus neither the Equity Transfer Contract nor the Debt Settlement Agreement was established. Regarding the fact that no arbitration clause can be established separately from the main contract, the arbitration clauses in the contract mentioned above have not been established either.

The SPC considered that the issue in dispute in this case was whether the arbitration clauses had been established. After Zhong Yuan Cheng applied for arbitration, Luck Treat Ltd. applied to a people's court to confirm that no valid arbitration clause existed between both parties on the ground that the arbitration clauses had not been

---

[2] (2019) Zui Gao Fa Min Te No. 1.

[3] In accordance with Paragraph 1 of Article 38 of the Civil Procedure Law and Paragraph 5 of Article 2 of the Provisions of the SPC on Several Issues Regarding the Establishment of the International Commercial Court.

established. Although this was different from a request for confirming the invalidity of an arbitration agreement, whether an arbitration agreement existed directly affected the dispute resolution method in the same way validity did. It was equally classified as a threshold question to be resolved. Therefore, a request to confirm the nonexistence of an arbitration agreement between the parties was an objection to the validity of an arbitration agreement in a broad sense. Paragraph 1 of Article 20 of the Arbitration Law stipulated that a party who objects to the validity of an arbitration agreement may apply to the arbitration institution for a decision or to a people's court for a ruling. Therefore, a request made by the party for confirming the nonexistence of an arbitration agreement on the ground that the arbitration clause has not been established was a case of an application to confirm the validity of an arbitration agreement, and thus a people's court shall accept the case and conduct hearing accordingly.

As mentioned above, the current legal norms do not clearly stipulate whether the existence of an arbitration agreement is within the scope of review for confirming the validity of arbitration agreements, and thus, there are different views and judicial practices.

Among them, those with negative views hold the opinion that the court should not accept the litigation filed by the parties regarding the existence of an arbitration agreement. The main reason is that the court's judicial review of arbitration should follow the principles of legal scope of review and legal procedures. No arbitration agreement is a circumstance of revocation of an arbitral award,[4] rather than a circumstance invalidating the arbitration agreement as stipulated in Article 17 of the Arbitration Law. The Arbitration Law and related judicial interpretations do not stipulate that the parties can file a separate lawsuit over whether there is an arbitration agreement between the parties. Pursuant to Article 4 of the Arbitration Law, the parties should submit a jurisdictional objection to the arbitration institution. Some cases holding this view are listed in Table 1.1.

In contrast, those with affirmative views consider that the application for confirming whether the arbitration agreement is binding shall be accepted as a case for confirming the validity of the arbitration agreement. The main reason is that the existence of an arbitration agreement is the prerequisite for confirming the validity of the arbitration agreement. Only when the parties have reached an arbitration agreement can the arbitration agreement be deemed invalid for certain reasons. Therefore, the court must first examine whether there is an arbitration agreement. Examples of related cases with affirmative views are listed in Table 1.2.

In addition, in the case of *Shenhua Coal Transportation and Marketing Co.v. Marinick Shipping Co.*, Shenhua Coal Transportation and Marketing Co. claimed that it had not concluded an arbitration agreement with Marinick Shipping Co. The SPC held in its Reply[5] that the Tianjin Maritime Court should accept Shenhua Coal Transportation and Sales Co.'s application. It can be seen from the reply that the SPC

---

[4] Paragraph 1 of Article 58 of the Arbitration Law.

[5] Reply of the SPC to the request for instructions regarding the arbitration clause between Shenhua Coal Transportation and Marketing Co. and Marinick Shipping Co., (2013) Min Si Ta Zi No. 4.

Table 1.1 Cases with negative views

No.	Applicant	Respondent	Court	Case number
1	Shibing Yuanxin Real Estate Development Co., Ltd. of Guizhou Province	Yingtan Fenghua Construction Engineering Co., Ltd.	The High People's Court of Chongqing City	(2018) Yu Min Zhong No. 568
2	Liao	Zhang		(2019) Yu Min Zhong No. 77
3	Huang	Yuanzheng Small Loan Co., Ltd., Wanzhou District, Chongqing City		(2018) Yu Min Zhong No. 386
4	Chongqing Bayue Construction and Installation Engineering Co., Ltd.	Chongqing Weiping Real Estate Development Co., Ltd.		(2018) Yu Min Zhong No. 569
5	Chongqing Highway Engineering Group Co., Ltd.	Chongqing Three Gorges Financial Guarantee Group Co., Ltd.		(2019) Yu Min Zhong No. 79
6	University of Science and Technology of China	Anhui Sanjian Engineering Co., Ltd.	The High People's Court of Anhui Province	(2018) Wan Min Te No. 1
7	Ge	Zhejiang Xinhua Commodity Exchange Center Co., Ltd	Ningbo Intermediate People's Court	(2019) Zhe 02 Min Te No. 20
8	Yue	Qian	Zhenjiang Intermediate People's Court	(2019) Su 11 Min Te No. 3
9	Guoji Construction Group Co., Ltd.	Shanghai Zhenxing Tourism Co., Ltd.	Haikou Intermediate People's Court	(2018) Qiong 01 Min Te No. 144
10	China Development Bank Securities Co., Ltd	Shanghai Huaxin International Group Ltd.	Beijing Third Intermediate People's Court	(2019) Jing 04 Min Te No. 387
11	Lin	Sifang Yufeng Investment Co., Ltd., et al.		(2019) Jing 04 Min Te No. 198
12	Pan	Beijing Xicheng Branch of Shenzhen Zhenai Information Technology Co., Ltd.		(2019) Jing 04 Min Te No. 180

(continued)

Table 1.1 (continued)

No.	Applicant	Respondent	Court	Case number
13	Wang	Shenzhen Chuangdongfang Fuben Investment Enterprise (L.P.), et al.		(2019) Jing 04 Min Te No. 174
14	Shanxi Gas Industry Group Co., Ltd.	Linklaters		(2015) Si Zhong Min (Shang) Te Zi No. 327
15	Hengfeng Real Estate Co., Ltd.	Beijing Urban Construction Real Estate Development Co., Ltd., et al.	Beijing Third Intermediate People's Court	(2014) San Zhong Min Te Zi No. 09095
16	Shanghai Zhongyun Asset Management Co., Ltd., et al.	Chen, et al.		(2015) San Zhong Min (Shang) Te Zi No. 10138
17	Shanghai Fengqing Chemical Co., Ltd.	Shanghai Branch of DBS Bank (China) Limited	Beijing Second Intermediate People's Court	(2016) Jing 02 Min Te No. 94
18	Yang	Yangpu China Railway Xinlong Trading Co., Ltd.	Beijing First Intermediate People's Court	(2013) Yi Zhong Min Te Zi No. 9618
19	Henan Yawen Hotel Co., Ltd.	Tengsheng Building Decoration Co., Ltd.	Zhengzhou Intermediate People's Court	(2019) Yu 01 Min Te No. 15
20	Huizhou International Container Terminal Co., Ltd.	Guangzhou Ronghaitai Dredging Engineering Co., Ltd.	Guangzhou Intermediate People's Court	(2018) Yue 01 Min Te No. 1220

also considers that the existence of an arbitration agreement is within the scope of review for confirming the validity of the arbitration agreement.

Similar to the spirit of the Reply, the SPC, in this subject case, also holds the opinion that the existence of an arbitration agreement is a prerequisite issue for confirming the validity of the arbitration agreement. Therefore, the existence of an arbitration agreement should be within the scope of review to confirm the validity of the arbitration agreement. If the parties request confirmation that the arbitration agreement does not exist on the grounds that there is no arbitration agreement or the arbitration clause is not established, the people's court shall accept the case for review.

The existence of an arbitration agreement is a precondition for the validity of the arbitration agreement. If there is no arbitration agreement between the parties, the arbitration agreement is not binding and invalid to the parties. From this perspective, the existence of an arbitration agreement should fall within the scope of review to confirm the validity of the arbitration agreement. Existing judicial practices with

Table 1.2 Cases with affirmative views

No.	Applicant	Respondent	Court	Case number
1	Guangzhou Baijiaxin Group Co., Ltd.	Guangzhou Zhujiang Sub-branch of Agricultural Bank of China Co., Ltd.	Guangzhou Intermediate People's Court	(2018) Yue 01 Min Te No. 1230
2	Huang	Guangzhou Zhongyong Small Loan Co., Ltd.		(2019) Yue 01 Min Te No. 555
3	Shenzhen Hongguangyang Vacuum Technology Co., Ltd.	Li	Shenzhen Intermediate People's Court	(2013) Shen Zhong Fa She Wai Zhong Zi No. 46
4	Shanghai Xiangfu Real Estate Development Co., Ltd.	Hangzhou Binjiang Real Estate Group Co., Ltd.	Shanghai Second Intermediate People's Court	(2018) Hu 02 Min Te No. 458
5	The People's Government of Hunan Province, et al	Triumph International Investment (Macau) Co., Ltd., et al..	Changsha Intermediate People's Court	(2015) Chang Zhong Min Wu Zhong Zi No. 01749
6	Fuzhou Haisheng Property Management Service Co., Ltd.	Shang	Fuzhou Intermediate People's Court	(2014) Rong Min Ren Zi No. 2
7	Huzhou Fengrun Real Estate Co., Ltd.	Li	Shaoxing Intermediate People's Court	(2016) Zhe 06 Min Te No. 23
8	Hangzhou Hanxin Machinery Manufacturing Co., Ltd.	Zhejiang Huanyu Construction Group Co., Ltd.		(2011) Zhe Shao Zhong Que Zi No. 6
9	Wuxi Wantong Real Estate Development Co., Ltd.	Changzhou Jiacheng Construction Engineering Co., Ltd., et al.	Wuxi Intermediate People's Court	(2015) Xi Min Zhong Shen Zi No. 00381
10	Xu	High-tech Sub-branch of Chongqing Three Gorges Bank Co., Ltd.	Chongqing FirstIntermediate People's Court	(2016) Yu 01 Min Te No. 1009
11	Shanghai Siemens High Voltage Switchgear Co., Ltd.	Wuxi Branch of China Pacific Property Insurance Co., Ltd.	Shanghai Financial Court	(2019) Hu 74 Min Te No. 10

negative opinions all believe that the absence of an arbitration agreement is a circumstance for revocation of arbitral awards. However, the challenging party can only apply to set aside an arbitral award after the arbitral award is rendered. Refusal to accept and review the application for confirming the existence of the arbitration agreement at an early stage is not conducive to determining the jurisdiction of the case as soon as possible. In fact, it may also cause a waste of judicial resources, affect the legitimate rights and interests of relevant parties, or result in excessive judicial costs for the parties involved.

1.2   Multi-tiered Disputes Resolution Clause

In commercial arbitration, there are often situations where the parties agree on a "multi-tiered dispute resolution clause", which refers to the provision where the parties agree that after disputes occur, the parties shall negotiate amicably or conduct mediation under the auspices of a specific subject, and the parties may initiate arbitration if negotiation or mediation fails. Sometimes the parties may also set a limitation on the period for negotiation or mediation. For example, the dispute resolution clause in the following case stipulated that "In the failure of negotiation, either party has the right to submit the dispute to CIETAC for arbitration in accordance with arbitration rules effective at that time within 60 days after the occurrence of disputes." This is equivalent to an agreed 60 day negotiation period.

From the wording of the "multi-tiered dispute resolution clause", it can be seen that the parties have agreed on more than one dispute resolution method in the same dispute resolution clause and agreed on the specific order in which the dispute resolution methods are applicable. The "multi-tiered dispute resolution clause" essentially means that the parties have agreed on the preconditions or pre-arbitration procedures.

Shandong Hongxingyuan Food Co., Ltd., et al. v. Suqian Zhongshan Tianrui Liding Venture Capital Center (L.P.)[6]

In May 2013, Shandong Hongxingyuan Food Co., Ltd. ("**Hongxingyuan Co.**"), Wang, Chen and Suqian Zhongshan Tianrui Liding Venture Capital Center (L.P.) ("**Tianrui Co.**"), Suqian Zhongshan Tiangui Liding Venture Capital Center (L.P.) ("**Tiangui Co.**"), etc. signed a Capital Increase and Share Expansion Agreement. Article 10.1 of the Agreement was the dispute resolution clause, which provided that any disputes arising from the interpretation or performance of this agreement shall be resolved through amicable negotiation. In the failure of negotiation, either party has the right to submit the dispute to CIETAC for arbitration in accordance with arbitration rules effective at that time within 60 days after the occurrence of disputes.

---

[6] (2018) Jing 04 Min Te No. 146 (1).

On September 29, 2016, Tianrui Co. and Tiangui Co. submitted their disputes under the Agreement to CIETAC for arbitration in accordance with the arbitration clause mentioned above against Hongxingyuan Co., Wang and Chen, and the application was accepted by CIETAC.

The requests of Tianrui Co. and Tiangui Co. were as follow: 1. to order Hongxingyuan Co., Wang and Chen to pay the original investment price of RMB 42 million in the amount of equity repurchase; 2. to order Hongxingyuan Co., Wang and Chen to pay the investment income of the amount of equity repurchase (based on the original investment price of RMB 42 million, calculated from June 5, 2013 to June 4, 2016 at an annual investment yield of 10%); 3. to order Hongxingyuan Co., Wang and Chen to pay the penalty interests arising from the overdue payment of the amount of equity repurchase (based on the unpaid amount of equity repurchase, calculated from March 29, 2016 to the date of actual repayment on the basis of 0.05% per day); 4. to order Hongxingyuan Co., Wang and Chen to pay arbitration fees and attorney fees.

On November 22, 2017, the arbitral tribunal issued the (2017) Jing Cai Zi No. 1408 Award, ruling that: 1. Wang and Chen should pay the amount of equity repurchase of RMB 54.6 million to Tianrui Co. and Tiangui Co. before February 4, 2018; 2. If Wang and Chen did not pay the amount of equity repurchase of RMB 54.6 million before February 4, 2018, they should pay the penalty interests arising from the overdue payment on the basis of 0.05% per day to Tianrui Co. and Tiangui Co. until the date of actual repayment; ... 6. Hongxingyuan Co. shall bear joint and several liabilities for the above payment obligations of Wang and Chen.

Later, the applicant filed a lawsuit with the Beijing Third Intermediate People's Court, requesting revoking the award. One of the reasons was that the respondent did not file for arbitration with the CIETAC within 60 days after the occurrence of the dispute, and thus, the arbitration agreement had become invalid.

The respondent stated that "within 60 days" stipulated in the arbitration agreement was intended to urge both parties to resolve the dispute as soon as possible. It cannot be understood that the right of both parties to file for arbitration has been eliminated after 60 days, thereby negating the validity of the arbitration agreement or determining that the arbitration agreement had become invalid.

Regarding the issue of the invalidity of the arbitration agreement, the Beijing Third Intermediate People's Court agreed with the respondent's view that the stipulation of "within 60 days" in the clause was originally intended to urge both parties to resolve the dispute as soon as possible. The arbitration agreement shall not be deemed invalid just because the party initiated arbitration 60 days after the occurrence of the dispute. In addition, the applicant did not raise an objection to the validity of the arbitration agreement before the first hearing of the arbitral tribunal. Therefore, the reason for setting aside the arbitral award was not upheld by the court.

In commercial practice, the "multi-tiered dispute resolution clause" raises some issues, such as whether the pre-arbitration procedure agreement in the clause is valid and enforceable, whether it is mandatory, and whether noncompliance will result in the lack of jurisdiction of the arbitral tribunal. Meanwhile, these issues themselves are closely related. If the agreement is not enforceable and compulsory, failure to comply with the pre-arbitration procedure agreement in the clause will not affect the jurisdiction of the arbitral tribunal.

Regarding the issues above, different arbitral tribunals, institutions and courts hold different views in different cases in the practice of commercial arbitration. Nevertheless, generally speaking, unless the parties clearly agree on the specific merits and procedural requirements for negotiation or mediation, so that the beginning, success or failure of negotiation or mediation can be effectively measured, arbitral tribunals and courts will generally consider this clause invalid and not enforceable due to lack of certainty.[7] Unless the parties explicitly agree that the pre-arbitration procedure agreement is mandatory, the arbitral tribunal and the court generally hold that the agreement is not mandatory, and failure to comply with the agreement will not lead to the lack of jurisdiction of the arbitral tribunal.[8]

For instance, the contract in *ICC Case No. 11490*[9] provided that any dispute between the parties will be settled in an amicable way. If the parties fail to agree over the said dispute, then it shall be referred for arbitration under the rules of the ICC in Paris under the law of England. The arbitral tribunal considered that, viewed from the parties' intention to agree on this clause, the parties did not intend to set negotiation as a precondition for arbitration; otherwise, the parties should clearly stipulate that friendly negotiation is a precondition for submission to arbitration. In contrast, the intention of the parties was to submit the dispute to arbitration, thereby precluding litigation in a court, and the wording of "friendly" merely expresses the parties' desire to avoid high litigation costs. Therefore, the arbitral tribunal believed that the clause did not constitute an effective pre-arbitration procedure of arbitration and therefore would not affect its jurisdiction over the dispute.

Another example is *ICC Case No. 14667*.[10] The parties in that case agreed that, in case of disputes, the parties will accept all measures to settle them by negotiations. Disputes on which no agreement could be reached were finally settled in accordance with the Reconciliatory and Arbitration Regulations of the International Chamber of Commerce, Geneva. The arbitral tribunal held the opinion that the parties did not regard reaching an agreement through negotiation as a precondition for arbitration but the failure to reach an agreement as a precondition for initiating arbitration. The initiation of arbitration by one party meant that the parties had failed to reach an agreement. Consequently, the precondition had been satisfied, and the party was entitled to initiate arbitration.

---

[7] Gary B. Born, *International Commercial Arbitration*, 917–918 (2nd ed., Kluwer Law International, 2014).

[8] Gary B. Born, *International Commercial Arbitration*, 922 (2nd ed., Kluwer Law International, 2014).

[9] *National Company (State X) v. (1) Company A (State Y), (2) Company B (State X), (3) Company C (State X)*, Final Award, ICC Case No. 11490, in Albert Jan van den Berg (ed.), Yearbook Commercial Arbitration 2012, Vol. 37.

[10] *State Joint Stock Company (Uzbekistan) v. State agency (India)*, Final Award, ICC Case No. 14667, 2011, in Albert Jan van den Berg (ed.), Yearbook Commercial Arbitration 2015, Vol. 40.

Similarly, in its Reply to the review report of Runhe Development Co., Ltd.'s application for non-enforcement of arbitral awards,[11] the SPC pointed out that the "friendly negotiation" and "the failure of negotiation" agreed upon by the parties were the form and result of negotiation, respectively, and one of the parties' applications for arbitration should be deemed a result of failure of negotiation. Therefore, in circumstances where "friendly negotiation" was difficult to define and "the failure of negotiation" had appeared, the arbitral tribunal had the right to accept cases on the basis of arbitration agreement.

In the case at hand, the parties agreed that any dispute arising from the interpretation or performance of this agreement shall be resolved through amicable negotiation. In the failure of negotiation, either party has the right to submit the dispute to the CIETAC for arbitration in accordance with arbitration rules effective at that time within 60 days after the occurrence of disputes. However, the parties did not clearly agree on the substantive meaning and procedures of "amicable negotiation" and how to determine "the failure of negotiation" and "the occurrence of disputes". At the same time, the parties did not explicitly stipulate that the negotiation procedure and the 60-day negotiation period are obligations that the parties must abide by, and the clause stipulated that any party had the "right" to initiate arbitration.

It can be seen that the parties' agreement on the pre-arbitration procedure is not mandatory, and the failure to comply with the agreement will not lead to the lack of jurisdiction of the arbitral tribunal. As stated by the Beijing Third Intermediate People's Court in this case, the intention to agree on the "within 60 days" in the clause was to urge both parties to resolve the dispute as soon as possible. Therefore, the arbitration agreement should not be deemed invalid just because the party initiated arbitration 60 days after the occurrence of disputes.

We may draw a conclusion here that when deciding whether the pre-arbitration procedure in the "multi-tiered dispute resolution clause" is enforceable and valid and whether it will affect the jurisdiction of the arbitral tribunal, the specific wordings of the clause must be examined. If the parties do not clearly agree on the specific merits and procedural requirements for negotiation or mediation, the agreement may lack certainty and enforceability; if the parties do not clearly stipulate that the pre-arbitration procedure agreement is mandatory, it is generally considered that the agreement is not mandatory, and noncompliance with the agreement will not lead to the lack of jurisdiction of the arbitral tribunal.

1.3   Transfer of Contract Rights

According to the difference of the object of the transfer, the transfer of contract can be divided into the transfer of contractual rights (credits), the transfer of contractual obligations (debts), and the overall transfer of contractual rights and obligations (credits and debts). Pursuant to Article 84 of the Contract Law, the transfer of debts

---

[11] (2018) Min Si Ta Zi No. 1.

requires the consent of the creditor. Pursuant to Article 555 of the Civil Code, the overall transfer of credits and debts also requires the consent of the counterparty to the original contract. Different from the previous circumstances, the transfer of credits does not require the debtor's consent. The creditor only needs to notify the debtor.[12] Accordingly, the transfer of credits will raise the issue of whether the arbitration clause of the original contract is transferred together with the credits.

Beijing Saiaotu Technology Development Co., Ltd. v. Zhang.[13]

On October 30, 2015, Beijing Saiaotu Technology Development Co., Ltd. ("**Saiaotu Co.**") as Party A and Jiangxi Tianmaizhiyin Technology Co., Ltd. ("**Tianmai Co.**") as Party B signed a Business Cooperation Agreement, of which Article 9 stipulates that "If there is any dispute between the two parties on the content of this agreement or its implementation, both parties shall conduct friendly negotiations. If the dispute cannot be resolved within three days after negotiation or one party is unwilling to negotiate, either party may submit the dispute to the Beijing Arbitration Commission for arbitration. The arbitral award is final and legally binding on both parties. During the arbitration, both parties will continue to perform the contractual clause other than the arbitration part."

On May 7, 2018, Tianmai Co. (the assignor of credits) and Zhang (the assignee of credits) signed the Credits Assignment Agreement, which stipulated that Tianmai Co. voluntarily transfers the principal of RMB 830,614.83 and the corresponding interests of the credits to Saiaotu Co. in the Business Cooperation Agreement to Zhang, and Zhang was aware and approved of the arbitration agreement between Tianmai Co. and Saiaotu Co. in the Business Cooperation Agreement.

After disputes occurred, Zhang filed an arbitration application against Saiaotu Co. at the Beijing Arbitration Commission on May 22, 2018. The Beijing Arbitration Commission accepted the case on May 23, 2018. Saiaotu Co. applied to the Beijing Third Intermediate People's Court to confirm that the arbitration agreement was invalid.

Saiaotu Co. took the view that the matters agreed for arbitration between it and Tianmai Co. were limited to the "content" and "execution" of the Business Cooperation Agreement. No written arbitration agreement had been reached with regard to the changes, assignments, and liabilities for breach of contract. Without a new arbitration agreement between the parties, the dispute cannot be resolved through arbitration. Additionally, Zhang could not obtain the independent right to submit the disputes with Saiaotu Co. to arbitration because of the conclusion of the Credits Assignment Agreement with Tianmai Co.

Zhang held that, in accordance with Article 19 of the Arbitration Law and Article 9 of the Arbitration Law Interpretation, the change of the contract subject did not affect the validity of the arbitration agreement, and the disputes involved in the case were within the scope of matters stipulated in the arbitration clause.

---

[12] Paragraph 1 of Article 80 of the Contract Law.

[13] (2018) Jing 04 Min Te No. 235.

The Beijing Third Intermediate People's Court ruled that, pursuant to Article 9 of the Arbitration Law Interpretation, Zhang was the assignee of credits between Tianmai Co. and Saiaotu Co., and Zhang knew and approved the arbitration agreement between Tianmai Co. and Saiaotu Co. Saiaotu Co. failed to provide evidence to prove the existence of the exceptions described in the provision, so the arbitration agreement involved in the case was binding on Zhang. Therefore, the court dismissed the application of Saiaotu Co.

In fact, regarding the issue of whether the arbitration clause of the original contract will be transferred together with the transfer of credits, Article 9 of the Arbitration Law Interpretation has provided an answer. Pursuant to the provision, where the creditor's rights and debts are transferred in whole or in part, the arbitration agreement shall bind the assignee in principle. However, there are two exceptions: the parties have agreed otherwise, the assignee expressly objected or was not aware of the existence of a separate arbitration agreement at the time of the transfer. If there are exceptional circumstances, the arbitration agreement will not be binding on the assignee. In addition, the "whole or partial transfer of creditor rights and debts" in the provision is not limited to the general transfer of creditor rights and debts but should also include the whole or partial transfer of creditors' rights and the whole or partial transfer of debts.[14]

The present case falls within the general situation. In this case, the original contract, Business Cooperation Agreement containing an arbitration clause, was signed between Tianmai Co. and Saiaotu Co. Afterwards, Tianmai Co. promised in the Credits Assignment Agreement to transfer the principal and corresponding interests of the creditor's rights to Saiaotu Co. in the Business Cooperation Agreement to Zhang. In addition, there exist no exceptions stipulated in Article 9 of the Arbitration Law Interpretation in this case. The assignee Zhang knew and recognized the existence of arbitration clauses in the original contract. Therefore, in accordance with Article 9 of the Arbitration Law Interpretation, the arbitration agreement involved in the case was binding on Zhang.

After the Arbitration Law Interpretation was promulgated, the judgments of the various courts on similar circumstances to this case were consistent.

For example, *Chongqing Bishan Jinchun Small Loan Co., Ltd. v. Chongqing Rail Transit (Group) Co., Ltd.,*[15] Chongqing Bishan Jinchun Small Loan Co., Ltd. ("**Jinchun Co.**") and Chongqing Yaowei Economic And Trade Co., Ltd. ("**Yaowei Co.**") signed two service supply contracts, which stipulated that disputes shall be arbitrated by the Chongqing Arbitration Commission. Later, Yaowei Co. and Chongqing Returnees Trading Co., Ltd. ("**Returnee Co.**") concluded the Contractual Credits Assignment Agreement, stipulating that Yaowei Co. transferred its credits under the above two Service Supply Contracts to Returnee Co. Returnee Co. and Jinchun Co. also signed the Credits Transfer Agreement, stipulating that Returnee Co. transferred its credits under the above two Service Supply Contracts to Jinchun Co. Both Yaowei Co. and Returnee Co. issued a Notice on Assignment of Credits to Chongqing Rail

---

[14] (2016) Zui Gao Fa Min Xia Zhong No. 273.

[15] (2017) Yu 0120 Min Chu No. 2096.

Transit (Group) Co., Ltd. ("**Rail Transit Co.**"). In this case, the court held that there was no evidence to prove that Jinchun Co. and Rail Transit Co. had an agreement to resolve disputes through litigation, or Rail Transit Co. had explicitly opposed the arbitration agreement when the credits were transferred and therefore confirmed that the arbitration agreement was valid.

In addition, *Kunshan Xingsheng Construction Development Co., Ltd. v. Shanghai Hengtai Law Firm*,[16] and the case *Weiming Composite Materials (Huai'an) Co., Ltd. v. Zhang*,[17] both courts drew a consistent conclusion in accordance with Article 9 of the Arbitration Law Interpretation.

However, when there is an exceptional circumstance, the arbitration agreement is not binding on the assignee. In the case of *Taiyuan Jinxiang Enterprise Management Consulting Co., Ltd. v. Xinjiang Daming Animal Husbandry Co., Ltd.*, et al.,[18] Article 10 of the Credits Assignment Agreement signed by the assignee and the assignor clearly stipulated that "the assignee does not agree, approve, or accept the arbitration jurisdiction agreement stipulated in the Convertible Notes Subscription Agreement and all parties have the right to settle related matters in the relevant courts of Shanxi Province."In view of the fact that this case fell within the exceptional circumstance as stipulated in Article 9 of the Arbitration Law Interpretation, the SPC held that the arbitration clause in the original contract was not binding on the assignee.

1.4   Standard Form Contract

The format contract, also known as the standard form contract or a fixed contract, refers to the contract where the terms are drawn up in advance by one of the parties for repeated use, and an unspecified counterparty generally agrees or rejects the contract and cannot bargain. Similarly, the format clause refers to the clause that is drawn up in advance by one of the parties for repeated use and is not negotiated with the other party when the contract is concluded.[19] It should be noted that not all terms in a format contract are format clauses. Therefore, arbitration clauses in format contracts are not certainly standard clauses.

Chen v. Beijing HB World Network Technology Co., Ltd.[20]

Beijing HB World Network Technology Co., Ltd. ("**HB**") is a trading platform that provides virtual currencies such as Bitcoin and Litecoin for online users. HB itself does not provide virtual currencies. Its main profit method is to charge corresponding fees when users trade virtual currencies or withdraw cash.

---

[16] (2017) Su 05 Min Te No. 61.

[17] (2017) Su 08 Min Te No. 75.

[18] (2016) Zui Gao Fa Min Xia Zhong No. 273.

[19] Paragraph 2 of Article 39 of the Contract Law.

[20] (2017) Jing 03 Min Te Jian No. 8.

On November 21, 2013, Chen registered on the Internet service platform provided by HB ("**HB Website**") and became an online user of the HB Website.

In February 2017, Chen filed a lawsuit against HB at the Beijing Haidian District People's Court ("**Haidian Court**") due to contractual disputes, requesting the Haidian Court to order HB to return Chen's Bitcoins in the amount of 52.8567 and Litecoins in the amount of 815.99731.

During the litigation process in the Haidian Court, HB submitted to the Haidian Court that both parties had concluded an HB User Agreement, which included a valid arbitration clause; thus, the dispute shall be resolved through arbitration, and the Haidian Court shall dismiss Chen's requests. Chen alleged that the arbitration clause proposed by HB should be deemed invalid. The Haidian Court held that the parties should first apply to the people's court to rule on the validity of the arbitration agreement due to the parties' disagreement regarding the validity of the arbitration clause.

On July 13, 2017, HB applied to the Beijing Third Intermediate People's Court to confirm the validity of the arbitration agreement. Since the result of the dispute over the validity of the arbitration agreement would directly determine whether the Haidian Court had jurisdiction over the case, the Haidian Court issued the (2016) Jing 0108 Min Chu No. 34671 civil ruling on July 21, 2017, ruling to suspend the trial of the case.

Pursuant to the (2017) Jing Xin De Nei Jing Zheng Zi No. 00661 Notarization rendered by the Beijing Xinde Notary Office, during the registration process of online users of HB Website, the registrant was required to tick the box in front of the sentence, that is, "I have read and agree to the HB Network User Agreement" in the registration page on the mobile phone, so that the registrant could click the "register" button. The HB Network User Agreement on this page was linkable, and the displayed name changed to the HB User Agreement after clicking it.

The HB User Agreement stipulated that HB and users hereby confirm the following: 1. When the user clicks the button of "consent to register" on the HB registration page, completes the registration process, and obtains the HB account and password, it is deemed that the user and HB have reached the HB User Agreement ("**Agreement**") regarding the user's entry into HB and the user's use of corresponding transaction services provided by HB. 2. HB and the user have carefully read all the terms in this HB User Agreement and the contents of the legal statements and operating rules issued by HB, have known, understood and accepted this Agreement and the foregoing service terms, legal statements and operating rules, and agreed that they serve as the basis for determining the rights and obligations of both parties......16.1 Disputes between the user and HB due to the performance of this Agreement shall be resolved through amicable negotiation. If the negotiation fails, either party has the right to submit the dispute to the Beijing Arbitration Commission for arbitration in accordance with its arbitration rules.

Pursuant to the (2017) Jing Xin De Nei Jing Zheng Zi No. 00662 Notarization rendered by the Beijing Xinde Notary Office, HB uploaded the Internet User Agreement through operations on October 28, 2013. Article 12 of the Agreement stated that disputes between users and HB Website due to the performance of this agreement shall be resolved through amicable negotiation. If the negotiation fails, either party has the right to submit the dispute to the Beijing Arbitration Commission for arbitration in accordance with its arbitration rules.

The Beijing Third Intermediate People's Court considered that on November 21, 2013, Chen became a user of HB Website by completing the user registration procedure. During the registration process, Chen, as a person with full civil capacity, voluntarily ticked the box in front of the sentence, that is, "I have read and agree to the HB Network User Agreement", proving that it had agreed to be bound by the Agreement. Therefore, both parties have a clear and specific intention of submitting disputes to arbitration. The relationship between HB and Chen was a service contract relationship between an online user and a service platform. Disputes arising under the contractual relationship between the two parties could be resolved through arbitration, which complied with the law. According to the agreement between the parties, the choice of the arbitration institution was unique and clear. Meanwhile, there were no circumstances that may invalidate the arbitration clause. As a result, the Beijing Third Intermediate People's Court made the (2017) Jing 03 Min Te No. 286 Ruling, confirming that the arbitration clause in the HB Website User Agreement agreed that Chen and HB was valid.

Chen disputed the Ruling and filed an objection to the Beijing Third Intermediate People's Court. The main reasons were: 1. The HB Website User Agreement was not fixed in any form, such as paper printing or screenshots, and the Agreement itself stated that the respondent could unilaterally modify any clause at any time. It was objectively impossible for HB to prove that the HB Website User Agreement Chen ticked at the time of registration contained the so-called arbitration clause nearly four years later. Therefore, the Ruling lacked basic evidence. 2. The HB Website User Agreement was a format contract. HB used its dominant position to force Chen to give up the right to choose dispute resolution methods and the right to choose arbitration institutions. This was a situation where the main rights of the other party were excluded by the use of a format contract, and no special notice was given. Therefore, the arbitration clause was invalid, and the Ruling was wrong in the applicable law.

Regarding the question of whether the arbitration clause existed, HB submitted the first notarized version of the HB Website User Agreement and provided a later modified version of the Agreement. Both versions contained the arbitration clause. Chen said that he "seems not to read" the content of the agreement when he checked the HB Website User Agreement. Based on the facts above, the Beijing Third Intermediate People's Court was convinced that there was an arbitration clause in the HB Website User Agreement ticked by Chen when he registered as the user at 8:32 on November 21, 2013. Without sufficient evidence to prove that there was no arbitration clause in the HB Website User Agreement Chen ticked, the Beijing Third Intermediate People's Court determined that the arbitration clause existed.

Concerning the validity of the arbitration clause, the Beijing Third Intermediate People's Court considered that according to general common sense, the public would see the precautions and risk warnings announced by the operator when registering as users on the Internet. When new users see the content of risk warnings, they should be aware of the risks of business behaviors. Among them, the choice of dispute resolution methods and the choice of arbitration institutions were crucial to the parties. It was extremely disproportionate between Chen's alleged behavior of not reading the content of the HB Website User Agreement when clicking it and his risk awareness as a legal educator. Additionally, there was no evidence to prove that the choice of the parties to submit disputes to arbitration would cause damage to their important rights thus far. Therefore, the objection that the arbitration clause was invalid was not supported by the court.

When determining the validity of the arbitration clause in a format contract, the issue that needs to be resolved first is whether the arbitration clause is a format clause. If the arbitration clause is the result of consensus between the parties, the arbitration clause is not a format clause. Generally, if the dispute resolution clause of a contract lists multiple options for the counterparty to choose or fill in, the court generally determines that the arbitration clause is not a format clause.

The case *Ya'an Dayuan Real Estate Development Co., Ltd. v. Ya'an Municipal Bureau of Land and Resources*[21] provides a good example. The stipulation of the dispute resolution method of the contract involved in the case was "Disputes arising from the performance of this contract shall be resolved through negotiation between the two parties. If the negotiation fails, it shall be resolved in accordance with the method agreed in item (1) of this Article: (1) submit to Ya'an Arbitration Commission for arbitration; (2) file a lawsuit to a people's court in accordance with the law."In this case, the SPC held that the article provided two options, that is, arbitration and litigation, and the parties agreed to choose arbitration by consensus, and there was no evidence to prove that the counterparty did not have the right to negotiate when choosing arbitration. Consequently, it cannot be regarded as a format clause.

Coincidentally, in the case *Qiu, et al. v. Kunming Bangsheng Real Estate Development Co., Ltd.*,[22] the Kunming Intermediate People's Court held that the parties' behavior to tick the box of "submit to Kunming Arbitration Commission for Arbitration" in the Dispute Resolution Methods in the contract involved had indicated that the parties have reached an agreement on the mechanism of resolving the disputes, and thus the clause did not constitute a format clause.

If the parties do not agree on the arbitration clause, the arbitration clause shall be regarded as a format clause. When determining the validity of the arbitration clause, it is necessary to further explore whether there are circumstances invalidating the arbitration clause.

Article 40 of the Contract Law provides for three situations where the format clause shall be deemed invalid: circumstances invalidating the contract stipulated in Article 52 of the Contract Law,[23] circumstances invalidating the exemption clause

---

[21] (2017) Zui Gao Fa Min Zhong No. 91.

[22] (2009) Kun Min Yi Chu Zi No. 1.

[23] The circumstances include: (1) one party concludes the contract through the use of fraudulent or coercive means, causing detriment to the interests of the State; (2) the contract involves a malicious conspiracy which is detrimental to the interests of the State, a collective or a third party; (3) illegal

in the contract stipulated in Article 53 of the Contract Law,[24] and where the clause operates to exclude the liabilities of the party proposing the format clause, to increase the liabilities of the other party, or to exclude main rights enjoyed by the other party.

In accordance with Article 497 of the Civil Code, a format clause is void under any of the following circumstances:

(1) existence of a circumstance under which the clause is void as provided in section 3 of Chapter VI of Book One and Article 506 of this Code;

(2) the party providing the standard clause unreasonably exempts or alleviates himself from the liability, imposes heavier liability on the other party, or restricts the main rights of the other party; or

(3) the party providing the standard clause deprives the other party of his mainrights.

According to the Civil Code regarding the invalidity of civil juristic acts, a format clause is void and invalid for the following reasons: (1) purely beneficial or unrecognized civil juristic acts performed by persons with no civil capacity or with limited civil capacity[25]; (2) civil juristic acts carried out with false intentions[26]; (3) civil juristic acts that violate mandatory provisions on effectiveness or violate public order and good customs[27]; (4) malicious collusion to damage the interests of others in civil jurisprudence.[28]

Among the situations listed above, the most common ones are that the invalidation of the format clause due to violation of the mandatory provisions of laws and administrative regulations and the situation where the party providing the format clause exempts its responsibilities increases the responsibilities of the other party and excludes the other party's main rights, which results in the invalidity of the format clause.

Regarding the first situation, the counterparty who accepts the format clause usually claims that the clause is invalid on the ground that the party providing the format clause failed to perform the obligation to draw attention stipulated in Article 39 of the Contract Law. In judicial practice, different courts hold different views on whether this situation will cause the invalidity of the format arbitration clause.

For instance, in the case *Li v. Jining Center Branch of AXA Tianping Property Insurance Co., Ltd.*,[29] both the Wulian County People's Court of Shandong Province in the first instance and the Intermediate People's Court of Rizhao City in the second instance considered the arbitration clauseinvalid on the ground that the insurance

---

intentions are concealed beneath an appearance of legality; (4) there is detriment to social and public interests; or (5) the mandatory provisions of laws and administrative regulations are violated.

[24] The circumstances include: (1) clauses relating to personal injuries sustained by the other party; and (2) clauses relating to property losses sustained by the other party either because of the first party's deliberate acts or its gross negligence.

[25] See Articles 144 and 145 of the Civil Code.

[26] See Article 146 of the Civil Code.

[27] See Article 153 of the Civil Code.

[28] See Article 154 of the Civil Code.

[29] (2016) Lu 11 Min Xia Zhong No. 90.

company did not provide evidence to prove that the arbitration clause involved was brought to the attention of the counterparty in a reasonable manner and the counterparty claimed that the arbitration clause was invalid.

In contrast, in the case *Qiu et al. v. Kunming Bangsheng Real Estate Development Co., Ltd.*,[30] the Kunming Intermediate People's Court clearly pointed out that the format clause should be deemed invalid only when it met the three conditions specified in Article 40 of the Contract Law. Following this logic, the obligation to draw attention stipulated in Article 39 of the Contract Law is not among the invalidating situations listed in Article 40 of the Contract Law, and thus, even a violation of Article 39 of the Contract Law does not necessarily result in the invalidation of a format clause.

Concerning this issue, first, the contents that Article 39 of the Contract Law requires the party to provide the format clause to take reasonable measures to draw the attention of the other party are "clauses which exempt or limit their liability". However, the arbitration clause only stipulates the dispute resolution method and does not fall within "clauses which exempt or limit their liability" of the party providing the format clause. Therefore, the party providing the format arbitration clause shall not bear the statutory obligation to draw attention and explain under Article 39 of the Contract Law. Second, even if the obligation exists, since Article 40 of the Contract Law does not include the breach of the obligation in situations invalidating the format clause, the arbitration clause shall not be invalidated since the provider has not drew attention and explained.

In addition, some parties cited Article 31 of the Civil Procedure Law Interpretation to allege that the arbitration clauses are invalid. For example, in *Bai v. Taiyuan Yingze Branch of the People's Insurance Company of China*,[31] Bai claimed that the arbitration clause involved in the case was invalid in accordance with Article 31 of the Civil Procedure Law Interpretation, and the claim was supported by the Luliang Intermediate People's Court. In the case *Chen v. Beijing HB World Network Technology Co., Ltd.*, Chen also raised this allegation.

This view is still open for discussion. The circumstance stipulated in Article 31 of the Civil Procedure Law Interpretation is that the operators use format clauses to enter into jurisdiction agreements with consumers. The jurisdiction agreement usually means that the parties to a contract or other property rights disputes choose the jurisdiction of the people's court in accordance with Article 34 of the Civil Procedure Law. However, the jurisdiction agreement is different from an arbitration agreement. Where the arbitration clause does not fall within the circumstances stipulated in Article 40 of the Contract Law and Article 17 of the Arbitration Law, it is unreasonable to apply Article 31 of the Civil Procedure Law Interpretation. With regard to the second situation, the counterparty who accepts the format clause will often claim that the arbitration clause excludes its right to choose the dispute resolution method, the right to choose an arbitration institution, or the right to resort to

---

[30] (2009) Kun Min Yi Chu Zi No.1.

[31] (2016) Jin 11 Min Xia Zhong No. 55.

litigation. The opinions of different courts are also not consistent on whether the claim can be supported.

In *Yang v. Huaihua Central Branch of the Bank of China Insurance Co., Ltd.*,[32] the Huaihua Intermediate People's Court found that the arbitration clause involved in the case was a clause that the insurance company created obstacles for the insured to claim contractual rights on the ground that the Changsha Arbitration Commission as stipulated in the arbitration clause involved was not related to the dispute and was far away from the place of residence of the parties and the place where the accident occurred, and determined that the arbitration clause was invalid in accordance with Article 40 of the Contract Law.

In *Luohe Branch of China XXXX Insurance Co., Ltd. v. Linying County Branch of Luohe City XX Company*,[33] Luohe Intermediate People's Court held that the arbitration clause involved "did not clearly state that the parties can choose to file a lawsuit before a people's court in accordance with the law, which restricted and deprived Linying County XX Company's right to choose the method of contractual dispute resolution", and thus ruled that the arbitration clause was invalid.

In contrast, *Ya'an Dayuan Real Estate Development Co., Ltd. v. Ya'an Municipal Bureau of Land and Resources*,[34] the SPC explicitly stated that "litigation and arbitration are both remedies for dispute resolution, and the choice of arbitration as the method of dispute resolution cannot be regarded as an exclusion of the main rights of the parties."

The choice of arbitration cannot be regarded as an exclusion of the main rights of the parties. The reasons include: (1) The choice of arbitration has equal binding force on both parties, which conforms to the principle of fairness; (2) Arbitration and litigation are both dispute resolution methods, and the choice of arbitration will not deprive the counterparty of the format clause of remedies; (3) The dispute resolution clause does not involve the distribution of substantive rights, and the arbitration clause of the format contract does not affect the substantive rights of the parties.

In this case, Chen ticked the HB Website User Agreement, which contained the arbitration clause stipulating that disputes between users and HB Website resulting from the performance of this Agreement shall be resolved through amicable negotiation. If the negotiation fails, either party has the right to submit the dispute to the Beijing Arbitration Commission for arbitration in accordance with its arbitration rules. Based on the analysis above, the arbitration clause is a format clause that was drafted by the HB Website in advance, and Chen could not negotiate and modify it. However, Chen did not provide evidence to prove that the arbitration clause fell within the invalidating situations under Article 40 of the Contract Law, and the choice of arbitration could not be considered an exclusion of the main rights of the parties. Therefore, the Beijing Third Intermediate People's Court rejected Chen's objection.

In summary, the judicial practice on the validity of the arbitration clause in the format contract of China is not consistent. To prevent the arbitration clause from

---

[32] (2014) Huai Zhong Min Er Zhong Zi No. 91.

[33] (2009) Luo Min Er Zhong Zi No. 147.

[34] (2017) Zui Gao Fa Min Zhong No. 91.

being invalidated as much as possible, the party providing the format contract should take active measures, such as listing multiple options in the dispute resolution clause of the contract for the counterparty to choose or fill in. At the same time, users should carefully read the relevant terms before ticking to agree to the relevant agreement to avoid ignoring some important terms.

1.5   The Dismissal of Law Suits *Ex Officio*

When the parties have agreed on an arbitration clause and one party files a lawsuit in the court, the other party usually submits an arbitration agreement to the court before the first hearing of the case and raises the objection that the case should be under the jurisdiction of the arbitration institution specified in the arbitration clause instead of the court. This approach is based on Article 26 of the Arbitration Law. Under such circumstances, there is no doubt that the court should dismiss the suit unless the arbitration agreement is invalid.

However, if the other party does not raise an objection to jurisdiction before the first hearing of the case, can the court dismiss the lawsuit on the basis of the existence of an arbitration agreement *ex officio*?

Hu v. Wang, et al.[35]

On November 3, 2013, Hu filed an action with the Hongshan District People's Court of Wuhan City, Hubei Province ("**Court of First Instance**"), requesting that:… 2. To confirm that the Wuhan City Stock House Sales Contract signed by the defendant Wang and the defendants Huang, et al. on August 30, 2017 was invalid, and the transfer was invalid; 3. To confirm that the Wuhan City Stock House Sales Contract signed by the defendant Huang and Wang and the defendant Li on September 23, 2017 was invalid, and the transfer was invalid; 4. To confirm that the Wuhan City Stock House Sales Contract signed by the defendant Li and the defendants Wang and Dai on October 23, 2017 was invalid, and the transfer was invalid; 5. To rule that the house in dispute shall belong to the plaintiff, and the defendants Wang and Dai shall cooperate to transfer the above mentioned house to the plaintiff; 6. The litigation costs in this case were jointly borne by the six defendants.

On March 1, 2018, Hu added the first claim, requesting that the Wuhan City Stock House Sales Contract signed by the third person Wang in the name of the plaintiff and the defendant Huang on March 1, 2018 was invalid, and the transfer was invalid.

Upon review, the Court of First Instance found that Article 5 of the Arbitration Law stipulates, "Where the parties reach an arbitration agreement and one party files a lawsuit in a people's court, the people's court shall not accept it, unless the arbitration agreement is invalid." Article 10 of the Wuhan Stock House Sales Contract signed by Hu and Wang stipulated that "If the parties fail to reach an agreement on the contractual disputes through negotiation, it shall be submitted to the Wuhan Arbitration

---

[35] (2018) E 01 Min Zhong No. 5438.

Commission for arbitration." This clause was an arbitration clause agreed between the two parties, and the agreed arbitration institution was clear and complied with Article 16 of the Arbitration Law. Consequently, the clause should be legal and effective. When Hu filed the case, the first request was deleted from the civil complaint submitted to the court of first instance. After the case was accepted, Hu applied to the Court of First Instance to add the first request. Hu's behavior obviously circumvented Article 5 of the Arbitration Law. In addition, upon Hu's application, the Court of First Instance retrieved the three agreements signed by Wang and Huang, et al., Huang, Wang and Li, Li and Wang, Dai. Article 10 of the Wuhan City Stock House Sales Contract also stipulates that "If the parties fail to reach an agreement on the contractual disputes through negotiation, it shall be submitted to the Wuhan Arbitration Commission for arbitration." Combined with Hu's litigation requests, pursuant to Article 19 of the Arbitration Law, the arbitration agreement exists independently. The invalidity of the contract does not affect the validity of the arbitration agreement. The arbitral tribunal has the right to confirm the validity of the contract. Therefore, the court did not have jurisdiction over the case, and Hu should apply to the Wuhan Arbitration Commission for arbitration. Thus, the Court of First Instance made the (2018) E 0111 Min Chu No. 1820 Civil Ruling, dismissing Hu's action.

Hu was dissatisfied with the ruling and appealed to the Wuhan Intermediate People's Court of Hubei Province, requesting revoking the original ruling and ruling that the Court of First Instance continue to hear the case.

Hu alleged that the six claims made by him in the trial were a whole. When filing the lawsuit, Hu did not obtain the house sale contracts signed by Wang and Huang, et al., Huang, Wang and Li, Li and Wang, Dai, which need to be retrieved by the court. Therefore, when Hu filed the lawsuit, the first claim with an arbitration clause was removed to meet the scope of the court's acceptance and facilitate the one-time trial of the case. After the first-instance case was accepted on November 3, 2017, Hu filed a petition for the change of litigation request and the Application for Investigation and Evidence Collection on March 1, 2018. The Court of First Instance retrieved evidence in accordance with the law and served the new complaint to all parties. The scheduled hearing date for the trial was May 4, 2018, and neither the defendants nor the third party submitted an arbitration agreement to the court before that date. Pursuant to Article 26 of the Arbitration Law, the people's court should not actively invoke the arbitration agreement to reject the suit after accepting the case. The people's court erroneously applied Article 5 of the Arbitration Law to reject the plaintiff's suit. The trial should continue to be heard.

Regarding the issue, the Wuhan Intermediate People's Court considered that Paragraph 2 of Article 124 of the Civil Procedure Law stipulated that "People's courts may deal with the following filing of lawsuits based on the respective circumstances: ...... (2) Where both parties to a lawsuit have entered into a written arbitration agreement to apply for arbitration pursuant to the provisions of the laws and are not allowed to file a lawsuit with a people's court, the people's court shall notify the plaintiff to apply to an arbitration organization for arbitration". Paragraph 3 of Article 208 of the Civil Procedure Law Interpretation stipulated that "After filing the case, if it is found that the conditions for lawsuit are not met or fall within the circumstances specified in Article 124 of the Civil Procedure Law, the lawsuit shall be rejected." Accordingly, the people's court had the legal right to actively review and handle the arbitration agreement after accepting the case. The Civil Procedure Law had the same level of effectiveness as the Arbitration Law, but the current effective Civil Procedure Law was revised lately. In accordance with the principle that the new law was superior to the old law, the old law was superior regarding the merits and the new law was superior regarding the procedures, the Civil Procedure Law and its Interpretation should take precedence over the Arbitration Law to be applied.

In addition, Article 26 of the Arbitration Law cited by Hu on the grounds of appeal was not fully applicable to the circumstances in this case. Article 26 of the Arbitration Law provides that "Where the parties have reached an arbitration agreement, but one of the parties initiates an action in a people's court without stating the existence of the arbitration agreement, the people's court shall reject the action if the other party submits to the court the arbitration agreement before the first hearing of the case unless the arbitration agreement is invalid. If the other party fails to object to the hearing by the people's court before the first hearing, the arbitration agreement shall be considered to have been waived by the party and the people's court shall proceed with the hearing." The "without stating" stipulated in the clause not only included not voluntarily notifying the existence of the arbitration clause but also included not reflecting on the evidence submitted. During the trial of this case, Hu intended to add the first claim after the case was filed and submitted the corresponding House Sales Contract. At the same time, Hu applied for the court to retrieve the House Sales Contracts pointed to by the second to fourth claims *ex officio*. This evidence should also be regarded as evidence submitted by Hu. Thus, the court has confirmed from the evidence submitted by Hu that the Sales Contract referred to in this case contained an arbitration clause. In view of this situation, the court did not need and should not wait passively for other parties to the contract to submit an arbitration agreement to the court. It should deal with it *ex officio*, respecting the parties' choice of dispute settlement methods when signing the contract, improving litigation efficiency and avoiding litigation delays.

Regarding the issue of whether the court can dismiss the lawsuit based on the existence of an arbitration agreement *ex officio* when the other party does not raise an objection to jurisdiction before the first hearing, there are two different views in practice.

One view is that the situation shall be regarded as the other party's waiver of the arbitration agreement, and the court shall continue to hear the case instead of dismissing the lawsuit based on the existence of an arbitration agreement *ex officio* in accordance with Article 26 of the Arbitration Law.

For example, in the case *Wang*, et al. *v. Hubei Chenggong Real Estate Development Co., Ltd.*, et al.,[36] Wuhan Jianghong Shunda House Expropriation Service Co., Ltd. (demolition unit), and Wang (the demolished person) signed a demolition agreement on the house involved in the case. He signed the Demolition Agreement and confirmed on behalf of Wang at the place where Party B should sign. After the house was

---

[36] (2018) E 01 Min Zhong No. 5174.

demolished, he received more than RMB 240,000 for demolition on behalf of Wang. Article 8 of the Demolition Agreement stipulated that "Disputes arising from the performance of this Agreement shall be resolved through negotiation between the parties. If the negotiation fails, both parties agree to submit disputes to the Wuhan Municipal Arbitration Commission for arbitration." Now Wang alleged that He, his mother-in-law, had no right to sign the Demolition Agreement on his behalf and filed a lawsuit to confirm the invalidity of the Demolition Agreement and request compensation for his loss. The court of first instance in this case considered that the dispute was a dispute arising from the performance of the Demolition Agreement, and the parties had clearly agreed to resolve the dispute by arbitration and thus dismissed the suit of Wang et al. in accordance with Item 2 of Article 124 of the Civil Procedure Law and Paragraph 3 of Article 208 of the Civil Procedure Law Interpretation. Later, Wang, et al. filed an appeal. The court of second instance held that pursuant to Article 26 of the Arbitration Law, the three defendants did not raise an objection to jurisdiction before the first hearing, and the court of first instance should continue to hear the case and therefore ruled to revoke the original ruling.

Another point of view is that even if the other party does not raise an objection to jurisdiction before the first hearing, the court has the right to reject the suit on the ground of the existence of an arbitration agreement *ex officio* in accordance with Item 2 of Article 124 of the Civil Procedure Law and Paragraph 3 of Article 208 of the Civil Procedure Law Interpretation.

Both courts of the first and second instance in the case held this view. In the case at hand, the several Wuhan Stock Housing Sales Contracts involved all provided that "If the parties fail to reach an agreement on the contractual disputes through negotiation, it shall be submitted to the Wuhan Arbitration Commission for arbitration." Hu filed an action before the court of first instance, and several defendants did not raise a jurisdictional objection before the first hearing. The court of first instance rejected Hu's suit on the ground of the existence of an arbitration agreement *ex officio*. Hu believed that after accepting the case, the court of first instance should not actively invoke the arbitration agreement to dismiss the lawsuit and thus appealed to the court of second instance. The court of second instance held that on the issue of whether the court can actively review the arbitration agreement *ex officio*, Article 26 of the Arbitration Law and Item 2 of Article 124 of the Civil Procedure Law were inconsistent. In accordance with the principle that the new law was superior to the old law, the old law was superior regarding the merits and the new law was superior regarding the procedures, the Civil Procedure Law which was revised lately should take precedence over the Arbitration Law to be applied. Therefore, the court of first instance had the power to review the arbitration agreement *ex officio* in accordance with Item 2 of Article 124 of the Civil Procedure Law and Paragraph 3 of Article 208 of the Civil Procedure Law Interpretation.

Coincidentally, in the case *Song v. Zhumadian Xinghai Real Estate Co., Ltd.,* et al.,[37] both courts of the first and second instance in the retrial procedure held that the parties involved had agreed on the arbitration clause in the Loan Contract,

---

[37] (2019) Yu 01 Min Zhong No. 4497.

although none of the defendants raised objections to the court's acceptance of the case before the first hearing, but the court still had the power to dismiss the action *ex officio* in accordance with Item 2 of Article 124 of the Civil Procedure Law and Article 215 of the Civil Procedure Law Interpretation.

Additionally, the court of second instance in the present case held that "one of the parties initiates an action in a people's court without stating the existence of the arbitration agreement" stipulated in Article 26 of the Arbitration Law not only included not voluntarily notifying the existence of the arbitration clause but also included not reflecting on the evidence submitted. In this case, the arbitration clause was included in the contract that Hu applied for the court to retrieve. Therefore, the court of second instance held that the case did not fell within the circumstance that "one of the parties initiates an action in a people's court without stating the existence of the arbitration agreement" stipulated in Article 26 of the Arbitration Law, and thus the clause was not fully applicable in this case.

1.6   The Principle of Independence of Arbitration Clauses

There are mainly two forms of arbitration agreement: separate arbitration agreement and arbitration clause contained in contracts.[38] Regardless of whether it is a separate arbitration agreement or an arbitration clause in a contract, whether the arbitration agreement is independent of the relevant underlying contract has been controversial.

If we view from the surface, since the arbitration clause is an integral part of the contract, when one party raises an objection to the validity of the contract, the validity of the arbitration clause is also uncertain, so the court may decide on the validity of the contract and the validity of the arbitration clause. However, the corresponding disadvantage is that this approach excludes the arbitration tribunal from hearing disputes over the validity of the contract and may allow one party to claim that the contract is invalid to avoid or delay arbitration.

With the development of arbitration, the principle of independence of arbitration clauses has been accepted by most countries, and it has been widely recognized that arbitration clauses do not lose their validity due to the invalidity of contracts. However, whether the arbitration clause is absolutely or relatively independent and to what extent the arbitration clause is independent are still disputed in practice.[39]

The independence of the arbitration clause means that although the arbitration clause is attached to the contract, it is separated from the other clauses of the contract and exists separately and does not become invalid due to the invalidity or cancellation of the contract. Regarding the basis underlying the independence of arbitration

---

[38] Article 16 of Arbitration Law provides: An arbitration agreement shall include the arbitration clause provided in the contract and any other written form of agreement concluded before or after the disputes providing for submission to arbitration. Additionally, see Article 21 of the Arbitration Law (Draft for Comments).

[39] Shen Deyong, Wan E, *Understanding and Application of Judicial Interpretation of the Arbitration Law of the Supreme People's Court*, 98 (2 ed., People's Court Press 2015).

clauses, academic circles have provided many theoretical viewpoints. For example, one of them is that arbitration clauses are different from other contract clauses[40]: First, they are different in nature. Other contract clauses stipulate the substantive rights and obligations that the parties "mutually" assume, that is, the obligations of one party to the other party, while the arbitration clause stipulates the rights and obligations that the parties "jointly" assume and will be borne by them in the event of a dispute; second, their purposes are different. The purpose of other contract clauses is to perform the contract to realize the benefits, while the arbitration clause stipulates the method of resolving disputes. The premise of the arbitration clause is that a dispute occurs.

China also accepts the principle of independence of arbitration clauses, holding the opinion that the change, cancellation, termination, invalidity, failure to take effect or revocation of the contract will not affect the validity of the arbitration clause. However, for the issue of whether the arbitration clause is valid when the contract is not established, China adopted a conservative view, considering that the principle of independence of arbitration clauses does not definitely apply to such situations. Article 19 of the Arbitration Law provides that "An arbitration agreement shall exist independently. Any changes to, rescission, termination or invalidity of the contract shall not affect the validity of the arbitration agreement."

Additionally, Article 10 of the Arbitration Law Interpretation stipulates that "Where a concluded contract has not taken effect or has been revoked, the provisions in the first paragraph of Article 19 of the Arbitration Law shall apply in the determination of the validity of the arbitration agreement. Where the parties reach an arbitration agreement at the time when concluding the contract, the validity of the arbitration agreement shall not be affected by the failure of the conclusion of contract."

Article 10 of the Arbitration Law Interpretation does not list the circumstance where "the contract has not been established" together with the circumstance where "the contract has not taken effect" and "the contract has been canceled" as a supplement of the circumstances that "does not affect the validity of the arbitration agreement" stipulated in Article 19 of the Arbitration Law. Rather, it lists a separate paragraph to clarify whether the parties reached a consensus on the arbitration agreement shall be reviewed when the contract is not established.

Different from the invalidity or cancellation of the contract, the validity of the arbitration clause may be affected if the contract has not been established. In a contract that contains an arbitration clause, there are actually two contracts concerning the rights and obligations of merits and the rights and obligations of dispute resolution.[41] In situations where the contract ceases to exist, such as invalidity and cancellation, although the contract ultimately loses its legal effect, the contract has been established, which means that the parties have reached an agreement on the contract,

---

[40] Liu Xiaohong, *Jurisprudence and Demonstration of International Commercial Arbitration Agreement*, 135 (1 ed., Commercial Press 2005).

[41] Shen Deyong, Wan E, *Understanding and Application of Judicial Interpretation of the Arbitration Law of the Supreme People's Court*, 98 (2 ed., People's Court Press 2015).

including the arbitration clause as part of the contract. In the case of the establishment of a contract, the establishment of an arbitration clause requires the process of an offer and an acceptance that has been completed together with the offer and acceptance to reach the contract.

In contrast, if the contract is not established, it means that the parties have not reached an agreement. Unless the parties specifically go through the process of offering and accepting the arbitration clause, that is, there is a situation of "the parties reach the arbitration agreement on the dispute", the arbitration clause in the unconcluded contract may not be established. If one party does not make a commitment to the other party's offer containing an arbitration clause, then the arbitration clause is only a unilateral expression of one party's intent and has no binding force on the other party.

Singapore Yideman Asia Pte.Ltd. v. Wuxi Huaxin Cocoa Food Co., Ltd.[42]

On January 12, 1999, Singapore Yideman Asia Pte. Ltd. ("Yideman") faxed a copy of Business Confirmation Letter ("Fax Dated January 12") to Wuxi Huaxin Cocoa Food Co., Ltd. ("Huaxin Company") through the intermediary agent of Malaysia Borneo Native Products Co., Ltd. ("Borneo Company").

The content of the Fax Dated January 12 were that: This letter confirmed that Yideman sold the following goods to Huaxin Company the goods as follow: 500 metric tons of Sabah SMC1A cocoa beans, 500 metric tons of SMC1B cocoa beans; Delivery Quality: SABAH SMC1A standard, SABAH SMC1B standard; Price: US$1,450 per metric ton, Conditions: The seller was responsible for paying the cost and freight and delivering the goods in Shanghai; Shipment: from January to February 1999; Weight: net shipping weight (1% deductible); Contract: according to C.A.L. Rules (London Cocoa Association); Payment: There was a 30-day irrevocable letter of credit issued by the First Bank of Singapore. The Fax also noted that the complete contract would wait later.

On January 13, 1999, Yideman faxed another letter to Huaxin Company ("Fax Dated January 13"), whose contents were as follows: For further explanation of the Business Confirmation Letter issued yesterday, please note the following contract number: 1. Contract S50502 for 500 metric tons of Sabah SMC1A cocoa beans; 2. Contract S50503 for 500 metric tons of SMC1B cocoa beans and indicated that "the details of all contracts will be described later" and "according to your instructions, we will arrange sampling before shipment for analysis on FFA indicators". In addition, the Fax Dated January 13 contained the requirement for Huaxin Company to issue a letter of credit and inform shipping instructions.

On January 14, 1999, Wang of Huaxin Company signed the faxes sent by Yideman on January 12 and 13. Among them, the Fax Dated January 12 was unchanged, and the analysis on FFA indicators in the Fax Dated January 13 ("We will arrange Singapore SGS to analyze the samples)" was changed to "Sampling and analysis before shipment shall be performed by Singapore SGS, and the FFA index is less

---

[42] (2001) Min Si Ta Zi No. 43.

than 1.75%." Later, Wang faxed to the intermediary agent, Borneo Company, which faxed to Yideman on the same day.

After receiving the fax, Yideman made a response to the issue relating to FFA on the same day that it would make sure that the FFA of the sample test before shipment is approximately 1.75%, but only the FFA index level of the samples obtained before shipment could be determined. In addition, Yideman informed Huaxin Company that it could ship the goods to Zhangjiagang in accordance with Huaxin Company's instruction, urgently ask Huaxin Company to issue a letter of credit, and informed the shipping procedures ("Reply Dated January 14").

On January 15, 1999, Yideman sent to Huaxin Company the official text of the two contracts ("Contract Dated January 15"), which had been unilaterally signed by Yideman. Huaxin Company returned them to Yideman without signatures on January 18.

On January 22, 1999, Huaxin Company faxed a reply to Yideman, stating that the FFA of not only the sampling before shipment but also the shipped sampling (tested by China Commodity Inspection Bureau) should be less than 1.75%, but Yideman could only guarantee the FFA level sampled before shipment, and thus the contracts received by Huaxin Company were inconsistent with its intent and could not be accepted.

On January 26, 1999, Yideman stated that it could only guarantee that the sample FFA before shipment was less than 1.75%, other requirements were acceptable, and again sent the contract text to Huaxin Company ("Contract Dated January 26").

After that, the parties continued to negotiate on the FFA level, SGS testing agency, payment terms, prices and other issues. Although an intermediary agent intervened, they failed to reach a consensus.

After the dispute arose, Yideman asked Huaxin Company to compensate for the losses caused to it due to Huaxin Company's failure to perform the Business Confirmation Letter signed on January 14 and said that it would initiate arbitration to resolve the dispute. Huaxin Company stated that the parties did not conclude the contract finally, there was no claim to discuss, and the parties did not agree to arbitrate.

Yideman then filed an application for arbitration with the London Cocoa Association Limited (C.A.L, hereinafter referred to as the "London Cocoa Association"). On April 30, 1999, after receiving the notice of arbitration from the London Cocoa Association, Huaxin Company replied on May 12 that it had received the relevant arbitration materials sent by the London Cocoa Association and stated that the two parties had not reached a contract.

On July 13, 1999, the London Cocoa Association made an arbitral award, ruling that there was a contract between the buyer (Huaxin Company) and the seller (Yideman). This contract was binding on the buyer and that the buyer should pay the seller's goods price difference of USD 106,645 and interests.

Since Huaxin Company failed to implement the arbitral award, Yideman applied to the Wuxi Intermediate People's Court for recognition and enforcement of the foreign arbitral award. During the review by the Wuxi Intermediate People's Court, Huaxin Company requested that the court not recognize and enforce it.

Regarding the present case, the SPC issued the Reply of [2001] Min Si Ta Zi No. 43, considering that the premise for the arbitration clause or arbitration agreement becomes effective independently was that the parties concerned reached a consensus on resolving disputes through arbitration. In this case, according to the faxes between Yideman and Huaxin Company, the two parties did not reach an agreement to resolve the dispute over the purchase of cocoa beans through arbitration. It lacked a factual and legal basis for the London Cocoa Association to accept the case based on the arbitration clause unilaterally drafted by Yideman. Consequently, the People's Court shall refuse to recognize and enforce the arbitral award in accordance with Article 269 of the Civil Procedure Law and the New York Convention China had acceded to.

In this case, the offers issued by Yideman to Huaxin Company included the Faxes Dated January 12 and 13, as well as the contracts unilaterally signed on January 15 and January 26. Huaxin Company signed the Fax Dated January 12 containing the arbitration clause, signed but substantively changed the Fax Dated January 13 which further explained the Fax Dated January 12, and rejected the Contracts Dated January 15 and January 26.

The Faxes Dated January 12 and 13 together constituted a complete offer, and Huaxin Company did not make a commitment to the offer but made a counteroffer. The two parties never reached a consensus. Therefore, the contract between Yideman and Huaxin Company was not established.

The Faxes Dated January 12 and January 13 were not two separate offers but a whole. The reasons are as follows: First, the Fax Dated January 13 itself was not an independent offer and did not include mandatory contractual clauses such as subject matter and quantity. Instead, it supplemented the Fax Dated January 12, indicating the contract number and cargo inspection agency not mentioned in the Fax Dated January 12. Second, although Huaxin Company's changes were marked on the Fax Dated January 13, the added "FFA index is less than 1.75%" was a modification of the quality clauses "SABAH SMC1A standard, SABAH SMC1B standard" in the Fax Dated January 12. Third, Huaxin Company signed the Reply Dated January 14, returning the two faxes together. Since Huaxin Company made a substantial change to the quality standard, it did not make a commitment to the offer dated January 12 and 13 but issued a new offer, while the two parties never reached an agreement on the quality clause and other contents, so the contract was not established.

Under the circumstance that the contract containing the arbitration clause was not established, the parties in this case did not specifically reach an agreement on the arbitration clause, so there was no arbitration agreement in this case. Although Huaxin Company signed the Fax Dated January 12 containing the arbitration clause sent by Yideman, part of the content marked on the Fax Dated January 13 by Huaxin Company had changed the quality clauses mentioned in the Fax Dated January 12, and the Faxes Dated January 12 and January 13 were a whole. Therefore, the Fax Dated January 12 signed by Huaxin Company was not a commitment, the two parties did not reach an agreement on the Fax Dated January 12, and the arbitration agreement contained in the Fax Dated January 12 was not established.

Although Huaxin Company did not object to the arbitration clause on Fax Dated January 12 and the contract was not established because the two parties failed to reach agreement on other clauses, the parties in this case did not go through the process of offering and committing to the arbitration clause. The arbitration clause was only a clause unilaterally drafted, the arbitration agreement did not exist, and the London Cocoa Association had no jurisdiction to hear the case.

However, if we consider from another perspective, whether the signature of Huaxin Company on the Fax Dated January 12 containing the arbitration clause and its subsequent series of behaviors can also be regarded as no objection to the arbitration clause, but only hold disagreements against the substantive issues? If so, based on the principle of independence of arbitration clauses, can the arbitration clause in this case be considered established and valid? Furthermore, it is also necessary to consider who is more appropriate to determine whether the arbitration clause is valid. Should the court exercise the power of judicial supervision or should it be included in the arbitral tribunal's self-adjudicating jurisdiction? This is another important issue related to this case.

Chapter 2
Multiple Contracts and Conflicting Dispute Resolution Provisions

2.1 "Arbitration or litigation" Clause

"Arbitration or litigation" clause refers to an agreement stipulated by the parties to resolve disputes by arbitration or litigation. It is generally believed that such an arbitration clause is invalid under Chinese law. Article 7 of the Arbitration Law Interpretation provides that "where the parties agree that a dispute may be submitted to an arbitration institution for arbitration or filed with the people's court for commencement of legal proceedings, the arbitration agreement shall be deemed invalid…".

However, if a party applies for arbitration according to an "arbitration or litigation" clause and the other party fails to raise an objection before the first hearing of the arbitration tribunal, the arbitration clause is deemed to be valid. Article 7 of the Arbitration Law Interpretation provides that "…one party has submitted an arbitration application to an arbitration institution but the other party failed to object within the time limit stipulated in the second paragraph of Article 20 of the Arbitration Law." Article 20 of the Arbitration Law stipulates that "party's challenge of the validity of the arbitration agreement shall be raised prior to the arbitration tribunal's first hearing." The reason for this exception is that the failure of other parties to raise an objection within the specified time limit is deemed that the parties have reached an agreement that their disputes should be solved by arbitration.[1]

A typical "arbitration or litigation" clause is agreed upon in a contract with content such as "all disputes arising from or in connection with the performance of this contract shall be settled by both parties through friendly negotiation. If the negotiation fails, one party may apply to A Arbitration Commission for arbitration or bring a lawsuit to B court." For example, in the *Reply of the SPC on the Request for Instructions on Determining the Validity of the Foreign Arbitration Clause between*

---

[1] Shen Deyong, Wan Erxiang, *Understanding and Application of the Supreme People's Court's Judicial Interpretation of the Arbitration Law*, 77, People's Court Press, (2nd., 2015).

This Chapter is coauthored with Gu Dai, partner of Yi & Partners Law Firm.

© The Author(s), under exclusive license to Springer Nature Singapore Pte Ltd. 2022
Y. Lin, *China Arbitration Yearbook (2021)*, China Arbitration Yearbook,
https://doi.org/10.1007/978-981-19-1284-9_2

Wang v. Dongguan Weiyang Sports Equipment Co., Ltd. et al.,[2] the arbitration clause stipulates that "if there is a dispute over the agreement, any party may apply for arbitration or bring a lawsuit to the people's court." The SPC held that the arbitration clause was invalid.

"Arbitration or litigation" clauses may also take the form of multiple clauses on arbitration and litigation agreed separately in a contract. For example, in the *Reply of the SPC on the Request for Instructions on the Validity of the Arbitration Clause in the Contract Termination Dispute between Yanzhou Haoke Weibo Mining Engineering Co., Ltd. v. A.WEBERS.A.*et al.,[3] Article 26 of the Manufacturing and Licensing Agreement stipulates that all disputes related to the contract shall be submitted to CIETAC for arbitration, while Article 29 of the Agreement provides for nonexclusive jurisdiction of Mainland court. The SPC held that the arbitration clause was invalid.

There are variations of "arbitration or litigation" clause. Here is an example:

Wuhan Weisidun Network Technology Co., Ltd. v. Shichuang Home Decoration Group (Lanzhou) Co., Ltd.[4]

The parties agreed in the Mobile Marketing Service Contract that "in case of any dispute over the content or performance of this contract, both parties shall negotiate with each other in a friendly manner; if the negotiation fails to solve the dispute, both parties may apply to Wuhan Arbitration Commission for arbitration; if the negotiation fails to solve the dispute or the written arbitration agreement is not formally submitted, either party may file a lawsuit to the people's court where Party B is located." The applicant filed an application to confirm the invalidity of the arbitration clause.

The Wuhan Intermediate People's Court of Hubei Province held that this case was about confirmation of the validity of the arbitration agreement. Article 7 of the Arbitration Law Interpretation provides that "where the parties agree that a dispute may be submitted to an arbitration institution for arbitration or filed with the people's court for commencement of legal proceedings, the arbitration agreement shall be deemed invalid…" In the instant case, the arbitration clause in the Contract belongs to the "arbitration or litigation" clause, and thus, the arbitration agreement was invalid.

When a dispute settlement clause could be an atypical "arbitration or litigation" clause, in the analysis, one needs to take the underlying causes for the invalidity of the "arbitration or litigation" clause into consideration.

The "arbitration or litigation" clause is invalid primarily for three reasons: first, arbitration and litigation, both of which are dispute resolution methods, are mutually exclusive in nature and cannot coexist; second, the parties who have chosen both arbitration and litigation as ways to resolve their disputes, should be deemed that their true intention is not yet certain; third, if the clause is found to be effective, it will lead to jurisdiction conflict between arbitration and litigation. Since no coordinated

---

[2] (2012) Min Si Ta Zi No. 52.

[3] (2009) Min Si Ta Zi No. 19.

[4] (2019) Er 01 Min Te No. 282.

legal mechanism exists between the two, there will be chaos, leaving human, material, financial and judicial resources wasted.[5]

In this case, the dispute resolution clause, which refers to arbitration and litigation at the same time, could be an "arbitration or litigation" clause. The clause that "if the negotiation fails to solve the dispute or the written arbitration agreement is not formally submitted, either party may file a lawsuit to the people's court" means that if arbitration is not applied, a party could bring a lawsuit to the court. Apparently, such clauses may result in jurisdiction conflict. For example, one party may not formally submit the arbitration agreement and file the case to the court, while the other party may apply for arbitration. Therefore, what the parties agreed here was an invalid "arbitration or litigation" clause.

The issue of an "arbitration or litigation" clause often arises in circumstances where the parties have not made a choice between arbitration and litigation in a standard contract. From the perspective of the SPC Research Office,[6] no "arbitration or litigation" clause exists in such cases since the parties have not reached any agreement on dispute settlement. Nonetheless, in judicial practice, some courts hold that such provisions are invalid "arbitration or litigation" clauses. For example, in *Xian v. Guangzhou Shangjian Decoration Design Co., Ltd.*,[7] the parties agreed in the Building Decoration Construction Contract that "any dispute arising from the performance of this contract shall be settled by both parties through negotiation. If the negotiation fails, it shall be settled in the following way: 1. Submit it to the local arbitration commission for arbitration; 2. File a lawsuit to the people's court in accordance with the law." The Guangzhou Intermediate People's Court of Guangdong Province concluded that it was an invalid "arbitration or litigation" clause. In summary, in both views, a party cannot apply for arbitration according to the dispute settlement clause in such a context.

2.2 "May" Apply for Arbitration

In drafting arbitration clauses, parties usually stipulate that disputes "shall" be submitted for arbitration, or each party "agrees" or "has the right" to apply for arbitration. For example, one of CIETAC's model clauses provides that "any dispute arising from or in connection with this Contract shall be submitted to CIETAC for arbitration which shall be conducted in accordance with the CIETAC's arbitration rules in effect at the time of applying for arbitration. The arbitral award is final and binding upon both parties." As another example, SCIA's model clauses provide that "any dispute arising from or in connection with this Contract shall be submitted to

---

[5] Shen Deyong, Wan Erxiang, *Understanding and Application of the Supreme People's Court's Judicial Interpretation of the Arbitration Law*, 76, People's Court Press, (2nd., 2015).

[6] Shen Deyong, Wan Erxiang, *Understanding and Application of the Supreme People's Court's Judicial Interpretation of the Arbitration Law*, 75, People's Court Press, (2nd., 2015).

[7] (2019) Yue 01 Min Xia Zhong No. 231.

SCIA Mediation Centre for mediation. If the mediation is successful, the parties agree to submit the settlement agreement to SCIA to request that an arbitral award be rendered in accordance with the Arbitration Rules and based on the terms of the settlement agreement", and "both parties agree that either party has the right to submit this settlement agreement to SCIA to request that an arbitral award be rendered in accordance with the Arbitration Rules and based on the terms of the settlement agreement."

However, it is common to find that parties agree in arbitration clauses that each of them "may" apply for arbitration. As mentioned in the previous section, the "arbitration or litigation" clause is invalid. Then, could the agreement that a dispute "may" be solved by arbitration be construed as an invalid "arbitration or litigation" clause? The question at issue is how to understand the word "may" here.

Licheng Yibo Aluminum Alloy Processing Plant v. Shenzhen Hongtao Decoration Co., Ltd.[8]

The parties agreed in the Construction Contract that if there is any dispute that cannot be solved through negotiation, either party may submit it to Jinan Arbitration Commission for arbitration.

The respondent argued that the arbitration clause was invalid. The word "may" in the arbitration clause only stipulated an optional way to solve the disputes and did not exclude the choice of litigation. It should be interpreted as "each party may apply to Jinan Commission Arbitration Commission for arbitration or bring a suit to the people's court." Therefore, the arbitration clause was invalid.

Regarding the respondent's defense of the "arbitration or litigation" clause, the Jinan Intermediate People's Court of Shandong Province held that the parties did not explicitly stipulate in the contract that disputes could be settled through litigation. The word "may" in the arbitration clause mainly modified the subject "each party", which means that "each party" may initiate arbitration rather than each party "may apply for arbitration and may bring a lawsuit." Therefore, the arbitration clause was valid.

In this case, the court recognized the validity of the arbitration clause that "the parties may apply for arbitration", holding that the word "may" modified the subject "each party" not the verb "apply for" arbitration or "bring" a lawsuit.

The case is not exceptional. As early as 2003, the SPC held the same position in a similar case. In the *Reply of SPC on the Request for Instructions on the Case of Anhui Hefei United Power Generation Co., Ltd. v. Alstom Power Generation Co., Ltd.,*[9] the SPC held that the parties did not specify in the clause that disputes may be resolved by litigation. "May" in the English arbitration clause mainly modified the subject, meaning that "any party" may institute an arbitration, and it cannot be construed as "any party may institute an arbitration or litigation."

---

[8] (2019) Lu 01 Min Te No. 46.

[9] (2003) Min Si Ta Zi No. 7.

For another example, in the *Beijing Branch of the People's Property Insurance Co., Ltd. v. Licheng Tongda Mining Co., Ltd.*,[10] the parties agreed that "any dispute arising from the execution of this Insurance Contract between the two parties shall be settled through friendly negotiation. If the negotiation fails, they may choose to apply to the Beijing Arbitration Commission for arbitration." The court of first instance held that the parties agreed that they could choose to apply for arbitration, that is, they could also choose to sue to the court, and therefore, the arbitration agreement was invalid. In this regard, the Changzhi Intermediate People's Court of Shanxi Province held a different view, found the trial court had applied the law improperly and corrected the judgment with the reasoning that "the arbitration clause here excluded the jurisdiction of the people's court over the case".

It is the adherence to the judicial principle of "making the arbitration agreement as effective as possible" in interpreting arbitration clauses that explains why the courts do not regard "may apply for arbitration" as an "arbitration or litigation" clause. Although it is not clearly stated in law or the SPC's interpretations, many courts implement the principle in judicial practice. For example, in *China Light Sanlian International Trade Co., Ltd. v. Tata International Metals(Asia)Limited*,[11] the Beijing Fourth Intermediate People's Court held "in light of the New York Convention, the development of international commercial arbitration and the SPC's judicial interpretations, relaxing the requirements on the validity of arbitration agreement and making it effective as far as possible not only respects the parties' intention to choose arbitration as a way to solve disputes but also promotes and supports the development of arbitration and creates a good legal environment for international commercial arbitration. In the judicial review of arbitration, courts should observe the judicial principle of supporting and encouraging arbitration, confirming the validity of arbitration agreement as far as possible in international commercial arbitration." Similarly, in *Zhongshan Ganghong Building Materials Co., Ltd., v. China Railway Seventh Bureau Group Zhengzhou Engineering Co., Ltd.*,[12] the Zhongshan Intermediate People's Court of Guangdong Province held that "in judicial review, courts should follow the principle of moderate review, that is, to respect the finality of arbitration award to make it as effective as possible."

Under the influence of "making arbitration agreements as effective as possible", the arbitration clause that mentions arbitration and litigation of some type at the same time should not be deemed an "arbitration or litigation" clause. Here are some examples:

1. Review of Arbitral Awards

   A clause relating to the "review of the arbitral award" is construed as "award subject to judicial supervision". In *Shanghai Hanshu Cosmetics Co., Ltd. v. NBA Ssports Culture Development (Beijing) Co., Ltd.*,[13] the parties agreed that any

---

[10] (2014) Chang Min Zhong Zi No. 00919.

[11] (2017) Jing 04 Min Te No. 23.

[12] (2018) Yue 20 Min Te No. 176.

[13] (2020) Jing 04 Min Te No. 20.

dispute "shall be submitted to CIETAC for arbitration. Review of the award may be filed to any competent court." One party claimed it was an invalid "arbitration or litigation" clause, arguing that what the parties had agreed here was duplicate trials of the case, first by arbitration commission and then by court. The Beijing Fourth Intermediate People's Court held that instead of being understood as a choice between arbitration and litigation, the arbitration clause should be construed that the parties agreed to submit the arbitral award to the competent court for judicial supervision, and the arbitration clause was effective.

2. Disputes Litigated by Arbitration Organ

An agreement that disputes shall be "litigated by arbitration organ" should not be construed as an "arbitration or litigation" clause. In *Tian v. Xiong*,[14] the parties agreed to "litigate disputes by the arbitration organ where the company's main body is located". The Zhengzhou Intermediate People's Court of Henan Province held that the arbitration clause should not be considered to express the intention that the agreement can be brought to a court was valid.

3. Seek Preliminary Injunctive Relief from Court

The parties that agree to seek preliminary injunctive relief from a court do not mean they have the intention to submit disputes for litigation. In *Liu v. Diantong Angel (Shanghai) Investment Co., Ltd.*,[15] the arbitration clause stipulated that the dispute shall be submitted to CIETAC for arbitration; any party may seek preliminary injunctive relief (if possible) from the competent court before the formation of the arbitration tribunal. The Beijing High People's Court held that the agreement did not reflect the parties' intention to resolve disputes through litigation, and the arbitration agreement was valid.

2.3 "First Arbitration then Litigation" Clause

The "first arbitration then litigation" clause refers to an agreement in which the parties mention arbitration and litigation to resolve their disputes at the same time, but unlike the "arbitration or litigation" clause, the parties have made clear the applicable order of dispute settlement methods, that is, to apply for arbitration first.

Here are some typical examples: "disputes shall be resolved by: 1. A Arbitration Commission; 2. B court"; "any party may submit disputes to A Arbitration Commission for arbitration, and if either party disagrees with the arbitration result or the award, it may file a lawsuit to B court"; and "a party may submit disputes to A Arbitration Commission for arbitration, and if the disputes cannot be resolved by arbitration, either party may file a lawsuit to B court".

The "first arbitration then litigation" clause makes it clear that the parties prefer arbitration as the way of dispute settlement, and litigation does not stand as a parallel

---

[14] (2020) Yu 01 Min Te No. 17.

[15] (2015) Er Zhong Min Te Zi No. 03923.

option. Thus, it seems that the clause does not fit the invalidity reasons for the "arbitration or litigation" clause. Considering that the parties have given preference to arbitration, does the "first arbitration then litigation" agreement fall into the scope of the "arbitration or litigation" clause? Chinese courts have not reached a consensus on this issue. Some hold such clause is invalid (such as No. 1 Case) while others confirm its validity (see No. 2 Case).

1. Jiangsu Jinxia Construction Group Co., Ltd., V. Shanxi Yirong Real Estate Development Co., Ltd.[16]

The parties agreed in the contract that "if there are differences between Party A and Party B, the parties may solve the differences through negotiation. If the negotiation fails, the parties can apply for mediation by relevant departments. If the mediation fails, the parties can apply to the Jinzhong Arbitration Commission. If the arbitration mediation fails, the parties can submit the disputes to the court where the contract was signed."

After one party applied for arbitration, the other party filed a suit to invalidate the arbitration clause.

The SPC held that although the parties agreed to apply for arbitration, they also agreed to resolve disputes through litigation if the arbitration mediation fails. Since the parties did not take arbitration as the final settlement of disputes, the arbitration clause was invalid.

In the instant case, the dispute settlement clause stipulated that if the arbitration mediation fails, the parties can bring a lawsuit to a court. The SPC held the arbitration clause invalid on the ground that the parties failed to choose arbitration as the final method of resolving disputes. In fact, it is the violation of arbitration finality and arbitration's exclusive effect on the jurisdiction of court that led the SPC to draw the conclusion. The SPC has made the point clear in the following case.

In *Inner Mongolia Jixiang Coal Industry Co., Ltd. v. Tianjin Metallurgical Group Trading Co., Ltd.*,[17] the parties agreed in the contract that "any party that disagrees with the award result may file a lawsuit to the court where the contract is signed". The SPC held that such agreement did not conform to the provisions of the first paragraph of Article 9 of the *Arbitration Law,* which provides "a system of a single and final award shall be practiced for arbitration", violated the basic principle that arbitration excludes the jurisdiction of court, and constituted an invalid "arbitration or litigation" clause.

Similarly, in *Sichuan Lanjun Land Industrial Co., Ltd. v. Zigong No. 1 Construction Engineering Company*,[18] the dispute settlement clause stipulates that "if the dispute cannot be solved through negotiation, the parties shall submit it to Mianyang Arbitration Commission for arbitration, and if the arbitration fails to solve the dispute, the parties shall file a lawsuit with the Mianyang People's Court. The result of the judgment is binding on both parties." The Mianyang Intermediate People's Court

---

[16] (2019) Zui Gao Fa Min Zhong No. 279.

[17] (2013) Min Er Zhong Zi No. 81.

[18] (2014) Mian Min Zhong Zi No. 26.

of Sichuan province held that the characteristics distinguishing arbitration from litigation are the finality of arbitration and arbitration's exclusion of court's jurisdiction. Although the parties agreed to apply for arbitration in the first half of the first sentence of the arbitration clause, in the second half, they agreed to bring a lawsuit if the dispute was not settled by arbitration. Moreover, the parties agreed in the second sentence that the court's judgment result shall be final. The above agreement denied the finality of arbitration awards and violated the principle that arbitration excludes the jurisdiction of courts. Therefore, the arbitration agreement was invalid.

However, not all courts hold the view that the "first arbitration then litigation" clause is invalid. Take the following case as an example:

2. *Anhui Dilong Pipeline Trenchless Engineering Co., Ltd. V. Nanjing Hongkun Telecom Engineering Design Co., Ltd.* [19]

The parties agreed in the construction contract that "any dispute arising from the performance of the contract shall be handled through friendly negotiation. If the negotiation fails, the dispute shall be transferred to the arbitration commission of the construction site for arbitration. If the arbitration fails, the parties shall bring a lawsuit to the people's court where the project is located."

One party argued that the arbitration clause, which stipulated that the parties can choose arbitration or litigation to solve the disputes, failed to select arbitration as the method for dispute settlement, violated the principle of the finality of arbitration and thus was invalid.

The Jiangsu High People's Court held that the parties' intention to choose arbitration as the method to settle disputes was quite clear. The arbitration clause, which was not an optional agreement between arbitration and litigation, was legal and effective.

In this case, with respect to the agreement that the parties shall sue to a court if the arbitration fails, the court held the arbitration clause, which manifested the parties' preference for arbitration and did not constitute an "arbitration or litigation" clause. In fact, it is the parties' clear intention to give priority to arbitration as the way to solve the disputes rather than the parallel option provided in Article 7 of the Arbitration Law Interpretation that the court confirms the validity of the "first arbitration then litigation" clause.

Likewise, in *Beijing Xinhua Multimedia Data Co., Ltd. v. Urumqi Shengshi Weimi Media Information Technology Co., Ltd.*,[20] the parties agreed that for any dispute that cannot be solved by negotiation, any party may submit it to Beijing Arbitration Commission for arbitration. If it still cannot be solved, the case can be brought to the people's court of the place where the defendant is located. The Beijing Fourth Intermediate People's Court held that although the arbitration clause mentioned litigation as a way for dispute settlement, it had not negated or altered the parties' intention to resolve disputes by arbitration first. Therefore, the arbitration clause did not belong to the invalid circumstances provided by Article 7 of the Arbitration Law Interpretation.

---

[19] (2017) Su Min Shen No. 4452.

[20] (2019) Jing 04 Min Te No. 382.

By comparing the above two opposite views on the "first arbitration then litigation" clause, we find that the opinions are based on different legal provisions. For those negating its effectiveness, the rationale is that the agreement violates the finality of arbitration provided in Article 9 of the Arbitration Law. For those confirming its validity, the reason is that the agreement here does not constitute the "arbitration or litigation" clause provided by Article 7 of the Arbitration Law Interpretation. The key to the differences are whether violation of the finality of arbitration affects the validity of the clause and whether Article 7 of the Arbitration Law Interpretation implies that a valid arbitration clause should completely exclude the jurisdiction of a court. However, with respect to the two issues, no consensus has been reached thus far.

2.4 Multiple Related Agreements

In commercial transactions, parties often sign more than one agreement, among which there could be conflicting dispute settlement clauses. Depending on whether they are about the same matter, the relationship of multiple agreements can be divided into three types: replacing, overall related and separable.

For the replacement type, unless otherwise agreed upon by the parties, the dispute settlement clause agreed upon in the latest contract shall prevail (such as case No. 1 below); for the overall related type, if arbitration and litigation are agreed upon in separate agreements, the arbitration clause may be held invalid due to the lack of parties' certain intention of choosing arbitration as the dispute settlement method (see case No. 2); and for the separable type, since each agreement is independent of each other, differences arising from each agreement are handled according to the dispute settlement clause provided in that agreement.

> *1. Jiangsu Suzhong Construction Group Co., Ltd., v. Handan JIAYE Real Estate Development Co., Ltd.*[21]

On April 10, 2013, the parties agreed in the Construction Supplementary Agreement that "in case of any dispute during the performance of this agreement, both parties shall solve it through friendly negotiation. If the negotiation fails, it shall be submitted to the local people's court for settlement."

On September 24, 2014, the parties executed a Registered Contract and filed it with the local construction administrative department. The dispute settlement clause stipulates that "both parties agree to settle the dispute in the following way: (1) apply to Handan Arbitration Commission for arbitration."

One party argued that the Registered Contract did not manifest the true intention of the parties, and thus the arbitration clause within is not binding.

The issue here is whether the parties are bound by the arbitration clause in the Registered Contract. In this regard, the SPC held that the dispute settlement clauses

---

[21] (2017) Zui Gao Fa Min Xia Zhong No. 76.

in the two contracts, which were agreed with the purpose of choosing a method to resolve disputes concerning the project construction, reflected the true intention of the parties and should both be valid. If parties have concluded several agreements on the same matter and there was inconsistency between them, the content agreed upon in the last contract shall prevail. Since the Construction Supplementary Agreement was signed before the Registered Contract, the arbitration clause in the Registered Contract should be regarded as the replacement of the litigation clause stipulated in the Construction Supplementary Agreement.

In the instant case, the parties signed two contracts for the project involved, one for actual performance and the other for filing requirements. The parties stipulated litigation and arbitration clauses in the two contracts, giving rise to the following question: which dispute settlement method should be adopted?

First, from the perspective of effectiveness, the dispute settlement clauses agreed upon in the two contracts were both valid. One party argued that the arbitration clause in the Registered Contract, which did not manifest the parties' true intention, was not binding. However, even if the Registered Contract was invalid, because of the independence of the arbitration clause, the binding force of the arbitration clause would not be affected. Article 19 of the Arbitration Law provides that "an arbitration agreement shall exist independently. The amendment, rescission, termination or invalidity of a contract shall not affect the validity of the arbitration agreement." Article 10 of the Arbitration Law Interpretation stipulates that "where a concluded contract has not taken effect or has been revoked, the provisions in the first paragraph of Article 19 of the Arbitration Law shall apply in the determination of the validity of the arbitration agreement." Hence, the arbitration law clause in the Registered Contract was valid.

Second, from the perspective of the priority of the two contracts, the latter contract shall prevail. Article 77 of the Contract Law stipulates: "the parties may modify the contract if they reach a consensus through consultation."[22] The so-called change is to replace the previous agreement with the later amendment, that is, the later agreement shall prevail. In this case, the Registered Contract and the Construction Supplementary Agreement were about the same matter. The execution of the Registered Contract was regarded as the change of the Construction Supplementary Agreement. Therefore, the arbitration clause in the Registered Contract shall prevail.

For another example, at *Zeng v. Xiamen Junhao Real Estate Development Co., Ltd.*,[23] the parties agreed to a litigation clause in the Commercial Housing Sales Contract. Later, they agreed in the Supplementary Agreement on the Settlement of Issues Related to Overdue Delivery to submit disputes to Xiamen Arbitration Commission for arbitration. The Xiamen Intermediate People's Court held that the Supplementary Agreement changed the agreement on overdue delivery in the original Commercial Housing Sales Contract, so the dispute settlement method agreed in the Supplementary Agreement should prevail.

---

[22] Article 543 of the Civil Code of the PRC.

[23] (2016) Min 02 Min Zhong No. 1303.

However, it should be noted that not in all cases would the dispute settlement clause specified in the later contract prevail. If the parties have special agreement on the priority, that agreement shall be observed. For example, at*Handan Second Construction and Installation Co., Ltd. v. Mingmen Real Estate (Anyang) Co., Ltd.*,[24] the Handan Intermediate People's Court of Hebei Province held that although the arbitration clauses agreed in the 2011 Construction Contract and 2012 Registered Construction Contract were inconsistent, it was clearly agreed in the final 2012 Agreement that the 2012 Registered Construction Contract was only for filing procedures, and all contract terms of the project were subject to the 2011 Construction Contract. Therefore, the dispute in this case should be submitted to the Shanghai Arbitration Commission for arbitration as stipulated in the 2011 Construction Contract.

2. Beijing Normal University Anbo Education Technology Co., Ltd. V. Changsha Yaxing Real Estate Development Co., Ltd.[25]

The parties agreed in the Cooperation Framework Agreement that Yaxing Company would transfer 70% of its operation rights, building property, equity and other rights and interests to Ambow Company. The agreement also stipulated that the parties would further clarify the details not covered in this contract in the Equity Transfer Agreement and the Equity Purchase Agreement.

To perform the Cooperation Framework Agreement, the parties signed a series of agreements, including the Project Cooperation Memorandum, the Equity Transfer Agreement and the Equity Purchase Agreement. The parties agreed in Project Cooperation Memorandum that "in case of any dispute arising from this memorandum, both parties shall settle it through friendly negotiation. If the negotiation fails, the case shall be submitted to CIETAC for arbitration". The Equity Transfer Agreement stipulated that "either party shall have the right to submit disputes to the people's Court of the place where the transferee (i.e., Ambow) is located". The Equity Purchase Agreement provided that any disputes between the parties "shall be subject to the jurisdiction of the California State Courts of the United States".

With respect to the jurisdiction issue, the SPC held that the Cooperation Framework Agreement was the basic agreement for the overall transaction, to which the Project Cooperation Memorandum, the Equity Transfer Agreement and the Equity Purchase Agreement affiliated. These ancillary agreements and the Cooperation Framework Agreement made a whole. As far as the whole contract was concerned, while the parties agreed in the Project Cooperation Memorandum that the dispute shall be submitted to arbitration, they decided in the Equity Transfer Agreement that disputes shall be governed by the court. That is, the parties' agreement on the dispute settlement clause included both arbitration and litigation. Under such circumstances, the parties' true intention should be deemed uncertain, and the arbitration clause was invalid.

In the instant case, the parties executed four contracts. Among them, the Cooperation Framework Agreement, which was about the cooperation intention and main

---

[24] (2015) Han Shi Zhi Yi Zi No. 00125.
[25] (2014) Min Yi Zhong Zi No. 24.

matters, laid the foundation for the transaction, and the Project Cooperation Memorandum, the Equity Transfer Agreement and the Equity Purchase Agreement, which contained details about rights and equity mentioned in the Cooperation Framework Agreement, worked as subsidiary agreements. Therefore, the four contracts together constituted a whole.

Hence, the four agreements could be deemed as a contract to which Article 7 of the Arbitration Law Interpretation applies. Given that the Project Cooperation Memorandum and the Equity Transfer Agreement stipulated arbitration and litigation clauses, respectively, the parties' intention to the method of dispute settlement cannot be determined, resulting in invalidity of the arbitration clause.

However, not all conflicting dispute settlement clauses in inseparable contracts, which make a whole, lead to invalid arbitration clauses. As long as the parties' true intention can be determined, the dispute settlement clause is effective. For example, in *Beijing Zhonghai Wobang Energy Investment Co., Ltd. v. Shaanxi Dingsheng Construction and Installation Engineering Co., Ltd.*,[26] while the parties agreed in the Pre-Drilling Project Contract to submit disputes to the "local arbitration commission" for arbitration, they later signed the Construction Safety Production and Environmental Protection Contract, which stipulated disputes shall be submitted to Xi'an Arbitration Commission for arbitration. Having noted that the Construction Safety Production and Environmental Protection Contract provided "this contract is an integral part of the main contract and has the same legal effect as the main contract" and the later signed Project Maintenance Contract also stipulated that the arbitration should be conducted by Xi'an Arbitration Commission, the Xi'an Intermediate People's Court held the Pre-Drilling Project Contract and the Construction Safety Production and Environmental Protection Contract were inseparable, and the latter clarified the arbitration commission mentioned in the former as Xi'an Arbitration Commission. Therefore, the arbitration clause was effective.

What we have discussed above are the replacement type and overall related type. For the independent separable type, since each document is relatively independent, differences arising from such documents are solved by the dispute settlement clause herein. For example, in *Hunan Huaxia Construction Co., Ltd. v. Changde Arts and Crafts School*,[27] the SPC held whether the arbitration clause agreed in the main contract also applies to the ancillary agreement depends on the relationship between the two contracts. Unless the parties agreed otherwise, if the main agreement and the ancillary contracts are mutually independent and separable, then the dispute settlement clause agreed in one contract shall apply to the document only. If the ancillary agreement supplements the main contract, must be attached to the main contract and cannot exist independently, the dispute resolution clause in the main contract also applies to the ancillary agreement.

---

[26] (2016) Shan 01 Min Te No. 270.

[27] (2015) Zhi Shen Zi No. 33.

2.5   Main Contract and Guarantee Contract

Whether the parties can submit the main contract as well as the guarantee contract to arbitration is a recurring question in judicial review and commercial arbitration practice in China. Chinese arbitration commissions have to address this issue in the case acceptance stage. For industries engaging in guaranteed businesses such as the banking industry, it is necessary to avoid the situation that disputes arising from a transaction need to resort to different dispute resolution methods.

If only litigation clauses are involved, disputes arising from the main contract and the guarantee contract can be tried together, considering the subordinate nature of the guarantee contract. Article 129 of the Interpretation of the Supreme People's Court on Certain Issues Concerning the Application of the "Guaranty Law of the People's Republic of China ("Guaranty Law Interpretation") provides that "the jurisdiction shall be determined on the basis of the main contract when a dispute of main and guarantee contracts is brought to court… Where the courts agreed upon in main and guarantee contracts are different, the one agreed in the main contract shall prevail."

However, the independent characteristics of arbitration agreement should be taken into consideration when arbitration procedures are involved. Article 19 of the Arbitration Law stipulates that "an arbitration agreement shall exist independently. The amendment, rescission, termination or invalidity of a contract shall not affect the validity of the arbitration agreement." Independence means that the validity of an arbitration agreement is not affected by other provisions in the same contract, not to mention by a separate guarantee contract. In addition, the principle of contract relativity is another factor to be considered. In short, independence is about the external relationship between the arbitration agreement and other rights and obligations, while contract relativity focuses on the internal relationship between the parties to the arbitration agreement.

Beijing Allianz Real Estate Development Co., Ltd. v. Beijing Anhengda Investment Co., Ltd. et al.[28]

On July 19, 2011, Beijing Allianz Real Estate Development Co., Ltd. ("Allianz Company") and Beijing Anhengda Investment Co., Ltd. ("Anhenda Company") signed a Transaction Framework Arrangement Agreement on equity transfer matters.

On July 26, 2011, Beijing Jinli Holding Group Co., Ltd. ("Jinli Company") issued an Irreversible Performance Guarantee to Allianz Company, promising to provide guarantee for Anhengda Company's performance of the obligations in the Transaction Framework Arrangement Agreement and bear joint and several liabilities. Article 8 of the Guarantee stipulated an arbitration clause.

After disputes arose among the parties, Allianz Company sued Anhengda Company based on the Transaction Framework Arrangement Agreement and Jinli Company according to the Irreversible Performance Guarantee.

During the defense period, Jinli Company raised the jurisdictional objection, alleging that the Irrevocable Performance Guarantee contained an arbitration clause

---

[28] (2014) Min Er Zhong Zi No. 00084.

and Allianz Company's claims against Jinli Company should be submitted to Beijing Arbitration Commission.

The SPC held that Jinli Company's jurisdictional objection on the ground of the arbitration clause in the Irrevocable Performance Guarantee issued to Allianz Company was tenable, and Allianz Company's claims against Jinli Company before a people's court should be rejected. However, according to the principle of contract relativity, the arbitration clause in the Irrevocable Performance Guarantee signed by Allianz Company and Jinli Company was binding only on the two parties. The arbitration clause should not apply to the disputes between Allianz Company and other parties.

In the literal sense, independence and subordination are contradictory. Since the guarantee contract is subordinate to the main contract, can the arbitration clause in the guarantee contract be treated differently? The answer is No. Although the guarantee contract has a subordinate nature, which is not absolute, it does not necessarily constitute an integral part of the main contract. Subordination is only relative to the rights and obligations under the main contract, so it is compatible with the relativity of contract. If a case involves both a main contract and a guarantee contract and the guarantee relationship can be separated, the settlement of the guarantee dispute can also be dealt independently.

What has been discussed above is the situation where the guarantee contract contains an arbitration clause. A more common circumstance involves the main contract with an arbitration clause, while the guarantee contract, which usually takes the form of a letter of guarantee or a separate guarantee contract, stipulates no arbitration clause. Can the disputes arising from the main contract and the guarantee contract be submitted to arbitration?

Although the SPC has already rendered some judgments involving the issue, judicial practice remains inconsistent. Some courts invoke Article 129 of the Guaranty Law Interpretation to deny separate jurisdiction over a subordinate contract. For example, in *China Construction Bank Co., Ltd. Zhejiang Branch Business Department v. Xue* et al.,[29] the Hangzhou Xiacheng District People's Court held "the purpose of Article 129 of the Guaranty Law Interpretation is to save litigation costs, the guarantee contract is subordinate to the main contract, and thus if the dispute settlement clauses of the two contracts are different, the one in the main contract shall prevail." Nonetheless, while Article 129 of the Guaranty Law Interpretation provides a clear rule when the parties agree litigation clauses in the main contract and the guarantee contract, it does not mention the situation when arbitration clauses are concerned.

As a matter of fact, the mainstream practice is to follow the SPC's view, that is, the main contract and the guarantee contract should be handled separately in the way of dispute settlement, since no provision stipulates that the dispute settlement clause in the main contract applies to the guarantee contract.[30]

---

[29] (2015) Hang Xia Shang Chu Zi No. 00953.

[30] This may be changed if final amended arbitration law comes into effect. The newly Arbitration Law (Draft for Comments) stipulates in Article 24 that "where arbitration agreements in the main contract and the subordinate contract conflict, the one in the main contract shall prevail. If the

For example, in the *Reply of the SPC on the Request of Yulin Intermediate People's Court for Instructions Not to Enforce the Foreign Arbitration Case of Dongxun Investment Co., Ltd.*,[31] Dongxun Company and Hengtong Company signed the Cooperation Contract, which contained an arbitration clause, and Yulin Municipal Government issued a Letter of Commitment as the guarantor without any arbitration clause. The arbitration tribunal rendered the award on the disputes arising from both the Cooperation Contract and the Letter of Commitment. The SPC made it clear that "there was no arbitration clause in the Letter of Commitment or between Yulin Municipal Government and Dongxun Company. As far as the guarantee dispute was concerned, the arbitration award had gone beyond the scope of the arbitration agreement in the Cooperation Contract."

For another example, in the *Reply of the SPC to the Request for Instructions on the Application of Chengdu Youbang Stationery Company and Wang Guojian for Revocation of Arbitral Award No. 601 [2011] of Shenzhen Arbitration Commission*,[32] Youbang Company and Chengdu Youbang Company reached the Trademark License Contract, which contained an arbitration clause, and Wang signed the Guarantee Letter with no arbitration agreement. Later, upon Youbang Company's application, the arbitral tribunal rendered an award regarding the disputes arising from the Trademark License Contract and the Guarantee Letter. The SPC held that the arbitration clause in the Trademark License Contract did not apply to the Guarantee Letter, and the arbitration tribunal had no legal basis to handle the dispute arising from the Guarantee Contract without an arbitration clause.

When dealing with the situation in which "the main contract has an arbitration clause while the guarantee contract has no arbitration agreement", Chinese commercial arbitration commissions and courts generally take the following factors into consideration:

1.   Relative Independence of the Guarantee Contract

   Although the guarantee contract is a subordinate contract of the main contract, its legal relation differs from that of the main contract. The guarantee contract possesses the characteristics of relative independence. The existence, validity and dispute settlement method of the guarantee contract are independent from that of the main contract. Therefore, the arbitration clause in the main contract does not directly bind the guarantee contract.

2.   Independence of Arbitration Agreement

   Pursuant to Article 19 of the Arbitration Law, the validity of an arbitration clause is not affected by the effectiveness of the main contract. The same is true for the judgment of existence, validity and applicable scope of the arbitration clause agreed upon in the guarantee contract. Hence, arbitration agreements' subordinate nature cannot override their independence.

---

subordinate contract does provide for arbiration, the arbitration agreement in the main contract shall be binding upon the parties.".

[31] (2006) Min Si Ta Zi No. 24.

[32] (2013) Min Si Ta Zi No. 9.

3. Relativity of contract

As a contract, arbitration agreements should follow the principle of contract relativity, which means that the arbitration agreement only binds the parties to it and that any third party cannot invoke it to exercise their rights. Pursuant to Article 129 of the Guarantee Law Interpretation, in terms of the court's jurisdiction, the subordinate guarantee contract can be considered to have overridden the relativity of the contract and constitute an exception. There could be a similar breakthrough in arbitration if there is new legislation or judicial interpretation. However, unlike a litigation clause, the independent nature of arbitration agreements constitutes a hard line to break. Under the current legal framework, only the parties to the arbitration agreement can become the parties to the arbitration.

4. Effective Elements of Arbitration Agreement

According to the Arbitration Law, a valid arbitration agreement must possess the effective elements required in Article 16 and be free from the conditions enumerated in Article 17. The arbitration agreement in the main contract must meet such legal requirements. If the arbitration agreement in the main contract is invalid, no valid arbitration clause exists in either the main contract or the guarantee contract, and disputes arising from both contracts are subject to the court's jurisdiction.

If the guarantee contract, issued by a third party or provided by the debtor itself, states clearly that it is bound by the arbitration clause of the main contract and no other party objects to it, disputes arising from the guarantee contract can be submitted to arbitration. However, if the provider of the guarantee contract is a third party and there is no evidence to show that it is bound by the arbitration clause in the main contract, the consequences could either be the arbitration commission's refusal to accept the case or the court's denial of the guarantee part in the arbitral award. Therefore, where a guarantee contract (whether it is guarantee, mortgage, pledge or other) is involved, all parties concerned and the creditor in particular should pay attention to the consistency of dispute settlement before signing the contract. Such factors should also be considered, and suggestions should be followed where a third party issues other types of unilateral documents.

In addition to what has been discussed above, we need to emphasize the position of pro-arbitration. For judges or arbitrators, in most cases, the process of applying law is the process of understanding and interpreting the law. The pro-arbitration position can be reflected in the following aspects: 1. to validate arbitration agreement as far as possible in literal interpretation; 2. to focus on the content of the parties' intention and to put less weight on the defects of other elements; and 3. to increase the burden of proof to the party that has not objected or refused arbitration in handling conflicts. This position is particularly important for the development of arbitration, whether it is about the main contract or the subordinate contract or for other problems discussed in this book.

2.6 Unilateral Document

Many unilateral documents contain no dispute settlement clause, and in such cases, it is not proper to mechanically copy and expand the application of some rules in similar cases, since it is hard to categorize what are these "similar cases".

Issuers of unilateral documents such as letter of commitment and letter of guarantee could be the debtor itself or a third party, and it is the former that this section focuses on. The following is an example concerning the jurisdiction issue represented by Yi & Partners during 2019 and 2020.

An Arbitration Case over Equity Transfer Contract and Commitment Letter

Party A and Party B concluded a Partnership Agreement with an arbitration clause. Since Party B could fulfill its obligation under the contract, Party B and Party C jointly issued a Letter of Commitment to Party A, stating that Party B would complete its performance of the contract after all its rights and interests were transferred to Party A. Otherwise, Party B would be liable for breach of contract. Later, Party A and Party C signed an equity transfer contract, whose main content reflected the letter of commitment and contained the arbitration clause to submit disputes to SCIA. One of the issues here is whether the arbitration clause also applied to the Letter of Commitment.

With respect to the issue, Yi & Partner's views are as follows:

The Letter of Commitment is a subordinate document to the Equity Transfer Contract, and the former is governed by the arbitration clause in the latter.

First, in terms of form, as a subordinate document of the Equity Transfer Contract, the Letter of Commitment stipulated subordinate obligations. Since Party C voluntarily issued the Letter of Commitment and Party A was a party to the Equity Transfer Contract, the Letter of Commitment differed from other guarantee documents provided by other third parties and would not undermine the rights and interests of third parties. In addition, the two documents, which shared coherent contents and were executed in short intervals, can be regarded as a complete set of documents.

Second, from the perspective of content, the Equity Transfer Contract encompassed the obligations in the Letter of Commitment, and the parties confirmed the Letter of Commitment through the execution of the Equity Transfer Contract. Therefore, the arbitration clause in the Equity Transfer Contract was not against Party B and Party C's original intention to issue the Letter of Commitment.

Finally, in light of performance, the fulfillment of the Letter of Commitment cannot be separated from that of the Equity Transfer Contract. Because the two contracts shared the same contents and the disputes between the parties shall be submitted to arbitration according to the arbitration clause in the Equity Transfer Contract, the Letter of Commitment, which specified parties' liabilities, should also be governed by arbitration clause.

It should be noted that the Letter of Commitment was issued by Party C to Party A, which involved no third party. Hence, it is not appropriate to apply the jurisdictional rules concerning third parties issuing guarantee documents. Otherwise, for the same disputes between the parties, the consequences of breach of contract should be handled by other procedures, which is not conducive to the distribution of judicial resources and the protection of the legitimate rights and interests of all parties.

Regarding the question of whether the Letter of Commitment fell into the scope of arbitration clause, the tribunal held that:

1. The dispute settlement method agreed that the equity transfer contract should prevail since the contract was signed after the letter of commitment.
2. To submit the disputes arising out of the Letter of Commitment to arbitration is in line with the intention of Party C and Party B. First, the Letter of Commitment did not contain dispute settlement method inconsistent with the arbitration clause in the Equity Transfer Contract. Second, both the Equity Transfer Contract and the Partnership Agreement were closely related to the Letter of Commitment that contained an arbitration clause. Last, the finding that Party B and Party C to the Letter of Commitment had the intention to solve their disputes in ways other than arbitration would violate the arbitration clause agreed also by Party B in the Partnership Agreement.
3. Incorporating the disputes arising from the Letter of Commitment into this case is conducive to saving the cost of dispute settlement, avoiding the waste of social resources, averting the possibility of conflicting results between different judicial organs, and better protecting the legitimate rights and interests of the parties.

This case, in which the provider of the unilateral document was also the party to the main contract, distinguishes it from the common unilateral guarantee disputes. The rule that "the guarantee contract is not bound by the arbitration clause in the main contract" did not apply here. In case analysis, one should not mechanically apply a certain formula but pay attention to the differences between cases.

Where there is no law or clear guidance from the SPC or guiding cases, the following factors should be taken into consideration:

1. Principle of Good Faith

   It is helpful to analyze transaction details, including contract execution background, to determine whether parties have the intention or motive to set up various methods to resolve disputes arising from different stages or programs. In most cases, it is unnecessary and unlikely for the parties to the main contract to resolve a single difference through multiple dispute settlement methods. It is unreasonable for parties to litigate product differences and arbitrate quality problems in China while submitting liquidated damage disputes for international arbitration. Contracts should be performed in good faith, and likewise, legal procedures should also be carried out in good faith. Unless there is contrary evidence, where the parties agree to adopt a certain way of dispute settlement for a transaction, it should be construed that the dispute settlement method provides a complete solution to all disputes arising from the transaction.

2. Principle of Reasonableness

Reasonableness is another factor to be taken into consideration. A reasonable dispute settlement method not only saves social and judicial resources but also avoids conflicting judgments. Legal experts do not have a monopoly on the principle of reasonableness. A reasonable person can draw the same conclusion by common sense or simple view of justice.

Reasonableness is a subjective concept, but this does not prevent it from becoming one of the most useful criteria for judges or arbitrators to exercise their discretion. Whether a judgment is reasonable is decided by judges' and arbitrators' experience as well as their inner conviction of the just value of law.

3. Purpose Principle

Just as parties reaching an agreement about a transaction aim to make the deal successful, the purpose of concluding a dispute settlement agreement is to resolve dispute rather than to create new differences. Where parties have different opinions, interpretation based on the purpose principle shall prevail.

Of course, the text of a dispute settlement clause should not be ignored. If a dispute resolution clause clearly excludes the settlement of a unilateral commitment, the principle does not apply.

4. Judicial Opinion

Although similar cases are limited, we can still find views of the SPC. For example, in *China National Complete Equipment Import and Export Tianjin Company v. Shandong Xinhua Pharmaceutical Group Co., Ltd.*,[33] the SPC held that "the Commitment should be regarded as a change to the relevant contents of the Cooperation Contract. Therefore, the disputes arising from the repayment of bank loans between the two parties should be classified as disputes during the performance of the Cooperation Contract, which belongs to the scope of arbitration agreement."

In drafting the Arbitration Law Interpretation, the SPC has studied the relationship between the main contract and the guarantee contract, especially when the arbitration clause is involved. However, whether the guarantee contract should be bound by the arbitration clause in the main contract is controversial. The general view is to distinguish the guarantee contract provided by the debtor from that offered by a third party. For the guarantee contract executed by a third party, if it is not clarified that it is bound by the arbitration clause of the main contract, the arbitration clause of the main contract cannot be deemed to apply to the guarantee contract. In contrast, for the guarantee contract provided by the debtor itself, if it has no arbitration clause, it

---

[33] (2013) Zhi Jian Zi No. 182.

is bound by the arbitration clause in the main contract unless the parties explicitly exclude the application of the arbitration clause of the main contract.[34]

Obviously, the case above falls into the category in which the guarantee contract with no arbitration clause was provided by the debtor. Since the parties had not explicitly excluded the application of the arbitration clause of the main contract, the guarantee contract was bound by the arbitration clause of the main contract.

2.7   Unilateral Commitment Letter

Unilateral documents such as letters of commitment, guarantees and understanding issued by one party are common in business transactions. Such documents are of subordinate nature. It would save resources to solve disputes arising from the main contract and unilateral documents together according to the dispute settlement clause in the main contract if such a clause is not stated in unilateral documents. However, whether it is feasible depends on who provides the unilateral documents. If it is issued by the debtor to the main contract, it is fine to apply the dispute settlement clause in the main contract to the unilateral document in both practice and theory. If the provider of such a unilateral document is a third party, there is uncertainty about the jurisdiction that requires a close analysis of the wording in the document. At present, disputes arising from unilateral documents provided by a third party are dealt with separately on the ground of the independence of arbitration agreement. Due to superior court cases, there has been a trend of expansion of such practice. However, this problem should not be treated mechanically but considered on a case-on-case basis.

This section focuses on the issue of whether other parties are bound by the dispute settlement clause stated in a unilateral document. In particular, can parties making claims based on substantive clauses in the unilateral document also invoke the dispute settlement clause?

Guangxi Investment Group International Co., Ltd. v. Guangxi Jiahe Investment Co., Ltd. and Guangxi Investment Group Hengyuan Trading Co., Ltd.[35]

Jiahe Company filed a lawsuit in the High People's Court of Guangxi Zhuang Autonomous Region against Hengyuan Company and Investment Group Company over contract disputes. Before the hearing, the Investment Group Company raised a jurisdiction objection on the ground of the existence of the arbitration clause in the Letter of Commitment it issued to Jiahe Company unilaterally, which states that "disputes shall be submitted to the Hong Kong International Arbitration Center for arbitration". Jiahe Company did not sign the Letter of Commitment but submitted it to the court as the evidence requiring the Investment Group Company to undertake the guarantee liability.

---

[34] Research Office of the SPC and the Fourth Civil Trial Tribunal of the SPC, *Understanding and Application of Judicial Interpretation of the Arbitration Law of the SPC*, 162–163, People's Court Press, 2016.

[35] (2019) Zui Gao Fa Min Xia Zhong No. 19.

Jiahe Company argued that the Letter of Commitment was issued by the Invest-ment Group Company unilaterally, and no arbitration agreement existed between the two companies. Its submission of the Letter of Commitment as evidence to the court only demonstrated its confirmation of the formation of a legal and effective guarantee contract relationship between the two parties and did not constitute an acceptance of the arbitration clause in the Letter of Commitment. Moreover, Jiahe Company's initiation of a lawsuit according to the dispute settlement clause in the main contract manifested its refusal to accept the arbitration clause in the Letter of Commitment.

The SPC held that according to Article 4 and paragraph 1 of Article 16 of the Arbitration Law, the parties shall reach a written arbitration agreement if they intend to submit their disputes to arbitration. In this case, the Letter of Commitment was issued by the Investment Group Company unilaterally without the signature and seal of Jiahe Company, so the two parties did not reach a written arbitration agreement. Although Jiahe Company submitted the Letter of Commitment to the court of first instance to claim Investment Group Company to bear guarantee liability, it did not submit the dispute to the Hong Kong International Arbitration Center for arbitration and made it clear that it would not accept the content. Therefore, Jiahe Company had not recognized the content of submitting the "dispute to the Hong Kong International Arbitration Center for arbitration" in the Letter of Commitment, and there was no arbitration agreement between the two parties.

Clearly, the SPC holds the position that if a unilateral document issued by one party states arbitration as the way of dispute settlement, an arbitration agreement is reached only if the other party has demonstrated its acceptance of this matter, such as in writing (signature or seal on the document) or actual action (submitting disputes to arbitration and accepting it in the lawsuit).

Where Party A issues a unilateral document containing an arbitration clause to Party B while a litigation clause exists in the main contract, there could be scenarios as follows:

(1) Party B Brings a Lawsuit

While there is an arbitration clause in the letter of commitment provided by Party A, Party B chooses not to submit the dispute to arbitration, although it relies on the substantive clause in the unilateral document, such as the case mentioned above. Due to the independence of the arbitration agreement, the validity of the arbitration agreement is considered separately and is not valid simply because the judicial organ deems the unilateral document effective. Since Party B has manifested its intention to reject arbitration through action, there is no valid arbitration agreement between Party A and Party B. Party B can bring a lawsuit.

Similarly, even if Party A now applies for arbitration, the basis for arbitration is insufficient, and the arbitration commission lacks the authority to accept the case.

(2) Party B Files a Lawsuit, Party A Raises an Objection, and Party B Accepts Arbitration

If Party B brings a lawsuit first and then agrees to arbitration either in words (such as agree to arbitration) or in action (such as withdrawing the lawsuit) after Party A's objection, an arbitration agreement should be deemed established and effective.

Party A's jurisdiction objection should be raised within the prescribed time limit, for example, "before the first hearing"; otherwise, the objection may not be effective. Article 26 of the Arbitration Law stipulates that "if the parties have concluded an arbitration agreement and one party has instituted an action in a people's court without declaring the existence of the arbitration agreement and, after the people's court has accepted the case, the other party submits the arbitration agreement prior to the first hearing, the people's court shall dismiss the case unless the arbitration agreement is null and void. If, prior to the first hearing, the other party has not raised an objection to the people's court's acceptance of the case, he shall be deemed to have renounced the arbitration agreement and the people's court shall continue to try the case." Article 14 of the Arbitration Law Interpretation provides that "the first hearing mentioned in Article 26 of the Arbitration Law means the first session of hearings organized by the people's court after the period for pleadings has expired and it shall not include the activities in prehearing procedures."

(3) Party B Files A Lawsuit, Party A Has No Objection, and Party B Proposed to Arbitrate Disputes

In some circumstances, after Party B brings a lawsuit to which Party A has no objection, Party B may change its mind to terminate the litigation procedure and turn to arbitration. For example, in the process of litigation, Party B may consider that it is likely to lose the case and thus accept arbitration as the way to solve disputes that it had previously rejected. In such cases, since Party B has already refused to arbitrate disputes proposed by Party A through the act of litigation, the two parties have not reached an agreement on arbitration, and Party B's claim to arbitration should not be supported.

Of course, if Party A also agrees to withdraw the lawsuit and submit the disputes for arbitration, which is the acceptance of the new offer made by Party B, the two parties have reached a new arbitration agreement.

Another situation is Party B brings a lawsuit to which Party A has no objection, the court makes a judgment against Party B, and Party B seeks to arbitrate the case. For example, in an unpublished case in 2019 by SCIA, having received an unfavorable judgment from a court in Taiwan region, the party attempted to submit the dispute to SICA in Mainland for arbitration according to the arbitration clause. In summary, once the expression of refusing to arbitrate is effectively made, it should be considered that the parties have changed their original intention of arbitration.

(4) Party B Applies for Arbitration and Party A Raises an Objection

If Party B applies for arbitration according to the arbitration clause in the letter of commitment, the arbitration agreement shall be deemed to have come into force. However, Party A may reject arbitration and claim that the disputes should be resolved through litigation since the arbitration clause is a unilateral statement to which Party B failed to respond in time. Unless there is a time limit for Party B's acceptance of the arbitration agreement in the letter of commitment, Party A's jurisdictional objection should not be supported. The rationale is the principle of good faith and estoppel in commercial practice and legal practice.

(5) Party B Applies for Arbitration and Then, Withdraws the Case

Usually, once Party B applies for arbitration, it will not turn to litigation. However, it is possible for Party B to do so if it considers that the arbitral tribunal may rule against it. As mentioned before, after Party applies for arbitration, the arbitration agreement is deemed to be effective. Without sound reasons such as Party A's agreement to litigate, Party B's turn to litigation on the ground that the arbitration clause is just a unilateral statement should not be upheld. Of course, Party B has the right to withdraw the arbitration case unless it is restricted by the arbitration rules.

(6) Party A Applies for Arbitration and Party B Raises an Objection Immediately

If Party A applies for arbitration according to the arbitration clause in the letter of commitment and Party B objects to arbitration at once, the arbitration agreement should be deemed not established. Similar to the rationale in the first scenario, since Party B has clearly rejected Party A's proposal to arbitrate their disputes, Party B is not bound by the arbitration clause.

(7) Party A Applies for Arbitration to which Party B Accepts

If Party A applies for arbitration and instead of raising objection Party B participates in arbitration proceedings, appoints arbitrators, files defenses or counterclaims, the arbitration agreement shall be deemed to be effective and binding on all parties. Neither party can bring a lawsuit afterwards unless both agree to litigate, which constitutes a waiver of effective arbitration agreement.

(8) Party A Applies for Arbitration and Party B Does Not Participate in the Arbitration

If Party A applies for arbitration and Party B is absent from the arbitration proceeding because of delivery failure (in terms of geography) or service in the legal sense, it is not appropriate to consider that the parties have reached an arbitration agreement since silence is not equivalent to implied consent.

(9) Party A Brings a Lawsuit While Party B Applies for Arbitration

Party A withdraws its intention to arbitrate through the behavior of bringing a lawsuit, and such withdrawal does not need the consent of Party B because both parties have not reached an effective arbitration agreement due to independence of arbitration agreement. Party B, which fails to accept the arbitration clause in the letter of commitment in time, should not claim that its nonobjection constitutes recognition or consent to arbitration in the letter of commitment, unless there are other circumstances sufficient to lead to the contrary conclusion.

Like the above scenario, silence does not mean implied consent. Therefore, both parties should settle disputes through litigation.

In summary, if Party A issues a unilateral document with an arbitration clause, the possible scenarios may be summarized as follows:

(1)   If Party B brings a lawsuit, the arbitration agreement should not be established.
(2)   If Party B files a lawsuit to which Party A raises an objection and Party B agrees with Party A, the arbitration agreement shall be deemed to be effective.
(3)   If Party B takes a claim to a court and Party A agrees to participate in the litigation, Party B's change to arbitration should not be upheld.
(4)   If Party B applies for arbitration, the arbitration agreement shall be deemed to be effective, and Party A's jurisdictional objection on the ground of unilateral intention to arbitrate should not be supported.
(5)   If Party B applies for arbitration, its change to litigation should not be upheld.
(6)   If Party A applies for arbitration and Party B raises objection at once, the arbitration agreement should be deemed to be not established.
(7)   If Party A applies for arbitration to which Party B accepts, the arbitration agreement shall be deemed to be effective, and neither party can unilaterally take a claim to a court.
(8)   If Party A applies for arbitration in which Party B fails to participate, no arbitration agreement should be deemed to have been reached.
(9)   If Party A files a lawsuit while Party B applies for arbitration, it is not appropriate to consider that the arbitration agreement is effective.

For any scenario in the above, the handling should take the parties' intention into consideration. An arbitration clause unilaterally made by one party usually does not bind the other party. In addition, due to the independence of arbitration agreement, the invocation of an arbitration clause is not affected by substantive clauses in the unilateral document.

Chapter 3
Arbitration Institution and Place

3.1 Nationality of Arbitral Awards Made by Foreign Arbitration Institutions in Mainland

In a commercial arbitration system, it is necessary to determine the nationality of an award because only those allowed by the domestic law of a specific country can be legally binding in that country. The determination of the nationality of an arbitral award is to find with which country the award is connected, which decides courts' right to revoke the award and the scope of the recognition and enforcement of the award.

Under China's arbitration law regime, arbitral awards are divided into two categories: domestic awards (including domestic and foreign-related arbitral awards) and foreign awards. This section focuses on arbitral awards made by arbitration institutions rather than *ad hoc* arbitral awards, although the same system applies.

The legal bases for annulment and non-enforcement of domestic awards differ from those of foreign awards. For domestic awards, the legal basis of vacating awards is Article 58 and Article 63 of the Arbitration Law and Article 237 of the Civil Procedure Law stipulating grounds for non-enforcement; for foreign-related awards, Article 70 of the Arbitration Law enumerates the circumstances for annulment, and the conditions for non-enforcement are provided in Article 71 of the Arbitration Law and Article 274 of the Civil Procedure Law. For foreign awards, mainland China's courts have no right to set them aside since China is not the country where the awards are made, and the legal basis for enforcement is Article 238 of the Civil Procedure Law, which further specifies the basis as either the New York Convention or reciprocal treaty.

Therefore, in mainland China's legal system, when an arbitral award enters the stage of judicial review, it is necessary to determine the nationality of the award first.

Brentwood Industries, Inc. (U.S.A) v. Guangdong Faanlong Machinery Equipment Engineering Co., Ltd.[1]

---

[1] (2015) Sui Zhong Fa Min Si Chu Zi No.62.

© The Author(s), under exclusive license to Springer Nature Singapore Pte Ltd. 2022
Y. Lin, *China Arbitration Yearbook (2021)*, China Arbitration Yearbook,
https://doi.org/10.1007/978-981-19-1284-9_3

The parties agreed in the Contract that "any dispute arising from or in connection with this contract shall be settled through friendly negotiation. If no settlement can be reached through negotiation, it shall be submitted to the ICC for arbitration in the place where the project is located in accordance with international practice. The award made by ICC is final and binding on both parties." The "project" mentioned in the clause refers to the "Guangzhou Liede Sewage Treatment Plant Phase IV Project" listed in the Supplementary Agreement. Therefore, the arbitration institution agreed that the arbitration agreement was ICC, and the agreed-upon place of arbitration was Guangzhou, China.

The applicant Brentwood Industries, Inc. (U.S.A) ("Brentwood Company") claimed that the applicable legal basis for the award here was the New York Convention or the Arrangements of the SPC on the Mutual Enforcement of Arbitral Awards by China's Mainland and Hong Kong. Under Chinese judicial practice, courts regard the location of the arbitration institution as the place of nationality of the arbitral award. Since the ICC was headquartered in Paris, France, the award should be recognized as a French arbitral award, and the New York Convention should apply, to which both China and France are parties. If the court considered that the award in the case was made by the Hong Kong Branch of ICC, the award was a Hong Kong arbitral award and shall be recognized and enforced in accordance with the provisions of the Arrangements of the SPC on the Mutual Enforcement of Arbitral Awards by China's Mainland and Hong Kong".

The respondent argued that the award in this case was neither domestic nor foreign and should not be recognized or enforced. Article 31 of the ICC Arbitration Rule provides that the nationality of the award is determined by the country where the award is made, and thus the nationality of the award was Chinese, considering the agreed place of arbitration was Guangzhou. Since the ICC was not a Chinese arbitration institution, determining the nationality of the award according to the place of arbitration institution as claimed by the applicant was unfounded. The ICC Arbitration Rules were contrary to Chinese law, and hence, the award here was neither domestic nor foreign-related. In addition, the award in this case was not made in the territory of another contracting state to the New York Convention, so the Convention was not applicable.

The Guangzhou Intermediate People's Court held that upon Brentwood Company's request, the ICC constituted an arbitration tribunal composed of the sole arbitrator to make the arbitration award in Guangzhou, China. According to this fact, the arbitral award involved in the case was an arbitral award made by a foreign arbitration institution in Mainland China and can be regarded as a foreign-related arbitral award of China.

The publication of the case has stirred much discussion and captured widespread attention among practitioners and academics. The case touched upon the tricky issue of how to determine the nationality of an award rendered by a foreign arbitration institution in Mainland under Chinese law and reflected the typical views on this topic.

In Chinese practice, there exist three standards to determine the nationality of arbitration awards: the place where the arbitration institution is located, the nondomestic award standard and the place where the award is made. Under the current legal framework, the third is optimal in my view.

1. The Standard of the Place Where the Arbitration Institution is Located

   The Arbitration Law does not clarify how to determine the nationality of an award; instead, it invokes relevant provisions of the Civil Procedure Law. The descriptions of "awards of arbitration institutions established by law", "awards made by the foreign-related arbitration institution" and "awards of foreign arbitration institutions" stipulated in Articles 237, 274 and 283 of the Civil Procedure Law correspond to the concepts of domestic awards, foreign-related arbitral awards and foreign awards in the Arbitration Law. It may be inferred that the legislators of the Arbitration Law and the Civil Procedure Law adopted the standard of the place where the arbitration institution is located to determine the nationality of arbitral awards.

   However, this standard not only deviates from the mainstream practices of international commercial arbitration but also causes many thorny problems. For example, it is impossible to determine the nationality of ad hoc awards since no arbitration institution is involved.

2. The Standard of Non-domestic Award

   Although in practice some courts regard awards made by foreign arbitration institutions in China as nondomestic awards, the main obstacle of this standard is that it is neither defined in the New York Convention nor clarified in judgments.

   Another barrier is the reciprocity reservation declaration made by China upon its accession to the New York Convention. Pursuant to the Notice of the SPC on Implementing the Convention on the Recognition and Enforcement of Foreign Arbitral Awards Acceded to by China,[2] China will only apply this Convention to the recognition and enforcement of arbitral awards made in the territory of another contracting state. In the instant case, the award made by ICC in Mainland does not satisfy the requirement of "in the territory of another contracting state", and thus even if it is considered a foreign award, it cannot be enforced in China under the New York Convention.

3. The Standard of the Place of Arbitration

   In 2009, the SPC stated in the Notice of the SPC on Issues concerning the Execution of Hong Kong Arbitral Awards in the Mainland[3] that the recognition and enforcement of ad hoc awards made in Hong Kong and awards made by ICC in Hong Kong should apply the Arrangements of the SPC on the Mutual Enforcement of Arbitral Awards by China's Mainland and Hong Kong rather than the New York Convention. That is, ad hoc awards made in Hong Kong and

---

[2] Fa [Jing] Fa [1987] No.5.

[3] Fa [2009] No.415.

awards made by the ICC in Hong Kong are regarded as Hong Kong awards. It can be seen that on the issue of determining the nationality of arbitral awards, the Notice adopts the standard of the place where the arbitral award is made.

According to the standard of the place of arbitration, awards made by the ICC in China are considered foreign-related awards. On the one hand, it conforms to the characteristics of foreign-related factors; on the other hand, it empowers Chinese courts to review such awards in accordance with the Arbitration Law and the Civil Procedure Law.

Chinese courts have not yet reached a consensus on the standards for the determination of the nationality of arbitral awards, but the trend is a shift from the place where the arbitration institution is located to the place where the award is made.

In 2004, the SPC expressly adopted the standard of the place where the arbitration institution is located to determine the nationality of awards in a reply,[4] which provided that "the award involved in this case is an institutional arbitral award made by ICC on the basis of the arbitration agreement concluded between the parties. Since the ICC is an arbitration institution established in France, both China and France are member states of the New York Convention, we should apply the provisions of this Convention for reviewing the recognition and execution of the award to this case rather than the Arrangements of the SPC on the Mutual Enforcement of Arbitral Awards by China's Mainland and Hong Kong."

In the same year, the Wuxi City Intermediate People's Court of Jiangsu Province stated in a case[5] that according to Article 1 of the New York Convention, the award made by ICC and confirmed by the seal of the Secretariat of its headquarters should be regarded as a nondomestic award, and the New York Convention should be applied. It can be seen from this case that the award made by the ICC in Shanghai is considered by the court a nondomestic award.

In 2015, the Guangzhou Intermediate People's Court held in the Brentwood case that the award made by the ICC in Guangzhou was a foreign-related award. This case shows that the criteria to determine the nationality of awards have changed from the standard of the place where the arbitration institution is located to the place where the arbitration award is made.

On July 30, 2021, the Arbitration Law (Draft for Comments) ("the Draft") was released. Article 27[6] of the draft defines the seat of arbitration as the place where the arbitral award is rendered. The Draft specifies the criterion of determining the seat of arbitration is that the parties can agree on the seat of arbitration in their arbitration agreement; if the contract entered into by the parties is silent or unclear in the seat of

---

[4] (2004) Min Si Ta Zi No.6.

[5] (2004) Xi Min San Zhong Zi No.1.

[6] Article 27 stipulates that: the parties can agree on the seat of arbitration in their arbitration agreement. If the parties fail to agree on the seat of arbitration or their agreement on the seat of arbitration is not clear, the seat of arbitration shall be the place where the arbitration institution that manages the case is located. The arbitral award is regarded to be rendered at the seat of arbitration. The determination of the seat of arbitration does not affect the arbitration activities such as panel discussion or hearing held by the parties or the arbitral tribunal in different places other than the seat of arbitration based on the agreement or they deem it appropriate.

arbitration, the seat of arbitration shall be the place where the arbitration institution that manages the case is located. The Draft also classifies the concepts of the seat of arbitration and the place of the hearing. The determination of the seat of arbitration does not affect the arbitration activities such as panel discussion or hearing held by the parties or the arbitral tribunal in different places other than the seat of arbitration based on the agreement or they deem it appropriate.

The Draft also specifies that the intermediate people's court of the seat of arbitration is entitled to determine the validity of arbitration agreement and jurisdiction (Article 28), whether to take the property preservation measures after the initiation of arbitration (Article 46), whether to set aside the arbitral award (Article 77), to determine the composition of special arbitral tribunal and the challenge of the arbitrators (Article 92), and take responsible for recording the arbitral awards rendered by the special arbitral tribunals (Article 93).

3.2 Inaccurate Arbitration Institution Name

In Chinese arbitration practice, it is common to find arbitration institution names agreed upon in arbitration clauses inaccurate, such as incorrect abbreviations or wrongful descriptions of the full name.

Whether the arbitration institution name is accurate is related to the validity of the arbitration agreement under Chinese laws.[7] A designated arbitration commission is one of the elements of a valid arbitration agreement. If the arbitration institution is not clearly agreed upon and supplementary agreement on this matter cannot be reached, the arbitration agreement should be invalid. Article 16 of the Arbitration Law provides that "an arbitration agreement shall contain the following particulars: (1) an expression of intention to apply for arbitration; (2) matters for arbitration; and (3) a designated arbitration commission"; and Article 18 stipulates that "if an arbitration agreement contains no or unclear provisions concerning the matters for arbitration or the arbitration commission, the parties may reach a supplementary agreement. If no such supplementary agreement can be reached, the arbitration agreement shall be null and void."

For example, in the Reply of the SPC to the Request for Instructions on Determining the Force of an Arbitral Agreement,[8] the parties agreed that "in the case of any dispute arising in the performance of this Contract, both parties shall resolve it through friendly negotiation. In case any negotiation fails, the dispute shall be presented to Beijing Economy and Trade Arbitration Commission for final ruling."

---

[7] This is the case under the framework of the current arbitration law. However, in the future, the case will be changed. The Arbitration Law (Draft for Comments) released in July 2021 does not take an arbitration institution as a necessary element of the arbitration agreement. Article 21 stipulates: The arbitration agreement includes the arbitration clause in the contract and the agreement with the intention to request arbitration, which is reached in other written forms before or after the dispute occurs. In this book, we only discuss relevant practices under the current arbitration law.

[8] (2005) Min Si Ta Zi No.52.

The SPC held that there was no such arbitration institution as stipulated by the parties in Beijing. Although there were three arbitration institutions in Beijing, namely, the Beijing Arbitration Commission, China International Economy and Trade Arbitration Commission and China Maritime Arbitration Commission, the true intent of the parties cannot be inferred therefrom. Where one party had applied with the people's court to confirm the invalidity of the arbitration clause, it could be deemed that both parties failed to conclude any supplement agreement with regard to the arbitration institution. According to Articles 16 and 18 of the Arbitration Law, the arbitration clause should be deemed invalid.

However, not all inaccurate descriptions of arbitration institutions will lead to the invalidation of the arbitration agreement. As long as the specific arbitration institution can be identified, the validity of the arbitration agreement will not be affected. Article 3 of the Arbitration Law Interpretation stipulates that "where the name of the arbitration institution provided in the arbitration agreement is inaccurate but is nevertheless identifiable, the arbitration institution shall be deemed to have been selected."

For example, in the *Reply of the SPC on the Validity of Arbitration Clauses in the Case of International Entertainment Overseas Co., Ltd. v. Hangzhou Little Donkey Sports Brokerage Co., Ltd.*,[9] the arbitration institution agreed upon by the parties was the "Hangzhou branch of China International Economic and Trade Arbitration Commission". The SPC held that although CIETAC did not have Hangzhou sub-Commission, Article 2 (6) of the applicable Arbitration Rules of CIETAC (2012) stipulated that "the parties may agree to submit their disputes to CIETAC or a sub-commission/arbitration center of CIETAC for arbitration…Where the sub-commission/arbitration center agreed upon by the parties does not exist or where the agreement is ambiguous, the Secretary Office of the Arbitration Commission shall accept the arbitration application and administer the case." Therefore, it can be concluded that the parties had chosen CIETAC for arbitration, and the arbitration clause was valid.

With the pro-arbitration approach, Chinese mainland courts do not deny the validity of the arbitration agreement simply because its contents are not clear, but it does not mean that the arbitration agreement will be supported in any case. Here is an example.

Jiujiang Hongbai Industry and Trade Co., Ltd., v. Jiujiang Shengchaoxinye Technology Co., Ltd.[10]

The parties agreed in the Equipment Sales and Installation Technical Service Contract that "in case of any dispute that cannot be settled through friendly negotiation, the parties shall file arbitration with the International Economic and Trade Arbitration Commission in accordance with the law. The place of arbitration may be Suzhou City, Jiangsu Province, and the arbitration result shall be final".

---

[9] (2013) Min Si Ta Zi No.53.

[10] (2018) Gan Min Zhong No.112.

As disputes arose, one party brought a lawsuit, and the other party raised jurisdictional objection claiming their differences should be resolved through arbitration according to the Equipment Sales and Installation Technical Service Contract.

The Jiangxi High People's Court held that according to Article 16 of the Arbitration Law, the arbitration agreement should specify the selected arbitration committee. In this case, the International Economic and Trade Arbitration Commission (or sub-Commission) in Suzhou City, Jiangsu Province, as agreed upon by both parties, did not exist. Since the arbitration agreement was not clear and the parties had not reached a supplementary agreement on the arbitration institution, the arbitration agreement was invalid.

In the instant case, the arbitration institution with the name of "International Economic and Trade Arbitration Commission" does not exist. Although CIETAC, SCIA and SHIAC all contain the word "International Economic and Trade Arbitration Commission" in their names, it is still impossible to determine the exact and sole arbitration institution agreed upon by the parties. Therefore, with no supplementary agreement, the arbitration clause was invalid.

It should be noted that the place of arbitration agreed upon by the parties in this case was Suzhou City, Jiangsu Province. If the place of arbitration agreed upon by the parties was the seat of the above three arbitration commissions, namely, Beijing, Shenzhen or Shanghai, the result might be different. In such cases, although the name of the arbitration institution remained inaccurate, the court may take into consideration the agreed place of arbitration when determining the specific arbitration institution, and might hold the arbitration agreement valid.

For example, in *Qingdao Antaixin Group Co., Ltd. v. Chalco International Engineering Equipment Co., Ltd.* et al.,[11] the parties agreed in the Guarantee Contract that "all disputes arising from or related to this contract shall be settled through friendly negotiation. If no settlement can be reached through consultation or one party is unwilling to settle the dispute through consultation, either party may submit the dispute to the China International Trade Arbitration Commission for arbitration in Beijing in accordance with its rules. The arbitration shall be final and legally binding on both parties." In this case, the court held that although the expression of the "China International Trade Arbitration Commission" was different from the accurate name of the China International Economic and Trade Arbitration Commission ("**CIETAC**"), since the place of arbitration was agreed upon in Beijing, it can be concluded that CIETAC was the only arbitration institution agreed upon by both parties, so the arbitration clause was valid.

For another example, in *National Technology Co., Ltd. v. Epekson Microelectronics Co., Ltd.*,[12] the parties agreed in the contract that "the case shall be submitted to China International Economic and Trade Arbitration Commission for arbitration In accordance with relevant laws. The place of arbitration shall be Shanghai, and the arbitration award shall be final and binding on both parties." The court held that although "China International Economic and Trade Arbitration" omitted the word

---

[11] (2017) Jing 02 Min Te No.228.

[12] (2014) Shen Zhong Fa She Wai Zhong Zi No.32.

"Commission" in the arbitration clause, it could be inferred as "China International Economic and Trade Arbitration Commission" ("CIETAC"). Given that the place of arbitration was Shanghai, that CIETAC had the right to accept the case and hold the hearing in Shanghai were in line with the agreement of both parties, and therefore the arbitration clause was valid.

Under the current Chinese legal framework, a designated arbitration institution is an important element of a valid arbitration agreement. When drafting contracts with arbitration clauses, parties are advised to pay attention to the name of the arbitration institution to avoid the invalidity of the arbitration agreement.

3.3 "Local" Arbitration Commission

In commercial practices, many parties agree to submit disputes to the "local" Chinese arbitration commission for arbitration. As mentioned in the previous section, according to Articles 16 and 18 of the Arbitration Law, if the arbitration institution is not clear and a supplementary agreement cannot be reached, the arbitration clause shall be invalid. Since "local" does not specify the name of the arbitration institution, parties are likely to disagree with the validity of the arbitration clause after their disputes occur.

By searching "China Judgment Online" with the key words of "local arbitration commission", a total of 1660 cases were found. Evidently, ambiguity in the "local arbitration commission" has given rise to many disputes. Among them, construction project contract disputes account for a considerable proportion. The case below serves as an example.

Du v. Jiangxi Tianma Investment Real Estate Co., Ltd.[13]

The parties agreed to jointly invest in a student apartment construction project in Nanchang, Jiangxi Province, and the Contract stipulated that "in the process of performing this Contract, both parties shall settle the dispute through consultation. If the negotiation fails, the parties may apply to the local arbitration commission for arbitration".

As disputes arose, one party filed a lawsuit, and the other party raised a jurisdictional objection, claiming that the differences should be submitted for arbitration.

The Jiangxi High People's Court summarized that the issue here was whether the arbitration institution in the arbitration clause was clear. The parties agreed to apply to the "local" arbitration committee for arbitration. Since the parties signed the contract on the construction project, the word "local" in the agreement naturally referred to the location of the construction project. It was against common sense to construe "local" as contract execution place, domiciles of the parties or other places. Because the construction project was located in Jiangxi Province and the Nanchang

---

[13] (2018) Gan Min Zhong No.460.

Arbitration Commission was the sole arbitration institution there when the contract was signed, the arbitration institution agreed upon by both parties was clear, and the arbitration agreement was valid.

In construction project contract disputes, if the parties agree in the contract to submit disputes to the "local arbitration committee" for arbitration, possible interpretations of "local" may include the location of the construction project, the domicile of both parties of the contract, etc. Depending on whether the construction project location and the residences of both parties are the same, cases involving the construction of "local" projects can be divided into two categories.

In the first scenario where the construction project location and the residences of both parties are the same, the courts generally consider that the parties' agreement on the location of the arbitration institution is clear. If there is sole arbitration institution in the place, the arbitration clause will be deemed to be valid in accordance with Article 6 of the Arbitration Law Interpretation.

For example, in *Gansu PetroChina Kunlun Gas Construction and Installation Investment Co., Ltd. v. Lanzhou Xiaoshaomenwai Central Heating Station*,[14] the parties agreed in the contract on construction project that "disputes arising from the performance of this contract shall be settled by both parties through negotiation or mediation by relevant competent authorities; in case of failure in negotiation or mediation, the dispute shall be submitted to the local arbitration commission for arbitration". In this case, the location of the construction project and the registration place of both parties were in Lanzhou City, Gansu Province, and there was only one arbitration institution in Lanzhou, namely, the Lanzhou Arbitration Commission. Therefore, the Gansu High People's court held that the arbitration clause was valid.

In the second case, where the location of the construction project differs from the domicile of both parties, there are two views.

It may be held that since the location of the construction project and the residences of both parties are different, the "local arbitration commission" is not clear, and the specific arbitration institution cannot be determined, leading to the invalidation of the arbitration agreement.

For example, in *Beijing Zhonghai Wobang Energy Investment Co., Ltd. v. Shaanxi Dingsheng Construction and Installation Engineering Co., Ltd.*,[15] the Predrilling Engineering Contract signed by the parties stipulated that "if the parties have disputes on the interpretation and implementation of this contract, they shall settle them through consultation. If they fail to reach an agreement, the dispute shall be submitted to the local arbitration committee." In this case, the construction project was in Linfen City, Shaanxi Province, and the two parties were domiciled in Beijing city and Xi'an City, Shaanxi Province. The Xi'an Intermediate People's Court held that the "arbitration by the local arbitration committee" agreed upon by the parties was not clear.

---

[14] (2018) Gan Min Zai No.5.

[15] (2016) Shan 01 Min Te No.270.

For another example, at *Sanya Lanwan Engineering Co., Ltd. v. Tianjin Xin'an Construction Engineering Co., Ltd.*,[16] considering the location of the construction project, the place of signing the contract and the domicile of the plaintiff were all located in Sanya City, Hainan Province, but the defendant's domicile was in Tianjin, the Hainan High People's Court held that the "local arbitration institutions" agreed by the parties did not specify the arbitration institution, and thus the arbitration clause was invalid.

From another perspective, in light of the characteristics of construction contract disputes, the word "local" of "local arbitration commission" naturally refers to the location of the construction project rather than the domicile of both parties or the execution place of contract. Therefore, the parties should be regarded as having specified the arbitration institution.

In the instant case, the Jiangxi High People's Court held this view. Both the location of the construction project and the domicile of the defendant were Nanchang City, Jiangxi Province, but the residence of the plaintiff was Tongcheng City, Anwei Province. Since the parties signed the Contract on the construction project, the word "local" in the agreement naturally referred to Nanchang, the location of the construction project, and there was only one arbitration commission in Nanchang. Therefore, the arbitration agreement was valid.

In summary, where the location of the construction project differs from the residences of both parties, whether the arbitration clause that stipulates disputes shall be submitted to the "local arbitration commission" is valid is uncertain. To be prudent, it is advised to avoid phrases such as "local" in drafting arbitration agreements.

3.4 The Scope of "Local"

This section proceeds to explore the validity issue of the arbitration clause in which parties agree to submit disputes to the "local" arbitration commission for arbitration. Article 6 of the Arbitration Law Interpretation provides that where the arbitration agreement stipulates that arbitration shall be conducted by an arbitration institution in a certain place and there is sole arbitration institution in that place, the arbitration institution shall be deemed as the agreed arbitration institution. However, under the current legal framework in China, there is no clear definition of the geographical scope of the "local place", which leads to differences in the validity of the arbitration agreement.

Jinghan Real Estate Group Co., Ltd. v. Langdu International Consulting (Beijing) Co., Ltd.

The parties agreed in the Entrustment Service Contract that any party has the right to apply for arbitration to the arbitration institution in the place where the event is

---

[16] (2015) Qiong Li Yi Zhong Zi No.106.

held in case of any dispute arising from the performance of this contract. The contract stated that the venue of the event was in Xiong'an New District.[17]

After disputes arose, one party filed a lawsuit while the other raised a jurisdictional objection, arguing that the case should be transferred to the Baoding Arbitration Commission.

The Beijing First Intermediate People's Court held that the parties agreed in the contract to submit disputes to the arbitration institution in the place where the activity was held, i.e., Xiong'an new district. Considering that there was no arbitration institution in the Xiong'an new area and no supplementary agreement was reached between the two parties, the arbitration agreement was invalid.

Concerning the meaning of "local", there are two types of problems: (1) horizontal region, i.e., whether it refers to the place where the contract is signed, where the contract is performed, where the object is located, or where both parties reside and (2) vertical region, i.e., Whether it refers to the area at the provincial, municipal or district level.

1. Horizontal Scope

Since "local" may include the places where the contract is signed or performed or the parties domicile, there may be three scenarios when the arbitration agreement fails to clarify which place is: (1) the places of contract execution, contract performance and parties' residences, etc. are the same, and there is sole arbitration institution in the place; (2) the parties domicile in different provinces and autonomous regions; (3) contract execution, contract performance and parties' residences, etc. are in different places.

Under the first circumstance, courts are likely to consider the arbitration agreement valid. For example, in *Northwest Construction Co., Ltd. v. Xi'an Shengjie Construction Engineering Co., Ltd.*,[18] the Xi'an Intermediate People's Court held that although the parties failed to point out the name of the arbitration institution using the phrases of "local arbitration institution", the domicile of the parties to the contract and the contract execution place were in Xi'an city, Shaanxi Province. In addition, the project involved was located in Shangluo city, Shaanxi Province. There was only one arbitration institution in Xi'an City, and the Shangluo sub-commission of Xi'an Arbitration Commission belongs to Xi'an Arbitration Commission. There was no ambiguity in understanding "local"; thus, the arbitration agreement was valid.

In the second case, the courts are likely to deem arbitration agreements invalid. For example, at *Liuzhou Longsheng Entertainment Management Co., Ltd. v. Guangxi Yingxuetang Pension Service Co., Ltd.*,[19] the parties agreed in the Lease Contract that if the dispute cannot be negotiated, it shall be submitted to the local arbitration committee for arbitration. The Liuzhou Intermediate People's Court in Guangxi Zhuang Autonomous Region held that since the

---

[17] (2020) Jing 01 Min Xia Zhong No.36.

[18] (2018) Shan 01 Min Te No.381.

[19] (2019) Gui 02 Min Xia Zhong No.9.

plaintiff and defendant domiciled in Nanning and Liuzhou city respectively, it was impossible to determine the "local" arbitration commission selected by the parties. In the absence of a supplementary agreement between the parties, the arbitration agreement was invalid.

For the third scenario, the court may hold that the arbitration agreement is invalid because the arbitration commission cannot be determined. For example, in *Sichuan Minzheng Construction Co., Ltd. v. Sichuan Taicheng Real Estate Development Co., Ltd.,*[20] the parties that domiciled in Wuhou District, Chengdu City, Sichuan Province, and Nanlong Town, Nanbu County, Sichuan Province, agreed that the dispute on contract performance shall be submitted to the local arbitration commission for arbitration. The Nanchong Intermediate People's Court held that "local" could be the place where the contract was signed, performed, the subject matter was located, or the parties were domiciled. In this case, such places were not in the same region, the "local" arbitration commission was not clear, and thus the arbitration clause was invalid without supplementary agreement between the parties.

2. Vertical Scope

The issue of vertical scope of "local" arbitration commission in arbitration agreements usually arises when the parties reside in the same province but in different areas. Most courts held "local" refer to the city at the municipal level, i.e., "local" municipalities directly under the central government, cities where the people's governments of provinces and autonomous regions are located, and other cities with subordinate districts.

For example, in *Pucheng Lvyuan Real Estate Co., Ltd. v. Pucheng County Bureau of Land and Resources of Shaanxi Province,*[21] the parties agreed to submit their dispute to the "local arbitration commission" for arbitration. The SPC held that although both parties domiciled in Pucheng County, Shaanxi Province, there was no factual or legal basis to limit the "local" to the area of the county to which the parties reside. There was only one arbitration institution in Weinan City, i.e., Weinan Arbitration Commission, where both parties were located. Therefore, the "local" arbitration commission agreed upon by the parties should be deemed the Weinan Arbitration Commission.

Article 10 of the Arbitration Law provides that "arbitration commissions may be established in municipalities directly under the Central Government and in cities that are the seats of the people's governments of provinces or autonomous regions. They may also be established in other cities divided into districts, according to need. Arbitration commissions shall not be established at each level of the administrative divisions."

In the instant case, the arbitration institution agreed upon by the parties was in Xiong'an New District. Xiong'an New District is a deputy provincial administrative unit, neither a district of Baoding city of Hebei Province nor a city at the municipal

---

[20] (2018) Chuan 13 Min Xia Zhong No.81.

[21] (2015) Min Yi Zhong Zi No.351.

level, as stipulated in Article 10 of the Arbitration Law. Considering that there was no arbitration institution in the Xiong'an New District, the court held that the arbitration agreement was invalid.

3.5   Arbitration Agreement with Arbitration Rules Only

Sometimes, parties only stipulate arbitration rules without mentioning the arbitration institution in the arbitration clause, which may run the risk of invalidation under Chinese law.[22]

Unless the arbitration commission can be inferred from the arbitration rule or clarified by the parties in their supplementary agreement, the arbitration clause with only the arbitration rule is invalid. Pursuant to Article 4 of the Arbitration Law Interpretation, where an arbitration agreement only provides the applicable arbitration rules, it shall be deemed that no arbitration institution is stipulated under the arbitration agreement, unless the parties have concluded a supplementary agreement, or an arbitration institution may be determined pursuant to the arbitration rules provided.

At present, China's main arbitration institutions stipulate in their arbitration rules that if the parties agree to apply their arbitration rules without specifying the arbitration institution, it shall be deemed that the parties agree to submit the dispute to the arbitration commission for arbitration. For example, Article 4 (4) of the CIETAC Arbitration Rules (2015) provides that "where the parties agree to refer their dispute to arbitration under these Rules without providing the name of the arbitration institution, they shall be deemed to have agreed to refer the dispute to arbitration by CIETAC." SCIA, BAC and SHIAC have similar provisions.

Panjin Liaohe Oilfield Kaite Petroleum Equipment Co., Ltd., v. Bohai Equipment Liaohe Heavy Industry Co., Ltd.[23]

The parties agreed in the Drilling Platform Construction Contract that "once the arbitration procedure is started, the arbitration clause of the current Chinese maritime organization shall be followed".

After disputes arose, one party filed a lawsuit, while the other argued that disputes should be submitted to the China Maritime Arbitration Commission for arbitration.

The SPC held that the parties did not specify the arbitration institution in the arbitration agreement. According to Article 4 of the Arbitration Law Interpretation, if the arbitration commission cannot be inferred from the arbitration rules agreed upon by the party, it should be deemed that no arbitration commission has been agreed upon, and the court can accept the case if one party brings a lawsuit. The parties mentioned "the arbitration clause of the current Chinese maritime organization" in the

---

[22] The requirement of arbitration institution for an arbitration agreement to be valid under Chinese law may be changed if ad hoc arbitration is allowed in the future in China arbitration. The Arbitration Law (Draft for Comments) provides for ad hoc arbitration in Article 91.

[23] (2017) Zui Gao Fa Min Xia Zhong No.255.

Drilling Platform Construction Contract, but no specific arbitration commission can be determined through such phrases, and the parties failed to reach a supplementary agreement on the arbitration institution. Therefore, since the arbitration commission agreed upon by the parties was unclear, the court of first instance had a legal basis to accept the case.

In the instant case, instead of specifying the arbitration commission, the parties stated "the arbitration clause of the current Chinese Maritime Organization" in the contract. From such agreement, it is impossible to determine the specific arbitration institution as China Maritime Arbitration Commission or any other institution. Therefore, without supplementary agreement on the arbitration institution by the parties, the arbitration clause is invalid according Article 18 of the Arbitration Law.

What if the parties stipulate the rules of a specific arbitration institution? It does not necessarily mean the arbitration commission can be determined and the arbitration agreement bound to be valid.

For example, *Hebei Zhongxing Automobile Manufacturing Co., Ltd. v. Automotive Gate FZCO*,[24] the parties agreed that "arbitration shall be conducted in China in accordance with the rules of ICC". The Shijiazhuang Intermediate People's Court held that it was impossible to determine that the arbitration institution agreed upon by the parties was an ICC according to the ICC Arbitration Rule (1998) applicable to this case. Therefore, without supplementary agreement on the arbitration institution by the parties, the arbitration clause was invalid.

Similarly, in the *Reply of the SPC to the Request for Instructions on the Case concerning the Application of Züblin International GmbH and Wuxi Woke General Engineering Rubber Co., Ltd. For Determining the Validity of the Arbitration Agreement*,[25] the parties agreed in the contract that "arbitration: applying arbitration rules of ICC, arbitration in Shanghai". The SPC held that although there was clear intention to arbitrate, arbitration rules and place of arbitration, the arbitration institution was not clearly designated. Therefore, the arbitration clause was invalid.

In the *Reply of the SPC to the Request for Instructions on the Validity of an Arbitration Clause in a Sales Contract Dispute between Cangzhou Donghong Packing Material Co., Ltd. and France DMT Ltd.*,[26] in 2003, the parties agreed in the contract that "any dispute in relation to the execution of this Contract shall be settled through friendly consultations between both parties. If such consultations fail, the dispute shall be submitted for arbitration. The arbitration shall be conducted under the relevant ICC rules..." The SPC held that because both parties in this case failed to agree upon the arbitral institution in the arbitration clause or reach a supplementary agreement, the arbitration clause was void.

In the *Reply of the SPC to the Request for Instructions* on *Contract Dispute between Taizhou Haopu Investment Company and Wicor Holding AG*,[27] in 1997, the parties agreed in the Joint Venture Contract that "in case no agreement can be reached

---

[24] (2011) Shi Min Li Cai Zi No.00002.

[25] (2003) Min Si Ta Zi No.23.

[26] (2006) Min Si Ta Zi No.6.

[27] (2012) Min Si Ta Zi No.6.

through negotiation, the dispute shall be submitted to arbitration. Arbitration shall be conducted in accordance with the rules of mediation and arbitration of ICC." The SPC held that the arbitration agreement did not stipulate an arbitration institution, which cannot be determined according to the arbitration rules of the ICC either. Since the parties had not reached a supplementary agreement on this matter, the arbitration clause was invalid.

Unlike the above cases, in the *Reply of the SPC to the Request for Instructions on the Validity of the Arbitration Clause in the Case concerning the Dispute over the Sale and Purchase Contract between Ningbo Beilun Licheng Lubricating Oil Co., Ltd. and Formal Venture Corp.,*[28] in 2013 the parties agreed that "all disputes or differences arising from or related to this contract shall be settled by arbitration in Beijing, and the arbitration rules of ICC and the awards based on them shall be binding on both parties…" The SPC held that the parties had agreed in the contract to apply the arbitration rules of ICC for arbitration, and whether they had agreed on an arbitration institution should be determined by the applicable arbitration rules of ICC at the time of the contract execution. Article 6 (2) of the ICC Rules effective from January 1, 2012, which was applicable in this case, provides that "by agreeing to arbitration under the Rules, the parties have accepted that the arbitration shall be administered by the Court". The ICC has jurisdiction over disputes between the parties only if they agree to apply its rule without mentioning other arbitration institutions. That was the case here. Since the arbitration institution can be determined according to the agreed arbitration rules, the arbitration clause in this case was valid.

---

[28] (2013) Min Si Ta Zi No.74.

Chapter 4
Parties

4.1 Nonsignatory to Property Service Contract

Parties' consensus is the basis of arbitration, and parties' autonomy is the cornerstone of arbitration. Article 4 of the Arbitration Law stipulates that "if the parties adopt arbitration to resolve their disputes, they shall reach an arbitration agreement on the voluntary basis. If no arbitration agreement is reached and a party applies for arbitration, the arbitration commission shall not accept the application." Based on the doctrines of parties' autonomy and relativity of contract, the arbitration agreements are only binding on the signatories but not the nonsigntories.

However, in some particular circumstances, an arbitration agreement can be binding on the nonsignatories. In international commercial arbitration, many theories are concerned with the extension of the effectiveness of arbitration agreements, such as Group of Company doctrine, doctrine of Piercing the Company Veil, the Exception of Relativity of Contract, Principle of Estoppel, Principle of Fair and Reasonable Expectation, and Principle of Good Faith.[1]

According to Chinese laws, there are four circumstances that reflect the effectiveness expansion of arbitration agreements.

I.   Broadly interpret the scope of "other written forms" of the arbitration agreement

Arbitration 16 (1) of the Arbitration Law provides "An arbitration agreement shall include arbitration clauses stipulated in a contract and agreements of submission to arbitration that are concluded in other written forms before or after disputes arise." According to Article 1 of the Arbitration Law Interpretation, "other written forms" comprise of agreements to arbitrate, which may

---

[1] Liu Xiaohong, *On Jurisprudence of Effectiveness Extension of Arbitration Agreements* (Volume 1, Beijing Arbitration Quarterly, 2004); Wang Hui, *The Extension of Arbitration Agreements to Nonsignatories by Good Faith Principle* (Volume 39, Arbitration Study).

This chapter is coauthored with Ma Huilian, partner of Yi & Partners Law Firm.

© The Author(s), under exclusive license to Springer Nature Singapore Pte Ltd. 2022
Y. Lin, *China Arbitration Yearbook (2021)*, China Arbitration Yearbook,
https://doi.org/10.1007/978-981-19-1284-9_4

take the form of written contracts, letters or electronic data texts (including tele-grams, telexes, facsimiles, electronic data interchanges, and emails). Pursuant to Article 11 of the Arbitration Law Interpretation, where a contract stipulates that an effective arbitration clause in another contract or document shall be applicable to dispute resolution, the parties shall, upon the occurrence of a dispute arising from the contract, apply for arbitration in accordance with the provisions of that arbitration clause.

II.   Merger or Division of a Legal Person

According to Article 8(1) and (3) of the Arbitration Law Interpretation, a party is merged or divided after the parities' conclusion of an arbitration agreement, and the arbitration agreement shall continue to be binding on the successors to the party's rights and obligations. Meanwhile, it is worth noting that Article 8 does not specify whether a successor is bound by the arbitration agreement after the legal person's cancellation of registration. In judicial practice, if a successor takes over all the rights and debts, Chinese courts tend to hold the view that, according to Article 9 of the Arbitration Law Interpretation, the successor is bound by the arbitration agreement.[2]

III.   Death of a Natural Person

According to Article 8(2) and (3) of the Arbitration Law Interpretation, where a party dies after the conclusion of an arbitration agreement, the arbitration agreement shall be binding upon the heir to the party's rights and obligations with regard to the arbitral matters. Please refer to another essay of this book "4.4 Heir" for more details.

IV.   Transfer of the Rights and Obligations

According to Article 9 of the Arbitration Law Interpretation, where all or part of the rights and obligations are transferred, the arbitration agreement shall be binding upon the transferee unless the parties agree otherwise or the transferee explicitly objects to or is unaware of the existence of a separate arbitration agreement when the rights and obligation are transferred.

Apart from the above four circumstances prescribed by the Arbitration Law and the Arbitration Law interpretation, some other Chinese laws also stipulate that arbitration agreements in some particular types of contracts are binding on nonsignatories. The property service contract for the early stage is one of them. According to Article 1 of the Interpretation of the SPC on the Specific Application of Law in Property Service Disputes ("Property Service Disputes Interpretation"), the property service contract signed by a construction company and a property service company at the early stage, as well as the property service contract signed by the owners' committee and the property service company selected by the owners, are binding on the owners. The Chinese courts shall reject it if an owner denies he or she is the competent party to such a property service contract. In judicial practice, if this type of property service

---

[2] (2015) Min Er Zhong Zi No. 381; (2019) Hu 01 Min Te No.439; (2020) Jing 01 Zhi Yi No. 70; (2020) Xin 01 Min Te No. 4–1.

contracts contains an arbitration clause, the arbitration clause is also binding on the nonsigntory. The below case will give more details.

C V. Shenzhen LM Property Management Co., Ltd.[3]

In February 2005, C, the Applicant in this set-aside of arbitral award case purchased a house from LM Industrial (Shenzhen) Co., Ltd. ("LM Industrial Company") for commercial use. C obtained the property ownership certificate on March 14, 2006.

The Respondent Shenzhen LM Property Management Co., Ltd. ("LM Property Company") and LM Industrial Company, signed a "Property Management Contract". Article 18 of the Property Management Contract provides that: This Contract shall take effect from the date of signature by the parties and shall be valid until the date of termination agreed by the parties or the date that owners' committee and LM Property Company (or another property management company) enters into another property management contract. Article 34 is the arbitration clause, under which either party can submit the dispute arising out of the Contract to Shenzhen Arbitration Commission for arbitration.

Disputes arose out of the Contract after it was signed, and LM Property Company filed an application to the Shenzhen Arbitration Commission for arbitration against C. In the arbitral proceedings, C argued that the Shenzhen Arbitration Commission lacked jurisdiction over this case. The Shenzhen Arbitration Commission rejected C's jurisdiction objection, continued to hear the case and rendered the arbitral award on September 30, 2017. C was dissatisfied with the award and applied to Shenzhen Intermediate People's Court to set it aside.

C argued that the C and LM Property Company had no arbitration agreement because the Property Management Contract was entered into by the LM Property Company and LM Industrial Company. Therefore, C was not bound by this Contract.

Because C was a Hong Kong resident, the Shenzhen Intermediate People's Court reviewed this case in accordance with Article 274 of the Civil Procedure Law. The Court held the main issue of this case was whether there was an arbitration agreement between C and LM Property Company. There was evidence showing that the owners' association had not yet been established. LM Industrial Company was the construction company from which C purchased the house. LM Property Company was the property service company chosen by LM Industrial Company to manage the properties of the owners at the early stage when the owners' association had not yet been established. The court further held that, according to Article 1 of Property Service Disputes Interpretation, the Property Management Contract entered into by LM Industrial Company and LM Property Company was binding on C, the owner of the house. The arbitration agreement contained in the Property Management Contract was also binding on C. Therefore, the court rejected C's argument.

The above case is not rare in judicial practice. For example, in *Fang v. Guangzhou Jinhe Property Co. Ltd.* ("Jinhe Company"),[4] Fang was the owner of a house located

---

[3] (2018) Yue 03 Min Te No. 245.

[4] (2014) Shui Zhong Fa Zhong Shen Zi No. 12.

in Jianzhen Garden. Jianzhen Garden was constructed by Guangzhou Lihe Real Estate Co., Ltd. ("Lihe Company"). Lihe Company and Jinhe Company entered into the Property Service Contract containing arbitration clause at the early stage when the owners' commission had not yet established. Afterwards, Jinhe Company applied for arbitration on the basis of this arbitration clause. Fang applied to Guangzhou Intermediate People's Court for confirmation there was no arbitration agreement between him and Jinhe Company, but the Court rejected his application. After the arbitral award was rendered, Fang was dissatisfied and applied to the Court to set aside the award, claiming there was no arbitration agreement. The Court did not support Fang's case on the grounds that the Property Service Contract at the early stage was binding on Fang according to Article 1 of Property Service Disputes Interpretation, so the arbitration clause contained therein was also binding on Fang. The courts in the following cases held similarly: *Jiao v. Beijing Kailai Property Management Co., Ltd. Guangzhou Branch*,[5] *Shi v. Guangzhou Panyu Junbang Property Management Co., Ltd.*,[6] *Liu v. Hainan Guanghua Jingrui Property Service Co., Ltd.*,[7] *Chen v. Fuzhou Rongqiao Property Management Co., Ltd.*,[8] *You v. Huaian Anzhongyuan Property Service Co., Ltd.*,[9] *Li v. Chongqing Yicai Property Management Co., Ltd.*[10]

4.2   Joint Venture Which is Nonsignatory to Joint Venture Contract

The basis for arbitration jurisdiction is party autonomy. In accordance with Article 4 of the Arbitration Law and on the basis of the principles of parties' autonomy and relativity of contract, an arbitration agreement is not effective on nonsignatories.

Articles 8 and 9 of the Arbitration Law Interpretation specify the four circumstances where the effectiveness of arbitration agreement can be extended to nonsignatories, including: after the conclusion of arbitration agreement, in case of any occurrence of merger, division, decease, as well as transfer of rights and obligation, the successors or the heirs are bound by the arbitration agreement.

In addition to the above four circumstances, property service contracts, as illustrated in Sect. 4.1, are also binding on nonsignatories. What are the other particular types of contracts? What about joint venture contracts? Please see the below case for more details.

U.S.A. Huaying Co., Ltd. v. Liaoning Haicheng Zhisheng Magnesium Products Co., Ltd.[11]

---

[5] (2018) Yue 01 Min Te No. 397, 398, 399, 400.

[6] (2017) Yue 01 Min Te No. 478.

[7] (2014) Hai Zhong Fa Zhong Zi No. 34.

[8] (2019) Min 01 Min Te No. 77.

[9] (2018) Su 08 Min Te No. 14.

[10] (2019) Yu 01 Min Te No. 91.

[11] (2017) Zui Gao Fa Min Zai No. 76.

In 1991, Liaoning Haicheng Yingluo Quartz Mineral Products Industrial Co. Ltd. ("Yingluo Company") and U.S.A Huaying Co., Ltd. ("Huaying Company") entered into a joint venture contract ("Joint Venture Contract") to set up the company called Haicheng Zhisheng Magnesium Products Co., Ltd. ("Joint Venture"). This Joint Venture Contract provided that any dispute arising out of this contract shall be submitted to CIETAC for arbitration.

Afterwards, Huaying Company brought a lawsuit against the Joint Venture before Dalian Intermediate People's Court, requesting invalidation of the board resolution made on December 18, 2006 with regard to the extension of the operation period. The Joint Venture raised jurisdictional objection on the ground that the Joint Venture Contract entered into by Huaying Company and Yingluo Company contained an arbitration clause, so this dispute shall be arbitrated.

Dalian Intermediate People's Court rejected the Joint Venture's jurisdiction objection and held that the Joint Venture Contract signed by Huaying Company and Yingluo Company was not binding on the Joint Venture.

The Joint Venture was dissatisfied with the judgment and filed an appeal with Liaoning High People's Court.

Liaoning High People's Court found that the Joint Venture Contract set forth that the operation period began on the date of the issuance of business license and lasted for 15 years, until January 27, 2007; if the parties agreed to extend the operation period, they shall follow the prescribed formalities to file for application 6 months prior to the expiration date, and obtained the approval of the competent governmental organs. On December 18, 2006, the board of the Joint Venture made the resolution, deciding to extend the operation period to 20 years. Huaying Company claimed that this resolution harmed its interests, requesting Dalian Intermediate People's Court to invalidate the resolution. Liaoning High People's Court held that the claims filed by Huaying Company for invalidation of the board resolution were bound by the arbitration clause contained in the Joint Venture Contract, so the Court overturned the verdict made by Dalian Intermediate People's Court.

Huaying Company was dissatisfied with this ruling and filed for review with the SPC. Huaying Company argued that: (1) The parties to the Joint Venture Contract and the parties to the board resolution disputes were not the same, so the arbitration agreement contained in the Joint Venture Contract should not be adopted to resolve this dispute over the board resolution. (2) The applicable laws were different because the disputes arising out of the Joint Venture Contract shall apply the Law on Sino-foreign Joint Ventures, while the Company Law should be applied to disputes over board resolution. (3) Although the Joint Venture Contract specified the arbitration clause, the resolution means regarding the dispute over the board resolution were not agreed upon, so this dispute shall be submitted to litigation. (4) The cause of action of the joint venture contract and that of the dispute over the board resolution were different.

The Joint Venture and Yingluo Company jointly argued that the purpose of the Joint Venture Contract was to set up the Joint Venture, and this Contract stipulated the names of the Joint Venture, as well as all the rights and obligations of the Joint Venture. In particular, Chapter 17 of this Contract sets forth the operation period.

The dispute claimed by Huaying Company fell within the scope of the rights and obligations stipulated in the Joint Venture Contract, so this dispute shall be resolved by arbitration.

The SPC held that, this was the case in which one party, also the shareholder, of the Joint Venture Contract requested the validity of the board resolution. The board of directors was the highest authority of the Joint Venture. The resolution made by the board of directors reflected the true will of the Joint Venture, and legal consequences shall also be borne by the Joint Venture. Therefore, the consequence of litigation regarding board resolution shall be undertaken by joint venture. The Joint Venture shall be defendant according to Article 22 of the Company Law.

The SPC further held that the basis for the jurisdiction of arbitration is party autonomy. In this case, the parties to the Joint Venture Contract were the shareholders of this Joint Venture, and the arbitral matters were the disputes arising out of the performance of this Joint Venture Contract, not the disputes over the board resolution between the shareholders and the Joint Venture. Therefore, the Joint Venture was not the party to the Joint Venture Contract and was not bound by the arbitration clause. The SPC supported Huaying Company by overturning the ruling made by the Liaoning High People's Court.

The issue of the case is whether a party is bound by the arbitration clause contained in the Joint Venture Contract where the dispute is intertwined with the rights and obligations of Joint Venture Contract, and the party, although it is not the signatory to the Joint Venture Contract, is closely connected with the Joint Venture Contract.

Specifically, the Joint Venture was invested and set up by Huaying Company and Yingluo Company in accordance with the Joint Venture Contract. Although the Joint Venture was not the signatory to the Joint Venture Contract, the terms and conditions of this Contract were mostly concerned with the Joint Venture. For example, the dispute of this case arose from the extension of the operation period stipulated by the Joint Venture Contract. The board of directors of the Joint Venture made the resolution arbitrarily extend the operation period from 15 to 20 years, failing to follow the formalities stipulated in the Joint Venture Contract. Therefore, Huaying Company brought the case before the court requesting invalidation of the board resolution, which gave rise to the question of whether the arbitration clause contained in the Joint Venture Contract is binding on the Joint Venture. In this case, the SPC took the view that the Joint Venture, which was not the signatory to the Joint Venture Contract, shall not be bound by the arbitration clause contained therein.

4.3 Insurance Subrogation Claimant

Regarding whether the arbitration clause reached by the insured and the third party in advance is binding on the insurer who obtains the right of insurance subrogation, Chinese laws and regulations are not very clear in this issue.

The SPC's views on this issue are mainly reflected in relevant judicial interpretations, judicial documents and judicial precedents, which will be elaborated below.

In short, in accordance with the SPC's guiding judicial documents and cases, the courts will first distinguish between nonforeign-related and foreign-related cases when hearing this issue. For nonforeign-related cases, the arbitration agreement reached between the insured and the third party before the insured event occurs is binding on the insurer. For foreign-related cases, such as disputes involving insurance subrogation claims based on contracts for the carriage of goods by sea, because the handling of foreign-related cases often involves the application of international treaties and international practices and related issues, the insurer obtains insurance subrogation claims after the insured's substantive rights to the third party are transferred to the insurer accordingly. However, if the insurer does not explicitly accept the arbitration agreement, the arbitration agreement reached in advance by the insured and the third party is not binding on the insurer.

PICC Guangzhou Branch v. Harbin Electric Company Limited[12]

Guangzhou Zhujiang Natural Gas Power Generation Co., Ltd. ("the Insured") entered into the project contract ("Project Contract") with Harbin Electric Co., Ltd. ("Harbin Electric Company") and General Electric Company of the United States("GE")(Collectively "the Third Parties"). Article 18 of the Project Contract stipulates "Any dispute arising from or related to the Contract between the parties shall be settled through amicable negotiation. If no settlement is reached, the dispute shall be submitted to CIETAC for arbitration in accordance with the arbitration rules of the ICC." After an insured incident occurred, PICC Guangzhou Branch ("the Insurer") compensated the Insured.

A dispute over the right of subrogation arose. The Insurer brought a lawsuit before Guangzhou Intermediate People's Court ("the Trial Court") in accordance with Article 60 of the Insurance Law. Harbin Electric Co. raised a jurisdictional objection, claiming that the court had no jurisdiction because the Project Contract had arbitration clause.

The Trial Court found that in this case, the Project Contract made by the Insured and the Third Parties had arbitration clause. The arbitration clause contained was not binding on the Insurer. Pursuant to Article 265 of the Civil Procedure Law, the Trial Court had jurisdiction over this case.

Harbin Electric Co. was dissatisfied and appealed to Guangdong High People's Court ("the Appellate Court"). The Appellate Court held that when the insurer exercised the right of the insured to request compensation from a third party, the jurisdiction was determined based on the legal relationship between the insured and the third party. Therefore, in this case, the Insurer should be bound by the Project Contract signed by the Insured and the third parties.

The Insurer was dissatisfied with the Appellate Court's ruling and applied to the SPC for a retrial. The Insurer argued that the Appellate Court confused the right of subrogation with the assignment of creditor's rights. It therefore wrongly determined the Insurer should, who in fact exercised the right of subrogation instead of the assignment of creditor's rights, be bound by the Project Contract. The assignment of

---

[12] (2019) Zui Gao Fa Min Shen No. 236.

creditor's rights was regulated by the principle of contract relativity, while the right of subrogation was regulated by the Insurance Law instead of the principle of contract relativity. Additionally, in judicial practice, the insurer's exercise of subrogation rights was not subject to the arbitration clause. The SPC's replies of (2005) Min Si Ta Zi No. 29 and (2009) Min Sita Zi No. 11 clearly stipulated that after an insurer obtains the right of subrogation, the arbitration clause stipulated in the original contract shall not apply to the insurer. The SPC's ruling of (2017) Zui Gao Fa Min Xia Jian No. 2 also agreed that the arbitration clause was not binding on the insurer if the insurer did not expressly accept the arbitration clause.

The SPC held that: This case was concerned with the insurer's right of subrogation in accordance with Article 60 of the Insurance Law, after the Insurer had reimbursed the Insured. The Project Contract containing arbitration clause was signed on September 25, 2004, and the insurance contract was signed on May 31, 2013. The Insurer should have been aware of the existence of the aforementioned arbitration clause when signing the insurance contract, and it did not explicitly oppose to the arbitration clause. Hence, the Appellate Court was correct for holding that the arbitration clause of the Contract was binding on the Insurer. In addition, all the cases cited by the Insurer applied for retrial were related to maritime cargo transportation contracts, so the facts and disputes involved were not the same as those of this case. The SPC did not take these cases for references.

It can be seen from the above case that if the contract between the insured and the third party contains a valid arbitration clause and the insurance contract is signed after the contract, unless there is evidence that the insurer expressly opposes the arbitration agreement, it should be presumed that the insurer should be aware of the existence of the aforementioned arbitration clause when signing the insurance contract. After the insurer compensates the insured, the insurer, as the insurance subrogation claimant, is bound by the aforementioned arbitration clause.

In addition to the above cases of the SPC, in judicial practice, different courts have different views on whether insurance subrogation claimants are bound by the arbitration clause. To present relevant cases more clearly, this article sorts out some relevant cases retrieved as follows:

1. **Cases in which the courts held insurance subrogation claimants are not bound by the arbitration clause**

No.	Complaint/appellant/claimant	Defendant/appellee/respondent	Court	Case no.	Cause of action	Foreign-related or not
1	Tongbao (Hong Kong) Oceanic co. Limited	China continent insurance Shanghai branch	SPC	(2017) Zui Gao Fa Min Xia Jian No.2	Objection to jurisdiction over maritime property damage liability disputes	Foreign-related

(continued)

(continued)

No.	Complaint/appellant/claimant	Defendant/appellee/respondent	Court	Case no.	Cause of action	Foreign-related or not
2	CPWorldPteLtd, Mitsui O.S.K.Lines, Ltd	Ping an property and casualty insurance company of China Shenzhen Branch	Guangdong High People's Court	(2015) Yue Gao Fa Li Min Zhong Zi No. 602	Disputes over maritime cargo transportation contracts	Foreign-related
3	Beijing Xiangheli International Shipping Co., Ltd	PICC Beijing Branch	Shandong High People's Court	(2015) Lu Min Xia Zhong Zi No. 28	Jurisdiction dispute over insurance subrogation rights based on contracts for the carriage of goods by sea	Foreign-related
4	Zhuhai Hengji Daxin International Chemical Storage Co., Ltd	Ping an property and casualty insurance company of China Guangdong branch	Guangdong High People's Court	(2014) Yue Gao a Li Min Zhong Zi No. 1875	Jurisdiction dispute over insurance subrogation rights based on port cargo custody contracts	Non-Foreign-related
5	China continent insurance Beijing Branch	China Pacific Shipping Co., Ltd.	Tianjin maritime court	(2014) Jin Hai Fa Shang Chu Zi No. 424–1	Jurisdiction dispute over insurance subrogation rights based on port cargo custody contracts	Non-Foreign-related
6	Beijing Xiangheli international shipping Co., Ltd	PICC Beijing branch	Shandong High People's Court	(2014) Lu Min Xia Zhong Zi No. 540	Jurisdiction dispute over insurance subrogation rights based on port cargo custody contracts	Foreign-related
7	TYANANAVIGATIONLTD	PICC Beijing branch	Shandong High People's Court	(2014) Lu Min Xia Zhong Zi No. 547	Jurisdiction dispute over insurance subrogation rights based on port cargo custody contracts	Foreign-related
8	Shenzhen Daguangfa Logistics Co., Ltd	PICC Shenzhen branch	Shenzhen Intermediate's People's Court	(2013) Shen Zhong Fa Shang Zhong Zi No. 2313	Jurisdiction dispute over insurance subrogation rights based on domestic cargo transportation contracts	Non-Foreign-related

(continued)

(continued)

No.	Complaint/appellant/claimant	Defendant/appellee/respondent	Court	Case no.	Cause of action	Foreign-related or not
9	Nondisclosed party	Nondisclosed party	Shenzhen Intermediate's People's Court	(2011) Shen Zhong Fa Min Si Zhong Zi No. 245	Jurisdiction dispute over insurance subrogation rights based on cargo transportation agreements	Hong Kong-related
10	Nondisclosed party	Nondisclosed party	Zhejiang High People's Court	(2008) Zhe Min Gao Zhong Zi No. 65	Dispute over jurisdiction over insurance subrogation rights in waterway cargo transportation contracts	Non-Foreign-related
11	Nondisclosed party	Nondisclosed party	Zhejiang High People's Court	(2008) Zhe Min Gao Zhong Zi No. 149	Jurisdiction dispute over insurance subrogation claims under time charter contracts	Foreign-related

2. Cases in which the courts held insurance subrogation claimants are bound by the arbitration clause

No.	Complaint/appellant/claimant	Defendant/appellee/respondent	Court	Case no.	Cause of action	Foreign-related or not
12	Chongqing ABB transformer Co., Ltd	Ping an insurance company of China Jiangsu Branch	Jiangsu High People's Court	(2015) Su Shang Xia Zhong Zi No. 00101	Jurisdiction dispute over insurance subrogation rights	Non-Foreign-related
13	Hubei Anjie logistics Co., Ltd	Zurich property insurance (China) Co., Ltd	Beijing Second Intermediate People's Court	(2015) Er Zhong Min Te Zi No. 10119	Jurisdiction dispute over insurance subrogation rights based on transportation service agreements	Non-Foreign-related
14	Shenzhen South China Shipping Freight Co., Ltd	Dubang Property Insurance Co., Ltd. Shenzhen Branch	Shenzhen Intermediate's People's Court	(2012) Shen Zhong Fa She Wai Zhong Zi No. 203	Jurisdiction dispute over insurance subrogation based on cargo transportation contract	Non-Foreign-related

From the above tables, most courts in the past held the view that insurance subrogation claimants are not bound by the arbitration clause. The main reasons for this view are as follows: On the one hand, from the perspective of the party autonomy of arbitration and the relativity of the contract, the insurance subrogation claimant is not a party to the contract that contains arbitration clauses signed by the insured and a third party. The insurance subrogation claimant itself does not choose arbitration; on the other hand, Article 9 of the Arbitration Law Interpretation does not apply to this situation. This clause stipulates that the creditor's rights shall be transferred on the consensus of both parties. However, the insurer's right to subrogation is obtained in accordance with Article 60 of the Insurance Law or Article 93 of the Special Procedure Law of the PRC on Maritime Procedures. The insurer shall not be bound by the arbitration clause.

The main reasons for these courts, which took the opposite view, are as follows: first, the insurer knows or should have known the existence of the arbitration clause when it is transferred with the creditor's rights without expressly objection to it. The SPC in the above case considered that the insurance subrogation claimant should be bound by the arbitration clause for this reason. Second, the insurance subrogation claimant should be in the same position as the insured in terms of substantive rights and procedural rights, and the arbitration agreement should not be an exception. Third, although the right of insurance subrogation is acquired by law, the provisions of Article 9 of the Arbitration Law Interpretation can also be applied as reference.

From the above cases, although the judicial views of the courts at all levels seem to be quite different, if subdivided, it can be seen that the courts hold quite consistent views to some degree in foreign-related cases as well as those in the nonforeign-related cases. That is, in nonforeign-related cases, the arbitration agreement reached between the insured and the third party before the insured event occurs is binding on the insurer. In foreign-related cases, after the insurer obtains the right of insurance subrogation, the insured's substantive rights to the third party shall be transferred to the insurer accordingly. However, if the insurer has not explicitly accepted the arbitration agreement, the arbitration agreement that the insured and the third party reached in advance is not binding on the insurer.

In addition to judicial cases, the development of the views of the SPC and other courts are also reflected in relevant judicial interpretations and judicial documents.

Article 12 of Interpretation (IV) of the SPC on Several Issues concerning the Application of the Insurance Law of the People's Republic of China provides the following: Where the insurer initiates a subrogation lawsuit against a third party that caused the insured accident, the legal relationship between the insured and the third party shall determine the court of jurisdiction. In judicial practice, this provision is applied in the determination of the court jurisdiction. It is yet to know whether it can be applied to determine the jurisdiction of arbitration clauses.

Several replies issued by the SPC all set forth that the insurer was not a party to negotiate a contract containing an arbitration clause, and the arbitration clause was not the true intention of the insurer and thus held that the arbitration clause is not binding on the insurer except that the insurer expressly accepts it. The aforementioned replies include the Letter of Reply of the SPC on Request for Instructions Re Arbitration Clause Validity in the Dispute over Insurance Subrogation under Contract for Carriage of Goods by Sea in the Case of *Beijing Branch of China Pacific Insurance*

(Group) Co., Ltd. v. China COSCO Logistics Co., Ltd., Tianjin Zhenhua Shipping Agency Co., Ltd. and Nile Dutch Africa Line B.V.[13] the Letter of Reply of the SPC on Request for Instructions on the validity of the arbitration clauses involved in the disputes over the insurance subrogation of the marine cargo transportation contract by *China Ping An Property Insurance Co., Ltd. Sichuan Branch v. Beijing Xiangheli International Shipping Co., Ltd. and Jifa Shipping Co., Ltd.*,[14] A Letter of Reply of the SPC on Request for Instructions on the Jurisdiction of the Insurance Subrogation Claim Dispute between *the Xiamen Branch of the People's Insurance Company of China v. the China-Poland Shipping Company*,[15] A Letter of Reply of the SPC on Request for Instructions on the Validity of the Arbitration Clause in the Case of *the Shenzhen Branch of the People's Insurance Company of China, Ltd. v. Guangzhou Ocean Shipping Co., Ltd.* on the Dispute over the Cargo Damage of the Maritime Cargo Transportation Contract.[16]

Article 127 of the SPC's Minutes of the Second National Foreign-Related Commercial Maritime Trial Work Conference[17] stipulates that after the insurer actually pays insurance compensation to the insured and obtains the right of subrogation, the jurisdiction agreement and the arbitration agreement reached by the insured and the third party to resolve the dispute are not binding on the insurer.

In judicial practice in China, courts may issue guiding opinions. The Answers to Several Questions about the Trial of Insurance Contract Dispute Cases by the Shanghai High People's Court (No. 2) (issued in 2015) distinguishes foreign-related cases and nonforeign-related cases. Foreign-related cases shall be handled in accordance with the provisions of the SPC on foreign-related cases. That is, after the insurer obtains insurance subrogation, the insured's substantive rights to the third party shall be transferred to the insurer accordingly; however, if the insurer does not explicitly accept the arbitration agreement, the arbitration agreement reached in advance between the insured and the third party is not binding on the insurer. For nonforeign-related cases, the provisions of Article 9 of the Arbitration Law Interpretation shall be applied. That is, the arbitration agreement reached by the insured and the third party in advance is binding on the insurer that exercising the insurance subrogation right, except as agreed or provided by law otherwise.

Article 98 of the Minutes of the National Civil and Commercial Trial Work Conference of the SPC ("Minutes of the Ninth Conference")[18] issued on November 8, 2019 clearly stipulates that: Insurance subrogation is a statutory assignment of claims; The arbitration agreement reached by the insured and the third party before the insured event occurs is binding on the insurer; however, there is an exception if the dispute involves foreign-related elements.

---

[13] (2009) Min Si Ta Zi No.11.

[14] (2009) Min Si Ta Zi No.39.

[15] (2004) Min Si Ta Zi No.43.

[16] (2005) Min Si Ta Zi No.29.

[17] Fa Fa[2005] No. 26.

[18] Fa[2019] No. 254.

From the Minutes of the Ninth Conference, the SPC has basically unified judicial views on the issues mentioned here. The trial of this issue needs to distinguish foreign-related and nonforeign-related cases and then apply relevant rules accordingly. Although this judicial document is not mandatory law, in future cases, the courts can refer to this judicial document when reasoning. Therefore, the Minutes of the Nine Conference are conducive to harmonizing the approach of Chinese judges regarding whether the insurance subrogation claimant is bound by the arbitration clause and enhancing the predictability of the trial results.

4.4 Heir

Arbitration agreement, as a type of contract, is subject to the doctrine of contract relativity. Based on the principle of party autonomy and the theory of contract relativity, arbitration agreements are effective between the signatories. The nonsignatories are not bound by the contract. However, there are exceptions. For example, according to the Arbitration Law Interpretation, when the parties merge, split, die, and transfer rights and debts after signing the agreement, under any of the aforesaid four circumstances, the arbitration agreement shall continue to bind the successors, heirs and transferees of the rights and obligations, unless otherwise agreed upon when the arbitration agreement was concluded.

This case will illustrate one of the above four circumstances: if a party enters an arbitration agreement, when this party dies, whether his or her heirs are the competent party in the arbitration case.

In accordance with Article 8(2) of the Arbitration Law Interpretation, where a party dies after the conclusion of an arbitration agreement, the arbitration agreement shall be binding upon the heir to the party's rights and obligations with regard to the arbitral matters. Therefore, the heir who inherits the rights and obligations of the arbitration matters is bound by the arbitration agreement.

When Article 8(2) of the Arbitration Law Interpretation were drafted, there were two views: One view is that the arbitration agreement has a certain degree of independence compared with the other clauses of the contract, and unless the successor is willing to be bound, the arbitration agreement cannot of course be considered binding on the successor; The other view is that after the arbitration agreement is reached, the parties shall abide by their commitments, and when the heir accepts the inheritance, he or she shall also accept the dispute resolution method agreed upon by the deceased and the counterparty to the contract.[19]

The second view is finally adopted because if the heir is allowed to arbitrarily deny the agreement reached between the deceased and the counterparty to the contract,

---

[19] Shen Deyong, *Understanding and Application of Judicial Interpretation of the Arbitration Law of the SPC*, 85 (2nd ed., People's Court Press 2015).

it will easily cause instability of commercial expectations and may trigger new disputes.[20]

In the practice of arbitral institutions, if a party dies in an arbitration case, the heir will continue the arbitration procedure. However, the determination of the identity of the heir is sometimes not easy, and it may involve the identification procedure.

In judicial practice, when applying the foregoing provisions, there are a series of questions related to how to understand "The heir to the party's rights and obligations with regard to the arbitral matters". On the issue of rights and obligations, where is the limit of the arbitral tribunal's power? Is it subject to the arbitration agreement as long as he or she is the heir and does not give up the right to inheritance? If there is an inheritance dispute, does it have to wait for an effective civil judgment to be issued, or otherwise it is impossible to determine who inherits the rights and obligations of the arbitration matters? Does the court have the right to review the arbitral tribunal's determination of this issue?

With regard to the above questions that some judicial cases have touched upon, the following are the views of the courts:

In a case involving multiple heirs, even though arbitral tribunal has not handled with the distribution of the inheritance among the heirs, the tribunal still has the power to hear the arbitration. See *Chen v. the Panyu branch of Guangzhou Rural Commercial Bank Co., Ltd.*.[21]

Heirs who have not given up their rights in relevant arbitration matters are bound by the arbitration agreement. In the case *Jin* et al. *v. Jianyin Cultural Industry Equity Investment Fund (Tianjin) Co., Ltd.*,[22] the Beijing Second Intermediate People's Court held that: After the death of Li A who was a party to the arbitration agreement, Jin and Li B were the first-tier beneficiaries. Although there were civil disputes over Li A's intestate estate with other heirs of Li A, both Jin and Li B made it clear that they would not give up the right of inheritance, including the right to inherit Li A's rights in arbitration matters. Therefore, the arbitration clause was binding on Jin and Li B.

For another example, *Li v. the Industrial and Commercial Bank of China Co., Ltd. Liaoyuan Dongfanghong Sub-branch,*[23] Liaoyuan Intermediate People's Court applied Article 20 of the Inheritance Law, which stipulates that after the inheritance begins, if the heir renounces the inheritance, he shall make an expression of giving up the inheritance before the disposal of the estate; If he remains silent, he shall be deemed to accept the inheritance. In this case, Li, as Wang's heir, did not expressly give up the right of inheritance after Wang died. In the trial, Li also made it clear that he would not give up the right to inherit Wang's estate. Therefore, it can be determined that Li agreed to accept the inheritance and that he was the legal heir

---

[20] Shen Deyong, *Understanding and Application of Judicial Interpretation of the Arbitration Law of the SPC*, 85 (2nd ed., People's Court Press 2015).

[21] (2019) Yue 01 Min Te No. 1179.

[22] (2015) Er Zhong Min Te Zi No. 00437.

[23] (2016) Ji 04 Min Te No. 3.

of Wang's estate. Therefore, Li was qualified as the respondent in the arbitration proceedings.

In the following case, the court held that according to Article 8(2) of the Arbitration Law Interpretation, if the parties die after entering an arbitration agreement, the arbitration agreement is binding on the heirs who inherit their rights and obligations in the arbitration; Whether the heirs inherit the rights and obligations in arbitration matters shall be determined by the arbitral tribunal, which does not fall within the scope of court review.

Zhu V. Li[24]

On February 9, 2017, Li filed arbitration with the Shanghai Branch of CIETAC against the first respondent Zhu, the second respondent Wu, the third respondent Zhang, the fourth respondent Liu and the fifth respondent Zhu (the fifth respondent shall have been Chen, but Chen died, so his surviving spouse Zhu was replaced as the respondent).

On November 15, 2017, CIETAC rendered the arbitral award which stated: The first to fifth respondents shall jointly compensate the claimant RMB 680,000, of which the fifth respondent's liability for compensation was limited to the actual value of the inheritance of Chen's properties.

Zhu claimed that although she was the heir to Chen after Chen died, it was yet to know whether she was entitled to inherit Chen's properties. In addition, she did not sign the Contract containing arbitration clause and knew nothing about it. Therefore, she was not the competent party to the arbitration case, and thus requested the court to set aside the arbitral award.

Li argued that Zhu was listed as the respondent in the arbitration because she was the heir to Chen's rights and obligations, and the arbitral award clearly stated Zhu's liability for compensation to be limited to the actual value of the inheritance of Chen's properties. Thus, the arbitral award did not exceed the scope provided by the law, and the court shall reject Zhu's application.

Beijing Third Intermediate People's Court held that, although Zhu claimed that she did not know about the signing of the arbitration agreement, she did not deny the authenticity of the arbitration agreement, and Zhu did not provide evidence to prove that she had objected to the validity of the arbitration agreement during the arbitration process. In addition, according to Article 8(2) of the Arbitration Law Interpretation, where the arbitration agreement is valid, whether the heirs inherit the rights and obligations in arbitration matters shall be determined by the arbitral tribunal, which was not subject to court's review. In conclusion, the court rejected Zhu's application for setting aside the arbitral award.

---

[24] (2018) Jing 04 Min Te No. 117.

4.5 Deregistered Enterprise

In some cases, a person does not sign the contract in his or her own name but in the name of a legal person or other organization that should be registered but not yet registered or canceled after being registered. In that case, is the contract still valid? If the contract contains arbitration clause, is the arbitration clause valid, and can it bind this person?

The Severability of Arbitration Agreements, also called Independence of Arbitration Agreements, is the basic doctrine in the field of commercial arbitration. Article 507 of the Civil Code stipulates that where a contract does not take effect or is void, revoked, or terminated, the validity of a clause concerning dispute resolution shall not be affected. Article 19 (1) of the Arbitration Law provides the following: An arbitration agreement shall exist independently; The amendment, rescission, termination or invalidity of a contract shall not affect the validity of the arbitration agreement. Even if a contract is invalid for the reason of being signed by a legal person or other organization that should have been registered but not registered or is canceled in accordance with the law, it will not affect the validity of the arbitration clause in the contract.

In addition, Article 62 of the Civil Procedure Law Interpretation stipulates that if a person or an entity signs a contract in the name of the legal person or other organization that shall have been registered but not registered or canceled according to law, this person or entity shall be regarded as the party to the contract. It comes to the question that: the contract is binding on the person, but is the arbitration clause in the contract equally binding on the person? The arbitration laws in China are not clear in this question.

On the basis of the doctrines of parties' autonomy and relativity of contract, an arbitration agreement is only binding on the signatories, not on the nonsignatories. However, in practice, the courts tend to adopt Article 62 of the Civil Procedure Law Interpretation and find that the arbitration clause contained in the contract is equally binding on the person. The below case will further illustrate this issue.

Li v. The Land Acquisition and Reserve Center of Zhijiang City[25]

The business license of Zhijiang Zhuli Cement Co., Ltd. ("Zhuli Company") was canceled on May 6, 2010. However, on June 20, 2011, Li, the legal representative of Zhuli Company, signed the Acquisition Contract of the State-owned Land Use Right ("Acquisition Contract") with the Land Acquisition and Reserve Center of Zhijiang City ("Land Reserve Center") in the name of Zhuli Company. Article 14 of the Acquisition Contract stipulated that if any dispute arises from the performance of this contract, it shall be resolved through negotiation between the parties. The parties who fail to reach the settlement through negotiation agree to apply to the Yichang Arbitration Commission for arbitration. Later, when a dispute occurred, Li filed a lawsuit against the Land Reserve Center and the Sanning Chemical Co., Ltd ("Sanning Company").

---

[25] (2017) Zui Gao Fa Min Shen No. 4911.

The Land Reserve Center raised an objection to jurisdiction, asserting that the Acquisition Contract contained arbitration clause, which should not be null and void even though the Acquisition Contract was invalidated. It argued further that the claims made by Li also arose from the Acquisition Contract because the claims were concerned about the return or the compensation based on the appraised value of the property after the invalidation of the Acquisition Agreement.

Regarding the objection, Hubei High People's Court ruled that although the Acquisition Contract contained the arbitration clause, Zhuli Company was deregistered on May 6, 2010, so it had no civil rights or civil capacity. In other words, Zhuli Company was not a competent party to the Contract. Since the Yichang Arbitration Commission had found that the Acquisition Contract was invalid in its award, the arbitration clause contained in this Contract shall accordingly be invalid based on the lack of competence of the party. On the basis of the aforementioned reasons, this Court overruled the objection of the Land Reserve Center.

The Land Reserve Center was dissatisfied with the ruling made by Hubei High People's Court and filed an appeal to the SPC. The SPC found that, in accordance with the doctrine of the severability of arbitration agreement stipulated in Article 10 of the Arbitration Law Interpretation and Article 19 of Arbitration Law, the arbitration clause contained in the Acquisition Agreement should not be regarded as invalid, although the Contract was invalid. In accordance with Article 62 (3) of the Civil Procedure Law Interpretation, because Li entered into the Contract in the name of Zhuli Company, whose business licenses were canceled, the liabilities resulting from the act of Li shall be borne by Li, who in fact acted as the party to the Contract. The Land Reserve Center and Li entered into the Acquisition Contract with the arbitration clause based on consensus. The arbitration agreement was independent from the contract. The parties were bound by the arbitration agreement reached in the contract. Therefore, the SPC rejected the lawsuit brought by Li and directed Li to apply for arbitration.

Li was dissatisfied and applied to the SPC for retrial on the grounds that: (1) In addition to against the Land Reserve Center, the lawsuit brought by Li was also against Sanning Company on the ground of tort, but this ruling was silent in the jurisdiction over Sanning Company that was not the party to the Contract, and therefore it constituted an omission of litigation claim; (2) This ruling was in error to take Li as the party to the Contract; (3) The presiding judge was changed at will without notifying the parties, and therefore the composition of the collegiate court bench was illegal; (4) This ruling was not binding on the nonsignatory, Sanning Company, which would made this ruling unenforceable; (5) Li brought this lawsuit for the cause of action of tort. Since Li and Sanning Company had no arbitration agreement, this case should be heard by the court.

The SPC found that:

1. With regard to the issue of whether the court was in error of applying the law to determine the invalidity of the arbitration agreement

   In accordance with Article 62 (3) of the Civil Procedure Law Interpretation, because Li signed the Contract in the name of Zhuli Company which was deregistered, it was not wrong for the court to find Li shall bear the consequence of jurisdiction. In addition, according to Article 57 of the Contract Law,[26] the invalidation of the Contract shall not affect the validity of the arbitration clause, which shall be independent from the Contract. The invalidity of the Contract shall not directly invalidate the arbitration clause contained therein. Therefore, this arbitration clause shall be valid according to Articles 16 and 17 of the Arbitration Law.

2. With regard to the issue of whether the composition of the collegiate court bench was illegal

   Li's assertion that "the presiding judge was changed at will without notifying the parties" was not the circumstance that could render the composition of the collegiate court bench illegal. In addition, Li failed to prove it with any evidence.

3. With regard to the issue of whether it was an omission of litigation claim for the ruling's failure to respond to the tort jurisdiction over Sanning Company.

   Li claimed that Sanning Company constituted illegal appropriation of land and house concerned in the Contract. In the opinion of the SPC, Li's tort claims were concerned with the disputes arose out of the Contract, and the findings of contractual disputes were the basis of determining whether Sanning Company committed a tort. The original ruling made by the SPC was the response to the appeal made by the Land Reserve Center, which did not constitute an omission of a litigation claim.

Based on the above reasoning, the SPC overruled Li's application for retrial on the ground that his application failed to satisfy the requirements set forth in Article 200 (6), (7)and(11) of the Civil Procedure Law.

Li signed the Contract in the name of Zhuli Company with the Land Reserve Center. Because Zhuli Company had no civil rights or civil capacity after its business license was canceled, Zhuli Company became an incompetent party to a contract. The Yuchang Arbitration Commission thus ruled the Contract invalid. However, the invalidation of the Contract did not mean its arbitration clause was also invalid. Based on the doctrine of Severability of Arbitration Agreement, the arbitration clause is an agreement on dispute resolution reached by the parties, which shall be independent from the contract.

Although Li argued that he in fact did not sign the contract with the Land Reserve Center in his own name, the court ruled that he was the party to the contract because he acted in the name of the deregistered legal person. According to Article 62(3) of

---

[26] Article 57 of Contract Law is rescinded and replaced by Article 507 of Civil Code since January 1, 2021.

the Civil Procedure Law Interpretation, Li shall take responsible for jurisdictional consequences that arose out of the Contract.

The case is a typical case where a person signs a contract containing an arbitration clause in the name of a deregistered company. However, on the issue of a person signing the contract in the name of a legal person or other organization that should be registered but not yet registered, the SPC has not issued any guiding case. In legal practice, the SPC may refer to this case on the basis of Article 62 of the Civil Procedure Law Interpretation.

4.6 Governmental Organ

In accordance with Articles 17 and 18 of the Arbitration Law, the following four circumstances may invalidate an arbitration agreement: (1) The agreed matters for arbitration exceed the scope of arbitrable matters as specified by law; (2) One party that concludes the arbitration agreement has no capacity for civil conduct or has limited capacity for civil conduct; (3) One party coerces the other party into concluding the arbitration agreement; and (4) An arbitration agreement contains no or unclear provisions concerning the matters for arbitration or the arbitration commission, and no such supplementary agreement was reached. For the first circumstance (the arbitrability of disputes), Articles 2 and 3 of the Arbitration Law have corresponding provisions.

Specifically, Article 2 of the Arbitration Law provides that contractual disputes and other disputes over rights and interests in property between individuals, legal persons and other organizations that are equal subjects may be arbitrated. Article 3 of Arbitration Law sets for the disputes that may not be arbitrated such as: (1) disputes regarding marital, adoption, guardianship, support and succession; (2) administrative disputes that shall be handled by administrative organs as prescribed by law.

Chinese laws and judicial interpretations are not clear about the concept and the applicable scope of "administrative disputes that shall be handled by administrative organs as prescribed by law". By reference to the case below, the court took the position that a contract signed by a governmental organ did not necessarily become an administrative contract. The nature of this type of contract shall be determined in consideration of the purposes, mutual rights and obligations, liabilities and so forth. If a contract is determined as a civil and commercial contract and there are no circumstances rendering it invalid, then the arbitration clause contained therein shall be valid.

Bazhong Municipal Government v. Sichuan Bawan Highway Co., Ltd.[27]

On November 6, 2013, the Bazhong Municipal Government and Dazhou Municipal Government signed the Bazhong-Wanyuan Highway BOT Project Concession Agreement ("Concession Agreement") with Sichuan Bawan Highway Co., Ltd.

---

[27] (2017) Jing 02 Min Te No. 11.

("Bawan Highway Company"). Article 13 "Dispute Resolution" of the Agreement stipulated that any dispute arises from the performance, violation, termination or invalidity of this Agreement, and either party can apply to CIETAC for arbitration. The arbitral award is final and binding on the parties.

When disputes between the parties arose, Bawan Highway Company applied to CIETAC for arbitration on September 22, 2016. CIETAC accepted the application on September 23, 2016. Afterwards, the Bazhong Municipal Government applied to Beijing Second Intermediate People's Court for confirming the arbitration clause (Article 13 of the Agreement) invalid.

The reasons for Bazhong Municipal Government to apply for invalidity of the arbitration clause are as follows:

(1)   According to current laws and regulations, disputes over government conces-sion agreements were subject to the exclusive jurisdiction of the courts;
(2)   The Concession Agreement was an administrative agreement;
(3)   The arbitration agreement involved in the case was invalid under Article 17 of the Arbitration Law.

Bawan Highway Company argued:

(1)   The Concession Agreement was a typical BOT agreement. This type of agree-ment had obvious characteristics of civil and commercial contracts. It should be characterized as a civil and commercial contract. It should not be regarded as an administrative contract under the Administrative Litigation Law and Administrative Litigation Law Interpretation;
(2)   The disputes concerned fell within the arbitrable scope prescribed in the Arbi-tration Law. The arbitration clause contained in the Concession Agreement was effective. Even if this type of dispute was subject to the acceptance scope of administrative litigation, it did not necessarily subject to the exclusive juris-diction of the court. In other words, the arbitrability of the disputes should not be denied.

The Dazhou Municipal Government held the same opinions as the Bazhou Municipal Government.

Beijing Second Intermediate People's Court held:

The BOT was the "build-operate-transfer" model. Its basic meaning was that the national or local government or its related functional departments signed a concession agreement with the investor or the project company established by the investor to authorize the project company to undertake the investment, construction, operation, management and maintenance, etc. The project company had the right to operate and manage the investment and construction of the infrastructure and to charge reasonable fees from the users of the infrastructure within the scope and time limit of the authorization to recover the cost of investment, operation and maintenance of the construction project, and the government and the investor will obtain corresponding benefits. Upon the expiration of the concession period, the project company will transfer the investment and construction of the infrastructure to the government or government-designated departments free of charge.

From the contents of the Concession Agreement, The Concession Agreement signed by the parties was a typical BOT agreement. The Bazhong Municipal Government and the Dazhou Municipal Government authorized the Bazhong Highway Company to implement the project's investment, construction, operation, maintenance and handover. On the one hand, its purpose was for the government to provide facilities to the public, and at the same time, it intended to obtain economic benefits for the parties. The project was not to provide the facilities at no charge. Although the Bazhong Municipal Government and Dazhou Municipal Government, as one of the parties to the Agreement, were governments, the Bawan Highway Company, as the counterparty of the Agreement, still enjoyed full autonomy in terms of signing contracts and deciding the contents of the contracts during the construction of the project. It was not subject to the unilateral administrative decision of the Bazhong Municipal Government and Dazhou Municipal Government. At the same time, the Agreement also stipulated that the Bazhong Municipal Government and Dazhou Municipal Government shall ensure to provide necessary policy support and assistance to the Bawan Highway Company. The Agreement also included the specific rights and obligations of the parties and liabilities for breach of contract, which all reflected that the parties reached this agreement on equal negotiations. Therefore, considering the purpose, liabilities, rights and obligations of the parties in the Concession Agreement, the Agreement shall not be regarded as an administrative contract under Article 12(11) of Administrative Litigation Law and Article 11(2) of the 2015 Administrative Litigation Law Interpretation. This Agreement should be regarded as civil and commercial contract.

Article 13 of the Concession Agreement provided that the parties agreed to submit any dispute to CIETAC for arbitration. Because this Agreement was a civil and commercial agreement, the arbitration clause contained shall be valid and binding on the parties. Beijing Second Intermediate People's Court thus rejected Bazhong Municipal Government's application.

In judicial practice, the courts' view on this issue can be divided as below:

I.   The courts which hold positive view:

The courts holding the positive view assert that a contract cannot be considered as an administrative agreement simply because one of parties of the contract is administrative organ. The courts should consider defining it from the perspectives of the purpose, responsibilities, rights and obligations of the contract, and the consensus of parties. In the case, Beijing Second Intermediate People's Court also held a positive view of the issue. When determining the nature of the contract, it took into consideration of the purpose of the agreement and the rights, obligations and responsibilities of the parties.

There are some other similar cases as below:

1.   Huixian Municipal Government v. Henan Xinling Highway Construction Investment Co., Ltd.[28]

---

[28] (2015) Min Yi Zhong Zi No. 244.

The agreement involved in this case was a concession agreement. The SPC held that the nature of the agreement should be analyzed from the purposes, contents, subjects and responsibilities:

(1)   Purposes: The main purpose of the agreement was the development and operation of Xinling Highway and the establishment of Xinling Highway toll stations. It provided public services for profits.

(2)   Contents: The contents of the contract included specific rights, obligations and liabilities for breach of contract, which reflected that the parties reached consensus after equal negotiations.

(3)   Subjects: Although one of the parties to the contract was the Huixian Municipal Government, the counterparty of the contract, Xinling Company, still enjoyed full autonomy in terms of signing the contract, determining the contents of the contract and was not subject to unilateral administrative decisions.

(4)   Responsibilities: The agreement not only stipulated administrative examination and approval or administrative licensing matters. The related administrative examination and approval and administrative licensing were the responsibilities and performance of the agreement.

Based on the above analysis, the court believed that the contract should be characterized as a civil and commercial contract, not an administrative agreement.

2.   Yilin Town Government of Funing County v. Kaifa Xinquan Sewage Treatment (Funing) Co., Ltd.[29]

The agreement involved in this case was a concession agreement. Beijing Second Intermediate People's Court held that to determine whether the disputes concerned were administrative disputes, it should consider the specific contents of the agreement, dispute matters and arbitration requests of the parties.

(1)   Contents: Kaifa Company enjoyed full autonomy in terms of signing the agreement and determining the contents of the agreement. The parties signed the agreement based on equal negotiations. The rights and obligations of the parties concerned and the compensation for breach of contract and other agreements can reflect the consensus of the parties through consultation.

(2)   Arbitration requests: Judging from the arbitration request submitted by Kaifa Company to the Arbitration Commission, it did not target the specific administrative actions of the administrative organ.

(3)   Subjects: the parties are in equal legal status.

Therefore, the court held that the disputes involved in the case were arbitrable and were not administrative disputes that should be handled by administrative organs in accordance with the law.

---

[29] (2017) Jing Min Te No. 272.

3. *Dalian Chunbin Wood Industry Co., Ltd. v. Dalian Jinpu New District Urban and Rural Construction Bureau*[30]

The contract involved in the case was a contract for the transfer of state-owned land use rights. Dalian Intermediate People's Court held that:

(1) The Contract for Transfer of State-owned Land Use Right was signed by the parties in accordance with the principles of equality and voluntariness.
(2) Regardless of whether the contract involved in the case was a civil contract or an administrative contract, disputes arising from the performance of the contract were not administrative disputes that should be handled by the administrative organs.
(3) The arbitration clause agreed upon by the parties was the true intention of the parties and did not breach the requirements stipulated in Article 17 of the Arbitration Law.

For the above reasons, the court held that the arbitration clause involved in the case was valid.

4. Mingfa Group Wuxi Real Estate Development Co., Ltd. v. Wuxi Municipal Bureau of Land and Resources[31]

The contract involved in the case was a contract for the transfer of state-owned land use rights. The Wuxi Intermediate People's Court held that:

(1) The contract involved in the case was an agreement signed by the parties based on the principles of equality, voluntariness, fairness, compensation for equal value, and good faith. The parties had equal legal status when signing the contract, which fell under Article 2 of the Contract Law. Therefore, the Contract was a civil contract rather than an administrative contract.
(2) The nature of the contract was a civil contract, and only part of the contents involved administrative measures. From the perspective of maintaining the validity of the contract clauses, when understanding the meaning of "all disputes" in the arbitration clause, a constrictive interpretation should be made to exclude disputes unrelated to civil disputes from "all disputes". Therefore, the agreement on arbitration in the Contract did not exceed the scope of arbitration provided by law. The arbitration clause should be deemed valid.

In addition, the arbitration clauses involved in the case complied with the requirements for the validity of the arbitration agreement stipulated in Article 16 of the Arbitration Law. The court determined that the disputes involved were arbitrable and that the arbitration clauses involved were valid.

---

[30] (2016) Liao 02 Min Te No. 78.
[31] (2017) Su 02 Min Te No. 209.

5. *Fuzhou Phoenix Housing Acquisition and Engineering Office v. Fuzhou
    Hengxing Binhai Real Estate Co., Ltd.*[32]

    The contract involved in the case was a house acquisition compensation and
    resettlement agreement. The Xiamen Intermediate People's Court analyzed the
    nature of the Contract from the subjects, contents and nature:

    (1) Subjects: Although one party to the contract was an administrative organ,
         not all actions taken by the administrative organ were administrative
         actions.
    (2) Contents: The contract was an agreement on the amount of compensation
         and the payment method. It was a dispute concerning property rights, and
         the contents of the contract were also the result of friendly negotiation
         between the parties.
    (3) In spirit of the SPC's Reply to the Issue of Acceptance by the People's
         Court,[33] if the dispute arose from the performance of the compensa-
         tion agreement reached between the parties, the litigation filed was civil
         litigation. That is, it was a civil contract dispute in nature.

II. The courts which hold negative views

     The courts with a negative attitude take their views that a contract signed by
     a governmental organ is an administrative contract, on the basis of Article
     12.1(11) of Administrative Litigation Law and Article 11 of the 2015 Adminis-
     trative Litigation Law Interpretation. The main reasons are the following. If one
     party to the contract is an administrative organ, the parties of the contract are
     not equal subjects. The act of signing the contract by the administrative organ
     is an act of exercising its powers in accordance with the law, so the contract is
     an administrative agreement, and therefore any dispute arising from adminis-
     trative agreements falls within the scope of administrative litigation and is not
     arbitrable.

     The following cases are some of the examples.

1. Zhangpu Zhonghuan Tianchuan Environmental Protection Water Co., Ltd. v.
    Zhangpu County Environmental Protection Bureau[34]

    The Contract involved is a concession agreement. The SPC held that:

    (1) One party to the Contract was the Chihu Town Government, the local
         government responsible for the environmental quality within its jurisdic-
         tion. The contract in this case was concerned with a sewage treatment
         project. Chihu Town Government signed and implemented the sewage
         treatment concession project agreement for exercising its power of public
         management. This behavior carried the characteristics of public power.

---

[32] (2016) Min 02 Min Te No. 52.

[33] (2007) Min Li Ta Zi No. 54.

[34] (2015) Min Shen Zi No. 3013.

(2) Article 26.3 of the Contract stipulates that Party A shall not take any action that violates laws and regulations or take any action other than those stipulated in this Contract to affect the construction and operation management of the project conducted by Party B and the project company. If such an impact occurs, Party A agrees to compensate for any direct loss caused by Party A, except for measures taken for public safety and health emergencies. This clause reflected the identity of the Chihu town government acting as a public affairs manager. Therefore, the court held that the Contract was an administrative contract.

2. Anqing Municipal Land and Resources Bureau v. Anqing Muncipal Yingchun Real Estate Development Co., Ltd.[35]

Anqing Intermediate People's Court held that Anqing Municipal Land and Resources Bureau had entered into the land use right transfer contract with Yingchun Company, which was an act of exercising state land administrative powers and satisfied the requirements of administrative contract defined under Article 11 of the 2015 Administrative Litigation Law Interpretation. Therefore, the arbitration clause contained in the administrative contract was null and void.

3. Xu v. Song[36]

The contract involved in the case was an agreement for the transfer of state-owned land use rights. The Jiaxing Intermediate People's Court directly applied the definition of the administrative agreement in Article 11 of the 2015 Administrative Litigation Law Interpretation and held it was an administrative dispute. Therefore, the arbitration clause was invalid and the court revoked the arbitral award concerned.

4. Jiaxing Municipal Bureau of Land and Resources v. Jiaxing Auchan Supermarket Co., Ltd.[37]

The contract involved in the case was an agreement for the transfer of state-owned land use rights. The Jiaxing Intermediate People's Court directly determined that the contract was an administrative agreement in nature, not a contractual dispute between equal parties. In addition, the administrative agreement disputes fell within the scope of administrative litigation. The arbitration clause shall be invalid.

5. Shanxi Kailaisike Yaoci Culture Co., Ltd. v. Tongchuan Municipal Bureau of Land and Resources[38]

The contract involved in the case is an agreement for the transfer of state-owned land use rights. The Tongchuan Intermediate People's Court analyzed the nature

---

[35] (2017) Wan 08 Xing Xia Zhong No.1.

[36] (2015) Zhe Jia Zhong Che Zi No. 16.

[37] (2016) Zhe 04 Min Te No. 4.

[38] (2018) Shan 02 Min Te No. 4.

of the Contract from the purposes of the Contract and the responsibilities of the parties:

(1) Purposes: The purpose was to rationally allocate land resources, promote land development, and achieve the administrative management goals of the Bureau of Land and Resources;

(2) Responsibilities: The contract was a manifestation of the administrative duties of the Tongchuan Municipal Bureau of Land and Resources.

Therefore, the court held that the Contract was an administrative agreement and that the parties were not equal subjects. Therefore, the arbitration clause did not comply with Article 2 of the Arbitration Law on equal subjects and should be deemed invalid.

From the above-listed cases, we can glimpse the different approaches in judicial practice regarding the validity of the arbitration clause in the contract in which the administrative organ is a party.

In our view, not all contracts in which the administrative organ is one of the parties are administrative contracts and thus shall not negate the validity of the arbitration clause in the contracts. To determine whether a contract is an administrative contract, the definition and characteristics of the administrative agreement should be taken into consideration. It is worth noting that the 2015 Administrative Litigation Law Interpretation was repealed on February 8, 2018. The new Administrative Litigation Law Interpretation implemented in 2018 deleted Article 11 of the 2015 Administrative Litigation Law Interpretation. The 2018 Administrative Litigation Law Interpretation is silent in the definition of administrative contracts. Since there is no definition of administrative agreement in the current laws and regulations, the concept of "administrative contract" in Article 11 of the 2015 Administrative Litigation Law Interpretation may continually be referred to when determining administrative contracts.

Specifically, pursuant to Article 11 of the 2015 Administrative Litigation Law Interpretation, an "administrative agreement" can be defined to carry the following characteristics: (1) The purpose of the agreement is for the administrative organ to achieve public interests or administrative management goals; (2) The signing of the agreement is made by the administrative organ within the scope of its statutory duties and powers; (3) The agreement contains rights and obligations prescribed in the administrative law.

In combination with the characteristics of the administrative agreement and the above-mentioned reasoning of the cases, the nature of the contract in which the administrative organ is one of the parties can be comprehensively judged from the objectives, responsibilities, duties, rights and obligations and other elements: (1) Purposes: whether the government organ provides public services completely at no charges? (2) Responsibilities: Does the agreement solely involve stipulations regarding the administrative examination and approval and the administrative license? (3) Rights and obligations: When market entities sign agreements with the government, do they have equal status and enjoy full autonomy?

4.7 Headquarters and Branch

Normally, in commercial arbitration proceedings, arbitration agreement is the sole source of jurisdiction of the arbitral tribunal. Therefore, in principle, if another person (whether as a coapplicant, corespondent or a third party) is added to the arbitration procedure, the premise is that the additional party has signed the same arbitration agreement or expressed its consensus to join the arbitration. Otherwise, the arbitral tribunal generally does not have the power to add a third party. Domestic arbitration rules have corresponding provisions, such as Article 18 (1) of the Arbitration Rules of the China International Economic and Trade Arbitration Commission,[39] Article 18 (1) of the Arbitration Rules of the Shenzhen Court of International Arbitration,[40] and Article 14(1) of the Arbitration Rules of the Beijing Arbitration Commission.[41]

If an arbitration agreement is entered into only with the branch of the headquarters, can the headquarters be added as the joint respondent of the arbitration? The general view of the courts is that although the branch is qualified as the subject of litigation according to the law, the branch does not have the status of a legal person, and its civil liability is borne by its headquarters. Therefore, the arbitration clause in the contract signed by the branch can bind its headquarters.

> ***Lanzhou New District Jiabo Cultural Development Co., Ltd. v. Guangzhou Boxia Architectural Design and Research Institute Co., Ltd. and Its Lanzhou Branch***[42]

Lanzhou New District Jiabo Cultural Development Co., Ltd. ("Jiabo Company") and Lanzhou Branch of Guangzhou Boxia Architectural Design and Research Institute Co., Ltd. ("Boxia Company Lanzhou Branch") signed the Construction Engineering Design Contract, which agreed to submit the dispute to arbitration. Jiabo Company brought lawsuit against Boxia Company. In face of jurisdiction objection, Jiabo Company defended itself that the contract concerned was signed by Boxia Company Lanzhou branch with Jiabo Company, and it had not agreed on any arbitration clause or reached any arbitration agreement with Boxia Company, so the dispute shall be tried by the court.

Gansu High People's Court held that although Boxia Company did not directly sign the Contract, Jiabo Company sued Boxia Company based on the Contract it

---

[39] Article 18 (1) of China International Economic and Trade Arbitration Commission (CIETAC) Arbitration Rules sets forth: During the arbitral proceedings, a party wishing to join an additional party to the arbitration may file the Request for Joinder with CIETAC, based on the arbitration agreement invoked in the arbitration that prima facie binds the additional party. Where the Request for Joinder is filed after the formation of the arbitral tribunal, a decision shall be made by CIETAC after the arbitral tribunal hears from all parties including the additional party if the arbitral tribunal considers the joinder necessary.

[40] Article 18 (1) of Shenzhen Court of International Arbitration (SCIA) Arbitration Rules sets forth: With the written consent by all parties, the SCIA may consolidate two or more pending arbitrations into a single arbitration to be decided by one arbitral tribunal.

[41] Article 14 (1) of Beijing Arbitration Commission Arbitration (BAC) Arbitration Rules sets forth: Before the Arbitral Tribunal is constituted, the parties may apply to join an additional party to the arbitration under the same arbitration agreement, subject to approval by the BAC.

[42] (2018) Gan Min Zhong No. 453.

signed with Boxia Company Lanzhou Branch. According to Article 14 of Company Law, a company can establish a branch, its branch does not have the status of a legal person, so its civil liabilities shall be borne by the company. Therefore, the contract signed by Boxia Company Lanzhou Branch shall be borne by Boxia Company. The arbitration clause agreed upon by the Boxia Company Lanzhou Branch shall have same legal effect on Boxia Company.

Other courts basically hold the same view.[43]

In contrast, adding a third party to the enforcement procedure of an arbitral award does not need to prove that the third party is the signatory of the arbitration agreement, the bearer of civil liabilities, or that the third party agrees to be added. After the arbitral award is rendered, if the losing party fails to perform the relevant obligations under the arbitral award, in accordance with Article 62 of the Arbitration Law and Article 237 (1) of the Civil Procedure Law, the winning party may apply to the court to enforce the arbitral award. The winning party applies to the court for enforcement of the arbitral award and initiate the court's enforcement procedure. Different from arbitration, litigation is backed by national coercive power, the court exercises national jurisdiction, and the source of its jurisdiction does not depend on the consent of the parties. Therefore, if the conditions stipulated by the law are met, the court can rule to add a third party. In the process of applying for enforcement of an arbitral award, if an entity subject to enforcement as a branch of a legal person cannot pay off debts, the entity applying for enforcement has the right to add the legal person as the entity subject to enforcement.

Zhuang v. Jiangsu Shuntong Construction Group Co., Ltd. Changzhou Branch[44]

On July 14, 2017, Changzhou Arbitration Commission rendered an arbitral award of *Zhuang v. Dai and Changzhou branch of Shuntong Company,* ruling: Dai should pay Zhuang RMB 5,852,161; Shuntong Company Changzhou branch paid Zhuang RMB 7,047,839; Dai compensated Zhuang's lawyer's fees of RMB 79,621, and Shuntong Company Changzhou branch compensated Zhuang's lawyers' fees of RMB 95,889; Zhuang's other arbitration requests were rejected.

Upon Zhuang's request, the Wuxi Intermediate People's Court accepted his enforcement application on August 25, 2017. During the enforcement procedure, it was found that Shuntong Company Changzhou branch had no property available for enforcement, and its whereabouts were unknown. Zhuang applied to the Wuxi Intermediate People's Court to add Shuntong Company as the enforced party.

Zhuang claimed: In the enforcement case against Shuntong Company Changzhou Branch, Wuxi Intermediate People's Court verified that Shuntong Company Changzhou Branch had no property for enforcement. According to Article 15 of Provisions of the SPC on Several Issues Concerning the Modification and Addition of Parties in Civil Enforcement, where the branch of a legal person subject to being enforced cannot pay off the debts, the applicant for enforcement has the right

---

[43] (2019) Jing 04 Min Te No. 170; (2018) Su 03 Min Te No. 73.

[44] (2017) Su Zhi Fu No.240.

in request to add the legal person as the enforced party, and therefore Zhuang was entitled to apply for adding Shuntong Company as the enforced party in the case.

Shuntong Company argued: The validity of the arbitral award cannot be traced back to the party, which was not a party to the arbitration agreement. There was no legal basis for the applicant to apply for adding Shuntong Company as the enforced party, and its Changzhou branch submitted the application for non-enforcement of the arbitral award on the date of receipt of the enforcement notice. Therefore, Zhuang's application shall be rejected.

Wuxi Intermediate People's Court held: In this case, Shuntong Company Changzhou branch was found to have no property available for enforcement, its whereabouts were unknown, and cannot pay off the debts determined by the effective arbitral award. Zhuang's application for adding Shuntong Company as the enforced party complied with the law, and the court granted its approval.

Compulsory enforcement of effective legal documents by the courts not only includes those that refer to civil, administrative judgments, rulings, mediation documents, civil sanctions, payment orders, civil judgments, rulings, and mediation documents issued by courts, but also include arbitral awards and mediation documents rendered by arbitral institutions. The application for non-enforcement of an arbitral award was not the reason for the suspension or termination of enforcement. Therefore, the Wuxi Intermediate People's Court ruled to add Shuntong Company as the enforced party of the case.

Shuntong Company refused to accept the ruling and applied to Jiangsu High People's Court for reconsideration, requesting revoking the ruling, and rejected Zhuang's application to add Shuntong Company as the enforced party.

In this case, Shuntong Company argued that the arbitral award was based on the willingness of the parties to arbitrate, and the arbitration agreement between Shuntong Company Changzhou Branch and Zhuang could not be traced back to be binding on Shuntong Company. The parties that could be enforced against were limited to the parties to arbitration agreement, and the parties which are not the parties to arbitration agreement shall not be subject to enforcement. This claim ignored the difference between the joinder of a third person in the enforcement procedure of the arbitral award and the joinder of a third person in the arbitration procedure, so it cannot be supported.

Jiangsu High People's Court held that: The issue of this case was whether the application for adding Shuntong Company as the enforced party complied with the law. In this case, the applicant for enforcement applied to the Wuxi Intermediate People's Court to enforce the arbitral award in accordance with the law. In the process of enforcement, pursuant to Article 15 of Provisions of the SPC on Several Issues Concerning the Modification and Addition of Parties in Civil Enforcement, the application for adding Shuntong Company as the enforced party had legal basis. Wuxi Intermediate People's Court's review of the application complied with the law.

In this case, the Wuxi Intermediate People's Court found that Changzhou Branch, as the enforced party, had no assets for enforcement and could not pay off the debts determined by the effective arbitral award and added its headquarters Shuntong Company as the party to the enforcement proceedings based on the application of the enforcer. There were factual and legal basis in support. Therefore, the Jiangsu High People's Court ruled to reject Shuntong Company's reconsideration application and maintain the Wuxi Intermediate People's Court's ruling.

Article 15 of Provisions of the SPC on Several Issues Concerning the Modification and Addition of Parties in Civil Enforcement clearly stipulates that "As a branch of a legal person subject to enforcement, in case of any failure to pay off the debts, if the enforcing party applies for changing or adding the enforced parties, the court shall grand its approval. If the properties directly managed by the legal person still cannot pay off the debts, the court may directly enforce the properties of other branches of the legal person." Article 78 of Provisions of the SPC on Several Issues Concerning the Enforcement of the People's Court (for Trial Implementation) also stipulates that "If the branch of an enterprise that is subject to enforcement cannot pay off debts, the enterprise may be ruled as the legal entity subject to enforcement. The properties directly managed by the enterprise still cannot pay off the debts, the court may rule to enforce the properties of other branches of the enterprise." These provisions are not only in line with the provisions of the Company Law that a branch does not have the status of a legal person, so the company assumes its civil liabilities. This regime is also conducive to promoting the effective enforcement of arbitral awards.

In this case, the Changzhou branch, as the party subject to enforcement, could not pay off the debts determined by the arbitral award. Zhuang applied for adding its headquarters Shuntong Company as the enforced party, which complied with legal requirements.

Similar to this case, in the case of *Beijing Huahong Integrated Circuit Design Co., Ltd. v. Chengdu Qidong Youshi Technology Co., Ltd,*[45] Beijing Huahong Company applied to Beijing First Intermediate People's Court to enforce the arbitral award rendered by Beijing Arbitration Commission against Chengdu Qidong Company Beijing Branch. During the enforcement procedure, the enforced party Chengdu Qidong Company Beijing Branch, had no property available for enforcement, so the applicant applied for adding Chengdu Qidong Company as the enforced party. This application was supported by the court.

Another similar case is *Huang v. Shanxi Fourth Construction Group Co., Ltd. Sichuan Branch.*[46] The Sichuan High People's Court also held a similar view that although a third party was not bound by the arbitral award, in the enforcement procedure of the case, both the *res judicata* and enforceability can be expanded in accordance with the law. That is, under statutory circumstances, even if the effective legal instrument did not specify the third party as the debtor, in the enforcement procedure, the enforced party can still be changed or added, creating rights and obligations in terms of enforcement for the third party. Article 78 of Provisions of the SPC on Several Issues Concerning the Enforcement of the People's Court (for Trial Implementation) is the legal basis for the expansion of *res judicata* and enforceability. A third party who is not subject to an arbitral award can be added as

---

[45] (2017) Jing 01 Zhi Yi No. 48.
[46] (2016) Chuan Zhi Fu No. 41.

the party to be enforced against in accordance with the law if it meets the statutory circumstances.

In modern transactions, headquarters and branches are common. It is necessary to take precautions before making a deal. Otherwise, once an arbitral award is rendered, in the process of applying for the enforcement of the arbitral award, if a party to be enforced against as a branch of a legal person cannot pay off the debts, the applicant has the right to add the legal person as the enforced party.

Chapter 5
Arbitrator and Tribunal

5.1 Colleagueship

Arbitrators are selected from among lawyers, judges, and scholars. This means that the arbitrators must have colleagues and former colleagues. However, if a party's agent is a former colleague of an arbitrator, should the arbitrator be challenged?

According to Article 34 of the Arbitration Law, "An arbitrator shall be withdrawn and the parties concerned have the right to request a withdrawal, whereas: (1) The arbitrator is a party involved in the case or the blood relation or relative of the parties concerned or their attorneys. (2) The arbitrator has vital personal interests in the case. (3) The arbitrator has other relations with the parties or their attorneys involved in the case that might affect the fair ruling of the case. (4) The arbitrator meets the parties concerned or their attorneys in private or has accepted gifts or attended banquets hosted by the parties concerned or their attorneys", the arbitrator should be challenged if he or she has vital personal interests in the case which may affect the impartiality of the arbitral award.

Since Article 34 does not clarify the meaning of "vital personal interests", the understanding of this sentence relies on the interpretation of the court. Chinese courts generally construe that the relationship of former colleagues does not constitute "vital personal interests".

Additionally, some arbitration institutions' rules provide more details on "vital personal interests". For example, Article 7 of the Rules for Evaluating the Behavior of Arbitrators (2021 Revision) formulated by CIETAC, specified that "other ties with the parties or their agents *ad litem*" refers to the following circumstances: (1) The arbitrator has previously advised on the same case to a party or its agent; (2) The arbitrator has recommended or introduced an agent to a party; (3) The arbitrator has served as a witness, appraiser, forensic examiner, defense lawyer or litigation/arbitration agent in the same case or a related case; (4) The arbitrator is currently a colleague of a party or its agent or used to be a colleague of the latter within the past two years; (5) The arbitrator is currently the legal adviser or agent of a party or has acted as the legal adviser or agent of a party within the past two years; (6) Any close relative of

Y. Lin, *China Arbitration Yearbook (2021)*, China Arbitration Yearbook,
https://doi.org/10.1007/978-981-19-1284-9_5

the arbitrator is colleague of a party or its agent; (7) The arbitrator or his or her close relatives might have the right to recourse against any of the parties; (8) The arbitrator, any of his or her close relatives, or his or her workplace are the joint holders of rights or obligations, or having any other common interests; (9) Any other circumstances that might affect the partiality of arbitration.

We notice that "past two years" is mentioned in the above CIETAC Rules. However, the majority of arbitration institutions in China do not have specific rules requiring that arbitrators and parties or their agents not be colleagues within the past two years.

Beijing Liumingju Catering Management Co., Ltd. v. Beijing Beiguang Electronic Group Co., Ltd.[1]

Beijing Liumingju Catering Management Co., Ltd. ("Liumingju Company") initiated a lawsuit to set aside the (2018) No. 2099 award ("Arbitration Award") of the BAC on the ground that the arbitration commission dismissed the challenge that the arbitrator Xie violated the arbitration rules and affected the impartiality of arbitration.

The court found that the BAC had served the notice of arbitration and other documents in accordance with the arbitration rules. On July 25, 2018, Liumingju Company raised an application to challenge the arbitrator Xie for a withdrawal. The reason was that the arbitrator Xie and the lawyer Qi who was the agent of the counterparty, had a close relationship on the grounds that they were both lawyers of some law firm and worked together at another law firm from 2011 to 2013. Arbitrator Xie submitted a personal statement to BAC about the challenge, claiming that he had no "close relationship" with Qi, and he referred to the decision of the arbitration commission on whether to withdraw himself. On July 27, 2018, Beijing Beiguang Electronic Group Co., Ltd. ("Beiguang Company") submitted a brief to BAC, alleging that although Xie and Qi had worked together, they had no "close relationship", and Xie and Qi were no longer colleagues after 2013. On July 31, 2018, BAC made a decision to dismiss the challenge.

The Beijing Fourth Intermediate People's Court held that the former colleague relationship between the arbitrator and the party's agent was not enough to determine that the arbitrator has vital personal interests with the agent. Liumingju Company failed to produce evidence to prove the existence of vital personal interests, and the application should not be supported. Other courts also hold the same position.

In *Guangzhou Mola Network Technology Co., Ltd. v. Tianjin Jiawu Warehousing Co., Ltd. & Guangzhou Yiruier Network Technology Co., Ltd.*,[2] Guangzhou Mola Company challenged the arbitrator on the ground that the arbitrator worked with the agent of the counterparty in the same law firm, and there was a vital personal interest between them. The Shanghai Second Intermediate People's Court held that Guangzhou Mola Company's application of withdrawal was based on the colleague relationship, which was not enough to determine whether this relationship may have affected the impartiality of arbitration.

---

[1] (2019) Jing 04 Min Te No. 227.

[2] (2015) Hu Er Zhong Min Si (Shang) Che Zi No. 1.

The Intermediate People's Court of Qingyuan City, Guangdong Province, in *Aba Prefecture Ciyun Ethnic Culture Co., Ltd. v. Dongguan Kaichuang Laser Technology Co., LTD.*,[3] held that "The application provided by the applicant that the arbitrator Liu should be withdrawn on the grounds that Arbitrator Liu and the lawyer Li, the agent of the respondent Dongguan Kaichuang Company, had worked in the same law firm… This fact does not satisfy the circumstances of challenge stipulated by Article 25 of the Qingyuan Arbitration Commission Rules."

The Intermediate People's Court of Chifeng, Inner Mongolia Autonomous Region, in *Chifeng Urban Construction Investment (Group) Co., Ltd. v. Beijing Ouandihezhong Architectural Design Consulting Co., Ltd.*,[4] held that "The applicant, Chifeng Urban Construction Investment (Group) Co., Ltd., alleged the arbitration award should be annulled on the grounds that the arbitrator and the respondent's agent were former colleagues, which violated the rules that 'the formation of the arbitration tribunal or the arbitration process has violated legal procedure'. The court did not support this position on the ground that the colleague relationship between the presiding arbitrator and the agent does not violate this rule."

The Intermediate People's Court of Hefei City, Anhui Province, in *Anhui Wanji Real Estate Group Co., Ltd. v. Anhui Anchao Construction Engineering Co., Ltd.*,[5] held that the application cannot be supported on the ground that the applicant did not challenge the arbitrator during the arbitration process, and the fact that the presiding arbitrator and his agent were colleagues before 2006 was not one of the circumstances stipulated by law for an arbitrator to be challenged, therefore did not violate due process rule.

5.2 Conflict of Identity Between Arbitrators and Agents

In the Chinese legal system and judicial practice, there are different views on the issue of whether an arbitrator may act as an agent for specific arbitration taken cognizance of by the arbitration institution in which he or she is listed as a panel arbitrator.

Paragraph 5 of Article 7 of the Measures for Punishing the Illegal Acts of Lawyers and Law Firms, promulgated by the China Ministry of Justice on June1, 2010, states that "A lawyer who has served as an arbitrator or is still serving as an arbitrator and who undertakes as an agent that in a case handled by the arbitration institution in which he or she formerly served or is currently serving falls within the scope of Article 47 Paragraph 3 of the Law of the PRC on Lawyers, which provides that a lawyer 'acting as an agent for both parties involved in the same case, or acting as agent where there is a conflicts of interest between himself or her close relatives and the legal affair he is handling'." The Measures prohibits an arbitrator from acting as an agent in an arbitral institution in which he or she was or currently serving. In

---

[3] (2017) Yue 18 Min Te No. 9.
[4] (2017) Nei 04 Min Te No. 23.
[5] (2015) He Min Zhong Zi No. 00124.

other words, literally, as long as a lawyer has served or is still serving as an arbitrator at an arbitration institution, the lawyer will not be allowed to act as an agent in this arbitration institution for any specific arbitration. This provision gives rise to controversy in the Chinese arbitration community.

After that, in 2016, other provisions came out. Paragraph 3 of Article 28 of the Measures for Administration of Legal Practice as Lawyers, which was amended and adopted by the China Ministry of Justice, stipulates that "A lawyer may not serve as an agent in a case in which another lawyer in his or her law firm is serving as an arbitrator. A lawyer who has served or is still serving as an arbitrator may not undertake legal affairs that have a conflict of interest with the cases that he or she has handled as an arbitrator." This provision lifts the restriction for arbitrators if he or she intends to act as an agent. It only prohibits the arbitrator from acting as an agent in the case that has a conflict with previous cases that he or she sat as an arbitrator.

Which rules should be applied to address identity conflict? Article 62 of the Measures for Administration of Legal Practice as Lawyers stipulates that "These Measures shall come into force as of November 1, 2016. If the previous regulations and normative documents formulated by the Ministry of Justice conflict with these measures, these Measures shall prevail." The Measures for Administration of Legal Practice as Lawyers shall prevail on the grounds that the Measures for Punishing the Illegal Acts of Lawyers and Law Firms came into force as of June 1, 2010, before the promulgation of the Measures for Administration of Legal Practice as Lawyers. Additionally, according to the principle of *Lex posterior derogat lex priori* provided by Article 92 of the Legislation Law, "if there is an inconsistency between the new provisions and the old provisions, the new provisions shall prevail", the Measures for Administration of Legal Practice as Lawyers shall prevail on the grounds that it is the new provision.

However, in China's judicial practice and arbitration practice, after the promulgation of the Measures for Administration of Legal Practice as Lawyers, there are still two different views referring to whether an arbitrator can act as an agent in the arbitration institution where he serves or is listed as a panel arbitrator.

Some courts held that the restriction on identity conflicts between arbitrators and agents stipulated by the Measures for Punishing the Illegal Acts of Lawyers and Law Firms is invalid because it violated the relevant provisions stated by the Measures for Administration of Legal Practice as Lawyers. Therefore, according to Paragraph 3 of Article 23 of the Measures for Administration of Legal Practice as Lawyers, one who is a panel arbitrator can act as an agent for arbitration conducted in the arbitration institution in which he or she is listed in the panel unless there is a conflict of interest. The following is an example.

Zhang v. Gu.[6]

In this case, after the Wuxi Arbitration Commission rendered an arbitral award, Zhang raised an application for non-enforcement of the arbitral award with the Wuxi Intermediate People's Court.

---

[6] (2017) Su 02 Zhi Yi No. 93.

One of the reasons for Zhang's application is that there was a legal circumstance that the arbitrators should be challenged because of the relationship between the agent of the respondent and the arbitrators. In addition, Zhang alleged that the three arbitrators and the defendant's agent, Hua, were both arbitrators of the Wuxi Arbitration Commission, and all of them were lawyers, which violated "the legal affairs with a conflict of interest" provided by Paragraph 5 of Article 7 of the Measures for Punishing the Illegal Acts of Lawyers and Law Firms: "the lawyer who has served as an arbitrator or is still serving as an arbitrator undertake a case handled by an arbitration institution in which he or she was or is currently serving."

For this application, the respondent, Gu, claimed that the defendant's agent, Hua, was an arbitrator of the Wuxi Arbitration Commission, and it should not be classified as a matter that can be challenged. According to Article 28 of the Measures for Administration of Legal Practice as Lawyers, a lawyer may not serve as an agent in a case in which another lawyer in his or her law firm is serving as an arbitrator, and a lawyer who has served or is still serving as an arbitrator may not undertake legal affairs that have a conflict of interest with the cases that he or she has handled as an arbitrator. Therefore, the arbitral award should be enforced because it did not violate the legal process.

The Wuxi Intermediate People's Court held that paragraph 3 of Article 28 of the Measures for Administration of Legal Practice as Lawyers stipulates that "A lawyer may not serve as an agent in a case in which another lawyer in his or her law firm is serving as an arbitrator. A lawyer who has served or is still serving as an arbitrator may not undertake legal affairs that have a conflict of interest with the cases that he or she has handled as an arbitrator", and Article 63 stipulates "These Measures shall come into force as of November 1, 2016. If the previous regulations and normative documents formulated by the Ministry of Justice conflict with these measures, these measures shall prevail". Therefore, the arbitrators and the agents in the case should not be challenged because it did not violate the legal process.

In this case, one of the reasons for the application is that the arbitrator should be challenged on the ground that the relationship between the arbitrator and the respondent's agent violated the legal process stipulated by paragraph 5 of Article 7 of the Measures for Punishing the Illegal Acts of Lawyers and Law Firms. The court held that according to Paragraph 3 of Article 28 and Article 62 of the Measures for Administration of Legal Practice as Lawyers, the fact that the respondent's agent was an arbitrator of the Wuxi Arbitration Commission should not be classified as an item subject to challenge. Therefore, this case does not violate the legal process.

In *Huaibei Changyuan Coal Gangue Comprehensive Utilization Co., Ltd. v. Suixi branch of Lianyungang East China Sea Construction and Installation Engineering Co., Ltd.*[7] and *China Oriental Minsheng Investment Co., Ltd. v. Wan & Meng*,[8] the courts also did not uphold an application for setting aside the arbitral award which claimed that the respondent's agent was an arbitrator of the arbitration institution.

---

[7] (2017) Wan 06 Min Te No. 29.

[8] (2017) Gan 01 Min Te No. 31.

However, some courts held that Paragraph 5 of Article 7 of the Measures for Punishing the Illegal Acts of Lawyers and Law Firms was valid, and according to the Measures for Punishing the Illegal Acts of Lawyers and Law Firms, it violated the legal process when the parties' agent did not disclose the fact that he had served or was still serving as an arbitrator in this arbitration institution and did not withdraw from the arbitral tribunal. This view also may be found in these cases, e.g., *Nanchang Huayu Building Industrial Co., Ltd. v. Jiangxi Dingchang Construction Engineering Co., Ltd.*, [9] and *Shanxi Construction Engineering (Group) Corporation v. Mengcheng Wanfo Shangping Co., Ltd.*[10] and *Huang & Guo v. Li.*[11]

On the one hand, from the perspective of legitimacy and according to Article 62 of the Measures for Administration of Legal Practice as Lawyers and the principle of *Lex posterior derogat lex priori* stated by Article 92 of the Legislation Law, the new provision, Paragraph 3 of Article 28 of the Measures for Administration of Legal Practice as Lawyers, shall prevail.

On the other hand, from the perspective of rationality, Paragraph 3 of Article 28 of the Measures for Administration of Legal Practice as Lawyers is more reasonable. First, the fact that the parties' agent is also listed as a panel arbitrator of the arbitration institution does not necessarily affect the impartiality and independence of the arbitrator when he or she serves as an arbitrator in other arbitration cases. Being an arbitrator is different from other legal professions, e.g., judges. Many arbitrators also have other professions, such as lawyers or university professors. It is impossible to infer that there is a conflict of interest between the two arbitrators based on the fact that they serve in or are listed in the arbitrator panel of the same arbitration institution. In fact, in Chinese arbitration institutions, there may often be hundreds of arbitrators in the panel. Second, Paragraph 5 of Article 7 of the Measures for Punishing the Illegal Acts of Lawyers and Law Firms will, to a large extent, discourage lawyers from serving as arbitrators. However, according to paragraph 2 of Article 13 of the Arbitration Law, lawyers are one of the main sources of arbitrators. Moreover, lawyers play an important role in arbitration practice, whether from domestic arbitration practice or international arbitration practice.

5.3 Time Limit for Challenge

If the parties fail to challenge the arbitrator within the prescribed time limit, does the party lose the right to set aside the arbitral award on that ground? Under China's legal arbitration system, there is no specific provision to regulate this issue.

The last opportunity required by the Arbitration Law for parties to challenge arbitrators seems to be prior to the end of the last hearing. Article 35 of the Arbitration Law provides that "In requesting withdrawal, the parties concerned shall state reasons

---

[9] (2016) Gan 01 Min Te No. 62.

[10] (2017) Wan 06 Min Te No. 59.

[11] (2017) Qiong 01 Min Te No. 7.

before the first hearing of the tribunal. If the reasons are known only after the first hearing, they may be stated before the end of the last hearing."

Arbitration institutions usually provide for more detailed regulations on the time limit for initiating a challenge against arbitrators. For example, Article 33 of the SCIA Arbitration Rules stipulates that "A party wishing to challenge the arbitrator on the grounds of the information disclosed by the arbitrator shall forward the challenge in writing within ten (10) days from the date of such receipt. Failing to file a challenge within the above time period, the party may not subsequently challenge the arbitrator on the grounds of the information disclosed by the arbitrator." Article 23 of the BAC Arbitration Rules and Article 32 of the CIETAC Arbitration Rules have similar provisions.[12]

If a challenge is initiated within the time limit but is not granted by the arbitral tribunal, the parties shall have the procedural right to set aside the award on the grounds of Article 58 of the Arbitration Law, which stipulates that "If parties concerned have evidence to substantiate one of the following, they may apply for the cancellation of arbitral award with the intermediate people's court at the place where the arbitration commission resides...3. The composition of the arbitration tribunal or the arbitration proceedings violates the legal proceedings...".

However, if a party fails to file a challenge within the time limit, does the party lose the right to set aside the arbitral award on the ground of arbitrator disqualification?

On this issue, neither the Arbitration Law nor the relevant judicial interpretations provide more details. To determine whether the composition of the arbitral tribunal or the arbitration proceedings violates the statutory procedures, one may refer to Article 14 of the Provisions of the SPC on Several Issues Concerning the Handling of Cases of Enforcement of Arbitral Awards by the People's Courts. It stipulates that the violation of arbitration proceedings provided in the Arbitration Law, the arbitration rules chosen by the parties concerned or the special agreement by the parties on arbitration proceedings, which may affect the fair judgment of the case, shall be identified as prohibited circumstances. Additionally, the arbitrators should withdraw but not withdraw under the Arbitration Law or the arbitration rules, which may affect fair judgment, and the people's court shall support the challenge. However,

---

[12] Article 23 of the BAC Arbitration Rules provides that "3. A challenge shall be raised before the first hearing. A challenge based on circumstances that become known after the first oral hearing may be raised prior to the closure of the final oral hearing. Without prejudice to Article 22(3), where no further oral hearing will be conducted, or in a documents-only arbitration, a challenge shall be raised within 10 days after the challenging party becomes aware of the circumstances giving rise to a challenge.".

Article 32 of the CIETAC Arbitration Rules states that "1. Upon receipt of the Declaration and/or the written disclosure of an arbitrator, a party wishing to challenge the arbitrator on the grounds of the disclosed facts or circumstances shall forward the challenge in writing within ten (10) days from the date of such receipt. If a party fails to file a challenge within the above time period, it may not subsequently challenge the arbitrator based on the matters disclosed by the arbitrator...3. A party may challenge an arbitrator in writing within fifteen (15) days from the date it receives the Notice of Formation of the Arbitral Tribunal. Where a party becomes aware of a reason for a challenge after such receipt, the party may challenge the arbitrator in writing within fifteen (15) days after such reason has become known to it, but no later than the conclusion of the last oral hearing.".

in the event that, with special reminders on the applicable arbitration proceedings or arbitration rules, a party knows or should have known the failure of complying with the arbitration proceedings or the arbitration rules it has chosen but still participates in or continues to participate in the arbitral proceedings without any objection, if the party applies for non-enforcement of the arbitral award on the grounds of violation of the legal procedures after the arbitral award is made, the people's court shall not support it.

Pursuant to the above-mentioned articles, if the parties knew or should have known the violation of the legal procedure but failed to file a challenge, they may not subsequently apply for non-enforcement of the award on this ground. However, the judicial interpretation also stipulates that the court should support the application for non-enforcement of the award in which the arbitrator should withdraw but not withdraw, which may affect the impartiality of the award.

Beijing Fuji Standard Dealer Circulation Information Technology Co., Ltd. and Tianjin Oriental Fuhai Equity Investment Fund Partnership (Limited partnership), et al.[13]

Beijing Fuji Standard Dealer Circulation Information Technology Co., Ltd. ("**Fuji Company**") requested the setting aside of the Arbitration Award of CIETAC [2019] China Mao Zhong Jing Cai Zi No. 1641.

The reason for the application was that, according to Article 31 and Article 32 of the Arbitration Rules (2015 edition) of the CIETAC, the arbitrator must sign a declaration and disclose any facts or circumstances likely to give rise to justifiable doubts as to his/her impartiality or independence. Fuji Company has the right to decide whether to challenge the arbitrator on the ground of the information disclosed by the arbitrator. The arbitrator Yang signed the declaration and claimed that there were no facts or circumstances that could cause reasonable doubt about his impartiality and independence. However, the Fuji Company alleged that the arbitrator violated the Arbitration Rule on the ground that the arbitrator failed to disclose the commercial relationship with Honghe Investment Co. and Oriental Fuhai Fund Partnership that might affect his impartiality and independence. The arbitrator made the award, which had the bias for Honghe Investment Co. And Oriental Fuhai Fund Partnership. Moreover, Yang was reappointed as an arbitrator in another case between Honghe Investment Co., Eastern Fuhai Fund Co., and Jiang, the legal representative of Fuji Company. These circumstances raised the suspicion that the arbitration committee or the arbitrator had interfered with the impartiality of the award. In conclusion, under Article 70 of the Arbitration Law, the award should be set aside.

The Beijing Fourth Intermediate People's Court held that Fuji Company's application that the arbitrator violated the Arbitration Rules by not disclosing the commercial relationship with Honghe Investment Co. and Oriental Fuhai Fund Co. should not be supported. Article 35 of the Arbitration Law stipulates that "in requesting withdrawal, the parties concerned shall state reasons before the first hearing of the tribunal. If the reasons are known only after the first hearing, they may be stated before the end of the last hearing." This is the legal basis for the party to challenge the arbitrator,

---

[13] (2020) Jing 04 Min Te No. 114.

and it is also a specific procedural requirement for the party to initiate the challenge procedure timely and reasonably after they have known the challenge reasons. In this case, Fuji Company should challenge Yang within the time limit stipulated in the Arbitration Law when it has known the existence of the circumstances that may affect the impartiality of the arbitrator, Yang. Therefore, the Fuji Company should bear the negative consequences of not challenging the arbitrator within the time limit.

Pursuant to Article 34 of the Arbitration Law, an arbitrator shall be withdrawn if the arbitrator is a party involved in the case or blood relation or relative of the parties concerned or their attorneys, or the arbitrator has vital personal interests in the case, or has other relations with the parties or their attorneys involved in the case. If the arbitrator meets the parties concerned or their attorneys in private or has accepted gifts or attended banquets hosted by the parties concerned or their attorneys, the arbitrator may be challenged and withdrawn.

The circumstances that should be disclosed by the arbitrator are the matters that the arbitrator is aware of, while the parties may not be aware of promptly without voluntary disclosure of the arbitrator, and being aware of these circumstances, the party may have justifiable doubts as to the arbitrator's impartiality and independence. In this case, Fuji Company produces evidence to prove that the arbitrator has some circumstances likely to give rise to justifiable doubts about his impartiality and independence, but these circumstances occurred before the end of the arbitration and were known by Internet research. There is no obstacle for Fuji Company to know these circumstances during arbitration. If Fuji Company held that arbitrator Yang should be withdrawn, it should raise an objection to CIETAC within the time limit. Additionally, the evidence produced by Fuji Company cannot prove that the arbitrator has a commercial relationship with the parties, which may affect impartiality. Therefore, this application cannot be supported by the court.

In this case, the Beijing Fourth Intermediate People's Court adopted the position that the court could review procedurally and substantively. The main reasons were that the parties had failed to exercise their procedural rights and did not apply for withdrawal under the Arbitration Law, and there was no evidence to prove that the arbitrator should be withdrawn from the case.

Furthermore, the Beijing Fourth Intermediate People's Court also adopted this position in other cases. For example, in *Tianjin Huawu Trading Co., Ltd. and Tianjin Branch of China Export Credit Insurance Co., Ltd.*,[14] the court held that "first, the evidence produced by the applicant Huawu Company is insufficient to prove that the arbitrator Zou has a vital personal interest with the respondent. Second, the arbitration procedure began on August 16, 2016, and ended on October 11, 2017. The evidence provided by the applicant Huawu Company can prove that: First, the facts and circumstances that may cause justifiable doubts as to the arbitrator's impartiality or independence have occurred before the end of the arbitration; Second, this evidence can be researched on the internet. There was no obstacle for the applicant Huawu Company to know these circumstances and facts, and it should initiate the challenge procedure within the time limit. Therefore, the applicant should bear the negative

---

[14] (2018) Jing 04 Min Te No. 42.

consequence because it never challenged the arbitrator during the arbitration and the court should not support its application."

It is common for courts to apply this approach that the court can make procedural and substantive reviews. Here are more examples. In *Chongqing Ganglong Industry and Trade (Group) Co., Ltd. v. Peng,*[15] the Intermediate People's Court of Zhanjiang City, Guangdong Province, held that "Regarding the application of Ganglong Company that the arbitration institution did not apply the rules of challenge…first in the case, the fact that the lawyer, He, participated in the arbitration as the agent of one party, does not fall within the scope of circumstances for challenging arbitrator…second, …during the arbitration, Ganglong Company did not apply for the withdrawal or raise objections to the composition of the arbitration tribunal. Therefore, the application was unreasonable, and the court should not support it."

In *Nanjing Runzhao New Energy Technology Co., Ltd. v. Jiangsu Huwu Construction Group Co., Ltd. & Jiangsu Longkun Group Co., Ltd.,* et al.,[16] the Intermediate People's Court of Yangzhou City, Jiangsu Province, held that "for the circumstance that 'the composition of the arbitration tribunal or the arbitration proceedings violates the legal proceedings'… Runzhao Company held that the arbitrator was unusually familiar with the agent of Longkun Company which may affect the impartiality of the arbitral award. However, the words 'unusually familiar' are the unilateral subjective judgment of Runzhao Company, and the evidence is insufficient to prove this. In addition, Runzhao Company did not challenge the arbitrator before the first hearing of the arbitration…".

However, some courts do not make substantive reviews. As long as the party has not initiated the challenge procedure within the time limit, the court does not support the further application that the arbitrator should be challenged.

For example, *Hengyang Hongyu Construction Engineering Co., Ltd. v. Hengyang Yiyuan Real Estate Development Co., Ltd. & Hunan Yinhai Real Estate Co., Ltd.,*[17] the Intermediate People's Court of Hengyang City, Hunan Province, held that "the applicant Hongyu Company did not challenge the arbitrator before the first hearing on the ground that the arbitrator, Xiao, slapped the table and glared at Hongyu Company when the hearing was held on November 23, 2018, the application should not be supported on the ground that the challenge was not initiated within the time limit."

In another case, *China Construction Seventh Bureau Construction Decoration Engineering Co., Ltd. v. Ningbo HongshanHigh-tech Panel Co., Ltd.,*[18] the Intermediate People's Court of Ningbo City, Zhejiang Province, held that the applicant, China Construction Seventh Bureau Company, never challenged the arbitrator during the hearing and expressly stated that it had received the statement of the arbitrator within the prescribed time limit. Therefore, the grounds were not substantiated, and

---

[15] (2018) Yue 08 Min Te No. 46.

[16] (2020) Su 10 Min Te No. 5.

[17] (2020) Xiang 04 Min Te No. 1.

[18] (2016) Zhe 02 Min Te No. 113.

the allegation that three remaining arbitrators may affect the impartiality of arbitration and the Ningbo Arbitration Commission did not serve a statement of arbitrators on the applicant were not the fact and could not be supported.

Chapter 6
Arbitral Procedures

6.1 Arbitral Procedures and Judicial Procedures

The Arbitration Law specifies only the framework of the arbitration procedure. The arbitration rules of specific arbitration institutions provide more detail on the arbitration procedure. However, the regulations of arbitration procedures are relatively simple compared with those provided for the litigation procedures in the relevant laws and judicial interpretations, e.g., Civil Procedure Law, the Interpretation of the SPC Concerning the Application of the Civil Procedure Law, the Several Provisions of the SPC on Evidence in Civil Procedures, and other regulations of judicial procedures. Therefore, if the Arbitration Law and arbitration rules do not stipulate on some specific matters, can civil procedure regulations be applied by analogy in the arbitration? For instance, when a party amends its claims and no arbitration rules exist in this respect, should the arbitral tribunal re-designate the time limit for the parties to produce evidence by referring to related evidence rules under the Civil Procedure Law?

Yangshuo Yuerong Hotel Co., Ltd. & Shanghai Zhongning Building Installation Senior Decoration Co., Ltd.[1]

Yangshuo Yuerong Hotel Co., Ltd. ("Yuerong Hotel") applied to set aside one CIETAC arbitral award.

Yuerong Hotel argued that Shanghai Zhongning Building Installation Senior Decoration Co., Ltd. ("Zhongning Company")'s claim to withdraw the application against Guangxi Construction No. 4 Company, one of the respondents, substantially amended its application after the hearing. However, the arbitral tribunal neither allowed Yuerong Hotel to respond to the amendment nor reorganize an oral hearing, which violated Article 15 of CIETAC Arbitration Rules (2015 edition). Therefore, the arbitral award should be set aside on the ground that it violated Article 15 of CIETAC Arbitration Rules (2015 edition), Paragraph 3 of Article 34 of the Several Provisions of the SPC on Evidence in Civil Procedures, "In case any party makes

---

[1] (2018) Jing 04 Min Te No. 43.

© The Author(s), under exclusive license to Springer Nature Singapore Pte Ltd. 2022   115
Y. Lin, *China Arbitration Yearbook (2021)*, China Arbitration Yearbook,
https://doi.org/10.1007/978-981-19-1284-9_6

additional or changes allegation or lodges a counterclaim, he shall do so prior to the expiration of the time limit for producing evidence.", and Article 35 of the Several Provisions "If, in the process of litigation, the nature of the legal relations alleged by the parties concerned or the validity of the civil acts are inconsistent with the findings of fact made by the court on the basis of the facts of the case, the provisions of Article 34 of the present Provisions shall not be applicable, and the court shall inform the parties concerned that the allegations litigation may be changed."

The Beijing Third Intermediate People's Court held that:

First, Yuerong Hotel claimed that the arbitration procedure violated the statutory proceeding as stipulated in Article 15 of CIETAC Arbitration Rules. However, the court stated that Article 15 of CIETAC Arbitration Rules shall not apply in this case because Article 15 did not specified under what circumstances the arbitral tribunal shall reorganize a hearing.

Second, Article 17 of CIETAC Arbitration Rules stipulates that the claimant may apply to amend its claim and the respondent may apply to amend its counterclaim. However, the arbitral tribunal may refuse any such amendment if it considers that the amendment is too late and may delay the arbitral proceedings. However, Article 17 does not specify whether the arbitral tribunal needs to re-conduct a hearing or organize a response. Therefore, after Zhongning Company withdrew the application against Guangxi Construction No. 4 Company, it did not violate the Arbitration Rules.

Third, regarding Yuerong Hotel's application claiming that the arbitral tribunal violated Article 35 of the Several Provisions of the SPC on Evidence in Civil Procedures, the court held that the provisions quoted by Yuerong Hotel were irrelevant to arbitration procedures.

Therefore, the Beijing Third Intermediate People's Court rejected the application to set aside the arbitral award.

The Arbitration Law only stipulates that the parties may amend the application but does not stipulate whether the arbitral tribunal shall re-designate the time limit for producing evidence or allow the respondent to reply to the amendments. However, some institutional arbitration rules may provide so. For example, Article 16 of the SCIA arbitration rules (2019) provides that "Amendments to the Claim or Counterclaim… (4) The provisions of Articles 11–14 of the Rules shall apply mutatis mutandis to the submission of, acceptance of, and defense to the amendments to the claim or counterclaim."

Furthermore, should the arbitral tribunal apply judicial interpretations related to litigation when the Arbitration Law and the arbitration rules do not have relevant stipulations concerning arbitration?

The main argument in favor of this position is that the China Arbitration Association or arbitration institutions should enact arbitration rules according to the Arbitration Law and the relevant provisions of the Civil Procedure Law. Therefore, the Civil Procedure Law should apply in the arbitration case when the Arbitration Law is silent in specific issues. According to Article 15 of the Arbitration Law, "The China Arbitration Association shall formulate arbitration rules according to this law and the Civil Procedure Law". Article 75 stipulates "Before the China Arbitration

Association has formulated arbitration rules, arbitration commissions may formulate interim rules for arbitration according to this law and the relevant provisions of the Civil Procedure Law." Additionally, in such situations, the Civil Procedure Law and relevant provisions based on the principle of procedural justice can guarantee the procedural rights of the arbitration party.

There are different opinions. For example, at *Guangdong Precious Metals Trading Center Co., Ltd. v. Guangdong Zhaoxin Precious Metals Trading Co., Ltd.*,[2] the applicant claimed that the arbitral tribunal should re-designate the time limit for producing evidence and re-conduct the hearing, and the applicant was deprived of such rights. In *Hexing Glass Aluminum (Shanghai) Co., Ltd. v. Suzhou Industrial Park Sudong Glass Technology Co., Ltd.*,[3] the applicant alleged that the arbitral tribunal did not re-designate the time limit for producing evidence and defense to the amendments to the claim. The arbitral tribunal violated the due process principle.

The opponents' arguments include the followings:

First, it is not stipulated in the Arbitration Law that the procedures should be governed by the Civil Procedure Law when the Arbitration rules are silent;

Second, one of the advantages of arbitration is flexibility. The main motivation for the party to choose arbitration is that they do not intend to refer their disputes to the courts. If judicial procedures are applied, they would deviate from the parties' intent.[4]

Third, the judicial interpretation of the SPC allows the parties to make a special agreement on the arbitration procedure. It indirectly rejects that the arbitration procedures must be regulated by the relevant interpretations of the Civil Procedure Law. According to Article 14 of the Provisions of the SPC on Several Issues Concerning the Handling of Cases of Enforcement of Arbitral Awards by the People's Courts,[5] "Upon being verified by the people's court, the violation of arbitration proceedings provided in the Arbitration Law, the arbitration rules are chosen by the parties concerned or the special agreement by the parties on arbitration proceedings, which may affect the fair judgment of the case, shall be identified as the circumstance that 'the composition of the arbitral tribunal or the arbitration proceedings violate the statutory procedures' specified in Item 3, Paragraph 2 in Article 237 of the Civil Procedure Law."

The Beijing Fourth Intermediate People's Court supported the opponents' view that the relevant provisions concerning litigation procedures should not be applied in the arbitration case. Therefore, in this case, Yuerong Hotel claimed that the withdrawal of the application by the respondent should be classified as "amendments to claims". According to Article 35 of Several Provisions of the SPC on Evidence in Civil Procedures, "Where the parties concerned change their allegations of litigation, the people's court shall prescribe the time period for producing evidence anew", the

---

[2] (2018) Yue 01 Min Te No. 638.

[3] (2015) Hu Yi Zhong Min Si (Shang) Che Zi No. 50.

[4] Lin Yifei, *International Commercial Arbitration Law and Practice* (2005), CITIC Press Corporation, 220.

[5] Fa Si (2018) No. 5.

arbitral tribunal violated statutory procedures because it should re-designate the time limit and organize the oral hearing in accordance with Article 15 of the Arbitration Rules. The court held that the Several Provisions of the SPC on Evidence in Civil Procedure only applies in civil litigation, not in arbitration procedure. The arbitral tribunal did not violate the statutory procedures because the Arbitration Rules did not provide for defense or hearing in case of amending claims. Therefore, the arbitral award should not be set aside.

In Chinese judicial practice, most courts adopt the same position as the Beijing Fourth Intermediate People's Court. For example, in *Chen v. Guiyang Baiyun Fuqiao Health Service Center*,[6] the Intermediate People's Court of Guiyang, Guizhou Province, held that although Paragraph 5 of Article 9 of the Several Provisions of the SPC on Evidence in Civil Procedure stipulates that "The facts as mentioned below need not be proved by the parties concerned by presenting evidence:...5. The facts affirmed in the award of the arbitration organ that has taken effect..." this article only regulates the evidence in civil procedure, and should not apply to arbitration.

6.2 The Service of Arbitral Award

According to Paragraph 1(b) of Article 5 of the New York Convention, recognition and enforcement of the award may be refused, where the party against whom the award is invoked was not given proper notice of the appointment of the arbitrator or of the arbitration proceedings or was otherwise unable to present his case. In Chinese judicial practice, defects in service are the main grounds for one party to challenge arbitration.

Fairdeal Supplies Ltd. v. Shanxi Coal Import & Export Group Co., Ltd.[7]

In an international goods sales contract dispute (case number: 14760/JEM), the sole arbitrator rendered an arbitral award for the applicant on 31 January 2008. The applicant applied to the Intermediate People's Court of Taiyuan City, Shanxi Province, for the recognition and enforcement of the arbitral award.

The respondent alleged: First, the respondent did not receive the arbitral award (case number: No. 14760/JEM) from ICC; Second, the applicant did not provide the written arbitration agreement required by Article 4 of the New York Convention; Third, the award should not be recognized and enforced on the ground that there was no binding written agreement between the applicant and the respondent, which violated Article V(1)(a) of the New York Convention; Fourth, in the arbitration procedure of ICC, the respondent did not respond to the application because the sole arbitrator failed to afford equal opportunity to both parties to present arguments; Fifth, the composition of the arbitral tribunal and the arbitration proceedings violated the "agreement" provided by the applicant; Sixth, the applicant did not apply for

---

[6] (2017) Qian 01 Min Te No. 97.

[7] (2018) Ji 01Minchu No. 921.

recognition and enforcement of the arbitral award within the time limit stipulated by the Arbitration Law. Since the date when the arbitral tribunal rendered the award was January 31, 2008, the applicant should apply to recognize and enforce the arbitral award within two years after the effective date of the award in accordance with the Arbitration Law. Therefore, the application should not be supported on the ground that it did not initiate the enforcement proceeding before the expiration of the period.

The court found that the communication address of the applicant and the agent is stated in No. 14760/JEMarbitral award: Room 707, Xianghai Building, No. 39 Xinjian Road, Taiyuan, Shanxi Province, China. Moreover, the address had been used for communication between the respondent and ICC in arbitration. On February 1, 2008, the ICC mailed the arbitral award to this address: Room F, Shengdaigong Building, No. 168 Nanneihuan Street, Taiyuan, Shanxi Province. On the same day, ICC mailed another notice to the other address stated in the arbitral award, notifying that the case has been closed, and any documents submitted by the parties will be destroyed. Therefore, the Intermediate People's Court of Taiyuan City, Shanxi Province held that the arbitral award could not be recognized because the court could not find that the arbitral award had been served on the respondent. Accordingly, the enforcement application cannot be supported.

Although Article 5 of the New York Convention is frequently invoked by parties to challenge the award, there are only a few successful cases in which the court refused to recognize and enforce the arbitral award on the ground of improper service. In this case, the applicant alleged that it had never received the arbitral award. However, it can be confirmed that the address where the ICC mailed the arbitral award was not the mailing address, as stated in the arbitral award, or the mailing address confirmed by the respondent to communicate with the ICC in arbitration. Therefore, the Intermediate People's Court of Taiyuan City held that the application for recognition and enforcement of the award should be dismissed on the ground that it cannot be verified that the arbitral award had been served on the respondent.

According to our statistics, among the cases in which applicants applied to Chinese courts for recognition and enforcement of foreign arbitral awards between 2008 and 2018, only 3 cases refused to be recognized and enforced on the ground of improper service.

Japan Shin-Etsu Chemical Industry Co. Ltd.v. Jiangsu Zhongtian Technology Co. Ltd. [8]

In this case, Article 53.2 of the Commercial Arbitration Rules of the Japan Commercial Arbitration Association provides that "The arbitral tribunal shall, upon conclusion of the examination pursuant to the preceding paragraph, notify the parties of the period of time during which it shall make an arbitral award." However, after announcing the award to be made on September 20, 2005, the arbitral tribunal did not notify the parties to extend the period of time again until February 23, 2006, when the award was actually rendered. Therefore, the SPC held that the arbitral award should not be recognized because this situation should fall within the grounds of Article 5, paragraph 1 (b), of the New York Convention.

---

[8] [2007] Min Si Ta Zi No. 26.

Japan Shin-etsu Chemical Industry Co.,Ltd. v. Tianjin Xinmao Science & Technology Co., Ltd.[9]

In this case, Article 20 of the Commercial Arbitration Rules of Japan Commercial Arbitration Association states that "The claimant (including counterclaimant) may, to the extent that the claim and counterclaim are covered by the same arbitration agreement, amend or supplement its claim (which shall hereinafter include a counterclaim for purposes of this rule) by submitting a written request for an amendment to the Association; provided that, after the establishment of the arbitral tribunal, such claimant or counterclaimant shall submit a written application for approval of such amendment to the arbitral tribunal and obtain its approval thereof. 2. The arbitral tribunal shall hear the other party's opinion before making a determination on the request for approval provided for in the preceding paragraph." The applicant submitted the application for amendments to the claims to Japan Commercial Arbitration Association on August 31, 2005. The respondent claimed that he did not receive the amendments, and the applicant did not provide any evidence to prove that the arbitral tribunal had mailed the amended application to the respondent. Therefore, the SPC held that, in this case, the respondent was deprived of the right and opportunity to present his case, which violated Article 5, paragraph 1 (b), of the New York Convention, and the arbitral award should not be recognized.

Mengadolado Co., Ltd. v. Zhejiang Zhancheng Construction Group Co., Ltd.[10]

In the case, the mail, No. 1677283941, which was signed by the party, did not refer to the notice of the arbitration procedure, and the mail, No. 1681469484, which includes "the procedure of resolution and the date of arbitration hearing", did not serve on the respondent, which resulted in the Respondent's failure to present his case. Therefore, the court refused to recognize and enforce the arbitral award on the ground that the arbitral award violated Article 5, paragraph 1 (b), of the New York Convention.

6.3 No Telephone Number

A default hearing occurs where one party fails to appear before the tribunal, and it often results in a negative result for the absent party. If one party does not receive the arbitration documents, for example, or notice of hearing, default hearing may take place. Arbitration rules established by arbitration institutions provide more details on service. Among the usual methods of service, mail is often used. The mailing details must include the address, name, and correct telephone number. Should the arbitral award be annulled on the ground that the arbitration institution fails to fill in the valid phone number when sending the arbitration documents by mail?

---

[9] [2007] Min Si Ta Zi No. 18.
[10] [2009] Min Si Ta Zi No. 46.

Tianjin Minghongjia Mechanical & Electrical Trading Co. Ltd. v. Qingdao Renyuan Environmental Equipment Co. Ltd.[11]

Tianjin Minghongjia Mechanical & Electrical Trading Co. Ltd. ("Minghongjia Company") requested to set aside an arbitral award of CIETAC on the grounds that the arbitration procedures violated the statutory procedures.

Minghongjia Company claimed that the arbitral award violated Article 8 "Service of Documents and Periods of Time" of the CIETAC Arbitration Rules on the ground that the arbitral tribunal neglected the special term of the contract concerning the representative of party A (Minghongjia Company) and only served the arbitration documents to the address provided by Qingdao Renyuan Environmental Equipment Co. Ltd. ("Renyuan Company"). Although both parties did not agree on a specific contact address or email address, the special term of the contract stated that "the representative of party A: Tong, telephone number: 158XX***XX". This means that the agreement stipulated the representative of party A, and the representative was the chief and the key contact person in charge of the whole project. However, the arbitral tribunal did not serve the arbitration documents to Tong, the key contact person, which directly resulted in the above-mentioned documents being returned by the post office on the ground that "no such recipient at the above address" and "telephone unanswered". Therefore, Minghongjia Company did not appear in the proceedings.

The court noted that on May 8, 2018, CIETAC mailed the arbitration application and its annexes to "Room 703–1, North and South Street, Hexi District, Tianjin", the last known address of Minghongjia Company provided by Renyuan Company, while these documents were returned by the post office on the grounds of "no such recipient at the above address" and "telephone unanswered". On May 30, 2018, CIETAC resent the arbitration document to the above-mentioned address through the notary service. Notices of hearing and other documents are also sent to the above-mentioned address through the notary service.

The Beijing Fourth Intermediate People's Court held that:

Article 8 of CIETAC concerning Service of Documents and Periods of Time stipulated that "…2. The arbitration documents referred to in the preceding Paragraph 1 shall be sent to the address provided by the party itself or by its representative(s) or to an address agreed upon by the parties. Where a party or its representative(s) has not provided an address or the parties have not agreed on an address, the arbitration documents shall be sent to a party's address as provided by the other party or its representative(s). 3. Any arbitration correspondence to a party or its representative(s) shall be deemed to have been properly serviced on the party if delivered to the addressee or sent to the addressee's place of business, place of registration, domicile, habitual residence or mailing address, or where after reasonable inquiries by the other party, none of the aforesaid addresses can be found, the arbitration correspondence is sent by the Arbitration Court to the addressee's last known place of business, place of registration, domicile, habitual residence or mailing address by registered or express

---

[11] (2019) Jing 04 Min Te No. 153.

mail, or by any other means that can provide a record of the attempt at delivery, including but not limited to service by a public notary, entrustment or retention,...."

In this case, both parties had filled the address in the contract, which shall be deemed the address agreed upon by the parties. The address left by Minghongjia Company Was Room 1–703, North and South Street, Hexi District, Tianjin, which was the registered address of Minghongjia Company until now. The service proceeding did not violate the relevant provisions of arbitration rules.

For an arbitral award to be set aside on the ground of violating statutory procedures, two conditions need to be satisfied: (1) Violating arbitration procedures provided in the Arbitration Law, the arbitration rules chosen by the parties concerned or the special agreements by the parties; (2) Affecting the impartial resolution of the disputes. Article 58 of the Arbitration Law stipulates that "If parties concerned have evidence to substantiate one of the following, they may apply for the cancellation of arbitral award with the intermediate people's court at the place where the arbitration commission resides...(3) The composition of the arbitration tribunal or the arbitration proceedings violates the legal proceedings..."Article 14 of Interpretation of the Supreme People's Court on Certain Issues Concerning the Application of the Arbitration Law of the People's Republic of China[12] provides that "The first hearing mentioned in Article 26 of the Arbitration Law means the first session of hearings organized by the people's court after the period for pleadings has expired and it does not include activities in pre-hearing procedures."

The Arbitration Law does not provide more details on service, and the requirements for service are regulated by the arbitration rules. In most Chinese arbitration institutions' rules,[13] the provision that "the arbitration documents shall be deemed to have properly delivered" only concerns the mailing address but not the telephone

---

[12] Fa Shi (2018) No. 5.

[13] Article 6 of SCIA Arbitration Rules stipulated that:

"3. Any arbitral document, notice or material sent by the SCIA to aparty or its representative shall be deemed to have been properlydelivered if:(a) delivered to the place of business, place of registration, placeof residence, address indicated on household registration oron the identification card, address confirmed with the SCIAorally or in writing, any effective address for external use,address provided under the parties' agreements or any othermailing address the SCIA considers appropriate;(b) delivered to the addressee's last known mailing addressby post or by any other means that provides a record ofdelivery, if none of the foregoing addresses can be found afterreasonable inquiries; or(c) the subsequent arbitral documents, notices or materials aredelivered to the original service address of the addressee ifa party or its representative changes its address after havingreceived the arbitral documents, notices or materials sent bythe SCIA yet did not notify the SCIA of such change.".

Article 71 of BAC Arbitration Rules provides that:

"(2) Arbitral documents, notices and materials shall be deemed to have been serviced if they have been delivered to the parties or their authorized representatives in person or by mail to the addressee's place of business, place of registration, place of residence, address indicated on ID card, Hukou address, address for service agreed by the parties or any other correspondence address provided by the addressee or the counterparty. (3)If, despite reasonable inquiries, the addressee's place of business, place of registration, place of residence, address indicated on ID card, Hukou address, address for service agreed by the parties, or other correspondence address cannot be found, service shall be deemed to have been affected if the document, notice or material is delivered to the

number. Therefore, if no phone number is indicated, that does not violate the statutory procedures, and the arbitral award shall not be set aside.

The address where CIETAC served the document was "Room 703–1, North and South Street, Hexi District, Tianjin". It was not only the address of the company agreed upon in the contract but also the address of registration. Therefore, the arbitration procedures did not violate Article 8 of CIETAC Arbitration Rules, and the arbitral award should not be set aside.

Other courts also held the same position. For example, at *Sichuan Tianzhihui Construction Engineering Co., Ltd. v. Chongqing Zhixiang Pavement Technology Engineering Co., Ltd.*,[14] the applicant, Tianzhihui Company, unsuccessfully argued that the arbitration procedures violated the statutory procedures on the ground that the Zhixiang Company concealed the valid telephone number and the arbitral tribunal neglected to correct the wrong number, which resulted in a default hearing.

In *Hainan Gusheng Industrial Investment Co., Ltd. v. Beijing Renji Real Estate Development Group Co., Ltd.*,[15] the applicant, Gusheng Company, applied unsuccessfully to set aside the arbitral award on the ground that the arbitration institution used the invalid address and wrong telephone number provided by Renji Company, which resulted in its absence from the hearing.

6.4 Negotiation

In practice, the parties often agree in the arbitration agreement to mediate or negotiate before arbitration. In such situations, if a party applies for arbitration without mediation or negotiation, does that affect the validity of the arbitral award?

Jiang v. Li.[16]

---

addressee's last known place of business, place of registration,place of residence, address indicated on ID card, Hukou address, address for service agreed by the parties or other correspondence address, whether by mail, courier or by any other means of delivery which allows for a record of delivery.".

Article 8 of the CIETAC Arbitration Rules provides that:

"3. Any arbitration correspondence to a party or its representative(s) shall be deemed to have been properly serviced on the party if delivered to the addressee or sent to the addressee's place of business, place of registration, domicile, habitual residence or mailing address, or where after reasonable inquiries by the other party, none of the aforesaid addresses can be found, the arbitration correspondence is sent by the Arbitration Court to the addressee's last known place of business, place of registration, domicile, habitual residence or mailing address by registered or express mail, or by any other means that can provide a record of the attempt at delivery, including but not limited to service by a public notary, entrustment or retention."

[14] (2019) Yu 01Min Te No. 308.

[15] (2018) Jing 03 Min Te No. 70.

[16] (2019) Jing 04 Min Te No. 310.

Jiang requested to set aside the arbitral award rendered by BAC on January 22, 2019, on the ground that the arbitration procedure violated the special agreement by the parties on arbitration proceedings.

Jiang alleged that according to Article 10.3 of the Equity Transfer Agreement, "If the dispute cannot be resolved through negotiation within thirty (30) days, the dispute shall be submitted to BAC in Beijing for arbitration in accordance with its rules of arbitration", Li should try to resolve the dispute through negotiation within 30 days. Therefore, Li violated the specific agreement because it applied for arbitration without negotiation. According to Article 2.1 of the BAC Arbitration Rules, the arbitral award should be revoked.

The Beijing Fourth Intermediate People's Court held that:

Jiang claimed that the agreement of "pre-arbitration procedures" stipulated by the Equity Transfer Agreement should prevail because this kind of agreement should be regarded as the specific provisions agreed upon by the parties on arbitration proceedings. However, according to Article 2.1 of the BAC Arbitration Rules, the parties may agree on certain procedural matters or the application of a different set of arbitration rules. However, this article only regulates the special agreement on arbitration proceedings, not the pre-arbitration procedures. Therefore, Article 2.1. should not apply to this case.

In this case, the applicant claimed that, according to the Equity Transfer Agreement, the arbitral award should be annulled on the ground that the respondent, Li, violated the special agreement on procedural matters. The court held that the pre-arbitration negotiation should not be regarded as procedural matters.

Obviously, the arbitral award should be revoked if the arbitration procedures violate the special agreement by the parties on arbitration proceedings. Article 14 of Provisions of the Supreme People's Court on Several Issues Concerning the Handling of Cases of Enforcement of Arbitral Awards by the People's Courts and Article 2.1 of BAC Arbitration Rules[17] both emphasize the importance of the special agreement by the parties on arbitration proceedings, which may be identified as the basis to determine whether the violation of the statutory procedure exists or not.

Nonetheless, "the arbitration proceedings" should be limited to the proceedings after the dispute is accepted by the arbitration institution. Section 1 of Chap. 4 of the Arbitration Law provides for matters relating to "Application and Acceptance". The parties concerned should meet the following requirements in applying for arbitration: an arbitration agreement, specific arbitration claims and arbitration matters falling into the limits of the authority of the arbitration commission.[18] The application

---

[17] Article 2.1 of BAC provides:

(1)The Rules shall apply where the parties have agreed to submit their dispute to the BAC for arbitration. Where the parties have agreed on certain procedural matters or the application of a different set of arbitration rules, their agreement shall prevail, unless the agreement is unenforceable or in conflict with the mandatory rules of law of the seat of arbitration. Where the parties have agreed on the application of a different set of arbitration rules, the BAC shall perform the corresponding administrative functions and duties.".

[18] See Article 21 of Arbitration Law.

submitted by the claimant and acceptance by the arbitration institution are both required for the initiation of arbitration proceedings. Therefore, the procedures before the arbitration institution accepts the arbitration application do not belong to the arbitration proceedings.

Therefore, the court did not regard the parties' agreement to negotiate as their agreement as to the arbitration procedures. In other words, there was no connection between the negotiation agreement and the violation of arbitration proceedings. The arbitral award should not be revoked on this ground of no negotiation.

In judicial practice, there are many cases in which the losing party claims unsuccessful for setting aside the arbitration award on the ground that no negotiation is conducted before the arbitration.

Some courts hold that, according to the Arbitration Law, negotiation is not the necessary pre-arbitration procedure. For example, in *Liqi Investment Co. Ltd. v. LI*,[19] the Guangzhou Intermediate People's Court so held. In this case, Article 17 of the Common Stock Subscription Agreement stipulated that the dispute shall be resolved by friendly negotiation and that any party can submit the dispute to the arbitration institution if the dispute cannot be settled through negotiation, and the arbitral award shall be final and binding on both parties. According to the agreement, it was not required that the parties try to resolve the dispute through negotiation or mediation before arbitration. The party failed to provide another legal basis to prove that mediation or negotiation was a mandatory pre-arbitration procedure in Hong Kong. Therefore, the claim that mediation or negotiation was mandatory before the arbitration procedure was not supported.

Other courts believe that it is not a restriction on an arbitration institution to accept the case if there exists an agreement to mediation or negotiation before arbitration. In *Gu v. Zhejiang Zhongke Donghai Venture Capital Partnership (Limited Partnership)*, etc.,[20] it was stipulated in Article 5.2 of the Capital Increase Agreement that any dispute arising from the Agreement shall be settled by friendly negotiation, and if the settlement cannot be reached, the dispute should be submitted to CIETAC for arbitration in Beijing. The Beijing Second Intermediate People's Court holds that this article did not limit or restrict the right that both parties enjoy submitting the dispute to arbitration; either party A or party B had the right to initiate the arbitration. This article was legal and valid.

In addition, some other courts hold that if the parties fail to negotiate before initiating the arbitration, as agreed upon, it will affect the validity of the arbitration agreement. However, if one party fails to challenge the validity of the arbitration agreement in arbitration proceedings, that party cannot apply to set aside the arbitration award thereafter on this ground. In *Cui v. Shanghai Guochun Venture Capital Co., Ltd.*,[21] the Shanghai First Intermediate People's Court held that even if the time

---

[19] (2014) Hui Zhong Fa Min Si Chu Zi No. 24.

[20] (2016) Jing 02 Min Te No. 78.

[21] (2019) Hu 01 Min Te No. 250.

limit of 30 days was not strictly followed, the applicant proceeded without challenging the validity of the arbitration agreement in the arbitration proceeding, which cannot justify the applicant's ground of violation of statutory arbitration procedures.

6.5 Delay in Amending the Claim or Producing Evidence

The time limit for amending the claims or producing evidence is helpful to urge the parties to proceed the procedures. In particular, the time limit of hearing is essential to avoid procedural delays and pursue efficient arbitration. However, if the arbitral tribunal admits the evidence produced by the parties after the specified time limit and rearranges the hearing, which may cause delay to some extent, should the arbitral award be revoked on the ground of the violation of statutory procedures?

Xia v. Beijing Yingsheng Asset Management Co., Ltd.[22]

Xia applied to set aside an arbitral award on the ground that the arbitral tribunal was unfair to one party and violated Article 12.2 of BAC Arbitration Rules. Xia claimed that the arbitral tribunal rendered the award in accordance with evidence produced by another party after the specified time period and rearranged hearing after the period.

The Beijing Fourth Intermediate People's Court held that the arbitral tribunal should have the power to decide whether to admit any evidence produced by the party or whether to hear the claim amended by the party after the specified time period, and the Arbitration Law and the arbitration rules do not have provisions otherwise. Therefore, the application alleged by Xia had no legal basis.

The issue of whether the arbitration procedure violates the Arbitration Law or the arbitration rules is the first step in judging whether there exists a violation of statutory procedures for an arbitral award. According to Article 20 of the Interpretation of the Supreme People's Court on Certain Issues Concerning the Application of the Arbitration Law of the People's Republic of China, "The phrase 'contravention of statutory procedures' as mentioned in Article 58 of the Arbitration Law refers to the circumstances where the violation of the arbitration procedures stipulated in the Arbitration Law and arbitration rules selected by the parties may affect the correct deciding of a case."

Therefore, since the Arbitration Law and the judicial interpretation have not made specific provisions on the time limit for amending the claim or producing evidence, specific arbitration rules shall be relied on to decide whether the procedures violate the "statutory procedure".

The majority of the arbitration institution rules do not provide more details on the time limit for amendments to the claim. Generally, an arbitral tribunal may refuse the amendments if it considers that the amendments will delay the arbitration proceedings. An arbitral tribunal also has the power to accept any amendment raised after

---

[22] (2018) Jing 04 Min Te No. 306.

that time period even if the time period is specified by the arbitration rules. Here are some examples.

Article 16 of SCIA Arbitration Rules states that "1.Any party may apply in writing to amend its claim or counterclaim. 2. The decision to grant the application for such amendments shall be made by the SCIA before the formation of the arbitral tribunal or by the arbitral tribunal after it is formed. The SCIA or the arbitral tribunal has the power to reject such amendments if it considers that the amendments will delay the arbitration proceedings, be unfair to the other party or result in other circumstances that may not be appropriate for such amendments."

Article 17 of CIETAC Arbitration Rules and Article 15 of SHIAC Arbitration Rules stipulate that "The Claimant may apply to amend its claim and the Respondent may apply to amend its counterclaim. However, the arbitral tribunal may refuse any such amendment if it considers that the amendment is too late and may delay the arbitral proceedings."

Article 12 of BAC Arbitration Rules provides that "(2) When determining whether to accept a late Counterclaim, the BAC or the Arbitral Tribunal, as the case may be, shall take into account the necessity to hear the late Counterclaim and the Claim at the same time in a single arbitration, the extent of the delay in lodging the Application for Counterclaim, unnecessary delay that will because to the arbitral proceedings and any other relevant factors."

Article 16 of the Arbitration Rules of Shanghai Arbitration Commission stipulates that "The Claimant may apply to amend its claim and the Respondent may apply to amend its counterclaim before the first oral hearing. If a party applies to amend its claim after the end of the first hearing and before the award is made, which is based on new evidence and facts, the arbitration can admit amendments to the claim."

Article 20 of the Arbitration Rules of China Guangzhou Arbitration Commission states that "(1) A party may request to amend its Claim or Counterclaim within fifteen (15) days after the day on which such Claim or Counterclaim has been accepted. In case it fails to make a request for doing so within the time limit, the decision on whether to accept the amended Claim or Counterclaim shall be made by the Arbitral Tribunal or, if no Arbitral Tribunal has been constituted, by China Guangzhou Arbitration Commission."

The arbitral tribunal has the power to decide whether to admit any evidence produced after the specified time period. For example, Article 42 of SCIA Arbitration Rules, Article 41 of CIETAC Arbitration Rules, Article 37 of SCIA Arbitration Rules and Article 37 of SHIAC Arbitration Rules all stipulate that "The arbitral tribunal may specify a time period for the parties to produce evidence and the parties shall produce evidence within the specified time period. The arbitral tribunal shall have the power to refuse to admit any evidence produced after that time period." Article 35 of Arbitration Rules of China Guangzhou Arbitration Commission states that "(2) A party shall complete its production of evidence within fifteen (15) days after the day on which it receives the Notice of Acceptance or the Notice of Arbitration. In case of any delay in doing so, whether the evidence produced by the party is acceptable shall be decided by the arbitral tribunal. In the event it is difficult indeed for a party to submit evidence within the period for submission of evidence, the party may file a written application for an extension prior to the expiration of the specified period. The Arbitral Tribunal shall decide whether such extension is to be allowed." Article 33 of BAC Arbitration Rules states that "(2) The arbitral tribunal may require the parties to produce their evidence within a specified period of time and the parties shall comply with any such order. The Arbitral Tribunal may reject any evidence not produced within the specified time period, unless the parties agree otherwise or the Arbitral Tribunal considers it necessary to accept the evidence."

In this case, the arbitral award was rendered by BAC. According to BAC Arbitration Rules, the arbitral tribunal "may" reject the late amendment to claims when it may cause the delay, not "must". The arbitral tribunal "may" rejects any evidence not produced within the specified period of time, not "must". Therefore, the arbitral tribunal has the power to decide whether to reject the late amendment or the evidence and not to reject it. In this case, the arbitral tribunal did not violate BAC Arbitration Rules, and the arbitration award should not be revoked.

It is important to note that the civil procedure law may provide different rules on the time limit of amending claims or producing evidence. In practice, the arbitration procedure may accord well with the arbitration rules but violate the civil procedure law.

For the amendments to the claim in civil proceedings, the latest time for the court to admit the amendments to the claim is before the end of the oral argument. Article 51 of the Civil Procedure Law states that "The plaintiff may relinquish or modify his claims. The defendant may admit or rebut the claims and shall have the right to file counterclaims." Article 34 of Provisions of the SPC on Evidence in Civil Procedures stipulates that "the party should add, amend its claim or counterclaim before the specific time period for the parties to produce evidence." Article 232 of Interpretation of the SPC concerning the Application of the Civil Procedure Law[23] stipulates that "Before the end of the oral argument and after the acceptance of the arbitration case, additional claims by the plaintiff, counterclaims by the defendant and third-party claims related to the case may be tried in combination."

For evidence produced after the specified time limit, according to the civil procedure laws, the court only accepts it on the ground that the evidence is produced beyond the prescribed time limit for the objective reason, other parties admit it, or the evidence relates to the fact of the case. The party that fails to produce the evidence within the prescribed time limit should state the reasons and may have to undertake the reprimand or fine. Article 65 of Civil Procedure Law states that "Where a party fails to provide the required evidence within the prescribed time limit, the people's court shall order the party to provide reasons for such failure; where the party refuses to provide reasons, or the reason provided is not tenable, the people's court may, in accordance with the actual circumstances, either reject the evidence or accept the evidence but with a reprimand or fine imposed on the party." Article 101 of Interpretation of the SPC concerning the Application of the Civil Procedure Law stipulates that "Where a party fails to provide the required evidence within the prescribed time limit, the people's court shall order the party to provide reasons for such failure. If

---

[23] Fa Si (2015) No. 5.

the party fails to provide the required evidence because of the objective reasons, or another party does not allege objection to the time limit, the evidence shall be deemed to be provided within the prescribed time limit." Article 102 stipulates that "Where the party who, intentionally or due to gross negligence, fails to provide the required evidence within the prescribed time limit, the court shall reject the evidence. If the evidence relates to the fact of the case, the court shall accept the evidence but with a reprimand or fine imposed on the party in accordance with Article 65 and Article 115.1 of the Civil Procedure Law. If the party fails to provide the required evidence and such failure is not based on the intention or the gross negligence, the court shall accept the evidence but with a reprimand imposed on the party."

6.6 Time Limit for Rendering the Award

Efficiency is one of the main advantages of arbitration. The arbitration rules of Chinese arbitration institutions usually stipulate a reasonable time limit for the award. Pursuant to the Arbitration Rules of SCIA,[24] CIETAC,[25] BIAC,[26] SHIAC,[27] for the

---

[24] Article 2, "Jurisdiction", of SCIA Arbitration Rules (2019) states that "1. The SCIA accepts arbitration cases related to contractual disputes and other disputes over property rights and interests, including:(a) international or foreign-related disputes;(b) disputes related to the Hong Kong Special Administrative Region, the Macao Special Administrative Region or Taiwan Region; and(c) Chinese Mainland disputes. 2. The SCIA accepts arbitration cases related to investment disputes between states and nationals of other states." Article 50, "Time-limit for the Award", states that "1. For cases under Article 2, Paragraph 1(a) and (b), the arbitral tribunal shall render an arbitral award within six (6) months from the date on which the arbitral tribunal is formed.2. For cases under Article 2, paragraph 1(c), the arbitral tribunal shall render an arbitral award within four (4) months from the date on which the arbitral tribunal is formed.3. For cases under Article 2, Paragraph 1 that may apply the Expedited Procedure under Chapter IX, the arbitral tribunal shall render an arbitral award within two (2) months from the date on which the arbitral tribunal is formed.4. Where there are special circumstances or adequate reasons justifying an extension of the duration of the arbitration, the SCIA may approve an appropriate extension upon the request of the arbitral tribunal.".

[25] Article 48, "Time Period for Rendering Award", of CIETAC Arbitration Rules (2015) states that "1. The arbitral tribunal shall render an arbitral award within six (6) months from the date on which the arbitral tribunal is formed.2. Upon the request of the arbitral tribunal, the President of the Arbitration Court may extend the time period if he/she considers it truly necessary and the reasons for the extension truly justified.".

[26] Article 47, "Time Limit for Rendering the Award", of BAC Arbitration Rules (2015) states that "The Arbitral Tribunal shall render its award within 4 months of its constitution. If there are special circumstances justifying an extension to this period, the Secretary-General may approve an extension of an appropriate time period at the request of the presiding arbitrator." Article 68, "Time Limit for Rendering the Award" of Chapter VIII "Special Provisions for International Commercial Arbitration" stated that "The Arbitral Tribunal shall render its award within 6 months (or 90 days where Article 54 applies) of the date of its constitution. If there are special circumstances justifying an extension of this period, the Secretary-General may approve an appropriate extension of time at the request of the presiding arbitrator or the sole arbitrator, as the case may be.".

[27] Article 4 "Jurisdiction" of SHIAC Arbitration Rules stated that "SHIAC accepts cases involving:1. international or foreign-related disputes;2. disputes relating to the Hong Kong Special Administrative Region, the Macao Special Administrative Region or the Taiwan region; and3. domestic

Chinese Mainland disputes, the arbitral tribunal shall render an arbitral award within four months from the date on which the arbitral tribunal is formed; For international or foreign related disputes, the arbitral tribunal shall render an arbitral award within six months from the date on which the arbitral tribunal is formed. However, the time period for rendering awards may be different on the ground that the circumstances of each case are different. If the arbitral tribunal exceeds the time limit for rendering the award, should the arbitral award be revoked based on the violation of statutory procedures?

Shenzhen Qianhai Jinshan Financial Services Co., Ltd. v. Shenzhen Tianyi Network Technology Co., Ltd.[28]

Shenzhen Qianhai Jinshan Financial Services Co., Ltd. ("Jinshan Company") requested the cancellation of an arbitral award rendered by SCIA. The reason was that the arbitration procedure violated statutory procedures because the arbitral tribunal did not render the award within two months, as stipulated in SCIA Arbitration Rules. However, according to Article 20 of the Interpretation of the SPC on Certain Issues Concerning the Application of the Arbitration Law states, the phrase "contravention of statutory procedures", as mentioned in Article 58 of the Arbitration Law, refers to the violation that may affect the correct finding of a case. The delay in rendering an arbitral award did not affect the correct finding, and the arbitral award should not be revoked.

Apart from the above-mentioned Article 20, Article 14 of Provisions of the SPC on Several Issues Concerning the Handling of Cases of Enforcement of Arbitral Awards by the People's Courts[29] also provides for circumstances violating statutory procedures.

When a court decides whether the case violates the statutory procedures or not, it considers the following questions:

1.   Do the arbitration procedures violate the arbitration rules?
2.   Do the arbitration procedures affect the correct finding?

For the first question, most of the arbitration institutions do provide as to the time limit for rendering an arbitral award, including the extension of the time limit.[30]

---

disputes." Article 44 "Time Limit for Rendering Award" stated that "1. For cases involving disputes referred to in Article 4.1 and Article 4.2 of these Rules, the tribunal shall render the award within six (6) months upon the date the tribunal is constituted.2. For cases involving disputes referred to in Article 4.3 of these Rules, the tribunal shall render the award within four (4) months upon the date the tribunal is constituted.3. Upon the request of the tribunal, the Secretary General of SHIAC may extend the aforesaid time limit if he/she considers it necessary with justifiable reasons.".

[28] (2013) Yue 03 Min Te No. 772.

[29] Fa Si (2018) No. 5.

[30] Article 50 of SCIA Arbitration Rules (2019) stipulates that "4. Where there are special circumstances or adequate reasons justifying an extension of the duration of the arbitration, the SCIA may approve an appropriate extension upon the request of the arbitral tribunal."Article 48 of CIETAC Arbitration Rules (2015) states that "2. Upon the request of the arbitral tribunal, the President of the Arbitration Court may extend the time period if he/she considers it truly necessary and the reasons

Therefore, the arbitral tribunal does not violate the arbitration rules if it extends the time period for rendering the award in accordance with the arbitration rules. In practice, there are many examples. In *Mohammed Enterprises (T) Ltd. v. Yiqi Africa Investment Co.Ltd.*,[31] the applicant held that the time for rendering the awards had been exceeded by 26 months, which violated the arbitration rules. The Beijing Fourth Intermediate People's Court held that, according to Article 46(1) of the Arbitration Rules, the arbitral tribunal shall render its award within 6 months from the date of its formation. According to Article 46(2), the secretary-general may approve an appropriate extension of time at the request of the presiding arbitrator. In the notice of extension of time sent by CIETAC to Mohammed Co., it stated that the Secretary-General of CIETAC approved that an extension of time was reasonable. Therefore, in this case, the extended time limit did not violate arbitration rules.

For the second question, whether the arbitration procedure affects the correct ruling, the Arbitration Law and the arbitration rules have many provisions regarding arbitration procedures. However, not all inconsistencies will definitely result in the revocation of the arbitral award. The arbitral award may be set aside only if the arbitration procedures may affect the correct decision of the case.

On the issue of whether the extension of the time limit for rendering the arbitral award will affect the correct ruling, as may be analyzed in *Shenzhen Qianhai Jinshan Financial Services Co., Ltd. v. Shenzhen Tianyi Network Technology Co., Ltd,*[32] the Shenzhen Intermediate People's Court clearly held that although the award was made after the time period, it did not affect the correct ruling and could not be deemed a violation of the statutory procedures.

On the issue of whether an extension will affect the validity of the award, the result may differ depending on whether the award is domestic or foreign-related. According to the New York Convention, if violation of the statutory procedures exists, the arbitral award may not be enforced or recognized regardless of the substantive result of the award. The SPC, in the reply of Non-enforcement of No. 04–05 award of Japan Commercial Arbitration Association in Tokyo,[33] states that the arbitral award should not be enforced on the ground that the time period for rendering the award exceeded the time limit stipulated by the Arbitration Rules of Japan commercial Arbitration Association which violated Article 5 of the New York Convention.

---

for the extension truly justified."Article 47 of BAC Arbitration Rules (2015) states that "…If there are special circumstances justifying an extension to this period, the Secretary-General may approve an extension of an appropriate time period at the request of the presiding arbitrator."Article 44 of SHIAC Arbitration Rules stated that "Upon the request of the tribunal, the secretary-general of SHIAC may extend the aforesaid time limit if he/she considers it necessary with justifiable reasons.".

[31] (2017) Jing 04 Min Te No. 41.

[32] (2013) Yue 03 Min Te No 772.

[33] (2007) Min Si Ta Zi No. 26.

Chapter 7
Evidence

7.1 Authenticity of Evidence

During the arbitration procedure, it is common that one party has no objection to the authenticity of the evidence but only objects to its relevance. Once losing the case, this party might apply to the court to set aside the award on the ground that the evidence produced by the counterparty on the same facts is in self-contradiction. In consideration of the party's confirmation on the authenticity of the evidence in arbitral proceedings, the court may not support its application for setting aside the award if the party fails to fully prove that the evidence concerned is fabricated, altered or obtained by any other illegal means.

In another circumstance, the tribunal has organized the examination and cross-examination in the arbitration procedure. If either party later seeks to set aside the award claiming in its application that the tribunal did not organize the parities to check the discrepancies between the evidence, the court may not support such an application.

> *Nanyang Real Estate (Nanjing) Co., Ltd. v. Nanjing Jianghong Property Development Co., Ltd.*[1]

With regard to the disputes between the claimant Nanyang Real Estate (Nanjing) Co., Ltd. ("Nanyang Company") and the respondent Nanjing Jianghong Property Development Co., Ltd. ("Jianghong Company"), the Nanjing Arbitration Commission rendered the arbitral award on August 10, 2018. Nanyang Company was dissatisfied with the arbitral award and applied to the Nanjing Intermediate People's Court to set aside it.

Nanyang Company claimed that the supplemental evidence submitted by Jianghong Company in the arbitration procedure was forged. Nanyang Company

---

[1] (2018) Su 01 Min Te No. 237.

This Chapter is coauthored with Ma Huilian, partner of Yi & Partners Law Firm.

Y. Lin, *China Arbitration Yearbook (2021)*, China Arbitration Yearbook, https://doi.org/10.1007/978-981-19-1284-9_7

further claimed that the arbitral procedure did not conform to the arbitral rules. First, during the arbitration procedure, Nanyang Company only recognized the authenticity of supplementary evidence on the surface but did not recognize its contents, and had required the counterparty to provide detailed and reliable evidence for verification. However, the arbitral tribunal ignored Nanyang Company's opinion and, directly and wrongly determined that Nanyang Company had no objection to the authenticity of the supplementary evidence. Second, the arbitral tribunal did not organize the verification of the discrepancies between supplementary evidence. Since there were self-contradiction in the evidence produced by the Jianghong Company, the supplemental evidence shall not be taken as the factual basis, and the award rendered should be set aside.

Nanjing Intermediate People's Court found that, according to the transcript of the arbitration hearing, Jianghong Company submitted supplemental evidence for cross-examination. Nangyang Co. had no objection to the authenticity of the supplemental evidence. According to Jianghong Company's arbitration requests, the arbitral tribunal held that the supplemental evidence were not related to the arbitration case. Hence, Nanjing Arbitration Commission rendered the arbitral award in favor of Jianghong Company.

In this case, regarding whether the award shall be set aside on the ground the evidence relied upon by the award was forged, Nanjing Intermediate People's Court held that during the arbitration hearing, Nanyang Company had confirmed the authenticity of the evidence submitted by Jianghong Company. During the review of this case, Nanyang Company asserted that supplemental evidence was in self-contradiction, but failed to produce sufficient evidence in support its claim the supplemental evidence was forged or obtained illegally. Even if the data contained in this piece of evidence were inconsistent with those in other pieces of evidence, it did not necessarily mean this piece of evidence was forged. The arbitral tribunal had taken the opinions of both parties into consideration before admitting the evidence. The admissibility of evidence fell within the scope of the arbitral tribunal's power of discretion. Therefore, the court did not accept Nanyang Company's argument.

Regarding whether the award shall be set aside on the ground that the arbitration procedure was not in conformity with the statutory procedure, Nanjing Intermediate People's Court held that, according to the transcript of the arbitration hearing, Nanyang Company Had been given full opportunity to defend itself, in particular giving opinions on the authenticity and relevance in terms of supplemental evidence. Additionally, Nanyang Company failed to prove that the tribunal was obliged to organize the parties to verify the specific differences between the evidence.

On the basis of the above reasoning, Nanjing Intermediate People's Court overruled Nanyang Co's application for setting aside the award.

From the case, the Chinese courts tend not to support the allegation where one party does not object to the authenticity of the evidence in the arbitration procedure but afterwards blames the arbitral tribunal for it. This essay will further discuss the issue which party shall bear the burden of proof that an award shall be set aside on the basis of forged evidence.

In the above case, the court held that it was the arbitral tribunal's discretion in terms of admissibility of evidence after taking into consideration all evidence submitted and all opinions issued by the parties.

First, forged evidence constitutes one of the grounds for setting aside an arbitral award on the premise that this piece of evidence shall be the "evidence on which the award is based." In most cases, the admissibility of evidence falls within the scope of the arbitral tribunal's power of discretion. If the court exercises its power to review the tribunal's admissibility of evidence, the court is suspected to exceed the limits of judicial review. Therefore, the judicial review of forged evidence is limited to the scope of evidence that has a substantial impact on the arbitral award.

Second, the differences in terms of the burden of proof between the inconsistent evidence and forged evidence are significant. There is no specific definition regarding forged evidence in Chinese civil laws. However, from a literal point of view, forgery of evidence reflects the intention to deceive; Inconsistency of evidence can be caused by negligence. According to Article 15 of Provisions of the SPC on Several Issues concerning the Handling of Cases regarding Enforcement of Arbitral Awards by the People's Courts, the court shall consider the following circumstances in determination of the forgery of "evidence on which the award is based": (1) The evidence has been accepted by the arbitral award; (2) The evidence is the principal evidence for determining the basic facts of the case; (3) The evidence is determined to be fabricated, altered, or illegally produced or obtained by any other illegal means, which violates objectivity, relevance, and legality as required by evidence.

In the case, Nanyang Company failed to prove the counterparty's intention to forge the evidence. In addition, the inconsistency of evidence should have been avoided if Nanyang Company had checked the discrepancies between the evidence submitted by the counterparty in the arbitration procedure. The judgment made by the court in the case can encourage the parties to take more active and full part in the arbitration procedure to verify the evidence and maintain the *res judicata* of arbitral awards.

"The arbitration procedure is not conformity with statutory procedure" and "the evidence on which the award is based is forged" are two grounds commonly adopted by an applicant for setting aside an arbitral award in Chinese judicial practice, but the applications are usually dismissed by the court due to a lack of factual evidence.

This case suggests that if an applicant fails to fully exercise its right to cross-examination in terms of evidence in the arbitration procedure, after the arbitral award is made, it may face the unfavorable consequences of its failure to exercise of the right, because the court may not support its application for setting aside the award in the judicial review.

7.2 Collection of Evidence

Each party shall bear the burden of proving the facts relied upon to support its claim or defense. However, when the relevant evidence is in the possession of the other party or a third party, the party faces difficulties in producing evidence. In this regard, the law gives the arbitral tribunal the power to collect evidence. Article 43 of the Arbitration Law stipulates that the arbitral tribunal may collect evidence where it deems necessary to collect. Most arbitration rules also have similar provisions. For example, Article 44(1) of the Arbitration Rules of Shenzhen Court of International Arbitration stipulates the following: Where the arbitral tribunal considers it necessary or where a party so requests and the arbitral tribunal agrees, the arbitral tribunal may undertake investigations and collect evidence on its own initiative. However, does this mean that the arbitral tribunal must collect evidence, or otherwise it would violate statutory procedures? The below case will address this issue. It can be seen that it is the arbitral tribunal's power of discretion to collect evidence on its own initiative, which shall not fall within the scope of judicial review.

Zhang et al. v. Wang et al.[2]

The applicants applied to Beijing Fourth Intermediate People's Court and requested the Court to set aside the arbitral award rendered by Beijing Arbitration Commission, on the ground that the arbitral tribunal violated the statutory procedure because the arbitral tribunal failed to collect the evidence as requested by the applicants during the arbitration procedure.

Beijing Fourth Intermediate People's Court held that:

Regarding the issue of whether the arbitration procedure violated the statutory procedure, according to Article 33(1) of the Arbitration Rules "If a party makes an application and the Arbitral Tribunal considers it necessary, or there is no such application but the Arbitral Tribunal considers it necessary according to the particular circumstances of the case, the Arbitral Tribunal may undertake investigations and/or collect evidence on its own initiative", the arbitral tribunal can exercise its discretion to decide whether to collect evidence. The arbitral tribunal did not grant approval to the applicants' application for the collection of evidence in the arbitral proceeding, which did not violate the requirement of the statutory procedure.

In the case, the Beijing Fourth Intermediate People's Court held that it was the arbitral tribunal's discretion to collect evidence, which was not within the scope of judicial review, and therefore did not support the applicants' application for setting aside the award.

Other courts also hold the same view. For example, in *Shanghai Shengjiu Investment Management Co., Ltd. v. Tianjin Jiajing Investment Consulting Co., Ltd.*,[3] the Beijing Second Intermediate People's Court held that: Regarding Shengjiu Company's request that the arbitral tribunal did not respond to its application for investigation and evidence collection and it was a violation of statutory procedures, the Court found that Shengjiu Company did not produce evidence to prove that it had submitted an application for evidence collection to the arbitral tribunal. In addition, according to the Arbitration Law and Arbitration Rules, whether to respond to and allow the parties to investigate and collect evidence were within the discretion of the arbitral tribunal, which did not fall within the scope of judicial review.

---

[2] (2019) Jing 04 Min Te No. 92.

[3] (2018) Jing 02 Min Te No. 2.

In practice, there are many cases where the parties apply for setting aside awards on the ground that the arbitral tribunals fail to collect evidence as requested in arbitral proceedings. In reality, it is actually difficult for arbitral institutions to successfully collect evidence. For example, in *Shanxi Yulongfeng Grain Purchase and Sale Co., Ltd. v. Beijing Huangcheng Cereals and Oils Co., Ltd.*,[4] the Beijing Second Intermediate People's Court held that: At the request of Shanxi Yulongfeng Company, the arbitral tribunal requested the inspection report from Beijing Grain, Oil and Food Inspection Institute, but the Institute refused to provide the inspection report, so the arbitral tribunal did not violate statutory procedure by not collecting evidence as requested.

Compared with the court, one of the reasons why it is more difficult for the arbitral tribunal to collect evidence lies in that: Arbitration Law only stipulates in principle that the arbitral tribunal is entitled to conduct investigation and collect evidence, as it considers necessary, but it fails to set out more details in terms of how to ensure the exercising of such power when the other party or a third party refuses to cooperate. The Civil Procedure Law has more detailed provisions in this regard for litigation procedures. The Civil Procedure Law not only provides that any entity or individual cannot reject the court's investigation and collection of evidence but also grants the court the power to discipline those entities or individuals who refuse to cooperate. Article 67 of the Civil Procedure Law sets forth that the court shall have the right to conduct investigation and collect evidence from the relevant entities or individuals; such entities or individuals may not refuse to provide information and evidence. Article 114 of the Civil Procedure Law provides that where an entity that is under an obligation to assist in investigation and execution commits any one of the following acts but refuses or obstructs the investigation and collection of evidence by the court, the court may, apart from enjoining it to perform its obligation, also impose a fine. With respect to an entity that commits the act specified above, the court may impose a fine on its principal heads or the persons who are held actually responsible for the act; It may detain them if they still refuse to perform the obligation to provide assistance, and it may, in addition, put forward a judicial proposal to the supervisory organ or the relevant organ that disciplinary sanctions are imposed on them.

In addition, unlike arbitral tribunals, who lack detailed rules in support of their power to collect evidence, there are supporting regulations and rules in ensuring the court's exercising the power to investigate and collect evidence. It can be seen that the courts also need assistance from other governmental agencies to collect evidence. For example, the Notice of the People's Bank of China, the SPC, the Supreme People's Procuratorate, and the Ministry of Public Security on Inquiring, Freezing, and Deducting Bank Deposits in Enterprises, Institutions, and Organizations[5] stipulate that banks shall actively cooperate with courts if the courts deem it necessary in a specific case to review or collect bank deposits, account books or other materials of the relevant entities.

---

[4] (2017) Jing 02 Min Te No. 171.

[5] Yinfa (1993) No. 356.

Notice on Some Issues concerning Regulating the Execution by the People's Courts and the Assistance in Execution by the Departments of Land, Resources and Real Estate Administration According to Law[6] stipulates that the Departments of Land, Resources and Real Estate Administration shall assist the courts in enforcement cases when the courts consider it necessary.

Several relevant governmental organs[7] stipulate that they shall assist the courts in handling administrative procedures and formalities when the courts deem it necessary according to law.

Despite the existence of the Arbitration Law, under the current legal framework, it is still difficult for arbitral tribunals to collect evidence from a third party as smoothly as the courts. It also explains why the Arbitration Law and the arbitration rules stipulate that the arbitral tribunal "can" but not "shall" collect evidence when it deems it necessary. Perhaps in the future, the legislature will consider it necessary to strengthen the power of arbitral tribunals to collect evidence.

7.3 Determination of Evidence

Regarding the determination of evidence, such as the admissibility, relevance and weight of the evidence, the arbitration laws of many countries recognize that the arbitral tribunal has discretion in this regard. For example, the English Arbitration Act of 1996 stipulates that, provided that it does not affect the parties' right to agree on any matter, the arbitral tribunal can decide all procedures and evidentiary matters, including that the arbitral tribunal can determine the facts or opinions submitted by the parties on any matter; Whether the admissibility, relevance or weight of materials (oral, written or other forms) are subject to strict evidence rules (or other rules), and the time, method and form of exchange and presentation of such materials, as well as whether and to what extent to determine the facts and laws.[8]

Mainstream international commercial arbitration rules also explicitly give the arbitral tribunal the power to determine evidence. For example, Article 19 of the UNCITRAL Model Law provides that the power conferred upon the arbitral tribunal includes the power to determine the admissibility, relevance, materiality and weight

---

[6] Fafa (2004) No. 5.

[7] Notice of the CPC Central Commission for Discipline Inspection, the Organization Department of the CPC Central Committee, the Publicity Department of the CPC Central Committee, the Office of the Central Committee for the Comprehensive Management of Public Security, the SPC, the Supreme People's Procuratorate, the National Development and Reform Commission, the Ministry of Public Security, the Ministry of Supervision, the Ministry of Civil Affairs, the Ministry of Justice, the Ministry of Land and Resources, the Ministry of Housing and Urban–Rural Development, the People's Bank of China, the State Administration of Taxation, the State Administration for Industry and Commerce, the Legislative Affairs Office of the State Council, the China Banking Regulatory Commission and the China Securities Regulatory Commission on Issuing the Opinions on Several Issues concerning Establishing a Sound Mechanism of Joint Efforts in Enforcement, Fafa (2010) No. 15.

[8] Song Lianbin (2010) Arbitration law, 200, 1st edn. Wuhan University Press.

of any evidence. Article 9 of IBA Rules on the Taking of Evidence in International Arbitration also states that the arbitral tribunal shall determine the credibility, relevance, materiality and weight of evidence.

However, the Chinese Arbitration Law does not clearly stipulate the power of the arbitral tribunal to determine evidence. Article 63 of the Arbitration Law (Draft for Comments) stipulates that the arbitral tribunal has the power to determine the effects and weight of evidence and allocate the burden of proof according to law. The power of the arbitral tribunal to determine evidence is mostly regulated by arbitration rules. For example, Article 38 of the BAC Arbitration Rules stipulates that the arbitral tribunal shall have the authority to assess the evidence. It shall also decide whether to adopt an appraiser's opinion. Chinese courts have recognized that the finding of facts in arbitration falls within the scope of the arbitration tribunal's power of discretion. Below is an example.

Beijing Heli Jinqiao System Integration Technology Co., Ltd. v. Beijing Xinli Hengfeng Technology Development Co., Ltd.[9]

The Applicant Beijing Heli Jinqiao System Integration Technology Co., Ltd. ("Heli Jinqiao Company") requested Beijing Fourth Intermediate People's Court to set aside the Arbitral Award on the ground of violation of statutory procedure.

In the applicant's opinion, according to Article 32(3) of the then applicable Arbitration Rules of the Beijing Arbitration Commission, if a party having the burden of proof fails to produce evidence within the specified period of time or if the evidence produced is insufficient to discharge its burden of proof, it shall bear the adverse consequences of such failure. In this case, the evidence submitted by Beijing Xinli Hengfeng Technology Development Co., Ltd. ("Xinli Hengfeng Company") after arbitration hearing was stamped with the seal of Heli Jinqiao Company, but none of the contents showed any relevance to Xinli Hengfeng Company. Therefore, the evidence cannot prove that Xinli Hengfeng Company had fulfilled the contract. However, the Arbitral Tribunal determined that the aforementioned evidence can prove that Xinli Hengfeng Company had already delivered all products to the end-user and passed the inspection of products. It can be seen that the Arbitral Tribunal had severely violated Article 32(3) of Arbitration Rules of Beijing Arbitration Commission and therefore the Arbitral Award rendered shall be set aside.

Beijing Fourth Intermediate People's Court held that the determination of evidence was subject to the arbitral tribunal's power of discretion, which was not a statutory ground for an arbitral award to be set aside according to Chinese law.

In this case, the applicant argued that the evidence submitted by the respondent cannot support its claims, but the arbitral tribunal still admitted the evidence. The Court dismissed the Applicant's application to set aside the Award on the ground that the determination of evidence was subject to the Arbitral Tribunal's power of discretion, which did not fall within the scope of judicial review.

Another related question is: what rules should the arbitral tribunal follow to determine evidence? Regarding how to determine evidence in litigation procedures, the

---

[9] (2018) Jing 04 Min Te No. 88.

Civil Procedure Law, the Civil Procedure Law Interpretation, and Evidence Rules of Civil Litigation stipulate detailed rules. However, the Arbitration Law and the Arbitration Law Interpretation have almost no provisions on the rules of evidence in arbitration procedures. Similarly, most other countries in their laws also do not separately stipulate the rules of evidence for arbitration procedures.

The laws do not stipulate the rules of evidence that must be applied to arbitration, which is conducive to distinguishing the arbitration procedure from the litigation procedure, and it also gives the arbitration procedure flexibility. Arbitration does not need to follow the strict rules of evidence as litigation does.[10] Perhaps for this reason, most arbitral institutions in China usually do not specify rules of evidence when formulating arbitration rules. Even if they do, they only stipulate principles instead of specific rules. For example, Article 38(2) of the Arbitration Rules of Beijing Arbitration Commission stipulates "When assessing any evidence, the Arbitral Tribunal may, in addition to referring to relevant laws, regulations and judicial interpretations, conduct its assessment by taking into consideration factors such as industry practices and trade usages, and shall consider the case in its totality."

However, considering that the facts found by the arbitral tribunal through the determination of evidence are critical in the arbitration procedure, if it is entirely subject to the arbitral tribunal's discretion based on its own experience and knowledge, uncertainty and unpredictability could arise. To resolve this problem, some arbitral institutions have formulated exemplary guidelines for adoption. The IBA has formulated IBA Rules on the Taking of Evidence in International Arbitration, which provides for the parties to choose and apply regulations in the areas of evidence discovery, witness testimony, expert reports, on-site inspections, admissibility and evaluation of evidence, etc. CIETAC also formulated the Guidelines on Evidence,[11] which were implemented on March 1, 2015. The guidelines consist of 26 articles, mainly including the burden of proof, examination of evidence, collection of evidence, exchange of evidence, cross-examination and determination of evidence. They do not form part of the arbitration rules of CIETAC. They can only be applied after the parties agree to apply them in specific cases.

7.4 Allocation of Burden of Proof

Regarding the burden of proof, the Arbitration Law and the arbitration rules of most arbitral institutions have relevant provisions. Article 43 of the Arbitration Law stipulates "The parties shall provide evidence for their claims." Article 33 of the Arbitration Rules of Beijing Arbitration Commission of 2019 stipulates the following: (1) Each party shall bear the burden of proving the facts relied upon to support its claim or defense....... (3) If a party having the burden of proof fails to produce

---

[10] Song Lianbin (2010) Arbitration law, 200, 1st edn. Wuhan University Press.

[11] CIETAC (2021) Guidelines on evidence. http://www.cietac.org.cn/index.php?m=page&a=index&id=107&l=en. Accessed 5 Feb 2021.

evidence within the specified period of time, or if the evidence produced is insuffi-cient to discharge its burden of proof, it shall bear the adverse consequences of such failure....... Article 42 of the Arbitration Rules of Shenzhen Court of International Arbitration of 2019 stipulates: ...... (2) Each party shall bear the burden of proving the facts upon which its claims, defenses or counterclaims are based. The arbitral tribunal shall have the power to assign the burden of proof between the parties. (3) If a party bearing the burden of proof fails to produce evidence within the specified time period or if the produced evidence is not sufficient to support its claims, defenses or counterclaims, it shall bear the consequences thereof.......

Can one party apply to set aside the arbitral award on the grounds that the arbi-tral tribunal violates the rules stipulated in Arbitration Law and relevant arbitration rules in terms of allocation of burden of proof? The burden of proof seems to be related to the arbitration procedure, and the Arbitration Law and the Arbitration Law Interpretation clearly stipulate that the arbitral award in violations of the arbitration procedure and arbitration rules affecting the fair award are subject to being set aside. Article 58 of Arbitration Law provides that if a party can produce evidence proving that the arbitral award is rendered under the circumstances that the composition of the arbitration tribunal or the arbitration procedure was not in conformity with the statutory procedure, the party may apply for setting aside an arbitral award to the intermediate people's court in the place where the arbitration commission is located. Article 20 of the Arbitration Law Interpretation stipulates that for the purposes of Article 58 of the Arbitration Law, "not in conformity with the statutory procedure" refers to circumstances where the arbitration proceedings under the Arbitration Law have been violated and where the arbitration rules selected by the parties are likely to affect the accurate ruling of the case. In the below case, Beijing Fourth Interme-diate People's Court held the opinion that the wrong allocation of burden of proof was not a ground for setting aside an arbitral award. Burden of proof was related to the substantive matters of the case, which does not fall within the scope of judicial review of the court.

Beijing Bei'ao Shengdian International Cultural Development Co., Ltd. v. Beijing Beite Shengdi Technology Development Co., Ltd. Second Branch[12]

Beijing Bei'ao Shengdian International Cultural Development Co., Ltd. ("Bei'ao Company") applied with Beijing Fourth Intermediate People's Court to set aside the arbitral award rendered by the Beijing Arbitration Commission on the ground of the arbitration proceedings was in violation of its arbitration rules.

Bei'ao Company argued that as Beijing Beite Shengdi Technology Develop-ment Co., Ltd. Second Branch ("Beite Company") claimed that the time for Bei'ao Company to affix its official seal was two months after the issuance of the Completion Acceptance Report, according to Article 32 of the Arbitration Rules, Beite Company should produce evidence to prove its claim, or otherwise it should bear the adverse consequences. The arbitral tribunal should have required Beite Company to bear the burden of proof for its claims to determine the facts. However, the arbitral tribunal

---

[12] (2019) Jing 04 Min Te No. 88.

did not require Beite Company to submit relevant evidence materials. The arbitral tribunal recognized, solely based on the expert's opinions in the Judicial Appraisal Opinion, the authenticity of the Completion Acceptance Report and further determined that the project had been inspected and accepted by both of the parties. The arbitral tribunal had seriously violated the evidence rule of "The party shall produce evidence for his claims" and made gross error in finding the facts.

Beijing Fourth Intermediate People's Court held that Bei'ao Co.'s claim that the arbitral tribunal made errors in both the allocation of the burden of proof and the determination of the statute of limitations was not within the scope of judicial review to set aside the arbitral award as prescribed in Article 58 of Arbitration Law.

The allocation of the burden of proof involves substantive matters, which are not within the scope of judicial review by the court. In another case, *China Construction Railway Construction Co., Ltd. v. Shanxi Rongquan Industrial Co., Ltd.,*[13] the court held that: When reviewing the cases applying for setting aside arbitral awards, the courts exercise the power of judicial review only conferred by Arbitration Law; The scope of judicial review shall be limited to provisions as prescribed by the Arbitration Law; With regard to domestic cases, the court shall focus on the review of procedural matters; The court shall not review the substantive matters such as the allocation of burden of proof, determination of evidence and facts, except for the review of those substantive matters limited to the authenticity of evidence and concealment of critical evidence.

This case involves two issues: (1) since the Arbitration Law does not clearly stipulate that the scope of judicial review of arbitral awards is limited to procedural matters, can it jump to the conclusion that the scope of judicial review is only limited to procedural matters? (2) The burden of proof is clearly stipulated in the procedures of the Arbitration Law. Why are substantive matters involved?

Regarding the scope of judicial review, there are different opinions of the different courts. Some views advocate that judicial review shall cover all contents of the arbitral award. Other views insist that only procedural matters should be reviewed. Although Chinese laws do not clearly stipulate that substantive matters shall be precluded in judicial review, the Arbitration Law sets forth that arbitration shall be carried out independently and that the arbitral award rendered thereof shall be final. If the courts are allowed to fully review the arbitral award including both procedural and substantive matters, then the independence of arbitration will be affected. In that case, the judicial review of the courts on the arbitral award is equivalent to trying the case for a second time, which is in conflict with the principle that the arbitral award shall be final and binding. Article 8 of the Arbitration Law provides that arbitration shall be carried out independently according to law and shall be free from interference of administrative organs, social organizations or individuals. Article 9 of the Arbitration Law provides that the arbitration shall strictly adopt the principle that an arbitral award shall be final and binding. If a party applies for arbitration with an arbitration commission or institutes an action in a court regarding the same dispute after an arbitral award has been made, the arbitration commission or the court shall

---

[13] (2019) Jing 04 Min Te No. 31.

not accept the case. However, if judicial review is limited to only procedural matters, it may impair justice. Therefore, on the basis of judicial review over procedural matters, it is appropriate to conduct limited judicial review over some substantive matters. For example, some jurisdictions conduct judicial review on applicable law or evidence.

Regarding the allocation of the burden of proof, there are also different views by the courts. For example, some views take the allocation of the burden of proof as substantive matter. Other views think otherwise that it is procedural matter. There is also another view trying to find balance and compromise. According to this view, the burden of proof not only involves which party produces evidence but also involves which party should bear adverse consequences if it is hard to determine the authenticity of evidence. Obviously, it touches upon the determination of facts, as well as impact on rights and obligations of the parties.

Moreover, allocation of the burden of proof is prescribed not only in procedural laws but also in substantive laws. For example, Article 1240 of Civil Code provides that where damage is caused to another person by a person engaging in work at a height, high voltage, or underground excavation activities, or by using high-speed rail transport vehicles, the operator shall bear tort liability, provided that the operator shall not assume any liability if it can be proven that the damage was intentionally caused by the victim or caused by *force majeure*. Where the infringed person is grossly negligent for the occurrence of the damage, the liabilities of the operator may be mitigated. More provisions can be found in other laws.[14]

The allocation of the burden of proof involves both procedural and substantive matters and plays the role of intersection of substantive laws and procedural laws. However, from the perspective of arbitration hearing, the allocation of the burden of proof is more concerned about the rights and obligations of the parties. Therefore, it is more appropriate to put it into the scope of substantive matters subject to arbitral tribunal power of determination.

---

[14] Article 1253 of Civil Code provides that where a building, structure, or another type of facility, or any object laid or hanged thereon, comes loose or falls down and thus causes damage to another person, the owner, manager, or user shall bear tort liability if it cannot be proven that he is notat fault. Where the damage is due to the fault of another responsible person, the owner, manager, or user who has paid compensation has the right to indemnification against the responsible person. Article 614 of Civil Code provides that where a buyer has a definite evidence to prove that a third person has a right over the subject matter, he may suspend payment therefor, unless the seller has provided an appropriate bond. Article 823 of Civil Code provides that a carrier shall bear the liability for compensation arising from the injury or death of a passenger occurring in the course of transportation, unless the injury or death is a result of the passenger's own health condition, or the carrier can prove that the injury or death is caused by the passenger's intentional or grossly negligent act.

7.5   Concealment of Evidence

In judicial review of an application for setting aside an arbitral award, the court can refer to the corresponding provisions as prescribed in those judicial interpretations by the SPC[15] to determine what constitutes the concealment of evidence by the counterparty sufficient to affect the impartiality of the arbitral award. When the following three conditions are met, the court will determine that the circumstance occurs and thus set aside the arbitral award: (1) The evidence is the principal evidence for determining the basic facts of the case; (2) The evidence is only in the possession of the counterparty, but has not been submitted to the arbitral tribunal; (3) During the arbitration process, the evidence is known to exist, and the counterparty is required to produce it or the arbitration tribunal is requested to order it to be submitted, but the counterparty fails to produce it or submit it without justified reasons.

Beijing Jinqiao Investment Co., Ltd. et al. v. Yishuo Holdings Co., Ltd. et al.[16]

Jinkuang Company, Yishuo Company, Sansheng Exchange and Jinqiao Company signed an equity transfer agreement. According to Article 2(2) of the Equity Transfer Agreement, Party A shall return the security deposit held in the joint account to Party B and Party C when the prescribed circumstances occur. Afterwards, the dispute arose relating to the return of the security deposit. Jinkuang Company and Yishuo Company applied to CIETAC for arbitration according to the arbitration clause in the Equity Transfer Agreement. CIETAC rendered the arbitral award on August 2017. Sansheng Exchange and Jinqiao Company (Collectively "the Applicants") were not satisfied with the arbitral award and applied to Beijing Fourth Intermediate People's Court for setting aside the award.

One of the arguments made by the Applicants to set aside the arbitral award was that Jinkuang Company and Yishuo Company (collectively "the Respondents") concealed critical evidence in the arbitration proceedings, which resulted in an unfair arbitral award. The Applicants alleged that the issue of this case was whether the condition for the return of security deposits was satisfied. However, the Respondents should have had the burden of proof but concealed the critical evidence that was sufficient to affect the impartiality of award, resulting in unfair arbitral award being rendered.

The Respondents argued that the application of the Applicants did not meet the requirements for concealing evidence that could affect the impartiality of the award. First, the Applicants did not clarify what the so-called concealed evidence was, including what the name and the contents of such evidence were. They simply argued that there was concealed evidence. Second, the Applicants stated that this evidence was in the hand of governmental organs. Obviously, according to their statement, this evidence was not only in the possession of the Respondents. Third, the Applicants did not submit any evidence during the entire arbitration process, nor did they request

---

[15] For example, Provisions of the SPC on Several Issues concerning the Handling of Cases regarding Enforcement of Arbitral Awards by the People's Courts.

[16] (2018) Jing 04 Min Te No. 23.

the arbitral tribunal to collect any evidence, nor did they require the Respondents to produce any evidence.

Beijing Fourth Intermediate People's Court decided that although the Applicants claimed the counterparty concealed the evidence regarding the filing of documents with the competent authorities during the arbitration proceedings, the filing of documents in itself was the joint obligation of the parties. During the arbitration, the Applicants had access to verify the specific circumstances of the document filing. Therefore, the court dismissed the Applicants' application for setting aside the arbitral award.

According to Article 58 of the Arbitration Law, "The counterparty has concealed evidence sufficient to affect the impartiality of the award" is one of the circumstances in which one party can apply for setting aside of an arbitral award. The Provisions of the SPC on Several Issues Concerning the Handling of Cases of Enforcement of Arbitral Awards by the People's Courts ("Enforcement Regulations"), which came into effect on March 1, 2018, stipulates in Article 16(1) that if the following conditions are met, the court shall determine the circumstances in which "the counterparty has concealed evidence sufficient to affect the fair award" as stipulated in Article 237 of Civil Procedure Law have occurred: (1) The evidence is the main evidence for determining the basic facts of the case; (2) The evidence is only in the possession of the counterparty, but has not been submitted to the arbitral tribunal; (3) During the arbitration submitting process, the evidence is known to exist, and the counterparty is required to produce it or the arbitration tribunal is requested to order it to be submitted, but the counterparty fails to produce it without it.

Although the determination of what constitutes "The counterparty has concealed evidence sufficient to affect the impartiality of the award" as stipulated in the Enforcement Regulations is concerned with the judicial review of non-enforcement of arbitral award, it can be seen from the above case that the provisions regarding non-enforcement of domestic arbitral awards as prescribed in Article 237 (2) of Civil Procedure Law are almost the same as those regarding setting-aside of domestic arbitral awards as prescribed in Article 58 of Arbitration Law. Therefore, the provisions of non-enforcement of arbitral awards can be referred to in the cases of setting aside arbitral awards.

The Enforcement Regulations stipulate stricter requirements for the determination of "The counterparty has concealed evidence sufficient to affect the impartiality of the award". That is, three requirements must be met. In this case, the applicants claimed that the counterparties "concealed" the evidence regarding the filing of the documents to the competent authorities during the arbitration, but the court held that the filing of documents in itself was the joint obligation of the parties. The applicants were fully capable of verifying the specific requirements of the filing of documents. Therefore, the application of the applicants in this case did not meet the second requirement, that is, "The evidence is only in the possession of the counterparty but has not been submitted to the arbitral tribunal", which could not prove that the respondents concealed the evidence sufficient to affect the impartiality of the arbitral award.

The concealment of evidence as a ground for setting aside an arbitral award could be easily abused. However, such concern may be alleviated to a certain extent if the three requirements stipulated in Article 16(1) of the Enforcement Regulations can be strictly applied.

Chapter 8
Arbitrability and Arbitral Scope

8.1 Arbitration Involving Criminal Case

In a litigation involving both criminal and civil case, depending on the specific circumstances, civil case may be dismissed or suspended until the criminal case were handled. If an arbitration case encounters a similar situation, can the arbitral tribunal refer to the same practice as litigation? The answer is no. There are no specific laws on how to handle arbitration cases related to criminal cases. The arbitral tribunal is not obligated to handle it in accordance with similar provisions in civil litigation cases. In the case, the party who applies for setting aside the award argues that the arbitral tribunal violates the statutory procedure because the arbitral tribunal has no power to hear the arbitration case involving a criminal case. The court does not support this argument.

***CITIC Securities Co., Ltd. v. Qian*[1]**

CITIC Securities Co. requested Beijing Fourth Intermediate People's Court to set aside the arbitral award on the grounds that the arbitral matters involved criminal matters, which exceeded the jurisdiction of an arbitral institution. In the arbitration filed by Qian against Xinsanban Co. and CITIC Securities Co., CITIC Securities Co. learned that the public security organ had accepted the criminal case and investigated Xinsanban Co. for the suspected crime of illegally absorbing public deposits. CITIC security Co. was applied with the arbitral tribunal to suspend the proceedings but was rejected by the arbitral tribunal. The arbitral tribunal was entitled only to try contractual disputes or other property disputes between the parties. It had no power to try any case that involved criminal cases. Therefore, the arbitral award shall be set aside. Second, the arbitral procedure was not in conformity with the statutory procedure. When arbitration involves a criminal case, the tribunal shall dismiss the arbitration application and transfer the case to a public security organ. However, in

---

[1] (2020) Jing 04 Min Te No. 187.

© The Author(s), under exclusive license to Springer Nature Singapore Pte Ltd. 2022
Y. Lin, *China Arbitration Yearbook (2021)*, China Arbitration Yearbook,
https://doi.org/10.1007/978-981-19-1284-9_8

this case, the tribunal directly rendered the arbitral award, which was in violation of the statutory procedure, and thus the award was set aside.

Beijing Fourth Intermediate People's Court held that, in accordance with Article 3 of the Arbitration Law, the disputes that cannot be arbitrated were those matters in relation to personal identity or administrative matters. In the arbitration, Qian's arbitral requests and arbitral matters were within the scope of the arbitration agreement entered into by the parties. Therefore, the court did not accept CITIC Securities Co.' first ground for setting aside the arbitral award.

The circumstance of "not in conformity with the statutory procedure" stipulated in Article 58 of the Arbitration Law referred to any violation of the arbitration procedures provided by the Arbitration Law and the arbitration rules agreed upon by the parties that may affect the impartiality of the award. Whether criminal offences were involved in arbitration cases, whether criminal acts affected the trial of arbitration cases, and whether arbitration should be conducted after the criminal case had been handled were all substantive matters subject to the arbitration tribunal's review of the case. CITIC Securities Co. cannot prove that the arbitral award violated the Arbitration Law and arbitration rules in terms of arbitral procedures. Therefore, this case did not meet the requirement of "not in conformity with the statutory procedure".

Under Chinese law, when the court hears a civil case that involves criminal case, the court can, depending on the factual connection between the civil case and criminal case, decide to continue, suspend, dismiss or overturn the civil case. In accordance with Several Specific Issues of the SPC on the Current Trial of Commercial Cases,[2] commercial cases and criminal proceedings under the same facts should be differentiated. First, if the facts involved in the commercial and criminal cases are exactly the same and the facts are fundamentally concerned with criminal cases, then the commercial case should not be accepted at the case filing stage. If the commercial case has accepted and the court finds during the civil procedure that this case involves criminal litigation with regard to the same facts, the court shall dismiss the commercial case. Second, if the commercial case is partially related to the facts involved in criminal case, then Article 150 (5) of Civil Procedure Law (that is, "The adjudication of the case pending is dependent on the results of the trial of another case that has not yet been concluded") shall be taken as the standard to determine whether to continue the hearing of the commercial case. Accordingly, if the hearing of commercial cases must be based on the outcome of another criminal case, the trial of commercial cases should be suspended until the criminal case has been concluded. Conversely, if the trial of commercial cases does not need to be based on the results of criminal cases, the trial of commercial cases should not be suspended.

According to Article 1 of Provisions of the SPC on Several Issues Concerning Suspected Economic Crimes in the Trial of Economic Dispute Cases,[3] if the same individual, legal person or other economic organization is involved in economic disputes and economic crime suspected cases due to different facts, the economic

---

[2] Several Specific Issues of the Supreme People's Court on the Current Trial of Commercial Cases was promulgated by SPC and took effect from December 24, 2015.

[3] Fashi (1998) No. 7.

dispute cases and economic crime suspected cases shall be heard separately. At the same time, Article 10 provides that in the trial of economic dispute cases, if the court finds clues and materials of economic crime suspected to be implicated in this case but not in the same legal relationship as this case, the court should transfer the clues and materials of suspected crimes to the relevant public security organs or procuratorial organs for investigation. Article 11 provides that the court accepts a case as an economic dispute but later finding out that it is not an economic dispute case and it may involve an economic crime, it shall rule to reject the case and transfer the relevant materials to the public security organs or the procuratorial organs.

However, for arbitration matters involving criminal cases, the laws and judicial interpretations do not have similar provisions. The Arbitration Law, the Arbitration Law Interpretation and other judicial interpretations related to arbitration do not mention the handling of criminal cases, and even the word "criminal" does not appear.

As for the arbitration rules, they are also silent in how to deal with criminal cases. Although most arbitration rules mention the suspension of arbitration proceedings, they basically do not specify the specific circumstances of suspension.[4]

In the absence of provisions in laws and arbitration rules, the provisions of litigation procedures do not apply to arbitration procedures. For example, in *Sinopec International Petroleum Exploration and Development Co., Ltd. v. UNI-TOP Asia Investment Limited*,[5] the court held that Article 248 of the Civil Procedure Law Interpretation ("Where new facts occur after a judgment/ruling comes into legal effect, and the party concerned files a new lawsuit, the competent people's court shall accept the new lawsuit pursuant to the law.") shall not apply to arbitration procedures.

---

[4] For example, Article 46 of SCIA Arbitration Rules of 2019 stipulates: (1) where parties request a suspension of the arbitration proceedings, or under circumstances where such suspension is necessary pursuant to relevant law or provisions of the Rules, the arbitration proceedings may be suspended by the arbitral tribunal. Where the arbitral tribunal has not yet been formed, such decision shall bemade by the SCIA. (2) The arbitration proceedings shall resume as soon as the reason for the suspension no longer exists.

Article 45of BAC Arbitration Rules of 2019 provides that: (1) If the parties jointly request, or if one party requests and the other parties do not object, the arbitral proceedings may be suspended. The arbitral proceedings may be resumed if one party so requests or the BAC or the Arbitral Tribunal deems this necessary. (2)The arbitral proceedings may be suspended if any exceptional circumstances occur that necessitate suspension. The arbitral proceedings shall be resumed once such circumstances cease to exist. (3)The suspension and resumption of the arbitral proceedings shall be decided by the Arbitral Tribunal, or if no Arbitral Tribunal has been constituted, by the BAC. Any period of time during which the arbitral proceedings were suspended shall not be taken into account for the calculation of the time limits provided for in Articles 48, 59 and 68.

Article 45 of CIETAC Arbitration Rules of 2015 provides that: (1) Where the parties jointly or separately request a suspension of the arbitral proceedings, or under circumstances where such suspension is necessary, the arbitral proceedings may be suspended. (2) The arbitral proceedings shall resume as soon as the reason for the suspension disappears or the suspension period ends. (3) The arbitral tribunal shall decide whether to suspend or resume the arbitral proceedings. Where the arbitral tribunal has not yet been formed, the decision shall be made by the President of the Arbitration Court.

[5] (2017) Jing 04 Min Te No. 39.

The laws are silent in how to handle arbitral matters involving criminal issues, so the arbitral tribunal is not required to handle those matters by reference to the similar provisions of civil cases in litigation.

8.2   Filing Litigation to Circumvent Arbitration Clause

In some litigation cases, the plaintiff may have multiple requests. If one of these litigation requests is based on other litigation requests and the disputes involved in other litigation requests do not fall within the jurisdiction of the court due to the existence of valid arbitration agreement, the court may be temporarily unable to hear the request directly.

Fuzhou Gulou District Housing Security and Real Estate Administration and Fuzhou Gulou District Construction Investment Management Center v. Fuzhou Hengxing Binhai Real Estate Co., Ltd. et al.[6]

On October 24, 2013, the Fuzhou Gulou Housing Administration and Fuzhou Gulou Construction Center entered the Expropriation Compensation and Resettlement Agreement ("the Agreement") with the Hengxing Company and Expropriation Office, in which the parties reached agreement on matters such as expropriation, compensation and resettlement, and the total monetary compensation for expropriated houses was RMB 233.99 million. On March 18, 2014, the parties reached Supplemental Agreement, which stipulated that any dispute arising out of the Agreement shall be submitted to the Xiamen Arbitration Commission for arbitration.

On May 20, 2016, the Expropriation Office filed with the Xiamen Intermediate People's Court to confirm the invalidity of the arbitration clause contained in Supplemental Agreement. The Xiameng Intermediate People's Court dismissed the Expropriation office's application and held that the arbitration clause was valid.

Fuzhou Gulou Housing Administration and Fuzhou Gulou Construction Center filed a lawsuit with Fujian High People's Court, requesting the court: (1) to dissolve the Agreement signed by the parties on October 24, 2013; (2) to order Hengxing Company to return Fuzhou Gulou Housing Administration and Fuzhou Gulou Construction Center the amount of compensation for expropriation RMB 100 million and interests; (3) The third parties Anfada Company, Shenglong Company and Lvde Company shall bear joint and several liabilities together with Hengxing Company for compensation and interests in the second request.

Hengxing Company and Anfada Company raised objects to jurisdiction on the ground that this case exceeded the jurisdiction of the court. With regard to the objection to jurisdiction, the Fujian High People's Court held that first, the effective ruling made by the Xiameng Intermediate People's Court had confirmed the validity of the arbitration clause contained in Supplemental Agreement. Second, the objection to jurisdiction was raised within the prescribed time of limit by law. Third,

---

[6] (2019) Zui Gao Fa Min Zhong No. 188.

regarding whether the arbitration clause can be applied to this case, from the litigation requests, it can be seen that the basis for the litigation was the Agreement entered into by the parties. The dispute arose out of the performance of this Agreement, where the Fuzhou Gulou Housing Administration and Fuzhou Gulou Construction Center found that Hengxing Company was not qualified to sign the Agreement and obtain expropriation compensation and thus required Hengxing Company to return the amount of RMB 100 million and interests. Therefore, the issue of this case was concerned with the performance of the Agreement. According to the arbitration clause, the dispute shall be submitted to Xiameng Arbitration Commission for arbitration beyond the jurisdiction of the court.

In addition, the Fuzhou Gulou Housing Administration and Fuzhou Gulou Construction Center claimed that Anfada Company, Shenglong Company and Lvde Company shall bear joint and several liabilities together with Hengxing Company for debts. Because the disputes arising from the performance of the agreement between the parties were not within the court's jurisdiction and the amount of compensation that Fuzhou Gulou Housing Administration and Fuzhou Gulou Construction Center required Anfada Company, Shenglong Company and Lvde Company to pay was uncertain, it did not satisfy the requirements for bringing a lawsuit. Therefore, the Fujian High People's Court dismissed the lawsuit filed by the Fuzhou Gulou Housing Administration and Fuzhou Gulou Construction Center against Hengxing Company, Anfada Company, Shenglong Company and Lvde Company.

Fuzhou Gulou Housing Administration and Fuzhou Gulou Construction Center objected to this ruling made by Fujian High People's Court and appealed to the SPC to revoke the ruling, on the grounds that: First, the parties of the lawsuit were not the parties of the Agreement. Fuzhou Gulou Housing Administration and Fuzhou Gulou Construction Center sued Anfada Company, Lvde Company and Shenglong Company to undertake the joint liabilities for Hengxing Company's debt. However, the Fuzhou Gulou Housing Administration and Fuzhou Gulou Construction Center did not enter into an arbitration agreement with the three companies Anfada Company, Lvde Company and Shenglong Company. Therefore, this case should be heard by the court instead of the arbitral tribunal. Second, the basic situation of Agreement and Supplemental Agreement changed. Because Hengxing Company was not qualified to sign the Agreement with Fuzhou Gulou Housing Administration and Fuzhou Gulou Construction Center, the Agreement and Supplemental Agreement are null and void for violating mandatory laws. Third, even if the Agreement and Supplemental Agreement were valid, in accordance with Article 11 of the Administrative Litigation Law Interpretation, any dispute in relation to or arising out of the compensation agreement of land or house expropriation shall be resolved through administrative litigation. Therefore, this case shall not be accepted by the arbitral institution.

The SPC held that the first request filed by Fuzhou Gulou Housing Administration and Fuzhou Gulou Construction Center was related to the Agreement and against Hengxing Company. Fuzhou Gulou Housing Administration and Fuzhou Gulou Construction Center argued that the Agreement and Supplemental Agreement were invalid because they violated mandatory laws. However, the validity of the arbitration clause contained in Supplemental Agreement was confirmed by the Xiamen Intermediate People's Court. According to Article 216 of the Civil Proce-dure Law Interpretation, before the commencement of the first court session, if the defendant raises objections to the acceptance of the civil case on the ground of having a written arbitration agreement, the competent court shall conduct the review. Where the relevant arbitral institution or a competent court had confirmed the validity of the arbitration agreement, the competent court shall render a ruling to dismiss the filing of the lawsuit. Therefore, the disputes in relation to the agreement were arbitrable matters, which should not be subject to the jurisdiction of the court. It was correct for the original court to dismiss the lawsuit.

In addition, regarding the third litigation request, this request was based on the second request, while the second request was not subject to the jurisdiction of the court, the court was temporarily unable to hear the third request. Therefore, the court dismissed the case, which did not affect the substantive rights of the Fuzhou Gulou Housing Administration and Fuzhou Gulou Construction Center. The Fuzhou Gulou Housing Administration and Fuzhou Gulou Construction Center can claim against Anfada Company, Lvde Company and Shenglong Company after disputes with Henglong Company were resolved through arbitration.

With regard to the Fuzhou Gulou Housing Administration and Fuzhou Gulou Construction Center's assertion, this case shall be resolved through administrative litigation. First, the Administrative Litigation Law Interpretation invoked by Fuzhou Gulou Housing Administration and Fuzhou Gulou Construction Center was promul-gated on May 1, 2015, which was repealed by the New Administrative Litigation Law Interpretation on February 8, 2018. Second, the plaintiff of administrative liti-gation shall only be the counterparty of administration. The Fuzhou Gulou Housing Administration and Fuzhou Gulou Construction Centerare governmental organs and cannot bring administrative cases as plaintiffs. Therefore, the court did not accept this argument made by the Fuzhou Gulou Housing Administration and Fuzhou Gulou Construction Center.

This case mainly involves two major issues: whether disputes arising from the land expropriation compensation agreement are arbitrable and how to handle the procedure for evading arbitration clauses. In the essay of Governmental Organ of this book, we have discussed the first issue. This essay only discusses the second issue.

In practice, when there is an arbitration agreement, some parties will adopt a liti-gation strategy of listing a nonsignatory to the arbitration agreement as codefendants or third parties to circumvent the arbitration agreement. Some courts have attempted to effectively regulate this practice.

In *Asia Optical Co., Inc. and Dongguan Xintai Optical Co., Ltd. v. Fujifilm Corpo-ration, Fujifilm (China) Investment Co., Ltd., Fujifilm (China) Investment Co., Ltd. Shenzhen Branch and Fujifilm Optoelectronics (Shenzhen) Co., Ltd.*,[7] the Plaintiffs Asia Optical Company and Dongguan Xintai Company entered into the agreement

---

[7] (2019) Zui Gao Fa Shang Chu No. 2.

containing an arbitration clause with Fujifilm Corporation. In addition to taking Fuji-film Corporation as defendant, the plaintiffs also brought the other three affiliated companies Fujifilm (China) Investment Co., Ltd., Fujifilm (China) Investment Co., Ltd. Shenzhen Branch and Fujifilm Optoelectronics (Shenzhen) Co., Ltd. as code-fendants, requesting them to assume joint liability. The SPC held that these three companies had no civil relationship with the plaintiffs. The plaintiff joining these three companies as codefendant was to circumvent the arbitration clause, so the court dismissed the lawsuit brought by the plaintiffs.

In *Zhao v. Shenzhen Construction Industry Group Co., Ltd. and Nanjing Dingzheng Real Estate Co., Ltd.,*[8] the actual constructor Zhao and the general contractor Shenzhen Construction Company signed the Project Leader Agree-ment containing an arbitration clause. After disputes arose, Zhao sued the general contractor Shenzhen Construction Company and the contractor Nanjing Dingzheng Company as codefendants and argued that he did not enter into any contract with the contractor Nanjing Dingzheng Company, so the disputes should not be resolved through arbitration. In this case, the Nanjing Intermediate People's Court held that, regarding the disputes between Zhao and the general contractor Shenzhen Construction Company, Zhao shall apply to the arbitral institution as agreed upon for resolution. Zhao shall not sue the contractor Nanjing Dingzheng Company as the codefendant to circumvent the arbitration clause.

In *BHMINGING & PETROLEUM PTE LTD v. Zhejiang Tianlu Energy Co., Ltd.,*[9] the plaintiff and the defendant entered into the Storage Tank Lease Agreement, which contained an arbitration clause. Afterwards, the dispute arose, the plaintiff sued Zhejiang Tianlu Energy Co., Ltd. in tort, and Zhejiang Tianlu Petrochemical Co., Ltd. as a codefendant. The plaintiff alleged the codefendants shall assume joint liabilities in the tort case. The Ningbo Maritime Court held that the disputes concerned arose from the Storage Tank Lease Agreement, which is subject to arbitration according to the arbitration clause. The plaintiff was not allowed to circumvent the arbitration clause by adding a codefendant. If the plaintiff insisted that Zhejiang Tianlu Petro-chemical Co., Ltd. is liable but cannot resolve the dispute through arbitration, the plaintiff can bring a separate lawsuit against Zhejiang Tianlu Petrochemical Co., Ltd.

In *Wang v. Qi,*[10] Qi sued Wang, Hinford International Limited and Beijing Global Jiaping Medical Investment Consulting Co., Ltd. and listed Handekang (Beijing) Medical Investment Management Consulting Co., Ltd. as the third party at the trial. Later, Qi withdrew the lawsuit against Hinford International Limited, Beijing Global Jiaping Medical Investment Consulting Co., Ltd. and Handekang (Beijing) Medical Investment Management Consulting Co., Ltd. The Equity Transfer Agree-ment entered by Qi and Wang contained an arbitration clause. In the appeal, Beijing Second Intermediate People's Court held that the trial court directly tried the case in the absence of the defendant Wang without notifying Wang of withdrawal of the lawsuit against the other parties, which deprived Wang's right to raise an objection

---

[8] (2019) Su 01 Min Zhong No. 686.

[9] (2017) Zhe 72 Min Chu No. 445.

[10] (2018) Jing 02 Min Zhong No. 8902.

to jurisdiction. The trial court had violated the statutory procedure, so its ruling was revoked.

In *Swiss Singapore Overseas Enterprises Pte Ltd v. Beijing Huitiansheng Agricultural Production Co., Ltd. and Li,*[11] the plaintiff and Qingdao Huitiansheng Agricultural Production Co., Ltd. entered Purchase and Sale Contract containing arbitration clause. Later, the plaintiff sued Qingdao Huitiansheng Company, Beijing Huitiansheng Co., and Li as codefendants before Qingdao Intermediate People's Court. Qingdao Huitainsheng Co. raised objections to jurisdiction on the grounds that arbitration clause existed. Qingdao Intermediate People's Court overruled the objection. Qingdao Huitiansheng appealed to Shandong High People's Court. Shandong High People's Court reversed the ruling made by Qingdong Intermediate People's Court and dismissed the lawsuit brought by the plaintiff against Qingdong Huitiansheng Co., but the lawsuit against Beijing Huitiansheng Co. and Li continued to be tried by Qingdao Intermediate People's Court. The Qingdao Intermediate People's Court held that the plaintiff had no contractual relationship with Beijing Huitiansheng Company and Li, so the plaintiff could submit to arbitration to resolve disputes with Qingdao Huitiansheng Company. After the arbitral award is rendered, the plaintiff can decide whether to sue Beijing Huitiansheng Company and Li based on the outcome of the arbitral award. Therefore, the Qingdao Intermediate People's Court dismissed the lawsuit against Beijing Huitiansheng Company and Li.

In Hua and Zeng v. Wen, Zhou, Shenzhen Litaihua Investment Management Co., Ltd. and Shenzhen Taikeyuan Trading Co., Ltd.,[12] Hua and Zeng entered the Real Estate Leasing Agreement containing arbitration clause with Wen and Zhou. Afterwards, disputes arose, Hua and Zeng brought Wen, Zhou, Shenzhen Litaihua Company and Shenzhen Taikeyuan Company as codefendants before the court. The Shenzhen Intermediate People's Court held that disputes arising from the Real Estate Leasing Agreement should be arbitrated by the agreed arbitral institution. Because one of the litigation requests of the plaintiffs was ordering Shenzhen Litaihua Company and Shenzhen Taikeyuan Co. to assume joint liabilities, a lawsuit against these two companies should be brought after the arbitral award has confirmed the amount and proportion of liabilities.

This case and the above-mentioned other cases are very significant for the parties who try to adopt the practice of adding parties who are nonsignatories to arbitration agreements to circumvent arbitration clauses in litigation cases.

---

[11] (2017) Lu 02 Min Chu No. 88.

[12] (2016) Yue 03 Min Zhong No. 12015.

8.3   Reasonable Expenses for Case Handling

Even if the contract does not specify which party takes responsible for the reasonable expenses for handling the case, such as attorney fees or notarization fees, the arbitration tribunal can render the award in this regard. Such an award is not considered exceeding the scope of the arbitration agreement.

Jia v. CITIC Securities Co., Ltd.[13]

CITIC Securities Co. and Jia signed the Stock Pledged Repurchase Agreement ("the Agreement"). The arbitration clause in the Agreement stipulates that any dispute arising from the Agreement shall be submitted to the BAC for arbitration. After the dispute between the parties occurred, CITIC Securities Co. submitted the dispute to the BAC in accordance with the above arbitration clause. The BAC accepted the arbitration case. The arbitral tribunal rendered the arbitral award in which Jia shall pay CITIC Securities Co. the amount of attorney's fee RMB 150,000 and notarization fee RMB 5010. Jia applied to the Beijing Fourth Intermediate People's Court to set aside the award.

One of the grounds for Jia's application to set aside the arbitral award was that the attorney's fees and notarization fees were not stipulated in the Agreement. Therefore, Jia asserted that these two fees were not within the scope of the arbitration agreement, and the arbitral tribunal had no right to arbitrate. CITIC Securities Co. argued that, in accordance with Article 51(4) of the Arbitration Rules, the arbitral tribunal had the right to arbitrate which party shall bear attorney fees and notarization fees.

The Beijing Fourth Intermediate People's Court held that the attorney's fees and notarization fees determined by the arbitral award were the expenses arising out of handling the disputes of the Agreement, and therefore they fall within the scope of the arbitration agreement. In addition, Article 51(4) of the BAC Arbitration Rules of 2015 stipulates that the Arbitral Tribunal may, pursuant to a party's request, order that the losing party shall bear the winning party's reasonable costs and expenses incurred from arbitration, including but not limited to attorney's fees, the costs of preservation measures, travel and accommodation expenses, and notarial fees. Where the arbitral tribunal determines the amount of these costs and expenses, it shall take into consideration the outcome of the case, its complexity, the actual workload of the parties or their attorneys, the amount in dispute, and any other relevant factors. The court held that the arbitral tribunal's adjudication of allocation of fees was in conformity with arbitration rules.

---

[13] (2018) Jing 04 Min Te No. 121.

According to Article 58(1) (2) of the Arbitration Law, "the matters decided in the award exceed the scope of the arbitration agreement or are beyond the arbitral authority of the arbitration commission" is one of the grounds for setting aside an arbitral award. In this situation, it is common that many applicants who apply to set aside an arbitral award will often argue that the contract does not stipulate the allocation of expenses such as attorney fees or notarization fees for handling the case, thus claiming that such expenses are not within the scope of the arbitration agreement and that the arbitral tribunal has no right to arbitrate.

Based on the legal research of the cases in recent years, the courts basically hold the same view on this issue. That is, even if the contract does not stipulate the allocation of the expenses to handle the case, such as attorney fees or notary fees, the arbitral tribunal's award in adjudicating the allocation of such expenses does not exceed the scope of the arbitration agreement, and the court will not set aside the arbitral award.

First, the arbitration rules of the arbitral institution selected by the parties have clearly stipulated that the arbitral tribunal has the power to rule that the losing party shall compensate the winning party for reasonable expenses incurred in handling the case. Therefore, the court held that the arbitral tribunal's award that the losing party should bear the winning party's attorney's fees or notarization fees does not violate the arbitration rules and does not exceed the scope of the arbitration agreement.

For example, in *He v. Chengliwei Industrial Co., Ltd., Zhuhai Zhu'ao Cross-border Industrial Zone*,[14] the parties agreed to submit the disputes to Guangzhou Arbitration Commission for arbitration. Article 74(6) of the Arbitration Rules stipulated that the arbitral tribunal may rule in the award that the losing party should compensate the winning party for reasonable expenses incurred in handling the case, but the amount of compensation shall not exceed 10% of the amount payable to the winning party. Therefore, the Guangzhou Intermediate People's Court held that the arbitral tribunal had the power to determine that the losing party should bear certain amount of attorney fees, so the arbitral award was not beyond the arbitration agreement and was not in violation of the arbitration rules.

For another example, in *Taixing Pharmaceutical Packaging Materials Co., Ltd. v. Air Products (Nanjing) Gas Co., Ltd.*,[15] the contract concerned stipulates that the disputes arising from the contract shall be submitted to CIETAC for arbitration. Article 52 of the CIETAC Arbitration Rules stipulates the arbitral tribunal has the power to determine in the arbitral award the arbitration fees and other expenses paid by which party or parties. Therefore, the Beijing Second Intermediate People's Court overruled the applicant's application for setting aside the award.

---

[14] (2016) Yue 01 Min Te No. 155.

[15] (2016) Jing 02 Min Te No. 85.

In fact, apart from the Guangzhou Arbitration Commission and CIETAC, SCIA,[16] BAC,[17] SHIAC[18] and CMAC[19] and other well-known arbitral institutions have similar provisions in their arbitration rules because it is common practice that the arbitral tribunal has the power to determine the reasonable expenses paid by the losing party to the winning party.

Second, even if the arbitration rules are silent in the allocation of reasonable expenses for case handling, the courts also hold that the disputes of the attorney's fees and notarization fees are covered by the arbitration agreement.

For example, in *Cao v. Chongqing Tanshi Finance Guarantee Co., Ltd.,*[20] the parties in the Agreement concerned stipulated that all disputes in relation to this Agreement shall be submitted to Chongqing Arbitration Commission for arbitration. Chongqing First Intermediate People's Court held that disputes about attorney fees were within the scope of "all disputes in relation to this agreement", so the award of determining the attorney fees was not beyond the arbitration agreement.

For another example, in *Sichuan Yuqiao Iron Tower Co., Ltd. v. Sichuan Guanghan Eleventh Construction Engineering Co., Ltd.,*[21] the contract concerned stipulated that any disputes arising out of the performance of the contract shall be referred to the Deyang Arbitration Commission for arbitration. The Deyang Intermediate People's Court held that although the parties failed to agree on which party shall bear the

---

[16] Article 64(4) of SCIA Arbitration Rules of 2019 provides that: The arbitral tribunal shall, at the request of a party, have the powerto determine in the arbitral award that the losing party bears the reasonable costs and expenses of the successful party incurred in relation to the arbitration proceedings, including but not limited to the attorney's fees, the costs of preservation measures, travel and accommodation expenses, notarial fees and witness expenses. While determining the amount of these costs and expenses, the arbitral tribunal shall take into account the outcome and complexity of the case, the actual workload of the parties or their representatives, the amount in dispute and any other relevantfactors.

[17] Article 52(4) of BAC Arbitration Rules of 2019 provides that: The Arbitral Tribunal may, pursuant to a party's request, order that the losing party shall bear the winning party's reasonable costs and expenses for the conduct of the arbitration, including but not limited to attorney's fees, the costs of preservation measures, travel and accommodation expenses, and notarial fees. Where the Arbitral Tribunal determines the amount of these costs and expenses, it shall take into consideration the outcome of the case, its complexity, the actual workload of the parties or their attorneys, the amount in dispute, and any other relevant factors.

[18] Article 47(2) of SHIAC Arbitration Rules of 2015 provides that: The tribunal has the discretion to decide in the award, according to the specific circumstances of the case, that the losing party shall compensate the winning party for the expenses reasonably incurred by it in pursuing its case. The tribunal shall consider the factors such as the outcome and complexity of the case, the workload of the winning party and/or its representative(s), and the amount in dispute, etc.

[19] Article 57(2) of China Maritime Arbitration Commission (CMAC) Arbitration Rules of 2020 provides that: The arbitral tribunal has the power to decide in the arbitral award, having regard to the circumstances of the case, that the losing party shall compensate the winning party for the expenses reasonably incurred by it in pursuing the case. In deciding whether or not the winning party's expenses incurred in pursuing the case are reasonable, the arbitral tribunal shall take into consideration various factors such as the outcome and complexity of the case, the workload of the winning party and/or its representative(s), and the amount in dispute, etc.

[20] (2017) Yu 01 Min Te No. 822.

[21] (2018) Chuang 06 Min Te No. 11.

attorney's fees, this dispute arose from the contract concerned, so the arbitral award's determination on this issue was not beyond the arbitration agreement.

In some cases, the courts will take both reasons as stated above into consideration. The above case *Jia v. CITIC Securities Co., Ltd.* is a typical example. On the one hand, the court held that the disputes of attorney fees and notarization fees were reasonable fees arising out of the agreement concerned, which shall be within the scope of the arbitration agreement. On the other hand, according to Article 51(4) of BAC Arbitration Rules, the arbitral tribunal had the power to determine the allocation of reasonable fees for handling cases such as attorney fees. Therefore, regardless of whether it is based on the arbitration clause or the arbitration rules, the arbitral tribunal's determination of reasonable expenses of case handling does not exceed the scope of the arbitration agreement.

8.4 Contracts in Which the Name and the Actual Legal Relationship Are Inconsistent

For a contract in which its name is inconsistent with the actual legal relationship, if the arbitral tribunal hears the case and renders an award based on the actual legal relationship, does it exceed the scope of the arbitration agreement stipulated in the contract? In the below case, the court held the view it did not exceed the scope of the arbitration agreement.

Hunan Tuotian Energy Saving Control Technology Co., Ltd. v. Changsha Machine Tool Co., Ltd.[22]

On April 3, 2013, Tuotian Company and Machine Tool Company signed the Technical Agreement, stipulating that this Technical Agreement was an attachment to the Purchase Order, and it was equally effective as the Purchase Order.

On June 18, 2013, Tuotian Company and the Machine Tool Company signed the Sales Contract in which the parties agreed the machine with electronic control system under the Contract shall observe the Technical Agreement. At the same time, the parties agreed in the Sales Contract that any dispute arising out of the performance of this Contract or in relation to this Contract shall be submitted to Changsha Arbitration Commission for arbitration.

Machine Tool Company, as the claimant, applied to Changsha Arbitration Commission for arbitration, requesting Tuotian Company to return the payment of the machine, compensate its losses and bear the arbitration costs and property preservation measure fees.

The Arbitral Tribunal ruled that Tuotian Company should return the payment of the machine to Machine Tool Company and rejected other arbitration requests of Machine Tool Company. The arbitral tribunal held that, because the Technical Agreement and the Sales Contract were both related to the research products of the

---

[22] (2016) Xiang 01 Min Te No. 26.

respondent, this Contract in its nature was Technical Service Contract although it was named Sales Contract.

Tuotian Company sought to set aside the arbitral award. Tuotian Company claimed the arbitral tribunal was in error of determining the cause of action as dispute of Technical Service Contract, so the award it rendered was beyond the claimant's submission and beyond the scope of the arbitration agreement.

Changsha Intermediate People's Court held that the determination of the cause of action of this case was subject to the arbitral tribunal's power of discretion. Such determination was not the adjudication in the matters at dispute. The award made by the arbitral tribunal was not beyond Machine Tool Company's submission, nor did it exceed the scope of the arbitration agreement. Therefore, the court dismissed Tuotian Company's application for setting aside the award.

The issue of this case was that, for a contract in which its name is different from the actual legal relationship, if the arbitral tribunal adjudicates the case and renders the arbitral award based on the actual legal relationship, does it exceed the scope of the arbitration agreement?

In Chinese legal practice, applicants usually take legal relationships as one of the grounds to set aside arbitral awards, and it is common for courts to support them. In *Huang and Mu v. Tianshui Hongye Real Estate Development Co., Ltd.*,[23] the Tianshui Intermediate People's Court found that the applicant's claim of "debt offsetting the house purchase price" was not based on the dispute arising from the performance of the House Purchase and Sale Contract. Therefore, the applicant's claim was related to another legal relationship, which should not be considered as the arbitration matters in this case. The arbitral award was beyond the scope of the arbitration agreement.

In another case, *Xianyang Guangyu Real Estate Development Co., Ltd. v. The 141 1st Division of the Shanxi Army Reserve Infantry of the Chinese People's Liberation Army*,[24] Xianyang Intermediate People's Court, held that although the contracting operation agreement with arbitration clause mentioned that consumption enjoyed specific discounts, this agreement was an agreement on the rights and obligations between the parties in terms of lease operation. The relationship arising from consumption in the restaurant contracted by the applicant should be a separate service contract relationship and not an arbitration matter agreed upon by the parties. The arbitral tribunal ruled on the consumption amount to deduct the applicant's rental fee, which exceeded the agreement of the parties. In other similar cases, the courts held that if the arbitral tribunal made an award on another legal relationship other than the legal relationship of the contract containing the arbitration clause, such an award is beyond the scope of the arbitration agreement.

The reason why the revocation of an arbitral award will consider legal relationship is that the legal relationship helps to define the scope of the contract thus helps determine whether the arbitral award exceeds the scope of the arbitration agreement.

Considering that most arbitration agreements adopt expressions such as "any disputes in relation to this contract" and "any disputes incurred in the performance

---

[23] (2012) Tian Zhi Zi No. 02.

[24] (2018) Shan 04 Min Te No. 5.

of this contract", the content of arbitration matters is closely related to the content of the contract. The legal relationship is one of the signs that distinguishes different contracts. The essence of legal relationships lies in the relationship of rights and obligations between the parties conferred by the laws.[25] For example, in an arbitration case initiated based on an arbitration clause in the sales contract, the arbitral tribunal should not rule on the lease relationship between the parties because the lease legal relationship already represents another lease contract, which exceeds the arbitration matters of the sales contract. That is, it is beyond the scope of the arbitration clause. However, depending on the specific provisions of the arbitration agreement, the adjudication of other contracts of other legal relationships in relation to the contract may not exceed the scope of the arbitration agreement, as stated in the Reply of the SPC on Request for Instructions Re Enforcement of Award No. 224 [2007] of the China International Economic & Trade Arbitration Commission.[26]

The legal relationship is one of the methods to define the scope of the contract. For the arbitration clause with general expressions as stated above, in determining whether the arbitral award exceeds the arbitration agreement or not, the key lies in the relationship between the arbitration matters and the contract with arbitration clause. Article 2 of the Arbitration Law Interpretation provides that if parties concerned generally agree that arbitrable matters shall be disputes arising from a contract, then all disputes arising from the formation, validity, modification, assignment, performance, liability for breach, interpretation, or rescission of the contract may be deemed arbitrable matters.

Based on the nature of the legal relationship, only when multiple legal relationships represent multiple contracts can the arbitral tribunal have the opportunity to adjudicate other contracts, which may result in the arbitral award rendered exceeding the arbitrable matters. With regard to the arbitration based on the contract in which its name and the actual legal relationship is inconsistent, no matter how many legal relationships are mentioned in one arbitral award, there is only one contract whose nature is determined. Under this situation, different relationships do not indicate the existence of different irrelevant contracts. Therefore, the arbitral tribunal is unable to adjudicate the matters outside the scope of one contract, and thus there exists no such issue that the arbitral award rendered thereof exceeds the scope of arbitration agreement.

In the case, Machine Tool Company filed an arbitration based on the arbitration clause in the Sales Contract. The arbitral tribunal ruled that the contract involved in the case was actually a technical service contract, and the actual legal relationship between the parties was a technical service contract dispute. The contract tried by the arbitral tribunal was still the sales contract and its appendix Technical Service Contract and did not involve any other contracts. The disputes dealt with as prescribed in the arbitration clause with the expression "any dispute arising out of the performance of this Contract or in relation to this Contract" were not beyond the scope of the arbitration clause.

---

[25] Liang Huixing (2017) General introduction to civil law, 58, 5th edn. Law Press China.

[26] (2008) Min Si Ta Zi No. 34.

8.5 Adjustment of Liquidated Damages

According to Article 585 of the Civil Code, the parties can request the court or the arbitral institution to adjust the amount of liquidated damages if the liquidated damages are lower or excessively higher than the losses incurred. However, if the parties do not make the request, can the court or the arbitral institution take the initiative to adjust the liquidated damages? In the case, the court held that it was subject to the arbitral tribunal's discretion to adjust the liquidated damage on its own initiative.

> *Hunan Lifeng Business Management Co., Ltd. v. Changsha Yangfan Real Estate Development Co., Ltd.* [27]

In May 2019, to resolve the dispute arising from the performance of the Lease Contract, Lifeng Company filed arbitration with Changsha Arbitration Commission, requesting Yangfan Company to compensate RMB 6.48 million.

On December 24, 2019, the Changsha Arbitration Commission rendered the arbitral award, ruling that Yangfan Company should compensate Lifeng Company for the losses of RMB 200,000.

Lifeng Company applied to set aside the arbitral award on the ground that the arbitral tribunal violated the statutory procedure by adjusting the amount of liquidated damages on its own.

Changsha Intermediate People's Court held that the adjustment of the amount of liquidated damages was within the discretion of the arbitral tribunal based on the faces as it deems necessary, which should not be considered procedural matters.

According to Chinese law, as far as the court is concerned, the adjustment of liquidated damages is based on the request of one party and cannot be adjusted on its own initiative. In *Guizhou Xinshengchang Real Estate Co., Ltd. v. Land and Resources Bureau of Dejiang County of Guizhou Province,* [28] the court held that the adjustment of liquidated damages should be based on the party's counterclaim or defense, and the court shall not adjudicate it on its own initiative. In *Hubei Jinliwu Real Estate Co., Ltd. v. Shenzhen Depusch Education Technology Co., Ltd.,* [29] the court held that the court shall fully respect the contract of the parties. Without the request of the parties, the court shall not take the initiative to adjust the amount of liquidated damages based on its own authorities.

The court's initiative to adjust liquidated damages may be corrected by High People's Court. In *Beijing Yuankun Law Firm v. Beijing Urban Construction Far East Construction Investment Group Co., Ltd.,* [30] the court held that the trial court of this case had clearly explained to Urban Construction Far East Co. whether it requested the court to adjust liquidated damages if it deemed it excessively high. However, the Urban Construction Far East Co. made it very clear that it did not

---

[27] (2020) Xiang 01 Min Te No. 66.

[28] (2017) Zui Gao Fa Min Shen No. 4029.

[29] (2017) Zui Gao Fa Min Shen No. 177.

[30] (2016) Jing Min Zai No. 11.

request the court to adjust the liquidated damages. Therefore, it was not appropriate for the trial court to take the initiative to adjust the agreed liquidated damages, and this court would grant the approval for a retry to correct the judgment.

The court may take the initiative to clarify when the party does not apply for adjustment of the liquidated damages. For example, the court may indicate the parties concerned by asking questions such as "Assuming the breach of contract is established, are the liquidated damages considered to be too high?" According to Article 8 of Guiding Opinions of the SPC on Several Issues concerning the Trial of Cases of Disputes over Civil and Commercial Contracts under the Current Situation,[31] in order to reduce the burden of litigation by the parties and properly resolve the disputes over liquidated damages, if the breaching party makes a defense that the contract is not signed, not yet come into effect, not valid or any other ground, but in failure of making a request for adjustment of liquidated damages, the court may clarify to this party whether it would like to make such request.

In judicial practice, both parties are often entangled in whether the contract is breached rather than whether the liquidated damages are too high or low. Where the parties do not request adjusting the amount of liquidated damages, the court can clarify whether the liquidated damages are too high or low based on the specific circumstances of the case.

However, the court has no obligation to take the initiative to explain the adjustment of liquidated damages. In *Xi'an Dapeng Biotechnology Co., Ltd. v. Shanxi Huayu Industrial Co., Ltd. and Xi'an Jingyi Property Management Co., Ltd.*,[32] the SPC held that the request for adjustment of liquidated damages is a right granted to the parties by the Contract Law, and the court cannot take the initiative to adjust liquidated damages without the request of the parties. The laws and judicial interpretations did not impose this obligation on the court.

Regarding whether the arbitral tribunal can take the initiative to adjust liquidated damages, there are no clear provisions in Chinese law. However, as this case shows, the arbitral tribunal's initiative to adjust liquidated damages is subject to the scope of its discretion, which is not a procedural matter and does not constitute a ground to set aside the arbitral award.

The applicant in the case argued that the arbitral tribunal's initiative to adjust the liquidated damages violated statutory procedures. In practice, it is common for an applicant to seek to set aside an arbitral award based on the ground that the award was beyond the arbitration agreement. For example, in the recent case *Chen v. Tang*,[33] Beijing Fourth Intermediate People's Court held that, according to the contract, Tang asked Chen to bear liabilities on the grounds of substantial breach of contract. The arbitral tribunal found that the liability for breach of contract claimed by Tang was established, but the degree of breach was not substantial and thus adjusted the amount of liquidated damages as requested by Tang. Such adjustment of the amount of liquidated damages fell within the scope of the arbitration tribunal's discretion.

---

[31] Fafa (2009) No. 40.

[32] (2014) Min Shen Zi No. 2159.

[33] (2020) Jing 04 Min Te No. 325.

Chen's assertion that the arbitral tribunal exceeding its jurisdiction was not sustained by the court.

8.6 Beyond the Scope of Arbitration

According to Article 7 of the Arrangements of the SPC on the Mutual Enforcement of Arbitral Awards by China's Mainland and Hong Kong ("the Arrangements"), beyond the scope of arbitration, also called *ultra petita*, is one of the grounds for the Mainland Courts to set aside or refuse the enforcement of an arbitral award rendered in Hong Kong. In the meantime, beyond the scope of arbitration is also one of the grounds for domestic arbitral awards being set aside or not being enforced, as well as one of the grounds for a foreign award being set aside or not be enforced by the contracting countries to New York Convention.

Beyond the scope of arbitration, from the point of its literal meaning, refers to the arbitral tribunal rendering an arbitral award beyond its power. However, according to the Arrangement and New York Convention, more than one circumstance is conducive to beyond the scope of arbitration, including: (1) The award deals with a difference not contemplated by or not falling within the terms of the submission to arbitration; and (2) The award contains decisions on matters beyond the scope of the submission to arbitration.

According to Article 58 of Arbitration Law and Article 237 of Civil Procedure Law, the circumstances are conducive to beyond the scope of arbitration, including: (1) The award deals with matters that are beyond the scope of arbitration agreement; and (2) The award deals with matters that are beyond the scope of arbitral institution authority. It is worth noting that the Chinese laws are silent in what circumstances an award contains decisions on matters beyond the scope of the submission to arbitration belongs to beyond the scope of arbitration. In judicial practice, courts may hold different views in this regard.

For example, in Reply of the SPC to the Request for Instructions on the Case Involving Wang Guolin's Application to Revoke Arbitral Award No. 3 [2012] of the China International Economic and Trade Arbitration Commission South China Sub-commission,[34] the SPC specified that the award contained decisions on matters beyond the scope of the submission to arbitration constituted beyond the scope of arbitration.

In *Ruihuan Education Investment Management Co., Ltd. v. Shanxi Dade Education Industry Development Co., Ltd. et al.*,[35] the arbitral award contained the decision on adjudicating the liquidated damages which was not claimed by the parties, and the court held that the arbitral tribunal had no power to adjudicate this matter.

---

[34] (2013) Min Si Ta Zi No. 8.
[35] (2017) Jing 02 Min Te No. 14.

In *Liu and Gao v. Zhongjing Industry (Group) Co., Ltd.,*[36] the court pointed out that the arbitral award contained decisions on matters beyond the submission to arbitration was not a ground for setting aside the award.

The Provisions of the SPC on Several Issues Concerning the Handling of Cases of Enforcement of Arbitral Awards by the People's Courts ("Enforcement Regulations") promulgated on March 1, 2018 has clarified in Article 13 that the following circumstances, once verified by the competent people's court upon examination, shall be deemed as the circumstance "where the matters decided in an arbitral award are beyond the scope of the arbitration agreement or the arbitral institution's authority" prescribed by Item (2) of Paragraph 2 of Article 237 of the Civil Procedure Law: (1) The matters decided in an arbitral award are beyond the scope of the arbitration agreement; (2) The matters decided in an arbitral award are nonarbitrable as prescribed by law or the arbitration rules chosen by the parties; (3) The decisions contained in an arbitral award are beyond the scope of the arbitration request of the party; or (4) The arbitral institution that has rendered an arbitral award is not agreed in arbitration agreement. On the basis of the enforcement regulations, the matters decided in an arbitral award are beyond the scope of the arbitration agreement and can constitute beyond the scope of arbitration in judicial review of domestic arbitral awards.

Among the four circumstances prescribed in enforcement regulation, the most common circumstance is that decisions contained in an arbitral award on matters are beyond the scope of the arbitration request of the party. An award beyond the scope of the arbitration requests can be further divided into (1) contents beyond the arbitration requests and (2) subjects beyond the arbitration requests.

First, that the contents are beyond the arbitration requests is mainly reflected in that the arbitral award exceeds the specific contents proposed by the parties in the arbitration requests. In *CHENCO Chemical Engineering and Consulting GMBH v. DFD Chemical Co., Ltd.,*[37] CHENCO Company's arbitration requests were "to stop using unauthorized technology and to pay liquidated damages for unauthorized use", but the arbitral award did not distinguish between authorized technology and unauthorized technology. Instead, the arbitral award ruled that if DFD Company continued to use the technology of CHENCO Company, it shall pay CHENCO Company liquidated damages of 100,000 euros per month on the 23rd of each month, and DFD Company cannot use CHENCO Company's technology until the amount of the liquidated damages was paid off.

In another case, *Bright Morning Limited v. Yixing Leqi Textile Group Co., Ltd.,*[38] neither of the parties mentioned anything regarding equity and its restriction and transfer in the arbitration request or the counterclaim. However, item (4) of the arbitral award ruled that "BM Company is prohibited from claiming its shareholder rights in the joint venture company, and shall transfer its equity upon request of Leqi Group Co.."

---

[36] (2018) Hu 01 Min Te No. 129.

[37] (2015) Xin Zhong Min San Chu Zi No. 53.

[38] (2016) Su 02 Xie Wai Ren No. 1.

Second, that the subjects are beyond the arbitration requests is mainly reflected in that the subjects who undertake the rights and obligations of the arbitral award are not those who are required to undertake the rights and obligation in the arbitration requests. The below case is one of those cases. If the subjects of an arbitral award required undertaking the obligations are beyond the scope of the subjects required in the arbitration requests, then this arbitral award is considered beyond the scope of arbitration and may face the risks of not being recognized, enforced or set aside.

IPCathayII L.P. v. Zhou et al.[39]

On June 30, 2011, IPCathayII L.P. entered the Class C Preferred Share Purchase Agreement ("the Agreement") with China Vocational Education Co., Ltd. ("the Target Company"), Beijing Ruiming Company, Ltd. ("Ruiming Company"), "Founders" (Zhou (1), Zhou (2), Zheng, Chen and Li) et al. IPCathayII L.P. paid a subscription payment of 10 million US dollars to purchase 87,303 Class C preferred shares of the Target Company (accounting for 5.686% of the total issued shares of the Target Company).

Article 13.1.1 of the Agreement stipulated that any disputes or claims arising from or related to this agreement or its interpretation, breach of contract, termination or validity shall be resolved in accordance with this clause. Once a dispute arises, the parties should first resolve the dispute through negotiation. Such negotiation should start within 7 days after the date when one party of this agreement submits a written request for such negotiation. If the dispute cannot be resolved within 30 days after the date of the written request, one party may submit the dispute to arbitration after sending a written notice to the other party. Article 13.1.2 stipulates that the arbitration will be conducted in HKIAC and be administered by the center.

After a dispute arose, IPCathayII L.P. filed a case against the Respondent, who was signatory to the Agreement other than Huizhi Co. who was nonsignatory. One of the arbitration claims of IPCathayII L.P. was to request the founder and/or Ruiming Company to perform the redemption or repurchase obligations under Article 9.1.1 and Article 9.1.2 of the Agreement. On August 24, 2015, the arbitral tribunal issued the HKIAC/A13027 arbitration award, ruling: (1) In terms of actual performance, the respondent of the award shall (a) repurchase all the shares of the company held by the applicant; (b) pay an investment of USD 10 million to the applicant; (c) pay the interests of the investment to the applicant (calculated at an annual interest rate of 20% from the date of initial issuance of Class C preferred stocks until the applicant receives all the money); (2) Alternatively, it is ruled that the respondents should pay the applicant the same amount of compensation as the amount listed in Article 1(b) and Article 1(c).

IPCathayII L.P. applied to the Beijing Fourth Intermediate People's Court for recognition and enforcement of the arbitration award. The respondents asserted that the arbitral award contained matters that should not be enforced under the arrange-ment. Among them, the respondents further argued that the first and second items of

---

[39] (2016) Jing 04 Ren Gang No. 2.

arbitral awards were not included inIPCathayII L.P.'s submission to arbitration and therefore should not be enforced according to Article 7 (1) (3) of the Arrangement.

The Beijing Fourth Intermediate People's Court held that 21 respondents were involved in arbitral awards. When the claimant IPCathayII L.P. filed arbitration, it only requested seven out of them to undertake redemption and repurchase obligations. However, the Item 1 and 2 of the arbitral award required all of respondents to undertake the repurchase obligations, which obviously exceeded the arbitration request made by IPCathayII L.P. The arbitral award met the circumstance stipulated in Article 7 (1) (3) of the Arrangement. Moreover, the arbitral award was rendered by taking all 21 respondents as a whole, and the matters of the award cannot be divided. Therefore, in accordance with the arrangement, the entire arbitral award should not be recognized and enforced.

This is the first case in which the Beijing Fourth Intermediate People's Court refused to recognize and enforce the HKIAC arbitral award. It reflects how Chinese courts review arbitral awards. Beyond the scope of arbitration does not mean overturning all decisions of the award. Only when decisions on matters beyond the scope of arbitration are inseparable from other arbitration matters in the award can the entire arbitral award not be enforced.

Chapter 9
Arbitral Awards and Decisions

9.1 Determination and Standards of Repeated Arbitration

The finality of arbitral awards, one of the basic characteristics of arbitration, provides a guarantee for the rapid resolution of disputes between the parties. This means that no repeated arbitration shall be allowed; that is, any party shall not apply to the arbitration institution for arbitration or bring a lawsuit to the court for disputes that have been heard and decided by the arbitral tribunal. Article 9 of the Arbitration Law stipulates that after an arbitral award is rendered, where the parties apply for arbitration or initiate an action to the people's court with respect to the same dispute, an arbitration commission or a people's court shall not accept the action.

Article 9 of the Arbitration Law is the sole provision on repeated arbitration. There is currently no clear and specific stipulation on the definition of the finality of arbitral awards and the "same dispute". Under such circumstances, does the arbitral tribunal have the power to refer to the relevant provisions of *ne bis in idem* in civil litigation when judging whether there is a repeated arbitration?

Guan v. CNBM Information Technology Co., Ltd.[1]

Guan requested to set aside the [2019] Zhong Guo Mao Zhong Jing Cai Zi No. 0089 ("No. 0089 Award") made by CIETAC. Guan's reason was that the No. 0089 Award violated Paragraph 1 of Article 9 of the Arbitration Law; that is, the No. 0089 Award violated the principle of the finality of arbitral awards. CIETAC rendered the [2017] Zhong Guo Mao Zhong Jing Cai Zi No. 1498 Award ("No. 1498 Award"), dismissing the claim of CNBM Information Technology Co., Ltd. to ask Guan to bear joint guarantee liability. The No. 1498 Award had come into effect. Regardless of any new facts, the same dispute should not be judged again. The No. 0089 Award conflicted with the finality of arbitral awards and thus should be set aside.

The Beijing Third Intermediate People's Court held that, in the No. 0089 Award, CIETAC heard the case, listing the issue raised by Guan of whether the No. 0089

---

[1] (2019) Jing 04 Min Te No. 159.

Award constituted a repeated arbitration with the No. 1489 Award and whether there is violation of the finality of arbitral awards as the core dispute. Since there was no detailed definition of the finality of arbitral awards in the laws, the arbitral tribunal referred to the standard of judging repeated litigation stipulated in Article 247 of the Civil Procedure Law Interpretation and analyzed and judged the dispute between the parties to the arbitration. Article 247 of the Civil Procedure Law Interpretation stipulated the principle and criteria of *ne bis in idem* in civil litigation. In essence, both the principle of the finality of arbitral awards and the principle of *ne bis in idem* negated the repeated litigation or arbitration the parties filed concerning the same dispute. Therefore, the reference of the arbitral tribunal was not improper. The No. 0089 Award was based on the new facts that occurred after the No. 1498 Award became legally effective, which did not violate the principle of the finality of arbitral awards. Guan's reason for Award No. 0089's violation of the principle of the finality of arbitral awards could not be supported.

Under the circumstance where there is no definition of the finality of arbitral awards and "same dispute" in the Arbitration Law, the arbitral tribunal shall have the power to refer to the relevant provisions of *ne bis in idem* in civil litigation when determining whether there is repeated arbitration. The reason is that both *bis in idem* in civil litigation and the finality of arbitral awards essentially negate the repeated litigation or arbitration the parties filed concerning the same dispute. Their purposes are to maintain *res judicata* and to prevent contradictory judgments rendered by the adjudicating institution on the same issue.

Moreover, it is common for the arbitral tribunal to refer to judicial interpretations in arbitration. For example, Article 37 of the Beijing Arbitration Commission Arbitration Rules stipulates that "when assessing any evidence, the arbitral tribunal may, in addition to referring to relevant laws, regulations and judicial interpretations, conduct its assessment by taking into consideration factors such as industry practices and trade usages, and shall consider the case in its totality."

In this case, the Beijing Third Intermediate People's Court made it clear that it was "not improper" for the arbitral tribunal to refer to the relevant provisions of *ne bis in idem*. Other courts also held the same view. For instance, in the case *Guangzhou Hongyang Bags Co., Ltd. v. Zhongshan Branch of Bohai Bank Co., Ltd.*,[2] the Guangzhou Intermediate People's Court held that "The arbitral tribunal rejected the application for arbitration of Hongyang Bags Co., Ltd. after analyzing referring to the conditions of the principle of *ne bis in idem* stipulated in Article 247 of the Civil Procedure Law Interpretation. The arbitral tribunal did not directly apply the Civil Procedure Law Interpretation, but within the scope of the arbitral tribunal to make an award *ex officio*."

For a situation to be considered repeated arbitration, the following conditions must be met: the parties in the two cases are the same, the subject matter of the arbitration are the same, the claims are the same, and there are no new facts.

Article 247 of the Civil Procedure Law Interpretation provides the criteria for a lawsuit to be deemed repeated: (1) The litigants in the latter lawsuit and the former

---

[2] (2018) Yue 01 Min Te No. 355.

lawsuit are identical; (2) The latter lawsuit and the former lawsuit have the same subject matter of lawsuit; or (3) The claims in the latter lawsuit and the former lawsuit are identical, or the claims in the latter lawsuit essentially negate the outcome of the ruling of the former lawsuit. Article 248 of the Civil Procedure Law Interpretation provides that if a litigant files another lawsuit due to the occurrence of new facts after a ruling has come into legal effect, the people's court shall accept the case pursuant to the law.

China Securities Co., Ltd. v. Yu.[3]

On September 21, 2012, Yu and China Securities Co., Ltd. concluded the Financing and Securities Lending Contract.

On June 30, 2015, Yu filed an arbitration request against China Securities Co., Ltd claiming that China Securities Co., Ltd. took mandatory liquidation measures without authorization, resulting in Yu's interruption of his investment behavior and economic losses.

The Beijing Arbitration Commission issued the (2017) Jing Zhong Cai Zi No. 1385 Award ("Former Award"), stating that the mandatory liquidation of China Securities Investment Co., Ltd. constituted negligence under the Contract in this case, and the Company should compensate Yu's losses.

Afterwards, Yu filed a request for arbitration on the ground that China Securities Co., Ltd. violated the agreement signed by the two parties by providing brokerage services in violation of laws and regulations and operating accounts on behalf of the client to extract funds, requesting China Securities Co., Ltd. to compensate for the economic losses caused by improper funds and services. The Beijing Arbitration Commission issued the (2018) Jing Zhong An Zi No. 4697 Award ("Latter Award") in support of Yu's request.

China Securities Co., Ltd. requested the court to set aside the latter Award. One of the reasons was that the latter Award in this case violated the finality of arbitral awards and the principle of *ne bis in idem*. The latter case was a repeated arbitration, and Yu's loss had been supported by the Former Award.

Regarding whether the two arbitration cases constituted repeated arbitration, the Beijing Fourth Intermediate People's Court held that repeated litigation in the sense of civil procedural law included the same parties, subject matters of lawsuit, and litigation claims. The subject matters of the two arbitration cases were not identical. The subject matter of the former arbitration was the claim for damages due to the behavior of mandatory liquidation of China Securities Co., Ltd., while the subject matter of the latter arbitration was the claim for damages due to the improper promotion and operation on behalf of customers of China Securities Co., Ltd. Therefore, the two arbitrations did not constitute repeated litigations (arbitrations) in the sense of procedural law. The ground of cancellation alleged by China Securities Co., Ltd. lacked factual or legal basis and thus shall not be upheld.

To determine whether there is repeated arbitration, we should not only focus on the facts of the case or the object of the claims, for example, whether the specific

---

[3] (2019) Jing 04 Min Te No. 439.

amounts of money requested are the same but also pay attention to whether the claims are the same. Even if the purposes of the claims are the same, the difference in legal reasons for the claim will result in different subject matters of the lawsuit. Of course, depending on the subject matters of litigation, the claims are often different. Therefore, the determination of litigation claims plays an important role in determining repeated arbitration.

"The subject matter of litigation (arbitration)" should be understood as the rights and obligations or legal relationship of the parties in substantive law. There are a variety of theories regarding the subject matter of litigation under Chinese law. Among them, the rights and obligations or legal relationship of the parties in substantive law is more in line with the actual situation of civil litigation in China. The SPC, in the cases *Liaoning Hexin Decoration Engineering Co., Ltd. v. Zhang et al.*[4] and *Li v. Lin*[5] defined the subject matter of litigation as "the relationship of civil rights and obligations in which a dispute arises between the parties and the court is requested to make a judgment in accordance with the law. It is the object of the court's trial and judgment and is also the basis for determining the cause of a civil case."

In the case at hand, there was a Financing and Securities Lending Contract between Yu and China Securities Co., Ltd. Yu filed a request for arbitration against China Securities Co., Ltd. for damages twice based on the same arbitration clause of the Contract. However, the legal relationships between Yu and China Securities Co., Ltd. in two cases were different. In the former case, Yu, based on the contractual relationship, claimed that China Securities Co., Ltd. should be liable for breach of contract for mandatory liquidation. In the latter case, Yu requested China Securities Co., Ltd. to bear tort liability due to the illegal act of China Securities Co., Ltd. of providing false statements when concluding the Contract. Accordingly, due to the difference in the subject matter of the two cases, the Beijing Third Intermediate People's Court held that the latter case did not constitute a repeated arbitration.

In judicial practice, multiple disputes arise between several parties in their transactions. Due to the difference in legal relationships between the parties in each case and the subject matter of arbitration, the latter case will not be deemed violating the principle of *ne bis in idem*. In the case *Chongqing Urban Construction Holdings (Group) Co., Ltd. v. Chongqing Qijiang Branch of Sichuan Tianxin Road and Bridge Engineering Co., Ltd.*,[6] the Chongqing First Intermediate People's Court held that "The legal relationship involved in the original case was the relationship resulting from improper gains and entrusted relationships, while the legal relationship involved in the present case was the relationship relating to credits and debt based on labor subcontracting contract, and thus the legal relationships were different. Therefore, the two cases do not belong to the "same matter" in *ne bis in idem*. This court does not support the claim of the applicant."

Similarly, if there are multiple contracts between the parties, arbitration initiated based on different contracts will naturally not constitute the same subject matter of

---

[4] (2016) Zui Gao Fa Min Zai No. 249.

[5] (2018) Zui Gao Fa Min Shen No. 3879.

[6] (2017) Yu 01 Min Te No. 761.

litigation (arbitration) due to different legal relationships. For example, in the case *Zhuzhou First General Machinery Factory of Hunan Province v. Crane Branch of Zoomlion Engineering*,[7] the claimant alleged that the dispute between the claimant's claim for processing reward and the respondent's claim for deduction of transportation expenses had been decided and the judgment had already taken effect. It violated the principle of *ne bis in idem* and constituted an illegal procedure for Changsha Arbitration Commission to continue to conduct the trial after acknowledging the outcome of the judgment of second instance rendered by the Changsha Intermediate People's Court and made an award. The respondent argued that the Yuelu District People's Court made a judgment on the matters related to the payment based on the Annual Purchase Contract signed by the two parties in 2012, and the Changsha Arbitration Commission made the award in the transportation fees in accordance with the Contracts signed by both parties in 2008, 2009 and 2010. The Yuelu District People's Court and Changsha Arbitration Commission did not hear the same matter. The Changsha Intermediate People's Court of Hunan Province agreed with the respondent.

9.2 Dismissal of Repeated Arbitration

Pursuant to Article 9 of the Arbitration Law, the arbitration commission shall not accept cases of repeated arbitration at the filing stage. However, can the arbitral tribunal dismiss the case if it discovers that the case constitutes repeated arbitration after the tribunal begins to hear the case? The Arbitration Law does not stipulate on the issue.

Shandong Charming Culture and Entertainment Management Co., Ltd. v. Goldstone China Investment 2 Co., Ltd.[8]

The Shandong Charming Culture and Entertainment Management Co., Ltd. ("Charming Company") requested the Beijing Third Intermediate People's Court to set aside [2017] Zhong Guo Mao Zhong Jing Cai Zi No. 0870 Award rendered by CIETAC. One of the grounds for cancellation was that the (2014) Zhong Guo Mao Zhong Jing Cai Zi No. 0786 Award rendered by CIETAC, which had come into effect, had determined that the statutory conditions for termination had not been met in that case, and Goldstone China Investment 2 Co., Ltd. ("Goldstone") was not entitled to terminate the contract. However, in this arbitration, Goldstone once again argued that the contract had been terminated. It violated the principle of *ne bis in idem*.

The Beijing Third Intermediate People's Court held that Goldstone changed its claims to terminate the Debt Assignment Agreement and the supplementary agreement. The arbitral tribunal accepted it based on the aforementioned reasons and the

---

[7] (2015) Chang Zhong Min Wu Zhong Zi No. 01994.
[8] (2017) Jing 04 Min Te No. 45.

arbitration rules, but the arbitral tribunal held that "There is no legal basis to support the argument that the parties can reopen their case and seek to rescind the Debt Assignment Agreement and the supplementary agreement again. Agreeing with the claimant's claim is equal to not recognizing the No. 0786 Award, which will violate the finality and legal effect of the arbitral award. Therefore, the arbitral tribunal cannot support the applicant's claim to terminate the contract, and this claim should be rejected." It could be seen that the arbitral tribunal also held that Goldstone should not again put forward a claim to terminate the contract, which violated the principle of *ne bis in idem* and thus rejected it. Obviously, the ground of Charming Company that the arbitral award violated *ne bis in idem* cannot be supported.

Regarding whether the arbitral tribunal has the power to dismiss cases of repeated arbitration, the Arbitration Law has no relevant provisions. Relevant provisions of the Civil Procedure Law may be referred to.

There are several provisions in the Arbitration Law that mention that the formulation of arbitration rules shall be in line with the relevant provisions of the Civil Procedure Law, reflecting that the Civil Procedure Law can be used for reference in arbitration. Paragraph 3 of Article 15 of the Arbitration Law stipulates that "The China Arbitration Association shall formulate arbitration rules in accordance with this Law and the Civil Procedure Law." Article 75 of the Arbitration Law provides that "The arbitration commission may formulate provisional arbitration rules in accordance with this Law and the relevant provisions of the Civil Procedure Law before the formulation of the arbitration rules by the China Arbitration Association." Article 73 of the Arbitration Law stipulates that "Foreign-related arbitration rules may be formulated by the China International Chamber of Commerce in accordance with this Law and the relevant provisions of the Civil Procedure Law."

Pursuant to the Civil Procedure Law and other provisions, the court shall not accept repeated lawsuit. If it has already been accepted, the lawsuit shall generally be rejected. Paragraph 2 of Article 247 of the Civil Procedure Law Interpretation provides that if a litigant files repeated lawsuit, the people's court shall rule on nonacceptance, and if it has been accepted, the people's court shall rule to reject the lawsuit, unless otherwise stipulated by laws or judicial interpretations.

Both nonacceptance and rejection of lawsuits result from the failure to meet the acceptance conditions. The core difference between the two lies in the different stages. The decision of nonacceptance should be made at the filing stage, and only after accepting the case is it found that the acceptance conditions are not met can the lawsuit be rejected.

Article 123 of the Civil Procedure Law stipulates that "People's courts shall protect the rights of litigants to file lawsuits pursuant to the provisions of the law. Lawsuits that comply with Article 119 of this Law shall be accepted. Article 208 of the Civil Procedure Law Interpretation provides that when a people's court receives a statement of claim from a litigant, which complies with the provision of Article 119 of the Civil Procedural Law and does not fall under the circumstances stipulated in Article 124, the people's court shall register and accept the lawsuit. When the filing falls under the circumstances stipulated in Article 124 of the Civil Procedural Law, the people's court shall rule that the lawsuit should be rejected.

The reason why the dismissal of lawsuits is stipulated in addition to nonacceptance is that the stage of review on filing at the beginning is a formal review,[9] and errors are unavoidable. Dismissal of the lawsuit can be regarded as a corrective measure. Similarly, this problem also exists in arbitration proceedings. Where there is only one party's materials and the period of review is even shorter than that of the court, which is five days after receiving the request for arbitration and other materials,[10] an arbitration commission cannot completely determine whether it constitutes repeated arbitration correctly. As a consequence, it is necessary to refer to the practice in litigation to handle the case that constitutes repeated arbitration discovered after an arbitration case has been accepted.

In the present case, the arbitration commission held that the claimant's claims violated the principle of *ne bis in idem* and rejected it. The Beijing Third Intermediate People's Court held that the ground of Charming Company that the arbitral award violated *ne bis in idem* cannot be supported.

In addition, other courts also hold the same view; that is, if the arbitral tribunal considers that the case constitutes repeated arbitration, it may rule to reject the claimant's claims.

For instance, in the case *Guangzhou Hongyang Bags Co., Ltd. v. Zhongshan Branch of Bohai Bank Co., Ltd.*,[11] The Guangzhou Intermediate People's Court held that the analysis of Guangzhou Arbitration Commission by reference to the conditions of *ne bis in idem* in accordance with Article 247 of the Civil Procedure Law Interpretation and the rejection of the arbitration application were within the scope of the arbitral tribunal to make an award *ex officio*, which does not fall within the statutory circumstances where arbitral awards may be revoked.

In the case *Shen v. Zhao* et al.,[12] the Jiaxing Intermediate People's Court of Zhejiang Province held that it was sufficient in factual and legal basis for the Jiaxing Arbitration Commission to reject the claim of claimant due to the violation of the principle of *ne bis in idem*, and there was no circumstance where arbitral awards may be revoked.

In the case *Tengxun Entertainment Co., Ltd.* et al. *v. Shanghai Tianhong Real Estate Investment Co., Ltd.*,[13] the Shanghai Second Intermediate People's Court held that "in terms of the two cases above, it was in line with the provisions of the Arbitration Law and the principles of civil litigation for the arbitral tribunal of No. 013 Award to rule that the claims of the two applicants violated the principle of

---

[9] Shen Deyong, Wan E, *Understanding and Application of Judicial Interpretation of the Arbitration Law of the Supreme People's Court*, 638 (1 ed., People's Court Press 2015).

[10] Article 24 of the Arbitration Law stipulates that "The arbitration commission shall, within 5 days from the date of the receipt of an application for arbitration, notify the parties that it considers the conditions for acceptance have been fulfilled, and that the application is accepted by it. If the arbitration commission considers that the conditions have not been fulfilled, it shall notify the parties of acceptance in writing and state its reasons.".

[11] (2018) Yue 01 Min Te No. 355.

[12] (2012) Zhe Jia Zhong Che Zi No. 2.

[13] (2015) Hu Er Zhong Min Si (Shang) Che Zi No. 58.

the finality of arbitral awards and reject them. This Court agrees with the arbitral tribunal."

In the following arbitration case, the arbitral tribunal held that the contract disputed had been determined to be valid before, and the claimant's claim to confirm the invalidity of the contract in the arbitration case was a reapplication for arbitration of the same dispute and should be rejected.

A New Energy Development Co., Ltd. v. B Technology Co., Ltd.[14]

The two parties signed a contract concerning the sales of inverters. During the performance of the contract, disputes occurred between the two parties. One party submitted the disputes to arbitration. In the arbitration case filed in 2015, the arbitral tribunal determined that the contract was valid and made an award based on the contract ("2015 Award").

In 2019, the losing party filed a request for arbitration as the claimant again. The applicant argued that the Equipment Purchase Contract and the Supplementary Contract were invalid. The reason was that the inverters provided by the respondent had major quality defects, and the respondent signed the contract by fraudulent means, which harmed the interests of the enterprise, the public interest of the state and society, violated the mandatory stipulations of laws and regulations such as Article 40 of the Product Quality Law, and thus fell within the circumstances invalidating contracts stipulated in Paragraphs 1, 4 and 5 of Article 52 of the Contract Law.

The respondent argued that the claim in this case essentially negated the result of the 2015 Award, which violated the principle of *ne bis in idem*, and thus the claimant's claim should be rejected.

In this regard, the claimant alleged that the cause of the legal relationship and the basis for the claims in this case were different from the case involved in the 2015 Award. Moreover, the facts confirmed by the 2015 Award occurred when the equipment was not put into use before the power station was connected to the grid in 2015 and only involved the payment of the goods, while the facts involved in this case were major product quality flaws and defects that occurred after the equipment was put into use after the power station was connected to the grid in 2015. This case was not an overturn of the 2015 Award but an identification of new legal facts.

The arbitral tribunal noted that Article 9 of the Arbitration Law stipulated that "The system of final and binding arbitral award shall apply to arbitration. After an arbitral award is rendered, where the parties apply for arbitration or initiate an action to the people's court in respect of the same dispute, an arbitration commission or a people's court shall not accept the action."

When judging whether the dispute involved in two cases constituted the "same dispute", the arbitral tribunal has the power to refer to the relevant provisions of "repeated litigation" in civil litigation. First, there is no definition of the finality of arbitral awards and the "same dispute" in the Arbitration Law and related judicial interpretations. Second, both the "repeated litigation" in civil litigation and the finality

---

[14] This case was administered by SCIA in 2020.

of arbitral awards in arbitration essentially negate the situation where the two parties dispute repeat litigation or arbitration of the same dispute.

Unless the party files a lawsuit based on new facts that occur after a ruling has come into legal effect, it shall be considered to be repeated litigation if the parties, subject matter of litigation and claims of the latter case are identical to those of the former case. Article 247 of the Civil Procedure Law Interpretation provides for the criteria to be satisfied. Article 248 of the Civil Procedure Law Interpretation provides for the situation where the people's court shall accept another lawsuit.

The arbitral tribunal considered that the claimant's claim to confirm the invalidity of the contracts in this case was a second application for arbitration concerning the same dispute. The reasons were as follows:

First, the parties in this case were the same as those in the case of the 2015 Award. Pursuant to the 2015 Award, the claimant in this case was the respondent in that case, the respondent in this case was the claimant in that case, and the parties to the two cases were the same.

Second, the subject matter of litigation in this case was the same as that of the 2015 Award. The arbitral tribunal held that the so-called "subject matter of litigation" referred to the rights and obligations or legal relationship of the parties in substantive law. The legal relationship of the parties and the applicable legal provisions in both cases were the same. Regardless of whether in this case or in the case of the 2015 Award, the basis of the claims requested by the party was the Equipment Procurement Contract and the Supplementary Contract signed by one party as the supplier and the other party as the purchaser, the legal relationships between the parties were relationships of sales and purchase contract, and the Contract Law and the Product Quality Law shall apply. Therefore, regardless of which relief the claimant sought, the subject matters of litigation in the two cases were identical.

Third, the claimant in this case requested confirming the invalidity of the contracts, which essentially negated the result of the 2015 Award. In the case of the 2015 Award, the respondent requested the claimant to pay the contract price and liquidated damages, whose implicit premise was that the contracts were valid. In this regard, the claimant argued in that case that the contracts were invalid on the ground that the respondent had conducted fraudulent activities that harmed the national interests. However, the claimant's defenses were not adopted. The 2015 Award held that "the contracts in this case did not violate the prohibitive provisions of laws and administrative regulations in China and should be deemed valid, and both parties should perform in accordance with the contracts." Again, the aforementioned reasons and other reasons were claimed to invalidate the contracts in the present case. Obviously, the claimant essentially denied the determination of the validity of the contracts in the 2015 Award.

Fourth, the claimant's claim that the contract was invalid was not based on new facts that occurred after the 2015 Award took effect. The so-called "new facts" should be facts that occurred after the effective ruling had come into effect, rather than facts that were not ascertained or involved in the original effective ruling, nor facts that the parties did not raise in the previous case.

The claimant claimed that the new facts in this case were major product quality flaws and defects that occurred after the equipment was put into use after the power station was connected to the grid in 2015. However, the effective date of the 2015 Award was September 16, 2015, and the claimant did not prove that it found that the equipment involved in the case had major product quality problems after September 16, 2015.

In contrast, pursuant to the Distributed Power Project Grid Connection Acceptance Opinion Form submitted by the claimant, as early as February 12, 2015, the equipment involved in the case started grid connection acceptance and passed other grid connections except for island protection tests. In addition, according to the letter sent by the claimant to the respondent on March 16, 2015, the claimant stated that "At present, our company has found that the inverters provided by your company is not operating normally, so your company is required to arrange relevant technical personnel to the project site to provide technical support within 5 working days." Moreover, the claimant mentioned in the Request for Arbitration that it "had no choice but to purchase products and installations from elsewhere to pass the inspection, but it also delayed the grid connection for more than 10 months." The date when the claimant and the third party signed a separate Procurement Contract was October 30, 2015. The claimant was able to connect to the grid at the beginning of 2015. If the equipment involved did have quality problems, the claimant had also known before the 2015 Award took effect, but the claimant did not mention this fact in the case of the 2015 Award. Therefore, the claimant's claim that there existed new facts in this case could not be upheld.

9.3 Non-enforceability Due to the Nonspecific Content of Awards

In arbitration practice, a claimant might not specify the details of performance when requesting to continue to perform the contract. If the arbitral tribunal also ignores this issue and simply decides to continue the performance of the contract, the issue of whether the award can be enforced will arise. If the award cannot be enforced, can the claimant reapply for arbitration?

Lin v. Li.[15]

Lin, the respondent in the arbitration, applied to set aside the (2016) Sui Zhong An Zi No. 7032 Arbitral Award ("2016 Award") made by Guangzhou Arbitration Commission. One of the reasons was that there was violation of the statutory prohibited procedure of *ne bis in idem*.

Lin was of the opinion that Guangzhou Arbitration Commission had issued the (2013) Sui Zhong An Zi No. 2716 Award ("2013 Award") on May 30, 2014, regarding the dispute over the House Sales Contract between the two parties, ruling

---

[15] (2017) Yue 01 Min Te No. 273.

Lin to continue to perform the contract. However, Li, the claimant in the arbitration, requested again in the latter case to: (1) Rule that Lin continue to perform the House Sales Contract, conduct the house transfer procedures for the house involved in the case and transfer the house agreed in the contract to Li within 10 days from the effective date of the award; (2) Rule that Lin deliver the real estate involved to Li within 3 days from the effective date of the award. These two claims were the refinement of the previous ruling that Lin continued to perform the contract, and they were different expressions of the same thing. Pursuant to Article 247 of the Civil Procedure Law Interpretation, the claims of Li violated the statutory prohibited procedure of *ne bis in idem*.

Li argued that this case did not violate the principle of *ne bis in idem*. With reference to Article 248 of the Civil Procedure Law Interpretation, after the 2013 Award was made, the enforcement court issued a Notice of Settlement, clearly informing that the ruling of continuing to perform the contract had no content for enforcement and thus could not be enforced. Meanwhile, in October 2016, to ensure the execution of the contract, Li took the initiative to perform the contractual obligations and paid the house payment in a lump sum to complete the payment obligation. The performance of the contract changed significantly, resulting in new facts; thus, the present case did not constitute repeated lawsuits.

Regarding whether the 2016 Award made by Guangzhou Arbitration Commission violated the principle of *ne bis in idem*, the Guangzhou Intermediate People's Court held that: First, it can be seen from the claims of Li in two cases that Li's claim in the former case was to continue to perform the contract without specific content, while Li's claim in the latter case was to conduct transfer procedures and deliver the house for use, which was specific and clear. Therefore, the claims in the two cases were not identical. Second, after the 2013 Award was issued, the People's Court of Tianhe District of Guangzhou City implemented the content of the monetary payment but held that the ruling "Lin continues to perform the House Sales Contract" did not meet the requirements for execution. Since then, Li had notarized the deposit of RMB 1.36 million of the contractual purchase price involved in the case at the Guangzhou Notary Public Office. The execution of the court and the delivery of the house payment were all new facts after the issue of the 2013 Award. Therefore, the 2016 Award made by Guangzhou Arbitration Commission did not constitute repeated arbitration and did not violate the principle of *ne bis in idem*.

The contents of the instruments that are enforceable by the court must be specific. Article 463 of the Civil Procedure Law Interpretation stipulates that "In regard to a legal document that has come into legal effect, for which a litigant applies to a people's court for enforcement, the following criteria shall be satisfied:(1) The entities of rights and obligations are specific; and (2) The contents of payment are specific. Where the legal document confirms continued performance of a contract, the specific contents for continued performance shall be specified."

If the arbitral award only rules to continue performance of the contract, but does not specify the specific contents such as the rights and obligations, the performance method, and the time limit for the continued performance, resulting in the failure to enforce, the court may reject the application for enforcement of that part.

Article 3 of the Provisions of the SPC on Several Issues Concerning the Handling of Cases of Enforcement of Arbitral Awards by the People's Courts provides for partly rejecting of enforcement of arbitral award.[16]

To determine whether Li's claim can be supported, it is necessary to clarify what is meant by repeated arbitration and new facts. As discussed above, three conditions shall be met to constitute the so-called "repeated arbitration" with reference to the stipulation of *ne bis in idem* in Article 247 of the Civil Procedure Law Interpretation: the parties in the two cases are the same, the subject matters of the litigation are the same, and the claims are the same.

In accordance with Article 248 of the Civil Procedure Law Interpretation, the occurrence of new facts is an exception that meets those conditions but does not constitute repeated arbitration. Regarding the definition of new facts, the SPC had pointed out in the case *Wu (1) v. Wu (2)*[17] that "'New facts' should be facts that occurred after the effective ruling had come into effect, rather than facts that were not ascertained or involved in the original effective ruling, nor facts that the parties did not raise in the previous case."

In this case, Li claimed that the award was held as unenforceable by the enforcement court after the 2013 Award took effect, which satisfied the aforementioned requirement on time. Moreover, this fact was not ascertained by the original Award. In view of this, the Guangzhou Intermediate People's Court held that the enforcement of the enforcement court was a new fact, and thus, the 2016 Award did not constitute repeated arbitration.

It is noteworthy that the ambiguity of the content of the award is not the only reason why the award cannot be enforced. If the enforcement cannot be carried out for other reasons, the parties' reapplication for arbitration will not violate the principle of *ne bis in idem*.

For instance, in the case *Shanghai Miao Ma Car Rental Co., Ltd. v. Le,*[18] the Shanghai First Intermediate People's Court, held that "Although the parties involved in the (2016) Hu Zhong An Zi No. 1297 Case and the present case were the same, and the claims of Le both include the claim to ask Shanghai Miao Ma Car Rental

---

[16] Article 3 provides: Where an arbitral award or mediation statement has any of the following circumstances, resulting in failure of enforcement, the people's court may make a ruling of rejecting the application for enforcement. In the case of failure of enforcement of a part of the arbitral award or mediation statement, the people's court may make a ruling of rejecting the application for enforcement of such part. In the case of failure of enforcement of a part of the arbitral award or mediation statement, and such part is inseparable from other parts, the people's court may make a ruling of rejecting the application for enforcement: (1) The subject of rights and obligations are not clear;(2) The specific amount of payment is not clear or the calculation method is not clear, resulting that the specific amount cannot be figured out;(3) The particular thing to be delivered is not clear or cannot be determined; or(4) The standard, target and scope of performance of action are not clear.If the arbitral award or mediation statement only determines to continue to perform the contract, but does not specify such specific contents as the rights and obligations that are continued to be performed, the specific method of performance and the deadline, etc., resulting in the failure of enforcement, the case shall be handled under the provisions of the preceding paragraph.

[17] (2018) Zui Gao Fa Min Shen No. 5058.

[18] (2018) Hu 01 Min Te No. 471.

Co., Ltd. to return the purchase price, a new fact occurred after the (2016) Hu Zhong An Zi No. 1633 Award became legally effective, that is, during the process of the enforcement of (2016) Hu Zhong An Zi No. 1633 Award, the vehicle could not be forcibly transferred to Le due to the reasons of relevant departments. Le filed a request for arbitration based on the new fact, which did not constitute the situation of 'two suits on the same matter'". The acceptance of the Shanghai Arbitration Commission of the case and the issue of an award did not violate the principle of *ne bis in idem*.

9.4 Consequences of Revocation or Non-enforcement of Awards

Paragraph 2 of Article 9 of the Arbitration Law and Paragraph 5 of Article 237 of the Civil Procedure Law stipulate the parties' right to litigate after a court has ruled that the arbitral award shall be revoked or not enforced.

Specifically, Paragraph 2 of Article 9 of the Arbitration Law stipulates that "If the arbitral award is canceled or is not enforced as rendered by a people's court in accordance with the law, the parties may, in accordance with a new arbitration agreement between them in respect of the dispute, apply for arbitration or initiate legal proceedings with the people's court." Paragraph 5 of Article 237 of the Civil Procedure Law states that "If the arbitral award is not enforced as rendered by a people's court, the parties may, in accordance with a new arbitration agreement in written between them, apply for arbitration or initiate legal proceedings with the people's court."

Qingdao Yonghong Sports Tourism Resort Co., Ltd. v. Natural Resources Bureau of Huangdao District of Qingdao City.[19]

On September 25, 2016, Qingdao Yonghong Sports Tourism Resort Co., Ltd. ("Qingdao Yonghong Company") submitted a Request for Arbitration to Qingdao Arbitration Commission in accordance with the arbitration clause in the Assignment Contract of Right of Use of State-owned Land signed with Natural Resources Bureau of Huangdao District of Qingdao City ("Natural Resources Bureau").

After the Qingdao Arbitration Commission made an arbitral award in accordance with the law, the Natural Resources Bureau refused to perform the arbitral award, and thus Qingdao Yonghong Company applied to the Qingdao Intermediate People's Court of Shandong Province ("Qingdao Intermediate People's Court") for enforcement.

The Qingdao Intermediate People's Court ruled to reject the application for enforcement of the first item of the arbitral award on the ground that the standard of performance, objects, scope of the item of the arbitral award were not clear, specific, and not enforceable. Qingdao Yonghong Company was unsatisfied with the Ruling

---

[19] (2019) Zui Gao Fa Min Zhong No. 1893.

and applied for reconsideration, which was also rejected by the Qingdao Intermediate People's Court.

Afterwards, Qingdao Yonghong Company filed a lawsuit with the High People's Court of Shandong Province, which was rejected by the (2018) Lu Min Chu No. 223 Civil Ruling issued by the High People's Court of Shandong Province.

Dissatisfied with the Ruling, Qingdao Yonghong Company appealed to the SPC, requesting revoking the original Ruling and instructing the High People's Court of Shandong Province to hear the case. The facts and reasons on which the appeal was based were as follows.

On the one hand, it was an error in the application of law for the court of first instance to reject Qingdao Yonghong Company's lawsuit. First, the original arbitration clause was not binding on this case. The dispute in this case arose from Qingdao Yonghong Company's request for the Natural Resources Bureau to pay the repurchase price and the loss of delayed payment. The two parties did not reach an arbitration clause on the issue of land repurchase. Second, even if this case was bound by the original arbitration clause, since the Natural Resources Bureau did not raise an objection, the court should continue to hear the case. Third, because the main contents of the award could not be implemented, the dispute between the two parties could not be fundamentally resolved. Under such circumstances, Qingdao Yonghong Company was entitled to seek relief through litigation procedures in accordance with Paragraph 2 of Article 9 of the Arbitration Law. Fourth, it was wrong in the application of law for the court of first instance to reject the lawsuit of Qingdao Yonghong Company on the ground of the existence of the arbitration clause after the acceptance of the case.

On the other hand, since the repurchase of right of use of land involved in the case was the result of the agreement of the parties and not an administrative act, it was improper for the court of first instance to characterize the repurchase as a governmental act and rejected the lawsuit on this ground.

The SPC was of the opinion that since Qingdao Yonghong Company and Natural Resources Bureau did not conclude an arbitration agreement, Qingdao Yonghong Company may file a lawsuit with the people's court in accordance with Paragraph 2 of Article 9 of the Arbitration Law. Moreover, after Qingdao Yonghong Company filed a lawsuit, the Natural Resources Bureau did not raise any objection to the acceptance of the case by the court of first instance before the first hearing. Pursuant to Article 26 of the Arbitration Law, the court of first instance shall continue to hear the case. Therefore, the SPC revoked the original Ruling and ordered the High People's Court of Shandong Province to hear the case.

The core issue in the present case is whether the parties can initiate legal proceedings with the people's court after the court rules that the arbitral award shall not be enforced. In the case at hand, the first item of the arbitral award was ruled not to be enforced by the Qingdao Intermediate People's Court. Dissatisfied with the Ruling, Qingdao Yonghong Company applied for reconsideration, which was rejected by the Qingdao Intermediate People's Court. The SPC considered that, under such circumstance, Qingdao Yonghong Company was entitled to file a lawsuit with the court in accordance with Paragraph 2 of the Arbitration Law, and the court of first instance should not reject the lawsuit of Qingdao Yonghong Company on the ground of the arbitration clause in the Contract.

Similarly, in the case of *Inner Mongolia Huineng Coal Chemical Co., Ltd. v. Shanghai Blower Works Co., Ltd.*,[20] the two parties agreed in the Procurement Contract that disputes shall be arbitrated by Ordos Arbitration Commission. After the parties resorted to arbitration, the arbitral award made by the Ordos Arbitration Commission was revoked by the Ordos Intermediate People's Court. The court finally determined that Inner Mongolia Huineng Coal Chemical Co., Ltd. had the right to file a lawsuit with the court in accordance with Paragraph 2 of Article 9 of the Arbitration Law.

It is worth mentioning that numbers of disputes may arise under a contract. For disputes that have been arbitrated under the contract, the parties can either reach an arbitration agreement again or bring a lawsuit to the court. However, for other disputes that have not been arbitrated under the contract, can the parties absolutely apply for arbitration based on the original arbitration agreement?

With regard to this issue, the Tongchuan Intermediate People's Court held in the case *Wang v. Liu*[21] that "Under normal circumstances, for other disputes that have not been arbitrated through arbitration under the contract, the parties may apply for arbitration based on the original arbitration agreement or arbitration clause. However, if multiple claims of the parties under the same contract are inseparable and the arbitral award concerning one of the disputes is revoked by the people's court in accordance with the law, the court may also hear other indivisible related disputes if the parties file a lawsuit with the people's court in accordance with Paragraph 2 of Article 9 of the Arbitration Law."

The case *Wang v. Liu* fell within the circumstance where the disputes were inseparable. In that case, the arbitral award that was revoked by the court involved a rent payment dispute. Liu's request in the lawsuit was to cancel the House Lease Contract signed by both parties and to order Wang to pay rent and house occupancy fees. The court held that the request for termination of the contract was inseparable from the payment of rent and house occupancy fees and other matters, and thus the court can handle the case together.

In addition, do Paragraph 2 of Article 9 of the Arbitration Law and Paragraph 5 of Article 237 of the Civil Procedure Law apply to the situation where the results of judicial review on the same arbitral award made by different courts are completely different?

In the case *Huatong Electromechanical Group Co., Ltd. v. Ye*,[22] Ye applied to the Wenzhou Intermediate People's Court of Zhejiang Province to revoke the arbitral-ruling and the application was rejected. However, when Huatong Electromechanical Group Co., Ltd. applied to the Heze Intermediate People's Court of Shandong Province to enforce the arbitral award, Ye filed an objection based on the same reason, and the court ruled not to enforce the award. The High People's Court of Zhejiang

---

[20] (2017) Nei 06 Min Zhong No. 1144.

[21] (2017) Shan 02 Min Zhong No. 218.

[22] (2017) Zhe Min Zai No. 345.

Province held that this situation was not completely consistent with the situation stipulated in Paragraph 2 of Article 9 of the Arbitration Law and Paragraph 5 of Article 237 of the Civil Procedure Law and that the Heze Intermediate People's Court of Shandong Province had initiated the trial supervision procedure and the rights and interests of Huatong Electromechanical Group Co., Ltd. could be remedied through this procedure. Therefore, it was ruled that the original ruling to reject the lawsuit should be maintained.

9.5 Cancellation of Mediation Statement

Pursuant to Article 51 of the Arbitration Law, a mediation statement is a document produced by the arbitral tribunal with the same legal effect as the arbitral award after the parties reach an agreement through the mediation of the arbitral tribunal during the arbitration process. However, the Arbitration Law[23] only provides for certain circumstances in which an arbitral award can be revoked and does not specify whether the mediation statement can be revoked. Therefore, the issue arises: do the parties have the right to apply for cancellation of the mediation statement?

Xinyu Zhongchuang Mining Co., Ltd. v. Ganxi Geological and Mineral Exploration and Development Institute of Jiangxi Geological Exploration Bureau.[24]

After disputes between Xinyu Zhongchuang Mining Co., Ltd. ("Zhongchuang Company") and Ganxi Geological and Mineral Exploration and Development Institute of Jiangxi Geological Exploration Bureau ("Ganxi Development Institute") arose, Zhongchuang Company submitted disputes to the Xinyu Arbitration Commission for arbitration.

The Xinyu Arbitration Commission issued the Yu Zhong Tiao Zi [2018] No. 16 Mediation Statement on July 25, 2018, confirming the settlement agreement reached by both parties on the same day. Afterwards, Zhongchuang Company applied to the Xinyu Intermediate People's Court of Jiangxi Province to cancel the Mediation Statement.

---

[23] Article 58 of the Arbitration Law stipulates that "The parties may apply to the intermediate people's court at the place where the arbitration commission is located for cancellation of an award if they provide evidence proving that the award involves one of the following circumstances: (1) there is no arbitration agreement between the parties; (2) the matters of the award are beyond the extent of the arbitration agreement or not under the jurisdiction of the arbitration commission; (3) the composition of the arbitral tribunal or the arbitration procedure is in contrary to the legal procedure; (4) the evidence on which the award is based is falsified; (5) the other party has concealed evidence which is sufficient to affect the impartiality of the award; or (6) the arbitrators have demanded or accepted bribes, committed graft or perverted the law in making the arbitral award. The people's court shall rule to cancel the award if the existence of one of the circumstances prescribed in the preceding clause is confirmed by its collegiate bench.The people's court shall rule to cancel the award if it holds that the award is contrary to the social and public interests.".

[24] (2019) Gan Min Te No. 2.

The Xinyu Intermediate People's Court considered that the Mediation Statement was a legal document produced by the arbitration institution in accordance with the agreement reached by both parties voluntarily, was the result of the unanimous expression of the true intentions of both parties, and was legally binding and effective. The Arbitration Law only stipulated the specific circumstances under which the parties can apply to the people's court to revoke the arbitral award. The party's application for revoking the Mediation Statement lacked a legal basis and did not fall within the scope of the people's court of accepting cases. Therefore, the Xinyu Intermediate People's Court issued the (2019) Gan 05 Min Te No. 18 Civil Ruling, ruling to reject the application of Zhongchuang Company.

Dissatisfied with the Ruling, Zhongchuang Company made an appeal to the High People's Court of Jiangxi Province, requesting revoking the Ruling made by the Xinyu Intermediate People's Court and revoking the Mediation Statement rendered by the Xinyu Arbitration Commission.

Zhongchuang Company claimed that the application for revocation of the Mediation Statement fell within the scope of the court of accepting cases Pursuant to Paragraph 2 of Article 51 of the Arbitration Law. When a settlement agreement is reached by mediation, the arbitral tribunal shall produce the mediation statement or the award on the basis of the results of the settlement agreement, and a mediation statement shall have the same legal force as that of an award. On this basis, after the parties reached a mediation agreement, the arbitral tribunal could choose to make a mediation statement or an award. The mediation statement or award was the same as the settlement method of mediation in the arbitration. They were just different in their titles, but they had the same legal effect. Since the Arbitration Law stipulated that the parties who disagreed with the arbitral award could apply for cancellation, the parties who disagreed with the mediation statement could also apply for cancellation in accordance with legal principles and legislative intents. The procedures and applicable laws followed by the court when conducting judicial review on the mediation statement shall comply with the relevant legal provisions for judicial review on the arbitral award. Therefore, the application for revocation of the mediation statement shall be within the scope of the court of accepting cases. Judging from the legislative intents of the Civil Procedure Law and the Arbitration Law and the judicial practice of the SPC and some local courts in recent years, it was also recognized that the mediation statement was subject to revocation.

The Ganxi Development Institute replied that the application for revocation of the mediation statement did not fall within the scope of the court of accepting cases. Although Paragraph 2 of Article 51 of the Arbitration Law stipulated that the mediation statement had the same legal effect as the award, the documents that could be ruled to be revoked were the arbitral award made by the arbitration institution, rather than the mediation statement in accordance with Paragraph 1 of Article 58 of the Arbitration Law. There was no legal basis for Zhongchuang Company to apply for revocation of the mediation statement. Meanwhile, Article 17 of the Arbitration Law Interpretation stipulated that "Where a party applies to set aside an arbitral award for reasons that are not stipulated in Article 58 of the Arbitration Law or Article 258 of the Civil Procedural Law, the people's court shall not uphold the application." Article

28 of the Arbitration Law Interpretation stated that "If a party requests not to execute the mediation statement or the arbitral award made in accordance with the settlement agreement between the parties, the people's court shall not support it." It could be seen from these provisions that the current laws, regulations and judicial interpretations had adopted a strict attitude to the parties' application to cancel the mediation statement, that is, without an explicit legal basis, the application for cancellation of the mediation statement did not fall within the scope of the court of accepting cases. Finally, the mediation statement was the result of the autonomy of the parties and was binding on both parties. The application of Zhongchuang Company to revoke the mediation statement was a waste of judicial resources and caused burdensome litigation. The reduction of the court's intervention in the autonomy of the parties was more conducive to saving judicial resources and achieving the effect of dropping suits and settling disputes.

Regarding the issue, the High People's Court of Jiangxi Province considered that Article 51 of the Arbitration Law stipulated that "Before rendering an award, an arbitral tribunal may first attempt to conciliate. If the parties apply for mediation voluntarily, the arbitral tribunal shall conduct mediation. If mediation is unsuccessful, an award shall be made promptly. When a settlement agreement is reached by mediation, the arbitral tribunal shall produce the mediation statement or the award on the basis of the results of the settlement agreement. A mediation statement shall have the same legal force as that of an award." It can be viewed that both mediation statements and arbitral awards were methods for arbitration to handle disputes. If the parties raised objections to the legality of the mediation statement, the people's court should accept such cases and conduct procedural review with reference to the relevant provisions on applications for revocation of arbitral awards. Therefore, it was improper for the court of first instance to rule out that the case did not fall within the scope of the people's court of accepting cases and did not hear the case accordingly. The Ruling should be corrected. Consequently, the High People's Court of Jiangxi Province ruled to revoke the (2019) Gan 05 Min Te No. 18 Civil Ruling made by the Xinyu Intermediate People's Court and ordered the Xinyu Intermediate People's Court to hear the case.

Regarding whether the parties have the right to apply for cancellation of the mediation statement, that is, the admissibility of the application for cancellation of the mediation statement, there are two different views in judicial practice.

One of the views is the opinion held by the Xinyu Intermediate People's Court and Ganxi Development Institute in this case. It is believed that Article 58 of the Arbitration Law is only applicable to the circumstance in which the parties apply for revocation of the arbitral award and does not include the application for revocation of the mediation statement. Therefore, there is no legal basis for the parties to apply for cancellation of the mediation statement, and the people's court should not accept the application.

This view was also reflected in the Research Opinion of the Research Office of the SPC on whether the people's court should accept the litigation filed by the parties to cancel the mediation statement.[25] The main reasons included:

(1)　The issue of whether the people's court should accept certain types of cases involved the exercise of the judicial power of the people's court, and there should be an explicit legal basis. If the law did not authorize the people's court to exercise the power to cancel the mediation statement, the people's court shall not exercise it beyond the legal provisions.

(2)　From the perspective of reducing interference in the autonomy of the parties and adhering to the principle of limited judicial supervision of arbitration, strict restrictions should be adopted for the circumstances in which the parties apply to revoke the mediation statement; that is, the people's court should not accept such a case without an explicit legal basis.

(3)　From the perspective of the design of the system, Article 52 of the Arbitration Law stipulated that "If the parties fall back on their words before the mediation statement is signed and accepted by them, an award shall be made by the arbitral tribunal promptly." If there are specific circumstances with the award, the parties could apply for revocation or non-enforcement in accordance with Article 58 of the Arbitration Law and Article 237 of the Civil Procedure Law. Article 17 of the Provisions of the SPC on Several Issues Concerning the Handling of Cases of Enforcement of Arbitral Awards by the People's Courts also empowered the parties to apply for non-enforcement of the mediation statement when the mediation statement violated social public interests. Therefore, the current regulations had already achieved a balance between adequately relieving the parties and maintaining the efficiency requirements of arbitration as an independent dispute resolution method.

Additionally, in judicial practice, many courts also agree with this view, and the application filed by the parties to cancel the mediation statement is often ruled to be rejected or nonaccepted. These cases are shown in Table 9.1.

Another view is that although the Arbitration Law does not stipulate whether the mediation statement can be revoked, it should be reviewed by reference to the provisions of the application for revoking an arbitral award. The main reasons are as follow:

On the one hand, in accordance with Article 51 of the Arbitration Law, the mediation statement, which has the same impact on the parties as the arbitral award, may determine the rights and obligations between the parties and can be enforced by the court. It constitutes different treatments of two legal documents with the same effect if the parties are not allowed to apply to the people's court for judicial review on the mediation statement, while they can only apply for judicial review on the arbitral award, which will obviously damage the systematization of law.

On the other hand, Article 17 of the Provisions of the SPC on Several Issues Concerning the Handling of Cases of Enforcement of Arbitral Awards by the People's

---

[25] Published in Shen Deyong, *Judicial Research and Guidance*, Vol. 2 (People's Court Press 2012).

Table 9.1

No	Applicant	Respondent	Court	Case number	Result(s)
1	Cui	Xu	High People's Court of Shandong Province	(2017) Lu Min Zhong No. 659	Dismissal of the prosecution and the appeal
2	Hongtai Real Estate Development Co., Ltd. of Hanzhong City	Hanshui Construction Engineering Co., Ltd. of Hanzhong City	Hanzhong Intermediate People's Court	(2017) Shan 07 Min Te No. 5	Dismissal of the prosecution
3	Li	Liu	High People's Court of Shanxi Province	(2016) Jin Min Zhong No. 438	Nonacceptance of the prosecution and dismissal of the appeal
4	Li	Ma et al.	Zhaotong Intermediate People's Court	(2018) Yun 06 Min Zhong No. 1441	Dismissal of the prosecution and the appeal
5	Lishui Liming Specialized Middle School	Luo et al.	Lishui Intermediate People's Court	(2017) Zhe 11 Min Te No. 3	Dismissal of the application
6	Ren et al.	Neihuang Forest Farm of Henan	Anyang Intermediate People's Court	(2015) An Zhong Min Yi Chu Zi No. 87	Dismissal of the application
7	Wei	Liu	Huaibei Intermediate People's Court	(2016) Wan 06 Min Te No. 13	Dismissal of the prosecution
8	Xiaoyi Jinda Coal Coke Co., Ltd.	Wu	High People's Court of Shanxi Province	(2015) Jin Min Zhong Zi No. 416	Dismissal of the application and the appeal
9	Qin	Li	High People's Court of Hubei Province	(2015) E Min Li Shang Zi No. 00337	Nonacceptance of the prosecution and dismissal of the appeal
10	Zhejiang XX Construction Engineering Co., Ltd.	Zhejiang XX Clothing Co., Ltd.	High People's Court of Zhejiang Province	(2012) Zhe Min Zai Zi No. 49	Nonacceptance of the prosecution and dismissal of the appeal

Courts stipulates that "The people's court shall not support the application of the person subject to enforcement for non-enforcement of the mediation statement or arbitral award made in accordance with the mediation agreement and conciliation agreement between the parties, with the exception that the mediation statement or the arbitral award violates social public interests." With reference to the non-enforcement of the mediation statement, the parties should also be allowed to apply for cancellation of the mediation statement.

In addition, in its Reply to the Request for Instructions on the Case Concerning the Application of Nanfang International Leasing Co., Ltd. for Cancellation of the (2007) Shen Zhong Tiao Zi No. 20–1 Supplementary Mediation Statement made by Shenzhen Arbitration Commission,[26] the SPC held that "With regard to Shenzhen Arbitration Commission's act of correcting the [2007] Shen Zhong Tiao Zi No. 20 Mediation Statement by the [2007] Shen Zhong Tiao Zi No. 20–1 Corrected Mediation Statement, the review shall be conducted by reference to the provisions concerning the correction of the award in the Arbitration Law and the Arbitration Rules of Shenzhen Arbitration Commission", and set aside the Corrected Mediation Statement in that case in accordance with the provisions of Article 70 of the Arbitration Law[27] on the ground that there existed the circumstance specified in Item 3, Paragraph 1 of Article 258 of the Civil Procedure Law.[28] It can be seen from this Reply that the SPC seems to be inclined to review applications for revocation of mediation statement by referring to the provisions on applications for revocation of arbitral awards.

There are also several relevant cases holding this view. These cases are shown in Table 9.2.

Among them, it is worth noting that even if the admissibility of the application for revocation of the mediation statement is recognized, different courts hold different views on whether the person not involved in the case has the right to apply for the cancellation of the mediation statement.

---

[26] (2010) Min Si Ta Zi No. 45.

[27] Article 70 of the Arbitration Law stipulates that "A people's court shall, after examination and verification by its collegiate bench, rule to cancel an award if a party to the case provides evidence proving that the arbitral award involves one of the circumstances prescribed in Paragraph 1, Article 260 of the Civil Procedure Law.".

[28] The Article was changed to Article 274 when amending the Civil Procedure Law in 2017, which stipulates that "For an arbitral award made by a foreign-related arbitration organization of the People's Republic of China, where the respondent presents evidence to prove that the arbitral award falls under any of the following circumstances, upon examination and verification by the collegiate formed by the people's court that the assertion is true, the people's court shall rule on non-enforcement: (1) The parties concerned have not included an arbitration clause in the contract or reached a written arbitration agreement subsequently; (2) The respondent has not received a notice from the designated arbitrators or notice on arbitration procedure, or the respondent is unable to make representation due to any reason not attributable to the respondent; (3) The composition of the arbitral tribunal or the arbitration procedure does not comply with the arbitration rules; or (4) The arbitration matter does not fall under the scope of the arbitration agreement or the arbitration organization has no right to carry out arbitration. Where a people's court deemed that enforcement of the arbitral award violates public interest, the people's court shall rule on non-enforcement.".

Table 9.2

No	Applicant	Respondent	Court	Case number	Result(s)
1	Zunyi Oriental Construction and Installation Co., Ltd.	Guizhou Zhongjie New Energy Development Co., Ltd.	High People's Court of Guizhou Province	(2018) Qian Min Zhong No. 1149	The application was rejected in the first instance, and the court of second instance considered that the procedural review should be conducted in accordance with the relevant provisions of the application for revocation of the arbitral award, and ruled to revoke the original ruling and instruct the court of first instance to retry
2	Han	Jin	Jilin Intermediate People's Court	(2015) Ji Zhong Min Zhong Zi No. 4	The applicant's application was rejected because the applicant failed to provide evidence to prove that there existed the circumstances specified in Article 58 of the Arbitration Law with the mediation statement involved

(continued)

(continued)

No	Applicant	Respondent	Court	Case number	Result(s)
3	Liao	/	High People's Court of Guangdong Province	(2018) Yue Min Zhong No. 1868	The court of first instance did not accept the application, and the court of second instance considered that the mediation statement could be included in the scope of judicial review. However, the applicant in this case was a person not involved in the case and did not have the right to apply for revocation of the arbitral award or the mediation statement, so the appeal was rejected and the original ruling was maintained
4	Residents Committee of Lianhu Community, Dongdajie Street Office, Hantai District	Hanzhong Hongtai Real Estate Development Co., Ltd., et al.	Hanzhong Intermediate People's Court	(2017) Shan 07 Min Te No. 16	The court of first instance rejected the claims, and the court of second instance ruled to revoke part of the mediation statement
5	Wang	Hanzhong Hongtai Real Estate Development Co., Ltd., et al	Hanzhong Intermediate People's Court	(2017) Shan 07 Min Te No. 15	The court of first instance rejected the claims, and the court of second instance ruled to revoke part of the mediation statement

(continued)

(continued)

No	Applicant	Respondent	Court	Case number	Result(s)
6	Chen	Zeng	Shenzhen Intermediate People's Court	(2015) Shen Zhong Fa She Wai Zhong Zi No. 154	The court ruled to revoke the mediation statement involved
7	Ningming County Jiade Jinghua Real Estate Co., Ltd	Fourth Construction Engineering Company of Dianbai County, Guangdong Province	Guangzhou Intermediate People's Court	(2017) Yue 01 Min Te No. 792	The court ruled to revoke the mediation statement involved
8	Zhuhai Guojia Education Investment Co., Ltd	Zhuhai Campus of Beijing Normal University	Zhuhai Intermediate People's Court	(2014) Zhu Zhong Fa Min Si Zhong Zi No. 7	The applicant's application was rejected because the applicant failed to provide evidence to prove that there existed the circumstances specified in Article 58 of the Arbitration Law with the mediation statement involved

For example, in the cases *Liao v. Wen* et al.[29] and *Shanxi Ruida Real Estate Development Co., Ltd. v. Dacheng Property Management Co.*,[30] the courts held that the subjects who may apply for revocation of the arbitral award or mediation statement were limited to the parties, that is, the claimant and the respondent who participated in the arbitration procedure, and the person not involved in the case who did not participate in the arbitration procedure had no right to apply for the cancellation of the arbitral award or mediation statement. If the person not involved in the case believed that the mediation statement was wrong and damaged his civil rights and interests, he may apply to the people's court for non-enforcement of the mediation statement in accordance with the Provisions of the SPC on Several Issues Concerning the Handling of Cases of Enforcement of Arbitral Awards by the People's Courts.

In contrast, in the cases *Residents Committee of Lianhu Community of Dongdajie Street Office of Hantai District v. Hanzhong Hongtai Real Estate Development Co., Ltd.*, et al.[31] and *Wang v. Hanzhong Hongtai Real Estate Development Co., Ltd.*, et al.,[32] the courts held that the person not involved in the case had the *standing* to apply for the cancellation of the mediation statement, and ruled to cancel part of the mediation statement in accordance with Item 2 of Article 52 of the Contract Law and Item 5, Paragraph 1 of Article 58 of the Arbitration Law.

Specifically, Item 2 of Article 52 of the Contract Law stipulated that "In any one of the following situations, a contract shall be without effect: ......(2) the contract involves a malicious conspiracy which is detrimental to the interests of the State, a collective or a third party;" In the two cases above, the courts held that the respondents had reached a settlement agreement to compensate the construction fund for the disputed house in this case when the respondents knew that the applicant had contractual rights and interests in the house involved in the case, which harmed the applicant's legitimate rights and interests, and thus the part of the settlement agreement to use the house to pay off the debt of Hongtai Co. was invalid.

Pursuant to Item 5, Paragraph 1 of Article 58 of the Arbitration Law, if the party provides evidence proving that the other party has concealed evidence that is sufficient to affect the impartiality of the award, it may apply to the intermediate people's court at the place where the arbitration commission is located for cancellation of an award, the people's court shall rule to cancel the award if the existence of one of the circumstances prescribed in the preceding clause is confirmed by its collegiate bench. In the cases above, the courts held that the respondents deliberately concealed to the arbitral tribunal that it had signed relevant agreements on the disputed house with the applicant, which caused the arbitration commission to make an incorrect mediation statement. Therefore, the invalid part of the mediation statement should be revoked.

---

[29] (2018) Yue Min Zhong No. 1868.

[30] (2018) Shan Min Zhong No. 628.

[31] (2017) Shan 07 Min Te No. 16.

[32] (2017) Shan 07 Min Te No. 15.

In summary, current laws in China have not yet clarified whether the parties and the person not involved in the case are entitled to apply to the court to revoke the mediation statement. There are different approaches in practice, which require further clarification by legislations or judicial interpretations to enhance certainty. If the parties reach an agreement through mediation organized by the arbitral tribunal, they must carefully choose the settlement document.

9.6 Application of Persons Not Involved in the Case of Non-enforcement of the Arbitral Award

The application for non-enforcement of arbitral awards by persons not involved in the case was first stipulated in the Provisions of the SPC on Several Issues Concerning the Handling of Cases of Enforcement of Arbitral Awards by the People's Courts. Prior to this, in accordance with the provisions of Article 63 of the Arbitration Law and Article 237 of the Civil Procedure Law, only the respondent against the enforcement has the right to apply for non-enforcement of the arbitral award, and the persons not involved in the case have no right to apply for non-enforcement of the arbitral award. In addition, due to the confidentiality of arbitration and the finality of the arbitral award, it is difficult for persons not involved in the case of seeking relief when faced with false arbitration that harms their interests.

In judicial practice, to protect the interests of persons not involved in the case in good faith from false arbitration, some courts have continuously tried to explore to break through the restriction that persons not involved in the case may not apply for non-enforcement of arbitral awards.

For example, the High People's Court of Shanxi Province formulated the Provisions on the Trial of Certain Issues Involving Domestic Civil and Commercial Arbitration Cases (for Trial Implementation) in 2010. Article 28 and Article 29 of the Provisions stipulate that the person not involved in the case may apply to the people's court for non-enforcement if he claims rights to the subject matter of execution determined by the arbitral award or mediation statement, and the court shall form a collegial panel to review.

In the case *Guo v. Jiangsu Horse Club Real Estate Co., Ltd.*,[33] the High People's Court of Jiangsu Province considered that malicious arbitration not only harmed the interests of third parties but also hindered the implementation of the law and the judicial order. The courts should not be subject to the limitations of the current laws but should apply Paragraph 3 of Article 58 of the Arbitration Law and Paragraph 3 of Article 237 of the Civil Procedure Law (that is, the composition of the arbitral tribunal or the arbitration procedure violated legal procedures) by analogy and should not confirm the validity of the arbitral award based on the violation of social public interests.

---

[33] (2014) Su Min Zhong Zi No. 203.

In the (2014) Zhu Zhong Fa Min Si Zhi Zhong Zi No. 1 and No. 2 Rulings, the Zhuhai Intermediate People's Court also ruled not to enforce the Zhu Zhong Cai Zi (2013) No. 145 Award on the ground that the parties to the arbitration had maliciously colluded to damage the lawful rights and interests of others and the execution of the arbitral award would obviously violate social public interests.

However, the impact of individual courts is limited. To prevent and combat false arbitration more effectively, the SPC issued the Provisions of the SPC on Several Issues Concerning the Handling of Cases of Enforcement of Arbitral Awards by the People's Courts on February 23, 2018, which took effect on March 1, 2018.

The provisions created a system for the non-enforcement of arbitral awards by persons not involved in the case. Specifically, the provisions provide stipulations on the legal effects, procedural elements, examination form, examination period, substantive elements, and remedies after the ruling made by the court, as well as disposal of the dispute after the award was ruled not to be enforced.

Among them, the procedural elements include: (1) There is evidence to prove that the party to the arbitration case maliciously applies for arbitration or fictitious arbitration, undermining its legitimate rights and interests; (2) The subject matter of enforcement involved in the lawful rights and interests claimed by the person not involved in the case has not yet been enforced and concluded; and (3) The application shall be filed within 30 days from the date when the person not involved in the case gets to know or should have known that the people's court has taken enforcement measures against the subject matter.

The substantive elements are as follows: (1) The person not involved in the case is a subject of the rights or interests; (2) The rights or interests claimed by the person not involved in the case are legitimate and true; (3) There is a fictitious legal relationship between the parties to the arbitration case and the facts of the case are fabricated; or (4) Part or all of the results concerning the handling of the civil rights and obligations of the parties concerned in the main text of the arbitral award or mediation statement are wrong, which damages the legitimate rights and interests of the person not involved in the case.

The elements for the application for non-enforcement of the arbitral award are different for the person not involved in the case and the respondent. The person not involved in the case needs to prove that the parties to the arbitration case maliciously apply for arbitration or false arbitration, while the respondent needs to prove the circumstances stipulated in Article 237 of the Civil Procedure Law, including: (1) The parties concerned have not included an arbitration clause in the contract or have not entered into a written arbitration agreement subsequently; (2) The arbitration matter does not fall under the scope of the arbitration agreement or the arbitration organization has no power to carry out arbitration; (3) The composition of the arbitral tribunal or the arbitration procedures is in violation of statutory procedures; (4) The evidence on which the arbitral award is based is forged; (5) The counterparty has concealed evidence which has an impact on making a fair arbitral award from the arbitration organization; or (6) The arbitrators have committed bribery award.

In other words, if the person not involved in the case fails to prove the existence of false arbitration or malicious arbitration, even if the person not involved in the case provides evidence to prove the circumstances specified in Article 237 of the Civil Procedure Law, the court cannot rule not to enforce the arbitral award involved.

Siemens Financial Leasing Co., Ltd. et al. v. Bankruptcy Liquidation Group of Jiangxi Hongwang Automobile Brake Manufacturing Co., Ltd., et al.[34]

On June 24, 2013, Siemens Financial Leasing Co., Ltd. ("Siemens Company") concluded a Lease Agreement with Jiangxi Hongwang Automobile Brake Manufacturing Co., Ltd. ("Hongwang Company") and Zhonghengtong (Fujian) Machinery Manufacturing Co., Ltd. ("Zhonghengtong Company").

According to the Lease Schedule attached to the Lease Agreement, Hongwang Company and Zhonghengtong Company leased several vehicles from Siemens Company. The parties also agreed on the price of rental equipment, down payment, deposit, lease term, the method of payment of rent, and so on. Hongwang Company and Zhonghengtong Company should pay the down payment, handling fees, deposits and other funds under remarks to Siemens Company within 5 days after the conclusion of the Lease Agreement.

Because Hongwang Company and Zhonghengtong Company were in arrears, Siemens Company applied to CIETAC for arbitration, requesting: (1) To terminate the Lease Agreement and its attachments; (2) To Confirm that Siemens Company had the ownership of the leased equipment under the Lease Agreement, and Hongwang Company should return the equipment under the Lease Agreement on the day when the award became effective; (3) Hongwang Company and Zhonghengtong Company shall compensate Siemens Company for all losses and corresponding overdue interests caused by the termination of the Lease Agreement; (4) Hongwang Company and Zhonghengtong Company shall pay Siemens Company all the costs and expenses of Siemens Company incurred to facilitate the fulfillment of the terms and conditions of the Lease Agreement, including but not limited to the legal fees, the property preservation fees and all arbitration fees in this case; (5) Siemens was entitled to discount the leased equipment under the Lease Agreement with Hongwang Company by agreement, or auction, or sell the equipment, and the proceeds would be used to settle the payment obligations of Hongwang Company if the proceeds were insufficient to pay off the debts, Hongwang Company would continue to pay off. If the proceeds exceeded the debts, the excess would be owned by Hongwang Company (6) The other respondents should bear joint and several guarantee responsibilities for the obligations of Hongwang Company and Zhonghengtong Company under the claims.

CIETAC issued the (2017) Zhong Guo Mao Zhong Jing Cai Zi No. 0162 Arbitral Award and supported all the other claims except for the fifth claim of Siemens Company The reason why the arbitral tribunal did not rule on the fifth claim of Siemens Company was that the arbitral tribunal had confirmed the ownership of the leased equipment under the Lease Agreement in this case, and Hongwang Company should return them to Siemens Company on the effective date of the award. Therefore, how to dispose of the leased equipment under the Lease Agreement in this case was

---

[34] (2018) Gan Zhi Fu No. 52.

a matter of Siemens Company's own consideration. The claim of Siemens Company did not require the arbitral tribunal to make an award.

Afterwards, Siemens Company applied to the Xinyu Intermediate People's Court of Jiangxi Province to enforce the (2017) Zhong Guo Mao Zhong Jing Cai Zi No. 0162 Arbitral Award. During the execution process, Xinyu Branch of Bank of China, a person not involved in the case, requested that the arbitral award not be enforced.

Xinyu Branch of Bank of China claimed that:

(1)   The failure of the Arbitral Award to rule on the fifth claim made by the claimant Siemens Company seriously violated legal procedures, obviously damaged the legitimate interests of Hongwang Company, and further harmed the mortgage rights of Xinyu Branch of Bank of China.

(2)   Siemens Company concealed relevant evidence during the hearing of arbitration, which led to the error of the fact determined in the arbitration. Siemens Company requested Hongwang Company to pay the expired rent without providing evidence, concealing the actual payment that Hongwang Company had already paid to Siemens Company, and the arbitral tribunal failed to verify the payment of both parties in the arbitral award, resulting in the wrong amount of rent arrears in the award.

(3)   Siemens Company failed to pay the supplier the corresponding purchase price as stipulated in the Financial Lease Contract, actually only paid 70% of the contract price and could not obtain the ownership of all leased equipment in accordance with the law. However, Siemens Company collected the financial leasing fee back from Hongwang Company, concealing the relevant evidence of the unpaid payment. It resulted in the arbitral award to ruling that the claimant had the ownership of the equipment, which obviously violated the principle of fairness.

(4)   The equipment suppliers Baoji Zhongcheng Machine Tool Company, Ltd. ("Baoji Co."), the claimant and Hongwang Company had malicious collusion and signed the "Yin Yang Contract" to inflate the equipment price, which led to an error in the arbitral award and directly harmed the applicant's legal rights.

The Xinyu Intermediate People's Court considered that:

Judging from the agreement signed with Hongwang Company provided by Xinyu Branch of Bank of China, it could be proved that it issued a loan to Hongwang Company, and Hongwang Company also mortgaged the equipment in the factory under its name (including the equipment under arbitration) as a guarantee. Although Hongwang Company concealed that the equipment used for mortgage was financial lease equipment, which had rights restrictions, or the person not involved in the case was negligent in handling the mortgage, it could not be denied that the person not involved in the case was a related party to the subject matter of enforcement (that is, the leased equipment) in the (2017) Gan 05 Zhi No. 607 Case. Therefore, it was legal for the person not involved in the case to claim rights.

According to relevant laws and regulations, Siemens Company, as the lessor of the financial lease, had the right to exercise the ownership of the leased equipment when Hongwang Company failed to perform its obligations. However, the Leasing Agreement signed by both parties also stipulated that Hongwang Company had the right to jointly dispose of the leased equipment with the claimant, but Siemens Company can be paid by the price after the disposal first after the liquidation of both parties. Therefore, the failure to initiate the disposal measure in a timely manner harmed the interests of Hongwang Company in terms of procedures and in turn harmed the legitimate rights and interests of the third party (the person not involved in the case) Xinyu Branch of Bank of China.

In summary, it was improper for CIETAC not to make a ruling on the fifth claim raised by the claimant in the arbitration. This meant that the rights and obligations of both parties were wrong, which damaged the legitimate rights and interests of Xinyu Branch of Bank of China, and thus the claims of the person not involved in the case should be supported. Therefore, the Xinyu Intermediate People's Court ruled not to enforce the (2017) Zhong Guo Mao Zhong Jing Cai Zi No. 0162 Award made by CIETAC.

Unsatisfied with the Award, Siemens Company applied to the High People's Court of Jiangxi Province for reconsideration, requesting revoking the ruling and rejecting the request of Xinyu Branch of Bank of China of not to enforce the arbitral award. Siemens Company held that the Xinyu Intermediate People's Court's acceptance of the application for non-enforcement by Xinyu Branch of Bank of China did not fulfill the requirement that the person not involved in the case "shall submit evidence to prove that the parties to the arbitration case maliciously applied for arbitration or false arbitration", and there were serious procedural defects.

The High People's Court of Jiangxi Province held that the focus of the dispute in this case was whether the arbitral award in the present case had fulfilled the statutory conditions for non-enforcement.

Pursuant to Articles 9 and 18 of the Provisions of the SPC on Several Issues Concerning the Handling of Cases of Enforcement of Arbitral Awards by the People's Courts, the three procedural requirements specified in Article 9 and the four substantive requirements specified in Article 18 should be satisfied if a person not involved in the case applied to the people's court for not executing an arbitral award. Among them, the determination of whether "there is evidence to prove that the parties to the arbitration case have maliciously applied for arbitration or false arbitration, harming their legitimate rights and interests" stipulated in Item 1, Article 9 of the Provisions shall be based on the substantive standards provided in Item 3 and Item 4 of Article 18.

In the case at hand, Xinyu Branch of Bank of China applied for non-enforcement of the arbitral award. Although the claimed legitimate rights and interests (mortgage) existed and the subject matter of execution (lease equipment) had not yet been enforced and concluded, Xinyu Branch of Bank of China did not submit evidence to prove that the parties to the arbitration in this case had maliciously applied for arbitration or false arbitration, nor did it submit evidence to prove that there was a fictitious legal relationship between the parties in this case, and the facts of the case were fabricated. The procedural and substantive conditions for the application for non-enforcement of the arbitral award by the person not involved in the case had not been fulfilled. Xinyu Branch of Bank of China may seek relief through other methods in accordance with the law if it considered that Hongwang Company's improper performance had harmed its legitimate rights and interests.

Regarding the allegation that Xinyu Branch of Bank of China maliciously colluded and concealed relevant evidence in the hearing of the arbitration in this case, the arbitral award of this case did not rule on the fifth claim of the claimant, Siemens Company, which violated statutory procedures, and that the facts determined in the arbitral award were wrong, the High People's Court of Jiangxi Province held that, pursuant to Article 63 of the Arbitration Law and Item 3, 4, 5, Paragraph 2 of Article 237 of the Civil Procedure Law, if it was believed that there was malicious collusion between the parties to the arbitration, that is, Siemens and other parties in this case, and the parties concealed evidence sufficient to affect the fairness of the award from the arbitration institution, or the composition of the arbitral tribunal or the arbitration procedure in this case violated legal procedures, and the evidence on which the arbitral award was based is forged, and other statutory circumstances, only the respondent of the arbitration, Hongwang Company, Zhongheng Co., Liu and Lu, had the right to provide evidence and apply for a ruling of non-enforcement by the people's court. Xinyu Branch of Bank of China, as a person not involved in the case, did not have the *standing* to apply for non-enforcement of the arbitral award on this ground, and Xinyu Branch of Bank of China may claim rights through other methods in accordance with the law.

In addition, the alleged violation of legal procedures by Xinyu Branch of Bank of China due to failure of the arbitral award in this case to rule on the fifth claim raised by Siemens Company did not fell within the circumstance "violation of legal procedures", as stipulated in the judicial interpretation above. It lacked a legal basis for Xinyu Branch of Bank of China to claim that the arbitral award in this case should not be enforced on this ground.

Therefore, the High People's Court of Jiangxi Province ruled to revoke the (2018) Gan 05 Zhi Yi No. 4 Ruling made by the Xinyu Intermediate People's Court and rejected the application for non-enforcement of Xinyu Branch of Bank of China, and the case was resumed.

It can be seen from the case above that Xinyu Branch of Bank of China, the party not involved in the case, provided evidence to prove that the arbitration involved violated legal procedures, the facts determined by the arbitration were wrong, or the arbitral award was wrong, but failed to provide evidence to prove that the parties to the arbitration involved maliciously applied for arbitration or false arbitration, or there was a fictitious legal relationship between the parties in this case, and the facts of the case were fabricated. Therefore, the requirements for the application for non-enforcement of the arbitral award by the person not involved in the case stipulated by the Provisions of the SPC on Several Issues Concerning the Handling of Cases of Enforcement of Arbitral Awards by the People's Courts had not been fulfilled, and thus the application should be rejected.

To conclude, a person not involved in the case applying for non-enforcement of an arbitral award must provide evidence to prove that the parties to the arbitration case have maliciously applied for arbitration or false arbitration or that there is a fictitious legal relationship between the parties to the arbitration case and the facts of the case are fabricated. In contrast, if the person not involved in the case only provides evidence to prove the circumstances specified in Article 237 of the Civil Procedure Law, the application for non-enforcement will be rejected.

9.7 Application of Persons Not Involved in the Case for Non-enforcement of Mediation Statement

Pursuant to Paragraph 2, Article 51 of the Arbitration Law, a mediation statement shall have the same legal force as that of an award. Paragraph 1, Article 14 of the Measures for the Payment of Litigation Costs also stipulates the application fee to be paid when applying to the people's court for the enforcement of the mediation statement.

It can be concluded from the provisions above that the mediation statement can be enforced as the arbitral award. If the debtor fails to perform its obligations under the mediation statement, the creditor has the right to apply to the people's court for the enforcement of the mediation statement. Therefore, do the person subject to enforcement and those not involved in the case have the right to apply to the court for non-enforcement of the mediation statement as an application for non-enforcement of an arbitral award?

Zhen v. Hefei Anbang Property Management Co., Ltd.[35]

Based on the arbitration clause in the mediation agreement signed between Hefei Anbang Property Management Co., Ltd. ("Anbang Company") and Li, Luan Arbitration Commission accepted the arbitration case between the parties.

On August 21, 2016, the two parties reached an agreement under the auspices of the Luan Arbitration Commission. Luan Arbitration Commission issued the (2016) Liu Zhong Cai Zi No. 102 Mediation Statement on the same day, confirming that (1) Li confirmed that the principal he owed to Anbang Company was RMB 5,711,993; (2) Li agreed to pay RMB 5,711,993 to Anbang Company in installments......; (3) The arbitration fee of this case is RMB 25,942 and should be borne by Li, and Li shall pay to Anbang Company before September 1, 2016; (4) If Li failed to repay any sum of money in the above agreed time and method, it was deemed that Li had breached the contract, and Anbang Company was entitled to request Li to pay all the money immediately; (5) After Li had paid off the loan according to the agreed time, the credits and debts between both parties would come to an end, there was no other utes.

After the aforementioned Mediation Statement took effect, Anbang Company applied to the Hefei Intermediate People's Court for enforcement on October 26, 2016. After lodging the case, the Hefei Intermediate People's Court issued the (2016)

---

[35] (2018) Wan 01 Zhi Yi No. 80.

Wan 01 Zhi No. 519 Execution Ruling on November 11, 2016, and assigned the case to the Hefei Railway Transportation Court for execution.

During the enforcement process, Anbang Company applied to the Hefei Railway Transportation Court for the addition of Zheng, the person not involved in the case, as the person subject to enforcement on December 12, 2016, but the application was not approved.

On January 17, 2017, the Hefei Railway Transportation Court seized three houses jointly owned by Zheng and Li. After seizing the abovementioned houses and deducting RMB 8,962 from Li's bank deposits, the Hefei Railway Transportation Court found that Li had no other property that could be enforced. Therefore, the court considered that after exhaustive enforcement measures, although Li had property, it was not suitable for disposal, and Anbang Company also agreed to wait for the division between Li and Zheng before disposing. Considering that the court did not temporarily dispose of the properties and there was no need to continue the case, the court made the (2016) Wan 8601 No. 202–2 Execution Ruling to terminate the execution procedure on May 16, 2017.

During the execution of the case, Anbang Company submitted a written application to the Hefei Railway Transportation Court on May 4, 2017, requesting postponement of the listing of Li in the list of dishonest persons subject to enforcement.

On September 6, 2018, Zheng applied to the Hefei Intermediate People's Court for the non-enforcement of the Mediation Statement. The main reason was that both Anbang Company and Li had concealed evidence from the arbitration institution that could affect the fairness of the award. Li was a major shareholder of Anbang Company, who had maliciously colluded with Li, fabricated debts, and infringed Zheng's lawful rights.

The Hefei Intermediate People's Court held that Article 18 of the Provisions of the SPC on Several Issues Concerning the Handling of Cases of Enforcement of Arbitral Awards by the People's Courts empowered the person not involved in the case to apply for non-enforcement of the mediation statement and that the people's court should support it when the four requirements were met.

In this case, after Anbang Company's first lawsuit was ruled to be rejected by the court on the ground that it failed to provide evidence to prove that it was the will of the legal person on June 16, 2016, Li highly cooperatively completed the procedures of changing the company's legal person on June 27, 2016. Anbang Company filed a lawsuit in the court again on July 1, 2016, and withdrew the lawsuit on August 4, 2016 on the ground that the two parties reached an out-of-court settlement agreement. After that, the two parties reached a settlement agreement again under the auspices of the Luan Arbitration Commission on August 21, 2016.

For a large amount of RMB 5,711,993, the cooperation between Anbang Company and Li was too tacit during the abovementioned litigation and arbitration process. Many IOUs had passed the limitation of prosecutions. In the case of *Anbang Company v. Li*, Li could have made the defense based on the limitation of prosecutions, but Li did not argue, but reached an arbitration clause in the settlement agreement with

Anbang Company, and fully recognized all the claims of Anbang Company in the arbitration procedure, without any refutation, which was contrary to common sense.

Moreover, many borrowings occurred during the period when Li served as the legal representative of Anbang Company. As the legal representative and the shareholder, Li had absolute control over Anbang Company during this period. The company's office had always been in real estate jointly owned by Zheng and Li. There was an interest relationship between Li and Anbang Company In addition, the remarks of some of the transfer receipts from Anbang Company to Li were labor fees, rather than loans, and the amount of the transfer receipts did not match the amount of the IOUs. In addition to the funds involved in the Mediation Statement, there were a large number of frequent and huge account transactions between Anbang Company and Li. Not only did Anbang Company transfer money to Li's account, but Li also transferred money to Anbang Company's account dozens of times. In the arbitration case, neither Anbang Company nor Li mentioned these current accounts. It was not reviewed whether these current accounts were related to borrowings in the Mediation Statement or whether they would affect borrowings. The authenticity of the loan involved in the Mediation Statement could not be determined.

The relationship between Li and Zheng was that of a husband and wife, and Li stated in many IOUs that the loans were used for family consumption and the purchase of real estate. However, the agreement reached between Anbang Company and Li in the arbitration was a mediation agreement. The authenticity of these debts was not confirmed by the court or arbitral award by the arbitration institution. The divorce litigation in which Li sued Zheng was currently being heard by the People's Court of Yaohai District of Hefei City. In that case, Li claimed the joint debt of RMB 5.8 million based on the Mediation Statement, and the Hefei Railway Transportation Court had already sealed the three properties jointly owned by Zheng and Li. Anbang Company also applied to the court to add Zheng as the person subject to enforcement. All of the above caused damage to Zheng's legitimate rights and interests.

In summary, the Hefei Intermediate People's Court held that the reason for the non-enforcement of the (2016) Liu Zhong Cai Zi No. 102 Mediation Statement by Zheng, who was not involved in the case, was established and thus ruled not to enforce the (2016) Liu Zhong Cai Zi No. 102 Mediation Statement rendered by the Luan Arbitration Commission.

There is a considerable difference in the judicial attitude toward the right of the person not involved in the case to apply for non-enforcement of the mediation statement before and after the Provisions of the SPC on Several Issues Concerning the Handling of Cases of Enforcement of Arbitral Awards by the People's Courts came into effect (i.e., March 1, 2018).

Before the provisions came into effect, relevant laws, regulations and judicial practices were more inclined to deny the right of persons subject to enforcement and persons not involved in the case to file an application for non-enforcement of the mediation statement.

At the level of judicial documents, Article 28 of the Arbitration Law Interpretation stipulates that "If a party requests not to execute the mediation statement or the arbitral award made in accordance with the settlement agreement between the parties, the people's court shall not support it." Item (1) Paragraph 2 of Article 4 of the Several Provisions of the High People's Court of Guangdong Province on Handling Applications for Non-Enforcement of Arbitral Awards (for Trial Implementation) provides that "The case-filing court shall make a decision not to lodge a case under the following circumstances after review: (1) The parties request not to execute the mediation statement or the arbitral award made in accordance with the settlement agreement between the parties;"

At the level of judicial practice, most of the applications for non-enforcement of the mediation statements filed by the parties were rejected by the courts. In the cases, *Tianjin Hengzeng Real Estate Development Co., Ltd. v. Zhang*,[36] *Guangzhou Hongsheng Solar Technology Co., Ltd. v. Guangzhou Youqing Daily Chemical Industry Co., Ltd.*,[37] *Bai v. Handan Rongbang Industrial Group Co., Ltd.*, et al.,[38] the persons subject to enforcement applied for non-enforcement of the mediation statements involved in the case, and the courts rejected their applications in accordance with Article 28 of the Arbitration Law Interpretation.

Meanwhile, there were also some views that the "mediation statement" mentioned in Article 28 of the Arbitration Law Interpretation only referred to a legal and effective mediation statement. The parties shall be entitled to apply for non-enforcement of a mediation statement made illegally, and the court shall rule on non-enforcement.[39]

For example, Article 4 of the Notice of the High People's Court of Hainan Province on Strengthening the Judicial Review of the Enforcement of Civil and Commercial Arbitral Awards and Mediation Statements stipulates that "……After the case is transferred for execution, if the parties and interested parties file an application for non-enforcement or a defense during the process of execution, the enforcement department shall form a collegiate panel to carefully examine whether there are circumstances where the arbitral award or mediation statement cannot be enforced, and reply to the parties and interested parties within two months. When necessary, the arbitration files shall be obtained, and the time limit for obtaining the arbitration file shall not be calculated in the execution period."

Article 5 of the Notice also stipulates that "After review, if there exist the following circumstances in the arbitral award or the mediation statement, it shall be ruled not to be enforced: (1) There exists one of the circumstances specified in Paragraph 2 of Article 237 of the Civil Procedure Law in the arbitral award or the mediation statement; (2) There exists one of the circumstances specified in Paragraph 1 of Article 274 of the Civil Procedure Law in the foreign-related arbitral award or the mediation statement; (3) Enforcement of the arbitral award or mediation statement violates the social public interest."

---

[36] (2016) Zui Gao Fa Zhi Jian No. 443.

[37] (2016) Yue 01 Zhi Yi No. 290.

[38] (2015) Han Shi Zhi Yi Zi No. 00135.

[39] Huo Wei, *"Mediation" is on the Embarrassing Way——Research on the Cancellation and Non-enforcement of Mediation Statement*, http://www.zhonglun.com/Content/2016/10-11/1429464426.html (accessed 3 Dec. 2020).

It can be viewed from the above provisions that the Notice reviewed the application for non-enforcement of the mediation statement with reference to the non-enforcement of the arbitral award.

Similarly, in the case of *Beijing Jingdeyuan Real Estate Development Co., Ltd.* ("Jingdeyuan Company") *v. Taiyuan Daidler Enterprise Management Consulting Co., Ltd.* ("Daidler Company"),[40] the person subject to enforcement, Jingdeyuan Company, applied for non-enforcement of the (2012) Ji Zhong Cai Zi No. 3012 Mediation Statement issued by Jinan Arbitration Commission, and the enforcement court, the Beijing Second Intermediate People's Court rejected Jingdeyuan Company's application based on Article 28 of the Arbitration Law Interpretation mentioned above. Jingdeyuan Company applied to the High People's Court of Beijing City for reconsideration. After review, the High People's Court of Beijing City held that the mediation agreement in this case was signed by both parties before applying for arbitration. There was no mediation process during the arbitration process. Therefore, the legal basis for the Jinan Arbitration Commission to render the Mediation Statement was lacking, and the arbitration procedure violated the law. Therefore, Jingdeyuan Company's application for not implementing the Mediation Statement complied with the legal provisions and arbitration rules and should be supported, and the original ruling should be revoked.

It can be concluded that before the Provisions of the SPC on Several Issues Concerning the Handling of Cases of Enforcement of Arbitral Awards by the People's Courts came into effect, there were different approaches to the issue of whether the court should accept applications filed by the parties and the person not involved in the case for nonapplication of the mediation statement, and the mainstream view seems to be more inclined to deny the admissibility of the application.

After the provisions came into effect, this situation changed. The provisions stipulate that the person subject to enforcement and the person not involved in the case have the right to apply to the people's court for non-enforcement of the mediation statement under certain circumstances.

For the person subject to enforcement, Article 17 of the Provisions provides that "The people's court shall not support the application of the person subject to enforcement for non-enforcement of the mediation statement or arbitral award made in accordance with the mediation agreement and conciliation agreement between the parties, with the exception that the mediation statement or the arbitral award violates social public interests." It can be viewed in conjunction with Article 24 of the Provisions, which stipulates that "The present Provisions shall come into effect as of March 1, 2018. In case of any inconsistence between judicial interpretations previously promulgated by this court and the present Provisions, the latter shall prevail", that Article 17 of the Provisions adds an exception to Article 28 of the Arbitration Law where the person subject to enforcement may apply for the non-enforcement of the mediation agreement, that is, the mediation agreement violates the social public interest. After the provisions came into effect, the court accepted all applications for non-enforcement of the mediation statement by the person subject

---

[40] (2013) Gao Zhi Fu Zi No. 104.

to enforcement and reviewed whether the mediation statement violated the social public interest.

For instance, in the cases *Lingshui Yunhai Investment Co., Ltd. v. Sun*[41] and *Liu v. Hou*,[42] the persons subject to enforcement applied for not executing the mediation statement on the ground that the mediation statement involved in the case violated the social public interest, but their applications were rejected due to the failure to provide sufficient evidence to prove the allegation.

Article 9 of the Provisions provides for some conditions to be met for the person not involved in the case to apply for non-enforcement of the arbitral award or mediation statement.[43] In this case, the court applied Article 18 of the Provisions and ruled not to enforce the (2016) Liu Zhong Cai Zi No. 102 Mediation Statement made by Luan Arbitration Commission.

9.8 Arbitral Awards Made by "Pre-arbitration"

There is no definition or relevant provisions of the "pre-arbitration" procedure in the existing laws of China. Referring to the Answers of the SPC's Executive Officer to Reporters' Questions on the Case Filing, Enforcement and Other Issues of Legal Application on "Pre-arbitration" ("Answers to Reporters' Questions"), "Pre-arbitration" means that to ensure that both parties perform their determined rights and obligations in the future, to ensure the realization of rights and interests in the future and to avoid arbitration or litigation in the future, when the parties sign and perform the online lending contract and no dispute occurs, the parties request the arbitration institution to make a binding and enforceable legal document in accordance with

---

[41] (2018) Qiong 72 Zhi Yi No. 33.

[42] (2018) Lu 01 Zhi Yi No. 82.

[43] Article 9 of the Provisions stipulates:

To apply for non-enforcement of the arbitral award or mediation statement to the people's court, any person not involved in the case shall submit a written application and evidence material supporting the establishment of its request, and the following conditions shall be met: (1) There is evidence to prove that the party to the arbitration case maliciously applies for arbitration or fictitious arbitration, undermining its legitimate rights and interests; (2) The subject matter of enforcement involved in the lawful rights and interests claimed by the person not involved in the case has not yet been enforced and concluded; and (3) The application shall be filed within 30 days from the date when the person not involved in the case gets to know or should have known that the people's court has taken enforcement measures against the subject matter." Article 18 of the Provisions provides that "Where the following conditions are met, the people's court shall support an application filed by any person not involved in the case for non-enforcement of an arbitral award or mediation statement in accordance with Article 9 of the present Provisions: (1) The person not involved in the case is a subject of the rights or interests; (2) The rights or interests claimed by the person not involved in the case are legitimate and true; (3) There is a fictitious legal relationship between the parties to the arbitration case and the facts of the case are fabricated; or (4) Part or all of the results concerning the handling of the civil rights and obligations of the parties concerned in the main text of the arbitral award or mediation statement are wrong, which damages the legitimate rights and interests of the person not involved in the case.

its existing agreement, including a mediation statement and an arbitral award made based on the mediation agreement. The "pre-arbitration" procedure generally applies to online lending contracts.

"Pre-arbitration" may have the following characteristics:

First, the parties sign the mediation agreement on the day when the loan contract is concluded, and the arbitration matters are stipulated in the two agreements.

Second, the parties apply for arbitration when the contract has not been performed or has not been fully performed, the arbitration institution makes an arbitral award or mediation statement based on the previous mediation agreement and at the same time issues an effective certificate. The signing and delivery of relevant documents are all conducted online.

Third, the lender of the loan contract is unknown. In some contracts, there are only the borrower and the intermediary (i.e., the online loan platform) without specifying the lender.

Fourth, the claimant in the mediation agreement is an online lending platform, whose business scope does not include financial lending business. The online lending platform claims to obtain credits through transfer and apply for arbitration and enforcement.

Fifth, the mediation agreement imposes several restrictions on the rights of the borrower. For example, it is clearly agreed that the case will not be publicly heard, the trial will not be held and the trial will be completed on the Internet; the borrower has no objection to the loan contract or other payment vouchers and other relevant evidence submitted by the applicant; the borrower waives to provide evidence; the borrower waives right of defense against the claims of arbitration and other rights.

Sixth, the arbitration institution stipulates in the arbitration rules that in the process of conclusion or performance of the contract, regardless of whether a substantive or public dispute occurs, it is considered to be an arbitration case, and the arbitration legal document made in accordance with the mediation agreement cannot be applied for cancellation or non-enforcement.

Here comes the question of whether the arbitral award made in such "pre-arbitration" is valid and can be enforced.

Huizhong Litong Investment Management (Beijing) Co., Ltd. v. Chou.[44]

On June 12, 2017, Chou signed the Loan Agreement through Huizhong Litong Investment Management (Beijing) Co., Ltd. ("Huizhong Litong Company"), stipulating that the total loan principal is RMB 60,947.94 and the loan period is 24 months with monthly repayment of principal and interest of RMB 2,860.5.

On the same day, the credit was transferred to Huizhong Litong Company, and Huizhong Litong Company signed a Mediation Agreement with Chou, which stipulated the repayment time, interest and overdue interest.

On the same day, the Zhanjiang Arbitration Commission accepted the private lending case. A sole arbitral tribunal was established, and the arbitral tribunal privately reviewed the case on the Internet without holding a hearing on the same day.

---

[44] (2018) Yue Zhi Fu No. 206.

The arbitral tribunal issued the (2017) Zhan Zhong Zi No. E00344261 Arbitral Award on the same day, ruling that: (1) It was confirmed that Chou still owed Huizhong Litong Company the loan principal of RMB 60,947.94; (2) Chou was requested to repay loan principal and interest of RMB 2,860.5 to Huizhong Litong Company on a monthly basis before the 10th of each month from July 10, 2017 to June 10, 2019; (3) If Chou failed to perform any period of repayment obligation on time and in full in accordance with the second ruling above, Huizhong Litong Company shall have the right to request Chou to pay overdue liquidated damages from the date of overdue on the basis of the outstanding loan amount with a monthly interest rate 2% until the payment was paid off......; (4) The arbitration of RM182.8 Huizhong Litong Company paid the arbitration fee in advance, and the arbitration fee would not be refunded. Chou was required to pay the arbitration fee to Huizhong Litong Company when performing the abovementioned obligations.

Huizhong Litong Company applied to the Foshan Intermediate People's Court for compulsory enforcement on the ground that Chou did not perform the obligations determined in the aforementioned Award.

The Foshan Intermediate People's Court held that it lacked legal basis for Zhanjiang Arbitration Commission to make the Award on the assumed disputes that may arise between the parties in the future under the circumstance where there is no dispute between the parties. The behavior of the Zhanjiang Arbitration Commission violated the legislative design of arbitration to resolve disputes so that the specific execution amount could not be calculated based on the contingent facts it identified. Pursuant to Item (2), Paragraph 1, Article 3 of the Provisions of the SPC on Several Issues Concerning the Handling of Cases of Enforcement of Arbitral Awards by the People's Courts, if the specific amount of payment is not clear or the calculation method is not clear, resulting that the specific amount cannot be figured out, the people's court may rule to reject the application for enforcement.

On May 16, 2018, the Foshan Intermediate People's Court issued (2018) Yue 06 Zhi No. 450 Execution Ruling, ruling to reject Huizhong Litong Company's application for enforcement.

Unsatisfied with the Ruling above, Huizhong Litong Company applied for reconsideration to the High People's Court of Guangdong Province, requesting (1) to revoke the (2018) Yue 06 Zhi No. 450 Execution Ruling; (2) to order the Foshan Intermediate People's Court to enforce the (2017) Zhan Zhong Zi No. E00344261 Arbitral Award.

Huizhong Litong Company alleged that there was no restriction in the laws on when mediation could be made, and mediation legal documents in arbitration should be implemented as long as they were true. The Award of the arbitration institution was made in accordance with the mediation agreement between the applicant and the person subject to enforcement, which complied with the law. Relevant laws had clear provisions on non-enforcement of arbitration legal documents, and only when the statutory circumstances were met can the court rule on non-enforcement. There were no legal circumstances for non-enforcement in this case, and the court should not ignore the existence of arbitration rules. It did not violate the law and the wishes of the parties for the two parties to voluntarily use mediation at the beginning of the civil act to resolve the issue through arbitration. "Pre-arbitration" had many advantages and should be supported.

The High People's Court of Guangdong Province considered that the core issue of this case was whether the Arbitral Award made by the arbitration institution before the dispute between the parties actually occurs should be filed for enforcement. Article 2 of the Arbitration Law stipulated that "Contractual disputes and other disputes arising from property rights and interests between citizens, legal persons and other organizations of equal status in law may be submitted for arbitration."

According to the facts ascertained in this case, Chou signed the Loan Agreement through Huizhong Litong Company, and on the same day, Huizhong Litong Company received credit and signed the Mediation Agreement with Chou. On the day when the agreement was signed, the Zhanjiang Arbitration Commission accepted the private lending case, privately reviewed the case on the Internet without holding a hearing, and issued the Arbitral Award. That is, the mediation statement was made directly in advance before the dispute had occurred, which deviated from the basic principles and systematic objectives of arbitration. It was not improper for the ruling made by the Foshan Intermediate People's Court to reject Huizhong Litong Company's application for enforcement.

Therefore, the High People's Court of Guangdong Province ruled to reject Huizhong Litong Company's request for reconsideration and to maintain the (2018) Yue 06 Zhi No. 450 Execution Ruling made by the Foshan Intermediate People's Court.

On June 5, 2018, the SPC issued its Reply on Case Filing, Enforcement and Other Issues of Legal Application on "Pre-arbitration" of Arbitration Institutions,[45] making it clear that if a party to an online lending contract applied for enforcement of an arbitral award or mediation statement made by an arbitration institution before the dispute occurs, the people's court shall rule not to accept it; if it had already accepted it, the people's court shall rule to reject the application for enforcement.

In addition, the Reply also pointed out that the situation where the arbitration institution failed to hear disputes or preside over mediation in accordance with the procedures prescribed by the Arbitration Law and simply made an arbitral award or mediation statement based on the settlement or mediation agreement signed by the parties to the online lending contract before the dispute occurred, or the situation where the arbitration institution fails to protect the basic procedural rights stipulated by the Arbitration Law, such as the application of arbitrators to withdraw, provide evidence, and make defense in the arbitration process, shall be deemed as the situation where "the composition of the arbitral tribunal or the arbitration procedure violates legal procedures" stipulated in Item 3, Paragraph 2, Article 237 of the Civil Procedure Law. Under such circumstances, the people's court should not support it if the parties to the online lending claim that the arbitration procedure does not violate the legal procedure on the ground of the agreed waiver clause.

Before the release of thereply, there were different practices of each court regarding whether arbitral awards made by "pre-arbitration" should be enforced.

---

[45] Fa Shi [2018] No. 10.

For instance, *Shenzhen Xiaoniu Online Internet Information Consulting Co., Ltd. v. Bie*,[46] The Jingzhou Intermediate People's Court ruled to enforce the (2016) Zha Zhong Zi No. 14764 Mediation Statement made by Zhanjiang Arbitration Commission.

In contrast, *Shenzhen Xiaoniu Online Internet Information Consulting Co., Ltd. v. Zhang*,[47] the Huludao Intermediate People's Court, held that the mediation agreement between the parties excluded the parties' statutory procedural rights, thereby excluding judicial supervision of arbitration through the provision that one party waived the right to apply for revocation or non-enforcement of the award by adopting standard clauses, which violated the principle of procedural review and the judicial principles of fairness and equal protection and thus should be invalid, and the lender is unknown. Therefore, it was ruled not to enforce the (2016) Zhan Zhong Zi No. 16280 Mediation Statement made by Zhanjiang Arbitration Commission.

In this case, the Foshan Intermediate People's Court held that "pre-arbitration" violated the legislative design of arbitration to resolve disputes so that the specific execution amount could not be calculated based on the contingent facts it identified. Hence, the Foshan Intermediate People's Court dismissed the application for enforcement in accordance with Item (2), Paragraph 1, Article 3 of the Provisions of the SPC on Several Issues Concerning the Handling of Cases of Enforcement of Arbitral Awards by the People's Courts.

After the reply was issued, the practices of each court were unified, and the arbitral awards made by "pre-arbitration" were ruled not to be enforced.

"Pre-arbitration" pursues the prevention of disputes and confirms the rights and obligations of the parties by an "effective award" before the occurrence of disputes. On the surface,"pre-arbitration" reduces the cost of arbitration, saves the time and energy for creditors such as online loan platforms to initiate arbitration after disputes, and meets the needs of parties in the financial sector for efficiency and convenience. However, "Pre-arbitration" deprives a party of the procedural rights in the arbitration procedure, including the rights to raise counterclaims,[48] apply for withdrawal,[49]

---

[46] (2017) E 10 Zhi No. 88.

[47] (2018) Liao 14 Zhi No. 38.

[48] Article 27 of the Arbitration Law stipulates that "A claimant may abandon or alter his arbitration claim. The respondent may accept the arbitration claim or object to it and has the right to lodge a counterclaim.".

[49] Article 34 of the Arbitration Law stipulates that "In any of the following circumstances, an arbitrator must withdraw from the arbitration, and the parties shall have the right to apply for his withdrawal if he: (1) is a party or a close relative of a party or of a party's representative; (2) is related in the case; (3) has some other relationship with a party to the case or with a party's agent which might affect the impartiality of the arbitration; (4) meets a party or his agent in private, accepts an invitation for dinner by a party or his representative or accepts gifts presented by any of them.".

cross-examination,[50] debate,[51] etc., and the right to apply for revocation[52] and non-enforcement[53] of the arbitral award. These rights are legal rights granted to the parties by the Arbitration Law and the Civil Procedure Law and cannot be arbitrarily excluded. In the case of violating legal procedures, "pre-arbitration" violates the principle of procedural justice. Pursuant to Item 3, Paragraph 2, Article 237 of the Civil Procedure Law, the court shall rule not to enforce the arbitral award if the composition of the arbitral tribunal or the arbitration procedure is in contrary to the legal procedure.

In addition, since "pre-arbitration" was conducted before the dispute actually occurred and there was still no dispute when conducting arbitration,"pre-arbitration" does not conform to the "arbitrable matters" defined in Article 2 of the Arbitration Law, that is, "contractual disputes and other disputes arising from property rights and interests between citizens, legal persons and other organizations of equal status". The arbitral award made through "pre-arbitration" is not an arbitral award in the sense of the Arbitration Law, which will result in other consequences.

For example, the specific amount of execution cannot be calculated based on the content of the award. In the case at hand, the (2017) Zhan Zhong Zi No. E00344261 Arbitral Award made by Zhanjiang Arbitration Commission ruled that Chou should repay the principle and the interests within the specified time, or Huizhong Litong Company should have the right to request Chou to pay overdue liquidated damages from the date of overdue on the basis of the outstanding loan amount with a monthly interest rate 2% until the payment was paid off. The calculation of liquidated damages

---

[50] Article 45 of the Arbitration Law stipulates that "Any evidence shall be produced at the start of the hearing. The parties may challenge the validity of such evidence.".

[51] Article 47 of the Arbitration Law stipulates that "The parties have the right to argue during arbitration procedures. At the end of the debate, the presiding arbitrator or the sole arbitrator shall ask for the final opinion of the parties.".

[52] Paragraph 1, Article 58 of the Arbitration Law stipulates that "The parties may apply to the intermediate people's court at the place where the arbitration commission is located for cancellation of an award if they provide evidence proving that the award involves one of the following circumstances: (1) there is no arbitration agreement between the parties; (2) the matters of the award are beyond the extent of the arbitration agreement or not under the jurisdiction of the arbitration commission; (3) the composition of the arbitral tribunal or the arbitration procedure is in contrary to the legal procedure; (4) the evidence on which the award is based is falsified; (5) the other party has concealed evidence which is sufficient to affect the impartiality of the award; or (6) the arbitrator(s) has (have) demanded or accepted bribes, committed graft or perverted the law in making the arbitral award.".

[53] Paragraph 2, Article 237 of the Civil Procedure Law stipulates that "Where the respondent presents evidence to prove that the arbitral award falls under any of the following circumstances, upon examination and verification by the collegiate formed by the people's court, a ruling on non-enforcement shall be made: (1) The parties concerned have not included an arbitration clause in the contract or have not entered into a written arbitration agreement subsequently; (2) The matters of the award are beyond the extent of the arbitration agreement or not under the jurisdiction of the arbitration commission; (3) The composition of the arbitral tribunal or the arbitration procedures is/are in violation of statutory procedures; (4) The evidence on which the arbitral award is based is forged; (5) The counterparty has concealed evidence which has an impact on making a fair arbitral award from the arbitration institution; or (6) The arbitrator(s) has (have) demanded or accepted bribes, committed graft or perverted the law in making the arbitral award.".

needs to be based on the amount of outstanding loan, which was not a specific figure, and thus it was impossible to calculate the specific amount of liquidated damages based on this unspecific amount. In other words, if the applicant and the respondent did not submit corresponding evidence on whether the principal and interest had been repaid, the court could not determine the amount of outstanding loans. Pursuant to Item 2, Paragraph 1 of Article 3 of the Provisions of the Supreme People's Court on Several Issues Concerning the Handling of Cases of Enforcement of Arbitral Awards by the People's Courts, the people's court may make a ruling of rejecting the application for enforcement if the specific amount of payment is not clear or the calculation method is not clear, resulting in the specific amount not be figured out.

It can be concluded that under the current legal framework of China, "pre-arbitration" does not comply with the legal provisions concerning arbitration, and arbitral awards or mediation statements made through "pre-arbitration" procedures cannot be enforced by the court.

Chapter 10
Public Policy

10.1 Violation of Mandatory Provisions of Laws

The violation of the social public interest is one of the situations in which parties may apply for setting-aside[1] and non-enforcement[2] of arbitral awards. It is also the main situation in which the court may review the setting-aside or non-enforcement of arbitral awards *ex officio*. Like most countries, there is no specific provision on the meaning and connotation of the social public interest in the current laws and regulations of China. In China's judicial practice, this Chinese concept is the same as public order or public policy.

Generally, in the practice of judicial review of arbitration, the courts have a comparatively consistent understanding of the meaning and connotation of the social public interest.

For instance, in the case of *Beijing Polestar Travel Technology Co., Ltd. v. Sichuan Jinlicheng Clothing Co., Ltd.*,[3] the Beijing Third Intermediate People's Court considered that "The social public interest refers to the general interests of the public involving the most fundamental laws and moralities of the entire society. It concerns the interests of all members of society and corresponds to private interests. It includes two aspects: public order and public morality. Public order mainly includes social public order and life order; public morality, that is, good customs, refers to the moral code generally recognized and followed by all members of society. The subject of the social public interests has social publicity and its content is universal." In the case *Beijing Zhongxin Zhirong Investment Fund Management Co., Ltd. v. Ma*,[4] the

---

[1] Paragraph 3 of Article 58 of the Arbitration Law stipulates that "The people's court shall rule to cancel the award if it holds that the award is contrary to the social public interests.".

[2] Paragraph 3 of Article 237 of the Civil Procedure Law stipulates that "The people's court shall rule not to enforce the award if it holds that the enforcement of the award is contrary to the social public interests.".

[3] (2018) Jing 03 Min Te No. 46.

[4] (2018) Jing 03 Min Te No. 113.

© The Author(s), under exclusive license to Springer Nature Singapore Pte Ltd. 2022   211
Y. Lin, *China Arbitration Yearbook (2021)*, China Arbitration Yearbook,
https://doi.org/10.1007/978-981-19-1284-9_10

Beijing Third Intermediate People's Court also held that "The subject of the social public interests has social publicity and its content is universal."

However, at the level of practical operation, there are still situations in which the identification of the social public interest is not consistent. For example, will the violation of mandatory provisions of laws violate social public interests?

Beijing Grand Metropark Hotel Co., Ltd. v. Qinhuangdao Bohai Aluminum Curtain Wall Decoration Engineering Co., Ltd.[5]

On July 15, 2013, China Travel Building Co., Ltd. (renamed Beijing Grand Metropark Hotel Co., Ltd. in 2015) and Qinhuangdao Bohai Aluminum Curtain Wall Decoration Engineering Co., Ltd. ("Bohai Company") signed a Professional Subcontracting Contract for Curtain Walls of China Travel Building Interior and Exterior Decoration Project.

Among them, Article 12 of the Subcontracting Contract stipulated that "Any dispute arising from the conclusion and performance of this Contract shall be settled through friendly negotiation. If the negotiation fails, either party has the right to apply to the Beijing Arbitration Commission for arbitration. The arbitration shall be conducted in accordance with the arbitration rules of the commission in effect at that time, and the seat of arbitration shall be Beijing. The arbitral award is final and binding on all parties."

After the dispute between the two parties arose, Bohai Company filed a Request for Arbitration with the Beijing Arbitration Commission.

On April 27, 2018, the Beijing Arbitration Commission made the (2018) Jing Zhong Cai Zi No. 0810 Award, ruling that (1) Beijing Grand Metropark Hotel Co., Ltd. ("Metropark Company") should pay the project funds in the amount of RMB 5,400,000 to Bohai Company; (2) Metropark Company should pay the interests to Bohai Company based on RMB 4,058,000 from April 1, 2016 to the date when the project funds was actually paid, which was temporarily calculated as RMB 267,744.62 on August 21, 2017; (3) Metropark Company should pay the attorney's fee in the amount of RMB 60,000 to Bohai Company; (4) Other claims of Bohai Company were dismissed; (5) Bohai Company should pay RMB 20,000 for losses to Metropark Company; (6) Other counterclaims of Metropark Company were dismissed; (7) In this case, the arbitration of RMB 70,316.68 for the claims should be borne by Bohai Company for whichRMB 21,09B,5. Seventy percent of the arbitration fee should be borne by Metropark Company, which was RMB 49,221.68. The arbitration fee for counterclaims in this case was RMB 26,550.Thirty percent of the arbitration fee should be borne by Bohai Company, which was RMB 7,965. Seventy percent of the arbitration fee should be borne by Metropark Company, which was RMB 18,585.

Afterwards, Metropark Company applied to the Beijing Third Intermediate People's Court to revoke the arbitral award. One of the reasons was that the award involved seriously violatedsocial public interests. Metropark Company alleged that it was a wholly state-owned enterprise, and the project involved was the exterior

---

[5] (2018) Jing 04 Min Te No. 250.

decoration project of Metropark Company's hotel, involving public places, and fell within the "large-scale infrastructure, public utilities and other projects related to the social public interests and public safety" stipulated in Item 1, Paragraph 1, Article 3 of the Bidding Law of the People's Republic of China ("Bidding Law") that must be tendered. However, the contract involved in the case was not tendered, and the arbitral tribunal made the Award based on the contract, which harmed the interests of the state-owned enterprise China Railway Co. The Award seriously violated the social public interest and thus should be set aside.

Bohai Company stated that the Award involved only resolved the dispute between Metropark Company and Bohai Company and did not involve the interests of persons not involved in the case, and China Railway Co. did not raise any objections. Moreover, the interests of state-owned enterprises were not equal to national interests or public interests, and the absence of bidding for a project did not equal the violation of social public interests. The public interests involved in the bidding law were mainly project quality and public safety, rather than the settlement or funds of a certain enterprise. Under the circumstance where the project was safe, the award on the settlement of project payments did not violate the public interests. The project in this case had been in normal use since it was accepted by Metropark Company National standards had been met by all technical indicators, and there was no harm to the public interests.

Regarding the issue of whether the Award involved in the case violated the social public interests, Beijing Third Intermediate People's Court considered that the social public interests were related to the interests of all members of society, were enjoyed by the public, were required by the development of the entire society, and had public and social influence, which were different from the interests of the parties to the contract. In the case at hand, the contract involved in the case was voluntarily concluded by the civil subjects, and its contents did not violate mandatory provisions of laws and administrative regulations. The two parties to the contract were Metropark Company and Bohai. Co. The disputes involved in the case were project payment and other related matters stipulated in the contract, which should fall within the disputes between equal civil subjects governed by the Contract Law. The result of this case only affected the parties to the contract and did not involve the public interest. Therefore, the reason for the cancellation of the application was not accepted.

In practice, different courts hold different opinions on whether the violation of mandatory provisions of laws will violate the social public interest.

In the present case, the contract involved in the case violated the provisions of the Bidding Law due to the failure to tender, but the court held that the dispute involved in this case was related to the project payment and other related matters between the two equal civil entities, Metropark Company and Bohai Company, while social public interests were related to the interests of all members of the society. The outcome of this case only affected the parties to the contract and therefore did not involve social public interests.

In contrast, *Dongying Jinmeng Construction & Installation Co., Ltd. v. Shandong Zhonghai Liqun Real Estate Co., Ltd.,*[6] the construction contract involved in the case also violated the Bidding Law due to the failure to conduct bidding. Pursuant to Article 1 of the Interpretation of the SPC on Issues Concerning the Application of Law for the Trial of Cases of Dispute over Contracts on Undertaking Construction Projects, the contract should be deemed invalid. The arbitral award in the case determined that the contract was valid and confirmed the rights and obligations of both parties accordingly. As a consequence, the court of the case considered that the award violated mandatory provisions of the Bidding Law and violated the social public interests, thus revoking the award involved.

Similar to this case, there are some cases where the violation of mandatory provisions of laws was deemed the violation of social public interest. We list some examples here.

In the case *Wuhan Chaofan Logistics (Ezhou) Co., Ltd., et al. v. CCCC Second Harbor Engineering Co., Ltd.,*[7] the award involved in the case, which determined that the delivery was qualified and awarded the payment for the project, violated the mandatory provisions concerning the completion of inspection and acceptance before being delivered for use in the Port Law and Measures for the Completion Check and Acceptance of Port Projects. Therefore, the court revoked the arbitral award on the ground of the violation of the social public interest.

Jiangsu Taishengda Construction Engineering Co., Ltd. v. Yancheng Dadi Real Estate Co., Ltd.,[8] the contract involved in the case, which involved illegal borrowing of building qualifications, violated Article 26 of the Construction Law regarding the prohibition of borrowing building qualifications by construction companies.The court found that the confirmation of the validity of the contract by the arbitral award violated the social public interest and should be set aside in accordance with the law.

In the case *Huaxin Petroleum (Guangdong) Co., Ltd. v. Guangdong Zhongyu Energy Development Co., Ltd.,*[9] the contract involved in the case, which covered up the true purpose of the refined oil transaction in the name of marine fuel oil, violated the mandatory provisions of the administrative regulations of the State Council on franchising. The court held that the confirmation of the validity of the contract by the arbitral award would have an undesirable demonstration effect and therefore violated the social public interests.

In fact, as to whether the violation of mandatory provisions of laws would constitute the violation of social public interests, the SPC had made it clear in its Reply on the Application for Recognition and Enforcement of the London Sugar Association Arbitral Award by ED & F Mans (Hong Kong) Co., Ltd.[10] that "The violation of mandatory provisions of laws of China cannot be completely equivalent to violation of public policy of China."

---

[6] (2016) Lu 05 Min Te No. 9.

[7] (2015) E Wu Han Zhong Zhong Jian Zi No. 00159.

[8] (2014) Yan Min Zhong Shen Zi No. 0015.

[9] (2013) Sui Zhong Fa Zhong Shen Zi No. 95.

[10] (2003) Min Si Ta Zi No. 3.

Although the reply was made for the recognition and enforcement of foreign arbitral awards, the meaning of public policy and social public interest should be the same. Paragraph 3, Article 7 of Arrangements of the SPC on the Mutual Enforcement of Arbitral Awards by the Mainland and Hong Kong stipulates that "If a court in the Mainland decides that to enforce the arbitral award in Mainland is contrary to the social public interests of the Mainland, or if a court of Hong Kong decides that to enforce the arbitral award in Hong Kong is contrary to public policy in Hong Kong, such a court may refuse to enforce the said award."In this provision, the social public interests and public policy are placed in corresponding positions, and both are situations where the arbitral award may not be enforced. Pursuant to the opinion of the SPC reflected in the aforementioned reply, the violation of mandatory provisions of law does not necessarily equal the violation of the social public interest of China.

10.2 Violation of Policy Documents

Pursuant to Paragraph 3, Article 58 of the Arbitration Law, the violation of social public interest is one of the situations where an arbitral award should be revoked. Different from the six situations stipulated in the first paragraph of Article 58 of the Arbitration Law, the violation of the social public interest does not depend on the proof of the subject applying for revocation of the arbitral award. The court may examine whether the arbitral award violates the social public interests *ex officio*.

Even so, in most applications for setting aside of arbitral awards, the applicant will claim that the arbitral award involved in the case violates the social public interests and thus shall be revoked. However, the claim is rarely supported by the courts. The reason is that the threshold for the court to find the violation of the social public interest is relatively high.

In practice, the applicant may claim that the arbitral award violates the social public interests based on the violation of a certain policy of the country.

Yang, et al. v. Ji.[11]

On February 10, 2015, Ji signed the Equity Investment Agreement with Yang, Shanghai Luban Financial Information Service Co., Ltd. ("Luban Company"), and Shanghai XX Co., Ltd., a person not involved in the case.

Afterwards, Shanghai XX Co., Ltd. transferred its shares of Luban Company to Shanghai Guangyun Technology Development Co., Ltd. ("Guangyun Company") and signed the Agreement on Transferring Luban's Equity.

Concerning the dispute arising from the performance of the Equity Investment Agreement, Ji applied to Shanghai Arbitration Commission for arbitration on January 2, 2019, and Shanghai Arbitration Commission accepted the case on January 4, 2019.

The requests of Ji included: (1) Yang and Guangyun Company should pay the equity repurchase price for the amount of RMB 14.4 million to Ji; (2) Yang and

---

[11] (2019) Hu 01 Min Te No. 639.

Guangyun Company should pay damages for breach of contract to Ji for overdue payment (calculated on the basis of the actual investment of Ji for the amount of RMB 12 million at 5% per day from October 31, 2018 until the date of actual payment); (3) Luban Company should pay liquidated damages to Ji for failing to provide quarterly operation reports and annual financial statements as contracted (calculated on the basis of the actual investment of Ji for the amount of RMB 12 million at 2% per day from August 1, 2016 until the date when the materials mentioned above had been actually provided); (4) Luban Company should cooperate with the audit of its operating status and financial status, respectively in 2015, 2016 and 2017; if it was audited that Luban Company had after-tax profits, it should distribute profits to Ji in proportion to its equity; (5) Yang should be jointly and severally liable for the third and fourth claims; (6) Yang, Guangyun Company and Luban Company should jointly bear attorney's fees for the amount of RMB 500,000 paid by Ji; (7) The arbitration costs should be jointly borne by Yang, Guangyun Company and Luban Company.

After the trial, the arbitral tribunal was considered as follows:

(1)   The Equity Investment Agreement was signed by all parties and reflected the true intention of the parties. Ji's participation in the operation and management of Luban Company was the autonomy of the internal shareholders of the company and a voluntary and reasonable sharing of business risks by all parties, which did not violate mandatory provisions of laws. Therefore, the Equity Investment Agreement was legal and valid.

(2)   Regarding the jurisdiction, Ji initiated arbitration on the basis of Article 8.2 of the Equity Investment Agreement concerning the repurchase of his shares and Article 29.2 concerning the dispute resolution clause. Therefore, the arbitral tribunal had jurisdiction over the dispute.

(3)   Regarding the equity repurchase price, pursuant to the clause involved, if Luban Company failed to complete the listing on schedule, Ji was entitled to request Yang and Guangyun Company to perform the equity repurchase obligations. Now that the repurchase conditions had been triggered, Yang and Guangyun Company should pay the equity repurchase price for the amount of RMB 14.4 million to Ji.

(4)   Regarding the starting time of liquidated damages, since Ji only proposed a repurchase plan with a 40% premium on the investment principal before the arbitration and a repurchase plan with a 20% premium on the investment principal was not proposed until the arbitration, the penalty for late payment should be calculated from the time when Yang, Guangyun Company and Luban Company submitted their Statements of Defense.

(5)   Ji raised no objection to the authenticity of the financial statement screenshots, audit reports and other evidence provided by Yang, Guangyun Company and Luban Company, and knew the content of these reports and the way to obtain them. Moreover, this right was never claimed during the period between the signing of the Equity Investment Agreement and the dispute between the two parties over the repurchase arose. Meanwhile, the conditions for profit distribution claimed by Ji were not yet available. Ji's request for liquidated damages

due to the failure of Luban Companyto provide quarterly operation reports and annual financial statements and profit distribution should not be supported by the arbitral tribunal.

(6) Regarding attorney fees, Ji provided proof of attorney fees, and this case was caused by the failure of Yang, Guangyun Company, and Luban Company to perform the agreed obligations under the Equity Investment Agreement, so the request for attorney fees claimed by Ji should be supported.

Shanghai Arbitration Commission issued the (2019) Hu Zhong An Zi No. 0032 Award on September 4, 2019, ruling that: (1) Yang and Guangyun Company should pay the equity repurchase price for the amount of RMB 14.4 million to Ji within 10 days from the date when the award was rendered; (2) Yang and Guangyun Company should pay damages for breach of contract to Ji for overdue payment (calculated on the basis of the actual investment of Ji for the amount of RMB 12 million at 5% per day from February 22, 2019 until the date of actual payment) within 10 days fromthe date when the award was rendered; (3) Luban Company should cooperate with the audit of its operating status and financial status, respectively in 2015, 2016 and 2017; (4) Yang, Guangyun Company and Luban Company should pay attorney's fees for the amount of RMB 500,000 to Ji within 10 days from the date when the award was rendered; (5) The arbitration costs in this case was RMB 156,636, Ji should bear RMB 156,636 and 140,972.40 should be jointly borne by Yang, Guangyun Company and Luban Company.

Yang, Guangyun Company, and Luban Company applied to the Shanghai First Intermediate People's Court to revoke the Award above because the Award violated social public interests. Pursuant to the Opinions on Doing a Good Job in the Classification and Disposal of Online Lending Institutions and Risk Prevention issued by the Office of the Leading Group for the Special Rectification of Internet Financial Risks and the Office of the Leading Group for the Special Rectification of P2P Online Lending Risks,[12] the responsibilities of the organization shall be consolidated, and the actual controller and senior management of the organization shall be required to promise the "Six Nos", including not changing the major shareholders. The Finance Office also inquired Luban Company several times. The Award in this case supported Ji's request for share repurchase, violating financial regulatory policies and social public interests.

Regarding the allegation of the applicant that the Award violated the social public interests, the Shanghai First Intermediate People's Court considered that: Generally, the social public interests refer to the interests of all members of society or an unspecified majority of people in society, mainly including social public order and social good customs, etc. The implementation of the Equity Transfer Agreement in this case only affected the rights and obligations between the parties involved, and the effect was not public or integral. For the supervisory opinions of financial service offices at all levels proposed by the applicant at online lending institutions, although social public interests were an important value goal of public policy formulation, not all policy documents could be covered by the scope of the social public

---

[12] Zheng Zhi Ban Han [2018] No. 175.

interests prescribed by laws. In this case, the evidence submitted by the applicant only showed that the country regulated the risk prevention and control of the online lending industry and the classification and disposal of online lending institutions, and the applicant stated that Luban Company had not currently been involved in any illegal activities. Therefore, the repurchase agreement between the parties did not involve the social public interests, and it did not violate the social public interests for the arbitral tribunal to make an award on this.

We can see from the results of the judgment that the court usually will not support the applicant's allegation that the arbitral award violates a certain state policy and thus violates the social public interests. In this case, the claimant alleged that the Arbitral Award, which ruled that Yang and Guangyun Company should repurchase the equity held by Ji, violated financial regulatory policies and thus violated social public interests. In this regard, the Shanghai First Intermediate People's Court held the opinion that although social public interests were an important value goal of public policy formulation, not all policy documents could be covered by the scope of the social public interests prescribed by laws. In other words, the violation of policy documents cannot be equal to the violation of social public interests.

Similarly, *Shenzhen Qianhai Chengyue Asset Management Co., Ltd. v. Wang, et al.,*[13] the applicant claimed that the arbitral award involved in the case, which ruled the applicant to pay all the investment funds and the loss of the income to investor Wang on the ground of the constitution of breach of contract due to its failure to redeem on time, constituted a rigid redemption, harmed the interests of other investors and the order of the financial market, and therefore violated social public interests. In this regard, the Beijing Third Intermediate People's Court held that the contract between the applicant and investor Wang was an agreement reached voluntarily by equal civil entities on the basis of equal consultation, and the civil disputes arising therefrom were disputes between private entities. The award did not involve social public interests.

From the above-mentioned court reasoning, it can be seen that not all policy documents can be covered by the scope of the social public interests prescribed by laws, and the violation of policy documents does not necessarily constitute the violation of the social public interests.

10.3   Conflicts with Effective Rulings of Courts

Pursuant to Paragraph 3 of Article 7 of Arrangements of the SPC on the Mutual Enforcement of Arbitral Awards by the Mainland and Hong Kong, the violation of the social public interest is a situation in which the courts in the Mainland may rule not to enforce the arbitral award made in Hong Kong *ex officio*.

Regarding the meaning of social public interests, the SPC had pointed out in its Reply to the Request for Instructions concerning the Applicant Castel Electronics Pty

---

[13] (2020) Jing 04 Jing Te No. 193.

Ltd.'s Application for Recognition and Enforcement of Foreign Arbitral Awards[14] that "The situation of the violation of public policy stipulated in Item B, Paragraph 2, Article 5 of the New York Convention should be understood as the situation where the recognition and enforcement of foreign arbitral awards will result in the violation of the basic principles of our country's laws, the infringement of our country's sovereignty, the detriment to social public security, the violation of good customs, etc., which will endanger the fundamental social public interest of our country."

In the Chinese context, the connotations of social public interests and public policy are often the same with relatively high applicable standards. Only when there is the violation of the basic principles of our country's laws, the infringement of our country's sovereignty, the detriment to social public security, the violation of good customs, etc., will it constitute the violation of the social public interests of China?

Automotive Gate FZCO, et al. v. Hebei Zhongxing Automobile Manufacturing Co., Ltd.[15]

The applicant and the respondent signed the Agency Agreement and the Technical Cooperation Agreement, respectively, in April and June 2007.

Among them, Article 14 of the Agency Agreement stipulated that "In case of breach of any of the Articles of this agreement by either of the parties, both Parties agree to put best efforts to remedy by negotiation. Otherwise, both parties agree to arbitration as per the International Chamber of Commerce and held in CHINA?" Article 10.4 of the Technical Cooperation Agreement stated that "Any dispute, controversy or difference which may arise between the parties out of or in relation to this Agreement or for the breach thereof shall be settled amicably by the parties, but in case of failure, it shall be finally settled in CHINA by arbitration pursuant to the Rules of the International Chamber of Commerce whose award shall bind the parties hereto."

In May 2011, the respondent filed an application with the Shijiazhuang Intermediate People's Court of Hebei Province ("Shijiazhuang Intermediate People's Court"), requesting confirmation that the arbitration clauses contained in the two agreements above were invalid.

On October 11, 2011, the applicant filed the No. 18228/CYK arbitration with ICC in Hong Kong.

In November 2011, the respondent informed the arbitral tribunal that it had made an application for confirmation of the invalidity of the arbitration clauses with the Shijiazhuang Intermediate People's Court.

On February 19, 2013, the sole arbitrator appointed by the ICC rendered a partial award, ruling that "a. The arbitral tribunal in this case has the power to deal with all disputes in the Terms of Reference; b. Although the respondent applied to the Shijiazhuang Intermediate People's Court, this arbitration procedure should not be suspended or stopped but should continue; c. The second, third and fourth applicants are parties to the CKD and Agency Agreement and Technical Cooperation Agreement and are eligible to participate in this arbitration procedure; d. Disputes arising from

---

[14] (2013) Min Si Ta Zi No. 46.

[15] (2017) Jing 04 Min Te No. 45.

or related to the CKD and Agency Agreement and Technical Cooperation Agreement listed in the Terms of Reference shall be consolidated into one case for processing; and ⑨. The claims relating to the CKD and Agency Agreement and after-sales services listed in the Terms of Reference agreed by all parties dated June 26, 2012 should not be submitted to CIETAC.

The applicant applied to the Yichang Intermediate People's Court of Hubei Province ("Yichang Intermediate People's Court") for recognition and enforcement of the Partial Award. The Yichang Intermediate People's Court made the (2015) E Yi Chang Zhong Min Ren Zi No. 00003 Ruling on March 20, 2017, ruling to suspend the lawsuit.

On July 6, 2018, the Shijiazhuang Intermediate People's Court made the (2011) Shi Min Li Cai Zi No. 00002 Ruling, confirming that the arbitration clauses in the CKD and Agency Agreement and Technical Cooperation Agreement were invalid. The case before the Yichang Intermediate People's Court was resumed.

In this case, of recognition and enforcement of the Partial Award, the respondent raised multiple defenses against the recognition and enforcement of the Partial Award. Among them, the respondent considered that there was a serious conflict between the Partial Award and the effective Ruling of the Shijiazhuang Intermediate People's Court, and the recognition and enforcement of the arbitral award would violate the social public interests of the Mainland; thus, the Partial Award should not be recognized and enforced.

The Yichang Intermediate People's Court held that:

The (2011) Shi Min Li Cai Zi No. 00002 case adjudicated by the Shijiazhuang Intermediate People's Court was accepted earlier than the ICC 18,228/CYK case, and the respondent filed a jurisdictional objection to ICC at the beginning of its defense and requested to suspend or terminate the arbitration procedure to wait for the Shijiazhuang Intermediate People's Court to make a ruling on the validity of the arbitration clauses. The ICC was aware of the existence of the (2011) Shi Min Li Cai Zi No. 00002 case but still made the No. 18228/CYK Partial Award, ruling that the arbitral tribunal had jurisdiction over the case. The Partial Award was made by the arbitral tribunal on the premise that both the arbitration clauses in the CKD and Agency Agreement and the Technical Cooperation Agreement were valid.

The Shijiazhuang Intermediate People's Court made the (2011) Shi Min Li Cai Zi No. 00002 Ruling on July 6, 2018 and determined that the arbitration clauses in the CKD and Agency Agreement and Technical Cooperation Agreement were invalid. The Ruling had come into legal effect. On the premise that the people's court had made a negative judgment on the validity of the arbitration clauses between the parties, the recognition and enforcement of the arbitral award based on the abovementioned arbitration clauses would conflict with the abovementioned effective Ruling of the people's court, which would violate the social public interest of the mainland.

Paragraph 3, Article 7 of Arrangements of the SPC on the Mutual Enforcement of Arbitral Awards by the Mainland and Hong Kong stipulates that "If a court in the Mainland decides that to enforce the arbitral award in the Mainland is contrary to the social public interests of the Mainland, or if a court of Hong Kong decides that to enforce the arbitral award in Hong Kong is contrary to public policy in Hong Kong, such a court may refuse to enforce the said award."

Therefore, the Yichang Intermediate People's Court made the (2015) E Yi Chang Zhong Min Ren Zi No. 00002 and No. 00003 Rulings ruling not to recognize and enforce the Partial Award.

Judging from the judicial practice of Chinese courts of the recognition and enforcement of foreign arbitral awards or arbitral awards made in Hong Kong, Macao and Taiwan Region in recent years, applications that are rejected due to the violation of the social public interest or the violation of public policy are often related to the judicial sovereignty of China and the judicial jurisdiction of Chinese courts.

For example, in the case of *Hemofarm DD, et al. v. Jinan Yongning Pharmaceutical Co., Ltd.*,[16] the parties signed the Joint Venture Contract and established Jinan-Hemofarm Pharmaceutical Co., Ltd. Afterwards, the respondent sued the joint venture company before the Jinan Intermediate People's Court, demanding the payment of rent and the return of part of the leased property, and submitted an application for property preservation to the court, which obtained the court's permission. After the dispute over the Joint Venture Contract between the parties arose, the applicant applied to the ICC for arbitration. In the third part of the arbitral award, the arbitral tribunal heard the lease agreement between the respondent and the joint venture company and ruled that the claimant could obtain 30% of the litigation costs for defending the joint venture in the lease dispute. In this case, the SPC held that under the circumstance where the relevant Chinese courts had ruled on the preservation on the property of the joint venture company and made a judgment on the lease agreement dispute between the respondent and the joint venture company, the hearing and adjudicating of the arbitral award on the lease agreement dispute had violated the judicial sovereignty of China and the judicial jurisdiction of Chinese courts, and thus the arbitral award involved should notbe recognized and enforced.

Similarly, in the case *Wicor Holding AG v. Taizhou Hope Investment Co., Ltd.*,[17] the joint venture contract signed by both parties contained an arbitration clause. The respondent filed a lawsuit with the Taizhou Intermediate People's Court on May 20, 2011, and the applicant filed an objection to the jurisdiction on the ground of the existence of an arbitration agreement between the parties. The Taizhou Intermediate People's Court made the (2011) Tai Zhong Shang Wai Chu Zi No. 0012 Civil Ruling, considering that the arbitration clause did not stipulate an arbitration institutionand the parties did not reach a supplementary agreement afterwards, and thus the arbitration clause involved in the case was invalid and rejecting the objection to the jurisdiction. The applicant made an appeal against the Ruling, but the original Ruling was maintained by the (2012) Su Shang Wai Xia Zi No. 0012 Civil Ruling rendered by the High People's Court of Jiangsu Province. Later, the Taizhou

---

[16] Reply of the SPC to the Request for Instructions on the Non-Recognition and Non-Enforcement of the ArbitralAward of ICC, [2008] Min Si Ta Zi No. 11.

[17] (2015) Tai Zhong Shang Zhong Shen Zi No. 00004; Reply of the SPC to the Request for Instructions on the Non-Enforcement of the No. 18295/CYK Arbitral Award of ICC, (2016) Zui Gao Fa Min Ta No. 8.

Intermediate People's Court notified the ICC of the invalidity of the agreement by mail, and the respondent also raised an objection concerning the invalidity of the arbitration clause in the arbitration proceedings. However, the ICC still accepted the applicant's request for arbitration and made a ruling, determining that the arbitration agreement was valid, and ruling that the respondent should bear a series of liabilities. Afterwards, the applicant applied to the Taizhou Intermediate People's Court for recognition and enforcement of the arbitral award. In its reply, the SPC held that the arbitral award was made by the arbitrators on the premise that the arbitration clause involved in the case was valid, the enforcement of the arbitral award in the Mainland would conflict with the effective ruling made by the High People's Court of Jiangsu Province and violate the social public interest of the Mainland, and thus, the arbitral award should not be enforced.

The same situation occurred in the case at hand. In this case, the CKD and Agency Agreement and the Technical Cooperation Agreement signed by the applicant and the respondent contained arbitration clauses. After the dispute occurred, the respondent first applied to the Shijiazhuang Intermediate People's Court to confirm that the above arbitration clauses were invalid, and the applicant applied to the ICC for arbitration. Afterwards, the arbitral tribunal made a partial award and considered that it had jurisdiction over the case. The Shijiazhuang Intermediate People's Court made the (2011) Shi Min Li Cai Zi No. 00002 Ruling on July 6, 2018, ruling that the arbitration clauses above were invalid. Later, the applicant applied to the Yichang Intermediate People's Court for recognition and enforcement of the Partial Award. The Yichang Intermediate People's Court considered that on the premise that the people's court had made a negative judgment on the validity of the arbitration clauses between the parties, the recognition and enforcement of the arbitral award based on the arbitration clauses would conflict with the effective Ruling of the people's court, which would violate the social public interests of the Mainland.

It is worth noting that the inconsistency between the determination of a certain matter (such as the validity of the arbitration agreement) in the arbitral award and the effective judgment of the Chinese courts does not necessarily constitute a violation of social public interest or public policy of China. It is still necessary to conduct an analysis based on the specific circumstances of each case.

For instance, in the case *Castel Electronics Pty Ltd. v. TCL Air Conditioner (Zhongshan) Co., Ltd.*,[18] although there were inconsistencies between the arbitral award involved in the case and the determination of the validity of the arbitration clause involved in the case by the Chinese court, the application for enforcement and recognition was not dismissed on the ground of the violation of the social public interests. On the one hand, the arbitral award involved in the case was issued earlier than the effective time of the ruling by the Chinese court. On the other hand, the respondent failed to raise an objection to the invalidity of the arbitration clause in the arbitration procedure. Instead, it filed a counterclaim to the arbitral tribunal. Based on these two reasons, the SPC held the position that it was in accordance with the law

---

[18] Reply of the SPC to the Request for Instructions on the Application of Castel Electronics Pty Ltd. of Recognition and Enforcement of Foreign Arbitral Award, [2013] Min Si Ta Zi No. 46.

of the seat of arbitration and the arbitration rules for the arbitral tribunal to determine the validity of the arbitration clause and its jurisdiction, and there was no violation of the judicial sovereignty of China.

This case was substantially different from the Castel case. Although the time when the arbitral tribunal made the Partial Award was earlier than the effective time of the Ruling made by the Shijiazhuang Intermediate People's Court in this case, the time when Shijiazhuang Intermediate People's Court accepted the case for confirming the validity of the arbitration agreement was earlier than the ICC 18,228/CYK case, and the respondent raised an objection to the jurisdiction of ICC and requested the suspension or termination of the arbitration procedure to wait for the Shijiazhuang Intermediate People's Court to make a ruling on the validity of the arbitration clause at the very beginning of its defense. These factors played an important role in the rejection of the Yichang Intermediate People's Court to the recognition and enforcement of the Partial Award.

Chapter 11
Main China Arbitration Institutions and Judicial Review Decisions

In recent years, arbitration in China has entered the stage of rapid development. In 2017, 253 arbitration institutions in China accepted 239,360 cases.[1] In 2018, arbitration institutions in China handled 544,536 cases, and the growth rate was 127%. The total disputed amount reached RMB 695 billion, which increased by 30% from 2017.[2] In 2019, arbitration institutions in China accepted 486,955 cases, and the total disputed amount was RMB 759.8 billion.[3]

With the substantial growth in the number of arbitration cases, the number of arbitration judicial review cases in China has increased correspondingly. In 2019, there were 11,029 applications to the courts in China to set aside arbitral awards, with 637 successfully or partly granted. Thirty-two applications for the recognition or enforcement of foreign arbitral awards were decided by China's courts in 2019, with only one partly refused.[4] The judicial review cases usually involve confirmation of the validity of arbitration agreement, application for setting aside the arbitral award, application for enforcement of domestic or foreign arbitral awards, etc. These cases can help us understand the practice of judicial review, clarify the judicial approach toward arbitration, and supplement, improve, or amend the practice of arbitration institutions.

---

[1] See *Annual Report on International Commercial Arbitration in China (2017)*.

[2] See *Annual Report on International Commercial Arbitration in China (2018–2019)*.

[3] CIETAC, *CIETAC releases Annual Report on International Commercial Arbitration in China (2019–2020)*, http://www.cietac.org/index.php?m=Article&a=show&id=17194 (accessed November 13, 2020).

[4] See *Annual Report of Judicial Review of China Arbitration (2019)* issued by SPC on December 23, 2020.

© The Author(s), under exclusive license to Springer Nature Singapore Pte Ltd. 2022
Y. Lin, *China Arbitration Yearbook (2021)*, China Arbitration Yearbook,
https://doi.org/10.1007/978-981-19-1284-9_11

Currently, there are 258 arbitration institutions in China.[5] To better understand the relationship between the arbitration institutions and the judicial review, we take some cases involving major arbitration institutions in China, such as SCIA, CIETAC, SHIAC, Guangzhou Arbitration Commission, BIAC, etc., to introduce and analyze those decisions and opinions concerning the arbitration agreement, arbitration parties, arbitration institutions, arbitration procedures, the scope of judicial review, the scope of arbitration and beyond the scope of submission to arbitration, arbitrability, and public policy, etc.

11.1   Arbitration Agreements

According to the Arbitration Law, to initiate arbitral proceedings, an arbitration agreement is required.[6] For an arbitration agreement to be valid, parties' consent to arbitration is required.[7] For the arbitration institution or the court conducting judicial review of arbitration, they need to make sure that there exists a valid arbitration agreement. Provisions concerning the arbitration agreement may also be found in the main arbitration institution rules, *i.e.*, Article 8 of the SCIA Arbitration Rules,[8] Article

---

[5] The data comes from the official website of the *Ministry of Justice of the PRC*, http://12348.moj. gov.cn/#/publicies/zc/zcfw (accessed May 14, 2020).

[6] Article 4 of the Arbitration Law provides that, "In settling disputes through arbitration, an agreement to engage in arbitration should first of all be reached by parties concerned upon free will. Without such an agreement, the arbitration commission shall refuse to accept the application for arbitration by any one single party.".

[7] Article 16 of the Arbitration Law provides that, "An agreement for arbitration shall include the arbitration clauses stipulated in the contracts or other written agreements for arbitration reached before or after a dispute occurs. An arbitration agreement shall contain the following: 1. The expression of application for arbitration. 2. Matters for arbitration. 3. The arbitration commission which has been chosen.".

[8] Article 8 of SCIA Arbitration Rules provides that, "1. An arbitration agreement means an arbitration clause in a contract or any other form of written agreement concluded between the parties providing for arbitration. 2. An arbitration agreement may be concluded between the parties either before or after the occurrence of the dispute.3. An arbitration agreement shall be in writing, which includes but not limited to, a memorandum of contract, letter or electronic message (including telex, facsimile, electronic mail and electronic data interchange), etc. which is capable of expressing its contents in a tangible form. 4. It shall be deemed that there is an arbitration agreement in writing: (a) where its existence is asserted by one party and not denied by the other during the exchange of the Request for Arbitration and the Statement of Defense; (b) where one party submits the dispute to SCIA for arbitration and the other party expresses its agreement on arbitration in writing; (c) where one party undertakes in writing to submit the dispute to SCIA for arbitration and the other party submits the dispute to SCIA for arbitration; or (d) where the parties sign the record of oral hearings or other documents jointly during the arbitration proceedings, stating their agreement to arbitrate in SCIA.".

5 of the CIETAC Arbitration Rules,[9] Article 5 of the SHIAC Arbitration Rules,[10] and Article 10 of the Arbitration Rules of Guangzhou Arbitration Commission.[11]

The primary issue that courts need to consider when deciding the validity of an arbitration agreement is whether the parties have expressed an intention to settle their dispute through arbitration. For each arbitration institution, the question is whether the parties have expressed an intention to resolve disputes for arbitration in this institution? Generally, the expression of the intention to arbitrate is easy to identify (as in the first case below), but sometimes it needs to be analyzed in combination with

---

[9] Article 5 of CIETAC Arbitration Rules provides that, "1. An arbitration agreement means an arbitration clause in a contract or any other form of a written agreement concluded between the parties providing for the settlement of disputes by arbitration. 2. The arbitration agreement shall be in writing. An arbitration agreement is in writing if it is contained in the tangible form of a document such as a contract, letter, telegram, telex, fax, electronic data interchange, or email. An arbitration agreement shall be deemed to exist where its existence is asserted by one party and not denied by the other during the exchange of the Request for Arbitration and the Statement of Defense. 3. Where the law applicable to an arbitration agreement has different provisions as to the form and validity of the arbitration agreement, those provisions shall prevail. 4. An arbitration clause contained in a contract shall be treated as a clause independent and separate from all other clauses of the contract, and an arbitration agreement attached to a contract shall also be treated as independent and separate from all other clauses of the contract. The validity of an arbitration clause or an arbitration agreement shall not be affected by any modification, cancellation, termination, transfer, expiry, invalidity, ineffectiveness, rescission, or nonexistence of the contract.".

[10] Article 5 of SHIAC arbitration rules provides that, "1. SHIAC shall, upon the written application of a party, accept a case in accordance with the arbitration agreement concluded between the parties, either before or after the occurrence of the dispute, in which it is provided that a dispute is to be referred to SHIAC for arbitration. 2. An arbitration agreement means an arbitration clause in a contract concluded between the parties or any other form of the written agreement providing for the settlement of disputes by arbitration. 3. An arbitration agreement shall be in writing. An arbitration agreement is in writing if it is contained in a tangible form of a document such as, but not limited to, a contract, letter, telegram, telex, facsimile, EDI, or email. An arbitration agreement shall be deemed to exist where its existence is asserted by one party and not denied by the other during the exchange of the Request for Arbitration and the Statement of Defense. 4. Where there are different provisions on the form and validity of an arbitration agreement in the laws applicable to an arbitration agreement, such provisions shall prevail. 5. An arbitration clause contained in a contract shall be treated as a clause independent of and separate from all other clauses of the contract, and an arbitration agreement attached to a contract shall also be treated as independent of and separate from all other clauses of the contract. The validity of an arbitration clause or an arbitration agreement shall not be affected by any modification, rescission, termination, transfer, expiration, invalidity, ineffectiveness, revocation, or nonexistence of the contract.".

[11] Article 10 of the arbitration rules of Guangzhou Arbitration Commission provides that, "1. An arbitration agreement means the parties agree to provide disputes which occur or may occur in their contractual or noncontractual legal relationship to arbitration. 2. An agreement for arbitration includes the arbitration clauses stipulated in the contracts or other written agreements for arbitration reached before or after a dispute occurs. 3. An arbitration agreement shall be in writing. An arbitration agreement in writing which includes, but not limited to, a contract, letter, telegram, telex, facsimile, EDI, or email. An arbitration agreement shall be deemed to exist where its existence is asserted by one party and not denied by the other during the exchange of the Request for Arbitration and the Statement of Defense. 4. In the exchange of the statement of claim and the statement of Defense, an arbitration agreement shall be deemed to exist where its existence is asserted by one party and not denied by the other during the exchange of the Request for Arbitration and the Statement of Defense.".

the special circumstances of a particular case. For example, if the parties conclude some contracts together with other valid agreements at the same time or after, which stipulate different dispute resolution methods, the court needs to decide the real intention of the parties.

Arbitration clauses may be similar to the model clauses recommended by various arbitration institutions. However, parties may agree to add or delete some content in the model arbitration clause, subject to relevant provision of the *lex arbitri*. For example, parties may agree to add the place of arbitration, place of heraring, arbitration language or applicable law to the arbitration clause.

1. In practice, the parties often agree in the arbitration agreement to mediate or negotiate before arbitration. It is generally accepted that pre-arbitration procedures do not affect parties' intent to arbitrate

   Wang v. Shenzhen Petrochemical Exchange Co., Ltd. & Shenzhen Qianhai Oil Laifu Petrochemical Investment Co., Ltd. & Guangzhou Helibao Payment Technology Co., Ltd.[12]

   In this case, the contract stipulated that "All disputes between both parties arising from the contract shall be resolved by friendly negotiation. If the disputes cannot be resolved through negotiation, it may apply for mediation to the Shenzhen Petrochemical Exchange or Shenzhen Qianhai Oil Laifu Petrochemical Investment Co., Ltd. If mediation fails, the dispute shall be submitted to SCIA for Arbitration in accordance with the provisional rules at the time of arbitration." Both the court of first instance and the court of second instance held that the dispute should be submitted to SCIA for Arbitration. This agreement was a valid arbitration clause, and both parties were legally bound by it. Therefore, this case should not be resolved through litigation.

   Shi v. Shenzhen Qianhai Yixiang Times Business Service Co., Ltd.[13]

   In this case, the plaintiff initiated a lawsuit without providing the underlying Loan Contract as evidence. The court accepted the defendant's opinion that the plaintiff has been registered as member to some platform, of which the relevant document stipulated that any dispute should be resolved by friendly negotiation, and if the negotiation failed, the dispute should be submitted to SCIA for arbitration.

   Shenzhen Qianhai Yinghua Fund Management Partnership (L.P.) v. Zhu.[14]

   The dispute resolution clause in this case provided for mediation and then arbitration. Article 25 of the Fund Contract stipulated that "All disputes arising from or related to this contract shall be resolved by friendly negotiation and mediation. If the settlement cannot be reached, it shall be submitted to SCIA for

---

[12] (2018) Yue 03 Min Zhong No. 8900.

[13] (2018) Xiang 0111 Min Chu No. 443.

[14] (2018) Yue 03 Min Chu No. 616.

arbitration." The court held that this clause did include the intention to arbitrate and should not be considered to be among the invalid circumstances provided by Article 7 of the Arbitration Law Interpretation, "Where the parties agree that a dispute may be submitted to an arbitration institution for arbitration or filed with the people's court for commencement of legal proceedings, the arbitration agreement shall be deemed invalid." There was no legal ground for the applicant to claim that the arbitration clause was unclear and invalid.

2. However, the arbitration intention can be altered, deviated or added. Generally, the court will respect the parties' latest intention

Shenzhen Xingyang Chemical Co., Ltd. v. Suining Yingchuangli Electronic Technology Co., Ltd.[15]

In this case, the contract stated that "both parties shall resolve all disputes arising from this contract through friendly negotiation; if the dispute cannot be resolved by negotiation, it shall be arbitrated by the arbitration commission where the party B is located, and the PRC Law shall apply." Afterward, the two parties signed the Quality Assurance Agreement and expressly stated that "Any dispute arising from the matters and contents that did not agree upon in this Agreement, Party A and party B shall resolve the disputes through negotiation. If the settlement cannot be reached, they shall file a lawsuit with the local Court of party A (the appellee)." "This agreement is a mandatory term that both parties must abide…" The court held that the parties had changed the original dispute resolution method in the Quality Assurance Agreement and agreed that the case should be resolved by the court where the appellee was located. In accordance with the relevant provisions of the Civil Procedure Law, this alteration was lawful and valid. Moreover, the dispute was caused by product quality problems, and it should be resolved by the court. In similar cases, the more contentious issue is that if the latter dispute resolution method is not clear, other parties may claim the existence of another valid jurisdiction agreement because of the independence of the arbitration agreement.

3. The agreements may stipulate different jurisdictions, leading to the jurisdictional conflict between the court and the arbitration institution. In this situation, the jurisdiction of the dispute needs to be judged in combination with the fact of a particular case

Tianjin Zhongse International Trade Co., Ltd. v. Hongda International Trade Co., Ltd.[16]

In this case, the Sale and Purchase Agreement stated that "If any dispute or claim arising from the contract cannot be settled through friendly negotiation, the case should be submitted to the arbitration institution where the defendant is located (any branch of the CIETAC or the Hong Kong International Arbitral Tribunal). The arbitral award shall be final and binding on both parties." Afterward, the

---

[15] (2018) Chuang 09 Min Xia Zhong No.3.

[16] (2017) Jing Min Zhong No. 494.

appellant and appelleesigned the Supplementary Agreement on November 14, 2014, which specified that the disputes should be resolved by the people's court where the appellant is located. After that, when the appellee refused to pay the debts, the appellant filed a lawsuit. The appellee raised a jurisdictional objection, which wasdismissed in the first instance. The Tianjin High People's Court on appeal heldthat the case should be recognized as a Hong Kong civil case because defendants in the first instance were legal persons registered in Hong Kong. Accordingly, the dispute should be arbitrated by the arbitration institution where the defendant was located. The court found that the Cooperation Agreement referred to "resolving the remaining matters of 2012 as soon as possible", but it did not explicitly define these remaining matters. Therefore, the jurisdiction shall be decided based on the Agreement of Sale and Purchase.

Taoyun (Beijing) Investment Fund Management Co., Ltd. & Shenzhen Taoyun Equity Investment Fund Management Center (L.P.) v. Zhang.[17]

In this case, applicant A and the respondent signed an Admission Agreement on June 25, 2015, and specified that "the disputes arising from this agreement shall be submitted to SHIAC for arbitration". On May 22, 2017, the two applicants and the respondent signed a withdrawal agreement, which stated that the disputes should be submitted to BAC for arbitration. The applicant believed the arbitration clauseswere invalid on the ground that the parties appointed two institutions, SHIAC and BIAC. The court concluded that the two separate agreements involved different issues, and both of them were independent and valid. In this case, the dispute arose from the withdrawal matter; thus, BAC has jurisdiction over the withdrawal dispute.

4.   In foreign-related commercial disputes, the law applicable to determine the validity of the arbitration agreement is a primary issue that the court needs to decide. Depending on the relevant governing law, the validity of the results may sometimes be different

Tianjin Zhongse International Trade Co., Ltd. v. Hongda International Trade Co., Ltd.[18]

In this case, the Sale and Purchase Contract stated "If any dispute or claim arising from the performance of the contract cannot be settled through friendly negotiation, the case shall be arbitrated by the arbitration institution in the place where the defendant is located (any branch of CIETAC or the Hong Kong International Arbitral Tribunal). The arbitral award shall be final and binding on both parties." The Tianjin High People's court of second instance held that the Hong Kong International Arbitral Tribunal should be determined as the arbitration institution with jurisdiction because the arbitration agreement was qualified by "the arbitration institution in the place where the defendant is located", and the appellee was registered in Hong Kong. Although the agreement was not accurate regardingthe

---

[17] (2018) Jing 04 Min Te No. 215.

[18] (2017) Jing Min Zhong No. 494.

name of the institution, it did not give rise to confusion regarding whether the "arbitration institution" exists. Therefore, the Hong Kong law should be applied to determine the validity of the arbitration agreement. According to Article 19 of the Arbitration Ordinance of Hong Kong, "'Arbitration Agreement' is an agreement by the parties to submit to arbitration all or certain disputes which have arisen or which may arise between them in respect of a defined legal relationship, whether is contractual or not. An arbitration agreement may be in the form of an arbitration clause in a contract or the form of a separate agreement", the arbitration clause's validity depends on the parties' intention to arbitrate, and it does not depend on whether the arbitration institution is agreed upon, whether the arbitration institution is the only one, or whether the name of the arbitration institution is accurate. The court of first instance did not have jurisdiction because the parties had already expressed the arbitration intention. In conclusion, the appeal was dismissed, and the original decision was upheld.

5. Based on the independence principle of the arbitration agreement, the invalidity, revocation or termination of a contract shall not affect the validity of the dispute settlement clause in this contract

Cao v. Zheng.[19]

In this case, the Land Sale Contract stipulated that the parties should submit the dispute to CIETAC Hubei Sub-Commission for arbitration. The appellant claimed that the arbitration agreement was invalid because the Land Sale Contract violated the prohibitions of law. The court held that the arbitration clause was valid on the ground that Article 57 of the Contract law stipulated that "the invalidity, revocation or termination of a contract shall not affect the validity of the dispute settlement clause in this contract." Therefore, the arbitration clause was valid whether the contract was valid or not. The dispute should be arbitrated by the CIETAC Hubei Sub-Commission.

6. Once a valid arbitration agreement exists, no party may circumvent the arbitration clause by initiating a lawsuit of tort liability or listing the third party as a codefendant

Zhu v. Shenzhen Hehui Automobile Trade Co., Ltd. & Yougu (Shanghai) Information Technology Co., Ltd.[20]

In this case, the appellant and Yougu Company signed a Quality Assurance Service Agreement, which stipulated that both parties should resolve the dispute by friendly negotiation. If the settlement cannot be reached, either party should submit the dispute to CIETAC for arbitration. After that, the appellant initiated a lawsuit to require Hehui Company and Yougu Company to undertake the joint liability. The court of first instance dismissed the application the grounds that the liability was indivisible and there was an arbitration agreement between the appellant and Yougu Company. The court concluded that although the appellant

---

[19] (2018) Yu 13 Min Zhong No.4713.
[20] (2018) Yue 03 Min Zhong No.511.

initiated a product liability lawsuit, the case should be recognized as a contractual dispute because the appellant's claim was based on breach of the contract. There was a contractual relationship between the appellant and Yougu Company, and this case should be bound by the arbitration clause in the contract. For this reason, there was nothing unreasonable for the court of First Instance to dismiss the application.In contrast, the court of first instance should accept the dispute between the appellant and Hehui Company because there was no arbitration agreement applied to this dispute, and, if necessary, the Yougu Company could take part in the suit as a third party.

Shanmei Coal Import and Export Co., Ltd. v. SINOSTEEL International Macao Offshore Business Service Co., Ltd.[21]

In this case, SINOSTEEL Company, Shanmei Company and Guangnan Company have entered into separate contracts that stipulated that "Any dispute arising from or related to the performance of the contract shall be resolved by friendly negotiation between the parties. If the settlement cannot be reached, the dispute shall be submitted to the China International Economic and Trade Arbitration Commission of CCPIT for arbitration." "The parties agree to submit all disputes to CCPIT in Beijing for Exclusive jurisdiction."SINOSTEEL Company alleged that Qingdao Decheng Mining Co., Ltd. (**"Decheng Company"**) should bear unlimited joint liabilities with the Shanmei Company and Guangnan Company because Decheng Company was the actual controller of Guangnan Company, and it profited from this transaction. The court held the dispute should be resolved by the arbitration institution on the ground that the lawsuit was a contractual dispute, and SINOSTEEL Company had an arbitration agreement with others. In addition, there was no legal relationship between Decheng Company and SINOSTEEL Company. Therefore, after the contractual dispute had been resolved, SINOSTEEL Company could decide whether to sue Decheng Company.

Wenzhou Huazheng Packaging Co., Ltd. v. MARKENIMAS (Shanghai) Label Technology Co., Ltd.[22]

In this case, the general terms on the Sale Contract stipulated that the dispute should be submitted to SHIAC for arbitration. Afterward, the appellant initiated a lawsuit of tort. The court concluded that although the appellant had chosen to initiate a lawsuit of tort, this dispute should be arbitrated by SHIAC because the dispute was caused by theproduct's quality. Additionally, referring to Article 7 of the Summary of the Second National Conference on Maritime Trials in Foreign-related Commercial Matters issued by the SPC, if the parties have agreed upon that all disputes arising from or related to the contract shall be settled by arbitration regardless of whether the party chooses to initiate a lawsuit base on the breach of contract or the tort, the dispute shall be arbitrated.

---

[21] (2018) Lu Min Xia Zhong No.402.

[22] (2017) Zhe 03 Min Zhong No. 5536.

7. However, if the party sues others based on the ground of unjust enrichment, the result of jurisdiction may be different from that of torts

   Greenland Holding Group Co., Ltd. v. Beijing Dongfangjinhong Real Estate Co., Ltd.[23]

   In this case, Beijing Dongfang Jinhong Real Estate Co., Ltd. (renamed Puxiang Real Estate (Beijing) Co., Ltd. in 2017, hereinafter "PuxiangReal Estate Company") signed a Basic Framework Agreement with Greenland Group in 2012 and stipulated that "If the dispute cannot be reached through negotiation, either party shall submit the dispute to CIETAC for arbitration in Beijing." After the transaction was completed, Puxiang Real Estate Company found that the Greenland Group Company and its subsidiary, Beijing Greenland Jingcheng Real Estate Co., Ltd. ("Greenland Jingcheng Company"), had overcharged on payment. Puxiang Real Estate Company initiated a lawsuit on the ground of unjust enrichment. Greenland Group Company raised a jurisdictional objection, claiming that the dispute should be resolved by CIETAC, and there were two causes of action. The court of first instance dismissed the jurisdictional objection, and Greenland Company filed an appeal. The court of second instance dismissed the appeal and upheld the original decision on the ground that this case was a dispute of unjust enrichment based on the fact that defendants had obtained unjust enrichment.

11.2 Party to Arbitration

Under Chinese law, the relativity of contracts also applies to arbitration agreements. In principle, the arbitration agreement binds only the parties to the arbitration agreement, not the nonparties.

1. When insurance subrogation rights are concerned, will parties by bound by the arbitration agreement?

   Harbin Electric Co., Ltd. ("Harbin Electric Company") v. the Guangzhou Branch of People's Property Insurance Co., Ltd.[24]

   In this case, the insurance company, after compensating for the insured's loss, initiated a subrogation lawsuit with the court of first instance pursuant to the arbitration clause in the Project Contract. Therefore, Harbin Electric Company raised jurisdictional objection, and the court of second instance dismissed it. Harbin Electric Company appealed. The court of second instance reversed the decision and dismissed the suit on the ground that the arbitration clause should be binding upon the insurer. The insurer refused to accept this ruling and applied for a retrial with the SPC. The SPC concluded that the date of signing the insurance

---

[23] (2018) Jing Min Xia Zhong No.41.

[24] (2019) Zui Gao Fa Min Shen No.236.

contract was later than the date of signing the project contract. Hence, the insurer should have known the existence of the arbitration agreement when he signed the insurance contract. Additionally, there existed no evidence to prove that the insured had raised objection to the arbitration agreement. Therefore, the retrial application of the insurer should be rejected.

2. The following cases involve the issue of whether the creditor in a subrogation dispute is bound by the arbitration agreement signed by the debtor and the third party

> **Henan Xinxiang Comprehensive Trade Co., Ltd. v. Guotou Coal Co., Ltd. & Henan Xinxing Coal Industry Co., Ltd.[25]**

In this case, the asset transfer agreement signed by the plaintiff and the third party stipulated that the plaintiff transferred the assets to the third party, and the transfer price should be paid in three installments. Each installment should be regarded as the investment payment to be paid by the defendant under the Capital Increase Agreement. After paying the first two installments, the third party and the defendant refused to pay the last installment. However, according to the defendant, both the Asset Transfer Agreement and the Capital Increase Agreement stipulated that the dispute should be submitted to SHIAC for arbitration, and the plaintiff's exercise of the subrogation right should not alter the dispute resolution method agreed upon by the parties. The court held that arbitration only applies to contractual disputes and other disputes over rights and interests in property between equal subjects. In this case, although the arbitration clauses were stipulated in both agreements, there was no contractual relationship between the plaintiff and defendant. Moreover, this dispute was based on the creditor's subrogation, and the plaintiff initiated the lawsuit on the ground of the creditor's right to subrogation. Therefore, the application that the dispute should be arbitrated did not have facts and legal bases.

11.3 Arbitration Institution

Pursuant to the Arbitration Law of PRC, a validity arbitration agreement shall specify the chosen arbitration institution.[26] The Arbitration Law Interpretation further provides that "Where the name of an arbitration institution as stipulated in the agreement for arbitration is inaccurate, but the specific arbitration institution can be determined, it shall be ascertained that the arbitration institution has been

---

[25] (2017) Jing 0101 Min Chu No.14520.

[26] Article 16 Paragraph 2 of the Arbitration Law: "An arbitration agreement shall contain the following: 1. The expression of application for arbitration. 2. Matters for arbitration. 3. The arbitration commission which has been chosen." This rule may be changed in the future because in the newly published Arbitration Law (Draft for Comments), the element of chose arbitration commission has been deleted.

selected."[27] For example, where the name of the arbitration institution chosen by the parties differs from the correct name of the arbitration institution only by the addition or subtraction of words, courts will hold that the defects do not affect the validity of the arbitration agreement. In contrast, if the name of the chosen arbitration institution is too vague and refers to more than one institution, Article 12 of Interpretation of the Arbitration Law shall be applied, and the chosen arbitration institution might be ascertained as an unidentified institution. Therefore, the intermediate people's court where the arbitration agreement was signed or the place of the respondent was domiciled had jurisdiction over this dispute.

1. The common agreement is "all disputes shall be submitted to the arbitration commission in _____ (place) for arbitration". Furthermore, there are plenty of arbitration clauses stipulating that the dispute arising from the contract can only be submitted to arbitration in one place

   Guangzhou Xingyi Exhibition Service Co., Ltd. v. Shanghai Junjue Exhibition Service Co., Ltd.[28]

   In this case, the dispute resolution clause stipulated that "All disputes arising from the performance of the contract shall be settled through friendly negotiation. If the settlement cannot be reached, either party has the right to submit the dispute to the Shenzhen City Arbitration Commission for arbitration in accordance with the provisional rules at the time of arbitration." Although the name of the "Shenzhen City Arbitration Commission" stipulated in the contract was not accurate, it only had one word different from the name of Shenzhen Arbitration Commission, it can be inferred that the arbitration institution agreed upon by both parties was Shenzhen Arbitration Commission. Therefore, the arbitration agreement was valid.

   Li v. Shenzhen Hongde Mingjiang Decoration Design Engineering Co., Ltd.[29]

   In this case, the dispute resolution clause stated that "All disputes are to be arbitrated in Shenzhen". More specifically, this clause stipulated that "if a dispute arises from the performance of the contract, it shall be resolved by negotiation or submitted to relevant organizations for mediation. If the settlement cannot be reached, it shall be submitted to arbitration in Shenzhen". The court held that Shenzhen has several arbitration institutions, such as the SCIA and CIETAC South China Sub-Commission, and the parties did not agree upon the specific arbitration institution. According to Article 5 of the Arbitration Law,"Whereas the parties concerned have reached an agreement for arbitration, the people's court shall not accept the suit brought to the court by any one single party involved, except in the case where the agreement for arbitration is invalid", the

---

[27] Article 3 of the Interpretation of the SPC on Certain Issues Concerning the Application of the Arbitration Law.

[28] (2018) Yue 01 Min Zhong No. 2811.

[29] (2018) Yue 03 Min Zhong No. 19616.

court held that this case should be heard by the court. In practice, the arbitration tribunal can hear the dispute in various places; thus, the validity of those arbitration clauses that refer to more than one institution relies on the interpretation of the court. If the court adopts the strict interpretation, these arbitration clauses without specifying arbitration institutions might be ascertained to be invalid.

2.   If there is a local arbitration institution[30] and a branch of a nonlocal arbitration institution located in the place agreed upon by the parties, Chinese courts may not consider that the parties "failed to specify the choice of arbitration commission" provided by Article 18 of the Arbitration Law

> *Chongqing Education Construction (Group) Co., Ltd. v. Chongqing Meijing Fireproof Material Co., Ltd.*[31]

In this case, Paragraph 3 of Article 10 of the Procurement Contract stated that "All disputes arising from or related to this contract shall be settled through friendly negotiation, if the settlement cannot be reached, the dispute shall be submitted to the arbitration commission where the project is located." Afterward, the applicant submitted the dispute to the China Chongqing Arbitration Commission for arbitration on the ground that the project was located in Chongqing. The defendant sought to invalidate the arbitration agreement in the court of law because Chongqing city has two arbitration institutions, the China Chongqing Arbitration Commission and CIETAC Southwest Sub-Commission. Therefore, the arbitration agreement was invalid because the two parties did not reach a supplementary agreement for the specific arbitration institution. The court held that Paragraph 3 of Article 2 of the CIETAC Arbitration Rules stipulates that "CIETAC is based in Beijing. It has sub-commissions or arbitration centers. The sub-commissions or arbitration centers are CIETAC branches, which accept arbitration applications and administer arbitration cases with CIETAC authorization. CIETAC Southwest Sub-Commission is the sub-commission of CIETAC", and Article 2 of the Arbitration Rules of China Chongqing Arbitration Commission stipulates that "Chongqing Arbitration Commission is the only legal arbitration institution in the administrative region of Chongqing to handle civil and commercial disputes." Although there is no arbitration institution in the Shapingba District of Chongqing City, the arbitration institution agreed upon by the parties shall be determined to be Chongqing Arbitration Commission because the only independent arbitration institution in Chongqing was the Chongqing Arbitration Commission. Therefore, the arbitration institution was Chongqing Arbitration Commission, and the defendant's application to invalidate the arbitration agreement cannot be supported.

---

[30] Local arbitration institution refers to the arbitration commission established pursuant to the Arbitration Law, i.e., established in the municipalities directly under the Central Government, in the municipalities where the people's governments of provinces and autonomous regions are located or, if necessary, in other cities divided into districts. Local arbitrations may operate some other branches in other place where they are not regarded as local.

[31] (2018) Yu 05 Min Te No. 125.

Dongfang Rili (Chengdu) Electronic Control Equipment Co., Ltd. v. Guangzhou Shengying Automatic Control System Co., Ltd.[32]

In this case, the Purchase Contract stated that "If the settlement cannot be reached, the dispute shall be submitted to the arbitration commission where the applicant is located for arbitration, and the Arbitration Rules of this Commission shall be applied." The court held that CIETAC Sichuan Sub-Commission (the arbitration center of the Sichuan Pilot Free Trade Zone) had not been established when the contract was concluded, and the CIETAC Sichuan Sub-Commission was a branch of CIETAC. In addition, the China Council for the Promotion of International Trade Sichuan Council is not an arbitration institution, and neither the CIETAC Southwest Sub-Commission nor Qinzhou arbitration commission is located in Chengdu. Therefore, there was just one arbitration institution in that place when the parties signed the Purchase Contract, and the applicant's argument that the arbitration agreement was invalid cannot be supported.

11.4 Arbitration Proceedings

The arbitration procedure involves the application for arbitration, service of all kinds of documents, constitution of the arbitral tribunal and oral hearing, rendering of the arbitral award, etc. Arbitration rules usually provide for more detailed arbitration procedures. The arbitration rules of arbitration institutions are the established and comprehensive rules about the arbitration proceedings.

1. Among various arbitration proceedings, the service of arbitration documents is the crucial issue that must be addressed carefully by the arbitration institution or the arbitral tribunal in practice and is also a frequently encountered issue in the case of judicial review

   Yang & Ye v. Chen & Shenzhen Puyi Battery Technology Co., Ltd.[33]

   In this case, according to Article 64 of the Arbitration Rules of South China International Economic and Trade Arbitration Commission[34] stated: "…2. Unless otherwise agreed upon by the parties, all written documents, notices, and materials concerning the arbitration proceedings may be delivered in person or sent by mail, facsimile, electronic mail, or any other means of electronic data interchange that can provide a record of delivery, or by any other means the arbitration institution considers appropriate. 3. Any arbitral document, notice, or material sent by the arbitration institution to a party or its representative shall be deemed to have been properly delivered: (a) delivered to the place of business, place of registration, place of residence, address indicated on household registration or

---

[32] (2018) Chuan 01 Min Te No. 21.

[33] (2018) Yue 03 Min Te No. 214.

[34] Now renamed as Shenzhen Court of International Arbitration (SCIA).

the identification card, address confirmed with the arbitration institution orally or in writing, any effective address for external use, address provided in accordance with the parties' agreements or any other mailing address the arbitration institution considers appropriate…",

The court held that the Arbitration commission had served the notice of Arbitration and other documents to the address stated on Yang's ID card. Yang's application to set aside the arbitral award on the ground that he had not received the notice could not be upheld.

Nanjing Natural Garments Co., Ltd. v. Shenzhen Yidatong Enterprise Service Co., Ltd.

In this case, the court held that Article 108 of the applicable arbitration rule stipulated that the arbitration documents, notices, and other materials should be served to the parties or their agents, and the parties or their agents should sign or affix their seals to the service receipt and indicate the date of receipt. Additionally, arbitration documents, notices, and other case materials can also be submitted by post, fax, telegram, or telex to the place of business, place of residence, address indicated on registration or on the identification card, domicile place, address agreed upon by the parties or address notified in writing by the served person. The date of receipt or return by post or telegram should be regarded as the date of service. In this case, the arbitral tribunal had delivered those materials to the place of registration and the place agreed upon by the parties. The service proceeding was lawful.

2. In the event of a clerical error in the service address, the validity of the service depends on the substantial impact of the clerical error

Puhua Youke (Beijing) Technology Co., Ltd. v. ILAC systems (Hong Kong) Co., Ltd.[35]

In this case, "Haidian District" in the address was mistaken as "Haidi District" when the arbitration institution filled in the address for mailing the materials to the respondent's place of business. The court held that the clerical error did not have a substantial impact on the validity of service, with the telephone number of the respondent's office filled in. The respondent did not receive the notice of the arbitration proceedings for its own reasons and should undertake the adverse legal consequences. In addition, the arbitral tribunal sent the relevant documents to the place of registration, but the documents were not delivered on the ground that the respondent did not have its actual office at that place. According to the relevant provisions governing enterprise registration, the registration of the company has the effect of public disclosures. Therefore, the service proceeding was lawful.

3. For some arbitration conducted according to the simplified arbitration procedures agreed upon by the parties, the losing party may later raise an objection on the ground of the irregularity of the proceedings. The court will decide the

---

[35] (2017) Jing 04 Min Te No. 47.

validity in accordance with the Arbitration Law, arbitration agreement or arbitration rules chosen by the parties. If a party participates in the hearing substantively without raising an objection or neglects to exercise the defense right and raises an objection after the hearing, the courts usually do not uphold their objection. Even if a party's objection is not raised after the hearing, as long as the summary procedures do not violate the due process or infringe on the parties' legitimate rights, the court usually concludes that the summary procedures are valid and lawful.[36]

Nanchang Zhongqun Garment Co., Ltd. v. Shenzhen Yidatong Enterprise Service Co., Ltd.[37]

In this case, the applicant claimed that the arbitration procedure was illegal. The court held that Article 6.4 of the Basic Financial Services Agreement stated that "To expedite the arbitration proceedings, the three parties have agreed to apply the summary procedures to resolve the dispute, and the case shall be arbitrated by an arbitrator appointed by the president of the Court of International Arbitration." The agents of the parties attended the hearing and expressed no objection to the jurisdiction of the Court of International Arbitration, the composition of the arbitral tribunal, and the arbitral proceedings that had been conducted. The composition of the arbitral tribunal was in accordance with the agreement between the parties. On this ground, the court did not support the applicant's claim that the arbitration violated the due process. Moreover, this case also involved the issue of the number of arbitration agents. The court held that there was no restriction on the number of agents in the Arbitration Law and arbitration rules; thus, the respondent's appointment of four agents did not violate the due process.

Dongguan Haichuan Chemical Co., Ltd. & Chen v. Shenzhen Jiasheng Supply Chain Co., Ltd.[38]

In this case, the parties also raised a plea as to whether the arbitration proceedings were lawful. The plea involved the permission to submit the supplementary evidence and the examination of evidence in writing. The court held that this case should be reviewed in accordance with Article 58 of the Arbitration law by which the party may seek to vacate the domestic arbitral award. Therefore, the violation of legal proceedings refers to the violation of the arbitration proceeding stipulated in the Arbitration Law or the arbitration rules chosen by the parties, which may affect the impartiality of ruling. In the case, the applicant raised an objection on the ground that the respondent produced the evidence of the legal fee at the hearing. Therefore, the arbitral tribunal's request for the

---

[36] It is necessary to pay attention to the relevant simplified clauses in Official Reply of the SPC on the Application of Law on Placing the "Advance Arbitral" Awards or Mediations of Arbitration Institutions on File for Enforcement. The arbitral award may be denied in these circumstances or similar circumstances.

[37] (2018) Yue 03 Min Te No. 228.

[38] (2018) Yue 03 Min Te No. 46.

respondent to produce supplementary evidence after the hearing did not violate the arbitration rules, which stipulated that "The arbitral tribunal may specify a time period for the parties to produce evidence". Additionally, according to Paragraph 2 of Article 40 of the applicable Arbitration Rules, "Where a case is to be decided on the basis of documents only, or where the evidentiary materials are to be submitted after the hearing, and the parties agree to examine the evidentiary materials in writing, the parties shall submit their written opinions on the documents or the evidentiary materials within the time period specified by the arbitral tribunal",the applicant should be responsible for being unable to provide the written opinions on supplementary evidence produced by the respondent. Therefore, the arbitral tribunal can exercise its power to decide whether to adopt supplementary evidence. Accordingly, there was no factual or legal basis on which the arbitral proceedings violated the due process.

4. Evidence is related to both substantive and procedural issues. The validity of the evidence is within the scope of substantive review of the arbitral tribunal.However, the burden of proof, the method of presenting the evidence, the organization of the examination of evidence, etc., may be regarded as procedural issues. According to the Arbitration Law, "if the opposite party conceals the evidence that may affect the impartiality of award", the party may apply to set aside the award to the intermediate people's courtwhere the arbitration commission is located. However, how can the evidence that may affect the impartiality of awards be defined?

Xiamen Tuoyuan Import & Export Co., Ltd. & Gong v. Shenzhen Yidatong Enterprise Service Co., Ltd.[39]

In this case, the arbitral award held that there were two mutually independent legal relationships, the insurance relationship that arose from the Insurance Contract and the Guarantee Slip and the lending relationship that arose from the Financing Agreement. For the insurance dispute, the parties shall find methods otherthan arbitration to resolve it. The court held this case should be reviewed pursuant to Article 58 of the Arbitration Law because the party applied to set aside the arbitration award. The first question decided by the court was whether the respondent concealed evidencethat may affect the impartiality of the award. The court held that this claim could be satisfied under two conditions. First, the evidence was occupied by the opposing party, and the applicant cannot obtain the evidence from other public sources. Second, the evidence must affect the impartiality of the award. The tribunal held the Insurance Contract, Guarantee Slip, and other shreds of evidence were not direct evidence related to the dispute, andthe evidence did not affect the impartiality of the award. Therefore, there was no factual or legal basis for the applicant to claim the other party has concealed evidence and affected the impartiality of the award.

Hebei Huamao Asset Management Co., Ltd. v. Zhang.[40]

---

[39] (2018) Yue 03 Min Te No. 204.
[40] (2018) Ji 01 Zhi Yi No. 319.

In this case, the party applied for non-enforcement of the arbitral award on the ground that the applicant has concealed the evidence that may affect the impartiality of the award. According to Paragraph 1 of Article 16 of the Provisions of the SPC on Several Issues Concerning the Handling of Cases of Enforcement of Arbitral Awards by the People's Courts: "Where the following conditions are met, the people's court shall identify the establishment of the circumstance that 'the other party has concealed any evidence to the arbitration institution that is sufficient to affect fair judgment' prescribed in Item 5 of Paragraph 2 of Article 237 of the Civil Procedure Law: (1) The evidence is the main evidence for identifying the basic facts of the case; (2) The evidence is only available to the other party, but the other party did not submit to the arbitral tribunal; and (3) It is learned of the existence of the evidence during the arbitration, and the other party is required to produce it or the arbitral tribunal is requested to order the other party to produce it, but the other party fails to produce or provide it without justifications," the court held that during the hearing, the respondent did not object to the evidence and did not request the arbitral tribunal to order the applicant to produce the relevant evidence. In addition, the arbitral tribunal had heard the facts and made the related determination. Hence, this application should not be upheld.

5. The fact that arbitral tribunal heart-related cases concurrently do not automatically constitute a violation of the Arbitration Law, as the following cases illustrate

   Beijing Hongan Construction Decoration Engineering Co., Ltd. v. Shibaishi (Shanghai) Construction Engineering Co., Ltd.[41]

   In this case, the two parties signed the Material Installation Contract and Material Supply Contract on March 6, 2014, which involved the same project.Afterward, SHIAC accepted the disputes arising from the two contracts on April 26 and 27, 2016. The same arbitrator heard the two cases.Three oral hearings were conducted for these two cases. The arbitrator made awards separately on September 20, 2017.The applicant sought to set aside one arbitral award on the ground of the violation of the Arbitration Law because the arbitral tribunal combined different cases and dismissed the claimant's challenge against the arbitrator. The court held that both parties, in this case, are legal persons of the PRC and that the award was a domestic arbitral award. Therefore, the case should be reviewed according to Article 58 of the Arbitration Law. Although the two cases were heard together based on the relationship between them, the two arbitration cases were initiated separately, each one had its own case number, the relevant documents were sent to the parties separately, and two hearing transcripts were signed by the parties. The hearings of the two cases were not considered consolidation of arbitrations in accordance with Article 30 of the

---

[41] (2018) Hu 02 Min Te No. 1.

Arbitration Rules of SHIAC. Moreover, the applicant did not raise any objection to the two cases being heard concurrently. The applicant has already exercised his rights to defend, present evidence, cross examine and other arbitration procedures. Therefore, the application should not be upheld.

6. The fact that an applicant initiates arbitration by listing a third party as one of the respondents does not mean that the arbitral tribunal accepts the third party to participate in the arbitration proceedings.

> **Zhongshan Century Tuoda Advertising Co., Ltd. v. Zhongshan Kangda Clinic & Wang.**[42]

In this case, the Advertising Contract stipulated that all disputes arising from the formation, performance or interpretation of the contract should be settled through negotiation, and if the settlement cannot be reached, any party should submit the dispute to the Zhongshan Arbitration Commission for arbitration. According to this clause, the Century Toda Company initiated arbitration with the Guangzhou Arbitration Commission Zhongshan Branch and listed Kangda Clinic and Wang as corespondents. After the arbitration commission rendered the award, Century Toda Company applied to the court to set aside the award on the grounds that century Toda Company listed Wang, who was not a party to the contract, as the corespondent, andWang did not participate in the hearing. Century Toda Company therefore could not have reached a supplementary arbitration agreement with Wang. The arbitral tribunal violated Article 24 of the Arbitration Rules "Joinder of a Non-Party with No Arbitration Agreement in Arbitration Proceedings". The court held that although the Century Toda Company listed Wang as a correspondent, the arbitral tribunal did not accept Wang as the corespondent on the grounds that Wang was not the party to the contract. Therefore, the application for setting aside the award should not be supported.

7. The parties may apply to set aside an arbitral award on the grounds that the arbitral tribunal has exceeded the time limit for rendering the arbitral award

> **Harbin Aowu Mechanical and Electrical Equipment Co., Ltd. v. Harbin Aowu Mechanical and Electrical Equipment Co., Ltd., et al.**[43]

In this case, the respondent raised an application for setting aside the arbitral award, claiming that the arbitral tribunal violated the provision that it should render an arbitral award within 75 days from the date on which the arbitral tribunal was formed. The court held that, according to Article 20 of Interpretation of the SPC on Certain Issues Concerning the Application of the Arbitration Law, "'The phrase "contravention of statutory procedures' as mentioned in Article 58 of the Arbitration Law refers to the circumstances in which the violation of the arbitration procedures stipulated in the Arbitration Law and arbitration rules selected by the parties may affect the correct ruling of a case", the Arbitration

---

[42] (2018) Yue 20 Min Te No. 13.
[43] (2018) Jing 04 Min Te No. 212.

Law and the arbitration rule should be taken as the criteria to review the case. Therefore, because the summary procedures applied, according to Article 62 of the Arbitration Rules, "1. The arbitral tribunal shall render an arbitral award within 3 months from the date on which the arbitral tribunal is formed. 2. Upon the request of the arbitral tribunal, the President of the Arbitration Court may extend the time period if he/she considers it truly necessary and the reasons for the extension truly justified", there was no further specific provision to regulate the time limit for rendering the award. In this case, the President of the Arbitration Court, based on the application of the arbitral tribunal, decided to extend the time limit to April 23, 2018, and the award was rendered on April 13, 2018. It was within the time period extended by the President of the Arbitration Court. Therefore, the respondent's claim should not be accepted.

8. Additionally, the fact that the arbitral tribunal's failure to verify the original evidence and to organize the cross-examination does not necessarily constitute a violation of the due process.

> ***Shanghai Pujing Chemical Technology Co., Ltd. v. Henan Shunda New Energy Technology Co., Ltd.***[44]

In this case, one party claimed that the arbitrator violated the arbitration proceeding stipulated in Article 45 of the Arbitration Law because the arbitrator did not verify the original evidence and did not organize the cross-examination. The court held that the presiding arbitrator had asked the parties for their opinion on the evidence, and both parties indicated that they had no objection, which meant that both had no objection to the authenticity of the evidence. Therefore, the presiding arbitrator did not violate the due process by deciding not to examine the evidence or to require the parties to present the original evidence.

11.5 The Scope of Judicial Review: Substances and Procedures

1. According to the Arbitration Law, it is generally construed that for judicial review of foreign-related arbitration, the court should not review substantive issues. For domestic arbitration without foreign elements, the court should review substantive issues to a limited extent. The arbitration rules of specific arbitration institutions sometimes also tend to make a distinction between substances and procedures. For example, the Arbitration Rules of Shenzhen Arbitration Commission, which entered into force in 2008, provide for foreign-related arbitration proceedings in one chapter, Chapter XII applying only to this kind of arbitration. The Arbitration Rules of SCIA also contain provisions concerning foreign-related arbitration

---

[44] (2018) Jing 04 Min Te No. 352.

Shanghai Yuanpu Investment Management Co., Ltd. v. Li[45]

In this case, the issue is whether the judicial review for setting aside an arbitral award involves merits and public interest. The court held that the case was a domestic arbitration. The arbitral tribunal determined the damages and the proportion of the damages from the infringing act, the damages, fault, causation, and the fact that the stock price fluctuated violently. It is not within the scope of the judicial review of arbitration. The court should not review it.

Dongguan Haichuan Chemical Co., Ltd. & Chen v. Shenzhen Jiasheng Supply Chain Co., Ltd.[46]

Inthis case, the court held that the issue regarding the arbitral award deciding the applicant to undertake the arbitration fees, preservation fees, security fees and attorney's fees fell within the scope of the tribunal's decision as to the merits of the case. The issue of whether the penalty is too high isalso related to the merits of the case, which the court should not review in the judicial review proceedings.

Shenzhen YapaiOpto Electronic Devices Co., Ltd. v. Shenzhen Xinfeitong Optoelectronics Technology Co., Ltd. & Dongguan Xinfeitong Optoelectronics Technology Co., Ltd.[47]

This case also involved the scope of the court's review in a foreign-related arbitration. In this case, the subject matter of the Asset Transfer Agreement involved the transfer of assets outside of China. Therefore, the dispute that arose from the Asset Transfer Agreement was a foreign-related civil and commercial dispute, and the arbitral award, in this case, was a foreign-related arbitral award. The court should review this case in accordance with Article 274[48] of the Civil Procedure Law. The application that the arbitral award was erroneous in fact-finding and concealing evidence did not constitute the legal circumstances for which the court could set aside the award, and the court should not examine it.

---

[45] (2018) Yue 03 Min Te No. 80. Similar cases: (2018) Yue 03 Min Te No. 78 and (2018) Yue 03 Min Te No. 79.

[46] (2018) Yue 03 Min Te No. 46.

[47] (2018) Yue 03 Min Te No. 254.

[48] Article 274 of the Civil Procedure Law (2017) provides that, "A people's court shall, after examination and verification by a collegial panel of the court, not to allow the enforcement of the award rendered by an arbitral organ of the People's Republic of China handling cases involving foreign element, if the party against whom the application for enforcement is made furnishes proof that: (1) the parties have not had an arbitration clause in the contract or have not subsequently reached a written arbitration agreement; (2) the party against whom the application for enforcement is made was not given notice for the appointment of an arbitrator or for the inception of the arbitration proceedings or was unable to present his case due to causes for which he is not responsible; (3) the composition of the arbitration tribunal or the procedure for arbitration was not in conformity with the rules of arbitration; or (4) the matters dealt with by the award fall outside the scope of the arbitration agreement or which the arbitral organ was not empowered to arbitrate. If the people's court determines that the enforcement of the award goes against the social and public interest of the country, the people's court shall make a written order not to allow the enforcement of the arbitral award.".

This is the difference between the judicial review of the domestic arbitral award and the judicial review of foreign-related arbitral award.

2. Moreover, in the case of an application for enforcement of an arbitral award, the court shall not, on its initiative and *ex officio*, decide not to enforce the arbitral award without the application of the party against whom the application for enforcement is made

Guangzhou branch of Minsheng Banking Co., Inc. v. Zhang.[49]

In this case, the applicant and the party against whom the application for enforcement is made signed a Financial Loan Contract, and the Guangzhou Arbitration Commission had rendered an award over their dispute on April 12, 2017. Furthermore, on November 5, 2017, the applicant applied to the court for enforcement of the award because that person did not fulfill the obligations within the time limit.According to Article 29 of the Arbitration Law Interpretation, this case should be heard by the intermediate people's court in the place where that person is domiciled or where his property is located. However, after the property investigation by the departments of Real Estate, Land, Industry and Commerce, that person did not have enforceable property within the jurisdiction of the court. The court of first instance decided not to enforce the award in accordance with Article 237 of the Civil Procedure Law and Article 29 of the Arbitration Law Interpretation. The applicant claimed that this arbitral award could be enforceable and appealed to a higher court. The High People's Court in Guangdong held that Article 237 of the Civil Procedure Law has a special regulation for the non-enforcement of an arbitral award, and the court can only review the application when the respondent, who has the obligation of performance, applies not to execute the award. In this case, the respondent did not apply for non-enforcement of the arbitral award. Therefore, the decision should be annulled because the court of first instance applied the incorrect law.

3. The following case involves the issue of whether mediation in arbitration proceedings can be included in the scope of judicial review

Liao v. Wen.[50]

The appellant, who was not a party to the award, claimed that the parties entered into a false agreement and applied for arbitration to reach a false mediation statement to confirm that the property in dispute should belong to one party. However, real estate was the common property of marriage, which could not be arbitrated pursuant to the Arbitration Law. The appellant, as an interested person, applied unsuccessfully for setting aside the mediation statement to the court of first instance. Hence, the appellant appealed to the court of second instance. The court of second instance held that, this was a case in which the party applied to set aside the mediation statement. In accordance with Article 58 of the Arbitration Law, the parties may apply to the intermediate people's

---

[49] (2018) Yue Zhi Jian No. 63.

[50] (2018) Yue Min Zhong No. 1868.

court at the place where the arbitration commission is located to set aside an award. In addition, pursuant to Article 51 of the Arbitration Law, which provides that the mediation statement has the same legal effect as the arbitral award, the mediation statement should be included in the scope of judicial review. The ruling of the first instance, which decided the party could not apply for setting aside the mediation statement, was wrong and should be corrected.

11.6   Arbitral Scope and Beyond the Scope of Submission to Arbitration

Arbitration should be conducted in accordance with the arbitration agreement and should not exceed the scope of the arbitration agreement. Under Chinese law, the award shall be set aside or not be enforced when the matters of the award are beyond the extent of the arbitration agreement or the jurisdiction of the arbitration commission.[51] The dispute falling outside of the jurisdiction of the arbitration commission is generally considered to be an arbitrability issue in China. The excess of the arbitration agreement can usually be included in the scope beyond the scope of submission to arbitration. There are different views on whether the award based on grounds other than those raised by parties can be considered beyond the scope of submission to arbitration.

1. When the arbitral tribunal renders an award, they need to take notice of whether the award exceeds the scope of the arbitration, particularly when the case involves multiple contracts

    Shenzhen-Shantou Special Cooperation Zone Dianjin Technology Co., Ltd. v. Shenzhen-Shantou Special Cooperation Zone Management Service Co., Ltd.[52]

    In this case, the applicant claimed that the dispute exceeded the scope of the arbitration agreement and should be heard by the people's court. The court held that the applicant and the respondent signed the Lease Contract on July 30, 2015, and Paragraph 1 of Article 12 of this Contract expressly provided that "All disputes between both parties arising from the contract shall be resolved by friendly negotiation. If the dispute cannot be resolved by negotiation, it should be submitted for arbitration in South China International Economic and Trade Arbitration Commission." The award also stipulated that only disputes arising from the Lease Contract had been heard, and the disputes arose from the Plant Lease Contract or the Agreement of Rent Arrears, which did not contain arbitration agreements, had not been heard in the proceedings. Therefore, the applicant's claim that the dispute heard by the arbitration commission exceeded the scope of the arbitration agreement and should be heard by the people's court could not be supported.

---

[51] Article 58 of the Arbitration Law and Article 274 of the Civil Procedure Law.

[52] (2017) Yue 03 Min Te No. 904.

2. At present, a large number of cases handled by arbitration institutions have an "all disputes" clause, which means that all disputes arising from the contract should be submitted to arbitration, such as the following cases

> **Shenzhen Dajiayi Industrial Development Co., Ltd. v. Guangzhou Chuangxi Property Management Co., Ltd.**[53]

In this case, Shenzhen Dajiayi Company claimed that the dispute decided by the arbitral tribunal was beyond the scope of the arbitration agreement, and the SCIA did not have the right to take cognizance of it. According to the Supplementary Agreement stipulated by the parties, "All disputes between both parties arising from the contract's performance or related to the Rental Property shall be resolved by friendly negotiation. If the disputes cannot be resolved by negotiation, it shall be submitted for arbitration in South China International Economic and Trade Arbitration Commission". Therefore, the court held that it's arbitrable for Guangzhou Chuangxi Property company's to claim that Shenzhen Dajiayi company should move out of the leased land immediately, restore the land and pay the occupancy fees. This case also involves the payment of legal fees that had not been paid. In accordance with Article 66 of the Arbitration Rule of South China International Economic and Trade Arbitration Commission, "the arbitral tribunal has the jurisdiction to determine the costs of arbitration and other costs that are borne by the parties, including the costs which should be paid by the parties in accordance with the rule of costs of arbitration, actual disbursements, and legal costs or other costs that incurred for arbitration reasonably." Therefore, the reasonable legal fees incurred for arbitration are not limited to the fees paid by the parties before the award, and the decision did not violate the arbitration rules, although the Guangzhou Chuangxi Property Company did not actually pay the legal fees before the award.

11.7 Arbitrability and Public Policy

Arbitrability can be understood as the scope of arbitration provided by law. Under the current Chinese law, some kinds of disputes cannot be resolved by means of arbitration. Article 3 of the Arbitration Law stipulates: "The following disputes may not be arbitrated: (1) Disputes arising from marriage, adoption, guardianship, bringing up of children and inheritance; (2) Disputes that have been stipulated by law to be settled by administrative organs." In addition, some kinds of disputes depend on other laws or regulations to determine whether they are arbitrable or not. For example, Article 77 of the Arbitration Law stipulates, "The arbitration of labor disputes and disputes arising from the farm work contract inside the collective agricultural organizations shall be formulated separately." Labor arbitration and commercial arbitration,

---

[53] (2017) Yue 03 Min Te No. 773.

according to Chinese laws, belong to two different dispute settlement systems[54] with different dispute resolution institutions, arbitration procedures and judicial review procedures

1. It is usually easy to identify the specific labor arbitration or commercial arbitration. However, with the diversification and innovation of businesses, there sometimes exists avague line between commercial disputes and labor disputes or disputes of other natures. The court may be requested to determine and distinguish the nature of the disputes to decide which arbitration procedures may be followed

    Tan v. Zhang, et al.[55]

    The case involves a distinction between a Labor Agreement and the Equity Transfer Agreement. The main reason Tan applied to annul the arbitral award was that the disputes between Tan and Zhang were labor disputes, and SCIA had no jurisdiction to arbitrate it under Chinese law.

    Between July and September 2014, Fangdi Technology Company signed a three-year labor contract with Zhang and other people, all of whom confirmed the existence of labor relations between Zhang and Fangdi Technology Company, and the labor contracts had expired. During the period of labor relations, Tan and other people signed an agreement entitled an equity incentive plan with Zhang and others. Tan and other people claimed that this agreement was consistent with the work and proposal of labor contracts. Zhang and other people argued that the agreement was different from the labor contracts. Although the Agreement was entitled an equity incentive plan, it is in nature an equity transfer agreement.

    The Shenzhen Intermediate People's Court held that although the agreement was entitled an Equity Incentive Plan, it was an Equity Transfer Agreement that enabled Zhang and others to acquire a certain amount of equity when they completed the tasks required by Fangdi Technology Company. Thus, the Agreement was consistent with the work and proposal of the Labor Contracts and was the supplementary agreement for the Labor Contracts as to work requirements and labor remunerations. The equity that was acquired by Zhang and other people when they completed their tasks was labor remunerations, and the disputes were labor disputes and should be dealt with first by the labor dispute resolution organization. SCIA, as a commercial arbitration institution, has no right to arbitrate, so the award should be set aside.

---

[54] Article 79 (Mediation and Arbitration) of the Labor Law of the PRC stipulates: "After the occurrence of a labor dispute, the parties may apply to the labor dispute mediation committee of the unit for mediation; If mediation fails and one of the parties requests arbitration, it may apply to the Labor dispute arbitration committee for arbitration. Either party may also directly apply to the labor dispute arbitration committee for arbitration. Those who refuse to accept the Arbitral award may bring a suit in a people's court.".

[55] (2018) Yue Min Zai No. 271.

Guangdong High People's Court, in the second instance, held that the Agreement was an Equity Transfer Agreement that ruled Zhang and others to acquire a certain amount of equity when they completed the tasks required by Fangdi Technology Company. The legal relationship between Tan, Zhang, and other people based on the agreement was commercial. The agreement should not be regarded as similar to employment contracts or as one part of labor contracts. In conclusion, the court decided to override the original ruling and rejected Tan's application to set aside the arbitral award.

In different countries, the criteria for determining arbitrability vary according to the applicable laws. However, as a preliminary issue, arbitrability must be resolved before the beginning of the arbitration procedures or the rendering of the award. Otherwise, it may affect the efficiency of the arbitration. In addition to labor relations, there are other disputes likely to arouse controversy. For example, under Chinese law, some disputes concerning antitrust, land transfer, public private partnership or other issues involving administrative relations may lead to a dispute over arbitrability. Another example is the dispute to dissolve the company. Pursuant to the opinion of the SPC in its Reply to the Application for the Setting Aside (2009) CIETAC Arbitral Award No. (0355),[56] "In accordance with Article 181 of the Company Law of the PRC, there is no legal basis for the arbitration institution to decide to dissolve the company, and it is a circumstance that the arbitration institution did not have the jurisdiction." Since the dissolution of a company may involve the company's affairs and other interested parties, the parties can only request the dissolution of the company to the people's court.

2. Public policy is often mentioned together with arbitrability. Although there is an overlap between the two concepts, public policy is more comprehensive and difficult to define. As the court held at *Shanghai Yuanpu Investment Management Co., Ltd. v. Li*,[57] the public interest is the interests of all members of society. The manifestation of violating the social public interest usually means that the violation of the basic system or the norms of the law of China, the violation of the basic morality and ethics of society, etc.

Beijing Pengyucheng Technology Development Co., Ltd. ("Pengyucheng Co., Ltd.") v. Jianwei Software Technology (Shanghai) Co., Ltd.[58]

In this case, after the arbitral award was made, Pengyucheng Company applied for non-enforcement of the award because the award was contrary to the public interest. Pengyucheng Company argued that the applicant told the third party to make up the fictional brokerage business and fictional VAT invoice. The arbitral award legalized the applicant's behavior for tax evasion and false VAT invoices, which caused the loss to the state's tax income and violated the public interest. The court held that the arbitral award was to decide the right and

---

[56] (2011) Min Si Ta Zi No. 13.

[57] (2018) Yue 03 Min Te No. 80. Similar cases: (2018) Yue 03 Min Te No. 78, (2018) Yue 03 Min Te No. 79.

[58] (2018) Jing 01 Zhi Yi No.53.

obligation between two equal civil subjects and that the public interest was not involved in the enforcement of the award. Therefore, this ground could not be supported, In conclusion, the court rejected Pengyucheng Company's application for non-enforcement of the arbitral award.

11.8 Others

In addition to the above cases of judicial review of arbitration involving several major arbitration institutions, many other cases involve various aspects, e.g., time limits or other procedural issues.

1. If the law stipulates the time for applying for judicial review, the provisions shall be strictly followed

    ***Zhang, et al. v. Shenzhen Zhonghe Chunsheng Yihao Equity Investment Fund Partnership (L.P.)*[59]**

    The case involved the parties' application for the invalidating an arbitration agreement in the course of the arbitration. The court held that Article 20 of the Arbitration Law Stipulates: "If the parties challenge the validity of the arbitration agreement, they request the arbitration commission to make a decision or apply to the people's court for a ruling. If one of the parties submits to the arbitration commission for a decision and the other party applies to a people's court for a ruling, the people's court shall give the ruling. If the parties contest the validity of the arbitration agreement, the challenge of the validity of the arbitration agreement shall be raised before the arbitration tribunal's first hearing." The case of Jiangsu Hi-tech Investment Group Co., Ltd., and Zhang concerning the investment agreement heard by the SCIA was heard on December 8, 2017, and after the first hearing of the arbitration tribunal, Zhang applied for confirmation of the validity of the arbitration agreement on December 26, 2017, which did not comply with the abovementioned legal provisions. Therefore, Zhang's application for confirmation of the validity of the arbitration agreement was rejected by the court.

2. According to China's legal arbitration system, the setting aside and non-enforcement procedures may be concurrent. To avoid procedural abuse by the parites, Article 26 of the Interpretation of the SPC on Certain Issues Concerning the Application of the Arbitration Law stipulates, "Where the application of a party concerned to a people's court to vacate an arbitration is dismissed, and subsequently, the party raises a defense during the enforcement proceedings to deny the enforcement with the same reason as the basis for such defense, the people's court shall not uphold that defense"

---

[59] (2017) Yue 03 Min Chu No. 2618.

Shenzhen-Shantou Special Cooperation Zone Dianjin Technology Co., Ltd. v.
Shenzhen-Shantou Special Cooperation Zone City Integrated Service Co., Ltd.[60]

In that case, the applicant applied for non-enforcement in the enforcement proceedings after applying for setting aside the award. One of the reasons for the court's rejection of the applicant was that the applicant's application for non-enforcement was on the same grounds as the application for setting aside the arbitral award.

---

[60] (2018) Yue 15 Zhi Yi No. 3.

Chapter 12
Recognition and Enforcement of New York Convention Awards in China

The New York Convention is undoubtedly one of the most successful international commercial treaties. To some extent, it is no exaggeration to call it the most successful international commercial convention to date. The year 2019 marks its 60th anniversary since it was adopted by the United Nations in June 1958 and entered into force in June 1959. In the past 60 years, many treaties have been adopted, endorsed, abrogated, or terminated, and yet, in the area of international dispute resolution, the New York Convention has been keeping on attracting increasingly contracting states and playing increasingly important roles. It has had a significant impact on the legislation of domestic commercial arbitration and the theory and practice of judicial review of arbitration in many countries, offering a strong safeguard for the order of international commerce. The number of its contracting states has increased from 24 countries 60 years ago to 166[1] today, covering almost all states where major international commercial entities are located.

China[2] adopted the New York Convention on December 2, 1986, at the 18th session of the Standing Committee of the 6th National People's Congress, and the New York Convention came into force in China as of April 22, 1987.[3] In the process of applying the New York Convention for more than 30 years, the practice of Chinese courts has been constantly developing. Although there are occasionally some cases in dispute, Chinese courts have generally adopted a pro-arbitration approach. We first summarize the overview regarding the applications for recognition and enforcement of foreign arbitral awards in China and then analyze approximately 100 relevant

---

[1] See New York Convention, List of Contracting States, at http://www.newyorkconvention.org/list+of+contracting+states, November3, 2020.

[2] In the context of this article, "China" only refers to the Mainland of China, not including Hong Kong, Macau and Taiwan Region.

[3] When acceding to the New York Convention, China made reciprocity reservation and commercial reservation.

This Chapter is coauthored with Ye Shanshan, Associate of Yi & Partners Law Firm.

© The Author(s), under exclusive license to Springer Nature Singapore Pte Ltd. 2022   253
Y. Lin, *China Arbitration Yearbook (2021)*, China Arbitration Yearbook,
https://doi.org/10.1007/978-981-19-1284-9_12

cases heard by Chinese courts from 2008 based on the type of defenses enumerated in the New York Convention.[4]

12.1 General Introduction

The legal basis for applying for recognition and enforcement of foreign arbitral awards in China includes the New York Convention, the Civil Procedure Law and the judicial interpretations made by the SPC. There are explicit regulations on the recognition and enforcement of foreign arbitral awards in China. The Civil Procedure Law[5] provides that "If an award made by a foreign arbitration institution needs to be recognized and enforced by a people's court of China, the party concerned shall directly apply to the intermediate people's court of the place where the party subject to enforcement is domiciled or where his property is located. The people's court shall handle the matter pursuant to international treaties concluded or acceded to by China or in accordance with the principle of reciprocity."

The most frequently cited international treaty in the application for recognition and enforcement of foreign arbitral awards is the New York Convention. To some extent, recognition and enforcement of foreign arbitral awards in China are mostly applied based on the New York Convention. It is extremely rare for parties to make such applications based on the principle of reciprocity or on other treaties.

The New York Convention did not prescribe circumstances where foreign arbitral awards shall be recognized and enforced. Instead, Article V of the New York Convention listed several circumstances where the court may refuse to recognize and enforce such awards. The listed circumstances encompass arbitration agreement, arbitration proceedings, scope of arbitration, composition of arbitral tribunal, effect of the award, arbitrability and public policy. Generally, for the five circumstances stipulated in Paragraph 1 of Article V, the court cannot voluntarily conduct review unless a party (usually the respondent) cites these circumstances, while the court may *ex officio* review the case from the two perspectives prescribed in Paragraph 2 of Article V. Although the wording of each circumstance is simple, the implementation of these provisions still rests with the understanding and interpretation of the courts of the contracting states.

---

[4] For the analysis of the legal practice by Chinese courts in the recognition and enforcement of foreign arbitral awards before, please refer to Lin Yifei,*Recognition and Enforcement of Foreign Arbitral Awards: The Judicial Practice of China in the Past Twenty Years*, Journal of International Economic Law, Vol. 1, 2009; Lin Yifei, *The Recognition and Enforcement of Foreign Arbitral Awards in China: The Judicial Practice between 1987–2007*, Commercial Arbitration Review, Vol. 1.

[5] In the 1991 edition of the Civil Procedure Law, it was Article269; in the 2017 edition of the Civil Procedure Law, it is Article 283, with the wording unchanged.

In general, Chinese courts have adopted a pro-arbitration approach. On April 10, 1987, the SPC released the Notice on Implementing the Convention on the Recognition and Enforcement of Foreign Arbitral Awards Acceded to by China,[6] which was aimed at encouraging Chinese courts to research and get prepared before the New York Convention came into effect in China. The Notice deals with reciprocity reservation, commercial reservation, the appropriate court to accept the applications, the application of Article V of the New York Convention, the time limit to file an application, etc. According to the Notice, the court accepting the case shall dismiss the application or recognize the arbitral award based on the provisions of Article V of the New York Convention.

Afterwards, the SPC promulgated various official judicial interpretations or documents with the effect of judicial interpretations to regulate the judicial review of foreign arbitral awards. Among them, it is particularly important to note that the SPC promulgated the Notice on Issues Concerning the People's Courts' Dealing of Foreign-Related Arbitration and Foreign Arbitration[7] on August 28, 1995, establishing a reporting regime for the refusal to recognize and enforce foreign arbitral awards. According to the regime, if one of the parties applies to the people's court for recognizing and enforcing an arbitral award made by a foreign arbitral institution and the court intends to dismiss the application, it shall report to the High People's court within the area for review; if the High People's court agrees with the lower court, the High People's court shall report to the SPC for review. Only after the SPC replies can the lower court refuse to recognize and enforce the award. As it is in essence an internal reporting system within the judiciary system, the regime has been playing a significant role in practice.

On December 26, 2017, the SPC released the Relevant Provisions on Issues Concerning Applications for Verification of Arbitration Cases under Judicial Review,[8] establishing the verification regime for the judicial review of arbitration cases in the form of judicial interpretation. Compared to the previous internal notice, the provisions gave the regime a higher level of legal effect. The provisions came into effect on January 1, 2018.[9]

In addition, the SPC has made some provisions on the harmonization of the procedures for the recognition and enforcement of foreign arbitral awards. On January 30, 2015, the SPC issued the Civil Procedure Law Interpretation,[10] providing further guidance regarding the recognition and enforcement of foreign arbitral awards. Such guidance is mainly contained in the provisions of Articles 546 to 548: Article 546 distinguishes the proceedings for recognition from those for enforcement[11]; Article

---

[6] Fa (Jing) Fa [1987] No. 5.

[7] Fa Fa [1995] No. 18.

[8] Fa Shi [2017] No. 21.

[9] The former reporting system only applies to foreign-related arbitration cases under judicial review, while the new Provisions include all arbitration cases under judicial review in the scope of the verification system.

[10] Fa Shi [2015] No. 5.

[11] Article 546 of the Civil Procedure Law Interpretation provides that, "Where a legally binding judgment/ruling rendered by a foreign court or a foreign arbitral award needs to be enforced by

547 regulates the time limit for making such applications[12]; and Article 548 defines the binding effect of the ruling rendered by the collegiate panel.[13] On December 26, 2017, the SPC issued the Provisions on Several Issues Concerning Deciding Cases of the Judicial Review of Arbitration,[14] which came into effect on January 1, 2018, consolidate the previous provisions and providing more standardized regulations on the procedure of the review.

In addition, the SPC has issued a large number of replies concerning judicial review of arbitration. According to the reporting regime, the cases in which the lower courts tend to dismiss the application shall be reported to the SPC, which will make replies to the lower courts. Such replies have also become indispensable references when conducting research or practicing in the area of arbitration in China. We may characterize these replies as part of the "case law" in this area. In this part, we mainly focus on the cases, without further discussions over the provisions mentioned above.

In this research, we take 127 cases of application for recognition and enforcement of foreign arbitral awards as the sample of our analysis, excluding cases where the party withdrew the application, where the accepting court lacked jurisdiction or where the application materials were insufficient.[15] To provide an overview of the application of recognizing and enforcing foreign arbitral awards in China in the past 10 years, the following table summarizes the relevant cases.

---

a court of the People's Republic of China, the party concerned shall first apply to the competent people's court for recognition of the said judgment/ruling or arbitral award. The people's court shall enforce the said judgment/ruling or arbitral award pursuant to Part 3 of the Civil Procedure Law after rendering a ruling to recognize the same upon review. Where a party concerned only applies for recognition of a legally binding judgment/ruling rendered by a foreign court or a foreign arbitral award, and does not apply for enforcement at the same time, the competent people's court shall only review, and render a ruling on, whether to recognize the said judgment/ruling or arbitral award.".

[12] Article 547 of the Civil Procedure Law Interpretation provides that, "The time period for a party concerned to apply for recognition and enforcement of a legally binding judgment/ruling rendered by a foreign court or a foreign arbitral award shall be governed by Article 239 of the Civil Procedure Law. Where a party concerned only applies for recognition of a legally binding judgment/ruling rendered by a foreign court or a foreign arbitral award, and does not apply for enforcement at the same time, the period for applying for enforcement shall be recalculated from the date when the ruling rendered by the people's court on the recognition application comes into effect.".

[13] Article 548 of the Civil Procedure Law Interpretation provides that, "A people's court shall form a collegiate panel to review a case for recognition and enforcement of a legally binding judgment/ruling rendered by a foreign court or a foreign arbitral award. The people's court shall serve the written application on the respondent who may state its opinions. The ruling rendered by the people's court upon review shall come into legal effect once served.".

[14] Fa Shi [2017] No. 22.

[15] The sources of research mainly consist of China Judgments Online, cnarb.com, itslaw.com, and the series of Guide on Foreign-Related Commercial and Maritime Trialexplain that it is an SPC publication.

No	Year	Applicant	Respondent	Seat	Enforcing court	Arbitration authority	Case no	Ruling
1	2008	First Investment Corp. (Marshall Island)	Fujian Mawei Shipbuilding Ltd.,Fujian Shipbuilding Industry Group Co., Ltd.	UK	Xiamen Maritime Court	ad hoc Tribunal	(2006) Xia Hai Fa Ren Zi No. 1	Reply of the SPC: dismiss[1]
2	2008	Shin-Etsu Chemical Co., Ltd.	Jiangsu Zhongtian Technology Co., Ltd.	Japan	Nantong Intermediate People's Court	JCAA	(2007) Su Min San Ta Zi No. 0002[2]	Reply of the SPC: dismiss[3]
3	2008	China Shipping Development Co., Ltd. Freighter Co.	Anhui Technology Imp. & Exp. Co., Ltd.	UK	Wuhan Maritime Court	ad hoc Tribunal	(2006) Wu Hai Fa Shang Zi No. 13	Reply of the SPC: dismiss[4]
4	2008	Shin-Etsu Chemical Co., Ltd.	Tianjin Xinmao Science & Technology Co., Ltd.	Japan	Tianjin High People's Court	JCAA	(2006) Jin Gao Min Ta Zi No. 0006[5]	Reply of the SPC: dismiss[6]
5	2008	Hemofarm DD, MAG International Trade Holding DD, Suramu Media Ltd.	Jinan Yongning Pharmaceutical Co., Ltd.	France	Jinan Intermediate People's Court	ICC	(2007) Lu Min Si Ta Zi No. 12[7]	Reply of the SPC: dismiss[8]
6	2009	Lifu Candy (Shanghai) Co., Ltd.	Shanghai Lianfu Food Co., Ltd.	Singapore	Shanghai Second Intermediate People's Court	SIAC	(2008) Hu Er Zhong Min Wu (Shang) Chu Zi No. 19	Recognize and enforce
7	2009	Voest-Alpine International Trading USA Corp.	Jiangsu Provincial Foreign Trade Corp.	Singapore	Nanjing Intermediate People's Court	SIAC	(2008) Ning Min Wu Chu Zi No. 43	Dismiss the application of recognition

(continued)

(continued)

No	Year	Applicant	Respondent	Seat	Enforcing court	Arbitration authority	Case no	Ruling
8	2009	Samyoung system	Li	Korea	Shanghai Second Intermediate People's Court	KCAB	(2009) Hu Er Zhong Min Ren (Wai Zhong) Zi No. 1	Recognize and enforce
9	2009	GRDMinproc Ltd.	Shanghai Flyingwheel Industry Co., Ltd.	Sweden	Shanghai First Intermediate People's Court	SCC	(2007)HuYi Zhong Min Wu (Shang) Chu Zi No. 116	Reply of the SPC: recognize and enforce[9]
10	2009	I. Schroeder KG. (GmbH & Co.)	Jiangsu Huada Food Industry Co., Ltd.	Germany	Jiangsu High People's Court	Waren-Verein Der Hamburger Borse E.V	(2009) Zhen Min San Zhong Zi No. 2	Recognize and enforce
11	2009	East Land Property Pte. Ltd.	Zhejiang Xinxing Rubber Co., Ltd.	Singapore	Zhejiang High People's Court	SICOM	(2009) Zhe Tai Zhong Que Zi No. 4	Recognize and enforce
12	2009	Noble Resource Pte. Ltd.	Zhoushan Zhonghai Grain and Oil Industry Co., Ltd.	Hong Kong	Ningbo Intermediate People's Court	HKIAC	(2007) Zhe Zhi Ta Zi No. 4[10]	Reply of the SPC: recognize and enforce[11]
13	2009	Concordia Trading B.V.	Nantong Gangde Grease Co., Ltd.	UK	Nantong Intermediate People's Court	FOSFA	(2009) Su Min San Zhong Shen Zi No. 0001[12]	Reply of the SPC: dismiss[13]

(continued)

(continued)

No	Year	Applicant	Respondent	Seat	Enforcing court	Arbitration authority	Case no	Ruling
14	2009	American Foreign Trading Corp.	Shenzhen Lionda Group Co., Ltd., et al.	USA	Shenzhen Intermediate People's Court	ICDR	(2008) Yue Gao Fa Min Si Ta Zi No. 11[14]	Reply of the SPC: recognize and enforce[15]
15	2009	Wu	Zhang	Mongolia	Binzhou Intermediate People's Court	Court of Arbitration of Mongolia	(2009) Lu Min Si Ta Zi No. 2[16]	Reply of the SPC: dismiss[17]
16	2009	Lehua MeilanHolding Co., et al.	Tianjin Jiashijie Group Co., Ltd., et al.	Swiss	Tianjin Second Intermediate People's Court	ICC	(2008) Jin Gao Min Si Ta Zi No. 0004[18]	Reply of the SPC: dismiss[19]
17	2009	Addax Bv	China-Base Ningbo Foreign Trade Co., Ltd.	Hong Kong	Ningbo Intermediate People's Court	HKIAC	(2009) Zhe Zhi Ta Zi No. 2[20]	Reply of the SPC: recognize and enforce[21]
18	2010	Tianrui Hotel Investment Co., Ltd.	Hangzhou Yiju Hotel Management Co., Ltd.	UK	Hangzhou Intermediate People's Court	LCIA	(2010) Zhe Shang Wai Ta Zi No. 3[22]	Reply of the SPC: recognize and enforce[23]
19	2010	Tianrui Hotel Investment Co., Ltd.	Hangzhou Heju Hanting Hotel Management Co., Ltd.	UK	Hangzhou Intermediate People's Court	LCIA	(2010) Zhe Shang Wai Ta Zi No. 2	Recognize and enforce[24]
20	2010	Tianrui Hotel Investment Co., Ltd.	Hangzhou Heting Hotel Management Co., Ltd.	UK	Hangzhou Intermediate People's Court	LCIA	(2010) Zhe Shang Wai Ta Zi No. 1	Recognize and enforce[25]
21	2010	Mon Eldorado Co., Ltd.	Zhejiang Zhancheng Construction Group Co., Ltd.	Mongolia	Shaoxing Intermediate People's Court	Court of Arbitration of Mongolia	(2009) Zhe Shao Min Que Zi No. 1	Reply of the SPC: dismiss[26]

(continued)

(continued)

No	Year	Applicant	Respondent	Seat	Enforcing court	Arbitration authority	Case no	Ruling
22	2010	Shin-Etsu Chemical Co., Ltd.	Jiangsu Zhongtian Technology Co., Ltd.	Japan	Nantong Intermediate People's Court	JCAA	(2010) Su Zhi Min Zhong Shen Zi No. 0002[27]	Reply of the SPC: dismiss[28]
23	2010	DMT S.A.	Chaozhou Huaye Packaging Materials Co., Ltd., et al.	Singapore	Chaozhou Intermediate People's Court	ICC	(2010) Yue Gao Fa Min Si Ta Zi No. 2[29]	Reply of the SPC: recognize and enforce (only for arbitral awards against the second Respondent)[30]
24	2010	Louis Dreyfus Commodities Asia Co., Ltd.	Guangdong Fuhong Oil Products Co., Ltd.	UK	Zhanjiang Intermediate People's Court	FOSFA	(2009) Yue Gao Fa Min Si Ta Zi No. 10[31]	Reply of the SPC: recognize and enforce[32]
25	2011	Subway International B.V.	Beijing Tepu Food Co., Ltd.	USA	Beijing Second Intermediate People's Court	ICDR	Jing Gao Fa [2011] No. 157[33]	Reply of the SPC: depends on the facts after investigation[34]
26	2012	Western Bulk Pte. Ltd.	Beijing Sinosteel Tiantie Iron & Steel Trading Co., Ltd.	UK	Tianjin Maritime Court	ad hoc Tribunal	(2010) Jin Hai Fa Que Zi No. 6	Reply of the SPC: dismiss[35]
27	2012	ALSTOM Technology Ltd.	Zhejiang University New Technology Co., Ltd.	Singapore	Hangzhou Intermediate People's Court	SIAC	(2012) Zhe Shang Wai Que Zi No. 1[36]	Reply of the SPC: dismiss[37]

(continued)

(continued)

No	Year	Applicant	Respondent	Seat	Enforcing court	Arbitration authority	Case no	Ruling
28	2013	Beijing Chaolai Xinsheng Sports &Leisure Co., Ltd.	Beijing Suowang Zhixin Investment Consulting Co., Ltd.	Korea	Beijing Second Intermediate People's Court	KCAB	Jing Gao Fa [2013] No. 388[38]	Reply of the SPC: dismiss[39]
29	2013	"Angfohuapin" Joint Venture Co., Ltd.	Henan Haofeng Chemical Co., Ltd.	Belarus	Zhengzhou Intermediate People's Court	BelCCI	(2012) Zheng Min San Chu Zi No. 37	Reply of the SPC: Recognize and enforce[40]
30	2013	Royal Food Import Co.	Ningbo Youngor International Trade and Transportation Co., Ltd.	USA	Ningbo Intermediate People's Court	AFI	(2012) Zhe Yong Zhong Que Zi No. 3	Recognize and enforce
31	2013	Proton Motors (China) Co., Ltd.	Jinxing Heavy Industry Manufacturing Co., Ltd.	Singapore	Dongguan Intermediate People's Court	SIAC	(2012) Yue Gao Fa Zhong Fu Zi No. 3[41]	Reply of the SPC: depends on the facts after investigation[42]
32	2013	Ruierma Food Co., Ltd.	Zhanjiang Guanya Food Co., Ltd.	USA	Zhanjiang Intermediate People's Court	AFI	(2011) Yue Gao Fa Min Si Ta Zi No. 15[43]	Reply of the SPC: depends on the facts after investigation[44]
33	2013	Castel Electronics Pty Ltd.	TCL Air Conditioner (Zhongshan) Co., Ltd.	Australia	Zhongshan Intermediate People's Court	ad hoc Tribunal	(2012) Yue Gao Fa Zhong Fu Zi No. 7[45]	Reply of the SPC: recognize and enforce[46]
34	2014	Allenberg Cotton Co.	Ningbo Youngor International Trade and Transportation Co., Ltd.	UK	Ningbo Intermediate People's Court	ICA	(2014) Zhe Shang Wai Que Zi No. 1[47]	Reply of the SPC: dismiss[48]

(continued)

(continued)

No	Year	Applicant	Respondent	Seat	Enforcing court	Arbitration authority	Case no	Ruling
35	2014	Daewoo Shipbuilding & Marine Engineering Co., Ltd.	AlphaElephantInc., et al.	UK	Xiamen Maritime Court	LMAA	(2014) Xia Hai Fa Ren Zi No. 14	Recognize and enforce
36	2014	CAI International Inc.	Daxinhua Logistics Holdings (Group) Co., Ltd.	USA	Tianjin Maritime Court	ad hoc Tribunal	(2014) Jing Hai Fa Que Zi No. 1	Recognize and enforce
37	2014	Jess Smith & Sons Cotton, LLC	Wuxi Natural Textile Industry Co., Ltd., et al.	UK	Wuxi Intermediate People's Court	ICA	(2013) Xi Shang Wai Zhong Shen Zi No. 0007	Dismiss
38	2014	Ksenja Pte. Ltd.	Guan	Finland	Shenzhen Intermediate People's Court	FAI	(2014) Shen Zhong Fa She Wai Chu Zi No. 119	Recognize and enforce
39	2014	SK Networks Co., Ltd.	Shanghai Pan Pacific Group Co., Ltd.	Singapore	Shanghai First Intermediate People's Court	SIAC	(2014) Hu Yi Zhong Min Ren (Wai Zhong)Zi No. S1	Recognize and enforce
40	2014	Rick Steven Brouman	Beijing Yadu Indoor Environmental Protection Technology Co., Ltd.	USA	Beijing First Intermediate People's Court	AAA	(2014) Yi Zhong Min Te Zi No. 878	Recognize and enforce

(Continued)

(continued)

No	Year	Applicant	Respondent	Seat	Enforcing court	Arbitration authority	Case no	Ruling
41	2014	Spring Maritime Ltd.	Shandong Haina Real Estate Co., Ltd.	UK	Qingdao Maritime Court	ad hoc Tribunal	(2013) Qing Hai Fa Hai Shang Chu Zi No. 1032	Recognize and enforce
42	2014	Gloria Jones Co..	Wuxi Dongxiang Knitting Textile Co., Ltd.	Russia	Wuxi Intermediate People's Court	RFCC	(2014) Xi Shang Wai Zhong Shen Zi No. 0004	Recognize and enforce
43	2014	Xiamen Hongxin Shipping Co., Ltd.	Wuhan Iron and Steel Group International Economic and Trade Corporation	UK	Wuhan Maritime Court	ad hoc Tribunal	(2014) Wu Hai Fa Ta Zi No. 00042	Recognize and enforce
44	2014	Marumo Corp.	Beijing Delin Golf Sports Development Co., Ltd.	Japan	Beijing Second Intermediate People's Court	JCAA	(2013) Er Zhong Min Te Zi No. 12593	Recognize and enforce
45	2014	Summer Maritime Ltd.	Shandong Haina Real Estate Co., Ltd.	UK	Qingdao Maritime Court	ad hoc Tribunal	(2014) Qing Hai Fa Hai Shang Chu Zi No. 721	Recognize and enforce
46	2014	Trust Bridge Pte. Ltd.	Qingdao Yongxinda Petrochemical Co., Ltd.	Singapore	Qingdao Intermediate People's Court	ICC	(2014) Qing Ren Zhi Zi No. 1	Recognize and enforce
47	2014	Allenberg Cotton Co.	Anhui Yuhua Textile Co., Ltd.	UK	Hefei Intermediate People's Court	ICA	(2014) He Min Te Zi No. 00001–3	Recognize and enforce

(continued)

(continued)

No	Year	Applicant	Respondent	Seat	Enforcing court	Arbitration authority	Case no	Ruling
48	2014	Olam International Ltd.	Jingshan Weijia Textile Enterprise Co., Ltd.	UK	Jingmen Intermediate People's Court	ICA	(2013) Ejing Men Min San Chu Zi No. 00019	Recognize and enforce
49	2014	Australia CBH Grain Co., Ltd.	Hebei Sihai Development Co., Ltd.	UK	Shijiazhuang Intermediate People's Court	GAFTA	(2013) Shi Min Wu Chu Zi No. 00525	Recognize and enforce
50	2014	German Schuleda Co.	China Dandong Junao Food Co., Ltd.	Germany	Dandong Intermediate People's Court	Waren-Verein Der Hamburger Borse E.V.	(2012) Dan Min San Te Zi No. 00001	Reply of the SPC: recognize and enforce[49]
51	2014	Toyoshima & Co., Ltd.	Shandong Zouping Shenghe Textile Co., Ltd.	UK	Binzhou Intermediate People's Court	ICA	(2014) Bin Zhong Min Er Wai Zi No. 1	Recognize and enforce
52	2014	Queensland Cotton Corporation Pty Ltd.	Jiangyin Huafu Textile & Clothing Corporation Ltd.	UK	Wuxi Intermediate People's Court	ICA	(2013) Xi Shang Wai Zhong Shen Zi No. 0002	Recognize and enforce
53	2014	TactCommunications, Inc.	Quanzhou Cardinu Travel Products Co., Ltd.	Japan	Quanzhou Intermediate People's Court	JCAA	(2013) Quan Min Ren Zi No. 35	Recognize and enforce
54	2015	JacobsonGolfCourseDesign,Inc.	Sihui Zhenhuiyuan Property Development Co., Ltd., et al.	USA	Zhaoqing Intermediate People's Court	ICDR	(2015) Zhao Zhong Fa Min Yi Zhong Zi No. 26	Recognize and enforce

(continued)

(continued)

No	Year	Applicant	Respondent	Seat	Enforcing court	Arbitration authority	Case no	Ruling
55	2015	Jess Smith & Sons Cotton, LLC.	Jihua 3509 Textile Co., Ltd.	UK	Xiaogan Intermediate People's Court	ICA	(2014) EXiao Gan Zhong Min Wai Chu Zi No. 00001	Recognize and enforce
56	2015	MinajHoldingsLimited	Rizhao Qihan International Import & Export Trade Co., Ltd.	UK	Rizhao Intermediate People's Court	ICC	(2014) Ri Min San Chu Zi No. 10	Recognize and enforce
57	2015	Allenberg Cotton Co.	Jiangsu Nijiaxiang Group Co., Ltd.	UK	Wuxi Intermediate People's Court	ICA	(2013) Xi Shang Wai Zhong Shen Zi No. 0009	Dismiss
58	2015	Super Sonic Imagine S.A.	Beijing Huaxing Yuanda International Technology Co., Ltd	France	Beijing Fourth Intermediate People's Court	ICC	(2015) Si Zhong Min (Shang)Te Zi No. 00195	Recognize and enforce
59	2015	Arkitema K/S	Cui	Denmark	Beijing Fourth Intermediate People's Court	ad hoc Tribunal	(2015) Si Zhong Min (Shang)Te Zi No. 57	Recognize and enforce
60	2015	Erasilnikov Sergei Vitalyevich	Heilongjiang Xinghe Dadao Automobile Trade Co., Ltd.	Russia	Heihe Intermediate People's Court	RFCC	(2015) Hei Zhong She Wai Shang Cai Zi No. 1	Recognize and enforce
61	2015	Noble Resources Pte. Ltd.	Carrad Holding Co., Ltd.	UK	Dezhou Intermediate People's Court	ICA	(2015) De Zhong Min Chu Zi No. 3	Recognize and enforce

(continued)

(continued)

No	Year	Applicant	Respondent	Seat	Enforcing court	Arbitration authority	Case no	Ruling
62	2015	Li	Yanshan County Yonghui Steel Pipe Co., Ltd.	Korea	Cangzhou Intermediate People's Court	KCAB	(2015) Cang Min Te Zi No. 13	Recognize and enforce
63	2015	LouisDreyfus Australia Ltd.	Jiangsu Nijiaxiang Group Co., Ltd.	UK	Wuxi Intermediate People's Court	ICA	(2013) Xi Shang Wai Zhong Shen Zi No. 0003	Dismiss
64	2015	Ostin Ltd.	Zhejiang Huateng Clothing Co., Ltd.	Russia	Shaoxing Intermediate People's Court	RFCC	(2015) Zhe Shao Zhong Que Zi No. 3	Recognize and enforce
65	2015	Siemens International Trading (Shanghai) Co., Ltd.	Shanghai Golden Land Co., Ltd.	Singapore	Shanghai No.1 Intermediate People's Court	SIAC	(2013) Hu Yi Zhong Min Ren (Wai Zhong)Zi No. 2	Reply of the SPC: Recognize and enforce[50]
66	2015	Trinity Bulk Shipping Ltd.	Jiangsu Huihong International Group Native Product Import & Export Co., Ltd., et al.	UK	Wuhan Maritime Court	ad hoc Tribunal	EGao Fa [2015] No. 283[51]	Reply of the SPC: partial recognition and enforcement[52]
67	2015	FSG Automotive Holding AG	Wuhan Fanzhou Machinery Manufacturing Co., Ltd.	Austria	Wuhan Intermediate People's Court	Arbitration Center of the Austrian Federal Economic Association	EGao Fa [2015] No. 405[53]	Reply of the SPC: partial recognition and enforcement[54]

(continued)

(continued)

No	Year	Applicant	Respondent	Seat	Enforcing court	Arbitration authority	Case no	Ruling
68	2015	Spliethoff's Bevrachtingskantoor B.V.	China Electronics Import &Export Shandong Co.,et al.	UK	Qingdao Maritime Court	ad hoc Tribunal	(2015) Lu Min Si Ta Zi No. 6[55]	Reply of the SPC: partial recognition and enforcement[56]
69	2015	COSCO Bulk Transport Co., Ltd.	Jiangsu Fumet International Trade Co., Ltd..	UK	Wuhan Maritime Court	ad hoc Tribunal	(2014) Wu Hai Fa Ta Zi No. 00038	Recognize and enforce
70	2015	Trafigura Pte. Ltd.	Guangzhou China Coal South China Sales Co., Ltd.	Singapore	Guangzhou Intermediate People's Court	LCIA	(2015) Sui Zhong Fa Min Si Chu Zi No. 4	Recognize and enforce
71	2015	Toyoshima & Co., Ltd.	Qingdao Yinxia Trading Co., Ltd.	UK	Qingdao Intermediate People's Court	ICA	(2014) Qing Ren Zhi Zi No. 2	Recognize and enforce
72	2015	GEA Heat Exchangers,Inc.	Guangdong Changying Heavy Industry Co., Ltd.	USA	Foshan Intermediate People's Court	ICDR	(2015) Fo Zhong Fa Min Er Zhong Zi No. 7	Recognize and enforce
73	2015	Fukui Bank Co.	Shanghai Yekao Optical Co., Ltd.	Japan	Shanghai No.2 Intermediate People's Court	JCAA	(2014) Hu Er Zhong Min Ren (Wai Zhong)Zi No. 1	Recognize and enforce

(continued)

(continued)

No	Year	Applicant	Respondent	Seat	Enforcing court	Arbitration authority	Case no	Ruling
74	2015	Ecom Agroindustrial Asia Pte. Ltd.	Qingdao Jinchangjiang Group Penglai Textile and Garment Co., Ltd.	UK	Yantai Intermediate People's Court	ICA	(2015) Lu Min Si Ta Zi No. 1[57]	Reply of the SPC: depends on the facts after investigation[58]
75	2015	Toyoshima & Co., Ltd.	Gaomi Luyuan Textile Co., Ltd.	UK	Weifang Intermediate People's Court	ICA	(2015) Lu Min Si Ta Zi No. 2[59]	Reply of the SPC: Recognize and enforce[60]
76	2015	Toyoshima & Co., Ltd.	Changyi Kunfu Textile Co., Ltd.	UK	Weifang Intermediate People's Court	ICA	(2015) Lu Min Si Ta Zi No. 3[61]	Reply of the SPC: Recognize and enforce[62]
77	2016	Paul Reinhart AG	Hubei Qinghe Textile Co., Ltd.	UK	Yichang Intermediate People's Court	ICA	EGao Fa [2015]No. 518[63]	Reply of the SPC: Recognize and enforce[64]
78	2016	Glencore Grain B.V.	Shandong Jinhe Cotton & Linen Co., Ltd.	UK	Jinan Intermediate People's Court	ICA	(2015) Ji Shang Wai Chu Zi No. 8	Recognize and enforce
79	2016	Olam International Ltd.	Wuxi Natural Textile Industry Co., Ltd.	UK	Wuxi Intermediate People's Court	ICA	(2015) Xi Shang Wai Zhong Shen Zi No. 4	Recognize and enforce
80	2016	Noble Resource Pte. Ltd.	Hubei Qinghe Textile Co., Ltd.	UK	Yichang Intermediate People's Court	ICA	(2015) EYi Chang Zhong Min Ren Zi No. 00001	Reply of the SPC: Recognize and enforce[65]

(Continued)

(continued)

No	Year	Applicant	Respondent	Seat	Enforcing court	Arbitration authority	Case no	Ruling
81	2016	Plexus Cotton Ltd.	Carrad Holding Co., Ltd.	UK	Dezhou Intermediate People's Court	ICA	(2016) Lu 14Xie Wai Ren No. 1	Recognize and enforce
82	2016	LH Asian Trade Finance Fund Ltd.	Zhengzhou Aluminum Co., Ltd.	Singapore	Zhengzhou Intermediate People's Court	SIAC	(2014) Zheng Min San Chu Zi No. 50	Recognize and enforce
83	2016	Singapore Huacheng Holdings Co., Ltd.	Anhui Huantai Metal Mineral Import &Export Co., Ltd.	Singapore	Hefei Intermediate People's Court	SIAC	(2015) He Min Te Zi No. 00004	Recognize and enforce
84	2016	ADM Asia–Pacific Trading Pte. Ltd	Shandong Yahe Agriculture Co., Ltd	Singapore	Rizhao Intermediate People's Court	GAFTA	(2017) Lu 11Xie Wai Ren No. 2	Recognize and enforce
85	2016	AOT Trading AG	Jiangsu Huihong International Group Zhongding Holding Co., Ltd.	Singapore	Nanjing Intermediate People's Court	ad hoc Tribunal	(2016) Su 01Xie Wai Ren No.2	Recognize and enforce
86	2016	BBC Chartering & Logistic GmbH & Co. KG	Shanghai Furui International Freight Forwarding Co., Ltd.	UK	Shanghai Maritime Court	LMAA	(2015) Hu Hai Fa Min Ren Zi No. 2	Recognize and enforce
87	2016	WicorHoldingAG	Taizhou Haopu Investment Co., Ltd.	Hong Kong	Taizhou Intermediate People's Court	ICC	(2015) Tai Zhong Shang Zhong Shen Zi No. 00004	Reply of the SPC: dismiss[66]

(continued)

(continued)

No	Year	Applicant	Respondent	Seat	Enforcing court	Arbitration authority	Case no	Ruling
88	2016	J & D IB Co.	Tian, et al.	Korea	Intermediate People's Court of Yanbian Korean Autonomous Prefecture	KCAB	(2015) Yan Zhong Min San Chu Zi No. 858	Reply of the SPC: recognize and enforce[67]
89	2016	Olam International Ltd.	Zibo Yinhua Cotton & Linen Co., Ltd.	UK	Zibo Intermediate People's Court	ICA	(2015) Zi Min Te Zi No. 1	Recognize and enforce
90	2016	Glencore International AG	Zhejiang Qiying Energy Chemical Co., Ltd.	UK	Ningbo Intermediate People's Court	LCIA	(2014) Zhe Yong Zhong Que Zi No. 1	Recognize and enforce
91	2016	Jiangyin Huacheng Industrial Co., Ltd.	Pipavav Defense and Offshore Engineering Co., Ltd.	Singapore	Wuhan Maritime Court	SIAC	(2016) E72Xie Wai Ren No. 4	Recognize and enforce
92	2016	Clavon Engineering Pte. Ltd	Pipavav Defense and Offshore Engineering Co., Ltd	Singapore	Wuhan Maritime Court	SIAC	(2016) E72Xie Wai Ren No. 3	Recognize and enforce
93	2016	Noble Resource Pte. Ltd.	Zhejiang Xiongsheng Industrial Co., Ltd.	UK	Shaoxing Intermediate People's Court	ICA	(2014) Zhe Shao Zhong Que Zi No. 1	Recognize and enforce
94	2016	United Company for Ginning and Cotton Export Co	Wuxi Natural Green Fiber Technology Co., Ltd.	Egypt	Wuxi Intermediate People's Court	Alexandria Cotton Exporters Association	(2013) Xi Shang Wai Zhong Shen Zi No. 0005	Recognize and enforce

(continued)

(continued)

No	Year	Applicant	Respondent	Seat	Enforcing court	Arbitration authority	Case no	Ruling
95	2016	Schiffahrts-GesellschaftMS "MENTOR" mbh & Co. KG	Da Xinhua Shiping (Yantai) Co., Ltd.	UK	Qingdao Maritime Court	LMAA	(2015) Qing Hai Fa Hai Shang Chu Zi No. 1552	Recognize and enforce
96	2016	Tajco A/S	JanSzklany	Denmark	Shenyang Intermediate People's Court	ad hoc Tribunal	(2015) Shen Zhong Min Si Te Zi No. 29	Recognize and enforce
97	2016	Remote Wireless Information Technology Co., Ltd.	Beijing Guangxin Jiashi Technology Co., Ltd.	Canada	Beijing Third Intermediate People's Court	ICC	(2014) San Zhong Min (Shang)Te Zi No. 12398	Recognize and enforce
98	2016	Johanm.K.Blumenthal GmbH & Co. KG	Jiangsu Rongsheng Heavy Industry Co., Ltd.	UK	Shanghai Maritime Court	LMAA	(2015) Hu Hai Fa Min Ren Zi No. 3	Recognize and enforce
99	2016	Compass Cotton B.V.	Shandong Yanggu Shunda Textile Co., Ltd.	UK	Liaocheng Intermediate People's Court	ICA	(2014) Liao Min Wu Chu Zi No. 4	Recognize and enforce
100	2017	BBC Chartering & Logistic GmbH & Co. KG	Zhenjiang Aihai Ship Industry Co., Ltd.	UK	Wuhai Maritime Court	LMAA	(2016) E72Xie Wai Ren No. 2	Recognize and enforce
101	2017	BrightMorningLimited	Yixing Leqi Textile Group Co., Ltd.	Singapore	Wuxi Intermediate People's Court	SIAC	(2016) Su 02Xie Wai Ren No. 1	Reply of the SPC: partial recognition and enforcement[68]

(continued)

(continued)

No	Year	Applicant	Respondent	Seat	Enforcing court	Arbitration authority	Case no	Ruling
102	2017	SPS European Chemicals Co.	Panjin Heyun Industrial Group Co., Ltd.	Sweden	Dalian Intermediate People's Court	SCC	(2016) Liao 02Xie Wai Ren No. 12	Recognize and enforce
103	2017	Oman Shipping Co. Soac	Jiangsu Rongsheng Heavy Industry Co., Ltd.	UK	Wuhan Maritime Court	ad hoc Tribunal	(2017) E72Xie Wai Ren No.1	Recognize and enforce
104	2017	Chenco Chemical Engineering and Consulting GmbH	Do-Fluoride Chemicals Co., Ltd	Swiss	Xinxiang Intermediate People's Court	ICC	(2015) Xin Zhong Min San Chu Zi No. 53	Reply of the SPC: partial recognition and enforcement[69]
105	2017	Russian Season Ltd.	Yongkang Tefan Import & Export Co., Ltd.	Russia	Jinhua Intermediate People's Court	RFCC	(2016) Zhe 07 Xie Wai Ren No. 3	Recognize but not enforce (the responcent has been cancelled)
106	2017	Rich Islands Ltd.	Jiangsu Rongsheng Heavy Industry Co., Ltd.	UK	Wuhan Maritime Court	ad hoc Tribunal	(2017) E72Xie Wai Ren No. 2	Recognize and enforce
107	2017	Royal Food Import Corp.	Suqian Canned Food Co., Ltd.	USA	Suqian Intermediate People's Court	AFI	(2016) Su 13 Xie Wai Ren No. 1	Recognize and enforce
108	2017	Caravel Shipping Ltd.	Shandong Yahe Agriculture Co., Ltd., et al.	UK	Qingdao Maritime Court	ad hoc Tribunal	(2017) Lu 72 Xie Wai Ren No. 1	Recognize and enforce
109	2017	Rhine Star Ltd.	Jiangsu Rongsheng Heavy Industry Co., Ltd.	UK	Wuhan Maritime Court	ad hoc Tribunal	(2017) E 72 Xie Wai Ren No. 5	Recognize and enforce

(continued)

(continued)

No	Year	Applicant	Respondent	Seat	Enforcing court	Arbitration authority	Case no	Ruling
110	2017	Plexus Cotton Ltd.	Jiangsu Jinfang Industrial Co., Ltd.	UK	Yancheng Intermediate People's Court	ICA	(2014) Yan Shang Wai Zhong Shen Zi No. 00001	Reply of the SPC: dismiss[70]
111	2017	Rex Commodities Pte. Ltd.	Qingdao Haiyunda Economic and Trade Co., Ltd.	Singapore	Qingdao Intermediate People's Court	SIAC	(2017) Lu 02 Xie Wai Ren No. 4	Recognize and enforce
112	2017	Subway International B.V.	Hangzhou Jiazhong Trading Company	USA	Hangzhou Intermediate People's Court	ICDR	(2017) Zhe 01Xie Wai Ren No. 1	Recognize and enforce
113	2017	Top Grand Ltd.	Jiangsu Rongsheng Heavy Industry Co., Ltd.	UK	Wuhan Maritime Court	ad hoc Tribunal	(2017) E 72 Xie Wai Ren No. 4	Recognize and enforce
114	2017	Valmet, Inc.	Zhejiang Purek Special Paper Co., Ltd.	Swiss	Jiaxing Intermediate People's Court	ICC	(2017) Zhe 04 Xie Wai Rem No. 1	Recognize and enforce
115	2017	Season Navigation Ltd.	Jiangsu Rongsheng Heavy Industry Co., Ltd.	UK	Wuhan Maritime Court	ad hoc Tribunal	(2017) E72Xie Wai Ren No. 6	Recognize and enforce
116	2017	HyundaiGlovisCo., Ltd.	Zhejiang Qiying Energy Chemical Co., Ltd.	Singapore	Ningbo Intermediate People's Court	SIAC	(2015) Zhe Yong Zhong Que Zi No. 3	Recognize and enforce
117	2017	Xinhe Marine Co., Ltd.	Dalian Xinhe Ship Material Supply Co., Ltd.	Singapore	Dalian Intermediate People's Court	SIAC	(2016) Liao 02 Xie Wai Ren No. 2	Recognize and enforce

(continued)

(continued)

No	Year	Applicant	Respondent	Seat	Enforcing court	Arbitration authority	Case no	Ruling
118	2017	Columbia Grain Trading Inc.	Shandong Shenying Coal Trading Co., Ltd.	USA	Rizhao Intermediate People's Court	FOSFA	(2017) Lu 11 Xie Wai Ren No. 1	Recognize and enforce
119	2017	West Ocean Shipping Co., Ltd.	Shenzhen Nanhai Shipping Co., Ltd.	UK	Guangzhou Maritime Court	ad hoc Tribunal	(2017) Yue 72 Xie Wai Ren No. 1	Recognize and enforce
120	2017	China Aviation Oil (Singapore) Co., Ltd.	Chengdu Xinhuaxin Chemical Materials Co., Ltd.	Singapore	Chengdu Intermediate People's Court	SIAC	(2017) Chuan 01 Xie Wai Ren No. 1	Recognize and enforce
121	2017	Wollema-absalia Movo Ltd., Republic of Tatarstan, Russian Federation	Jinzhou Dongfeng Machinery Co., Ltd.	Russia	Shijiazhuang Intermediate People's Court	RFCC	(2016) Ji Xie Wai Ren Zi No. 1[71]	Reply of the SPC: further investigate[72]
122	2017	Semimaterials Co., Ltd.	Henan GCL Solar Technology Co., Ltd.	Hong Kong	Luohe Intermediate People's Court	HKIAC	(2016) Yu Min Ta No. 2[73]	Reply of the SPC: enforce[74]
123	2017	Core White Ltd.	Jiangsu Rongsheng Heavy Industry Co., Ltd.	UK	Wuhan Maritime Court	ad hoc Tribunal	(2017) E 72 Xie Wai Ren No. 3	Recognize and enforce
124	2017	Noble Resources International Pte. Ltd..	Shanghai Xintai International Trade Co., Ltd.	Singapore	Shanghai No.1 Intermediate People's Court	SIAC	(2016) Hu 01 Xie Wai Ren No. 1	Dismiss
125	2018	Golden Agriculture International Pte. Ltd.	Shandong Changhua Industrial Development Co., Ltd.	Singapore	Rizhao Intermediate People's Court	SIAC	(2017) Lu 11 Xie Wai Ren No. 4	Recognize and enforce

(continued)

(continued)

No	Year	Applicant	Respondent	Seat	Enforcing court	Arbitration authority	Case no	Ruling
126	2018	Louis Dreyfus Commodities Suisse SA	Ningbo Qiancheng Import & Export Co., Ltd.	UK	Ningbo Intermediate People's Court	ICA	(2015) Zhe Yong Zhong Que Zi No. 5	Recognize and enforce
127	2018	China Land Shipping Pte. Ltd.	Conor Shipping Co., Ltd.	UK	Tianjin Maritime Court	LMAA	(2018) Jin 72 Min Te No. 2	Recognize and enforce

[1] The Reply of the SPC on the Application of First Investment Corp. (Marshall Island) for the Recognition and Enforcement of the Arbitral Award rendered by an ad hoc Tribunal in London of the UK, [2007] Min Si Ta Zi No. 35

[2] As the case number of the case in the Nantong Intermediate People's Court could not be found, the number of the Report of Jiangsu High People's Court on Non-Recognition of the No. 04–05 Tokyo Arbitral Award rendered by the JCAA was filled here

[3] Reply of the SFC to the Report on Non-Recognition of the No. 04–05 Tokyo Arbitral Award rendered by the JCAA, [2007] Min Si Ta Zi No. 26

[4] Reply of the SPC to the Request for Instructions of the Case Concerning the Application of China Shipping Development Co., Ltd. Freighter Co. for Recognition and Enforcement of London Arbitral Award, [2008] Min Si Ta Zi No. 17

[5] As the case number of the case in the Tianjin High People's Court could not be found, the number of the Report of Tianjin High People's Court on Non-Recognition and Non-Enforcement of the No. 05–03 Tokyo Arbitral Award rendered by the JCAA was filled here

[6] Reply of the SFC on Non-Recognition of the No. 05–03 Tokyo Arbitral Award rendered by the JCAA, [2008] Min Si Ta Zi No. 18

[7] As the case number of the case in the Jinan Intermediate People's Court could not be found, the number of the Request for Instructions of Shandong High People's Court on the Non-Recognition and Non-Enforcement of an Arbitral Award of ICC was filled here

[8] Reply of the SFC to the Request for Instructions on the Non-Recognition and Non-Enforcement of an Arbitral Award of ICC, [2008] Min Si Ta Zi No. 11

[9] Reply of the SFC to the Request for Instructions of the Case Concerning the Application of GRDMinproc Ltd. for Recognition and Enforcement of Arbitral Award rendered by the SCC, [2008] Min Si Ta Zi No. 48

[10] As the case number of the case in the Ningbo Intermediate People's Court could not be found, the number of the Report of Request for Instruction of Jiangsu High People's Court on the Case Concerning the Application of Zhoushan Zhonghai Grain and Oil Industry Co., Ltd. for Non-Enforcement of the Arbitral Award rendered by the HKIAC was filled here

[11] Reply of the SPC to the Request for Instructions of the Case Concerning the Application of Zhoushan Zhonghai Grain and Oil Industry Co., Ltd. for Non-Enforcement of the Arbitral Award rendered by the HKIAC, [2009] Min Si Ta Zi No. 2

[12] As the case number of the case in the Nantong Intermediate People's Court could not be found, the number of the Request for Instruction of Jiangsu High People's Court on the Case Concerning the Application of Concordia Trading B. V. for Recognition and Enforcement of the No. 3948Arbitral Award rendered by the FOSFA was filled here

13 Reply of the SPC to the Request for Instruction of Jiangsu High People's Court on the Case Concerning the Application of Concordia Trading B. V. for Recognition and Enforcement of the No. 3948 Arbitral Award rendered by the FOSFA, [2009] Min Si Ta Zi No. 22

14 As the case number of the case in the Shenzhen Intermediate People's Court could not be found, the number of the Request for Instruction of Guangdong High People's Court on the Case Concerning the Application of American Foreign Trading Corp. for Recognition and Enforcement of the Arbitral Award rendered by the ICDR was filed here

15 Reply of the SPC to the Request for Instruction on the Case Concerning the Application of American Foreign Trading Corp. for Recognition and Enforcement of the Arbitral Award rendered by the ICDR, [2009] Min Si Ta Zi No. 30

16 As the case number of the case in the Binzhou Intermediate People's Court could not be found, the number of the Request for Instruction of Shandong High People's Court on the Case Concerning the Application of Non-Recognition and Non-Enforcement of the Arbitral Award rendered by the Court of Arbitration of Mongolia was filed here

17 Reply of the SPC to the Request for Instruction on the Case Concerning the Application of Non-Recognition and Non-Enforcement of the Arbitral Award rendered by the Court of Arbitration of Mongolia, [2009] Min Si Ta Zi No. 33

18 As the case number of the case in the Tianjin Second Intermediate People's Court could not be found, the number of the Request for Instruction of Tianjin High People's Court on the Non-Recognition and Non-Enforcement of the 12,330/TE/MW/AVH Arbitral Award rendered by the ICC in Lausanne was filed here

19 Reply of the SPC to the Request for Instruction of Tianjin High People's Court on the Non-Recognition and Non-Enforcement of the 12,330/TE/MW/AVH Arbitral Award rendered by the ICC in Lausanne, [2009] Min Si Ta Zi No. 38

20 As the case number of the case in Ningbo Intermediate People's Court could not be found, the number of the Request for 21 Instruction of Zhejiang High People's Court on the Case Concerning the Application of China-Base Ningbo Foreign Trade Co., Ltd. for Non-Enforcement of the Arbitral Award rendered by the HKIAC was filed here

21 Reply of the SPC to the Request for Instruction of Zhejiang High People's Court on the Case Concerning the Application of China-Base Ningbo Foreign Trade Co., Ltd. for Non-Enforcement of the Arbitral Award rendered by the HKIAC, [2009] Min Si Ta Zi No. 42

22 As the case number of the case in Hangzhou Intermediate People's Court could not be found, the number of the Request for Instruction on the Case Concerning the Application of Tianrui Hotel Investment Co., Ltd. for Recognition of Arbitral Award against Hangzhou Yiju Hotel Management Co., Ltd. was filed here.

23 Reply of the SPC to the Request for Instruction of on the Case Concerning the Application of Tianrui Hotel Investment Co., Ltd. for Recognition of Arbitral Award against Hangzhou Yiju Hotel Management Co., Ltd., [2010] Min Si Ta Zi No.18

24 The Zhejiang High People's Court made a request for instruction concerning this case to the SPC, but the SPC's reply to the case has not been made public and cannot be accessed. In view of the high similarity in the subject and content between this case and the case Tianrui Hotel Investment Co., Ltd. v. Hangzhou Yiju Hotel Management Co., Ltd., this article reasonably speculates that the content of the reply of the SPC in this case is to recognize and enforce the arbitral award involved in either

25 The Zhejiang High People's Court made a request for instruction concerning this case to the SPC, but the SPC's reply to the case has not been made public and cannot be accessed. In view of the high similarity in the subject and content between this case and the case Tianrui Hotel Investment Co., Ltd. v. Hangzhou

Yiju Hotel Management Co., Ltd., this article reasonably speculates that the content of the reply of the SPC in this case is to recognize and enforce the arbitral award involved either

[26] Reply of the SPC to the Report Concerning the Non-Recognition of the No. 73/23–06 Arbitral Award rendered by the Court of Arbitration of Mongolia, [2009] Min Si Ta Zi No. 46

[27] As the case number of the case in Nantong Intermediate People's Court could not be found, the number of the Request for Instruction of Jiangsu High People's Court on the Case Concerning the Non-Enforcement of the No. 07–11 Arbitral Award rendered by the JCAA in Tokyo was filed here

[28] Reply of the SPC to the Request for Instruction on the Case Concerning the Non-Enforcement of the No. 07–11 Arbitral Award rendered by the JCAA in Tokyo, [2010] Min Si Ta Zi No. 32

[29] As the case number of the case in Chaozhou Intermediate People's Court could not be found, the number of the Request for Instruction of Guangdong High People's Court on the Case Concerning the Application of DMT S. A. (France) for Recognition and Enforcement of Foreign Arbitral Award against Chaozhou Huaye Packaging Materials Co., Ltd. was filed here

[30] Reply of the SPC to the Request for Instruction on the Case Concerning the Application of DMT S. A. (France) for Recognition and Enforcement of Foreign Arbitral Award against Chaozhou Huaye Packaging Materials Co., Ltd., [2010] Min Si Ta Zi No. 51

[31] As the case number of the case in Zhanjiang Intermediate People's Court could not be found, the number of the Request for Instruction of Guangdong High People's Court on the Case Concerning the Application of Louis Dreyfus Commodities Asia Co., Ltd. for Recognition and Enforcement of Foreign Arbitral Award against Guangdong Fuhong Oil Products Co., Ltd. was filed here

[32] Reply of the SPC to the Request for Instruction on the Case Concerning the Application of Louis Dreyfus Commodities Asia Co., Ltd. for Recognition and Enforcement of Foreign Arbitral Award against Guangdong Fuhong Oil Products Co., Ltd., [2010] Min Si Ta Zi No. 48

[33] As the case number of the case in Beijing Second Intermediate People's Court could not be found, the number of the Request for Instruction of Beijing High People's Court on the Case Concerning the Recognition and Enforcement of No. 26–435-08 Arbitral Award rendered by the American Dispute Resolution Centre was filed here

[34] Reply of the SPC to the Request for Instruction on the Case Concerning the Recognition and Enforcement of No. 26–435-08 Arbitral Award rendered by the American Dispute Resolution Centre, [2011] MSTZ No. 21.

[35] Reply of the SPC to the Request for Instruction on the Case Concerning the Application of Western Bulk Pte. Ltd. for Recognition and Enforcement of a UK Arbitral Award, [2012] Min Si Ta Zi No. 12

[36] As the case number of the case in Hangzhou Intermediate People's Court could not be found, the number of the Request for Instruction of Zhejiang High People's Court on the Case Concerning the Application of ALSTOM Technology Ltd. for Recognition and Enforcement of Foreign Arbitral Award against Zhejiang University New Technology Co., Ltd. was filed here

[37] Reply of the SPC to the Request for Instruction on the Case Concerning the Application of ALSTOM Technology Ltd. for Recognition and Enforcement of Foreign Arbitral Award against Zhejiang University New Technology Co., Ltd., [2012] Min Si Ta Zi No. 54

[38] As the case number of the case in Beijing Second Intermediate People's Court could not be found, the number of the Request for Instruction of Beijing High People's Court on the Case Concerning the Application of Beijing Chaolai Xinsheng Sports & Leisure Co., Ltd. for Recognition of No. 12113–0011 and No. 12112–0012 Artitral Awards rendered by the KCAB was filed here

[39] Reply of the SPC to the Request for Instruction on the Case Concerning the Application of Beijing Chaolai Xinsheng Sports & Leisure Co., Ltd. for Recognition of No. 12113–0011 and No. 12112–0012 Arbitral Awards rendered by the KCAB, [2013] Min Si Ta Zi No. 64

[40] Reply of the SPC to the Request for Instruction on the Case Concerning the Application of "Angfohuapin" Joint Venture Co., Ltd. for Recognition and Enforcement of the Arbitral Award rendered by the BelCCI, [2012] Min Si Ta Zi No. 42

[41] As the case number of the case in Dongguan Intermediate People's Court could not be found, the number of the Request for Instruction of Guangdong High People's Court on the Case Concerning the Application of Proton Motors (China) Co., Ltd. for Recognition and Enforcement of Foreign Arbitral Awards against Jinxing Heavy Industry Manufacturing Co., Ltd. was filed here

[42] Reply of the SPC to the Request for Instruction on the Case Concerning the Application of Proton Motors (China) Co., Ltd. for Recognition and Enforcement of Foreign Arbitral Awards against Jinxing Heavy Industry Manufacturing Co., Ltd., [2013] Min Si Ta Zi No. 28

[43] As the case number of the case in Zhanjiang Intermediate People's Court could not be found, the number of the Request for Instruction of Guangdong High People's Court on the Case Concerning the Application of Ruierma Food Co., Ltd. for Recognition and Enforcement of Foreign Arbitral Awards against Zhanjiang Guanya Food Co., Ltd. was filed here

[44] Reply of the SPC to the Request for Instruction on the Case Concerning the Application of Ruierma Food Co., Ltd. for Recognition and Enforcement of Foreign Arbitral Awards against Zhanjiang Guanya Food Co., Ltd., [2013] Min Si Ta Zi No. 40

[45] As the case number of the case in Zhongshan Intermediate People's Court could not be found, the number of the Request for Instruction of Guangdong High People's Court on the Case Concerning the Application of Castel Electronics Pty Ltd. for Recognition and Enforcement of Foreign Arbitral Awards was filed here

[46] Reply of the SPC to the Request for Instruction on the Case Concerning the Application of Castel Electronics Pty Ltd. for Recognition and Enforcement of Foreign Arbitral Awards, [2013] Min Si Ta Zi No. 46

[47] As the case number of the case in Ningbo Intermediate People's Court could not be found, the number of the Request for Instruction of Zhejiang High People's Court on the Case Concerning the Application of Allenberg Cotton Co. for Recognition and Enforcement of Foreign Arbitral Awards against Ningbo Youngor International Trade and Transportation Co., Ltd. was filed here

[48] Reply of the SPC to the Request for Instruction on the Case Concerning the Application of Allenberg Cotton Co. for Recognition and Enforcement of Foreign Arbitral Awards against Ningbo Youngor International Trade and Transportation Co., Ltd., [2014] Min Si Ta Zi No. 32

[49] Reply of the SPC to the Request for Instruction of Liaoning High People's Court on the Case Concerning the Non-Recognition and Non-Enforcement of No. 2/11 Arbitral Award rendered by the Waren-Verein Der Hamburger Borse E. V., [2014] Min Si Ta Zi No. 31

[50] Reply of the SPC to the Request for Instruction on the Case Concerning the Application of Siemens International Trading (Shanghai) Co., Ltd. for Recognition and Enforcement of Foreign Arbitral Award, [2015] Min Si Ta Zi No. 5

[51] As the case number of the case in Wuhan Maritime Court could not be found, the number of the Request for Instruction of High People's Court of Hubei Province on the Case Concerning the Application of Trinity Bulk Shipping Ltd. for Recognition and Enforcement of London Arbitral Award against Jiangsu Huihong International Group Native Product Import & Export Co., Ltd. and Yangzhou Huamei Shipping Industry Co., Ltd. was filed here

[52] Reply of the SPC to the Request for Instruction on the Case Concerning the Application of Trinity Bulk Shipping Ltd. for Recognition and Enforcement of London Arbitral Award against Jiangsu Huihong International Group Native Product Import & Export Co., Ltd. and Yangzhou Huamei Shipping Industry Co., Ltd., [2015] Min Si Ta Zi No. 34

[53] As the case number of the case in Wuhan Intermediate People's Court could not be found, the number of the Request for Instruction of High People's Court of Hubei Province on the Case Concerning the Application of FSG Automotive Holding AG for Recognition and Enforcement of No. SCH-5239 Arbitral Award rendered by the Arbitration Center of the Austrian Federal Economic Association against Wuhan Fanzhou Machinery Manufacturing Co., Ltd. was filed here

[54] Reply of the SPC to the Request for Instruction on the Case Concerning the Application of FSG Automotive Holding AG for Recognition and Enforcement of No. SCH-5239 Arbitral Award rendered by the Arbitration Center of the Austrian Federal Economic Association against Wuhan Fanzhou Machinery Manufacturing Co., Ltd., [2015] Min Si Ta Zi No. 46

[55] As the case number of the case in Qingdao Maritime Court could not be found, the number of the Request for Instruction of High People's Court of Shandong Province on the Case Concerning the Application of Spliethoff's Bevrachtingskantoor B. V. for Recognition and Enforcement of Foreign Arbitral Award against China Electronics Import & Export Shandong Co. and Rongcheng Xixiakou Ship Industry Co., Ltd. was filed here

[56] Reply of the SPC to the Request for Instruction on the Case Concerning the Application of Spliethoff's Bevrachtingskantoor B. V. for Recognition and Enforcement of the HULL XXK06-039 Foreign Arbitral Award rendered by a Tribunal in London, UK, [2015] Min Si Ta Zi No. 48

[57] As the case number of the case in Yantai Intermediate People's Court could not be found, the number of the Request for Instruction of High People's Court of Shandong Province on the Case Concerning the Application of Ecom Agroindustrial Asia Pte. Ltd. for Recognition and Enforcement of the Arbitral Award rendered by the ICA was filed here

[58] Reply of the SPC to the Request for Instruction of High People's Court of Shandong Province on the Case Concerning the Application of Ecom Agroindustrial Asia Pte. Ltd. for Recognition and Enforcement of the Arbitral Award rendered by the ICA, [2015] Min Si Ta Zi No. 29

[59] As the case number of the case in Weifang Intermediate People's Court could not be found, the number of the Request for Instruction of High People's Court of Shandong Province on the Case Concerning the Application of Toyoshima & Co., Ltd. for Recognition and Enforcement of Foreign Arbitral Award against Gaomi Luyuan Textile Co., Ltd. was filed here

[60] Reply of the SPC to the Request for Instruction of High People's Court of Shandong Province on the Case Concerning the Application of Toyoshima & Co., Ltd. for Recognition and Enforcement of Foreign Arbitral Award against Gaomi Luyuan Textile Co., Ltd., [2015] Min Si Ta Zi No. 30

[61] As the case number of the case in Weifang Intermediate People's Court could not be found, the number of the Request for Instruction of High People's Court of Shandong Province on the Case Concerning the Application of Toyoshima & Co., Ltd. for Recognition and Enforcement of Foreign Arbitral Award against Changyi Kunfu Textile Co., Ltd. was filed here

[62] Reply of the SPC to the Request for Instruction of High People's Court of Shandong Province on the Case Concerning the Application of Toyoshima & Co., Ltd. for Recognition and Enforcement of Foreign Arbitral Award against Changyi Kunfu Textile Co., Ltd., [2015] Min Si Ta Zi No. 31

[63] As the case number of the case in Yichang Intermediate People's Court could not be found, the number of the Request for Instruction of High People's Court of Hubei Province on the Case Concerning the Application of Paul Reinhart AG for Recognition and Enforcement of Foreign Arbitral Award against Hubei Qinghe Textile Co., Ltd. was filed here.

[64] Reply of the SPC to the Request for Instruction on the Case Concerning the Application of Paul Reinhart AG for Recognition and Enforcement of Foreign Arbitral Award against Hubei Qinghe Textile Co., Ltd., (2016) Zui Gao Fa Min Ta No. 11

[65] Reply of the SPC to the Request for Instruction on the Case Concerning the Application of Noble Resource Pte. Ltd. for Recognition and Enforcement of Foreign Arbitral Award against Hubei Qinghe Textile Co., Ltd., (2016) Zui Gao Fa Min Ta No. 12

[66] Reply of the SPC to the Request for Instruction on the Case Concerning the Non-Enforcement of No. 18295/CYK Arbitral Award rendered by the ICC, (2016) Zui Gao Fa Min Ta No. 8

[67] Reply of the SPC to the Request for Instruction on the Case Concerning the Application of J & D IB Co. for Recognition of Foreign Arbitral Award, (2016) Zui Gao Fa Min Ta No. 38

[68] Reply of the SPC to the Request for Instruction of High People's Court of Jiangsu Province on the Case Concerning the Application of Bright Morning Limited. for Recognition and Enforcement of ARB130/11/MJL Arbitral Award rendered by the SIAC against Yixing Leqi Textile Group Co., Ltd., (2017) Zui Gao Fa Min Ta No. 44

[69] Reply of the SPC to the Request for Instruction of High People's Court of Henan Province on the Case Concerning the Application of Chenco Chemical Engineering and Consulting GmbH for Recognition and Enforcement of Foreign Arbitral Award against Do-Fluoride Chemicals Co., Ltd., (2016) Zui Gao Fa Min Ta No. 66

[70] Reply of the SPC to the Request for Instruction of High People's Court of Jiangsu Province on the Case Concerning the Application of Plexus Cotton Ltd. for Recognition and Enforcement of the UK Arbitral Award rendered by the ICA, (2016) Zui Gao Fa Min TaNo. 31

[71] As the case number of the case in Shijiazhuang Intermediate People's Court could not be found, the number of the Request for Instruction of High People's Court of Hubei Province on the Case Concerning the Application of Wollema-absalia Movo Ltd., Republic of Tatarstan, Russian Federation for Recognition of Russian Arbitral Award was filed here

[72] Reply of the SPC to the Request for Instruction on the Case Concerning the Application of Wollema-absalia Movo Ltd., Republic of Tatarstan, Russian Federation for Recognition of Russian Arbitral Award, (2016) Zui Gao Fa Min Ta No. 97

[73] As the case number of the case in Luohe Intermediate People's Court could not be found, the number of the Request for Instruction of High People's Court of Henan Province on the Case Concerning the Application of Henan GCL Solar Technology Co., Ltd. for Non-Enforcement of Hong Kong Arbitral Award against Semimaterials Co., Ltd. was filed here

[74] Reply of the SPC to the Request for Instruction on the Case Concerning the Application of Semimaterials Co., Ltd. for Enforcement of Hong Kong Arbitral Award, (2016) Zui Gao Fa Min Ta No. 75

In the following sections, we analyze the Chinese courts' judicial review of foreign arbitral awards by applying the New York Convention based on the grounds and perspectives involved. Add something more about this.

12.2 Validity of Arbitration Agreements

Under Chinese law, there will be no arbitration in the absence of a valid arbitration agreement. The arbitration agreement shows that the parties choose to submit their disputes that might arise or have already arisen for arbitration. Such an expression of intent is the prerequisite and basis for initiating the arbitration proceedings, as well as the source of the jurisdiction of an arbitral tribunal. Considering the importance of the arbitration agreement, the New York Convention listed the defects in arbitration agreement as the first circumstance that the court may refuse to recognize and enforce foreign arbitral awards.

Specifically, pursuant to Article V(1)(a) of the New York Convention, if the respondent can provide evidence to prove that the parties to the arbitration agreement were, under the law applicable to them, under some incapacity, or the said agreement is not valid under the law to which the parties have subjected it or failing any indication thereon, under the law of the country where the award was made, then the court may refuse to recognize and enforce the award.

In practice, it also happens that the respondent claims that there exists no arbitration agreement. Since the existence of an arbitration agreement is a prerequisite for the validity of the arbitration agreement,[16] if the respondent can provide evidence to show that there is no arbitration agreement between the parties, the court may refuse to recognize and enforce the said arbitral award as well.

A. The Defense of No Arbitration Agreement

Whether there is an arbitration agreement between the parties often involves the finding of relevant facts. Generally, pursuant to Article II of the New York Convention, the parties need to reach an arbitration agreement in writing, which can be reflected by an arbitration clause in a contract concluded by the parties, a separate arbitration agreement, or those contained in an exchange of letters or telegrams.

[a] Cases where the Applications were Refused Due to No Arbitration Agreement

Among the 127 cases about the application for recognition and enforcement of foreign arbitral awards, there were 7 cases in which the courts refused to recognize or enforce the awards based on the finding that there existed no arbitration agreement between the parties. We listed these cases as follows.

---

[16] Reply of the SPC to the Request for Instruction of High People's Court of Jiangsu Province on the Case Concerning the Application of Plexus Cotton Ltd. for Recognition and Enforcement of the UK Arbitral Award rendered by the ICA, (2016) Zui Gao Fa Min Ta No. 31.

Voest-Alpine International Trading USA Corp. v. Jiangsu Provincial Foreign Trade Corp.[17]

In this case, the respondent did not either sign or affix its seal in the Sales Confirmation Letter, which contained an arbitration clause. Although the applicant twice authorized its attorney to deliver mails containing a notice of arbitration to the respondent, the respondent did not reply to the first mail. The court considered that the notices above cannot ensure that the respondent receives overseas legal documents in a timely manner. In addition, when the applicant authorized its Chinese attorney to deliver the notice of arbitration once again, the respondent replied on December 22, 2004, denying the existence of an arbitration agreement. The court ruled that there was no time limit specified in the notices sent by the applicant, nor was there the requirement of "a reasonable period of time" in the relevant provisions of Singaporean law, so there was no legal basis for the arbitral tribunal to assume that there was a valid arbitration agreement, as the respondent did not reply within a reasonable period of time. Therefore, the court dismissed the application for recognition of the arbitral award rendered by the SIAC based on the finding that the parties did not reach an arbitration agreement over the dispute involved in the case.

Concordia Trading B. V. v. Nantong Gangde Grease Co., Ltd.[18]

In this case, the respondent did not sign or affix its seal in the three contracts containing the dispute resolution clause, which provided that the disputes shall be submitted to FOSFA for arbitration upon receiving the contracts. Neither did the respondent send them back to the applicant. In addition, according to the following correspondence between the parties, although the letter of guarantee issued by the respondent involved the numbers of the above copies of contracts, the amount of goods, the prices and the terms and conditions for futures margin stated in the letter of guarantee were apparently different from the content of the three contracts. Based on those facts, the SPC stated in its reply that there is insufficient evidence to prove that the parties had reached an arbitration agreement in writing and that the New York Convention did not accept implied arbitration agreement, and thus the arbitral award involved in this case should not be recognized or enforced.

Allenberg Cotton Co. v. Ningbo Youngor International Trade & Transportation Co., Ltd.[19]

In this case, the applicant could prove the authenticity of the respondent's seal in the Cotton Purchase Agreement, which contained an arbitration clause. Neither could the applicant prove that Wu, the respondent's senior representative, was properly

---

[17] (2008) Ning Min Wu Chu Zi No. 43.

[18] Reply of the SPC to the Request for Instruction on the Case Concerning the Application of Concordia Trading B.V. for Recognition and Enforcement of the No. 3948 Arbitral Award rendered by the FOSFA, [2009] Min Si Ta Zi No. 22.

[19] Reply of the SPC to the Request for Instruction on the Case Concerning the Application of Allenberg Cotton Co. for Recognition and Enforcement of Foreign Arbitral Awards against Ningbo Youngor International Trade and Transportation Co., Ltd., [2014] Min Si Ta Zi No. 32.

authorized to represent the respondent. Therefore, the SPC, in its reply, was of the opinion that there was insufficient evidence to show that the parties had reached an arbitration agreement regarding the dispute arising out of the Cotton Purchase Agreement, and there was no factual or legal basis for the ICA to accept the case. Therefore, the SPC approvedtheHigh People's Court of Zhejiang Province's ruling to refuse to recognize the arbitral award.

Jess Smith & Sons Cotton, LLC ("Jess Smith") v. Wuxi Natural Textile Industry Co., Ltd. ("Wuxi Natural") and Wuxi Natural Green Fiber Technology Co., Ltd.("Wuxi Green Fiber").[20]

In this case, Jess Smith (the seller) and Wuxi Natural (the buyer) signed a cotton sales contract, which was revised five times on November 26, 2010, November 29, 2010, November 16, 2011, May 11, 2012, and May 22, 2012. The aforementioned contract texts were standard contract format provided by Jess Smith. When applying for recognition and enforcement of the foreign arbitral award, Jess Smith submitted the last four revised contract versions to the court. Among them, the buyer stipulated in the version on May 22, 2012 was Wuxi Green Fiber, whilethe buyers stipulated in the remaining three versions were Wuxi Natural. In addition, the corporate seal of Wuxi Natural and the signature of its legal representative Zhu appeared only on November 29, 2010, while none of the other three versions contained the seal or signature of Wuxi Natural or Wuxi Green Fiber.

The court held that Wuxi Natural and Wuxi Green Fiber were two separate legal entities. Although their legal representative and vice president were identical and Wuxi Green Fiber issued the Letter of Credit in the order of Wuxi Natural, it could not be properly inferred that the two companies were the same. Additionally, Wuxi Natural had, in its two mails to Jess Smith, expressly confirmed that Wuxi Natural and Wuxi Green Fiber were not the same company. Consequently, the signature by Wuxi Natural on the contract version of November 29, 2010, cannot be taken as the expression of intention of Wuxi Green Fiber. In addition, there was no seal or signature by Wuxi Green Fiberin the contract version of May 22, 2012, which listed Wuxi Green Fiber as the Buyer. As Jess Smith was not able to provide evidence to show that implied agreement had been the business practice between the parties, it could not be concluded based on the unilateral provisions of Jess Smith's formatted contract text thatthe acquiescence of Wuxi Green Fiber was a commitment to the contract. Therefore, the court ruled that there existed no valid contract between Jess Smith and Wuxi Green Fiber, let alone an arbitration agreement, and thus the arbitral award rendered against Wuxi Green Fiber shall not be recognized or enforced.

Allenberg Cotton Co. v. Jiangsu Nijiaxiang Group Co., Ltd.[21]

In this case, there was no official seal of the respondent on the Cotton Purchase Contract containing the arbitration clause, and Zhang, the person whose name

---

[20] (2013) Xi Shang Wai Zhong Shen Zi No. 0007.

[21] (2013) Xi Shang Wai Zhong Shen Zi No. 0009.

appeared in the purchaser column of the said contract, denied that he had ever signed the said contract. The court held that the applicant shall prove that the respondent has agreed to the arbitration clause. Although the applicant provided the original fax copy of the contract, the applicant could not further prove the authenticity of the signature by Zhang while expressly refusing to identify the signature. In addition, the four contracts between the respondent and Jiangyin Tiangong Textile Co., Ltd. ("**Jiangyin Textile**") signed through Louis Dreyfus (Beijing) Trade Co., Ltd., were all in the form of hard copies and signed by Zhang with the official seal of the applicant. However, the contract in this case was concluded by fax with only the signature of Zhang, which was significantly different from the practices before. The applicant could not prove that it had concluded any other contract by fax with either the respondent or Jiangyin Textile. Therefore, the court concluded that the evidence provided by the applicant could not sufficientlyprove that the parties had reached an arbitration agreement.

Even if the signature of Zhang on the said contract was real, it could not be inferred that the respondent had the intention to submit the disputes for arbitration. According to the agency law of the UK, the seat of arbitration, the arbitration agreement was valid only when the agent was specifically authorized to sign an arbitration agreement. Such authorization included the actual authorization (explicit and implied) and the apparent authorization. In this case, the applicant failed to prove that Zhang had been duly authorized by the respondent to sign the contract. Therefore, there was no explicit authorization. By requiring the court not to recognize and enforce the said arbitral award, the respondent had shown that it had no intention of ratifying such an act. Consequently, based on the currently available evidence, the applicant was unable to prove that it was reasonable to believe that Zhang had the proper authorization to sign the arbitration agreement on behalf of the respondent. In summary, the court ruled that there was no valid arbitration agreement between the parties, and thus, the arbitral award made by the ICA shall not be recognized or enforced.

Louis Dreyfus Australia Ltd. v. Jiangsu Nijiaxiang Group Co., Ltd.[22]

This case is almost identical to the case of *Allenberg Cotton Co. v. Jiangsu Nijiaxiang Group Co., Ltd.* in terms of the facts and grounds of refusal for recognition and enforcement.

Plexus Cotton Ltd. v.Jiangsu Jinfang Industrial Co., Ltd.[23]

There was no signature of the respondent in the Sales Contract based on which the applicant submitted the dispute to arbitration. Based on the currently available facts, it could not be concluded that the parties had reached an arbitration agreement. According to the law of the UK, the seat of the arbitration, the arbitration agreement of the parties was the prerequisite for the arbitration agreement to be valid. Therefore, the court refused to recognize and enforce the arbitral award rendered by the ICA.

---

[22] (2013) Xi Shang Wai Zhong Shen Zi No. 0003.

[23] (2014) Yan Shang Wai Zhong Shen Zi No. 00001.

[b]   **Cases where the Subsequent Act of the NonsigningParty MakesIt Subject to Contractand the Arbitration Clause Contained Therein.**

In the remaining several cases, the defense that the arbitration agreement did not exist was not supported. Among them, it is noteworthy that although one party did not sign the contract, the subsequent act of the nonsigning party might make it subject to the contract and the arbitration clause contained therein. We list three cases here.

Western Bulk Pte. Ltd. v. Beijing Sinosteel Tiantie Iron & Steel Trading Co., Ltd.[24]

Although there was no signature of the respondent on the contract involved in the case, the liquidation group of the respondent acknowledged the signature and partial fulfillment of the contract when sending the notice to the applicant. The SPC held that it should be considered that there was an arbitration agreement between the parties in the case where the respondent did not provide sufficient evidence to the contrary.

Australia CBH Grain Co., Ltd. v. Hebei Sihai Development Co., Ltd.[25]

Although the respondent did not sign the contract, the minutes of the meeting signed by the parties afterwards expressly revised the contract, and such revision only covered the amount of goods, letter of credit and prices. Therefore, the court held that, as the respondent did not expressly exclude the application of other clauses of the contract (including the arbitration clause), the contract, together with the minutes of the meeting, constituted the contractual basis between the parties. Correspondingly, the arbitration clause in the contract constituted an arbitration agreement in writing between the parties.

Louis Dreyfus Commodities Suisse SA v. Ningbo Qiancheng Import & Export Co., Ltd.[26]

The applicant sent the Letter of Termination to the respondent on October 8, 2012, attaching the list of the contract numbers including the 22 Cotton Sales Contracts involved in the case. The respondent, in its reply on October 26, 2012, did not raise any objection to the validity of the 22 contracts and only asked for further negotiations in view of the difficulties in its performance of such contracts. The court considered that such a reply by the respondent not only proved that the 22 contracts had been duly concluded but also proved that the parties had reached an arbitration agreement.

B.   **The Defense of Invalid Arbitration Agreement**

Among the cases retrieved, there was no case where the court refused to recognize or enforce a foreign arbitral award due to the invalidity of the arbitration agreement. This also reflects the position of the Chinese courts in supporting arbitration anddenying foreign arbitral awards. Nevertheless, we still list some noteworthy issues concerning the validity of arbitration agreement here.

---

[24] Reply of the SPC to the Request for Instruction on the Case Concerning the Application of Western Bulk Pte.Ltd. for Recognition and Enforcement of a UK Arbitral Award, [2012] Min Si Ta Zi No. 12.

[25] (2013) Shi Min Wu Chu Zi No. 00525.

[26] (2015) Zhe Yong Zhong Que Zi No. 5.

[a]   **The Applicable Law for Determining the Validity of Arbitration Agreements**

Mon Eldorado Co., Ltd. v. Zhejiang Zhancheng Construction Group Co., Ltd.[27]

The Construction Contract involved in this case stipulated that"If negotiation fails, the dispute shall be resolved by the court or arbitral tribunal in the state of registration." The High People's Court of Zhejiang Province proposed in its request for instruction that the court shall apply *lex fori*, i.e., the law of China, to determine the validity of the arbitration clauses above, and such arbitration clauses shall be held as voids according to the law of China. The SPC was of the opinion that only when the arbitration agreement was invalid according to the applicable law that the parties have agreed upon or, in the absence of such agreement, according to the law of the seat of arbitration can the court refuse to recognize or enforce the award, and the courts shall not determine the validity of arbitration agreement according to *lex fori*.

Toyoshima & Co., Ltd. v. Changyi Kunfu Textile Co., Ltd.[28]

The parties agreed on "ICA Rules and Arbitration" in the Cotton Sales Contract but did not agree upon the applicable law to determine the validity of arbitration agreement. The respondent was unable to provide evidence to show that according to the law of the seat of arbitration, i.e., the law of the UK, this arbitration agreement was invalid. Therefore, the SPC held that there was no legal ground to rule that the arbitration agreement was void in accordance with the law of China.

Olam International Ltd. v. Jingshan Weijia Textile Enterprise Co., Ltd.,[29] *Jess Smith v. Jihua 3509 Textile Co., Ltd.,*[30] *and Compass Cotton B.V. v. Shandong Yanggu Shunda Textile Co., Ltd.*[31]

The contracts in the three cases all stipulated that "The disputes shall be submitted for arbitration in accordance with the rules of the ICA and the law of UK shall apply." The respondents in the cases above all raised the objection that an arbitration agreement without specifying the arbitration institution was void in accordance with the law of China. The courts in the three cases all held that according to the law of the UK agreed upon by the parties, there was no mandatory requirement to specify the arbitration institution; thus, it did not constitute the circumstance specified by Article V(1)(a) of the New York Convention.

---

[27] Reply of the SPC to the Report Concerning the Non-Recognition of the No. 73/23–06 Arbitral Award made by the Court of Arbitration of Mongolia, [2009] Min Si Ta Zi No. 46.

[28] Reply of the SPC to the Request for Instruction of High People's Court of Shandong Province on the Case Concerning the Application of Toyoshima & Co., Ltd. for Recognition and Enforcement of Foreign Arbitral Award against Changyi Kunfu Textile Co., Ltd., (2015) Min Si Ta Zi No. 31.

[29] (2013) E Jing Men Min San Chu Zi No. 00019.

[30] (2014) E Xiao Gan Zhong Min Wai Chu Zi No. 00001.

[31] (2014) Liao Min Wu Chu Zi No. 4.

[b]   **The Validity of the Arbitration Agreement That Submits Disputes without Foreign-Related Factors to Overseas Arbitral Institutions for Arbitration**

Beijing Chaolai Xinsheng Sports & Leisure Co., Ltd. v. Beijing Suowang Zhixin Investment Consulting Co., Ltd.[32]

In this case, both parties were Chinese entities, and the contract involved the transfer of the applicant's share of a golf course within the territory of China. The subject matter was also within the territory of China, and the contract was signed and performed within Chinese territory either. The contract involved provided that "If there is any dispute, the parties shall try to resolve such disputes through friendly negotiation and reach an agreement. For matters that cannot be agreed upon, the parties may submit such disputes to the KCAB for arbitration. The arbitration outcome shall be equally binding on both parties."

The SPC held that, regardless of whether the parties had made an explicit agreement, both the contract and its arbitration clause were subject to the law of China. Pursuant to Article 271 of the Civil Procedure Law[33] and Paragraph 2 of Article 128 of the Contract Law,[34] the law of China did not authorize the parties to refer disputes without foreign factors to an overseas arbitration institution or ad hoc tribunal outside China for arbitration. Therefore, the arbitration clause where the parties agreed to submit the dispute to the KCAB was invalid, and the flaw of validity could not be corrected just because the parties did not raise objections in the arbitration proceedings.

[c]   **The Identification of Foreign-Related Factors**

Siemens International Trading (Shanghai) Co., Ltd. v. Shanghai Golden Land Co., Ltd.[35]

---

[32] Reply of the SPC to the Request for Instruction on the Case Concerning the Application of Beijing Chaolai Xinsheng Sports & Leisure Co., Ltd. for Recognition of No. 12113–0011 and No. 12112–0012 Arbitral Awards rendered by the KCAB, (2013) Min Si Ta Zi No. 64.

[33] Article 271of the Civil Procedure Law stipulates that "Where disputes arising from economic, trade, transport or maritime activities involve foreign parties, if the parties have included an arbitration clause in their contract or subsequently reach a written arbitration agreement that provides that such disputes shall be submitted for arbitration to an arbitration institution of the People's Republic of China for foreign-related disputes or to another arbitration institution, no party may institute an action in a people's court.".

[34] Paragraph 2 of Article 128 of the Contract Law stipulates that "Where the parties do not wish to, or are unable to, resolve such dispute through settlement or mediation, the dispute may be submitted to the relevant arbitration institution for arbitration in accordance with the arbitration agreement between the parties. Parties to a foreign-related contract may apply to an arbitration institution in China or another arbitration institution for arbitration……".

[35] (2013) Hu Yi Zhong Min Ren (Wai Zhong) Zi No. 2.

The focus of the dispute in this case was whether the arbitration clause where the parties agreed to submit the disputes relating to the contract to the SIAC for arbitration was valid. Regarding this issue, the court held that although the contract did not appear to have typical foreign-related factors (including the subject, the place of delivery, the subject matter), the contract, which was significantly different from ordinary domestic contract in its subject and characteristics of performance, shall be considered a foreign-related civil legal relationship.

On the one hand, although the parties were Chinese entities, their places of registration were the Shanghai Pilot Free Trade Zone, and they were wholly foreign-owned enterprises. Since the sources of capital, ultimate benefit ownership, and operating decisions of such enterprises were generally closely related to their foreign investors, such enterprises had more obvious foreign-related factors than ordinary domestic enterprises.In the context of the reform of the pilot free trade zone to promote investment and trade facilitation, the aforementioned foreign-related factors should be given more attention.

On the other hand, although the subject matter under the contract was eventually delivered at the domestic construction site, the subject matter was first transported from the territory outside China to the Shanghai Pilot Free Trade Zone for supervision, the customs clearance procedures were completed in a timely manner, and the goods were transferred from inside to outside of the Zone. Thus, the circulation ofthe subject matter also had certain characteristics of international sales goods from the perspectives of the signature and performance of the contract involved, and the performance of the contract in this case was significantly different from the ordinary domestic contract due to the application of special customs supervision measures in the pilot free trade zone.

Based on the situations above, the court held that the contractual relationship in this case fell within the scope of "other circumstances under which the civil relationship may be determined as foreign-related civil relationship"stipulated in Article 1 of the Interpretations of the SPC on Several Issues Concerning Application of the Law of China on Choice of Law for Foreign-Related Civil Relationships (I), and thus the dispute related to the contract had foreign-related factors, and the arbitration agreement of the parties to submit the disputes to the SIAC for arbitration was valid.

2. *Lifu Candy (Shanghai) Co., Ltd. V. Shanghai Lianfu Food Co., Ltd.*[36]

In this case, the respondentalleged that one of the parties did not bear any rights and obligations stipulated in the contract, and the other parties were all Chinese enterprises;thus, the contract involved in the case did not have foreign factors, and the arbitration clause where the parties agreed to submit disputes to overseas arbitration institutions for arbitration was invalid.

The court held that although the signatory party did not bear any rights and obligations, it was still a signatory party of the contract, and the arbitral award still listed it as the party to arbitration. As a consequence, the contract involved in the case had foreign factors.

---

[36] (2008) Hu Er Zhong Min Wu (Shang) Chu Zi No. 19.

[d] Whether the Validity of Arbitration Agreement will beAffected by Other Factors

GRD Minproc Ltd. v. Shanghai Flyingwheel Industry Co., Ltd.[37]

The respondent arguedthat it did not have the right to engage in foreign trade when signing the contract and did not have the qualifications to sign the foreign trade contract;thus, the contract and the arbitration clause contained therein were invalid. In response to the defense, the court held that the disputed contract was jointly signed by the applicant (the seller), Shanghai Foreign Trade Corporation (the buyer), and the respondent (the user). It was precisely because the respondent did not have the right to operate foreign trade that Shanghai Foreign Trade Corporation would participate in the conclusion of the contract as the buyer. Therefore, the contract and the arbitration clauses contained therein were legal and valid.

Proton Motors (China) Co., Ltd. v. Jinxing Heavy Industry Manufacturing Co., Ltd.[38]

Concerning this case, the SPC clearly stated in its reply that "In accordance with Article 57 of the Contract Law regarding the independence of dispute resolution clauses[39] and Article 2 of the Provisions of the SPC on Several Issues concerning the Trial of Disputes Involving Foreign-Funded Enterprises (I),[40] the validity of the jurisdictional clauses in the Memorandum shall not be affected by the fact that the Memorandum had not been approved by the examination and approval organ.

3. Tact Communications, Inc. V. Quanzhou Cardinu Travel Products Co., Ltd.[41]

The respondent argued that the contract involved in this case was not actually performed, and thus the arbitration clause in the contract was not binding on either party.The court was of the opinion that based on the independence of the arbitration clause, whether the contract is actually performed would not affect the validity of the arbitration clause.

---

[37] (2007) Hu Yi Zhong Min Wu (Shang) Chu Zi No. 116.

[38] Reply of the SPC to the Request for Instruction on the Case Concerning the Application of Proton Motors (China) Co., Ltd. for Recognition and Enforcement of Foreign Arbitral Awards against Jinxing Heavy Industry Manufacturing Co., Ltd., [2013] Min Si Ta Zi No. 28.

[39] Article 57 of the Contract Law stipulates that "If a contract is null and void, revoked or terminated, it shall not affect the validity of the dispute settlement clause which is independently existing in the contract.".

[40] Article 2 of the Provisions of the SPC on Several Issues concerning the Trial of Disputes Involving Foreign-Funded Enterprises (I) stipulates that "Where a supplemental agreement reached by the parties on the issues concerning a foreign-funded enterprise does not constitute any significant or substantial change to the approved contract, the people's court shall not determine the supplemental agreement as ineffective on the ground that it has not been approved by the foreign-funded enterprise examination and approval organ. The term "significant or substantial change" as mentioned in the preceding paragraph shall include changes in registered capital, corporate form, business scope, business term, investment contribution of the shareholders, form of contribution, merger of the company, split of the company, equity transfer, etc.".

[41] (2013) Quan Min Ren Zi No. 35.

C.   The Defense of Incapacity of the Parties

It is rare for the respondent to argue that the parties to the arbitration agreement are under some incapacity. Incapacity was raised in only one of the 127 cases set out above.

Spring Maritime Ltd. v. Shandong Haina Real Estate Co., Ltd.[42]

The respondent filed an objection to the recognition and enforcement of the arbitral award involved in this case, arguing that the parties and the person using the seal did not have the capacity for civil conduct to issue the Letter of Guarantee without the approval of the respondent's board of directors or shareholders' meeting, which made the Letter of Guarantee and the arbitration clause contained therein invalid.

The court held that, in accordance with Paragraph 1 of Article V of the New York Convention, the respondent was a legal person registered in China, and thus its capacity for civil conduct should be determined in accordance with the law of China. Pursuant to Article 36 of the General Principles of the Civil Law of China, a legal person's capacity for civil conduct shall begin when the legal person was established and shall end when the legal person terminates. Consequently, the respondent had the capacity for civil conduct to provide external guarantees during its duration. In addition, the court would not review whether the parties had been approved by the board of directors or shareholders' meeting since it was not a statutory circumstance stipulated in the New York Convention.

12.3   Due Process

Procedural justice is an indispensable part of achieving legal justice. It also applies to the recognition and enforcement of foreign arbitral awards. Article V(1)(b) of the New York Convention stipulates that if the respondent proves that it was not given proper notice of the appointment of the arbitrator or of the arbitration proceedings or was otherwise unable to present his case, then the court can refuse to recognize and enforce the arbitral award. In practice, the flaw in service is one of the objections frequently raised by the respondent.

A.   Basis for Determining whether the Service of Arbitration Notice is Appropriate

"Angfohuapin" Joint Venture Co., Ltd.v. Henan Haofeng Chemical Co., Ltd.[43]

Both the Zhengzhou Intermediate People's Court and the High People's Court of Henan Province held that the act of serving the notice of arbitration proceedings by

---

[42] (2013) Qing Hai Fa Hai Shang Chu Zi No. 1032.

[43] Reply of the SPC to the Request for Instruction on the Case Concerning the Application of "Angfohuapin" Joint Venture Co., Ltd. for Recognition and Enforcement of the Arbitral Award rendered by the BelCCI, [2012] Min Si Ta Zi No. 42.

the BelCCI by mail to the respondent did not have legal effects and fell within the circumstance stipulated in Article V(1)(b) of the New York Convention in accordance with the Convention on the Service Abroad of Judicial and Extra Judicial Documents in Civil or Commercial Matters and the Treaty between China and the Republic of Belarus on Civil and Criminal Judicial Assistance.

The SPC clearly pointed out in its reply that whether the service in arbitration proceedings was proper should be determined in accordance with the parties' agreement or the applicable arbitration rules, rather than the Convention on the Service Abroad of Judicial and Extra Judicial Documents in Civil or Commercial Matters and the Treaty between China and the Republic of Belarus on Civil and Criminal Judicial Assistance. Pursuant to Chapter 20 of the Rules of BelCCI, request for Arbitration, statement of defenses, notices, awards and other decisions made by the arbitral institution on the case shall be sent by registered mail or receipt to the recipient. Unless otherwise agreed upon by the parties, if the documents above were mailed to habitual residence, place of business or mailing address of the recipient, it shall be deemed that the documents have been delivered. Therefore, the act of BelCCI to send documents to the place of residence of the respondent by mail did not violate the parties' agreement or the provisions of the arbitration rules.

Subway International B.V. v. Beijing Tepu Food Co., Ltd.[44]

In the case at hand, the American Dispute Resolution Centre mailed the notice of the appointment of arbitrators to the respondent, and the mailing address was "D-901, Jiarun Garden, Guangshun Street, Wangjing, Chaoyang District, Beijing." However, the mail was returned on the ground that the respondent was "relocated". After that, the arbitration institution no longer served the respondent with the notice of the appointment of arbitrators. The parties agreed in the arbitration agreement to conduct arbitration in accordance with the UNCITRAL arbitration rules. Article 2(1) of the UNCITRAL arbitration rules in force at that time provided that "For the purpose of these Rules, any notice, including a notification, communication or proposal, is deemed to have been received if it is physically delivered to the addressee or if it is delivered at his habitual residence, place of business or mailing address, or, if none of these can be found after making reasonable inquiry, then at the addressee's last-known residence or place of business. Notice shall be deemed to have been received on the day it is so delivered."

Therefore, the SPC held in its reply that the High People's Court of Beijing City should further investigate whether the mailing address above was the habitual residence, place of business or place of communication of the respondent, or the last-known residence or place of business. If so, the notice shall be deemed to have been effectively delivered even if the mail was not signed.

B. Cases where the Arbitral Awards Were Refused to be Recognized and Enforced Due to Improper Services

---

[44] Reply of the SPC to the Request for Instruction on the Case Concerning the Recognition and Enforcement of No. 26–435-08 Arbitral Award rendered by the American Dispute Resolution Centre, [2011] Min Si Ta Zi No. 21.

Among the 127 sample cases, the respondents in many cases argued that the service procedure was improper, which made them unable to present their cases. However, there were only 3 cases where the arbitral awards refused to be recognized and enforced by the courts due to improper service.

Shin-Etsu Chemical Co., Ltd.v. Jiangsu Zhongtian Technology Co., Ltd.[45]

In this case, Article 53.2 of arbitration rules of the JCAA, which was chosen by the parties, stipulated that "The arbitral tribunal shall notify the parties of the time limit for rendering the award when the hearing proceeding mentioned in the preceding paragraph concludes."

However, the arbitral tribunal did not renew the extension and notify the parties in accordance with the arbitration rules from September 20, 2005 (the date when the arbitral tribunal promised to render the award), to February 23, 2006 (the date when the award was actually rendered).Therefore, the SPC considered in the reply that the act constituted the circumstance specified in Article V(1)(b) of the New York Convention, and the arbitral award in this case should not be recognized.

Shin-Etsu Chemical Co., Ltd. v. Tianjin Xinmao Science & Technology Co., Ltd.[46]

Article20[47] of arbitration rules of the JCAA involved in this case provide that "1.The claimant may amend its claim under the same arbitration agreement by submitting a request for amendment to JCAA. If the amendment is made after the constitution of the arbitral tribunal, the claimant should submit a request for amendment to the arbitral tribunal and obtain approval from the arbitral tribunal. 2. The arbitral tribunal shall give the other Party an opportunity to comment before granting approval of an amendment."

In this case, the applicant filed the request for amendment to the arbitral tribunal on August 31, 2005. However, the respondent denied that it had received the request for comments sent by the arbitral tribunal, the applicant did not provide evidence, and there was no evidence to prove that the arbitral tribunal had mailed such documents to the respondent.

Therefore, the SPC held that the respondent was deprived of his right and opportunity to make a defense, which constituted the circumstance specified in Article V(1)(b) of the New York Convention, and the arbitral award should not be recognized.

---

[45] Reply of the SPC to the Report on Non-Recognition of the No. 04–05 Tokyo Arbitral Award rendered by the JCAA, [2007] Min Si Ta Zi No. 26.

[46] Reply of the SPC on Non-Recognition of the No. 05–03 Tokyo Arbitral Award rendered by the JCAA, [2008] Min Si Ta Zi No. 18.

[47] The number of this Article has amended to 21 in the present arbitration rules of the JCAA 2019.

Mon Eldorado Co., Ltd. v. Zhejiang Zhancheng Construction Group Co., Ltd.[48]

In the present case, it was shown that the signed express mail with the number of 1,677,283,941 did not involve the notice of arbitration proceedings, and the express mail with the number of 1,681,469,484, including the notice of Resolution Process and the Date of the Arbitration Hearing", did not reach the respondent, resulting in the failure of the respondent to present his case before the arbitral tribunal in the hearing proceeding. Consequently, the court refused to recognize and enforce the arbitral award on the ground that there existed the circumstance specified in Article V(1)(b) of the New York Convention.

C. Cases where the Notice cannot be Delivered because of the Respondent

East Land Property Pte.Ltd. v. Zhejiang Xinxing Rubber Co., Ltd.[49]

In this case, the respondent claimed that it had not received the notice of arbitration since its address had changed. In response to the defense, the court held that the respondent had neither informed the applicant norconducted registration of changes in the industry and commerce department, so the act of the arbitral tribunal to send the notices to the respondent's business registration address should be regarded as effective.

Addax Bv v. China-Base Ningbo Foreign Trade Co., Ltd.[50]

Inthis case, the HKIAC sent a notice of the appointment of arbitrators by fax and double registered mail to the respondent according to the fax number and address specified in the contract. The respondent claimed that the fax number was no longer used when the HKIAC sent the notice and therefore it had not received the notice.In this regard, the SPC held in its reply that, in accordance with Article 2 "Notice, calculation of periods of time" of UNCITRAL arbitration rules, since the fax number of respondents specified in the contract was the final communication method it assured in this case, the notice sent by the HKIAC according to the fax number should be deemed to have been received by the respondent.

GEA Heat Exchangers, Inc.v. Guangdong Changying Heavy Industry Co., Ltd.[51]

The arbitration institution delivered the arbitration materials to the respondent by express according to the address indicated in the contract, but the feedback mail provided by the express delivery company showed that the recipient refused to accept

---

[48] (2009) Zhe Shao Min Que Zi No. 1; Reply of the SPC to the Report Concerning the Non-Recognition of the No. 73/23–06 Arbitral Award made by the Court of Arbitration of Mongolia, [2009] Min Si Ta Zi No. 46.

[49] (2009) Zhe Tai Zhong Que Zi No. 4.

[50] Reply of the SPC to the Request for Instruction on the Case Concerning the Application of China-Base Ningbo Foreign Trade Co., Ltd. for Non-Enforcement of the Arbitral Award rendered by the HKIAC, [2009] Min Si Ta Zi No. 42.

[51] (2015) Fo Zhong Fa Min Er Zhong Zi No. 7.

it.The court held that the respondentshall bear the corresponding adverse consequences for its refusal to receive the arbitration materials sent by the arbitration institution

D.   Whether the Failure to Specify the Arbitration Document in the Mailing List Will Affect the Validity of Service

Ruierma Food Co., Ltd. v. Zhanjiang Guanya Food Co., Ltd.[52]

In this case, the arbitration institution, AFI, sent a registered mail to the respondent. The mailing address was the same as the respondent's address. However, the mailing list did not indicate the arbitration notice, arbitral award or other arbitration documents. The SPC held in its reply that the act was not improper, and the court shall not refuse to recognize and enforce the arbitral award on the ground that the arbitration notice was not received by the respondent.

E.   Whether the Correspondence Address Specified in the Contract Need to be Explicitly Agreed Before it can be Applied to the Arbitration Proceedings

Western Bulk Pte.Ltd. v. Beijing Sinosteel Tiantie Iron & Steel Trading Co., Ltd.[53]

Article 49 "Notice" of the contract involved in the case stipulated the method, language, and correspondence address that should be used for mutual notification during the performance of the contract. The High People's Court of Tianjin City held that the clause should not be applicable to the arbitration procedure due to the independence of the arbitration clause and the failure of the clause to explicitly stipulate that it can also be applied to the arbitration procedure;thus, it was inappropriate for the applicant to send the arbitration notice and other documents to the mailing address specified in the clause.

The SPC held in the reply that the parties had been in contact with each other in accordance with the clause before the respondent's cancellation. It lacked a factual basis for the court to consider that the parties did not agree on the method of correspondence due to the failure of the parties to explicitly stipulate that the clause can also be applied to the arbitration procedure.

In addition, the SPC made it clear in this case that it did not violate the relevant laws and regulations for the claimant and the arbitrator to send documents related to the arbitration to the respondent, the company's shareholders, members of the liquidation group and the legal adviser of the liquidation group by fax, e-mail, express mail, and personal delivery after the respondent entered the liquidation procedure.

---

[52] Reply of the SPC to the Request for Instruction on the Case Concerning the Application of Ruierma Food Co., Ltd. for Recognition and Enforcement of Foreign Arbitral Awards against Zhanjiang Guanya Food Co., Ltd., [2013] Min Si Ta Zi No. 40.

[53] Reply of the SPC to the Request for Instruction on the Case Concerning the Application of Western Bulk Pte.Ltd. for Recognition and Enforcement of a UK Arbitral Award, [2012] Min Si Ta Zi No. 12.

12.4   The Scope of Arbitration

As to the arbitral award rendered by the arbitral tribunal exceeding its powers, pursuant to Article V(1)(c) of the New York Convention, the court may refuse to recognize and enforce the award if the award deals with a difference not contemplated by or not falling within the terms of the submission to arbitration, or it contains decisions on matters beyond the scope of the submission to arbitration, and if the decisions on matters submitted to arbitration can be separated from those not so submitted, that part of the award which contains decisions on matters submitted to arbitration may be recognized and enforced.

In view of the fact that the authority of the arbitral tribunal mainly comes from the arbitration agreement between the parties and the claimant's claim (or the respondent's counterclaim), the grounds of defense the respondent may raise on the scope of arbitration can be roughly divided into defenses concerning the arbitration agreement and defense concerning the scope of the submission to arbitration.

A.   Cases where the Arbitral Awards Were Refused to be Recognized and Enforced Due toan "Excessive Award"

Among the cases concerning the application for recognition and enforcement of foreign arbitral awards from 2008 to 2018, there were 7 cases in total where the arbitral awards were partially or wholly refused to be recognized and enforced due to "excessive award".

Hemofarm DD, MAG International Trade Holding DD, Suramu Media Ltd. v. Jinan Yongning Pharmaceutical Co., Ltd.[54]

In this case, Article 58 of the Joint Venture Contract stated that "All disputes arising from or related to the performance of the contract shall be resolved by friendly negotiation; if the disputes cannot be resolved through negotiation, it shall be submitted to the ICC in Paris for arbitration in accordance with the provisional rules of the arbitration procedure of the institution." However, the arbitral tribunal reviewed the Lease Agreement between the respondent and the joint venture company and ruled that the applicant was entitled to receive 30% of the litigation costs incurred in making defenses for the joint venture company in the lease dispute.

The SPC pointed out in its reply that the arbitration clauses in the Joint Venture Contract only referred to the disputes between the parties to the Joint Venture Contract over matters of the joint venture, instead of the disputes relating to the Lease Contract between the respondent and the joint venture company. It was beyond the scope of the arbitration agreement in the Joint Venture Contract for the ICC arbitral tribunal to review and rule the dispute relating to the Lease Contract.

Jess Smith v. Wuxi Natural& Wuxi Green Fiber.[55]

---

[54] Reply of the SPC to the Request for Instructions on the Non-Recognition and Non-Enforcement of an Arbitral Award of the ICC, [2008] Min Si Ta Zi No. 11.

[55] (2013) Xi Shang Wai Zhong Shen Zi No. 0007.

In this case, the arbitral institution accepted the case in accordance with the arbitration clause in the Sales Contract concluded between Jess Smith and Wuxi Natural. However, the arbitral tribunal listed Wuxi Green Fiber, who did not sign arbitration agreements with Jess Smith, as one of the respondents according to the application of Jess Smith and rendered the arbitral award on Wuxi Green Fiber. The court was of the opinion that the arbitral award was clearly beyond the scope of the arbitration agreement.

In addition, the arbitral award required Wuxi Natural and Wuxi Green Fiber to assume joint and several liabilities for the performance of the contract. The main body of the award also used the term "buyer" to refer to Wuxi Natural and Wuxi Green Fiber throughout the award. There was no clear distinction between the responsibilities of these two companies. Therefore, the court held that it was impossible to separate the decisions on matters submitted to arbitration from those not so submitted, so the court refused to recognize and enforce all the arbitral award involved in the case.

Trinity Bulk Shipping Ltd. v. Jiangsu Huihong International Group Native Product Import & Export Co., Ltd., Yangzhou Huamei Shipping Industry Co., Ltd.[56]

In this case, the arbitral tribunal dealt with the legal costs incurred by the applicant in response to the lawsuit filed by the respondent before a domestic court of China. The SPC held in the reply that "As the cost award in this case was a ruling on how to account and share the arbitration fees incurred in the London arbitration process, the loss the applicant may suffer resulting from the respondent's violation of the arbitration clause, i.e., the behavior to file a lawsuit in a Chinese court, whose nature was damages for breach of contract, was not included in the arbitration fees incurred in the London arbitration process. It was beyond the scope of the cost award for the arbitral tribunal to directly deal with the loss incurred by the applicant in the Chinese court proceedings." Therefore, the SPC considered that this part of "excessive award" shall not be recognized and enforced.

Spliethoff's Bevrachtingskantoor B.V. v. China Electronics Import& Export Shandong Co., Rongcheng Xixiakou Ship Industry Co., Ltd.[57]

In this case, the applicant and the respondent concluded the Ship Construction Contract, which contained an arbitration clause. After the dispute arose, the applicant resorted to arbitration in London. Afterwards, the arbitral tribunal rendered the arbitral award.

The SPC stated in its reply that "Although the Shandong Branch of the Bank of China provided a repayment guarantee for the return of the buyer's advance payment

---

[56] Reply of the SPC to the Request for Instruction on the Case Concerning the Application of Trinity Bulk Shipping Ltd. for Recognition and Enforcement of London Arbitral Award against Jiangsu Huihong International Group Native Product Import & Export Co., Ltd. and Yangzhou Huamei Shipping Industry Co., Ltd., [2015] Min Si Ta Zi No. 34.

[57] Reply of the SPC to the Request for Instruction on the Case Concerning the Application of Spliethoff's Bevrachtingskantoor B.V. for Recognition and Enforcement of the HULL XXK06-039 Foreign Arbitral Award rendered by a Tribunal in London, UK, (2015) Min Si Ta Zi No. 48.

under the Ship Construction Contract, the bank was not a party to the Ship Construction Contract, nor did it sign a written arbitration agreement with the contracting parties, nor was it a claimant or respondent in the arbitration.The rights and obligations of the letter of guarantee should not be subject to the arbitral award involved in the case. The fifth decision of Part A of the award made by the London arbitral tribunal was beyond the scope of the arbitration agreement. Therefore, this part of the award should not be recognized, but it did not affect the recognition of other divisible parts of the award."

BrightMorningLimited v. Yixing Leqi Textile Group Co., Ltd.[58]

In this case, neither party mentioned the equity and its restrictions and transfers in the claims and counterclaims, while the fourth decision of the arbitral award ruled that the applicant was prohibited from claiming its shareholder's rights in the joint venture company and should transfer its equity at the request of the respondent.

The court held the opinion that "the shareholders' rights were statutory rights arising from the legal system of the company, rather than contractual rights. The disputes the parties submitted to arbitration were disputes related to the performance, breach of contract, termination, etc. of the Joint Venture Contract or the dispute arising therefrom. That is, the disputes resolved by the arbitral tribunal were limited to the disputes between the parties related to the Joint Venture Contract, and the arbitral tribunal could not extend its jurisdiction to the joint venture company itself. To balance the interests of the parties and avoid the applicant from obtaining so-called "double compensation", the arbitral tribunal voluntarily interfered with the shareholder's rights of the applicant in the joint venture company, which was not only beyond the scope of the dispute submitted to arbitration by the partiesbut also beyond the scope of the matters submitted to arbitration by the parties.

Chenco Chemical Engineering and Consulting GmbH v. Do-Fluoride Chemicals Co., Ltd.[59]

In this case, the applicant's claim was "to stop using unauthorized technology and to pay liquidated damages due to unauthorized use". However, Paragraph 414 of the arbitral award did not distinguish authorized technology from unauthorized technology and ruled that "as long as the respondent continues to use the technology of Chenco Company, it shall pay a monthly fine of 100,000 Euros to the applicant on the 23rd of each month". Paragraph 415 of the arbitral award ruled that "the respondent is prohibited from using the applicant's technology until all the amounts awarded in Paragraph 414 of this Final Award have been fully paid". Paragraph 417

---

[58] (2016) Su 02 Xie Wai Ren No. 1; Reply of the SPC to the Request for Instruction of High People's Court of Jiangsu Province on the Case Concerning the Application of Bright Morning Limited for Recognition and Enforcement of ARD130/11/MJL Arbitral Award rendered by the 3IAC against Yixing Leqi Textile Group Co., Ltd., (2017) Zui Gao Fa Min Ta No. 44.

[59] (2015) Xin Zhong Min San Chu Zi No. 53; Reply of the SPC to the Request for Instruction of High People's Court of Henan Province on the Case Concerning the Application of Chenco Chemical Engineering and Consulting GmbH for Recognition and Enforcement of Foreign Arbitral Award against Do-Fluoride Chemicals Co., Ltd., (2016) Zui Gao Fa Min Ta No. 66.

ruled that "the monthly due penalty thereafter shall also bear interest at 5% per annum and the interest shall be calculated until the payment is completed."

Since those parts of the arbitral award above could be separated from the remaining part of the arbitral award, the court dismissed the application to recognize and enforce Paragraphs 414, 415, 417 of the arbitral award.

B.   **Whether the Behavior of the Arbitral Tribunal to Render a Cost Award When the Parties do not Claim Constitutes an "Excessive Award"**

GRD Minproc Ltd. v. Shanghai Flyingwheel Industry Co., Ltd.[60]

The respondent made a defense that the claimant never filed a counterclaim on the arbitration fee during the arbitration proceeding, and thus the dispute dealt with by the arbitral award was not the subject matter the parties submitted to arbitration.

The court held that, according to the parties' agreement in the contract, the arbitration fee should be borne by the losing party. Meanwhile, the arbitration rules also stipulated that the arbitral tribunal may require the losing party to bear the other party's relevant costs at the request of a party. However, the arbitration rules did not specify that the above-mentioned "the request of a party" must be submitted in the form of a counterclaim. Therefore, it was in line with the agreement of the parties and the arbitration rules for the arbitral tribunal to make a cost award under the circumstance where the arbitral tribunal had determined that the respondent had lost the case on the substantive issues, and the applicant had submitted the list of relevant fees to the arbitral tribunal. Thus, the behavior of the arbitral tribunal to render a cost award when the parties do not claim did not constitute an "excessive award".

12.5 Composition of Arbitral Tribunal and Arbitration Proceedings

In practice, the defense of the composition of arbitral tribunal and arbitration procedures is one of the objections frequently raised by the respondent. Pursuant to Article V(1)(d) of the New York Convention, if the respondent can prove that the composition of the arbitral authority or the arbitral procedure was not in accordance with the agreement of the parties or failing such agreement was not in accordance with the law of the country where the arbitration took place, the court may refuse to recognize and enforce the award.

It can be seen from the provision that the standard of examining the legality of the composition of the arbitral tribunal or the arbitration procedure is the arbitration agreement of the parties or the law of the seat of arbitration. Generally, the arbitration rules agreed upon by the parties in the arbitration agreement also become a part of the arbitration agreement, and thus, the arbitration rules are also one of the standards.

---

[60] (2007) Hu Yi Zhong Min Wu (Shang) Chu Zi No. 116.

A. **Whether the IBA Guidelines on Conflict of Interest in International Arbitration and Other Regulations that Do Not have Mandatory Effects are Standards of Examining the Legality of the Composition of Arbitral Tribunal or Arbitration Procedure**

Bright Morning Limited. v. Yixing Leqi Textile Group Co., Ltd.[61]

The respondent claimed that the two arbitrators in this case violated the disclosure obligation stipulated in the IBA Guidelines on Conflicts of Interest in International Arbitration, which led to the violation of the arbitration rules of the composition of the arbitral tribunal. The Court held that the guidelines were not mandatory legal norms, and the violation of such guidelines did not necessarily violate the arbitration rules. Hence, the court did not support the defense.

Marumo Corp. v. Beijing Delin Golf Sports Development Co., Ltd.[62]

The respondent alleged that the nondisclosure of the arbitrator of the fact that the company in which the arbitrator worked as a director was associated with the applicant and the arbitrator had been a good friend of the agent of the applicant for years violated the IBA Guidelines on Conflicts of Interest in International Arbitration. The court held that the issue of the disclosure of arbitrators only needs to be examined by the arbitration rules involved in the case, so the provisions on the obligation of disclosure of arbitrators in the Guidelines did not apply to this case.

B. **The Defense of Illegal Composition of Arbitral Tribunal**

[a] **Cases where the Defense of Illegal Composition of Arbitral Tribunal was Upheld**

Among the cases researched, there were 6 cases in which the defenses of the respondents of the illegal composition of arbitral tribunal were supported by the Court.

First Investment Corp. (Marshall Island) v. Fujian Mawei Shipbuilding Ltd.&Fujian Shipbuilding Industry Group Co., Ltd.[63]

In this case, the applicant and the respondent signed an Option Agreement on shipbuilding and agreed that "Any dispute arising out of or related to the agreement shall be submitted to arbitration in London; The arbitration procedure, including the enforcement of the arbitral award, shall be in accordance with the Arbitration Act 1996 of UK or any amendment or reenactment currently in force thereof, and the rules of LMAA for the time being in force; Each party shall appoint one arbitrator and the third arbitrator shall be selected by the two arbitrators appointed." After providing

---

[61] (2016) Su 02 Xie Wai Ren No. 1.

[62] (2013) Er Zhong Min Te Zi No. 12593.

[63] (2006) Xia Hai Fa Ren Zi No. 1; Reply of the SPC on the Application of First Investment Corp. (Marshall Island) for the Recognition and Enforcement of the Arbitral Award rendered by an ad hoc Tribunal, [2007] Min Si Ta Zi No. 35.

opinions on the first draft of the arbitral award, one of the arbitrators was detained under criminal law and did not participate in the remaining process of arbitration including the deliberation of arbitral award.

The Court held that the composition of the arbitral tribunal was inconsistent with the arbitration agreement and the law of UK where the arbitration took place. Consequently, the Court ruled that the award shall not be recognized and enforced.

China Shipping Development Co., Ltd. Freighter Co. v. Anhui Technology Imp. & Exp. Co., Ltd.[64]

In this case, the parties agreed that "the arbitration shall take place in Hong Kong and the law of UK shall apply"in the Charter Agreement. After the disputes arose,the applicant submitted the disputes to arbitration and appointed WP as the arbitrator. Upon notice of the applicant, the respondent did not appoint an arbitrator. As the sole arbitrator, WP reviewed the case and rendered the arbitral award. Afterwards, the applicant applied to the Chinese court for recognition and enforcement of the arbitral award. The respondent claimed that the sole arbitrator did not conform to the provisions of the Law of Hong Kong on the composition of the arbitral tribunalor the New York Convention.

The SPC considered that since the arbitration clause stipulated that the seat of arbitration is Hong Kong without stipulating the applicable law of the arbitration clause, the Arbitration Ordinance of Hong Kong where the arbitration took place and the Model Law shall apply. Pursuant to Article 34C (5) of the Arbitration Ordinance of Hong Kong, if the parties fail to reach an agreement on the number of arbitrators, the parties shall first apply to the HKIAC for a decision on the number of arbitrators to be one or three. If the HKIAC decides to appoint a sole arbitrator and the parties fail to reach an agreement on the arbitrator, the procedure stipulated in Article11 (3) (B) of the Model Law shall be applied to determine the sole arbitrator, i.e.,the sole arbitrator shall be appointed by the HKIAC upon the request of a party. The appointment of the sole arbitrator in the case violated the procedures above and therefore should not be recognized and enforced.

Lehua Meilan Holding Co., et al. v. Tianjin Jiashijie Group Co., Ltd., et al.[65]

In this case, the parties agreed in the arbitration agreement that "The disputes will be submitted to three arbitrators appointed in accordance with the arbitration rules of ICC". Pursuant to Articles 27 and 28 of the arbitration rules of the ICC, an award approved by the arbitration institution shall be signed by the arbitral tribunal. However, one of the arbitrators did not participate in the whole process of arbitration, and the arbitral tribunal did not send the award to the arbitrator for signature. Therefore, the SPC replied that the composition of the arbitral tribunal in this case was

---

[64] Reply of the SPC to the Request for Instructions of the Case Concerning the Application of China Shipping Development Co., Ltd. Freighter Co. for Recognition and Enforcement of London Arbitral Award, [2008] Min Si Ta Zi No. 17.

[65] Reply of the SPC to the Request for Instruction on the Non-Recognition and Non-Enforcement of the 12,330/TE/MW/AVH Arbitral Award rendered by the ICC in Lausanne, [2009] Min Si Ta Zi No. 38.

not only inconsistent with the arbitration agreement but also violated the arbitration rules;thus, the arbitral award shall not be recognized and enforced.

Western Bulk Pte.Ltd. v. Beijing Sinosteel Tiantie Iron & Steel Trading Co., Ltd.[66]

In this case, Article 39 of the Voyage Chartering Contract stipulated that "The disputes shall be settled by a sole arbitrator appointed by both parties; or if one party fails to reply to the other party's notice of the appointment of the arbitrator, the arbitrator shall be the sole arbitrator settling the disputes. If the parties fail to agree on the appointment of a sole arbitrator within 14 days after receivingthe notice of arbitration, the disputes shall be settled by two arbitrators, and each party shall appoint one arbitrator. If the two arbitrators fail to reach an agreement on any issue, they shall appoint a third arbitrator."

After receiving the notice of appointing MBH as the sole arbitrator from the applicant, the respondent rejected the appointment of MBH as the sole arbitrator but appointed Chen as the other arbitrator. Therefore, the condition of a sole arbitrator stipulated in the arbitration clauses was not fulfilled, and the arbitral tribunal was composed of two arbitrators. Since Chen resigned as an arbitrator afterwards, the issue involved in this case was how to fill the vacancy in the arbitral tribunal.

In accordance with Article 27 (2) (3), Article 16 (7) and Article 18 (2) of the Arbitration Act 1996 ofthe UK where arbitration took place, the applicant shall apply to the Court to make the decision on the composition of the arbitral tribunal after informing the respondent. However, the applicant did not apply to the Court. The case was reviewed by MBH, the sole arbitrator appointed by the applicant.

Therefore, the SPC held that the composition of the arbitral tribunal was inconsistent with the law of the seat of arbitration, and thus,the arbitral award shall not be recognized and enforced.

ALSTOM Technology Ltd. v.Zhejiang University New Technology Co., Ltd.[67]

In this case, Article 18 (c) of the License Agreement concluded by both parties stated that "Disputes arising from this Agreement shall be arbitrated by the SIAC in accordance with the arbitration rules of the ICC". Article 8.4 of the arbitration rules of the ICC stipulated that "Where the dispute is to be referred to three arbitrators, each party shall nominate in the Request and the Answer, respectively, one arbitrator for confirmation. If a party fails to nominate an arbitrator, the appointment shall be made by the Court. The third arbitrator, who will act as the chairman of the Arbitral Tribunal, shall be appointed by the Court unless the parties have agreed upon another procedure for such appointment, in which case the nomination will be subject to confirmation pursuant to Article 9. Should such procedure not result in a

---

[66] (2010) Jin Hai Fa Que Zi No. 6; Reply of the SPC to the Request for Instruction on the Case Concerning the Application of Western Bulk Pte.Ltd. for Recognition and Enforcement of a UK Arbitral Award, [2012] Min Si Ta Zi No. 12.

[67] Reply of the SPC to the Request for Instruction on the Case Concerning the Application of ALSTOM Technology Ltd. for Recognition and Enforcement of Foreign Arbitral Award against Zhejiang University New Technology Co., Ltd., [2012] Min Si Ta Zi No. 54.

nomination within the time limit fixed by the parties or the Court, the third arbitrator shall be appointed by the Court."

However, the presiding arbitrator in this casewas nominated by one of the arbitrators without objection of the other. The composition of the arbitral tribunal of the SIAC in accordance with its arbitration rules was not in conformity with the provisions of the arbitration rules of the ICC on the appointment of the presiding arbitrator. In addition, the respondent had expressed its opposition to the decision of the SIAC, alleging that such practice did not reflect the true will of both parties, and the respondent reserved all rights that could be exercised to the arbitral tribunal with respect to the matter to indicate that it had not waived its right of objection.

Therefore, the SPC held that the composition of the arbitral tribunal in this case was inconsistent with the agreement of the parties and thus shall not be recognized and enforced.

Noble Resources International Pte. Ltd. v. Shanghai Xintai International Trade Co., Ltd.[68]

The parties reached the arbitration clause in the Iron Ore Trade Agreement signed by them: "16.1 All disputes and claims arising out of or in connection with the transaction and/or this agreement, including any question relating to its existence, validity or termination, shall be settled by arbitration under arbitration rules of the SIAC for the time being in force. Such rules shall be regarded as being quoted and incorporated in this clause. 16.1.1 The arbitral tribunal shall consist of three arbitrators……".

Afterwards, a dispute arose between the parties, and the applicant filed a Request for Arbitration to the SIAC in accordance with the arbitration clause and applied for the application of Expedited Procedure. The respondent had repeatedly indicated to the SIACrefusing to apply the Expedited Procedure. The SIAC approved the application of the applicant, decided to arbitrate the case according to the Expedited Procedure, and appointed DX as the sole arbitrator.

With regard to Expedited Procedures, Article 5.2 of the 5th Edition of the arbitration rules of the SIAC 2013 stipulates that "When a party has applied to the Registrar under Rule 5.1, and when the President determines, after considering the views of the parties, that the arbitral proceedings shall be conducted in accordance with the Expedited Procedure, the following procedure shall apply:……; b. The case shall be referred to a sole arbitrator unless the President determines otherwise;……".

The Court held that the provisions above did not exclude the possibility of applying other ways of composition of the arbitral tribunal in the Expedited Procedure, nor did they provide that the President was authorized to forcibly apply Article 5.2(b) relating to sole arbitration when the parties had agreed to apply other ways of composition of the arbitral tribunal. Applying the Expedited Procedure did not affect the parties' essential procedural right to compose a three-arbitrator arbitral tribunal in accordance with the arbitration clause. Under the circumstance that the arbitration clause provided that the arbitral tribunal shall consist of three arbitrators and the respondent had explicitly objected to sole arbitration, the SIAC still adopted sole

---

[68] (2016) Hu 01 Xie Wai Ren No. 1.

arbitrator in accordance with Article 5.2 of its arbitration rules, which violated the agreement of the arbitration clause involved, and thus the arbitral award involved shall not be recognized and enforced.

[b] Whether the Circumstance Where the Arbitrator Has the Corresponding Qualifications When Accepting the Commission but Loss the Corresponding Qualifications When Making the Award Constitutes anIllegal Composition of Arbitral Tribunal

Toyoshima & Co., Ltd. v. Gaomi Luyuan Textile Co., Ltd.[69]

There was an arbitration agreement between the parties that stipulated that the arbitration rules of the ICA shall apply. The respondent alleged that two arbitrators of the arbitral tribunal had the relevant technical qualification when accepting the commission, but they did not have the qualification when making the arbitral award, which made the composition of the arbitral tribunal illegal.

The SPC held that there was no stipulation on how to deal with the situation in the arbitration rules of the ICA, so it could not be concluded that the composition of the arbitral tribunal was inconsistent with the arbitration rules.

In addition, according to the principle established by the Reply of the SPC Regarding the Enforcement by the People's Court of an Arbitral Award Signed by the Original Arbitrator who is No Longer Appointed,[70] the loss of the qualification of two arbitrators only restricted the cases accepted by the arbitration institution afterwards but would not affect the trial work of the previously legally established arbitral tribunal.

C. Defense of Improper Arbitration Procedure

[a] Cases where the Defense of Improper Arbitration Procedurewas Upheld

Among 127 cases, there were 4 cases where the courts refused to recognize and enforce arbitral awards due to improper arbitration procedures.

Shin-Etsu Chemical Co., Ltd. v. Jiangsu Zhongtian Technology Co., Ltd. (2008).[71]

The parties in the case concluded a Sales Contract and agreed that "All disputes arising out of this Agreement and related to this Agreement shall be arbitrated in Tokyo, Japan, governed by the commercial arbitration rules of the JCAA in the event that both parties fail to settle through negotiation. The arbitral award shall be final and binding on both parties." Regarding the time limit for making an award, Article 53.1 of the commercial arbitration rules of the JCAA stipulates that "Upon determining that the arbitral proceedings have been conducted fully and the tribunal

---

[69] Reply of the SPC to the Request for Instruction of High People's Court of Shandong Province on the Case Concerning the Application of Toyoshima & Co., Ltd. for Recognition and Enforcement of Foreign Arbitral Award against Gaomi Luyuan Textile Co., Ltd., (2015) Min Si Ta Zi No. 30.

[70] Fa Shi [1998] No. 21.

[71] Reply of the SPC to the Report on Non-Recognition of the No. 04–05 Tokyo Arbitral Award rendered by theJCAA, [2007] Min Si Ta Zi No. 26.

is able to make an award and therefore decides to conclude the hearing proceedings, the tribunal shall render the award within five weeks from the date of the decision; if the case is especially complex or there are other relevant reasons, the tribunal may extend the said period if necessary, but it shall be no more than eight weeks."

On July 7, 2005, the arbitral tribunal decided to accept the request of the applicant for the amendments to its claims and conclude the hearing proceeding. On August 31, 2005, the arbitral tribunal announced that it would delay the rendering of the award by 20 days to September 20, 2005. However, the award was actually rendered on February 23, 2006. Hence, the arbitral tribunal did not render the award within the time limit stipulated in the commercial arbitration rules of the JCAA.

The SPC also pointed out in its reply that since the parties clearly agreed on the application of the commercial arbitration rules of the JCAA in the arbitration clause, the content of the arbitration rules had become a part of the parties' agreement, and thus, the violation of the arbitration rules constituted the circumstance where the arbitration procedure was inconsistent with the parties' agreement, and the arbitral award should not be recognized and enforced.

Shin-Etsu Chemical Co., Ltd. v. Tianjin Xinmao Science &Technology Co., Ltd.[72]

The parties in the case concluded the Long-term Sales Agreement and agreed that "All disputes arising out of this Agreement and related to this Agreement that cannot be resolved by mutual agreement shall be submitted for arbitration in Tokyo, Japan, in accordance with the rules and procedures of the JCAA; the arbitral award shall be final and binding on both parties." Article 53.2 of the commercial arbitration rules of the JCAA stipulates that "After the arbitral tribunal decides to conclude the hearing proceeding according to the provisions of the preceding paragraph, it shall notify the parties of the period of time for making arbitral award."

However, the arbitral tribunal of the case did not notify the respondent of the period of time for making arbitral award after the conclusion of hearing proceeding. As a consequence, the SPC held that such behavior violated the mandatory regulations of the arbitration rules, which shall be deemed an improper arbitration procedure.

It is worth noting that there also existed a situation in which the arbitral tribunal did not inform the parties of the time limit for making an award in accordance with the commercial arbitration rules of the JCAAin the case *Shin-Etsu Chemical Co., Ltd. v. Jiangsu Zhongtian Technology Co., Ltd. (2008).* However, in that case, the SPC considered that the situation constituted"The party against whom the award is invoked was not given proper notice of the appointment of the arbitrator or of the arbitration proceedings or was otherwise unable to present his case", as stipulated in Article V(1)(b)of the New York Convention.[73]

---

[72] Reply of the SPC on Non-Recognition of the No. 05–03 Tokyo Arbitral Award rendered by the JCAA, [2008] Min Si Ta Zi No. 18.

[73] Reply of the SPC to the Report on Non-Recognition of the No. 04–05 Tokyo Arbitral Award rendered by the JCAA, [2007] Min Si Ta Zi No. 26.

Shin-Etsu Chemical Co., Ltd. v. Jiangsu Zhongtian Technology Co., Ltd. (2010).[74]

In the previous arbitration procedure, the applicant had applied to the JCAAt o confirm that the Long Term Sales and Purchase Agreement between January 2004 and December 31, 2008 could be performed, but this claim was rejected by the arbitral tribunal in the No. 04-05arbitral award. In this arbitration, the applicant applied to the JCAA to claim damages for breach of contract from August 2005 to March 2008, which implied that the Agreement of the time period could be performed.

Therefore, the SPC held that the arbitration matter in this case was the same as the applicant's claim in the previous arbitration procedure, which constituted a repeated acceptance. Since the parties had clearly agreed on the binding effect of the arbitration in the arbitration clause, the arbitral award involved in the case was inconsistent with the agreement. Thus, the arbitration procedure in this case was held to be inconsistent with the agreement of the parties.

Lehua Meilan Holding Co., et al. v. Tianjin Jiashijie Group Co., Ltd., et al.[75]

In this case, the parties agreed in the arbitration agreement that "Disputes shall be submitted to three arbitrators appointed in accordance with the arbitration rules of the ICC". Pursuant to Article 12 of the arbitration rules of the ICC, when the arbitrator fails to perform his duties, whether the arbitrator should be replaced and whether the arbitration can be continued without replacement in certain circumstances should be decided by the ICC. The arbitral tribunal does not have the discretion.

However, in this case, the remaining two arbitrators continued to constitute an arbitral tribunal, signed and made an arbitral award without the authorization of the ICC. Therefore, the SPC held that the arbitration procedure in this case was in violation of the arbitration rules of the ICC, and thus, the arbitral award involved in the case shall not be recognized and enforced.

[b] **Cases where the Arbitration Procedures Do Not Violate the Arbitration Rules and the Laws of the Country Where the Arbitrations Took Place**

As mentioned above, generally, the criteria for examining whether the arbitration proceedings are improper are whether there are violations of the arbitration rules chosen by the parties and the laws of the country where the arbitration take place. If the arbitration procedures do not violate the arbitration rules and the laws of the seat of arbitration, the court will usually deem the arbitration procedures legal.

Gloria Jones Co. v. Wuxi Dongxiang Knitting Textile Co., Ltd.[76]

---

[74] Reply of the SPC to the Request for Instruction on the Case Concerning the Non-Enforcement of the No. 07–11 Arbitral Award rendered by the JCAA, [2010] Min Si Ta Zi No. 32.

[75] Reply of the SPC to the Request for Instruction on the Non-Recognition and Non-Enforcement of the 12,330/TE/MW/AVH Arbitral Award rendered by the ICC in Lausanne, [2009] Min Si Ta Zi No. 38.

[76] (2014) Xi Shang Wai Zhong Shen Zi No. 0004.

In the case at hand, the respondent argued that the notice of arbitration issued by the arbitral tribunal only used Russianwithout Chinese translation, resulting in the failure to achieve the purpose of the notice. The court held that the arbitration rules of the RFCC agreed that the parties stipulated that the arbitration procedure shall be conducted in Russia, and the parties did not make any other agreement on the choice of arbitration language. Consequently, the defense raised by the respondent did not constitute a violation of the arbitration rules and correspondingly the ground for not recognizing the arbitral award in the case.

Jess Smith & Sons Cotton, LLC v. Jihua 3509 Textile Co., Ltd.[77]

The respondent alleged that the ICA, the arbitration institution involved in the case, did not deliver the arbitral award to it. Pursuant to Article 55 (3) and Article 56 (1) of the Arbitration Act 1996 ofthe UK and Article 308 (7) of the bylaws and rules of the ICA, the arbitral award will be served only after the parties have paid the relevant fees. The court held that the fact that the ICA did not serve the arbitral award to the respondent due to the respondent's failure to pay the relevant fees did not violate the Arbitration Act 1996 of the UK and the bylaws and rules of the ICA.

Glencore International AG v. Zhejiang Qiying Energy Chemical Co., Ltd.[78]

One of the defenses raised by the respondent in this case was that the arbitral tribunal directly communicated with the parties, which violated the arbitration rules. The court found that Article 13.2 of the arbitration rules of the LCIA involved in the case stipulated that "Following the formation of the Arbitral Tribunal, all communications shall take place directly between the Arbitral Tribunal and the parties (to be copied to the Registrar), unless the Arbitral Tribunal decides that communications should continue to be made through the Registrar."

It could be seen from the rules above that the arbitral tribunal had the power to communicate directly with the parties on the premise of giving instructions in advance. On July 7, 2012, the arbitral tribunal in this case sent instructions to both parties requiring the arbitral tribunal to directly communicate with the parties, which were sent to both parties by email and copied to the Registrar at the same time. Therefore, the direct communication between the arbitral tribunal and the parties did not violate the relevant provisions of the arbitration rules.

[c]   **Whether the Failure to List All the Parties to the Contract as the Parties to the Arbitration Constitutes an Improper Arbitration Procedure**

Ksenja Pte. Ltd. v. Guan Ke.[79]

In the present case, the respondent claimed that the agreement involved multiple parties that were not listed as parties in the arbitral award, and it violated the agreement between the parties. The court considered that the parties to the contract could

---

[77] (2014) E Xiao Gan Zhong Min Wai Chu Zi No. 00001.

[78] (2014) Zhe Yong Zhong Que Zi No. 1.

[79] (2014) Shen Zhong Fa She Wai Chu Zi No. 119.

not be equal to the parties of the arbitration. The parties involved in the arbitration were listed according to the request for arbitration submitted by the applicant, and there existed an arbitration clause between the parties. Hence, the arbitration procedure in the case did not violate the agreement between the parties.

[d] **Whether the Arbitration Period Exceeds the Agreed Period of the Arbitration Agreement Constitutes an Illegal Arbitration Procedure**

Tajco A/S v. Jan Szklany.[80]

The respondent made a defense that the period of arbitration in the case exceeded the agreed period of arbitration stipulated in the contract and thus shall not be recognized and enforced. In view of this, the court held that the time limit for making an arbitral award shall be determined by the arbitral tribunal in accordance with the laws of the country where the arbitration took place, arbitration rules and the specific circumstances of the case, which was not within the scope of the agreement between the applicant and the respondent. Therefore, the situation alleged by the respondent did not fall within the circumstance stipulated in Article 5 of the New York Convention, and thus, the defense should not be supported.

[e] **Whether the Failure to Serve the Award in Time Constitutes the Illegality of Arbitration Procedure**

Oman Shipping Co. Soac v. Jiangsu Rongsheng Heavy Industry Co., Ltd.[81]

The respondent claimed that it had not received the arbitral award and that the arbitral award was not effective before it was served. The court held that although the arbitral award involved in the case was not delivered to the respondent in time, it had been delivered and confirmed by the respondent in writing by the time of the court's ruling, so this situation did not constitute an improper arbitration procedure.

[f] **Cases where the Parties Do Not Raise Objection to the Inconsistency of the Arbitration Procedure with Arbitration Agreement, Arbitration Rules or the Law of the Seat of Arbitration**

Chenco Chemical Engineering and Consulting GmbH v. Do-Fluoride Chemicals Co., Ltd.[82]

Although the language of the arbitration procedure agreed upon by the parties was English, the respondent did not raise an objection and issued its opinion on the evidence when the applicant did not submit the English evidentiary documents. At the same time, Article 33 of the arbitration rules of the ICC applicable to the

---

[80] (2015) Shen Zhong Min Si Te Zi No. 29.

[81] (2017) E 72 Xie Wai Ren No.1.

[82] Reply of the SPC to the Request for Instruction of High People's Court of Henan Province on the Case Concerning the Application of Chenco Chemical Engineering and Consulting GmbH for Recognition and Enforcement of Foreign Arbitral Award against Do-Fluoride Chemicals Co., Ltd., (2016) Zui Gao Fa Min Ta No. 66.

case stipulated that "A party which proceeds with the arbitration without raising its objection to a failure to comply with any provision of the Rules, or of any other rules applicable to the proceedings, any direction given by the arbitral tribunal, or any requirement under the arbitration agreement relating to the constitution of the arbitral tribunal or the conduct of the proceedings, shall be deemed to have waived its right to object." Based on this, the SPC held that the failure of the applicant to submit the English documents of the evidence did not constitute an improper arbitration procedure.

Hyundai Glovis Co., Ltd. v. Zhejiang Qiying Energy Chemical Co., Ltd.[83]

The court in this case also took whether the respondent submitted an objection as an important factor when analyzing the legality of the composition of the arbitral tribunal and the arbitration procedure.

12.6   Validity of the Arbitral Award

The effectiveness of arbitral awards is one of the prerequisites for the recognition and enforcement of arbitral awards. Pursuant to Article V(1)(e) of the New York Convention, if the respondent can prove that the award has not yet become binding on the parties, has been set aside or suspended by a competent authority of the country in which, or under the law of which, that award was made, the court may refuse to recognize and enforce the award.

A.   **Whether the Court May Conduct Review on the Validity of the Arbitral Award** *ex officio*

It can be viewed from the provision above that the effect of the award, similar to the other circumstances stipulated in Article V(1) of the New York Convention, isnot a circumstance that the court may review *ex officio* but a circumstance that should be reviewed at the defense of the respondent. The SPC was expressly stated in the cases of *Paul Reinhart AG v. Hubei Qinghe Textile Co., Ltd.*[84] and *Noble Resource Pte. Ltd. v. Hubei Qinghe Textile Co., Ltd.*[85] that "The review of the people's court on whether there were circumstances for refusing recognition and enforcement stipulated in Article V(1) of the New York Convention must be conducted at the request of the parties. If the parties do not request, the people's court should not review."

However, in practice, some courts still took the initiative to review the effect of arbitral awards without objection raised by the respondent.

---

[83] (2015) Zhe Yong Zhong Que Zi No. 3.

[84] Reply of the SPC to the Request for Instruction on the Case Concerning the Application of Paul Reinhart AG for Recognition and Enforcement of Foreign Arbitral Award against Hubei Qinghe Textile Co., Ltd., (2016) Zui Gao Fa Min Ta No. 11.

[85] Reply of the SPC to the Request for Instruction on the Case Concerning the Application of Noble Resource Pte. Ltd. for Recognition and Enforcement of Foreign Arbitral Award against Hubei Qinghe Textile Co., Ltd., (2016) Zui Gao Fa Min Ta No. 12.

Ksenja Pte. Ltd. v. Guan Ke.[86]

In this case, the respondent did not raise any objection to the validity of the arbitral award. The court took the initiative to review the effect of the arbitral award *ex officio*, holding the opinion that "Although the arbitral award involved in this case allowed both parties to appeal against the arbitrator's decision on the amount of compensation within 60 days from the date of receipt of a copy of the award, neither party appealed, and there was no evidence to prove that the award was set aside or not enforced in Finland, the country where the award was rendered. Therefore, the award in the case had come into effect and was binding on both parties."

Noble Resource Pte.Ltd. v. Zhejiang Xiongsheng Industrial Co., Ltd.[87]

The respondent did not submit any defense relating to the invalidity of the arbitral award. The court ruled that both parties did not appeal concerning the arbitral award involved in this case within the period of appeal, and thus the arbitral award was final and binding on all parties.

B. Cases where the Respondent's Objections on the Effect of the Arbitral Award Were Dismissed

Among the cases of applying for recognition and enforcement of foreign arbitration awards before Chinese courts from 2008 to 2018, the respondents in only 3 cases objected to the validity of the arbitral award. However, all these objections were dismissed by the courts.

Olam International Ltd. v. Jingshan Weijia Textile Enterprise Co., Ltd.[88]

In this case, the respondent alleged that there existed the circumstance stipulated in Article V(1)(e) of the New York Convention, and thus the arbitral award should not be recognized.The court held that the arbitral award had stated that the arbitral award had entered into force on January 11, 2013, and the respondent did not provide evidence to prove that the arbitral award was set aside or not enforced by the competent authority of theUK;thus, the allegation could not be supported.

Olam International Ltd. v. Zibo Yinhua Cotton & Linen Co., Ltd.[89]

In the case at hand, the respondent claimed that it had not received the arbitral award, so the award did not have legal effect on it.After reviewing the record of expressdelivery of the arbitral institution serving the arbitral award to the respondent, the court found that the delivery address was the registered address of the respondent and was the same as the address where the respondent received the request for arbitration and hearing notice in this lawsuit. Therefore, the allegation made by the respondent that the arbitral award was not received and thus not effective was rejected.

---

[86] (2014) Shen Zhong Fa She Wai Chu Zi No. 119.

[87] (2014) Zhe Shao Zhong Que Zi No. 1.

[88] (2013) E Jing Men Min San Chu Zi No. 00019.

[89] (2015) Zi Min Te Zi No. 1.

Rex Commodities Pte. Ltd. v. Qingdao Haiyunda Economic and Trade Co., Ltd.[90]

In this case, the respondent claimed that it had not received the arbitral award, so the award did not have legal effect on it either. The court held that pursuant to Article 28 of the arbitration rules of the SIAC, "the parties further agree that an award shall be final and binding on the parties from the date it is made." Therefore, the defense shall not be supported.

12.7 Arbitrability and Public Policy

As mentioned above, the five circumstances stipulated in Paragraph 1 of Article V of the New York Convention that the courts may refuse to recognize and enforce foreign arbitral awards must be reviewed at the request of the parties (usually the respondent). Meanwhile, Paragraph 2 of Article V of the New York Convention provides for two matters that the Courts may review *ex officio*, namely, the arbitrability of the disputes and whether the awards violate public policy.

Specifically, in accordance with the clause, recognition and enforcement of an arbitral award may also be refused if the competent authority in the country where recognition and enforcement is sought finds that (a) the subject matter of the difference is not capable of settlement by arbitration under the law of that country or (b) the recognition or enforcement of the award would be contrary to the public policy of that country.

A. Arbitrability

In accordance with the law of China, there are two main provisions concerning the arbitrability of disputes.

First, pursuant to Article 3 of the Arbitration Law, marital, adoption, guardianship, support and succession disputes, as well as administrative disputes that shall be handled by administrative organs as prescribed by law, may not be arbitrated.

Second, pursuant to Notice of the SPC on the Implementation of the "Convention on the Recognition and Enforcement of Foreign Arbitral Awards" Acceded to by China, China made a commercial reservation declaration upon its accession to the New York Convention, i.e., China would apply the Convention only to differences arising out of legal relationships, whether contractual or not, which are considered commercial under the national law of China. "Legal relationships, whether contractual or not, which are considered commercial" means the economic rights and obligations arising from contracts, torts or relevant legal provisions, such as purchase and sale of goods, lease of property, project contracting, processing, technology transfer, equity or contractual joint adventure, exploration and development of natural resources, insurance, credit, labor service, agersal, consultation, marine investors and civil aviation, railway or road utenger cargo transportation, environment liability,

---

[90] (2017) Lu 02 Xie Wai Ren No. 4.

pollution pollution, credit, labor service, agersal disputency, except service between foreign investors and the government.

Among the 127 cases retrieved in this article, only one application for recognition and enforcement of foreign arbitral awards was dismissed since the dispute was not capable of settlement by arbitration.

Wu Chunying v. Zhang Guiwen.[91]

The dispute in this case arose from the claim of the applicant, the legal heir of her deceased husband, of her rights under the contract before Court of Arbitration of Mongolia according to the arbitration clause in the contract. After accepting the applicant's request for arbitration, the arbitral tribunal finally ruled: "1. The case falls within the jurisdiction of arbitration; 2. According to the provisions of Article 520.1.1 of the Civil Law of China, Wu Chunying, the wife of the deceased Zhao Xinshuang and a citizen of China, isthe legal Heir to property......".

The SPC held in its reply that"The main content of the arbitral award is to confirm Wu Chunying's status as the legal heir and the rights of investment property due to that status. The award did not deal with commercial disputes such as the company's continued operation and cancellation. Therefore, the arbitral award was an award mainly dealt with succession matter." In view of the fact that the Arbitration Law clearly stipulated that succession disputes cannot be arbitrated, the SPC considered that the arbitral award involved in this case should not be recognized and enforced.

B. Public Policy

Public policy is the last "safety valve" for the contracting state of the New York Convention to review and decide whether a foreign arbitral award shall be recognized and enforced. If the court considers that the recognition and enforcement of the foreign arbitral award would violate the public policy of the country where the court is located, the court may refuse to recognize or enforce the award *ex officio*.

[a] The Meaning of "Public Policy"

The New York Convention did not expound on it. Instead, it is an area reserved for the discretion of the courts of each contracting state. From the judicial practice of the Chinese courts, we can see that the standard of violating public policy of China is comparatively high. Only on rare occasions did the Chinese courts find recognition and enforcement contrary to China's public policy.

In the Reply to the Request for Instruction on the Case Concerning the Application of Castel Electronics Pty Ltd. For Recognition and Enforcement of Foreign Arbitral Awards,[92] the SPC pointed out that "The circumstance of violation of public

---

[91] Reply of the SPC to the Request for Instruction on the Case Concerning the Application of Non-Recognition and Non-Enforcement of the Arbitral Award rendered by the Court of Arbitration of Mongolia, (2009) Min Si Ta Zi No. 33.

[92] Reply of the SPC to the Request for Instruction on the Case Concerning the Application of Castel Electronics Pty Ltd. for Recognition and Enforcement of Foreign Arbitral Awards, [2013] Min Si Ta Zi No. 46.

policy specified in Article V(2)(b) of the New York Convention, shall be interpreted as that recognition and enforcement of a foreign arbitral award would violate the fundamental principles of the law of China, infringe upon the state sovereignty of China, undermine the social order and the good customs, etc., which would endanger the fundamental social and public interest of China."

It is noteworthy that in the context of China, "public policy" is often used almost as the equivalent of "social public interest". For instance, in the Reply to the Request for Instructions of the Case Concerning the Application of Zhoushan Zhonghai Grain and Oil Industry Co., Ltd. For Non-Enforcement of the Arbitral Award rendered by the HKIAC, the SPC used the wording "social public interest" when determining whether there existed the circumstance stipulated in Article V(2)(b) of the New York Convention.

[b] Cases Which Were Refused Due to Public Policy

Among the 127 cases of application for recognition and enforcement of foreign arbitral awards before the courts of China between 2008 and 2018, only 2 applications were denied due to public policy.

Hemofarm DD, MAG International Trade Holding DD, Suramu Media Ltd. v. Jinan Yongning Pharmaceutical Co., Ltd.[93]

In this case, the parties signed a Joint Venture Contract with the aim of establishing a pharmaceutical company named "Jinan-Hemofarm". Afterwards, the respondent filed a lawsuit against the Joint Venture Company at the Jinan Intermediate People's Court, asking the latter to pay the rent and return some of the leased property. The respondent also filed an application for property preservation order, which was approved by the Jinan Intermediate People's Court. After disputes arose among the parties regarding the Joint Venture Contract, the applicant submitted such disputes to the ICC for arbitration. The arbitral tribunal, in the third part of its award, reviewed the Lease Agreement between the respondent and the joint venture company and ruled that the applicant should be compensated for 30% of the litigation fees it has paid for defending the joint venture company in the lawsuit about the lease.

The SPC held that in the case that the relevant Chinese court has ruled on the preservation of the property of the joint venture company and made a judgment on the dispute concerning the lease contract between the respondent and the joint venture company, the arbitral tribunal still reviewed and ruled over the same issue on the award. Such behavior infringed upon the judicial sovereignty of China and the judicial jurisdiction of the Chinese courts, and thus the arbitral award shall not be recognized or enforced.

Wicor Holding AG v. Taizhou Haopu Investment Co., Ltd.[94]

---

[93] Reply of the SPC to the Request for Instructions on the Non-Recognition and Non-Enforcement of an Arbitration Award of the ICC, [2008] Min Si Ta Zi No. 11.

[94] (2015) Tai Zhong Shang Zhong Shen Zi No. 00004; Reply of the SPC to the Request for Instruction on the Case Concerning the Non-Enforcement of No. 18295/CYK Arbitral Award rendered by the ICC, (2016) Zui Gao Fa Min Ta No. 8.

In this case, the parties signed a joint venture contract containing an arbitration clause. The respondent filed a lawsuit at Taizhou Intermediate People's Court on May 20, 2011. The applicant raised an objection to the jurisdiction of the court because there was an arbitration agreement between the parties. The Taizhou Intermediate People's Court made the (2011) Tai Zhong Shang Wai Chu Zi No. 0012 civil ruling, finding that, as the arbitration clause did not specify an arbitral institution and the parties did not enter into any supplementary agreement afterwards, the arbitration agreement was void and rejecting the objection to the jurisdiction raised by the applicant. Afterwards, the applicant appealed against the ruling, while the (2012) Su Shang Wai Xia Zhong Zi No. 0012 civil ruling made by the High People's Court of Jiangsu Province still found the arbitration clause invalid.

Later, the Taizhou Intermediate People's Court notified the ICC of the findings above, and the respondent also raised an objection against the validity of the arbitration agreement during the arbitral proceedings. However, the ICC accepted the submission for arbitration by the applicant and rendered an award confirming the validity of the arbitration agreement and holding the respondent liable for a series of matters. Now, the applicant applied to the court of China for recognizing and enforcing the award.

The SPC held in its reply that the arbitral award was made by the arbitral tribunal on the premise that the arbitration clause was valid, and the enforcement of such an arbitral award in mainland China would conflict with the effective ruling made by the High People's Court of Jiangsu Province and thus violated the social and public interest of mainland China. Therefore, the arbitral award could not be enforced.

[c]   **Whether Inconsistencies between the Arbitral Award and Effective Judgment of Courts Necessarily Constitute a Violation of Public Policy**

Although the applications for recognition and enforcement of foreign arbitral awards in the two cases above, which were denied based on public policy concerns, are both related to judicial sovereignty and the jurisdiction of the courts, the inconsistencies between the arbitral award and the effective judgments of courts in specific matters, such as the validity of the arbitration agreement, do not necessarily constitute a violation of public policy in China. Whether it constitutes a violation of public policy still needs to be analyzed based on the specific facts of each case.

Castel Electronics Pty Ltd. v. TCL Air Conditioner (Zhongshan) Co., Ltd.[95]

Although there were inconsistencies between the arbitral award and the Court of China on the validity of the arbitration agreement involved in the case, the date when the said award was rendered was earlier than the effective date of the judgment of the Court of China, and the respondent did not raise any objection against the validity of the arbitration clause during the arbitral proceedings. Instead, the respondent submitted a counterclaim to the arbitral tribunal.

---

[95] Reply of the SPC to the Request for Instruction on the Case Concerning the Application of Castel Electronics Pty Ltd. for Recognition and Enforcement of Foreign Arbitral Awards, [2013] Min Si Ta Zi No. 46.

Based on the reasons above, the SPC held that it was in compliance with the law of the seat of arbitration and the relevant arbitration rules for the arbitral tribunal to determine the validity of the arbitration clause and its jurisdiction accordingly, and thus there existed no circumstance that the judicial sovereignty of China had been infringed upon in this case.

[d]   Whether the Violation of the Laws and Regulations of China Equals the Violation ofthe Public Policy of China

The most common reason cited by the respondent who asserts that the arbitral award is contrary to public policy is that the award has violated the laws and regulations of China. However, none of the allegations has been supported by the courts.

Tianrui Hotel Investment Co., Ltd. v. Hangzhou Yiju Hotel Management Co., Ltd.[96]

The agreement signed by both parties was by nature a commercial franchise contract. According to the commercial franchise management regime effective at the time of signing the contract, the engagement of commercial franchise business within China of foreign companies must be conducted by establishing a foreign-invested enterprise and subject to the approval of the administrative authority in charge. However, the Regulation on the Administration of Commercial Franchises promulgated by the State Council, which came into effect on May 1, 2007, only stipulates that commercial franchise contracts should be recorded with the competent administrative authority after its conclusion, without approval requirements.

The SPC pointed out in its reply that "The recording regime above belongs to the regulatory regulation of mandatory regulation in the administrative regulations, which does not affect the validity of the civil contract. The arbitral award's handling of the Unit System Agreement involved in this case does not violate China's mandatory laws and regulations, nor does it constitute a violation of China's public policy."

Spring Maritime Ltd. v. Shandong Haina Real Estate Co., Ltd.[97] & *Summer Maritime Ltd. v. Shandong Haina Real Estate Co., Ltd.*[98]

In these two cases, although the respondents provided a guarantee to a foreign party without approval or registration of the administrative authority in charge violated the laws and regulations concerning foreign-related guarantees of China, the courts considered that the act did not constitute a violation of the public policy of China.

Jacobson Golf Course Design Inc. v. Sihui Zhenhuiyuan Property Development Co., Ltd. & Sihui Huiguan Investment Co., Ltd.[99]

---

[96] Reply of the SPC to the Request for Instruction of on the Case Concerning the Application of Tianrui Hotel Investment Co., Ltd. for Recognition of Arbitral Award against Hangzhou Yiju Hotel Management Co., Ltd., [2010] Min Si Ta Zi No.18.

[97] (2013) Qing Hai Fa Hai Shang Chu Zi No. 1032.

[98] (2014) Qing Hai Fa Hai Shang Chu Zi No. 721.

[99] (2015) Zhao Zhong Fa Min Yi Zhong Zi No. 26.

In this case, the respondent claimed that the arbitral award violated the mandatory regulations of the Construction Law and the Bidding Law of China. The court held that the violation of the mandatory regulations of the laws of China should not be deemed completely equal to the violation of the public policy of China, and the recognition and enforcement of the award did not constitute a violation of the fundamental social interest and legal principles of China. Therefore, the respondent's argument that the recognition and enforcement of the arbitral award should be dismissed on the ground of violation of public policy should not be supported.

China Aviation Oil (Singapore) Co., Ltd. V. Chengdu Xinhuaxin Chemical Material Co., Ltd.[100]

Although the conduct of the parties violated China's foreign exchange management policies and relevant provisions of the Foreign Trade Law of China, the court also held that the situation did not absolutely constitute a violation of the public policy of China.

In addition, the defense that the outcome of the arbitration is apparently unfair cannot be supported either.

[e] Defense that the Arbitration Outcome is Obviously Unfair

Western Bulk Pte.Ltd. v. Beijing Sinosteel Tiantie Iron & Steel Trading Co., Ltd.[101]

The High People's Court of Tianjin City ruled that the outcome of the arbitration in this case was obviously unfair, so it would be contrary to the public policy of China to recognize this arbitral award. The SPC stated in its reply that, "……the court shall apply strict interpretation and application to the provision concerning the public policy……It is inappropriate to refuse to recognize and enforce the arbitral award on the ground that the outcome of the arbitration is obviously unfair and violates the social and public interest of China."

GRD Minproc Ltd. v. Shanghai Flyingwheel Industry Co., Ltd.[102]

Both the Shanghai First Intermediate People's Court and the High People's Court Shanghai City ruledthat the outcome of the arbitration involved in the case was contrary to the spirit of fairness and justice and objectively not conducive to the social and public interest of China. Hence, both courts suggested not recognizing or enforcing the said award based on public policy concerns.

However, the SPCstated in its reply that "Whether the substantive outcome of the arbitration is fair and just should not be considered as the criteria for examining whether the award would violate the public policy of China. As the recognition and

---

[100] (2017) Chuan 01 Xie Wai Ren No. 1.

[101] Reply of the SPC to the Request for Instruction on the Case Concerning the Application of Western Bulk Pte.Ltd. for Recognition and Enforcement of a UK Arbitral Award, [2012] Min Si Ta Zi No. 12.

[102] Reply of the SPC to the Request for Instructions of the Case Concerning the Application of GRD Minproc Ltd. for Recognition and Enforcement of Arbitral Award rendered by the SCC, [2008] Min Si Ta Zi No. 48; (2007) Hu Yi Zhong Min Wu (Shang) Chu Zi No. 116.

enforcement of the arbitral award in the present case does not violate the fundamental interest, the fundamental legal principles and good customs of China, there exists no such circumstance as prescribed in Article 5(2)(b) of the New York Convention in this case."

Noble Resource Pte.Ltd. v. Zhejiang Xiongsheng Industrial Co., Ltd.[103]

There were miscalculations in the arbitral award. However, the court held that although there were imperfections in the award, the party who was disadvantaged did not raise an objection, and thus, the recognition and enforcement of such an award would not harm the public order of China.

12.8   Conclusion

We can see from the judicial practice of Chinese courts in the period of 2008–2018 that although there were issues of the courts voluntarily reviewing the effectiveness of arbitral awards *ex officio*, the Chinese court system has, in general, adopted a pro-arbitration approach and a prudent attitude toward the judgment of refusing to recognize or enforce foreign arbitral awards. Meanwhile, regarding the cases wherethe seven circumstances stipulated in Paragraph 1 and Paragraph 2 of Article V of the New York Convention exist, Chinese courts have also duly refused to recognize and enforce such foreign arbitral awards in accordance with the New York Convention.

We have also noticed that some intermediate people's courts, High People's courts and the SPC differ in their perspectives and interpretations in some controversial cases. The reporting regime established by the Notice on Issues Concerning the People's Courts' Dealing of Foreign-Related Arbitration and Foreign Arbitration and the Relevant Provisions on Issues Concerning Applications for Verification of Arbitration Cases under Judicial Review has been of great help in avoiding conflicting judgments made by different courts in China and maintaining the consistency of the judicial standards and perspectives in practice. It not only increases the predictability of the outcomes for the application for recognition and enforcement of foreign arbitral awards in China but also facilitates the harmonization of arbitration as a dispute resolution mechanism in China and the world. It lives up to commercial expectations as well.

Of course, it should be pointed out that the judicial review of arbitral awards is closely related to the development of arbitration itself, the legal environment of a country, the attitude toward arbitration and understanding of arbitration of its judiciary. Such practice and attitudes always evolve with nothing remaining unchanged.

---

[103] (2014) Zhe Shao Zhong Que Zi No. 1.

Official Replies by the Supreme People's Court Concerning Arbitration in China

1. **Reply of the Supreme People's Court to the Request for Instructions of the High People's Court of Hunan Province on the Case Concerning the Application of the People's Government of Hunan Province and theDepartment of Transportation of Hunan Province for Confirmation of the Validity of the Arbitration Agreement against Victory International Investment (Macau) Co., Ltd. and Hunan Victory Changtan West Line Highway Co., Ltd.**
   September 28, 2016, [2016] Zui Gao Fa Min Ta No. 70.

To the High People's Court of Hunan Province:

The Request for Instructions on the Case Concerning the Application of the People's Government of Hunan Province and the Department of Transportation of Hunan Province for Confirmation of the Validity of the Arbitration Agreement against Victory International Investment (Macau) Co., Ltd. and Hunan Victory Changtan West Line Highway Co., Ltd. [(2016) Xiang Min Ta Zi No. 3]submitted by your courthas been received. After deliberation, our reply is as follows:

The applicants in the present case requested the people's court to confirm whether the arbitration agreement was binding to the disputes between the applicants and the respondents. The people's court shall acceptthis type of case as the case of confirmation of the validity of the arbitration agreement. Your court shall, first of all, determine the validity of the arbitration agreement and then review the request of the applicant. If the arbitration agreement is null and void, then it shall not be binding on any of the parties. If the arbitration agreement is valid, the court shall continue to examine whether the agreement is binding on the person who is not aparty to the arbitration agreement.

Based on the facts stated in the Request for Instructions of your court, the arbitration agreement involved was reflected as the arbitration clause in the Franchise Agreement. First, the People's Government of Hunan Province was not a party to the Franchise Agreement. There were no civil relationships such as authorization or delegation between it and the Department of Transportation of Hunan Province, nor was there any relationship of assignment of rights and obligations. Therefore,

© The Editor(s) (if applicable) and The Author(s), under exclusive license to Springer Nature Singapore Pte Ltd. 2022
Y. Lin, *China Arbitration Yearbook (2021)*, China Arbitration Yearbook,
https://doi.org/10.1007/978-981-19-1284-9

the arbitration agreement involved was not binding to the People's Government of Hunan Province. Second, although Hunan Victory Changtan West Line Highway Co., Ltd. did not exist when the Franchise Agreement was signed, the Department of Transportation of Hunan Province and Victory International Investment (Macau) Co., Ltd. agreed to the establishment of Hunan Victory Changtan West Line Highway Co., Ltd. as well as the new company's rights and obligations. After its foundation, Hunan Victory Changtan West Line Highway Co., Ltd.participated in the performance of the Agreement in accordance with the Agreement, filed the request for arbitration after disputes arose and declared that it agreed to be bound by the arbitration clause in the Agreement by issuing an Explanation Letter in writing. Therefore, the arbitration agreement involved shall be binding on Hunan Victory Changtan West Line Highway Co., Ltd.

It is so replied.

2.   **Reply of the Supreme People's Court to the Request for Instructions on the Case Concerning the Application of China United Communications (Holdings) Co., Ltd. for the Recognition and Enforcement of an Arbitral Award Made by Hong Kong International Arbitration Center.**
September 19, 2016, [2016] Zui Gao Fa Min Ta No. 63.

To the High People's Court of Beijing:

The Request for Instructions on the Case Concerning the Application of China United Communications (Holdings) Co., Ltd. for the Recognition and Enforcement of an Arbitral Award Made by Hong Kong International Arbitration Center [Jing Gao Fa (2016) No. 166] submitted by your court. After deliberation, the replies are as follows:

1.   The present case concerns the application for recognition and enforcement of an arbitral award made in the Hong Kong Special Administrative Region. Pursuant to Article 1 of the Arrangement of the Supreme People's Court on Mutual Enforcement of Arbitral Awards between the Mainland and the Hong Kong Special Administrative Region, for an arbitral award made in the Mainland or Hong KongSpecial Administrative Region, if one party refuses to comply with it, the other party may apply to the competent court where the respondent is domiciled or where the property is located. Based on the materials sent by your court, the registered owner of the property involved in the application for enforcement was VIA Technologies (China) Co., Ltd. The relationship between the respondent and VIA Technologies (China) Co., Ltd. was a relationship of indirect investment. Existing evidence cannot prove that Beijing is the location of the respondent's property. Consequently, the Beijing Third Intermediate People's Court does not have jurisdiction over the present case.

2.   The Arrangement of the Supreme People's Court on Mutual Enforcement of Arbitral Awards between the Mainland and the Hong Kong Special Administrative Region only stipulates the content of the reciprocal enforcement between the Mainland and Hong KongSpecial Administrative Region. A review on recognition still needs to be conducted for the mutual enforcement of arbitral awards.

Taking Article 8 of Provisions of the Supreme People's Court on the Recognition and Enforcement of Arbitral Awards Issued in Taiwan (Fa Shi [2015] No. 14) as a reference, i.e., "if the application does not meet the conditions, the people's court shall, within 7 days, rule not to accept the application and give an explanation on the reasons thereon; if the applicant is unsatisfied with the ruling, it may appeal against the ruling", a decision of not accepting the case shall be made in the present case.

It is so replied.

3. **Reply of the Supreme People's Court to the Request for Instructions of the High People's Court of Beijing on the Case Concerning the Application of COFCO Wines Co., Ltd. for Confirmation of the Validity of Arbitration Agreement.**
    September 14, 2016, [2016] Zui Gao Fa Min Ta No. 87.

To the High People's Court of Beijing:

The Request for Instructions Concerning the Application of COFCO Wines Co., Ltd. for Confirmation of the Validity of Arbitration Agreement (three cases) [Jing Gao Fa [2016] No. 266] submitted by your courthas been received. After deliberation, the replies are as follows:

Regarding the applicable law to the three arbitration agreements, among the three arbitration agreements, one was signed before the Law of the People's Republic of China on Choice of Law for Foreign-related Civil Relationships came into effect, and two were signed after the Law came into effect. Pursuant to Article 2 of the Interpretations of the Supreme People's Court on Several Issues Concerning Application of the Law of the People's Republic of China on Choice of Law for Foreign-Related Civil Relationships, for foreign-related civil relationships that came into existence before the Law on Choice of Law for Foreign-related Civil Relationships came into force, the court shall apply relevant laws that were in force when such relationships came into existence to determine the law applicable to the arbitration agreement. Therefore, the bases to determine the applicable law to the three arbitration agreements were different. As the arbitration agreement involved in this case was signed on February 24, 2011, before the Law on Choice of Law for Foreign-related Civil Relationships came into effect, the applicable law shall be determined in accordance with Article 16 of the Interpretation of the Supreme People's Court on Certain Issues Concerning the Application of the Arbitration Law of the People's Republic of China. Although the parties did not agree upon the choice of law, they had agreed that the arbitration should be conducted in Switzerland. Therefore, the Swiss law shall be applied to the determination of the validity of the arbitration agreement in the case at hand.

Two criteria should be satisfied for the "International arbitration" stipulated in Chap. 12 of Switzerland's Federal Code on Private International Law. First, the seat of the arbitration is Switzerland. Second, when the arbitration agreement was signed, the domicile, habitual residence or place of business of at least one of the parties was outside Switzerland. The arbitration agreement involved in the present case complied with the stipulations above.

The disputes arising from the Sales Contract were disputes regardingproperty between the partiesand were arbitrable. Although the arbitration agreement involved did not specify an arbitral institution, Chap. 12 of Switzerland's Federal Code on Private International Lawstipulates that, in the absence of an agreement on the constitution of the arbitral tribunal, the parties may request the court in the seat of arbitration to appoint arbitrators in accordance with Article 179. This means that Switzerland recognized ad hoc arbitration. Therefore, the arbitration agreement involved in the present case does not violate the mandatory rules of Switzerland's Federal Code on Private International Lawand shall be recognized as valid.

4. **Reply of the Supreme People's Court to the Request for Instructions of the High People's Court of Shandong Province Regarding the Validity of the Arbitration Agreement in the Sales Contract between Shandong Huarui Road Materials Co., Ltd. and Mabong Co., Ltd.**

   May 26, 2016, [2016] Zui Gao Fa Min Ta No. 60.

To the High People's Court of Shandong Province:

The Request for Instructions Regarding the Validity of the Arbitration Agreement in the Sales Contract between Shandong Huarui Road Materials Co., Ltd. and Mabong Co., Ltd. [(2016) Lu Li Han Zi No. 3]submitted by your courthas been received. After deliberation, the replies are as follows:

Based on the facts stated in the Request for Instructions of your court, one party in this case was a Korean company, and the contract involved that contained the arbitration agreement was signed on November 12, 2014, after the Law of the People's Republic of China on Choice of Law for Foreign-related Civil Relationships came into effect. Therefore, the Law of the People's Republic of China on Choice of Law for Foreign-related Civil Relationships and its judicial interpretations shall be applied to determine the applicable law on examining the validity of the arbitration agreement involved. Since the parties in this case did not select the applicable law and neither did they agree upon a specific arbitration institution or the seat of arbitration, the law of the People's Republic of China shall be applied todetermine the validity of the arbitration agreement in accordance with Article 14 of the Interpretations of the Supreme People's Court on Several Issues Concerning Application of the Law of the People's Republic of China on Choice of Law for Foreign-Related Civil Relationships (I).

Article 18 of the Arbitration Law of the People's Republic of China stipulates that "If the arbitration matters or the arbitration commission are not agreed upon by the parties in the arbitration agreement, or if the relevant provisions are not clear, the parties may supplement the agreement. If the parties fail to agree upon the supplementary agreement, the arbitration agreement shall be invalid." Based on the facts stated in the Request for Instructions of your court, the agreement of the parties on the arbitration institution in this case was not clear, and the parties did not reach a supplementary agreement. Therefore, pursuant to the provisions above, the arbitration agreement involved in the case is invalid.Therefore, Supreme People's Court agrees with your court's opinion that the arbitration agreement is null and void.

It is so replied.

5. **Reply of the Supreme People's Court to the Request for Instructions Regarding the Establishment of the Arbitration Agreement in the Disputes Arising from the Inspection Contract between ACE O.C.T.G Co., Ltd., Wuhan Branch of General Standard Technical Service Co., Ltd. and General Standard Technical Service Co., Ltd.**
   May 27, 2016, (2016) Zui Gao Fa Min Ta Zi No. 53.

To the High People's Court of Hubei Province:

The Request for Instructions Regarding the Establishment of the Arbitration Agreement in the Disputes Arising from the Inspection Contract between ACE O.C.T.G Co., Ltd. ("**ACE**"), Wuhan Branch of General Standard Technical Service Co., Ltd. and General Standard Technical Service Co., Ltd. [(2016)E Min Xia Zhong No. 20]submitted by your courthas been received. After deliberation, the replies are as follows:

ACE entrusted Wuhan Branch of General Standard Technical Service Co., Ltd. to inspect the products it ordered via email, while the relevant email did not specify the dispute resolution method. Afterwards, General Standard Technical Service Co., Ltd. ("**SGS**") sent the invoice to ACE, demanding the payment of testing fees. At the bottom of the said invoice, it read that "Important notice: The acceptance of all orders and the issuance of all reports and certificates are subject to the General Service Clauses (copies may be provided upon request)." Article 8 of the Service Clauses stipulated that "Unless otherwise agreed, all disputes arising from or in connection with the contractual relationship under this General Clauses shall be governed by Swiss substantive law (except for any regulations related to conflict of laws), and shall be finally settled under the Arbitration Rules of ICC by one or more arbitrators appointed in accordance with the said rules. The arbitration shall be conducted in Paris, France, in English." As an invoice is the financial proof produced by one party, rather than agreement between the parties, there is no evidence to prove that ACE has accepted the arbitration clause in the Service Clauses. Therefore, the court cannot, solely based on the invoice, conclude that there is a valid arbitration agreement between the parties.

After disputes arose between the parties, the ACE submitted the request for arbitration to the ICC but also declared in writing to the ICC that "We raise objection to the standard terms and conditions, i.e., the aforementioned General Service Clauses. If SGS only deems the clause as an invitation to ad hoc arbitration under the ICC rules, we would like to accept the invitation. If SGS disagrees with our assertion that the General Service Clauses do not apply to the contractual relationship between the parties and considered that it did not send the invitation to ad hoc arbitration by ICC, then this request for arbitration shall be deemed the invitation to arbitration of ACE. Wuhan Branchof SGS stated in writing to ICC that "as ACE claimed that there was no arbitration clause between the parties, except an invitation to arbitration, and such an invitation had not been accepted thus far, it would be meaningless to discuss the constitution of the arbitral tribunal at this moment." It showed that Wuhan Branch of SGS had denied the existence of an arbitration agreement between the parties and refused to accept the invitation to arbitration. Under suchcircumstances, ACE withdrew its request for arbitration and brought the case to the court of first instance. After the court accepted the case, Wuhan Branch of SGS and SGS raised the jurisdictional objection, alleging that the case should be arbitrated by ICC and the court did not have the proper jurisdiction since there was a valid arbitration agreement between the parties and ICC shall retain the jurisdiction, and thus the court should dismiss the action. Such behavior obviously ran counter to the principleof good faith.

In summary, the parties of this case have not reached the arbitration agreement, which was further clarified when the parties submitted their statement to the ICC. We therefore agree with your court's opinion that the decision by the court of first instance to dismiss the action shall be cancelled and your court instructs the court of first instance to hear the case.

It is so replied.

6. **Reply of the Supreme People's Court to the Request for Instructions on the Case Concerning the Application of Paul Reinhart AG for Recognition and Enforcement of Foreign Arbitral Award against Hubei Qinghe Textile Co., Ltd.**

> May 26, 2016, (2016) Zui Gao Fa Min Ta No. 11.

To the High People's Court of Hubei Province:

The Request for Instructions on the Case Concerning the Application of Paul Reinhart AG for Recognition and Enforcement of Foreign Arbitral Award against Hubei Qinghe Textile Co., Ltd. [E Gao Fa (2015) No. 518] submitted by your courthas been received. After deliberation, the replies are as follows:

This case is a case of application for recognition and enforcement of a foreign arbitral award. Pursuant to Article 283 of the Civil Procedure Law of the People's Republic of China, the international treaties ratified or acceded to by the People's Republic of China shall apply to this case. As the arbitral award involved was made within the territory of the United Kingdom, another contracting state of the Convention on the Recognition and Enforcement of Foreign Arbitral Awards (hereinafterreferred to as the "**New York Convention**"), stipulations of the New York Convention shall be applied when examining this case.

Pursuant to the stipulation of Paragraph 1 of Article 5 of the New York Convention "Recognition and enforcement of the award may be refused, at the request of the party against whom it is invoked, only if that party furnishes to the competent authority where the recognition and enforcement is sought, proof that…" and Paragraph 2 of Article 5that "Recognition and enforcement of an arbitral award may also be refused if the competent authority in the country where recognition and enforcement is sought finds that...",for the issue whether there exists a situation of refusal of recognition and enforcement listed in Paragraph 1 of Article 5 of the New York Convention, the people's court can only review it upon the request of the party. If the party does not request, the people's court shall not conduct the review; for the issue of whether there exists the situation of violating arbitrability and public policy as are listed in Paragraph 2 of Article 5 of the New York Convention, the people's court may review *ex officio*. In this case, the respondent Hubei Qinghe Textile Co., Ltd. did not raise the allegation of nonrecognition and enforcement of the arbitral award based on the situation listed in Paragraph 1 of Article 5 of the New York Convention. It lacks acorresponding legal basis for your court to conduct the review *ex officio* and intends to refuse to recognize and enforce the award in accordance with Paragraph 1 of Article 5 of the New York Convention. As the situations provided in Paragraph 2 of Article 5 of the New York Convention do not exist, the people's court shall rule to recognize and enforce the award.

It is so replied.

7. **Reply of the Supreme People's Court to the Request for Instructions of the High People's Court of Jiangsu Province Regarding the Validity of the Arbitration Agreement in the Case on Disputes Arising from Sales Contract between Hong Kong Baiteng Trading Co., Ltd. and Yunnan Jiahui Import and Export Co., Ltd.**

May 25, 2016, (2016) Zui Gao Fa Min Ta No. 10.

To the High People's Court of Jiangsu Province:

The Request for Instructions Regarding the Validity of the Arbitration Agreement in the Case on Disputes Arising from Sales Contract between Hong Kong Baiteng Trading Co., Ltd. and Yunnan Jiahui Import and Export Co., Ltd. [(2015) Su Shang Wai Zhong Shen Xiao Ta Zi No. 00001] submitted by your court has been received. After deliberation, the replies are as follows:

One party in the present case is a Hong Kong company, so the arbitration agreement concerned is a Hong Kong-related arbitration agreement. According to the principle identified in Article 19 of the Interpretations of the Supreme People's Court on Several Issues Concerning Application of the Law of the People's Republic of China on Choice of Law for Foreign-Related Civil Relationships (I), relevant regulations about foreign-related civil relations shall be referred to for the determination of the applicable law. The evidence attached to the report of your court and the arbitration agreement involved were signed after the Law of the People's Republic of China on Choice of Law for Foreign-Related Civil Relationships came into effect. Therefore, Article 18 of the Law of the People's Republic of China on Choice of Law for Foreign-Related Civil Relationships shall apply to this case to determine the applicable law of reviewing the validity of the arbitration agreement.

The arbitration agreement signed by the parties did not specify an arbitration institution, and they only agreed that the seat of arbitration shall be Beijing(any dispute arising out of or in connection with this contract, including any question regarding its existence, validity or termination, shall be referred to and finally resolved by arbitration in BEIJING, CHINA). In addition, the parties did not choose the applicable law to the validity of the arbitration agreement. Hence, in accordance with Article 18 of the Law of the People's Republic of China on Choice of Law for Foreign-Related Civil Relationships, the law of the agreed seat of arbitration, i.e., the law of People's Republic of China shall apply to determine the validity of the arbitration agreement.

Article 18 of the Arbitration Law of the People's Republic of China stipulates that "Where an arbitration agreement contains no or unclear provisions concerning the matters for arbitration or the arbitration commission, the parties may reach a supplementary agreement. Where no such supplementary agreement can be reached, the arbitration agreement shall be null and void." Article 6 of Interpretation of the Supreme People's Court on Certain Issues Concerning the Application of the Arbitration Law of the People's Republic of China stipulates that "Where the arbitration agreement stipulates that arbitration shall be conducted by an arbitration institution in a certain place and there is only one arbitration institution in that place, the arbitration institution shall be deemed as the agreed arbitration institution. Where there are more than two arbitration institutions in the place, the parties may agree to choose one of the arbitration institutions for arbitration; if the parties cannot agree on the choice of arbitration institution, the arbitration agreement shall be deemed invalid." As the parties in the present case did not agree upon a specific arbitral institution, there are more than two arbitral institutions in Beijing, the agreed seat of arbitration, and now the parties have not reached an agreement on the selection of the arbitral institution, the arbitration agreement involved in the present case is null and void in accordance with the stipulations above. Therefore, the Supreme People's Court agrees with the opinion your court stated in the Request for Instructions.

It is so replied.

8. **Reply of the Supreme People's Court to the Request for Instructions on the Case Concerning the Application of J&D IB Co. for Recognition of a Foreign Arbitral Award.**
   May 17, 2016, [2016] Zui Gao Fa Min Ta No. 38.

To the High People's Court of Jilin Province:

The Request for Instructions on the Case Concerning the Application of J&D IB Co. for Recognition of a Foreign Arbitral Award [(2016) Ji Min Ta No. 1] submitted by your court has been received. After deliberation, the replies are as follows:

Based on the facts stated in the Request for Instructions of your court, as the guarantors of the present case, Tian (1) and Tian (2) signed the Joint Guarantee Contract Related to the Acquisition and Operation of the Aide Department Store Project (Advance Loan) on February 7, 2011. As citizens of the People's Republic of China, two guarantors did not go through the approval and registration process of overseas guarantees as required by relevant provisions of the State Administration of Foreign Exchange. Your court is of the opinion that the behaviors of two guarantors to provide external guarantees have violated the mandatory provisions of administrative regulations of China on the policies of foreign exchange management and further considered that the recognition and enforcement of the No. 14113–0021 arbitral award made by the Korean Commercial Arbitration Board on February 2, 2012 would violate the public policy of China. However, the behaviors of Tian (1) and Tian (2) to provide external guarantees do not violate the mandatory provisions of the laws and administrative regulations of China. This case is only an individual case, and the recognition and enforcement of this arbitral award shall not be deemed against the public policy of China. Moreover, Tian (1) and Tian (2), as guarantors, may claim rights from the relevant principal debtor after assuming the responsibility of the guarantee, and their legitimate rights and interests can be protected through other legal methods.

In summary, the circumstance stipulated in Article 5(2)(b) of the Convention on the Recognition and Enforcement of Foreign Arbitral Awards does not exist in this case. If no other statutory circumstances exist, the arbitral award made by the Korean Commercial Arbitration Board should be recognized and enforced in accordance with law.

It is so replied.

9. **Reply of the Supreme People's Court to the Request for Instructions in the Case Concerning the Non-Enforcement of the Arbitral Award Made by ICC.**

March 22, 2016, (2016) Zui Gao Fa Min Ta No. 8

To the High People's Court of Jiangsu Province:

The Request for Instructions on the Case Concerning the Non-Enforcement the Arbitral Award Made by ICC [(2015) Su Shang Wai Zhong Shen Zi No. 0002] submitted by your court has been received. After deliberation, the replies are as follows:

According to the case reported by your court, the arbitral award involved made bythe ICC is an arbitral award made by a sole arbitrator appointed by the ICC inthe Hong Kong Special Administrative Region. Wicor Holding AG applied to the Intermediate People's Court of Taizhou for enforcement of the arbitral award. Pursuant to the Notice of the Supreme People's Court on the Enforcement of Hong Kong Arbitral Award in the Mainland (Fa [2009] No. 415), the people's court shall reviewin accordance with theArrangements of the Supreme People's Court on the Mutual Enforcement of Arbitral Awards by the Mainland and Hong Kong Special Administrative Region ("**Arrangements**"). When hearing another dispute between Wicor Holding AG and Taizhou Hope Investment Co., Ltd. over the same Joint Venture Contract on Sino-foreign Joint Venture Taizhou Warwick Insulation Material Co., Ltd., your court made the (2012) Su Shang Wai Xia Zhong Zi No. 0012 Ruling on December 11, 2012, determining that the arbitration agreement involved was void. The Ruling has come into effect. The arbitral award involved in the present case was made on the premise that the arbitration agreement was valid. Enforcement of the arbitral award in themainland will conflict with the effective ruling of the people's court and violate the public policy of themainland. The people's court may refuse to enforce the arbitral award involved in accordance with Paragraph 3 of Article 7 of the Arrangements. Therefore, the Supreme People's Court agrees with your court's opinion of refusing the enforcement of the arbitral award involved.

It is so replied.

10. **Reply of the SPC to the Request for Instructions on the Case Concerning the Application of Spliethoff's Bevrachtingskantoor B.V. for Recognition of the HULL XXK06-039 Arbitral Award rendered by an Arbitral Tribunal in London, UK.**

December 25, 2015, (2015) Min Si Ta Zi No. 48.

To the High People's Court of Shandong Province:

The Report of Request for Instructions on the Case Concerning the Application of Spliethoff's Bevrachtingskantoor B.V. for Recognition and Enforcement of a Foreign Arbitral Award against China Electronics Import and Export Shandong Corporation and Rongcheng Xixiakou Ship Industry Co., Ltd. [(2015) Lu Min Si Ta Zi No. 6] submitted by your court has been received. After deliberation, the replies are as follows:

This is a case of application for recognition of an arbitral award made by an arbitral tribunal in London, UK. Both China and the United Kingdom are contracting states of the Convention on the Recognition and Enforcement of Foreign Arbitral Awards. Whether the arbitral award involved shall be recognized and enforced shall be reviewed in accordance with the provisions of the Convention. According to the situations stated in the Report of Request for Instructions of your court, the focus of review is whether there are circumstances violating the public policy of China, exceeding the scope of arbitration agreement and other procedural problems with the HULL XXK06-039 arbitral award made by an arbitral tribunal in London, UK.

First, regardingwhether the arbitral award involved violated the public policy of China, the arbitral award involved was made by an arbitral tribunal in London over the disputes arising from the Shipbuilding Contract between Spliethoff's Bevrachtingskantoor B.V., China Electronics Import and Export Shandong Corporation and Rongcheng Xixiakou Ship Industry Co., Ltd.Regarding litigation,Rongcheng Xixiakou Ship Industry Co., Ltd. filed on tort disputes over ship equipment sales against Wärtsilä Finland Co., Ltd., Spliethoff's Bevrachtingskantoor B.V. and Wärtsilä Engine (Shanghai) Co., Ltd.concerning the quality of the main engine purchased during the construction of the same ship, the Qingdao Maritime Court made the (2011) Qing Hai Fa Hai Shang Chu Zi No. 361 Civil judgment of the firstinstance on April 9, 2013, and your court has made the (2013)Lu Min Si Zhong Zi No. 88 Civil Judgment of second-instance on April 2, 2014. Now,this court has issued the (2014)Min Shen Zi No. 1723 Civil Ruling on December 14, 2015, deciding to file the retrial of the case. The parties concerned, the subject matter, the legal relationship and the specific claims between two cases of arbitration and litigation are different. In addition, both the delivery of the main engine of the ship and the dispute thereof occurred after the fact that the ship involved was overdue (210 days after the delivery date agreed in the Shipbuilding Contract on January 31, 2009) and was still not delivered. The termination of the Shipbuilding Contract has nothing to do with the problem of the main engine, there is no implication of the two cases in their causes of actions, and there is insufficient evidence showing that recognition of the arbitral award involved will conflict with the judicial sovereignty of China or violate the public policy of China.

Second, we examined whether the arbitral award involved exceeded the scope of the arbitration agreement to resolve technical disputes. Pursuant to the agreement in the Shipbuilding Contract involved, the procedure, where the seller and the buyer shall jointly appoint a third-party expert to issue opinions, shall apply to "the resolution of technology related disputes before the deliver and acceptance of the ship, and the resolution of technology related disputes during the warranty period after the delivery of the ship", i.e., apply to the resolution of technical disputes in the delivery and warranty phase after delivery under the condition of (normal)continued performance of the contract. While the arbitral award involved dealt with issues of delayed shipbuilding, reasons for such delays, whether the contract was terminated, etc., and finally the award determined that the contract was terminated due to the seller's inability to deliver the ship within the agreed period. The dispute resolved was whether the Shipbuilding Contract could continue to be performed, rather than involving the technical dispute that should be resolved through the issuance of opinions by a thirdparty expert. Therefore, it cannot be determined that the arbitral award involved exceeded the scope of the arbitration agreement.

Third, regarding the issue of whether the arbitral award involved exceeded the scope of arbitration agreement to deal with the assumption of liabilities, Item 5 of Part A of the arbitral award involved in the case was that "if the seller fails to return the amount to the buyer, the buyer shall be entitled to demand payment from Shandong Branch of Bank of China." Although Shandong Branch of Bank of China provided a repayment guarantee the return of the buyer's deposit under the Shipbuilding Contract, the bank itself was not a party to the Shipbuilding Contract. Neither did the bank sign a written arbitration agreement jointly with the parties, nor was the bank the claimant or the respondent of the arbitral award involved. The rights and obligations under the guarantee should not be a matter of award subject to the said arbitration, so Item 5 of Part A of the arbitral award made by the arbitral tribunal in London exceeded the scope of arbitration agreement. Consequently, this section shall not be recognized, but it does not affect the recognitionof other sections in the award that are separable from the above section.

Fourth, regarding the issue of whether there are any other procedural defects in the arbitral award involved in the case, the respondents of the present case, China Electronics Import and Export Shandong Corporation and Rongcheng Xixiakou Ship Industry Co., Ltd., also raised other defenses, such as the overdue award made by the arbitral tribunal in London. Both the Qingdao Maritime Court and the collegial panel of your court considered that such defenses cannot be supported. After examination, our court agrees with the relevant analysis opinions of the Qingdao Maritime Court and the collegial panel of your court.

Fifth, regarding the request that the applicant, Spliethoff's Bevrachtingskantoor B.V., withdrew the application for recognition, Item 6 of Part A of the arbitral award was that "Upon receiving the notice of termination from the buyer, the seller shall, without delay, return all the amount of 16,392,000 US dollars and any interests produced therefrom to the buyer."Spliethoff's Bevrachtingskantoor B.V. withdrew the application for recognition of Item 6 of Part A of the arbitral award in written to the Qingdao Maritime Court on the ground that it had received the relevant amount 16,392,000 US dollars and interests paid by the guarantor, Bank of China. The disposal of its rights in litigation shall be permitted, and correspondingly, the item of the award shall not be reviewed.

In conclusion, except Item 5 of Part A, which exceeded the scope of arbitration agreement,and Item 6 of Part A, which shall not be reviewed as the applicant withdrew the application for recognition, other Items of the HULL XXK06-039arbitral award made by the arbitral tribunal in London shall be recognized. Therefore, our court basically agrees with the majority opinion and unanimous opinion of the collegial panel of your court and disagrees with the opinion of the Qingdao Maritime Court, which considered that there were problems relating to violations ofthe public policy of China and exceeding the scope of arbitration agreement to resolve technical disputes. Please send a copy of the civil ruling to our court after the case is closed.

It is so replied.

11. **Reply of the Supreme People's Court to the Request for Instructions on the Case Concerning the Application of FSG Automotive Holding AG for Recognition and Enforcement of No. SCH-5239 Arbitral Award rendered by the Arbitration Center of the Austrian Federal Economic Association against Wuhan Fanzhou Machinery Manufacturing Co., Ltd.**
    December 24, 2015, (2015) Min Si Ta Zi No. 46.

To the High People's Court of Hubei Province:
    The Request for Instructions on the Case Concerning the Application of FSG Automotive Holding AG for Recognition and Enforcement of No. SCH-5239 Arbitral Award rendered by the Arbitration Center of the Austrian Federal Economic Association against Wuhan Fanzhou Machinery Manufacturing Co., Ltd. ([2015] E Gao Fa No. 405) submitted by your court has been received. After deliberation, the replies are as follows:
    This is a case concerning the application for recognition and enforcement of an arbitral award made by the Arbitral Center of the Austrian Federal Economic Association. As both China and Austria are contracting states of the Convention on the Recognition and Enforcement of Foreign Arbitral Awards ("**New York Convention**"), the relevant regulations of the New York Convention shall be applied to the review in this case pursuant to Article 283 of the Civil Procedure Law of the People's Republic of China.

Regarding the issueof whether Sect. 5 and Sect. 9 of the arbitral award involved in this case exceeded the scope of the arbitration agreement, in accordance with the materials sent by your court, the scope of arbitration agreed by the arbitration agreement, i.e., Article 27.3 of the Joint Venture Contractincludes any dispute arising from or in connection with the Joint Venture Contract. Article 29.1 and Article 29.2 of the Joint Venture Contract stipulate the obligations of the shareholders to cooperate with each other to perform the Joint Venture Contract in good faith, including trying their best to urge employees to perform the relevant provisions of the Joint Venture Contract. Section 5 of the award-ordered Wuhan Fanzhou Machinery Manufacturing Co., Ltd. ("**Fanzhou Co.**") to urge the representatives it sent to the joint venture to comply with the Joint Venture Contract and the Articles of Association, dealing with the disputes arising fromArticles 29.1 and 29.2. The obligated party under Sect. 5 is Fanzhou Co., rather than the joint venture. However, in terms of specific matters that the item of award ordered to complete, Item I to Item III, which dealt with the issue that Fanzhou Co. hindered FSG Automotive Holding AG ("**FSG**") from exercising the shareholder's right to know, was essentially a dispute over the Joint Venture Contract. Item IV dealt with the dispute on the settlement of account receivables between FSG and the Joint Venture, which was not a dispute over the Joint Venture Contract, and the joint venture was not a party to the arbitration agreement. Therefore, this part of the award fell within the circumstance of exceeding the scope of arbitration agreement as prescribed in Article 5(1)(c) of the New York Convention, and thus Item IV of Sect. 5 was *ultrapetita*. As this part was separable from Items I to III of Sect. 5, in accordance with the relevant provisions of the New York Convention, the *ultrapetita* part shall not be recognized or enforced.

Section 9 of the said award ordered Fanzhou Co. through the representative, it sent to the joint venture to finish the necessary steps for the application for dissolution and the nomination of members of the liquidation team. Pursuant to Article 90 of Regulations for the Implementation of the Law of the People's Republic of China on Chinese-Foreign Equity Joint Ventures, if the joint venture contract is terminated due to one party's fundamental breach of contract, the party performing the contract shall submit an application for dissolution and submit it to the examination and approval authority for approval. Article 2 of Guiding Opinions of the General Office of the Ministry of Commerce on Doing a Good Job in the Dissolution and Liquidation of Foreign-invested Enterprises According to Law stipulates that, upon receipt of the dissolution application and effective legal documents and other relevant materials, the examination and approval authority shall issue an approval document to approve the dissolution of the enterprise. The enterprise shall set up a liquidation team within 15 days from the date of approval of the dissolution and start liquidation according to law. Therefore, the dissolution of joint ventures under the circumstance where the joint venture contract is terminated due to breach of contract does not involve the issue of shareholders' assistance in performing the obligation to submit for approval. Disputes over the type of dissolution and liquidation fell outside the scope of the arbitration agreement in the Joint Venture Contract. Our court agrees with your court's opinion that Sect. 9 of the said award was *ultrapetita*.

In summary, in accordance with Article 283 of the Civil Procedure Law of the People's Republic of China and Article 5(1)(c) of the New York Convention, Item IV of Section 5 and 9 of the arbitral award involved in the case shall not be recognized or enforced, while the rest of the award shall be recognized and enforced.

It is so replied.

12. **Reply of the Supreme People's Court to the Request for Instructions on the Case Concerning the Application of Dong Cheng International Trade Co., Ltd.for Enforcement of a Foreign-Related Arbitral Award.**
    December 9, 2015, (2015) Min Si Ta Zi No. 53.

To the High People's Court of Tianjin:

The Request for Instructions on the Case Concerning the Application of Dong Cheng International Trade Co., Ltd. for Enforcement of a Foreign-Related Arbitral Award ([2015] Jin Gao Min Si Ta Zi No. 3) submitted by your court has been received. After deliberation, the replies are as follows:

AlthoughTianjin Port Free Trade Zone Tiangong International Trade Co., Ltd. submitted the application for non-enforcement of the (2014) Zhong Guo Mao Zhong Jing Cai Zi No. 0468 arbitral award made by CIETAC on June 11, 2014 based on the assertion that "the arbitral proceedings in this case were inconsistent with the arbitration rules", its reason is that Dongcheng International Trade Co., Ltd. did not provide a quality inspection report for the goods or provide evidence to prove that it had performed the contract and deceived the tribunal by using false evidence. It violated Article 39 of the Arbitration Rules of CIETAC, i.e., "Each party shall bear the burden of proving the facts on which it relies to support its claim, defense or counterclaim and provide the basis for its opinions, arguments and counterarguments; if a party fails to produce evidence within the specified time period, or if the produced evidence is not sufficient to support its claim, the party bearing the burden of proof shall assume the consequences thereof", for the arbitral tribunal to order it to assume the responsibility of compensation. These assertions were made by Tianjin Port Free Trade Zone Tiangong International Trade Co., Ltd. involve the admission of evidence, findings of facts and the determination of liabilities, which are not the procedural aspects of the arbitration, are beyond the scope of judicial review by the people's court. As a result, the present case does not fall within the situation stipulated by Article 274(1)(c) of the Civil Procedure Law of the People's Republic of China, i.e., "Thearbitration proceedings are inconsistent with the arbitration rules." In addition, after the dismissal of its application for setting aside the arbitral award involved in the case before the Beijing Second Intermediate People's Court, Tianjin Port Free Trade Zone Tiangong International Trade Co., Ltd.raised a defense of non-enforcement on the same ground in the enforcement procedure. Pursuant to Article 26 of the Interpretation of the Supreme People's Court on Certain Issues Concerning the Application of the Arbitration Law of the People's Republic of China, the defense shall not be supported by the people's court.

To summarize, our court agrees with the first opinion listed in the Request for Instructions of your court.

It is so replied.

13.   **Reply of the Supreme People's Court to the Request for Instructions on the Case Concerning the Application of Trinity Bulk Shipping Ltd. for Recognition and Enforcement of London Arbitral Award against Jiangsu Huihong International Group Native Product Import & Export Co., Ltd. and Yangzhou Huamei Shipping Industry Co., Ltd.**
      November 27, 2015, (2015) Min Si Ta Zi No. 34.

To the High People's Court of Hubei Province:

The Request for Instructions on the Case Concerning the Application of Trinity Bulk Shipping Ltd. for Recognition and Enforcement of London Arbitral Award against Jiangsu Huihong International Group Native Product Import & Export Co., Ltd. and Yangzhou Huamei Shipping Industry Co., Ltd. [E Gao Fa(2015) No. 283] submitted by your court has been received. After deliberation, the replies are as follows:

First, in the Cost Award, there is no circumstance of nonrecognition and non-enforcement stipulated in Article 5 of the Convention on the Recognition and Enforcement of Foreign Arbitral Awards in the arbitral tribunal's award about the expenses incurred by the applicant for the London arbitration procedure, the fees and relevant interests charged by thearbitral tribunal. Therefore, the cost award should be recognized and enforced.

Second, as the cost awardwas mainly about the calculation and assumption of the relevant arbitration fees incurred by the London arbitration procedure, the possible damages caused to the applicant due to the violation of the arbitration clause in the contract and the filing of lawsuit before a Chinese court in Chinawere not included in the arbitration fees incurred by the London arbitration procedureand were by nature the damages for breach of contract. It exceeded the scope of the Cost Award for the arbitral tribunal to decide on the damages caused to the applicant incurred by the lawsuit before a Chinese court. Pursuant to Article 5(1)(c) of the Convention on the Recognition and Enforcement of Foreign Arbitral Awards, the part of damages in the amount of 33,815.42 pounds and interests in the Cost Award shall not be recognized and enforced.

To summarize, our court agrees with your court's opinion that the part of damages and interests caused to the applicant incurred by the lawsuit before a Chinese court in the Cost Award shall not be recognized or enforced, while the rest of the Cost Award shall be recognized and enforced.

It is so replied.

14.   **Reply of the Supreme People's Court to the Request for Instructions of the High People's Court of Beijing on the Case Concerning the Application of CGCOC Group for Revocation of the [2015] Zhong Guo Mao Zhong Jing Cai Zi No. 0377 Arbitral Award made by CIETAC.**
      October 26, 2015, (2015) Min Si Ta Zi No. 39.

To the High People's Court of Beijing:

The Request for Instructions concerning the Case Concerning the Application of CGCOC Group for Revocation of the [2015] Zhong Guo Mao Zhong Jing Cai Zi

No. 0377 Arbitral Award made by CIETAC (Jing Gao Fa [2015]No. 309) submitted by your court has been received. After deliberation, the replies are as follows:

This is a case where a party applies for the revocation of a foreign related arbitral award made by an arbitral institution in China. According to the facts stated in the Request for Instructions, the arbitral tribunal in the present case, while resolving the disputes under the Cooperation Agreement in a housing project between CGCOC Group and China Railway Construction Engineering Group, ruled on the expenses in the Jier Stadium project in the amount of RMB 360,000 and the dispute being heard by the people's court over a loan of RMB 2 million under the Funds Loan Certificate signed by the parties in this case which were unrelated with the disputes under the Cooperation Agreement. Such behavior falls within the situation "The arbitration matter does not fall under the scope of the arbitration agreement or the arbitration institution has no power to carry out arbitration" stipulated in Item 4, Paragraph 1 of Article 274 of the Civil Procedure Law of the People's Republic of China. After communication between the Beijing Second Intermediate People's Court and CIETAC, CIETAC expressly agreed to reaarbitrate the case. Therefore, your court may, in accordance with Article 61 of the Arbitration Law of the People's Republic of China, inform the arbitral institution toreaarbitrate the case. Your court's opinion in the Request for Instructions is agreed.

It is so replied.

15. **Reply of the Supreme People's Court to the Request for Instructions on the Case Concerning the Application of Siemens International Trading (Shanghai) Co., Ltd.for Recognition and Enforcement of a Foreign Arbitral Award.**
    October 10, 2015, (2015) Min Si Ta Zi No. 5

To the High People's Court of Shanghai:

The Request for Instructions on the Case Concerning the Application of Siemens International Trading (Shanghai) Co., Ltd. for Recognition and Enforcement of a Foreign Arbitral Award [(2013)Hu Gao Min Ren (Wai Zhong) No. 1] submitted by your court has been received. After deliberation, the replies are as follows:

Based on the facts reflected in the Request for Instructions, both the applicant, Siemens International Trading (Shanghai) Co., Ltd., and the respondent, Shanghai Golden Landmark Co., Ltd., in the present case are legal persons of China. There is no typical foreign-related factor in the Goods Supply Contract concluded by the two parties. However, the case at hand is related to FTZs, and both parties are subsidiaries of wholly foreign-owned enterprises. After Shanghai Golden Landmark Co., Ltd. filed the arbitration procedure as the applicant in the arbitration case, Siemens International Trading (Shanghai) Co., Ltd. first raised a jurisdictional objection, which was dismissed by the arbitral tribunal, and then brought counterclaims. Both parties have actually participated in the whole arbitration proceedings. Shanghai Golden Landmark Co., Ltd. also made partial performance of its obligations determined by the arbitral award after the arbitral award was issued. To implement the requirements of "promoting international commercial maritime arbitration to play an important role in the construction of the 'One Belt and One Road'" put forward in the Several Opinions of the Supreme People's Court on the People's Court Providing Judicial Guarantees for the Construction of the "One Belt and One Road", in the spirit of supporting the initiatives in building the rule of law in the free trade zone, and in consideration with the actual situations in the present case, as well as the legal principles of estoppel, good faith, justice and fairness, it can be determined that the arbitration agreement in this case falls within the circumstance "other circumstances that may be deemed as foreign-related civil relationships"as stipulatedin Item 5, Article 1 of the Interpretations of the Supreme People's Court on Several Issues Concerning the Application of the Law of the People'sForgnem 5, Article 1 of the Interpretations of the Supreme's People's vil Court (I). "Other circumstances that may be determined as foreign-related civil relations." Additionally, there is no evidence to prove that the recognition and enforcement of the arbitral award would be in violation of the public policy of China. Therefore, there is no circumstance as stipulated in Article 5 of 1958,the Convention on the Recognition and Enforcement of Foreign Arbitral Awards acceded to by China in the arbitral award in this case, and the arbitral award shall be recognized and enforced.

It is so replied.

16. **Reply of the Supreme People's Court to the Request for Instructions of the High People's Court of Shanghai on the Case Concerning the Revocation of the (2013) Hu Mao Zhong Cai Zi No. 415 Arbitral Award Made by Shanghai International Economic and Trade Arbitration Commission.**
     October 9, 2015, (2015) Min Si Ta Zi No. 8

To the High People's Court of Shanghai:

The Request for Instructions on the Case Concerning the Revocation of the (2013) Hu Mao Zhong Cai Zi No. 415 Arbitral Award Made by Shanghai International Economic and Trade Arbitration Commission [(2014)Hu Gao Min Er (Shang) Che Zi No. S1] submitted by your court has been received. After deliberation, the replies are as follows:

According to the Report of Request for Instructions and attached materials sent by your court, Article 11.6 of the Framework Agreement Regarding No. 688 Huaihai Middle Road, Luwan District, Shanghai, China ("**Framework Agreement**") signed by Union Investment Real Estate AG ("**Union AG**"), Whole Team Limited ("**W&T**") and Shanghai Huashi Zhongxing Shopping Mall Management Co., Ltd. ("**Huashi Co.**"), Article 3 of the Amendment Agreement of the Framework Agreement, and Article 13 of the supplementary provisions of the Shanghai Real Estate Purchase Contract annexed to the Framework Agreement signed by Union AG and Huashi Co. all stipulated that any dispute arisingfrom or in connection with the agreement (excluding the net profit guarantee, contract guarantee and purchase price guarantee attached to the Framework Agreement) should be submitted to the Shanghai International Economic and Trade Arbitration Commission for arbitration to be finally resolved. Those arbitration clauses, which comply with the governing law of the arbitration agreements, i.e., the law of China, are legal and valid and are legally binding on Union AG, W&T and Huashi Co.

Regarding the issueof whether Defa Shopping Mall Management (Shanghai) Co., Ltd. ("**Defa Co.**") was a party to the arbitration agreement, Defa Co. was not established when the above agreements were signed, nor did Defa Co. sign the agreements. However, viewed from the contents of the framework agreement and its appendixes, W&T and Huashi Co., etc., as the sellers, agreed that Union AG may buy itself or designate another company to purchase the shopping mall located at No. 688 Huaihai Middle Road, Luwan District, Shanghai. The sellers agreed to take all necessary measures and actions to ensure the sellers' promises and rights given to the buyer under the agreements. Article 2 of the supplementary provisions of the Shanghai Real Estate Purchase Contract annexed further stipulated that Union AG and Huashi Co. confirmed that when signing this agreement, it was the intent of both parties that Union AG would appoint an affiliate within the territory of Shanghai to purchase the shopping mall, and both parties shall fully cooperatewith each other to ensure that Union AG may set up the designated body as soon as possible after signing the agreements. Pursuant to the above agreements, Huashi Co. and W&T acknowledged and agreed that Union AGwould perform the framework agreement by appointing a newly established company as the buyer. Huashi Co. and W&T had fully anticipated that the disputes between them and the newly established company arising from the performance of the Framework Agreement shall be governed by the arbitration clauses. Viewed from the performance of the agreements, Union AG notified Huashi Co. and W&T through mails on November 2, 2006 and November 7, 2006 that it had applied for establishing a wholly foreign owned enterprise named Defa Co. in Shanghaiso that the new company could purchase the shopping mall. Meanwhile, in Huashi Co.'s Request for Arbitration filed in December 2007 against Union AG in another case, Huashi Co. also confirmed that Union AG had designated Defa Co. as the buyer. Therefore, Defa Co. had become a party to the arbitration clause contained in the Framework Agreement because it was designated by Union AG as the buyer, and there is no need to sign another arbitration clause. As Article 1.2.1 of the Framework Agreement stipulated that when Union AG appoints the buyer, it still has the right to exercise its rights within its own authority, and Article 11.4 stipulated that the obligations of Union AG and the buyer appointed by Union AGunder the agreements were joint and several, Union AG did not withdraw from the Framework Agreement due to the designation of Defa Co. as the buyer, and still had the standing to initiate arbitration. To summarize, according to the content of the agreements as well as the background and intention of the transaction, there exists a legal basis in the agreement, and it is conducive to resolvingdisputes for Union AG and Defa Co. to act asapplicants of arbitration.

The issues of whether the way of appointment of the buyer by Union AG complied with the specific requirements stipulated in Article 3.1 of the Framework Agreement, whether the notice and confirmation letter sent by Union AG reached Huashi Co. before the termination of contracts, whether Union AG had fulfilled the capital contribution obligation to Defa Co., and when the "exclusion period" in the contracts expired, etc., are disputes over the substantive rights and obligations in the case, which fall within the scope of arbitration matters as agreed in the arbitration clauses and shall be determined by the arbitral tribunal to determine substantively. It lacks corresponding legal basis for your court to conduct substantive review on matters mentioned above, which exceeds the scope of statutory grounds for review stipulated in Article 70 of the Arbitration Law of the People's Republic of China and Article 274 of the Civil Procedure Law of the People's Republic of China.

The issueof whether there is inconsistency between the arbitration proceedings and arbitration rules in the present case shall be determined in accordance with the Arbitration Rules of the China International Economic and Trade Arbitration Commission (version 2005). Article 42 of the Arbitration Rules provided that "Time Period for Rendering Award: 1. The arbitral tribunal shall render an arbitral award within six months from the date on which the arbitral tribunal is formed.2. Upon the request of the arbitral tribunal, the President of the Arbitration Commission may extend the time period if he/she considers it truly necessary and the reasons for the extension truly justified." The Shanghai International Economic and Trade Arbitration Commissionmade notices of extending the time period regarding the award involved in this case several times, some of which were made after the expiration of the extended periods. Nevertheless, as the Arbitration Rules did not specify when the extension notice shall be sent and the award in the case at hand was rendered within the extended period, the present case does not constitute the situation "the arbitral proceedings are inconsistent with the arbitration rules" stipulated in Item 3, Paragraph 1 of Article 274 of the Civil Procedure Law.

To conclude, the grounds for setting aside the award of Huashi Co. and W&T that there was no arbitration agreement between them and Defa Co., that Union AG and Defa Co. could not act as the applicants for arbitration at the same time, and that the arbitral proceedings violated the arbitration rules, could not be established, and the application shall be rejected.

It is so replied.

17. **Reply of the Supreme People's Court to the Request for Instructions of the High People's Court of Guangdong Province on the Case Concerning the Application of Dongguan Haoqing Paper Co., Ltd. et al., for Non-Enforcement of an Arbitral Award.**
    October 9, 2015, (2015) Min Si Ta Zi No. 35.

To the High People's Court of Guangdong Province:

The Request for Instructions on the Case Concerning the Application of Dongguan Haoqing Paper Co., Ltd., Dongguan Dingtian Industrial Investment Co., Ltd., Zhang Faming, and Zeng Nanjiao for Non-Enforcement of an Arbitral Award against-stShenzhen Hongxun Century Trading Co., Ltd. and Chen Gengsen, Chen Yedi and Ma Tingguo as the third parties[(2015)Yue Gao Fa Zhong Fu Zi No. 1] submitted by your court has been received. After deliberation, the replies are as follows:

Zeng Nanjiao, the applicant in the present case, is a resident of the Hong Kong Special Administrative Region. Therefore, this is a case involving the application for non-enforcement of a Hong Kong-related arbitral award made by an arbitral institution in the mainland. Pursuant to Article 551 of the Interpretation of the Supreme People's Court on the Application of the Civil Procedure Law of the People's

Republic of China, Article 71 of the Arbitration Law of the People's Republic of China and Article 274 of the Civil Procedure Law of the People's Republic of China shall be applied by reference to the review in the present case.

According to the facts stated in the Request for Instructions, Shenzhen Arbitration Commission rendered the [2014] Shen Zhong Tiao Zi No. 27 Mediation Statement upon the Request of ChenGengsen, etc. on the private lending dispute-between them and Dongguan Haoqing Paper Co., Ltd.("**Haoqing Co.**"). During the process of enforcing the Mediation Statement by the people's court, the applicants, Chen Gengsen, etc., assigned their creditor rights involved in this case to Shenzhen Hongxun Century Trading Co., Ltd. ("**Hongxun Co.**"). The Dongguan Intermediate People's Court ruled to change the applicant for enforcementto Hongxun Co. During this period, Hongxun Co. and Haoqing Co. reached a mediation agreement including an arbitration clause. Upon the request of Hongxun Co.,and based on the content of the aforementioned mediation agreement, the Shenzhen Arbitration Commission made the [2014] Shen Zhong Cai Zi No. 1287 Arbitral Award. The arbitral awards made by the Shenzhen Arbitration Commission upon the requests of different parties based on different arbitration agreements and on different arbitration requests do not constitute the repeated arbitration on the same dispute stipulated in Article 9 of the Arbitration Law of the People's Republic of China. Therefore, there does not exist the circumstance stipulated in Item 4, Paragraph 2 of Article 274 of the Civil Procedure Law of the People's Republic of China in the [2014] Shen Zhong Cai Zi No. 1287 Arbitral Award made the Shenzhen Arbitration Commission, so Haoqing Co.'s application for not enforcing the arbitral award on this ground cannot be established.

It is so replied.

18.   **Reply of the Supreme People's Court to the Request for Instructions of the High People's Court of Shandong Province on the Case Concerning the Application of Toyoshima Stock Co., Ltd. for Recognition and Enforcement of a Foreign Arbitral Award Against Gaomi Luyuan Textile Co., Ltd.**

September 24, 2015, (2015) Min Si Ta Zi No. 30.

To the High People's Court of Shandong Province:

The Request for Instructions Concerning the Case of the Application of Toyoshima Stock Co., Ltd. for Recognition and Enforcement of a Foreign Arbitral Award Against Gaomi Luyuan Textile Co., Ltd. [(2015) Lu Min Si Ta Zi No. 2] submitted by your court has been received. After deliberation, the replies are as follows:

This is a case concerning the application for recognition and enforcement of a foreign arbitral award. As the arbitral award involved in this case was made by the International Cotton Associationin the United Kingdom, and both China and the United Kingdom are contracting states of the Convention on the Recognition and Enforcement of Foreign Arbitral Awards ("**New York Convention**"), pursuant to Article 283 of the Civil Procedure Law of the People's Republic of China, the recognition and enforcement of the arbitral award involved shall be reviewed in accordance with the relevant provisions oftheNew York Convention.

The core issue in the Request for Instructions of your court is whether there exists the circumstance where the constitution of the arbitral tribunal is illegal and accordingly the recognition and enforcement shall be refused in accordance with Article 5(1)(d) of the New York Convention in the arbitral award involved. The circumstance stipulated in Article 5(1)(d) of the New York Convention is that "The composition of the arbitral authority or the arbitral procedure was not in accordance with the agreement of the parties, or failing such agreement, was not in accordance with the law of the country where the arbitration took place". As the parties to the present case have reached an arbitration agreement, which stipulated that the arbitration rules of the International Cotton Association shall apply, the review shall be conducted on whether the composition of the arbitral tribunal was in compliance with the arbitration rules the parties agreed to apply. The specific issue involved in the present case iswhether it constitutes the circumstance of illegal composition of arbitral tribunal that the two arbitrators of the arbitral tribunal, who were qualified as technical arbitrators and had been duly appointed as arbitration by the arbitral tribunal, did not have the qualifications of technical arbitrators when the arbitral award was rendered.According to your court's Request for Instructions, "There is no stipulation in the rules of the International Cotton Association Ltd. on the handling of situation where the arbitrator is qualified at the beginning of appointment but is disqualified as an arbitrator during the arbitration process". Based on this, it can be considered that there is no circumstance where the composition of the arbitral tribunal does not conform to the explicit provisions of the arbitration rules in this case. In addition, according tothe principle established by the Reply of this Court Regarding the Enforcement by the People's Court of an Arbitral Award Signed by the Original Arbitrator who is No Longer Appointed [Fa Shi (1998) No. 21], the majority opinion of your court that the two arbitrators were qualified when the arbitral tribunal was composed of, even if the two arbitrators had not been qualified as technical arbitrators when the arbitral award was rendered, the loss of the qualification of two arbitrators only restricted the cases accepted by the arbitration institution afterwards, but would not affect the trial work of the previously legally established arbitral tribunal.In contrast, the minority opinion of your courtis based on the testimony of Du Feng, the Chinese.

Liason Officer of the International Cotton Association Ltd., who considered that only technical arbitrators could be the member of the arbitral tribunal and heard this case and accordingly the composition of the arbitral tribunal in the present case was not in compliance with the relevant rules and thus the award should not be recognized or enforced, rather than the relevant arbitration rules. The minority opinion lacks legal basis.

In summary, the majority opinion of your court that the defense cannot be supported that the disqualification of two arbitrators as technical arbitrators when the arbitral award was rendered, the arbitration proceedings were illegal and thus the arbitral award shall not be recognized or enforced is agreed.

It is so replied.

19.   **Reply of the Supreme People's Court to the Request for Instructions of the High People's Court of Shandong Province on the Case Concerning the Application of ECOM AGROINDUSTRIAL ASIA PTE LTD for Recognition and Enforcement of the Arbitral Award Made by International Cotton Association.**
       September 24, 2015, (2015) Min Si Ta Zi No. 29.

To the High People's Court of Shandong Province:

The Request for Instructions Concerning the Application of ECOM AGROIN-DUSTRIAL ASIA PTE LTD for Recognition and Enforcement of the Arbitral Award Made by International Cotton Association [(2015) Lu Min Si Ta Zi No. 1] submitted by your court has been received. After deliberation, the replies are as follows:

This is a case concerning the application for recognition and enforcement of a foreign arbitral award. As the arbitral award involved in the case at hand was made by the International Cotton Association in the United Kingdom, and both China and the United Kingdom are contracting states of the Convention on the Recognition and Enforcement of Foreign Arbitral Awards ("**New York Convention**"), pursuant to Article 283 of the Civil Procedure Law of the People's Republic of China, the recognition and enforcement of the arbitral award involved shall be reviewed in accordance with the relevant provisions of the New York Convention.

When reviewing cases of application for recognition and enforcement of foreign arbitral awards, the court is empowered to examine and determine whether the parties have reached an arbitration agreement and whether such arbitration agreement is valid, etc., based on relevant evidence. According to the Request for Instructions of your court, the core issue in the present case is whether the parties have reached an arbitration agreement, which is a matter of fact finding. Article 2 of the Notice of the Supreme People's Court Concerning Issues on Request for Instructions in the Trial Work [Fa (1999) No. 13] stipulates that the High People's Court shall be responsible for the facts and evidence of cases in request for Instructions. Therefore, the factual issueofwhether the parties involved had signed an arbitration agreement shall be determined by the court,which accepted the case after hearing. If it is confirmed that the parties involved had not reached an arbitration agreement, the recognition and enforcement of the arbitral award involved shall be denied in accordance with relevant provisions of the New York Convention.

It is so replied.

20.   **Reply of the Supreme People's Court to the Request for Instructions of the High People's Court of Shandong Province on the Case Concerning the Application of Toyoshima Co., Ltd. for Recognition and Enforcement of a Foreign Arbitral Award against Shandong Changyi Kunfu Textile Co., Ltd.**
       September 24, 2015, (2015) Min Si Ta Zi No. 31.

To the High People's Court of Shandong Province:

The Request for Instructions on the Case Concerning the Application of Toyoshima Co., Ltd. for Recognition and Enforcement of a Foreign Arbitral Award against Shandong Changyi Kunfu Textile Co., Ltd. [(2015) Lu Min Si Ta Zi No. 3] submitted by your court has been received. After deliberation, the replies are as follows:

This is a case concerning the application for recognition and enforcement of a foreign arbitral award. As the arbitral award involved in the case at hand was made by the International Cotton Association in the United Kingdom, and both China and the United Kingdom are contracting states of the Convention on the Recognition and Enforcement of Foreign Arbitral Awards ("**New York Convention**"), pursuant to Article 283 of the Civil Procedure Law of the People's Republic of China, the recognition and enforcement of the arbitral award involved shall be reviewed in accordance with the relevant provisions of the New York Convention.

According to the Request for Instructions of your court, the core issue disputed in the present case is whether there exists the circumstance stipulated in Article 5(1)(a) of the New York Convention. Article 5(1)(a) of the New York Convention stipulates that "The parties to the agreementwere, under the law applicable to them, under some incapacity, or the said agreement is not valid under the law to which the parties have subjected it or failing any indication thereon, under the law of the country where the award was made." According to the facts stated in the Request for Instructions of your court, there was a clause stipulating "ICA RULES AND ARBITRATIONS" in the Raw Cotton Sales Contract signed by both parties, but the clause did not specify the applicable law to determine the validity of the arbitration agreement. The respondent did not provide any evidence to prove that the arbitration agreement was invalid in accordance with the law of the United Kingdom, i.e., the seat of arbitration, which falls within the circumstance denying recognition and enforcement stipulated in Article 5(1)(a) of the New York Convention. The minority opinion in the Request for Instructions of your court, which considered the arbitration agreement invalid in accordance with the law of China due to the failure of specifying arbitration institution, lacks legal basis.

In summary, the majority opinion of your court that the arbitral award involved in this case does not fall within the circumstance stipulated in Article 5(1)(a) of the New York Convention is agreed.

It is so replied.

21. **Reply of the Supreme People's Court to the Request for Instructions on the Case Concerning the Application of Haomei Co., Ltd. for Confirmation of the Validity of an Arbitration Agreement.**
    September 24, 2015, (2015) Min Si Ta Zi No. 36.

To the High People's Court of Guangdong Province:

The Request for Instructions on the Case Concerning the Application of Haomei Co., Ltd. for Confirmation of the Validity of an Arbitration Agreement against Shenzhen Guodi Construction Co., Ltd. [(2015) Yue Gao Fa Zhong Fu Zi No. 6] submitted by your court has been received. After deliberation, the replies are as follows:

This is a Hong Kong-related case of application for confirmation of the validity of an arbitration agreement. Based on the facts stated in the Request for Instructions of your court, there was an arbitration agreement in the Contract for Undertaking a Project signed on August 12, 2014 involved in the present case, which provided that all disputes arising out of or related to the contract shall be submitted to South China International Economic and Trade Arbitration Commission for arbitration. The parties did not specify the applicable law to determine the validity of the arbitration agreement. Pursuant to Article 18 of Law of the People's Republic of China on Choice of Law for Foreign-related Civil Relationships, the law of the place of South China International Economic and Trade Arbitration Commission for arbitration, i.e., the law of the People's Republic of China, shall apply. Article 4 of the Arbitration Law of the People's Republic of China stipulates that the parties settling disputes by means of arbitration shall reach an arbitration agreement on a mutually voluntary basis. Based on the facts stated in the Request for Instructions of your court, the signature of Ye Xinli, the director of Haomei Co., Ltd. ("**Haomei**") in the contract involved in the case was not signed by himself. Chen Liangsheng, the person who actually signed the contract, was not authorized by Haomei. Therefore, the contract, including the arbitration clause therein, did not reflect the true intention of Haomei. As Haomei and Shenzhen Guodi Construction Co., Ltd. did not reach a valid arbitration agreement voluntarily, the arbitration agreement involved in the case shall not be binding on Haomei. The opinion in the Request for Instructions of your court is agreed upon.

It is so replied.

22. **Reply of the Supreme People's Court to the Request for Instructions Concerning the Validity of a Foreign-Related Arbitration Agreement in the Voyage Charter Dispute between China North Shipping Logistics Co., Ltd. and Benxi Beiying Steel Group Import and Export Co., Ltd.**
September 21, 2015, [2015] Min Si Ta Zi No. 22.

To the High People's Court of Liaoning Province:

The Request for Instructions Concerning the Validity of a Foreign-Related Arbitration Agreement in the Voyage Charter Dispute between China North Shipping Logistics Co., Ltd. and Benxi Beiying Steel Group Import and Export Co., Ltd. [(2015)Liao Min San Ta Zi No. 2] submitted by your court has been received. After deliberation, the replies are as follows:

The SS Clauses in the Contract of the goods exports in the present case stipulated that"GENERAL AVERAGE/ARBITRATION IF ANY IN BENXI AND CHINESE LAW TO BE APPLIED. In the event of general average/arbitration, this agreement shall be governed by Chinese law, and the seat of arbitration shall be Benxi." Althoughthe Benxi Arbitration Commission is the only arbitration institution in Benxi, the Clauses were a special agreement between the two parties only on the place of arbitration and the applicable law when arbitrating the dispute involved. They did not constitute an agreement on the only way to resolve disputes between the parties and did not exclude litigation. Pursuant to Item 1, Paragraph 2, Article 16 of the Arbitration Law of the People's Republic of China, such Clauses shall be invalid.

Article 25 of the Chartering Agreement concerning the import of goods involved in the case stipulated that "Arbitration: Any disputes arising under the Charter Party shall be settled amicably. In case no such settlement can be reached, the matter in dispute shall be referred to three persons at Beijing and according to Chinese law. One chosen by each of the parties hereto and the third by the two so chosen; their decision or that of two of them shall be final, and for the purpose of enforcing the award, this agreement may be made a rule of the court. The arbitrators shall be commercial men." Although the arbitration clause specified that the seat of arbitration should be Beijing, it did not specify an arbitration institution. Nor is there any evidence to show that the two parties have reached a supplementary agreement on the selection of an arbitration institution. Pursuant to Item 3, Paragraph 2 of Article 16 and Article 18 of the Arbitration Law of the People's Republic of China, the arbitration clause is invalid due to the absence of an agreement on an arbitration institution.

The port of destination or port of departure for each voyage involved is within the jurisdiction of the Dalian Maritime Court, so the Dalian Maritime Court has jurisdiction over this case. The opinion in the Request for Instructions of your courtthat the arbitration agreement in the present case is invalid is agreed upon.

It is so replied.

23. **Reply of the Supreme People's Court to the Request for Instructions on the Case Concerning the Application of Petroleum Engineering General Contracting Branch of CNPC Bohai Drilling Engineering Co., Ltd. for Confirmation of the Validity of an Arbitration Agreement.**
    August 17, 2015, (2015) Min Si Ta Zi No. 23.

To the High People's Court of Beijing:

The Request for Instructions on the Case Concerning the Application of Petroleum Engineering General Contracting Branch of CNPC Bohai Drilling Engineering Co., Ltd. for Confirmation of the Validity of an Arbitration Agreement [(2015) Gao Min Ta Zi No. 3066] submitted by your court has been received. After deliberation, the replies are as follows:

Article 24.2 of the Master Service Contract signed between the Petroleum Engineering General Contracting Branch of CNPC Bohai Drilling Engineering Co., Ltd. and Far East Energy (Bermuda) Co., Ltd. on September 1, 2013 stipulated that "If the parties have failed to resolve their disputes through negotiation within sixty (60) days since the occurrence of such disputes or claims, any party may submit such disputes or claims to arbitration. The arbitration shall be conducted in accordance with the following provisions." Article 24.3 stipulated that "Any award in the arbitration shall be final and binding on Party A and Party B. Both parties shall respect and abide by the arbitral award. Such an award shall be enforceable in any relevant countries, including but not limited to the People's Republic of China." Viewed from the above content about dispute resolution in the Contract, although both parties expressed their intention to submit disputes to arbitration, they did not specify the arbitration institution or the seat of arbitration at the same time. Nor have they reached any supplementary agreement on that. Since the parties in the present case have not agreed on the applicable law to determine the validity of the arbitration agreement, pursuant to Article 14 of the Interpretations of the Supreme People's Court on Several Issues

Concerning Application of the Law of the People's Republic of China on Choice of Law for Foreign-Related Civil Relationships (I) and Article 16 of the Interpretations of the Supreme People's Court on Several Issues Concerning Application of the Arbitration Law of People's Republic of China, the law of the People's Republic of China shall be applied to determine the validity of the arbitration agreement. Pursuant to Article 18 of the Arbitration Law of the People's Republic of China, the arbitration agreement in the present case shall be ruled invalid. Therefore, the opinion in the Request for Instructions of your court is agreed upon.

It is so replied.

24. **Reply of the Supreme People's Court to the Request for Instructions on the Case Concerning the Application of Chongqing Pulefei Import & Export Co., Ltd. for Non-Enforcement of an Arbitral Award.**
    July 22, 2015, [2015] Min Si Ta Zi No. 11.

To the High People's Court of Chongqing:

The Request for Instructions on the Case Concerning the Application of Chongqing Pulefei Import & Export Co., Ltd. ("**Pulefei**") for Non-Enforcement of an Arbitral Award {[2014] Yu Gao Fa Zhi Shi Zi No. 174} submitted by your court has been received. After deliberation, the repliesare as follows:

This is a case concerning the application for non-enforcement of an arbitral award. According to the materials sent by your court, the parties agreed in Article 11 of the Basic Purchase Contract that "This Contract shall be governed by the law of the People's Republic of China (except for its conflict of laws). The parties shall resolve any dispute arising out of or in connection with this contractthrough negotiation in good faith. In the event of failure of negotiation, the parties agree to submit the disputes to the China International Economic and Trade Arbitration Commission Shanghai Sub-Commission for arbitration in accordance with the latest arbitration rules effective at the time of submission. All arbitration expenses shall be borne by the losing party." Pursuant to Article 16 of the Interpretations of the Supreme People's Court on Several Issues Concerning Application of the Arbitration Law of People's Republic of China, the validity of the arbitration agreement in the case at hand shall be reviewed in accordance with the law that the parties have agreed upon, i.e., the law of the People's Republic of China.

As the parties have clearly expressed their intention to arbitrate in the arbitration agreement and agreed upon the specific arbitration matters as well as the arbitration institution selected, the arbitration agreement is in compliance with Article 16 of the Arbitration Law of the People's Republic of China and thus is legal and valid.

The Basic Purchase Contract was signed on January 25, 2011. Pursuant to Article 3 of the Reply of the Supreme People's Court to the Request for Instructions of the High People's Court of Shanghai and Other Courts on Cases Involving Judicial Review of the Arbitral Awards Issued by the China International Economic and Trade Arbitration Commission, Former Sub-Commissionsthereof and Other Arbitration Institutions, after the China International Economic and Trade Arbitration Commission rendered the award in this case, if any party applies for non-enforcement based on the assertion that the arbitration institution does not have jurisdiction, the court shall not support such a claim. Therefore, the application of Pulefei does not fall within the situation stipulated in Paragraph 2, Article 273 of the Civil Procedure Law of the People's Republic of China, and shall be rejected.

After closing the case, please send the legal documents to our court for reference. It is so replied.

25. **Reply of the Supreme People's Court to the Request for Instructions on the Case Concerning the Application of Jiarui Shipping Co., Ltd. for Non-Enforcement of a Foreign-Related Arbitral Award in the Voyage Charter Dispute against Sichuan Beifang Qinyuan Bioengineering Co., Ltd.**

September 26, 2014, (2014) Min Si Ta Zi No. 41.

To the High People's Court of Hubei Province:

The Request for Instructions on the Case Concerning the Application of Jiarui Shipping Co., Ltd. for Non-Enforcement of a Foreign-Related Arbitral Award in the Voyage Charter Dispute against Sichuan Beifang Qinyuan Bioengineering Co., Ltd. [E Gao Fa (2014) No. 212] submitted by your court has been received. After deliberation, the replies are as follows:

The arbitral award involved in this case was a foreign-related arbitral award made by an arbitration institution in China. The issue of whether the said award shall be enforced shall be reviewed in accordance with Article 274 of the Civil Procedure Law of the People's Republic of China. The focus of the review in this case is whether there exist circumstances where the arbitration proceedings in the present case are inconsistent with Article 38 and Article 44 of the Arbitration Rules of the China Maritime Arbitration Commission ("**Arbitration Rules**").

According to the facts stated in the Request for Instructions of your court, the China Maritime Arbitration Commission Shanghai Sub-commission ("**Arbitral Tribunal**") held a hearing on November 19, 2012. After the hearing, Jiarui Shipping Co., Ltd. ("**Jiarui**") sent the Attorney's Opinions and a British precedent to the arbitral tribunal on November 26, 2012. The arbitral tribunal sent the materials above to Sichuan Beifang Qinyuan Bioengineering Co., Ltd. ("**Qinyuan**"). Qinyuan submitted its supplementary Attorney's Opinions to the arbitral tribunal on December 7, 2012, claiming that the British precedent submitted by Jiarui should not be admitted as the evidence as it carried no probative value. Afterwards, the arbitral tribunal rendered the award on December 17, 2012. Since the aforementionedBritish precedent was submitted by Jiarui after the hearing held by the arbitral tribunal, Qinyuan did not raise any objection regarding the cross-examination of evidence after receiving the British precedent sent by the arbitral tribunal. Instead, Qinyuan submitted supplementary Attorney's Opinions on theBritish precedent. Such behavior of Qinyuan showed that it had acknowledged written cross-examination. The arbitral tribunal did not violate Article 44 of the Arbitration Rules. Pursuant to Article 52 of the Arbitration Rules, Qinyuan's behavior of continuing to participate in the arbitration proceedingsshall be deemed as having waived its right to object.

Although the arbitral award in this case mentioned the assertion of Jiarui to quote the relevantBritish precedent while the arbitral award did not mention Qinyuan's allegation that the British precedent shall not be applied in its assertion, Qinyuan submitted a written Attorney's Opinions regarding this issue before the award was made. This situation means that the arbitral tribunal had given Qinyuan the opportunity to present its case and debate, and Qinyuan also exercised such rights. Consequently, there is no circumstance where the arbitral tribunal did not treat both parties fairly and impartially stipulated in Article 38 of the Arbitration Rules. In addition, in the arbitral award involved, the British precedent submitted by Jiarui was not taken as the basis of the award. Therefore, there is no substantive significance to the outcome of the arbitral award in this case with Qinyuan's assertion that its opinion that the British precedent should not be admitted as evidence was not contained in the arbitral award.

In conclusion, the ground of Qinyuan's application for non-enforcement of the arbitral award in the case does not fall within the circumstances prescribed in Article 274 of the Civil Procedure Law of the People's Republic of China. The second opinion of your court is agreed.

It is so replied.

26. **Reply of the Supreme People's Court to the Request for Instructions on the Case Concerning the Application of Hainan Lion City Tourism Development Co., Ltd. for Non-Enforcement of an Arbitral Award.**
    July 31, 2014, (2014) Min Si Ta Zi No. 37.

To the High People's Court of Hainan Province:

The Request for Instructions on the Case Concerning the Application of Hainan Lion City Tourism Development Co., Ltd. for Non-Enforcement of an Arbitral Award [Qiong Gao Fa Zhuan Bao (2014) No. 4] submitted by your court has been received. After deliberation, the replies are as follows:

The handling opinion put forward in your court's Request for Instructions is agreed upon. According to the facts described in the Request for Instructions, the domicile of Hainan Lion City Tourism Development Co., Ltd. was "Room 501, Building C, Lihua City, Yanjiang Sandong Road, Haidian Island, Haikou City, Hainan Province", rather than "Room 501, Building C, Yuhua City, Yanjiang Sandong Road, Haidian Island, Haikou City, Hainan Province". Grandall Law Firm used the former address to communicate with Hainan Lion City Tourism Development Co., Ltd. before initiating arbitration. However, whenGrandall Law Firm initiated arbitration beforethe China International Economic and Trade Arbitration Commission, it used the latter address, which was wrong, resulting in the fact that Hainan Lion City Tourism Development Co., Ltd. did not receive the arbitration documents, such as the notice of appointment of arbitrators, notice of hearings, and accordingly was unable to participate in the arbitration proceedings and present its opinions. Pursuant to Item 2, Paragraph 1 of Article 274 of the Civil Procedure Law of the People's Republic of China, the (2012) Zhong Guo Mao Zhong Jing Cai Zi No. 0502 arbitral award made byChina International Economic and Trade Arbitration Commission shall be ruled not to be enforced.

It is so replied.

27. **Reply of the Supreme People's Court to the Request for Instructions on the Case Concerning the Application of Allenberg Cotton Co., Ltd. for Recognition and Enforcement of a Foreign Arbitral Award against Ningbo Youngor International Trade&Transportation Co., Ltd.**
July 31, 2014, (2014) Min Si Ta Zi No. 32.

To the High People's Court of Zhejiang Province:

The Request for Instructions on the Case Concerning the Application of Allenberg Cotton Co., Ltd. for Recognition and Enforcement of a Foreign Arbitral Award against Ningbo Youngor International Trade & Transportation Co., Ltd. [(2014)Zhe Shang Wai Que Zi No. 1] submitted by your court has been received. After deliberation, the replies are as follows:

This is a case concerning the application for recognition and enforcement of an arbitral award made by the International Cotton Association in the United Kingdom. As both China and the United Kingdom are contracting states of the Convention on the Recognition and Enforcement of Foreign Arbitral Awards, the review in this case shall be conducted in accordance with the relevant provisions of the Convention.

According to the situation stated in the Request for Instructions of your court, Allenberg Cotton Co., Ltd. ("**Allenberg**") and Ningbo Youngor International Trade & Transportation Co., Ltd. ("**Youngor**") signed the No. 347450 and No. 347460 Cotton Purchase Agreements on August 152,008.The parties signed the No. 348990 Cotton Purchase Agreement on September 9, 2008. Cotton Purchase Agreements provided for the purchase of a total amount of 2,000 tons of cotton with Youngor as the buyer and Allenberg as the seller. The Agreements also stipulated that any dispute related to the Cotton Purchase Agreements shall be arbitrated in Liverpool, the United Kingdom, in accordance with the arbitration rules of International Cotton Association and the applicable law shall be the law of the United Kingdom. After signing the Agreements, disputes arose between the parties due to the failure of Youngor to perform its obligation to issue Letter of Credit under the Agreements. Allenberg submitted the dispute to the International Cotton Association for arbitration on December 14, 2009. However, Youngor raised an objection against the authenticity of the aforementioned three Cotton Purchase Agreements, claiming that the seal on the Agreements was not Youngor's corporate seal and neither did Youngor entrust the so-called senior representative Wu Yien to confirm the Agreements. According to the statements of Allenberg, the three Cotton Purchase Agreements were initially concluded orally and then confirmed by a senior representative of Youngor, who immediately sent the written confirmation letters afterwards. Allenberg claimed that the so-called written confirmation letters were in fact the three Cotton Purchase Agreements, which were signed by fax. However, Allenberg could not specify the specific fax number through which the agreements were signed, and neither could it prove connection between the fax number and Youngor. Allenberg alleged that the three Cotton Purchase Agreements were confirmed by the senior representative of Youngor, Wu Yien, without any evidence. There was no evidence to prove that

Wu Yien was authorized by Youngor and neither did Wu Yien sign the three Cotton Purchase Agreements. Regarding the authenticity of the seals, the attorney designated by the arbitral tribunal for professional opinion stated in the legal opinion that the issue should be reviewed by the arbitral tribunal and the legal opinion he/she issued was based on the assumption that the seals of Youngor were authentic. The arbitral tribunal concluded in the award that the seals of Youngor on the threeCotton Purchase Agreements were highlysimilar to the seals on the two pieces of documents submitted by Youngor and held accordingly that the two pieces of documents submitted by Youngor were evidenceagainst Youngor. The arbitral tribunal considered that the arbitration agreements were valid based on its knowledge and understanding of the law of the United Kingdom without clarifying detailed reasons or legal basis.

The premise of the validity of an arbitration clause or agreement is that the parties reached consensus on resolving disputes through arbitration. It is also the premise for an arbitration institution to accept arbitration cases. However, in the present case, Allenberg could not prove the authenticity of Youngor's seal on the three Cotton Purchase Agreements or that Wu Yien had the right to represent Youngor. Therefore, there is no valid evidence showing that Youngor and Allenberg have reached a consensus on resolving the disputes arising out of the Cotton Purchase Agreements. It lacked a factual and legal basis for the International Cotton Association to accept the case.

In summary, the opinion in the Request for Instructions of your court that the arbitral award issued byInternational Cotton Association on September 9, 2011 regarding Nos. 347450, 347,460 and 348,990 Cotton Purchase Agreements shall not be recognized was agreed upon.

It is so replied.

28. **Reply of the Supreme People's Court to the Request for Instructions on the Case Concerning Non-Recognition and Non-Enforcement of the No. 2/11 Arbitral Award rendered by the Waren-Verein Der Hamburger Borse E.V.**
    June 30, 2014, (2014) Min Si Ta Zi No. 31.

To the High People's Court of Liaoning Province:

The Request for Instructions on the Case Concerning Non-Recognition and Non-Enforcement of the No. 2/11 Arbitral Award rendered by the Waren-Verein Der Hamburger Borse E.V. [(2014) Liao Min San Ta Zi No. 00001] submitted by your court has been received. After deliberation, the replies are as follows:

This case concerns an application for recognition and enforcement of a foreign arbitral award. Pursuant to Article 183 of the Civil Procedure Law of the People's Republic of China, the people's court shall apply the relevant stipulations of the Convention on the Recognition and Enforcement of Foreign Arbitral Awards ("**New York Convention**") to examine the case.

According to the facts stated in the Request for Instructions of your court and the case materials, the arbitral tribunal sent documents including the appointment of arbitrators, Request for Arbitration, summons, etc., to the respondent, Dandong Junao Food Co., Ltd. by registered mail through Deutsche Post AG. The certificate issued by Deutsche Post AG stated that the mail has been "delivered to the legal recipient" but "have not received the receipt or any other form of confirmation of deliveryfrom the postal institution in the destination country." Dandong Junao Food Co., Ltd. only claimed that it had not received the materials without producing any evidence to prove that the procedure of the notice of the arbitral tribunal did not comply with the "proper notice" requirement prescribed in Article 5(1)(b) of the New York Convention, i.e., the arbitral tribunal did not properly inform the respondent of the appointment of the arbitrators, the arbitration proceedings, etc. or the means of notification were against the applicable arbitration rules or the laws of the place of arbitration, etc., and in consequence, the respondent was unable to present his case. Therefore, there are nocircumstances prescribed in Article 5(1)(b) of the New York Convention in the arbitral award in the present case. Under the situation where there are no other circumstances prescribed in other provisions of Article 5 of the New York Convention, the arbitral award involved in the present case shall be recognized and enforced.

It is so replied.

29. **Reply of the Supreme People's Court to the Request for Instructions on the Case Concerning the Application of Shi Dong Rubber Co., Ltd.for Non-Enforcement of a Foreign-related Arbitral Award against Triangle Tire Co., Ltd.**
    March 22, 2013, (2013) Min Si Ta Zi No. 12.

To the High People's Court of Shandong Province:

The Report of Request for Instructions on the Case Concerning the Application of Shi Dong Rubber Co., Ltd. for Non-Enforcement of a Foreign-related Arbitral Award against Triangle Tire Co., Ltd. [(2012) Lu Zhi Qing Zi No. 2] submitted by your court has been received. After deliberation, the replies are as follows:

This is a case concerning the application for non-enforcement of aforeign-related arbitral award made by a domestic arbitration institution. According to Article 7 of the Provisions of the Supreme People's Court on Several Issues Concerning the Application of Law to the Cases That Are Pending When the Civil Procedure Law as Amended Takes Effect, the case shall be reviewed in accordance with Article 258 of the Civil Procedure Law of the People's Republic of China (2007 Amendment).

According to the facts stated in the Report of Request for Instructions of your court, Shi Dong Rubber Co., Ltd. ("**Shi Dong**") only provided a copy of the contract that contained an arbitration clause, while Triangle Tire Co., Ltd. ("**Triangle**") did not acknowledge the authenticity of such a copy and denied that there was a valid arbitration agreement between the parties. Shi Dong failed to provide other corroborating evidence and was unable to prove that it had reached a valid arbitration agreement with Triangle. Even if the authenticity of the copy of the contract wasconfirmed, in terms of the process for concluding contract confirmed by the parties, after Triangle faxed the offer to Shi Dong, Shi Dong made material changes to the

contents, such as the parties, the amount of goods, the prices, etc., which constituted a new offer. Shi Dong also failed to prove that Triangle had accepted the offer.
Therefore, the contract was not established between the parties.To take a step back,
even if the contract is presumed to be established based on the behavior of the parties
to actually perform the contract, according to the written requirement of an arbitration agreement and the principle of independence of the arbitration agreement under
the law in China, it cannot be concluded that the parties had reached an arbitration
agreement on the method of dispute resolution. Moreover, based on the fact found
by the court of first instance, the contract that the parties actually performed was a
spot sales contract thatwas not involved in the present case and did not contain an
arbitration clause, rather than the contract containing an arbitration clause provided
by Shi Dong. Therefore, there was no valid written arbitration agreement between
Shi Dong and Triangle.

In summary, there exists the circumstance prescribed in Item 1, Paragraph 1 of
Article 258 of the Civil Procedure Law of the People's Republic of China with the
arbitral award involved in this case, and people's court shall not enforce it. The
opinion of the adjudication committee of your court is agreed upon.

It is so replied.

30.   **Reply of the Supreme People's Court to the Request for Instructions on
the Case Concerning the Application of Chengdu Youbang Stationery Co.,
Ltd. and Wang Guojian for the Revocation of the (2011) Shen Zhong Cai
Zi No. 601 Arbitral Award Made by Shenzhen Arbitration Commission.**
March 20, 2013, (2013) Min Si Ta Zi No. 9

To the High People's Court of Guangdong Province:

The Request for Instructions on the Case Concerning the Application of Chengdu
Youbang Stationery Co., Ltd. and Wang Guojian for the Revocation of the (2011)
Shen Zhong Cai Zi No. 601 Arbitral Award Made by Shenzhen Arbitration Commission [(2012)Yue Gao Fa Zhong Fu Zi No. 2] submitted by your court has been
received. After deliberation, the replies are as follows:

This is a case involving the application for revoking a Hong Kong-related arbitral
award made by a domestic arbitration institution. The Guarantee Contract involved
in the case did not contain an arbitration clause. The opinion of the arbitral tribunal
thatthere was an arbitration clause in the Master Contract, the Guarantee Contract as
an accessory contract shall be bound by the arbitration clause in the Master Contract
lacks legal basis. As the arbitral tribunal tried and made an award on the Guarantee
Contract that did not contain an arbitration agreement, the reason for the guarantor
Wang Guojian's application to revoke the part of arbitral award involving him as
the guarantor is established. Considering Wang Guojian, Qi Xiang and Chen Jianjun
were joint guarantors who shared the same legal status, and the award involving the
above three guarantors was stated in Item 4 of the award, the people's court shall
revoke this inseparable part.

In summary, pursuant to Article 70 of the Arbitration Law of the People's Republic of China and Item 1, Paragraph 1 of Article 274 of the Civil Procedure Law of the People's Republic of China, Item 4 of the award and part of Item 6, which required the three guarantors to jointly bear the arbitration expenses, shall be revoked.

It is so replied.

31. **Reply of the Supreme People's Court to the Request for Instructions on the Case Concerning the Application of Wang Guolin for the Revocation of the (2012) Zhong Guo Mao Zhong Shen Cai Zi No. 3 Arbitral Award Made by China International Economic and Trade Arbitration Commission South China Sub-commission.**
     February 26, 2013, (2013) Min Si Ta Zi No. 8

To the High People's Court of Guangdong Province:

The Request for Instructions on the Case Concerning the Application of Wang Guolin for the Revocation of the (2012) Zhong Guo Mao Zhong Shen Cai Zi No. 3 Arbitral Award Made by China International Economic and Trade Arbitration Commission South China Sub-commission [(2012)Yue Gao Fa Zhong Fu Zi No. 4] submitted by your court has been received. After deliberation, the replies are as follows:

This is a case involving the application for revoking a Taiwan-related arbitral award made by a domestic arbitration institution, which shall be reviewed in accordance with Article 70 of the Arbitration Law of the People's Republic of China and Paragraph 1 of Article 274 of the Civil Procedure Law of the People's Republic of China (2012 Amendment).

Regarding the validity of the arbitration clause, the parties have agreed to an explicit arbitration agreement in the contract involved in the present case. According to the principle of the independence of the arbitration clause, the invalidity of the contract involved does not affect the validity of the arbitration clause therein. Your court's opinion that the arbitration clause involved in the present case was valid is agreed upon.

Regarding the issue of whether the award is *ultrapetita*, in the present case, Wu Shuochen applied for arbitration,requesting Wang Guolin to pay the balance of equity transfer based on the validity of the contract. The arbitral tribunal was empowered to review the validity of the contract involved and to determine its own initiative. However, it indeed exceeded the scope of the parties' submissions and constituted *an ultrapetita* award for the arbitral tribunal to render the award on the return of property and liability for damages without clarifying the consequences of the invalidity of the contract and giving the parties the chance of modifying their claims. The people's court may revoke the arbitral award involved by reference to Article 70 of the Arbitration Law of the People's Republic of China and Item 4, Paragraph 1 of Article 274of the Civil Procedure Lawof the People's Republic of China. However, in view of the specific circumstances about the subject matter of the case and the arbitral tribunal's ability to rectify the aforementioned mistake, the people's court may provide an opportunity to rearbite to the arbitral tribunal. As a consequence, for the specific handling of this case, the people's court shall notify the arbitral tribunal to rearbitate in accordance with Article 61 of the Arbitration Law of the People's Republic of China. If the arbitral tribunal refuses to rearbite, the people's court may revoke the arbitral award involved.

It is so replied.

32. Reply of the Supreme People's Court to the Request for Instructions on the Case Concerning the Application of Ecom USA. Inc. for Enforcement of a Foreign-Related Arbitral Award.

February 6, 2013, (2013) Min Si Ta Zi No. 3

To the High People's Court of Guangxi Zhuang Autonomous Region:

The Request for Instructions on the Case Concerning the Application of Ecom USA.Inc.for Enforcement of a Foreign-Related Arbitral Award [(2012) Gui Qing Zi No. 19] submitted by your court has been received. After deliberation, the replies are as follows:

Although the quotation of the same kind of goods ascertained by the arbitral tribunal was not cross-examined by the parties, the quotation was a well-known price. The amount of compensation awarded by the arbitral award was far less than the amount requested, and the arbitral award did not exceed the scope of the arbitration request. When determining the assumption of attorney fees, the arbitral tribunal did not accept the evidence submitted by the applicant beyond the period of submitting evidence. Moreover, issues with evidence are not the same as issues with the arbitration proceedings. Therefore, the issue in your court's Request for Instructions does not fall within the circumstance where the arbitration proceedings are inconsistent with the arbitration rules. If there are no other statutory circumstances for not enforcing an arbitral award, the (2007) Zhong Guo Mao Zhong Jing Cai Zi No. 0161 arbitral award should be enforced. The opinion of your court is agreed.

It is so replied.

33. Reply of the Supreme People's Court to the Request for Instructions on the Case Concerning the Application of Northern Wanbang Logistics Co., Ltd. for the Revocation of the (2012) Hai Zhong Jing CaiZi No. 001Arbitral Award.

January 22, 2013, (2013) Min Si Ta Zi No. 5

To the High People's Court of Tianjin:

The Request for Instructions on the Case Concerning the Application of Northern Wanbang Logistics Co., Ltd. for the Revocation of the (2012) Hai Zhong Jing Cai Zi No. 001 Arbitral Award [(2012)Jin Gao Min Si Ta Zi No. 6] submitted by your court has been received. After deliberation, the replies are as follows:

According to the facts provided by your court,the International Transportation Agency Contract signed by Northern Wanbang Logistics Co., Ltd. ("**Wanbang**") and Zhuoyu Group Co., Ltd. ("**Zhuoyu**") stipulated that "Any disputes arising out of or in connection with this agreement shall be submitted to China Maritime Arbitration Commission for arbitration in Beijing in accordance with the arbitration rules effective when applying for arbitration." This agreement was the consensus the two parties have reached regarding the method of contractual dispute resolution, so it is not inappropriate for Zhuoyu to apply for arbitration before the arbitral institution. The counterclaims raised by Wanbang against Zhuoyu shall also be bound by the arbitration clause in the International Transportation Agency Contract concluded by the two parties. It is consistent with relevant laws for the arbitral tribunal to rule on such counterclaims. However, the arbitration clause can only bind the parties to the contract, i.e., Wanbang and Zhuoyu. As the first claimant, Jinyuan Mining Co., Ltd. ("**Jinyuan**") applied for arbitration before the arbitration institution against Wanbang. Jinyuan did not provide any evidence to prove that there was a valid arbitration clause between Jinyuan and Wanbang. After Wanbang raised an objection to jurisdiction, it lacked factual basis and legal basis for the arbitral tribunal to determine in accordance with Article 403 of the Contract Law of the People's Republic of China that it had jurisdiction over Jinyuan, and to rule that the arbitration proceedings shall continue between Jinyuan, Zhuoyu and Wanbang. The arbitral award involved in this case involves the rights and obligations of Zhuoyu, Wanbang and Jinyuan, but there is no valid arbitration agreement between the three parties. Therefore, the arbitral award involved violated Article 4 of the Arbitration Law, which stipulates, "The parties settling disputes by means of arbitration shall reach an arbitration agreement on a mutually voluntary basis. An arbitration commission shall not accept an application for arbitration submitted by one of the parties in the absence of an arbitration agreement."

Your court's opinion that the (2012) Hai Zhong Jing CaiZi No. 001 arbitral award made by China Maritime Arbitration Commission shall be revoked is agreed.

It is so replied.

34.   **Reply of the Supreme People's Court to the Request for Instructions on the Case Concerning the Application of "Angfohuapin" Joint Venture Co., Ltd. for Recognition and Enforcement of an International Arbitral Award Made by the Belarusian Chamber of Commerce and Industry.**
      November 2, 2012, (2012) Min Si Ta Zi No. 42.

To the High People's Court of Henan Province:

The Request for Instructions on the Case Concerning the Application of "Angfohuapin" Joint Venture Co., Ltd. for Recognition and Enforcement of an International Arbitral Award Made by the Belarusian Chamber of Commerce and Industry has been received. After deliberation, the replies are as follows:

Concerning whether there was the circumstancefornonrecognition and non-enforcementprescribed in Article 5(1)(b) in the New York Conventionin the arbitral award involved in the present case, i.e., whether the respondent in the arbitration was not given proper notice of the appointment of the arbitrator or of the arbitration proceedings, the arbitration rules agreedupon by the parties shall be applied to determine whether the service of the arbitration proceedings constitutes proper notice, rather than the Hague Service Convention or the Treaty between the People's Republic of China and the Republic of Belarus on Civil and Criminal Judicial Assistance. Pursuant to Chapter 20 of the Rules of the International Arbitration Court of the Belarusian Chamber of Commerce and Industry, Request for Arbitration, Statement of Defense, notification, arbitral award and other rulings made by the arbitral tribunal shall be delivered to the recipient by registered mail or mail with receipt from the recipient. Unless otherwise agreed upon by the parties, mailed to the recipient's usual residence, the corporate residence or postal address shall be deemed to have been received. Therefore, it does not violate the arbitration rules agreed upon by the parties for the International Arbitration Court of the Belarusian Chamber of Commerce and Industry to serve the domicile of the respondent in the arbitration by mail.

Concerning the evidence of mail, "Angfohuapin" Joint Venture Co., Ltd. provided the courier company's mailing slips and receipts copied from the arbitration file, which stamped with the official seal of the International Arbitration Court of the Belarusian Chamber of Commerce and Industry and the signature of the chairman. As these two pieces of evidence were made outside the territory of the People's Republic of China, in accordance with Article 11 of Several Provisions of the Supreme People's Court on Evidence in Civil Proceedings, a reasonable time period may be determined by the accepting court, and the applicant may handle notarization and certification or go through the corresponding certification procedures through judicial assistance to prove that the abovementioned evidence is consistent with the retained documents in the arbitration file.

In conclusion, the respondent bears the burden of proof regarding the existence of any circumstances for denying recognition and enforcement prescribed in Article 5(1) of the New York Convention. The evidence currently available cannot prove that the respondent was not given proper notice, so the denying reason alleged by the respondent cannot be established. If there is no other circumstance for nonrecognition and non-enforcement in the arbitral award involved in this case, the court shall rule to recognize and enforce the arbitral award.

It is so replied.

35. **Reply of the Supreme People's Court to the Request for Instructions on the Case Concerning the Application of Singapore Zhongtian Investment (Group) Co., Ltd. for Revocation of an Arbitral Award Made by China International Economic and Trade Arbitration Commission.**
    October 25, 2012, (2012) Min Si Ta Zi No. 47.

To the High People's Court of Beijing:

The Request for Instructions on the Case Concerning the Application of Singapore Zhongtian Investment (Group) Co., Ltd. for Revocation of an Arbitral Award Made by China International Economic and Trade Arbitration Commission [Jing Gao Fa (2012) No. 251] submitted by your court has been received. After deliberation, the replies are as follows:

This is a case concerning the application for revocation of a foreign-related arbitral award, so it shall be reviewed in accordance with Article 70 of the Arbitration Law of the People's Republic of China and Article 258 of the Civil Procedure Law of the People's Republic of China. The reasonfor the application for revocation by Singapore Zhongtian Investment (Group) Co., Ltd. is that the constitution of the arbitral tribunal in the present case is inconsistent with the arbitration rules. It held that there was a close personal relationship between the arbitrator Yang Song and Xu Shuangquan, the representative of the respondent (the applicant in the arbitration) Huludao Port Logistics Co., Ltd., and the said arbitrator did not disclose such personal relationship, which was inconsistent with the relevant provisions of Article 25 of the Arbitration Rules of China International Economic and Trade Arbitration Commission (2005).

According to the content of the Report of Request for Instructions, Xu Shuangquan graduated from Liaoning University and is the director of Beijing Yingke(Shenyang) Law Firm. The Arbitrator Yang Song is the dean of the Law School of Liaoning University and has delivered a guest speech at the opening ceremony of Beijing Yingke (Shenyang) Law Firm. Viewed from the actual situations available now, Xu Shuangquan and Yang Song only share the same education background and attend the same ceremony. There is no direct teacher-student relationship or any relation with significant interest between them. Such relationships are not sufficient to constitute the impact on the independence and impartiality of the arbitration. Therefore, the facts above are insufficient to determine that there is a close social relationship that may influence the independence and impartiality of arbitration between Xu Shuangquan and Yang Song. The reason for revocation asserted by Singapore Zhongtian Investment (Group) Co., Ltd., i.e., the constitution of the tribunal was inconsistent with the arbitration rules, does not fall within the statutory circumstance of revocation prescribed by Item 3, Paragraph 1 of Article 258 of the Civil Procedure Law of the People's Republic of China. Your court's opinion that the award involved shall be revoked is not agreed.

It is so replied.

36. **Reply of the Supreme People's Court to the Request for Instructions on the Case Concerning the Application of Western Bulk Pte. Ltd. for Recognition and Enforcement of an UK Arbitral Award.**
    May 21, 2012, (2012) Min Si Ta Zi No. 12.

The High People's Court of Tianjin:

The Request for Instructions on the Case Concerning the Application of Western BulkPte. Ltd. for Recognition and Enforcement of an UK Arbitral Award [(2001)Jin Gao Min Si Ta Zi No. 4] submitted by your court has been received. After deliberation, the replies are as follows:

First, regarding the validity of the arbitration clause, it was found in the Report of Request for Instructions of your court that the Voyage Charter Contract signed on August 1, 2008 and provided by Western Bulk Pte. Ltd. only had the seal and signature of Western Bulk Pte. Ltd. while those of Beijing Sinosteel Tiantie Steel Trading Co.,

Ltd. ("**Sinosteel Tiantie**") were missing. However, when sending a notice to Western Bulk Pte. Ltd.On March 13, 2009, the liquidation team acknowledged the signature of the Contract and the fact that it had performed the voyage charter in 2008 in accordance with the Contract and appointed Chen Bo as the arbitrator. Although raising the objection to the authenticity of theContract in present, Sinosteel Tiantie has not provided sufficient contrary evidence. The authenticity of the Voyage Charter Contract shall be recognized, and the arbitration clause in the said Contract shall be binding on both parties. It lacks sufficient factual basis for your court to hold that there is no sufficient evidence to prove that the two parties had reached the consensus on arbitration and reached a written arbitration agreement.

Second, regarding the constitution of the arbitral tribunal, Article 39 of the Voyage Charter Contract involved in the case stipulated that "The disputes shall be resolved by the sole arbitrator the parties agree to appoint; if one party fails to reply to the arbitrator appointed by the Notice of Arbitration sent by the other party, the arbitrator shall be the sole arbitrator adjudicating the disputes. If the parties cannot agree on the appointment of a sole arbitrator within 14 days after the service of notice, the disputes shall be resolved by two arbitrators with each party appointing one arbitrator. If the two arbitrators cannot reach a consensus on any issue, the two arbitrators shall appoint the third arbitrator." In the case at hand, after the claimant Western Bulk Pte. Ltd.sent the notice of appointing Michael Baker-Harber as the arbitrator, Sinosteel Tiantie did not agree with the appointment of Michael Baker-Harberand appointed Chen Bo as the other arbitrator. Therefore, the condition for the appointment of a sole arbitrator was not satisfied, and the tribunal was composed of two arbitrators. Afterwards, since Chen Bo resigned as the arbitrator, the issue involved in this case arose regarding how to fill the vacancy of the arbitral tribunal. Pursuant to Paragraph 2 and Paragraph 3 of Article 27, Paragraph 7 of Article 16 and Paragraph 2 of Article 18 of the Arbitration Act 1996 of the United Kingdom, the claimant shall apply to the court for the decision on the constitution of the arbitral tribunal after notifyingthe respondent. However, the claimant in the present case, Western Bulk Pte. Ltd., did not apply to the court, but the arbitrator appointed by it conducted a sole arbitration. The constitution of the arbitral tribunal was not consistent with the arbitration clause and the Arbitration Act 1996 of the United Kingdom. Pursuant to Article 5(1)(d) of the Convention on the Recognition and Enforcement of Foreign Arbitral Awards ("**New York Convention**"), if an arbitral award falls within the situation where "the composition of the arbitral authority or the arbitral procedure was not in accordance with the agreement of the parties, or, failing such agreement, was not in accordance with the law of the country where the arbitration took place", the arbitral award shall not be recognized or enforced.

Third, regarding the service method of arbitration documents and arbitration proceedings, the notice clause in Article 49 of the Voyage Charter Contract involved in the case agreed on the means, language and recipient addresses to be used for mutual notification during the performance of the Contract. Before the cancellation of Sinosteel Tiantie, the parties had been in touch with each other in accordance with the agreement. It lacks factual basis for your court to consider that the parties have not agreed on the means of communication to be used on the ground that the clause did not stipulate that it shall apply to the arbitration proceedings. On April 21, 2009, after the cancellation of Sinosteel Tiantie, Western Bulk Pte. Ltd. and the arbitrator have sent relevant arbitration documents to Sinosteel Tiantie, shareholders, the members and legal counsels of the liquidation team via fax, email, express courier service and delivery by designated person, etc., which did not violate the relevant laws and regulations. It lacks factual and legal basis for your court to hold that the arbitral award involved shall not be recognized or enforced on the ground that the method of service of arbitration documents is illegal and shall not be viewed as valid delivery and the arbitration proceedings are illegal.

Fourth, regarding the principle of public policy, pursuant to Article 5(2)(b) of the New York Convention, where the Chinese court considers that the arbitral award is contrary to the public policy of China, the court may refuse to recognize or enforce it. However, the public policy stipulated in the provision shall be strictly interpreted and applied. Only when the recognition and enforcement of foreign commercial arbitral awards will be contrary to the fundamental principles of the law of China, interfere in the sovereignty of China, threaten national and public social security, or harm the good customs and other fundamental values of China can the ground of public policy be cited for the refusal of recognition and enforcement. It is inappropriate for your court to refuse to recognize and enforce the arbitral award on the ground that the result of arbitration is grossly unfair and contrary to the social public interest of China.

In conclusion, your court's conclusion that the award shall not be recognized or enforced because the constitution of the arbitral tribunal is contrary to the law of the seat of arbitration is agreed.

It is so replied.

37. **Reply of the Supreme People's Court to the Request for Instructions on the Case Concerning the Recognition and Enforcement of the No. 26–435-08 Arbitral Award Made by Dispute Resolution Center of the United States.**
    June 30, 2011, [2011] Min Si Ta Zi No. 21.

To the High People's Court of Beijing:

The Request for Instructions on the Case Concerning the Recognition and Enforcement of the No. 26–435-08 Arbitral Award Made by Dispute Resolution Center of the United States {Jing Gao Fa [2011] No. 157} submitted by your court has been received. After deliberation, the replies are as follows:

This is a case concerning an application for recognition and enforcement of an arbitral award made by an arbitration institution in the United States. As China and the United States are contracting states of the Convention on the Recognition and Enforcement of Foreign Arbitral Awards, the relevant provisions of the Convention shall apply to the review in the present case.

According to the statements in your court's Report of Request for Instructions, the Dispute Resolution Center of the United States mailed the notice of appointment of arbitrators to Beijing Tepu Food Co., Ltd. ("**Tepu**") on September 9, 2008, with the address "D-901, Jiarun Garden, Guangshun Street, Wangjing, Chaoyang District, Beijing". However, the mail was returned on the ground of "moving". Afterwards, although theDispute Resolution Center of the United States mailed other documents to Tepu, it did not deliver the notice of appointment of arbitrators to Tepu again. Viewed from the two opinions requested for Instructions by your court, the focus of the present case is whether the respondent Tepu received the notice of appointment of arbitrators and whether there exists the situation stipulated in Article 5(1) (b) of the Convention on the Recognition and Enforcement of Foreign Arbitral Awards in this case, i.e., "The party against whom the award is invoked was not given proper notice of the appointment of the arbitrator or of the arbitration proceedings or was otherwise unable to present his case."

As the two parties have agreed in the arbitration agreement that the arbitration shall be conducted in accordance with the Arbitration Rules of the United Nations Commission on International Trade and Law ("**UNCITRAL Arbitration Rules**"), and Dispute Resolution Center of the United States also confirmed in the notices sent to Tepu that the arbitration shall be conducted in accordance with the UNCITRAL Arbitration Rules, the issue of whether the notice of appointment of arbitrators has been validly delivered shall be reviewed in accordance with the UNCITRAL Arbitration Rules. Paragraph 1 of Article 2 of the UNCITRAL Arbitration Rules stipulates that "For the purposes of these Rules, any notice, including a notification, communication or proposal, is deemed to have been received if it is physically delivered to the addressee or if it is delivered at his habitual residence, place of business or mailing address, or, if none of these can be found after making reasonable inquiry, then at the addressee's last-known residence or place of business. Notice shall be deemed to have been received on the day it is so delivered."

Your court's Report of Request for Instructions has not identified whether "D-901 Jiarun Garden, Guangshun Street, Wangjing, Chaoyang District, Beijing" was the habitual residence, place of business or mailing address, or its last-known residence or place of business of Tepu. Your court shall make further examinations into this issue. Pursuant to Paragraph 1 of Article 2 of the UNCITRAL Arbitration Rules, if the address "D-901 Jiarun Garden, Guangshun Street, Wangjing, Chaoyang District, Beijing"Dispute Resolution Center of the United States sent the notice of appointment of arbitrators to Tepu was the recipient's habitual residence, place of business or mailing address, or its last-known residence or place of business stipulated in the aforementioned Arbitration Rules, then even though such mail was not signed, it shall be deemed to have been validly delivered. The people's court shall not refuse to recognize and enforce the arbitral award based on Article 5(1)(b) of the Convention on the Recognition and Enforcement of Foreign Arbitral Awards. In contrast, if the address was not the habitual residence, place of business or mailing address, or its last-known residence or place of business of Tepu, and the mail was actually returned, then it shall be determined that Dispute Resolution Center of the United States did not appropriately serve upon the recipient the notice of appointment of arbitrators, and thus, the people's court shall refuse to recognize and enforce the arbitral award in accordance with Article 5(1)(b) of the Convention on the Recognition and Enforcement of Foreign Arbitral Awards.

It is so replied.

38. **Reply of the Supreme People's Court to the Request for Instructions on the Case Concerning the Revocation of the(2009) CIETACBJ No. 0355Award Made by China International Economic and Trade Arbitration Commission.**

April 22, 2011, [2011] Min Si Ta Zi No. 13.

To the High People's Court of Beijing:

The Request for Instructions on the Case Concerning the Revocation of the (2009) CIETAC BJ No. 0355 Award Made by China International Economic and Trade Arbitration Commission {Jing Gao Fa [2011] No. 67} submitted by your court has been received. After deliberation, the replies are as follows:

First, there is no valid arbitration clause in the Joint Venture Contract of Qingdao VEM Machinery Co., Ltd. signed by Qingdao Jiacheng Engineering Co., Ltd. and VEM Company. Qingdao Jiacheng Engineering Co., Ltd. did not agree to arbitrate in regard to contractual disputes, so the arbitral tribunal did not have jurisdiction over the disputes arising out of the Contract. The joint venture contract involved in the case was signed between Qingdao Jiacheng Engineering Co., Ltd., VEM Company and Simest S.P.A., and there was a clear and valid arbitration clause therein. Therefore, the arbitraltribunal may arbitrate the disputes over the Contract.

Second, pursuant to Article 181 of the Company Law of the People's Republic of China, there is no legal basis for an arbitration institution to render an award on dissolving a company, which is outside its authority to arbitrate.

Third, the arbitral award involved in the present case was made based on the determination that the two joint venture contracts were invalid and the dissolution of the joint venture company. Since the arbitral award was generally inseparable, the arbitral award shall be revoked in accordance with Article 70 of the Arbitration Law of the People's Republic of China and Item (a) and (d) of Paragraph 1 of Article 258 of the Civil Procedure Law of the People's Republic of China. Your court's opinion of request for Instructions is agreed.

It is so replied.

39. **Reply of the Supreme People's Court to the Request for Instructionson the Case Concerning the Revocation of the (2010) Zhong Guo Mao Zhong Jing Cai Zi No. 0159 AwardMade by China International Economic and Trade Arbitration Commission.**

December 2, 2010, [2010] Min Si Ta Zi No. 49.

To the High People's Court of Beijing:

The Request for Instructions on the Case Concerning the Revocation of the (2010) Zhong Guo Mao Zhong Jing Cai Zi No. 0159 Award Made by China International Economic and Trade Arbitration Commission {Jing Gao Fa [2010] No. 262} submitted by your court has been received. After deliberation, the replies are as follows:

This case involves a Hong Kong-related arbitral award made by the China International Economic and Trade Arbitration Commission, which shall be reviewed by reference to relevant foreign-related provisions in the Civil Procedure Law of the People's Republic of China and the Arbitration Law of the People's Republic of China.

According to the facts found in your court's Report of Request for Instructions, Article 54 of the Contract for Beijing Jingyuan Printing Co., Ltd. ("**Joint Venture Contract**") signed by Beijing Yiyuan Art Service Center ("**Yiyuan Center**") and Jiangyuan Cultural Enterprise Company ("**Jiangyuan**") on December 30, 1991 stipulates that "Any disputes arising out of or in connection with this Contract shall be resolved by both parties through friendly negotiation. In the failure of negotiation, such disputes shall be submitted to the China International Economic and Trade Arbitration Commission for arbitration in accordance with the interim rules of the arbitration procedure. The arbitral award is final and binding upon both parties. Unless otherwise agreed, the arbitration fees shall be borne by the losing party." On May 29, 2007, the Amendment Agreement to the Contract for Beijing Jingyuan Printing Co., Ltd. ("**Amendment Agreement**") concluded by Yiyuan Center and Jiangyuan made amendments to the Joint Venture Contract and did not provide for the dispute resolution method separately. Jiangyuan submitted the dispute for arbitration in accordance with the arbitration clause in the Joint Venture Contract. There is legal basis for the arbitral tribunal to render the award on both the Joint Venture Contract and the Amendment Agreement in accordance with the arbitration clause in the Joint Venture Contract.

Article 2 of the Interpretation of the Supreme People's Court on Certain Issues Concerning the Application of the Arbitration Law of the People's Republic of China stipulates that "Where the parties generally agree that the matters agreed upon for arbitration are contractual disputes, any dispute arising from the establishment, validity, modification, assignment, performance, liability for breach of contract, interpretation or termination of the contract may be deemed as a matter agreed upon for arbitration." The arbitration clause in the Joint Venture Contract above has generally agreed that the matters agreed upon for arbitration are "any disputes arising out of or in connection with this Contract". Although the Amendment Agreement did not contain an arbitration clause, its contents regarding "the reduction of registered capital and the transfer of investment" belong to relevant matters of the modification of the Joint Venture Contract and therefore fall within the scope of the arbitration clause in the aforementioned Joint Venture Contract. The act of the arbitral tribunal to arbitrate the disputes under the Amendment Agreement regarding the modification of the Joint Venture Contract together did not exceed the scope of the submission to arbitration.

As there is no legal basis for the application for revocation of the (2010) Zhong Guo Mao Zhong Jing Cai Zi No. 0159 Award Made by the China International Economic and Trade Arbitration Commission, the application shall be rejected.

It is so replied.

40. **Reply of the Supreme People's Court to the Request for Instructions on the Case Concerning the Application of DMT Co., Ltd. (France) for Recognition and Enforcement of a Foreign Arbitral Award against Chaozhou Huaye Packaging Materials Co., Ltd. and Chao'an Huaye Packaging Materials Co., Ltd.**

October 12, 2010.

To the High People's Court of Guangdong Province:

The Request for Instructions on the Case Concerning the Application of DMT Co., Ltd. (France) for Recognition and Enforcement of a Foreign Arbitral Award against Chaozhou Huaye Packaging Materials Co., Ltd. and Chao'an Huaye Packaging Materials Co., Ltd. {[2010] Yue Gao Fa Min Si Ta Zi No. 2} submitted by your court has been received. After deliberation, the replies are as follows:

This is a case concerning the application for recognition and enforcement of the 13,450/EC Arbitral Award made by ICC (Singapore)International Court of Arbitration. Both China and Singapore are contracting states of the Convention on the Recognition and Enforcement of Foreign Arbitral Awards ("**New York Convention**"). Therefore, the issue of whether to recognize and enforce the arbitral award involved in the case shall be reviewed in accordance with the New York Convention.

Regarding the issue of whether Chaozhou Huaye Packaging Materials Co., Ltd. was a qualified respondent in this case, although the Arbitral Award listed "Chaozhou Huaye Packaging Materials Co., Ltd." as the respondent, the tribunal rendered a Supplementary Arbitral Award to change it to "Chao'an Huaye Packaging Materials Co., Ltd."before the applicant applied for recognition and enforcement. Chaozhou Huaye Packaging Materials Co., Ltd. was not a party to this arbitration case involved,and there was no dispute between it and the applicant. Hence, there is no foreign arbitral award that needs recognition and enforcement. The application of DMTCo., Ltd. (France) against Chaozhou Huaye Packaging Materials Co., Ltd. shall be dismissed.

Regarding the issue of whether the presiding arbitrator appointed by the arbitral tribunal was in compliance with the parties' agreement on the presiding arbitrator, Chao'an Huaye Packaging Materials Co., Ltd. did not raise any objection to the presiding arbitrator's Singaporean citizenship during the arbitration process. There is also no sufficient evidence to prove that the presiding arbitrator was not familiar with Chinese laws and had lost its independence. As a consequence,Chao'an Huaye Packaging Materials Co., Ltd. that the presiding arbitrator appointed by the arbitral tribunal was inconsistent with the parties' agreement cannot be established. Other reasons for refusal of recognitionand enforcement of the Arbitral Award raised by Chao'an Huaye Packaging Materials Co., Ltd.fall within the scope of substantive reviewand are outside the scope of review on the recognition and enforcement of foreign arbitral awards under the New York Convention. Therefore, Chao'an Huaye Packaging Materials Co., Ltd. for not recognizing or enforcing the 13,450/EC Arbitral Award cannot be established.

To conclude, your court's opinion of request for Instructions is agreed upon.

It is so replied.

41. **Reply of the Supreme People's Court to the Request for Instructions on the Case Concerning the Application of Louis Dreyfus Commodities (Asia) Co., Ltd. for Recognition and Enforcement of the No. 3980 Arbitral Award Made by Federation of Oils, Seeds and Fats Associations.**
     October 10, 2010, [2010] Min Si Ta Zi No. 48.

To the High People's Court of Guangdong Province:

TheRequest for Instructions on the Case Concerning the Application of Louis Dreyfus Commodities (Asia) Co., Ltd. for Recognition and Enforcement of the No. 3980 Arbitral Award Made by Federation of Oils, Seeds and Fats Associations [2009] Yue Gao Min Si Ta Zi No. 10 submitted by your court has been received. After deliberation, the replies are as follows:

The No. 3980 Arbitral Award made by the Federation of Oils, Seeds and Fats Associations involved in the case at hand was rendered in London, the United Kingdom, and thus is a foreign arbitral award. Both China and the United Kingdom are contracting states of the Convention on the Recognition and Enforcement of Foreign Arbitral Awards (**"New York Convention"**). Pursuant to Article 267 of the Civil Procedure Law of the People's Republic of China, the issue of whether to recognize and enforce the Arbitral Award involved shall be reviewed in accordance with the New York Convention.

According to the facts found in the Report of Request for Instructions of your court, the applicant Louis Dreyfus Commodities (Asia) Co., Ltd. (**"Louis Dreyfus"**) cannot provide evidence to prove the exact date on which it received the Arbitral Award. It is not inappropriate for your court to use August 29, 2007,the effective date of the Award involved, as the starting date of the application for recognition and enforcement. The Zhanjiang Intermediate People's Court (**"Zhanjiang Intermediate People's Court"**) received materials for the enforcement of Louis Dreyfus on February 13, 2008, and confirmed that it immediately informed Louis Dreyfus to resubmit the application for recognition. Louis Dreyfus immediately applied orally for recognition. Pursuant to Article 219 of the Civil Procedure Law of the People's Republic of China effective then, Louis Dreyfus has made the application to the Zhanjiang Intermediate People's Court within the statutory time limit.

Although the goods concerned were mixed with toxic seed-coating soybeans, such soybeans were picked out before unloading. There was no evidence to prove that this batch of goods had caused serious sanitation and safety and had harmed public health. The arbitrators considered that there was an apparent gap between the provisions of Chinese laws and regulations and the application in practice, but this misunderstanding will not make the recognition and enforcement of theArbitral Award contrary to the public policy of China. Therefore, it lacksa sufficient basis to reject the recognition and enforcement of the Arbitral Award on the ground of public policy.

In addition, the issueofwhether the act of the independent arbitrator affected the impartiality of the Arbitral Award does not fall within the scope of review stipulated in the New York Convention.

In conclusion, the arbitral awardinvolved in the case should be recognized and enforced.

It is so replied.

42.   **Reply of the Supreme People's Court to the Request for Instructions on the Case Concerning the Non-Recognition of the No. 07-11Arbitral Award Rendered by Japan Commercial Arbitration Association in Tokyo.**
      June 29, 2010, [2010] Min Si Ta Zi No. 32.

To the High People's Court of Jiangsu Province:

The Request for Instructions on the Case Concerning the Non-Recognition of the No. 07–11 Arbitral Award Rendered by Japan Commercial Arbitration Association in Tokyo {[2010] Su Zhi Min Zhong Shen Zi No. 0002} submitted by your court has been received. After deliberation, the replies are as follows:

The present case concerns the application of Japanese party Shin-Etsu Chemical Co., Ltd. ("**Shin-Etsu**") for recognition and enforcement of the No. 07–11 Arbitral Award made by Japan Commercial Arbitration Association ("**07–11 Award**") in Tokyo before the Chinese court. Both China and Japan are contracting states of the Convention on the Recognition and Enforcement of Foreign Arbitral Awards ("**New York Convention**"), so the issue of whether to recognize and enforce the Arbitral Award involved in the case shall be reviewed in accordance with the relevant provisions of the New York Convention.

First, according to the materials sent by your court, before making the 07–11 Award, JCAA had made the No. 04–05 Award which dismissed Shin-Etsu's request to confirm that the Long Term Sales and Purchase Agreement from January 2004 to December 31, 2008 can be performed on the ground that there has been no trust between the parties since July 2005 and it would be unfair to allow Shin-Etsu to request for damages after August 2005. Shin-Etsu's request in this arbitration was the damages for breach of contract during August 2005 to March 2008, whichimpliedly included the request to confirm that the agreement during the above period can be performed. Therefore, the matters concerned in this arbitration were identical to Shin-Etsu's request to confirm that the agreement can be performed, which constituted repeated acceptance. The parties expressly agreed in the arbitration agreement (clause) on the principle of finality of arbitration. The 07–11 Award violated the principle, so the arbitration proceedings were consistent with the parties' agreement. The application for recognition shall be rejected in accordance with Article 5(1)(d) of the New York Convention.

Second, the violation of public policy shall be limited to situations in which the consequences of recognizing an arbitral award wouldviolate the fundamental legal system and harm the fundamental social interests of China. There exist other circumstancesforrefusal to recognize, and it is inappropriate to apply the principle of public policy to reject the recognition of the arbitral award involved.

In conclusion, there exists the circumstance prescribed in Article 5(1)(d) of the New York Convention in the 07–11 Award, and thus the Award shall not be recognized.

It is so replied.

43. **Reply of the Supreme People's Court to the Request for Instructions Regarding the Non-Enforcement of the [2008] Zhong Guo Mao Zhong Jing Cai Zi No. 0379 Arbitral Award Made by China International Economic and Trade Arbitration Commission**

May 27, 2010, [2010] Min Si Ta Zi No. 21.

To the High People's Court of Jiangsu Province:

The Request for Instructions Regarding the Non-Enforcement of the [2008] Zhong Guo Mao Zhong Jing Cai Zi No. 0379 Arbitral Award Made by China International Economic and Trade Arbitration Commission {[2010] Su Zhi Min Zhong Shen Zi No. 0001} submitted by your court has been received. After deliberation, the replies are as follows:

Jinhao Company is a corporate legal person registered in Hong Kong. Its application for enforcing the [2008] Zhong Guo Mao Zhong Jing Cai Zi No. 0379 Arbitral Award shall be examined by reference to Article 258 of the Civil Procedure Law of the People's Republic of China.

The first item of the Arbitral Award was that Qingtian Company shall repay to the joint venture the interests obtained by violating the Cooperation Contract. As the joint venture was the subject of such interests, it shall be the joint venture to claim against Qingtian Company. Jinhao Company had no right to request arbitration substituting the joint venture. Based on the application of Jinhao Company, the arbitration institution arbitrated the issue of the interests Qingtian Company should repay to the joint venture, which, in essence, conducted arbitration over the dispute between the joint venture and Qingtian Company. However, the cooperation contract was signed between Jinhao Company and Qingtian Company, and the scope of the arbitration clause therein was limited to the disputes arising out of or in connection with the cooperation contract between Jinhao Company and Qingtian Company. Therefore, the arbitral tribunal has no power to arbitrate the disputes between the joint venture and Qingtian Company, and this item of the Arbitral Award shall not be enforced.

The second item of the Arbitral Award was that Qingtian Company shall compensate Jinhao Company for all expenses incurred by its efforts to stop the breach of contract behavior. As this matter involved the disputes arising out of the Cooperation Contract between Jinhao Company and Qingtian Company, which fell within the scope of the arbitration clause in the Cooperation Contract, the arbitration institution had the power to arbitrate the dispute, and this Item of the Arbitral Award shall be enforced.

The third item of the Arbitral Award was to dismiss all other requests by Jinhao Company. There is no content that should be enforced in thisitem of the arbitral award.

The fourth item of the arbitral awardwas about the undertaking of the arbitration fees. The arbitration institution had the power to render the award on the undertaking of arbitration fees. Consequently, this item of the arbitral award shall be enforced.

It is so replied.

44.　**Reply of the Supreme People's Court to the Request for Instructions on the Case Concerning the Application of Tianrui Hotel Investment Co., Ltd.for Recognition of an Arbitral Award againstHangzhou Yiju Hotel Management Co., Ltd.**

May 18, 2010, [2010] Min Si Ta Zi No. 18.

To the High People's Court of Zhejiang Province:

The Request for Instructions on the Case Concerning the Application of Tianrui Hotel Investment Co., Ltd. for Recognition of an Arbitral Award against Hangzhou Yiju Hotel Management Co., Ltd. {[2010] Zhe Shang Wai Ta Zi No. 3} submitted by your court has been received. After deliberation, the repliesare as follows:

The Arbitral Award involved in this case was made by the London Court of International Arbitration in the United Kingdom. Both China and the United Kingdom are contracting states of the Convention on the Recognition and Enforcement of Foreign Arbitral Awards ("**New York Convention**"), so this case shall be reviewed in accordance with the relevant provisions of the New York Convention.

This is a case concerning an arbitral award made by the London Court of International Arbitration (LCIA). As both the People's Republic of China and the United Kingdom are signatory states of the Convention on the Recognition and Enforcement of Foreign Arbitral Awards (the New York Convention), the case shall be reviewed according to Article 267 of the Civil Procedure Law of the People's Republic of China (the "Civil Procedure Law") and the relevant provisions in the New York Convention.

The nature of the Unit System Agreement concluded by Tianrui Hotel Investment Co., Ltd. and Hangzhou Yiju Hotel Management Co., Ltd. on October 28, 2004 was a commercial franchise contract. According to the franchise management system effective then, foreign companies that conduct commercial franchise business in China should carry out such businesses by establishing foreign invested enterprises and was also subject to the approval of the administrative competent authority. However, the Regulation on the Administration of Commercial Franchisespromulgated by the State Council, which came into effect since May 1, 2007, only stipulates that the commercial franchise contract shall be filed with the administrative competent authority afterwards without approval requirements. The filing system above belongs to the administrative provisions in the mandatory norms of administrative regulations, which does not affect the validity of civil contracts between the parties. The handling of the Unit System Agreement in the Arbitral Award does not violate the mandatory legal provision of China, let alone contradicting the public policy of China. Therefore, there does not exist thecircumstance prescribed in Article 5(2)(b) of the New York Convention in the present case. Disputes arising from the Unit Service Agreement between Super 8 Hotels (China) Co., Ltd. and Hangzhou Yiju

Hotel Management Co., Ltd. involved another legal relationship between different parties. Whether the result of the latter disputes was consistent with the Arbitral Award involved in not within the scope of review stipulated in Article 5 of the New York Convention.

In conclusion, in the present arbitral award, there are no circumstances prescribed in Article 5 of the New York Convention in the Arbitral Award involved in this case. The people's court shall recognize theArbitral Award involved in this case.

It is so replied.

45. **Reply of the Supreme People's Court to the Request for Instructions on the Case Concerning the Application of McLane Group International Trading Company of the United States and its Beijing Representative Office for the Revocation of the [2008] Xia Zhong Cai Zi No. 0379Arbitral Award.**
December 16, 2009, [2008] Min Si Ta Zi No. 43.

To the High People's Court of Fujian Province:

The Request for Instructions on the Case Concerning the Application of McLane Group International Trading Company of the United States and its Beijing Representative Office for the Revocation of the [2008] Xia Zhong Cai Zi No. 0379 Arbitral Award {[2009] Min Min Ta Zi No. 42} submitted by your court has been received. After deliberation, the replies are as follows:

The applicantMcLane Group International Trading Company is a company registered in the United States. This is a case regarding the application for setting aside a foreign-related arbitral award. The key issue disputed in the present case is whether the arbitration agreements signed by the parties in the Agency Sales agreement and its Supplementary Agreement were valid. The parties agreed in the Agency Sales agreement and its Supplementary Agreement that, if negotiation fails in the event of disputes, "any party has the right to request for arbitration before the arbitration institution in the location." Article 16 of the Interpretation of the Supreme People's Court on Certain Issues Concerning the Application of the Arbitration Law of the People's Republic of China stipulates that "The applicable law for the determination of validity of a foreign-related arbitration agreement shall be the applicable law as agreed upon by the parties; where the parties have not agreed upon an applicable law but have agreed upon the seat of arbitration, the law of the seat shall apply; where the parties have neither agreed upon the applicable law nor the seat of arbitration or where they fail to clearly agree upon the seat of arbitration, the law of the place where the court is located shall apply." As the parties in the present case did not agreed upon the applicable law for the determination of validity of the arbitration agreement, and neither did they agree upon the seat of arbitration, in accordance with the above provision, the law of the place where the court is located, i.e., the law of China shall apply to determine the validity of the arbitration agreement. The arbitration institution agreed upon by the parties in the arbitration agreement is "the arbitration commission in the location", but the issue to which parties' location the "location" refers is not clear. Moreover, it is unclear whether the place refers to the city, province or country where the party resides. Therefore, the agreement of the parties on the arbitration institution was unclear,and they did not reach any supplementary agreement. Article 18 of the Arbitration Law of the People's Republic of China stipulates that "If the arbitration matters or the arbitration commission are not agreed upon by the parties in the arbitration agreement, or if the relevant provisions are not clear, the parties may supplement the agreement. If the parties fail to agree upon the supplementary agreement, the arbitration agreement shall be invalid." Pursuant to the provision, the arbitration agreement in the present case shall be deemed invalid.

Even if the "location" is identified as the location of the city where the parties reside, as McLane Group International Trading Company of the United States Beijing Representative Office and Xiamen Dalutong Marketing Co., Ltd. who affixed its corporate seal to the Agency Sales Contract and the Supplementary Agreement are located in Beijing and Xiamen, respectively, the arbitration institutions the parties have agreed on are more than two. Article 5 of the Interpretation of the Supreme People's Court on Certain Issues Concerning the Application of the Arbitration Law of the People's Republic of China stipulates that "Where an arbitration agreement provides for two or more arbitration institutions, the parties may negotiate to choose one of them for arbitration; where the parties are unable to agree on the choice of an arbitration institution, the arbitration agreement shall be deemed as invalid." Article 6 stipulates that "Where the arbitration agreement stipulates that arbitration shall be conducted by an arbitration institution in a certain place and there is sole arbitration institution in that place, the arbitration institution shall be deemed as the agreed arbitration institution. Where there are more than two arbitration institutions in the place, the parties may agree to choose one of the arbitration institutions for arbitration; if the parties cannot agree on the choice of arbitration institution, the arbitration agreement shall be deemed invalid." As the parties in the present case did not reach a consensus on the choice of the arbitration institution, in accordance with the provisions above, the arbitration agreement shall be void.

In conclusion, the arbitration agreement signed between the parties in the present case shall be deemedvoid. Pursuant to Article 18 of the Interpretation of the Supreme People's Court on Certain Issues Concerning the Application of the Arbitration Law of the People's Republic of China, if the arbitration agreement is deemed invalid or revoked, it shall be deemed that there is no arbitration agreement. In addition, the applicant McLane Group International Trading Company of the United States Beijing Representative Office raised objection to the jurisdiction of the arbitral tribunal at the first hearing. Therefore, in accordance with Article 70 of the Arbitration Law of the People's Republic of China and Item 1, Paragraph 1 of Article 258 of the Civil Procedure Law of the People's Republic of China, the arbitral award in this case shall be revoked. Your court's opinion of request for Instructions is agreed.

In addition, as the arbitral award in the case at hand is foreign-related, Article 70 of the Arbitration Law of the People's Republic of China shall apply to its revocation. Your court should pay attention to the fact that it was wrong for the Xiamen Intermediate People's Court to cite Article 58 of the Arbitration Law of the People's Republic of China.

It is so replied.

46. **Reply of the Supreme People's Court to the Report of Review on the Case Concerning the Application of China-Base Ningbo Foreign Trade Co., Ltd. for Non-Enforcement of an Arbitral Award Made by Hong Kong International Arbitration Center.**
December 9, 2009, [2009] Min Si Ta Zi No. 42.

To the Superior People's Court of Zhejiang Province:

The Report of Review on the Case Concerning the Application of China-Base Ningbo Foreign Trade Co., Ltd. for Non-Enforcement of an Arbitral Award Made by Hong Kong International Arbitration Center {[2009] Zhe Zhi Ta Zi No. 2} submitted by your court has been received. After deliberation, the replies are as follows:

This case was filed because Addax Bv applied to the Ningbo Intermediate People's Court for the enforcement of an arbitral award made by Hong Kong International Arbitration Center and China-Base Ningbo Foreign Trade Co., Ltd. ("**China-Base Ningbo**") filed a defense application for non-enforcement. Therefore, the case shall be reviewed in accordance with Article 7 of Arrangements of the Supreme People's Court on Mutual Enforcement of Arbitral Awards between the Mainland and the Hong Kong Special Administrative Region {Fa Shi [2000] No. 3}. The main reason that Ningbo Trade applied for non-enforcement is that it had not received the proper notice of appointment of arbitrators.

According to the facts stated in your court's report, Hong Kong International Arbitration Center sent the notice of appointment of arbitrators via fax and double registered mail to China-Base Ningbo according to its fax number and the address stipulated in the Mixed Aromatics Installment Supply Contract and requested it to "reply before August 1" on July 18, 2006. Regarding this fact, China-Base Ningbo alleged that the aforementioned fax number was no longer used when Hong Kong International Arbitration Center sent the fax and the double registered mail "was received on August 17, so that it was impossible to reply before August 1." With regard to the allegation mentioned above, first, pursuant to Article 2 of United Nations Commission on International Trade Law Arbitration Rules, "Notice, Calculation of Periods of Time", the fax number prescribed by China-Base Ningbo in the Contract was the last known communication method in the present case, and thus the notice of appointment of arbitrators sent by Hong Kong International Arbitration Center according to the fax number shall be deemed to have been received by China-base Ningbo. Second, China-Base Ningbo failed to provide sufficient evidence to prove that the double registered mail "was received on August 17". Therefore, China-basedNingbo's application for non-enforcement cannot be established.

In conclusion, there is no circumstance of non-enforcement of arbitral awards stipulated in Article 7 of the Arrangements of the Supreme People's Court on Mutual Enforcement of Arbitral Awards between the Mainland and the Hong Kong Special Administrative Region in the present case. The arbitral award made by the Hong Kong International Arbitration Centershould be enforced.

It is so replied.

47. **Reply of the Supreme People's Court to the Report Concerning the Non-Recognition of the No. 73/23-06Arbitral Award Made by Court of Arbitration of Mongolia.**
    December 8, 2009, [2009] Min Si Ta Zi No. 46.

To the High People's Court of Zhejiang Province:

The Report Concerning the Non-Recognition of the No. 73/23–06 Arbitral Award Made by Court of Arbitration of Mongolia {[2009] Zhe Shang Wai Ta Zi No. 1} submitted by your court has been received. After deliberation, the replies are as follows:

This is a case of application for recognition and enforcement of a foreign arbitral award. Since the arbitral award involved in this case was rendered by the arbitration institution of Mongolia and both China and Mongolia are contracting states of the Convention on the Recognition and Enforcement of Foreign Arbitral Awards ("**New York Convention**"), pursuant to Article 267 of the Civil Procedure Law of the People's Republic of China and Article 1 of the New York Convention, the recognition and enforcement of the arbitral award involved shall be reviewed in accordance with relevant provisions in the New York Convention.

First, regarding the issue of validity of the arbitration clause involved in the present case, pursuant to Article 5(1)(a) of the New York Convention, only when, under the law applicable to the parties, or failing any indication thereon, under the law where the award is made, the agreement is not valid, can the court refuse to recognize and enforce the award. It is inconsistent with the provision above to refuse to recognize the award involved in accordance with the law of China.

Second, regarding the issue of the service of notices of arbitration proceedings, according to the facts ascertained in the Report of Request for Instructions, the No. 1677283941 express did not contain any notice of arbitration proceedings, while the No. 1681469484 express, which containedthe "Resolution procedure and arbitration hearing date", was not properly delivered to Zhejiang Zhancheng Construction Group Co., Ltd. ("**Zhancheng**"). As a consequence, Zhangcheng was unable to present its case at the hearing. Therefore, the present case falls within the circumstancejustifying the refusal of recognition and enforcement prescribed in Article 5(1)(b) of the New York Convention.

Third, regarding whether there is an authentic arbitration agreement between the parties, it can be determined that there was no "written agreement" between the parties andthat the people's court may refuse to recognize and enforce the award in accordance with Article 2(2) of the New York Conventionif Zhancheng can provide evidence to prove that the corporate seal of "Zhejiang Yaojiang Construction Group Co., Ltd." (Zhancheng's predecessor) affixed to the Contract concerned is not authentic.

Your court's opinion is agreed.

It is so replied.

48.   **Reply of the Supreme People's Court to the Report of Request for Instructions on the Case Concerning the Application of Ningbo Yongxin Auto Component Manufacturing Co., Ltd. for the Revocation of the Yong Zhong Cai Zi[2007] No. 44Arbitral Award Made by Ningbo Arbitration Commission.**

December 8, 2009, [2009] Min Si Ta Zi No. 46.

To the High People's Court of Zhejiang Province:

The Report of Request for Instructions on the Case Concerning the Application of Ningbo Yongxin Auto Component Manufacturing Co., Ltd. for the Revocation of the Yong Zhong Cai Zi [2007] No. 44 Arbitral Award Made by Ningbo Arbitration Commission {[2009] Zhe Shang Wai Ta Zi No. 2} submitted by your court has been received. After deliberation, the replies are as follows:

This is a case of the party's application for setting aside a foreign-related arbitral award made by Ningbo Arbitration Commission before the people's court. Consequently, the people's court shall conduct judicial review on the arbitral award in accordance with Article 70 of the Arbitration Law of the People's Republic of China and Paragraph 1 of Article 258 of the Civil Procedure Law of the People's Republic of China.

In the case at hand, CENTRAL Corporation of Korea submitted disputes under the Joint Venture Contract for arbitration in accordance with the arbitration clause in the Joint Venture Contract. Its requests included a request to terminate the joint venture contract and to dissolve the joint venture through liquidation. During arbitration, Ningbo Yongxin Auto Component Manufacturing Co., Ltd. raised the defense that the arbitral tribunal did not have power to arbitrate the issues of dissolution and liquidation of the joint venture, and the arbitral award still contained the content "The joint venture Ningbo Sente Auto Components Co., Ltd. shall be dissolved and to be liquidated according to law". Strictly speaking, the arbitral tribunal shall only arbitrate the issue of whether to terminate the joint venture contract between the parties. However, the inevitable legal consequence of the termination of the Sino-foreign Joint Venture Contract is that the joint venture established by the parties in accordance with the Joint Venture Contract will be dissolved and enter intotheliquidation procedure. It is essentially a further interpretation of the legal consequences of terminating the Joint Venture Contract for the arbitral award to point out the dissolution and liquidation of the joint venture at the same time when ruling to terminate the Joint Venture Contract. Furthermore, the arbitral tribunal ruled on the dissolution and liquidation of the joint venture does not mean that the arbitral tribunal will arrange the liquidation matters of the joint venture. This part of the award only pointed out that after the termination of the joint venture contract, the joint venture was dissolved and entered intothe liquidation procedure. Details about liquidationshould be processed in accordance with the provisions of relevant laws and regulations. Therefore, it is inappropriate to conclude that the content "The joint venture Sente Company shall be dissolved and to be liquidated according to law" in the arbitral award involved in this case falls within the circumstance where the arbitral tribunal has no power to arbitrate or the circumstance where the scope of arbitration is exceeded. That is, there are nocircumstances prescribed by Item 4, Paragraph 1 of Article 258 of the Civil Procedure Law of the People's Republic of China in the arbitral award involved in the present case.

In addition, there are no other circumstances stipulated in Items 1, 2, 3, Paragraph 1 of Article 258 of the Civil Procedure Law ofthe People's Republic of China in the present case.

To conclude, the people's court shall rule to reject the application of Ningbo Yongxin Auto Component Manufacturing Co., Ltd. for the partial revocation of the arbitral award involved in this case.

It is so replied.

49.   **Reply of the Supreme People's Court to the Report of Request for Instructions on the Case Concerning the Application of Zhoushan Zhonghai Cereal & Oil Industry Co., Ltd. for Non-Enforcement of an Arbitral Award Made by Hong Kong International Arbitration Center.**
      March 18, 2009, [2009] Min Si Ta Zi No. 2

To the High People's Court of Zhejiang Province:

The Report of Request for Instructions on the Case Concerning the Application of Zhoushan Zhonghai Cereal & Oil Industry Co., Ltd. for Non-Enforcement of an Arbitral Award Made by Hong Kong International Arbitration Center {[2007] Zhe Zhi Ta Zi No. 4} submitted by your court has been received. After deliberation, the replies are as follows:

This case was filed because Noble Resources Co., Ltd. ("**Noble**") applied for enforcement of an arbitral award made by the Hong Kong International Arbitration Center and Zhoushan Zhonghai Cereal & Oil Industry Co., Ltd. ("**Zhongliang**") raised the defense application for non-enforcement. After review, your court holds the opinion that the enforcement of the arbitral award in this case will damage the authority of the administrative order and the health of the public and therefore decides not to enforce the arbitral award on the ground of violation of social public interests.

It can be viewed from the facts stated in your court's Report of Request for Instructions that, on May 10, 2004, the General Administration of Quality Supervision, Inspection and Quarantine of the People's Republic of China issued the [2004] No. 322 Urgent Warning Notice, deciding to halt the exportation of soybeans by Noble and three other Brazilian suppliers to China since that day. However, the Urgent Warning Notice expressly pointed out that soybeans already on the way that complied with the inspection and quarantine standards would still be allowed to be imported. In the present case, before the issuance of the Urgent Warning Notice, the goods concerned had already been loaded and were in fact goods on the way. On June 23 of the same year, the General Administration of Quality Supervision, Inspection and Quarantine of the People's Republic of China terminated the import restriction order and restored the qualifications of suppliers including Noble for importing goods into China. In July of the same year, Noble obtained a biosafety certificate for GMO soybeans, and Zhongliang also obtained a soybean import license. This batch of goods complied with the inspection and quarantine standards and did not fall into the category of import-prohibited products. Additionally, there is no evidence showing that the goods concerned would bring serious safety risks or undermine public health. Therefore, enforcing the arbitral award made bytheHong Kong International Arbitration Center will not violate social public policy. Pursuant to the Arrangement of the Supreme People's Court on Mutual Enforcement of Arbitral Awards between the Mainland and the Hong Kong Special Administrative Region, the arbitral award made by Hong Kong International Arbitration Center shall be enforced.

It is so replied.

50. **Reply of the Supreme People's Court to the Request for Instructions Concerning the Revocation of the[2008]Zhong Guo Mao Zhong Jing Cai Zi No. 0044 Award Made by China International Economic and Trade Arbitration Commission.**
    March 18, 2009, [2009] Min Si Ta Zi No. 1

To the High People's Court of Beijing:

The Request for Instructions Concerning the Revocation of the [2008] Zhong Guo Mao Zhong Jing Cai Zi No. 0044 Award Made by China International Economic and Trade Arbitration Commission {Jing Gao Fa [2008]No. 373} submitted by your court has been received. After deliberation, the replies are as follows:

Your court is of the opinion that Hong Kong Zhonghua Pharmaceutical Bioscience Co., Ltd. ("**Zhonghua Pharmaceutical**") did not sign the arbitration clause or the arbitration agreement before participating in the arbitration proceedings. The main reason is that the first and second copies of the Power of Attorney submitted by Zhonghua Pharmaceutical's attorney, lawyer Liu Huili of Beijing Zhongsheng Law Firm, to China International Economic and Trade Arbitration Commission ("**CIETAC**") did not go through the notarization procedures. Although the third copy of the Power of Attorney was notarized after hearing before the arbitral tribunal, Zhonghua Pharmaceutical did not ratify participation in arbitration of the lawyer Liu Huili. Based on the above facts, it was considered that Zhonghua Pharmaceutical did not accept the jurisdiction of CIETAC, and the arbitral award made by CIETAC shall be set aside.

The focus of the present case is whether Zhonghua Pharmaceutical hadaccepted the jurisdiction of the arbitral tribunal. Viewing from the facts stated in your court's Report of Request for Instructions, althoughZhonghua Pharmaceutical denied the validity of the Power of Attorney based on the reason that the first and second copy presented to the arbitral tribunal by Lawyer Liu Huili were not duly notarized, Lawyer Liu Huili stated at the hearing before the arbitral tribunal that he would finish the procedures after the hearing because Shantou Xinyuan Trading Co., Ltd. ("**Xinyuan**") raised an objection to the Power of Attorney submitted by Lawyer Liu Huili for not going through the notarization procedures. Lawyer Liu Huili did not object to the jurisdiction of the arbitral tribunal. Subsequently, Lawyer Liu Huili submitted the third notarized Power of Attorney as promised, which had been accepted by the arbitral tribunal after the fulfillment of the procedure. In this regard,Zhonghua Pharmaceutical ratified the participation of Lawyer Liu Huili in the arbitration proceedings.

Paragraph 2 of Article 20 of the Arbitration Law of the People's Republic of China stipulates that "If the parties object to the validity of the arbitration agreement, such objection shall be raised before the first hearing of the arbitral tribunal." When attending the hearing, Lawyer Liu Huili did not raise an objection to jurisdiction but made a substantive defense. Pursuant to Article 8 of the Arbitration Rules of China International Economic and Trade Arbitration Commission (2005), "A party shall be deemed to have waived its right to object where it knows or should have known that any provision of, or requirement under, these Rules has not be complied with and yet participates in or proceeds with the arbitral proceedings without promptly and explicitly submitting its objection in writing to such noncompliance." Accordingly, it can be held that Zhonghua Pharmaceutical had waived its right to object and the arbitral tribunal has jurisdiction over this case. In conclusion, the reason for the application of Zhonghua Pharmaceutical for setting aside the said award that the arbitral tribunal did not have jurisdiction over the case cannot be established.

It is so replied.

51. Reply of the Supreme People's Court to the Request for Instructions on the Case Concerning the Application of GRD Minproc Co., Ltd. for Recognition and Enforcement of an Arbitral Award Made by the Arbitration Institute of the Stockholm Chamber of Commerce.

March 13, 2009, [2008] Min Si Ta Zi No. 48.

To the High People's Court of Shanghai:

The Request for Instructions on the Case Concerning the Application of GRD Minproc Co., Ltd. for Recognition and Enforcement of an Arbitral Award Made by the Arbitration Institute of the Stockholm Chamber of Commerce {[2008] Hu Gao Min Si (Shang) Ta Zi No. 2} submitted by your court has been received. After deliberation, the replies are as follows:

This is a case in which one party applied for recognition and enforcement of an arbitral award made by a foreign arbitration institution before a Chinese court, while the other party made a defense of non-enforcement. Therefore, the people's court shall review the case in accordance with the relevant provisions of Article 267 of the Civil Procedure Law of the People's Republic of China and the Convention on the Recognition and Enforcement of Foreign Arbitral Awards ("**New York Convention**").

Regarding the issue of whether the recognition and enforcement of the arbitral award involved in the present case will be in violation of the public policy of China, the equipment purchased by Flywheel Company from abroad had been approved by the relevant competent authorities, and the equipment was not prohibited from import in China. The reasons for the environmental pollution caused by the equipment during the installation, debugging and operation phases may vary. Under the circumstance where Flywheel Company submitted the issue of the equipment's quality to arbitration based on the valid arbitration clause in the contract, the arbitral tribunal rendered its judgment on the equipment's quality, which is the power of the arbitral tribunal and the consequence that the parties shall bear for their agreement to resolve disputes through arbitration. Whether the substantive outcome of the arbitration is fair and just cannot be the criteria for examining whether the recognition and enforcement of the arbitral award involved will violate the public policy of China. The recognition and enforcement of the arbitral award in this case does not violate the fundamental interest of society, the fundamental legal principles and good customs of China. Therefore, there does not exist the circumstance prescribed in Article 5(2)(b) of the New York Convention.

There are no other circumstances stipulated in Article 5 of the New York Convention in the arbitral award involved. Thus, the court shall recognize and enforce the arbitral award involved.

It is so replied.

52. **Reply of the Supreme People's Court to the Request for Instructions on the Case Concerning the Application of Subway International B.V. for Recognition and Enforcement of the No. 50/114/T/00171/07 Arbitral Award Made by the International Arbitral Tribunal of International Center for Dispute Resolution.**
   February 26, 2009, [2008] Min Si Ta Zi No. 47.

To the High People's Court of Beijing:

The Request for Instructions on the Case Concerning the Application of Subway International B.V. for Recognition and Enforcement of the No. 50/114/T/00171/07 Arbitral Award Made by the International Arbitral Tribunal of International Center for Dispute Resolution {Jing Gao Fa [2008] No. 348} submitted by your court has been received. After deliberation, the replies are as follows:

The arbitral award involved in this case is a foreign arbitral award. Pursuant to Article 267 of the Civil Procedure Law of the People's Republic of China, this case shall be reviewed in accordance with the relevant provisions of the Convention on the Recognition and Enforcement of Foreign Arbitral Awards. However, according to the facts found by the Beijing Second Intermediate People's Court, the respondent Sabowei Food Service Co., Ltd. had not been duly registered at the Administration for Industry and Commerce of China. As a consequence, the Chinese court cannot recognize and enforce the arbitral award involved in accordance with the Convention on the Recognition and Enforcement of Foreign Arbitral Awards. Since the respondent does not exist, the application of SubwayInternational B.V. shall be rejected in this case.

It is so replied.

53. **Reply of the Supreme People's Court to the Request for Instructions in the Case Concerning the Application of Changsha Xinye Industrial Co., Ltd.for Revocation of an Arbitral Award against Metals Plus International Co., Ltd. of the United States.**
   November 18, 2008, [2007] Min Si Ta Zi No. 43.

To the High People's Court of Hunan Province:

The Report of Review in the Case Concerning the Application of Changsha Xinye Industrial Co., Ltd. for Revocation of an Arbitral Award against Metals Plus International Co., Ltd. of the United States {[2007] Xiang Gao Fa Min San Qing Zi No. 16} submitted by your court has been received. After deliberation, the replies are as follows:

First, there is no dispute over the existence of the agreement on arbitration between the two parties. The parties only disagree on the interpretation of the "country of defendant" in the arbitration clause. Regardless of how to interpret it, it does not affect the parties' intent to arbitrate in China. Therefore, pursuant to Article 16 of the Interpretation of the Supreme People's Court on Certain Issues Concerning the Application of the Arbitration Law of People's Republic of China, the validity of the arbitration clause involved in this case shall be reviewed in accordance with the law of the People's Republic of China.

Second, the term "country" will usually be translated as the "state", so translating the "country of defendant" as the "place where the defendant resides" cannot accurately define the special legal meaning of the legal term. As the two parties in the present case belong to two different countries, it would be more reasonable to translate the "country of defendant" as the "the country where the defendant resides".

Third, there are several arbitration institutions in China. After disputes arose, the parties did not reach a consensus on the choice of the arbitration institution in accordance with Article 6 of the Interpretation of the Supreme People's Court on Certain Issues Concerning the Application of the Arbitration Law of People's Republic of China. Therefore, the arbitration clause involved in the present case shall be determined as invalid.

Your court's opinion that the arbitral award involved in this case shall be set aside. It is so replied.

54. Reply of the Supreme People's Court to the Request for Instructions on the Case Concerning the Revocation of an Arbitral Award between Korea Daesung G-3 Co., Ltd. and Changchun Yuanda Auto Engineering Trade Co., Ltd.

October 21, 2008, [2008] Min Si Ta Zi No. 28.

To the High People's Court of Jilin Province:

The Request for Instructions on the Case Concerning the Revocation of an Arbitral Award between Korea Daesung G-3 Co., Ltd. and Changchun Yuanda Auto Engineering Trade Co., Ltd. {[2008] Ji Min San Ta Zi No. 1} submitted by your court has been received. After deliberation, the replies are as follows:

Paragraph 2 of Article 20 of the Arbitration Law of the People's Republic of China stipulates that "If the parties object to the validity of the arbitration agreement, they should raise such objection before the first hearing of the arbitral tribunal." According to the facts stated in your court's Report of Request for Instructions, the applicant Korea Daesung G-3 Co., Ltd. only raised objections to the validity of the arbitration agreement and the jurisdiction of the arbitral tribunal in the first and the fourth hearing. It did not raise the objection to the validity of the arbitration agreement before the first hearing of the arbitral tribunal. In addition, according to the facts reflected in the arbitral award attached to the case file, Korea Daesung G-3 Co., Ltd. appointed the arbitrator, entrusted its agent and submitted its statement of defense in written on the substantive matters of the case before the first hearing of the arbitral tribunal. Therefore, Korea Daesung G-3 Co., Ltd. acknowledged the jurisdiction of the Changchun Arbitration Commission over their dispute before the first hearing of the arbitral tribunal. The two parties in the arbitration case reached a consensus on submitting their disputes to the Changchun Arbitration Commission for arbitration, and the arbitration agreement was valid. Although Korea Daesung G-3 Co., Ltd. raised an objection to the validity of the arbitration agreement and the jurisdiction of the arbitral tribunal in the first hearing of the arbitral tribunal, the time limit stipulated by the law for the parties to raise an objection to the validity of arbitration agreement had been exceeded. Therefore, the arbitration agreement was valid, and the Changchun Arbitration Commission had the jurisdiction over the dispute in this case in accordance with the law. The objection to the validity of the arbitration agreement and the jurisdiction of the arbitral tribunal shall not be supported by. The opinion that "It can be determined that the two parties failed to reach a consensus on the choice of the arbitration institution, so the arbitration agreement was invalid and it shall be deemed that there is no arbitration clause between the parties" in the Report of Request for Instructions of Changchun Intermediate People's Court and your court cannot be established. The arbitral award shall not be revoked on the ground that there was no arbitration clause in the contract or the parties did not reach a written arbitration agreement afterwards.

It is so replied.

55. **Reply of the Supreme People's Court to the Request for Instructions Concerning the [2007] Zhong Guo Mao Zhong Hu Cai Zi No. 224 Arbitral Award Shall Not be Enforced.**
    September 12, 2008, [2008] Min Si Ta Zi No. 34.

To the High People's Court of Zhejiang Province:

The Report on Agreeing with the Ningbo Intermediate People's Court on the Non-enforcement of the [2007] Zhong Guo Mao Zhong Hu Cai Zi No. 224 Arbitral Award has been received. After deliberation, the replies are as follows:

First, your court's opinions that the law of China shall be applied to review the arbitral award involved in the present case, China International Economic and Trade Arbitration Commission Shanghai Sub-Commission had the jurisdiction over the dispute in this case, and substantive review shall not be conducted in the foreign-related arbitral award are agreed.

Second, the AQ7200 Project Technology Development Contract involved in the arbitral award in this case stipulated that "For any dispute arising out of or in connection with this Contract, the parties shall first resolve it through negotiation. If such negotiation fails…, such dispute shall be submitted to China International Economic and Trade Arbitration Commission Shanghai Sub-Commission for arbitration." It can be viewed from the agreement above that the scope of dispute submitted for arbitration includes "any dispute arising out of or in connection with this Contract". Regarding the issue of *ultrapetita* DVD production fees in the amount of 7,500 euros alleged by Aux Group Co., Ltd., viewing from the facts ascertained in your court's Report of Request for Instructions, the DVD was produced by Rick-Lipsar Co., Ltd. in order to enable Aux Group Co., Ltd. to clearly understand the effects of the completed vehicle and facilitate its external publicity.Although the DVD production did not fall within the scope of technology agreed upon in the contract, it was related to the performance of the AQ7200 Project Technology Development Contract. The arbitration authority had the power to arbitrate the disputes arising therefrom.

The issue alleged by Aux Group Co., Ltd., that the fact determined in the arbitral award that the legal representative of Aux Group Co., Ltd. watched the DVD in Spain and accepted the price of 7,500 euros did not conform to the facts and facts ascertained were unclear, falls within the scope of substantive review and the court has no power to review. Therefore, the reason of Aux Group Co., Ltd. for not enforcing the arbitral award cannot be supported.

In conclusion, the reason of Aux Group Co., Ltd. for its application to the Intermediate People's Court of Ningbo for not enforcing the arbitral award cannot be supported.The [2007] Zhong Guo Mao Zhong Hu Cai Zi No. 224 Arbitral Award made by theChina International Economic and Trade Arbitration Commission Shanghai Sub-Commissionshall be enforced.

It is so replied.

56. Reply of the Supreme People's Court to the Report Concerning the Ruling of Non-Recognition and Non-Enforcement of the No. 05–03 Arbitral Award Made by Japan Commercial Arbitration Association in Tokyo.
September 10, 2008, [2008] Min Si Ta Zi No. 18.

To the High People's Court of Tianjin:

The Report Concerning the Ruling of Non-Recognition and Non-Enforcement of the No. 05–03 Arbitral Award Made by Japan Commercial Arbitration Association in Tokyo {[2006] Jin Gao Min Si Ta Zi No. 0006} submitted by your court has been received. After deliberation, the replies are as follows:

This case concerns the application of Shin-Etsu Chemical Co., Ltd. ("**Shin-Etsu**") for recognition of an arbitral award made by the Japan Commercial Arbitration Association before a Chinese court. Both China and Japan are contracting states of the Convention on the Recognition and Enforcement of Foreign Arbitral Awards ("**New York Convention**"), so the relevant provision of the New York Convention shall apply for review.

Viewing from the situations stated in your court's Report of Request for Instructions, the procedure of notice in the arbitral award in this case was inconsistent with the Commercial Arbitration Rules of Japan Commercial Arbitration Association ("**Arbitration Rules**"), and there are circumstances stipulated in Articles 5(1)(b) and (d) of the New York Convention.

First, Article 53 of the Arbitration Rules above stipulated that "1. Upon determining that the hearing proceedings have been conducted fully and the arbitral tribunal is able to make an award and therefore decides to terminate the proceedings, the arbitral tribunal shall render the award within five weeks within 5 weeks from the date of making the decision; if the case is especially complex or there are other reasons, the arbitral tribunal may extend the said period if necessary, but it shall be no more than eight weeks. 2. After deciding to terminate the hearing proceedings based on the preceding paragraph, the arbitral tribunal shall notify the parties of the time limit for rendering the award."

After the termination of the hearing proceeding, the arbitral tribunal in this case did not perform its obligation to "notify the parties of the time limit for rending the award" stipulated in the Arbitration Rules. The arbitral tribunal did not inform Tianjin Xinmao Technology Co., Ltd. (formerly Tianjin Tianda Tiancai Co., Ltd., "**Xinmao**") of the time limit for rending the award. As the arbitration rules stipulate the time limit for the arbitral tribunal to notify the parties the time limit to render an arbitral award as a duty that the arbitral tribunal must perform, the arbitral tribunal does not have the right to choose whether to notify or not. Consequently, the arbitral tribunal's failure to inform Xinmaoof the time limit to render an award violated the mandatory stipulation of the Arbitration Rules. As the two parties had selected arbitration as the dispute resolution method and expressly agreed on the application of the Commercial Arbitration Rules of Japan Commercial Arbitration Association in the agreement, the relevant contents of the Arbitration Rules had become part of the parties' agreement. The tribunal's violation of such content of the Arbitration Rules falls within the circumstance "The composition of the arbitral authority or the arbitral procedure was not in accordance with the agreement of the parties" stipulated in Article 5(1)(d) of the New York Convention.

Second, Article 20 of the Arbitration Rules stipulates, "1.The claimant may amend the content of its claims by submitting an application for amending Request for Arbitration to the Association in writing on the same arbitration agreement. If such anapplication is made after the arbitral tribunal is constituted, the claimant shall submit the request to amend its request for arbitration to the arbitral tribunal and obtain the approval of the arbitral tribunal. 2. The arbitral tribunal shall hear the opinions of the opposing party before granting approval of the preceding paragraph."

Shin-Etsu claimed thatit had submitted the Application for Amending Claims to the arbitral tribunal on August 31, 2005, and the general affairs office of the Arbitration Association had sent the Request for Opinions to Xinmao via an international courier on October 21, 2005. However, Xinmao denied that it had received the relevant Request for Opinions sent by the arbitral tribunal. Shin-Etsu also failed to provide any evidence of the behavior of the arbitral tribunal to actually comply with the obligation to notify mentioned above. Meanwhile, there is no evidence showing that the arbitraltribunal had mailed the document involvingShin-Etsu's Request for Amendment to Xinmao on October 21, 2005. Neither did Xinmao put forward its opinions on Shin-Etsu's behavior to amend its claims.

Under the circumstance where Shin-Etsu made amendments to its claims, Xinmao was entitled toput forward its opinions on the amended claims. The Notice of such amendment shall be an important part of the arbitration proceedings. The tribunal's failure to notify Xinmao of such amendment had actually deprived Xinmao of the right and chance to make a defense, which falls within the circumstances "The party against whom the award is invoked was not given proper notice of the appointment of the arbitrator or of the arbitration proceedings or was otherwise unable to present his case"prescribed by Article 5(1)(b) of the New York Convention. It is alsoinconsistentwith the arbitration rules chosen by the parties.

In conclusion, your court's opinion that there exist the circumstances stipulated in Articles 5(1)(b) and (d) in the arbitral award involved in this case, and thus the award shall not be recognized.

It is so replied.

57.   **Reply of the Supreme People's Court to the Report of Request for Instructions on the Case Concerning the Application of China Shipping Development Co., Ltd. Freight Company for Recognition of an Arbitral Award Made in London.**
      August 6, 2008, [2008] Min Si Ta Zi No. 17.

To the High People's Court of Hubei Province:

The Report of Request for Instructions on the Case Concerning the Application of China Shipping Development Co., Ltd. Freight Company for Recognition of an Arbitral Award Made in London {[2008] E Min Si Ta Zi No. 1} submitted by your court has been received. After deliberation, the replies are as follows:

The Charter Agreement signed between China Shipping Development Co., Ltd. Freight Company and Anhui Technology Import and Export Co., Ltd. expressly stipulates "Arbitration in Hong Kong and the law of the United Kingdom shall apply". Therefore, this clause shall be identified as the arbitration clause in the present case.

The arbitration clause above shall be interpreted as choosing Hong Kong as the seat of arbitration and the law of the United Kingdom as the applicable law to resolve substantive disputes over the Charter Agreement. However, the clause did not specify the applicable law to the arbitration clause. Hence, the applicable law to the arbitration clause shall be the Arbitration Ordinance of Hong Kong, the seat of the arbitration, and the UNCITRAL Model Law on International Commercial Arbitration ("**Model Law**") that the Arbitration Ordinance referred to. The two parties had agreed that disputes shall be submitted for arbitration in writing in the Charter Agreement, which is in compliance with the Arbitration Ordinance and the Model Law, and thus the arbitration clause was valid.

Pursuant to Paragraph 5 of Article 43C of the Arbitration Ordinance of Hong Kong, when the parties fail to reach a consensus on the number of arbitrators, the parties shall first apply to Hong Kong International Arbitration Center ("**Arbitration Center**") to determine the number of arbitrators to be one or three. If the Arbitration Center decides to appoint a sole arbitrator and the parties fail to agree on one arbitrator, the sole arbitrator shall be decided in accordance with the procedure stipulated in Item B, Paragraph 3 of Article 11 of the Model Law, i.e., one of the parties shall apply to the Arbitration Center for the appointment of the sole arbitrator. The appointment of the arbitrator in the present case violated the procedures stipulated abovein the Arbitration Ordinance and the Model Law. Pursuant to Article 5(1)(d) of the New York Convention, the arbitral award involved shall not be recognized or enforced.

Your court's preference opinion that the arbitral award made by the English arbitrator William Packard on March 9, 2006 in London shall not be recognized and enforced.

It is so replied.

58. **Reply of the Supreme People's Court to the Request for Instructions on the Case Concerning the Application of Yang Zhihong for Revocation of a Hong Kong-Related Arbitral Award Made by Guangzhou Arbitration Commission.**
     July 24, 2008, [2008] Min Si Ta Zi No. 21.

To the High People's Court of Guangdong Province:

The Request for Instructions on the Case Concerning the Application of Yang Zhihong for Revocation of a Hong Kong-Related Arbitral Award Made by Guangzhou Arbitration Commission {[2007] Yue Gao Fa Min Si Ta Zi No. 22} submitted by your court has been received. After deliberation, the replies are as follows:

After deliberation, it is held that this is a case about the application for revocation of a Hong Kong-related arbitral award made by an arbitration institution in the Mainland. The review shall be carried out by reference to Article 70 of the Arbitration Law of the People's Republic of China and Article 258 of the Civil Procedure Law of the People's Republic of China.

According to the situation reflected in your court's Report of Request for Instructions and the attached case file, Article 97 of Chapter 8 "Expedited Procedures" of the Arbitration Rules of Guangzhou Arbitration Commission stipulates that "This chapter shall apply if the disputed amount is no more than RMB 200,000 unless the parties agree otherwise; for cases with the disputed amount higher than RMB 200,000, this chapter may also apply if the parties agree to it in writing." However, in this present case, the amount of the gold Guangzhou Arbitration Commission ordered Yang Zhihong to buy to the Jewelry Company exceeded RMB 200,000, and the parties did not agree in writing on the adoption of the expedited procedure by arbitration commission. Under such circumstances, the adoption oftheexpedited procedure of theGuangzhou Arbitration Commission on the review in the present case falls within the situation "the constitution of the tribunal or the arbitral proceedings was inconsistent with the arbitration rules" referred to by Item c, Paragraph 1 of Article 258 of the Civil Procedure Law of the People's Republic of China.

In addition, in the Application for Clarification of Arbitration Claims submitted by the Jewelry Company on May 25, 2004 to the arbitral tribunal, there existed the claim that "The Jewelry Company shall buy the gold stock from Yang Zhihong". However, the Application for Clarification of Arbitration Claims sent by the tribunal to Yang Zhihong on May 31 did not contain the above claim, plus that there was no record of such clarification of arbitration claim in the transcript of the hearing by the arbitral tribunal. The arbitral tribunal ruled to support the claim without informing Yang Zhihong of the above arbitration claim, resulting in the inability of Yang Zhihong to present her case against the said claim. Such circumstances fall within the situation "the person was unable to present his case due to reasons for which he is not responsible" referred to by Item b, Paragraph 1 of Article 258 of the Civil Procedure Law of the People's Republic of China.

In conclusion, the [2003] Sui Zhong An Zi No. 2761 Arbitral Award made by Guangzhou Arbitration Commission shall be revoked.

It is so replied.

59. Reply of the Supreme People's Court to the Request for Instructions on the Case Concerning the Application of Weibei Hongli Co., Ltd. for the Revocation of a Foreign-Related Arbitral Award Made by Zhuhai Arbitration Commission.

May 27, 2008, [2008] Min Si Ta Zi No. 2

The High People's Court of Guangdong Province:

The Request for Instructions on the Case Concerning the Application of Weibei Hongli Co., Ltd. for the Revocation of a Foreign-Related Arbitral Award Made by Zhuhai Arbitration Commission submitted by your court has been received. After deliberation, the replies are as follows:

I. Among the parties in the present case, Weibei Hongli Co., Ltd. ("**Hongli**") is a company incorporated in British Virgin Islands, Huasheng Paper Factory Co., Ltd. ("**Huasheng**") is a company incorporated in Hong Kong. Consequently, this is a foreign-related arbitration case. The review on the revocation ofthis arbitral award shall be conducted applying the provisions related to foreign arbitration in the Civil Procedure Law of the People's Republic of China and the Arbitration Law of the People's Republic of China.

II. Article 84 of Chapter 7 "Special Provisions for Foreign-related Arbitration" of the Arbitration Rules of Zhuhai Arbitration Commission stipulates that "Where one party or both parties is or are foreign person(s), stateless person(s), foreign enterprises or organizations and the disputes are over contract or other property rights and interests, this chapter shall apply. If there are no related provisions in this chapter, other relevant provisions shall apply." As the present case is foreign-related, relevant provisions from the aforementioned chapter shall apply. Article 89 of Chapter 7 of the Arbitration Rules of Zhuhai Arbitration Commission stipulates that "After the arbitral tribunal decides on the date of the first hearing, the arbitration commission shall notify the parties of the date of hearing 20 days before the hearing of the arbitral tribunal. The hearing may be held in advance if the arbitral tribunal agrees upon the parties' request." Viewed from the facts found in your court's report of request for Instructions, the date for the tribunal to notify the parties of the hearing was October 30, 2006, while the first hearing was held on November 15, 2006. The arbitral tribunal did not notify the parties 20 days before the hearing in accordance with the provision of the Arbitration Rules of Zhuhai Arbitration Commission above. There is no evidence proving that the arbitral tribunal agrees to hold the hearing in advance upon the parties' request. Therefore, the arbitration procedure of the arbitral tribunal has violated the provisions of the arbitration rules.

III. Pursuant to Article 84 of the Arbitration Rules of Zhuhai Arbitration Commission, if there are no related provisions in Chapter 7 concerning foreign-related arbitration, other relevant provisions shall apply. Article 20 of the Arbitration Rules of Zhuhai Arbitration Commission stipulates that "The amendment of claims by the claimant or the amendment of counterclaims by the respondent shall be put forward before the completion of investigation of the arbitral tribunal, and the arbitral tribunal may decide whether to accept such amendments. If the arbitral tribunal decides to accept, and the other party needs period of defense, the other party shall submit the defense in writing against the amended claims or counterclaims within 15 days upon receiving the application for amendments to the claims or application for amendments to the counterclaims." According to the facts found in your court's report of request for Instructions, Huasheng amended its claims at the second hearing. The arbitral tribunal rendered the award without notifying Hongli of such amendments and inquiring Hongli of whether it needs period of defense and providing 15 days as the period of defense. There indeed exists a situation where the arbitration procedures violated the relevant provisions of the arbitration rules.

In conclusion, the arbitration proceedings violated Articles 89 and 20 of the Arbitration Rules of Zhuhai Arbitration Commission in the present case. Pursuant to Item 3, Paragraph 1 of Article 260 of the Civil Procedure Law of the People's Republic of China and Article 70 of the Arbitration Law of the People's Republic of China, the Zhu Zhong CaiZi [2006] No. 168 Arbitral Award made by Zhuhai Arbitration Commission shall be revoked.

It is so replied.

60. **Reply of the Supreme People's Court to the Report of Review on the Case Concerning the Application of Runhe Development Co., Ltd. for Non-Enforcement of an Arbitral Award.**
     May 8, 2008, [2008] Min Si Ta Zi No. 1

To the High People's Court of Hunan Province:

The Report of Review on the Case Concerning the Application of Runhe Development Co., Ltd. for Non-Enforcement of an Arbitral Award {[2005] Xiang Gao Fa Zhi Qing Zi No. 1} submitted by your court has been received. After deliberation, the replies are as follows:

1. This is a case where a party applied for enforcement of an arbitral award. As one of the parties, Runhe Development Co., Ltd. ("**Runhe**") was incorporated in Hong Kong, the relevant provisions concerning the enforcement of foreign-related arbitral awards shall apply to the review in the present case.

2. According to the contents recorded in the arbitral award, the arbitral tribunal served Runhe the notice of arbitration, the arbitration rules, the list of arbitrators and the Request for Arbitration submitted by the claimant, etc., by mail according to the address provided by the claimant Shenzhen Mawan Power Co., Ltd. ("**Mawan**") in the Request for Arbitration. However, such

mails were returned on the ground that "No such a company exists". Afterwards, Mawan authorized an attorney through the CIETAC South China Sub-Commission to investigate the respondent's registered information, which shows that the respondent's registered address was "231 Wing Lok Street 3rd FLR". According to that registered address, the Secretariat of CIETAC South China Sub-Commission sent the documents above to Runhe again, plus the notice of the constitution of the arbitral tribunal and notice of hearing, etc. However, all such mails were returned on the ground that "no recipient found" or "no resident at the address". According to the industrial and commercial registration materials submitted by Runhe recorded in the case file, its legal registration address is "3/F 231 WING LOK STREET HK", and Runhe provided evidence showing that the respondent had received the mails sent by the Hong Kong government agencies in accordance with the registration address. As the address to which the arbitral tribunal sent the notifications was inconsistent with the respondent's registration address, Runhe was not able to receive relevant documents objectively. Therefore, the first reason for not enforcing the said award in your court's report of request for Instructions, i.e., "The arbitral tribunal did not properly serve the parties the arbitration documents" is established.

3.   Although the parties agreed in the arbitration agreement that disputes shall be resolved through negotiation, they did not specify a period of negotiation. As the content agreed is general, different understandings may arise regarding the issue of how to perform such clausesand define the relevant terms. The true meaning of the agreement shall be judged in combination with the purpose of the parties to enter into an arbitration agreement. Among the two conditions agreed upon by the parties, i.e., "friendly negotiation" and "failure of negotiation", the former is a form of negotiation procedurally, and the latter can be understood as thatthere must be the result of failure of negotiation. The behavior of Mawan to requestarbitration shall be deemed the occurrence of such a failure. Therefore, under the circumstance where it is hard to define the standard of the former condition while the latter condition has been established, the arbitral tribunal shall have the power to accept the case in accordance with the arbitration agreement. The second reason for non-enforcementin your court's report of request for Instructions, i.e., "Such disputes had not come to the stage of arbitration, the arbitration institution should not accept the case", cannot be supported.

4.   The arbitral tribunal has the power to render an award on matters such as the validity of the disputed contract between the parties, whether to terminate the contract, etc. In the case at hand, the arbitral tribunal held the opinion after deliberation that Mawan was entitled to terminate the contract and finally ruled that Runhe shall return the relevant amount and interests thereof to Mawan. The arbitral tribunal did not rule on issues including the validity of the approval certificate issued by the People's Government of Hunan Province and that of the Reply of the Business Promotion Bureau of Changsha City and whether to terminate the contract. Therefore, the third reason for non-enforcementin your court's report of request for Instructions, i.e., "It is illegal for the arbitral tribunal

to change the approvals by governmental administrative agencies", cannot be supported.

5. According to the content stated in the arbitral award, Mawan appointed Wang Pu as an arbitrator. As Runhe did not appoint or authorize an agent to appoint an arbitrator within the specified period, in accordance with the provisions of the Arbitration Rules, the chairman of CIETAC South China Sub-Commission appointed Luo Liwei as the arbitrator for the respondent. As both parties failed to jointly appoint or jointly authorize an agent to appoint the presiding arbitrator within the specified period, the chairman of CIETAC South China Sub-Commission appointed Guo Xiaowen as the presiding arbitrator. The facts found in your court's report of request for Instructions did not deny the authenticity of the contents stated in the arbitral award above. Pursuant to the transcripts of the investigation conducted by the Intermediate People's Court of Changsha City with the arbitration commission, the arbitration commission claimed that the reply to the report of the appointment of arbitrators was made orally. Articles 26 and 27 of the Arbitration Rules do not require such replies to be in writing. Therefore, the absence of the approval procedures in the case file of the present arbitration cannot indicate that the procedure of the appointment of arbitrators is illegal. The fourth reason for non-enforcement in your court's report of request for Instructions, i.e., "the procedures of appointing arbitrators is illegal", cannot be supported.

In conclusion, since the address of the service of the arbitral tribunal was wrong, the arbitral tribunal did not properly serve upon the party the arbitration documents in accordance with law, Runhe was unable to participate in the arbitration and present its case. As a consequence, in accordance with Item 2, Paragraph 1 of Article 260 of the Civil Procedure Law of the People's Republic of China, the present arbitral award shall not be enforced.

It is so replied.

61. **Reply of the Supreme People's Court to the Report Concerning the Non-Recognition of the Tokyo No.04-05Arbitral Award Made by Japan Commercial Arbitration Association.**

March 3, 2008, [2007] Min Si Ta Zi No. 26.

To the High People's Court of Jiangsu Province,

The Report Concerning the Non-Recognition of the Tokyo No. 04–05 Arbitral Award Made by Japan Commercial Arbitration Association {[2007] Su Min San Ta Zi No. 0002} submitted by your court has been received. After deliberation, the replies are as follows:

This is a case where the Japanese Shin-Etsu Chemical Co., Ltd. ("**Shin-Etsu**") applied to a court in our country for recognition of an arbitral award made by the Japan Commercial Arbitration Association. Both China and Japan are contracting states of the Convention on the Recognition and Enforcement of Foreign Arbitral Awards ("**New York Convention**"). Therefore, the case shall be reviewed in accordance with the relevant provisions of the New York Convention.

From thesituations reflected in your court's report, the time limit for rendering the arbitral award and the relevant procedures of notice in the present case were inconsistent with the relevant provisions of the Commercial Arbitration Rules of Japan Commercial Arbitration Association ("**Arbitration Rules**") and the Japan Arbitration Act, which fall within the circumstances stipulated by Article 5(1)(b) and (d) of the New York Convention.

First, the time limit for rendering the arbitral award in the present case was inconsistent with the arbitration rules. Article 53.1 of the said Arbitration Rules stipulates that "Upon determining that the hearing proceedings have been conducted fully and the arbitral tribunal is able to make an award and therefore decides to terminate the proceedings, the arbitral tribunal shall render the award within five weeks within 5 weeks from the date of making the decision; if the case is especially complex or there are other reasons, the arbitral tribunal may extend the said period if necessary, but it shall be no more than eight weeks." On July 7, 2005, the arbitral tribunal decided to accept the request by Shin-Etsu for the amendments to its claims and concluded the hearing process. On August 31, 2005, the arbitral tribunal announced that it would delay the date of rendering the award by 20 days to September 20, 2005, while the award was actually rendered on February 23, 2006. After deciding to conclude the hearing process, the arbitral tribunal did not render the arbitral award within the time limit in accordance with theCommercial Arbitration Rules of Japan Commercial Arbitration Association. The parties chose arbitration as the method of dispute resolution and specifically agreed on the application of the Commercial Arbitration Rules of Japan Commercial Arbitration Association. Hence, the relevant content of the Arbitration Rules has become part of the agreement between the parties. The above violations of the Arbitration Rules and the Japan Arbitration Act fall within the circumstance where "The composition of the arbitral authority or the arbitral procedures was not in accordance with the agreement of the parties, or failing such agreement, was not in accordance with the law of the country where the arbitration took place" stipulated in Article 5(1)(d) of the New York Convention.

Second, Article 53.2 of the Rules stipulates, "After deciding to terminate the hearing proceedings based on the preceding paragraph, the arbitral tribunal shall notify the parties of the time limit for rendering the award."After announcing that it would issue the arbitral award on September 20, 2005, the arbitral tribunal did not decide on the delay and notify the parties in accordance with the provisions of the Arbitration Rules until the award was actually issued on February 23, 2006, which constituted the circumstance where "The party against whom the award is invoked was not given proper notice of the appointment of the arbitrator or or the arbitration proceedings or was otherwise unable to present his case" stipulated in Article 5(1)(b) of the New York Convention.

In conclusion, your court's opinion that there were circumstances in the present case stipulated in Article 5 (1)(b) and (d) of the New York Convention and thus the arbitral award shall not be recognized is agreed upon.

It is so replied.

62. **Reply of the Supreme People's Court to the Request for Instructions Regarding the Non-Enforcement of the Arbitral Award between Hong Kong Euraslan Technology Co. v. Xinjiang Hops Co., Ltd.**
November 28, 2007, [2006] Min Si Ta Zi No. 18.

To the High People's Court of Xinjiang Uygur Autonomous Region:

The Request for Instructions Regarding the Non-Enforcement of the Arbitral Award between Hong Kong Eurasian Technology Co. v. Xinjiang Hops Co., Ltd. {[2006] Xin Zhi Jian Zi No. 97} submitted by your court has been received. After deliberation, the replies are as follows:

According to the materials attached to your court's report, after the negotiation regarding the purchase of a hops production line and joint check of equipment between the applicant Hong Kong Eurasian Technology Co. and the respondent Xinjiang Hops Co., Ltd., due to the lack of the qualification of import and export, Xinjiang Hops Co., Ltd. designated Xinjiang Agricultural Reclamation Import and Export Corporation to import the above equipment. On October 19, 1996, Xinjiang Agricultural Reclamation Import and Export Corporation and Hong Kong Eurasian Technology Co. signed the No. 96XK - 1015HK Contract (including two Exhibits A and B) in Urumqi City. The deputy general manager of Xinjiang Hops Co., Ltd. signed on the original copy of the Contract. The Contract provided that the law of the People's Republic of China shall apply to the Contract. If the parties cannot resolve their dispute through friendly negotiation, such disputes shall be submitted for arbitration in Hong Kong. On December 1, 1997, Xinjiang Hops Co., Ltd. and Hong Kong Eurasian Technology Co. signed the Amendment Agreement to No. 96XK - 1015HK Contract Singed in Urumqi City on October 19, 1996and Exhibit B. In the Amendment Agreement, the parties agreed that the Amendment Agreement shall be part of the original Contract. Afterwards, disputes arose between Xinjiang Hops Co., Ltd. and Hong Kong Eurasian Technology Co., and the latter submitted the said disputes for arbitration. On June 24, 2001, the Hong Kong International Arbitration Center rendered the final award. After Hong Kong Eurasian Technology Co. made an application to the Intermediate People's Court of Urumqi City for enforcing the said award, Xinjiang Hops Co., Ltd. made the defense claiming that there was no arbitration agreement between the parties and the said award shall not be enforced.

After review, this Court is of the opinion that, as Xinjiang Hops Co., Ltd. and Hong Kong Eurasian Technology Co. expressly agreed in the Amendment Agreement that such Amendment Agreement shall be part of the original Contract and that there was an arbitration clause in the original Contract. Therefore, the arbitration clause in the original Contract was binding upon the two parties. The enforcement of the arbitral award over the sales dispute between Xinjiang Hops Co., Ltd. and Hong Kong Eurasian Technology Co. made by Hong Kong International Arbitration Center on June 24, 2001 shall not be refused on the ground that there was no arbitration agreement between them. In addition, pursuant to Article 16 of the Interpretation of the Supreme People's Court on Several Issues on the Application of the Arbitration Law of People's Republic of China and Article 7(1)(a) of Arrangements of the SPC on the Mutual Enforcement of Arbitral Awards by China's Mainland and Hong Kong

Special Administrative Region, where the parties do not agree on the applicable law on the arbitration agreement but agree on the seat of arbitration, the law of the seat of arbitration, i.e., the law of Hong Kong Special Administrative Region, shall be appliedto determine the validity of the above arbitration clause. The respondent did not assert that the above arbitration clause was invalid in accordance with the law of the Hong KongSpecial Administrative Region. Neither did it assert that there were other circumstances prescribed by Article 7(1) of Arrangements of the SPC on the Mutual Enforcement of Arbitral Awards by China's Mainland and Hong Kong Special Administrative Region. If there are no circumstances as is prescribed by Article 7(2) and (3) of the Arrangement, the said award shall be enforced.

It is so replied.

Ingram Content Group UK Ltd.
Milton Keynes UK
UKHW020647060723
424661UK00006B/210

9 789811 912863